Sybase Sy
Management

MW01040993

Karen Hogoboom

Prentice Hall PTR
Upper Saddle River, New Jersey 07458
http://www.prenhall.com

Library of Congress Cataloging-in-Publication Data

Hogoboom, Karen.
 Sybase systems management / Karen Hogoboom
   p. cm.
 Includes index.
   ISBN 0-13-455353-5
   1. Relational databases. 2. Sybase I. Title.
 QA76.9.D3H642 1996
 005.75'65--dc20   96-18153
                                               CIP

Editorial/production supervision: *Joanne Anzalone*
Interior Design*: Gail Cocker-Bogusz*
Manufacturing manager: *Alexis R. Heydt*
Acquisitions editor: *Mark L. Taub*
Editorial assistant: *Kate Hargett*
Cover design: *Aren Graphics*
Cover design director: *Jerry Votta*

© 1997 Karen Hogoboom

 Published by Prentice Hall PTR
Prentice-Hall, Inc.
A Simon & Schuster Company
Upper Saddle River, New Jersey 07458

The publisher offers discounts on this book when ordered in bulk quantities.
For more information, contact:
Corporate Sales Department
Prentice Hall PTR
1 Lake Street
Upper Saddle River, NJ 07458

Phone: 800-382-3419, Fax: 201-236-7141
E-mail: corpsales@prenhall.com

Printed in the United States of America
10 9 8 7 6 5 4 3 2 1

    ISBN 0-13-455353-5

Prentice-Hall International (UK) Limited, *London*
Prentice-Hall of Australia Pty. Limited, *Sydney*
Prentice-Hall Canada Inc., *Toronto*
Prentice-Hall Hispanoamericana, S.A., *Mexico*
Prentice-Hall of India Private Limited, *New Delhi*
Prentice-Hall of Japan, Inc., *Tokyo*
Simon & Schuster Asia Pte. Ltd., *Singapore*
Editora Prentice-Hall do Brasil, Ltda., *Rio de Janeiro*

SQL-BackTrack—Trademark of DataTools, Inc.

SYBASE, INC. TRADEMARKS
(Effective April 10, 1996)

The following list sets forth certain of the trademarks used by Sybase, Inc. or its affiliates. This list is subject to change at any time. Applications for registration for many of these marks are pending and may become registered marks in the near future. ™ or ® indicates current U.S. status. Some marks, not registered yet in the U.S., may already be registered in foreign countries. If you have any questions regarding the current form of any mark please call Sybase at (510) 922-3500.

Notes:

ADA Workbench™
AnswerBase™
APT Workbench™
Backup Server™
Bit-Wise™
Certified SYBASE Professional℠
Client-Library™
DataServer℠
Datawindow™
Data Pipeline™
Data Workbench®
DB-Library™
DBA Companion®
Designor™
Embedded SQL™
Enterprise CONNECT™
Enterprise SQL Server Manager™
EMS™
EWA™
Gain Momentum®
GainExposure®
InfoMaker™
InformationCONNECT™

MainframeCONNECT™
MAP™
MDI™
MDI Database Gateway™
MethodSet™
Navigation Server Manager™
Net-Gateway™
Net-Library™
OASiS® (UK only)
OmniCONNECT™
OmniSQL Server™
Open Client™
Open Client/Server™
Open Server™
Open Solutions™
PowerBuilder®
PowerScript™
Powersoft®
Report Workbench™
Replication Agent™
Replication Driver™
Replication Server®
Replication Server Manager™

SAFE™

SDF™

Secure SQL Server™

SKILS™

SQL Anywhere™

SQL Debug®

SQL Server™

SQL Server Manager™

SQL Server Monitor™

SQL Solutions®

SQR Workbench™

SQR®

STEP^SM

Support*Plus*^SM

Sybase®

Sybase Development Framework™

Sybase Gateways™

Sybase Intermedia™

Sybase Interplay™

Sybase IQ™

SYBASE® (logo)

Sybase MPP™

Sybase OpenLine (no TM symbol)

Sybase Virtual Server Architecture™

SybaseWare™

SyBooks™

System 10™

System 11™

System XI™ (logo)

Tabular Data Stream™

Transact-SQL®

Warehouse WORKS™

Watcom™

Watcom™ SQL

Watcom SQL Server™

XA-Library™

XA-Server™

For my sweeties,

Bob, Harry, and Ginger

Contents

Preface
Why *Sybase Systems Management*?,   xv
    What's an Information System?,   xvi
    What's a Systems Manager?,   xvi
    How Do You Become a SQL Server Expert?,   xx
    How Is Sybase Systems Management Structured?,   xxi
    Conventions,   xxiii
    Acknowledgments,   xxv

Part 1 Sybase SQL Server,   1

Chapter 1
An External View of SQL Server Structure,   3
    Client/Server Architecture,   5
    Relational Database Management Systems,   8
    Databases,   15

Tables,   17

Rows,   20

Columns,   23

Indexes,   29

Schemas,   33

   Managing User-defined Datatypes,   33

Chapter 2

An External View of SQL Server Processing,   35

Data Protection,   35

Integrity Features,   37

Transactions,   44

Locking,   47

DBCC,   58

Backing up and Loading Databases,   60

Security,   66

The Transact-SQL Language,   73

SQL Server Utilities,   81

SQL Server Limits,   82

   Starting and Stopping SQL Server,   83
   Managing Database Objects,   83
   Backup and Recovery,   84
   Avoiding Hard-coded Limits,   84
   Managing Stored Procedures,   85
   Managing Roles,   85
   Managing Object Permissions,   85

Chapter 3

An Internal View of SQL Server Structure,   87

Terminology,   89

Device Types and Features,   90

Device Performance,   92

SQL Server Devices,   97

Configuring Disk Devices,   99

Disk Mirroring,   103

System Databases,   105

User Databases,   109
Database Objects,   111
Segments,   112
Partitions,   116
Allocation Units,   119
Extents,   120
Pages,   121
Rows,   126
   Managing the Model Database,   128
   Managing the Sybsecurity Database,   128
   Making Backups of System Databases,   129
   Disk Partition Use,   129
   Managing Space with Segments and Thresholds,   129

Chapter 4
An Internal View of SQL Server Processing,   131
SQL Server Files,   131
CPU Usage,   135
Memory Usage,   137
Network Usage,   151
Internationalization,   156
   Internationalization,   162

Chapter 5
The Sybase SQL Server System Catalogs,   163
Server Management Tables,   164
Object Management Tables,   181
Security and User Management Tables,   191
Direct Updates of System Tables,   201
Bitmapped Status Values,   203
   Managing User-defined Messages,   205

Chapter 6
SQL Server System-wide Configuration   207
Configuration Block,   209
sp_configure Command,   210

Server Management Configuration Values,   218

Object and Data Management Configuration Values,   234

Language and Localization Configuration Values,   241

Connection and Process Management Configuration Values,   242

Security Management Configuration Values,   252

Documenting a Standard Configuration,   253

Managing Server Configuration,   254

Chapter 7

Database and User Environment Configuration,   255

Database Options,   255

User Environment Configuration,   263

Managing Database Configuration,   273

Chapter 8

Performance Analysis and Tuning,   275

SQL Server Performance Factors,   278

Setting Performance Goals and Measuring Results,   281

Understanding the SQL Server Query Process,   289

Optimizing Indexes,   294

Optimizing Queries,   300

Optimizing Stored Procedures,   311

Optimizing Operating Environment,   315

Optimizing Design,   318

Minimizing Locking,   326

SQL Server Performance-related Commands,   329

Chapter 9

Enterprise Data Strategies,   335

Determining a Storage Management Strategy,   336

System Migration,   351

Data Conversion,   353

Data Replication,   354

Data Warehouses,   360

Decision Support Systems and Online Analytical Processing,   365

Distributed, Interoperable Systems,   371
The Standards Strategy,   380
Beyond Organizational Systems,   385
    Archiving Data,   387
    Managing Communication Between Servers,   387

Chapter 10
Preventing and Resolving Problems,   389
    Backup and Recovery,   389
    Improving Maintainability,   412
    Automating Logins,   418
    Managing Connections,   420
    Increasing Security,   424
    Upgrading SQL Server,   429
    Troubleshooting,   431
    SQL Server Errorlog,   436
        Notifying Users About Downtime,   440
        Reporting Errors,   440
        Disaster Recovery,   440
        Contacting Vendors,   441
        Passwords,   441
        Upgrades,   441

Part 2 Systems Management,   443

Chapter 11
Establishing System Goals,   445
    Information System,   446
    The Systems Manager's Job,   447
    System Vision,   448
    Organizational Goals,   452
    Technology-driven Goals,   463
    Personal Goals,   474
    The Right System for the Organization,   478
        Document System Goals,   483
        Information System Solutions,   483
        Organizational Structure,   484

Chapter 12
Implementing the Right Projects,   485
    Choosing What to Change,   485
    Choosing What Not to Change,   493
    Choosing When to Make Changes,   499
    Initiating Projects,   500
    Design,   515
    Validation and Verification,   526
    Implementation,   531
    Technical Support,   544
    Just Do It,   548
        Requests for Information Systems Changes,   548
        System Timing Considerations,   549
        Creating Proposals,   549
        Information System Project Standards,   549
        Consultant Arrangements,   550
        Programming Standards,   550
        Naming Conventions,   551

Chapter 13
Project Leadership,   553
    Leadership, Management, and Coordination,   553
    Selecting a Project Leader,   557
    Communication,   558
    Team Building,   560
    Motivation,   562
    Successful Meetings,   564
    Time Management,   567
    A Quick Time Management Lesson,   568
    Preventing and Recovering from Delays,   572
    Managing Expectations,   574
    Managing Resistance to Change,   575
    Communication,   576
        Notifying Users of System Changes,   578
        Recommended Communication Methods,   578
        Project Document Storage,   578

Chapter 14

Identifying the Costs, Benefits, and Functions of System Components,   579
>   Techniques of Cost/Benefit Analysis,   581
>   Evaluating Current and Future System Elements,   598
>>   *Format for Cost/Benefit Analysis,   625*
>>   *Evaluating Proposals,   626*
>>   *Hardware and Software Acquisition and Support,   626*

Appendix A

Sybase Products and Services Overview,   627
>   Server and Server Administration Products,   628
>   Tools,   634
>   Middleware,   637
>   Services,   643

Bibliography,   647
>   Favorites,   647
>   Becoming an Expert,   648
>   Sybase,   650

Index,   653

Preface

Why *Sybase Systems Management?*

Sybase publishes more manuals than you ever have time to read, including user guides, reference guides, administration guides, language reference manuals, and supplements, so why would anyone write yet another Sybase book? The answer lies in the typical Sybase professional's job description: "Fix it *now!*" And fixing "it" means finding out what "it" is. In the process of resolving problems, you first attempt to identify whether it's really SQL Server that's broken, or a hard drive, or a network node, or a user who inadvertently shared his coffee with his workstation. Ultimately, the root cause often lies in lack of user training, lack of sound design principles, or lack of proper investment in the system. Far beyond database administration, the typical job of a Sybase professional involves systems analysis, design, and management. The Sybase manuals describe technical details, but that's only half the story. Those who want their job descriptions to go beyond "technician," "administrator," and "burnout" and to go toward "professional," "management," and "fulfillment" need to learn to understand their systems from a managerial standpoint to get their organizations to invest in the right information system solutions. *Sybase Systems Management* provides both the technical and managerial insights to help you achieve professional success.

WHAT'S AN INFORMATION SYSTEM?

We do not operate software in a vacuum, yet much documentation is written as if we did. We can learn much from examining a computer component isolated in its ideal environment. However, we must also understand mission-critical software in the systems context to deploy it successfully. This book explains how to work with Sybase software as it exists in practice—as part of a real-world system with real-world problems, implemented by people who aren't always perfect. A well-designed Sybase database cannot perform as well as expected if the network is slow. Database integrity can be compromised if hard disks are not configured properly. SQL Server may not work properly with the latest release of an operating system due to changed system calls. Without proper investment in hiring and managing information systems personnel, computers can lower rather than increase organizational productivity. Finally, if the state of your data resembles the state of someone's closet, garage, or attic, no amount of CPU power, network bandwidth, or flair for politics will elevate your career past data archaeology.

Understanding Sybase software as part of an information system that consists of software, hardware, networks, people, and data will help you deliver solutions that work and stay working.

WHAT'S A SYSTEMS MANAGER?

Titles for people responsible for Sybase software vary. Depending on the size and the focus of the organization, people taking on this role could be called

- System Administrator (sa)
- Database Administrator (DBA)
- Database Owner (dbo)

- Systems Analyst
- Software Engineer
- Office Automation Specialist
- Secretary
- Student Intern
- Volunteer
- The stand-in until someone else is found
- Consultant

Regardless of the title, we can categorize the work of the typical information systems person roughly as follows:

- Answering questions about the system for users and management
- Fixing reported problems with the current system
- Changing the system to eliminate or minimize recurring problems
- Changing the system to make improvements that support business goals
- Constantly trying to find the time, money, and people to do all the above

To excel at these tasks, a person must have a blend of technical and political skills. Yet, few computer classes or books describe how or why to acquire this mix of talents. Somehow, to discuss technology and politics in the same conversation seems to dilute the theoretical purity of either topic. However, for computers to successfully solve real-world problems, we must embrace the integration of managerial expertise and deep technical understanding. For this reason, I refer to the person responsible for Sybase products as a Systems Manager. Your boss might not give you this title, and you might not think you want it, but to succeed you will be responsible for knowing and managing a variety of systems details.

Consider these fictional, yet typical scenarios:

- A system administrator doesn't realize he needs to "sell" a project to management in order to get resources to implement it. It's obvious to him that a particular technological approach is the way of the future, but he doesn't understand why its not obvious to his bosses. Meanwhile, the company's competition learns about the new development, bases a new product on it, and radically increases its market share.

■ A manager is frustrated with a software engineer who doesn't know how to manage his own time. She doesn't trust his proposed solution to a problem. She would prefer to have him work on a quick fix because he never sees a long-term fix through to its conclusion. The short-term fix causes new problems that set the whole project back 6 months.

■ A hardware technician replaces a disk without regard to the fact that it's the end of the quarter. He knows that whatever he's supposed to do, someone always wants it done yesterday, so it doesn't occur to him to check if it's a good time for the change. Because he's in a hurry (as usual), he fails to take necessary precautions and work is lost. The resulting delay causes 2 weeks of order processing to be deferred into the following quarter. Consequently, management's revenue projections are off by 15%.

A fundamental problem in these scenarios is not knowing what you don't know. It never occurs to the system administrator that management has an agenda he is unaware of, such as conserving cash so that another company can be acquired. The manager and the engineer in the second example are thoroughly frustrated with each other because each thinks the other has serious shortcomings to address. So focused on each others' failings, both are blind to their own. In the last example, the technician has been under so much pressure for so long that he is blind to the concept of different priority levels, and he doesn't really care any more. In each case, if someone had realized his or her own blind spot or someone else had pointed it out, disaster could have been averted.

Most experienced drivers know that a car has a blind spot, and when changing lanes, they check it. In contrast, the pace and complexity of today's computer technology have generated many constantly shifting blind spots. Very few people know where to find all of them, and even fewer are experienced enough to check for them when under pressure. These blind spots make the implementation of information systems risky. If I were an executive trying to hire a manager for my mission-critical information systems, I would try to minimize my risk by looking for someone to fit this profile:

■ Expertise with specific technology used by the organization

■ Commitment to staying current about technical issues that may affect future decisions about the information system

- Excellent research skills
- Experience with coordination, management, and leadership
- Effective working with everyone, from customers to executives
- Excellent diplomatic skills
- Effective at all forms of communication
- Ability to perform well under pressure
- Comfortable with change
- Highly self-disciplined
- Highly self-motivated
- Ability to identify, confront, and solve managerial and technical problems
- Ability to maintain objectivity when evaluating alternatives
- Manages time effectively
- Approaches work with integrity
- Finds creative solutions to problems
- Maintains appropriate long-term perspective
- Commitment to producing results on time and on budget
- Ability to learn new concepts quickly

So where would I find such a person? He may be working for another company for far more money than I expected to pay him. Or she may be running her own business. Most people don't graduate from Computer Science or MBA programs with this mix of skills. Reading a wide variety of books from the computer and management sections of the book store might give one a good start. However, it usually takes hard-won experience with solving daily problems to turn a computer enthusiast into a seasoned systems professional.

When a systems technology, such as Sybase database software, quickly gains broad market acceptance, the limited supply of seasoned professionals becomes a problem and demand rises for books and training. That realization motivated me to write this book. During my 12-year computer career, I have served in various roles, including systems manager and analyst, programmer, manager, consultant, teacher, writer, sales coordinator, office automation specialist, technical support engineer, and webmaster. I have observed systems successes and failures from many angles. In one of my roles at Sybase, I helped hundreds of customers recover from database disasters in the middle of the night. Consistently, I have seen failures within a systems manager's control having one of two common themes:

1. Technical failure to regard a software component as part of a system

2. Communication failure between engineers and management, resulting in a technology implementation that solved the wrong problems

This book addresses Sybase SQL Server from a perspective that will help avert these failures. Of course, one book cannot turn a novice into a guru. However, to become an expert, the first thing to learn is where the blind spots are—as quickly as possible. Toward that end, each chapter of this book introduces you to the broad scope of things to think about in relation to the topic. To give you the systems perspective, managerial and technical explanations are interwoven. While Sybase technical information not available elsewhere is presented in depth, most managerial information is summarized. It is assumed that you mostly need to know how to persuade your organization's managers to do what you want. You can find more thorough treatments of management issues in other texts if you are interested in becoming a full-fledged manager. Flip to the bibliography at the end of the book for suggestions on further reading.

If you are a working systems manager, you will not have time to master all the suggested tasks in each chapter. Instead, reading the chapter will give you a foundation for taking action. The material will help you set clear priorities and make informed decisions. If someone asks you why something wasn't done, you should be able to answer that you evaluated the options and chose another route, rather than stammering, "Well, I don't know. I didn't think of that."

■ HOW DO YOU BECOME A SQL SERVER EXPERT?

You can learn a lot about SQL Server functionality by reading the product documentation. However, to anticipate how reconfiguring your SQL Server will affect performance or to troubleshoot a mysterious problem, you will need to understand the role of Sybase software in your information system. By learning how Sybase interacts with hard disks, memory, networks, and CPUs, you will be able to guess "what the software is thinking" with reasonable accuracy. *Sybase Systems Management* is designed to help. If you read it straight through, you should know enough about Sybase so that you can think through most problems and proposed changes without relying on a consultant or calling technical support.

The discussion includes examples for Sybase SQL Server running on UNIX primarily, but alternative syntax for OpenVMS and Microsoft Windows is also given. Note that this book does not attempt to cover Microsoft SQL Server. While Sybase and Microsoft jointly developed SQL Server up to version 4.2, the two branches of the product have diverged significantly since then. Some of the information given here may apply to Microsoft SQL Server, but don't rely on that. This book spends a lot of time talking about the internals of the Sybase Server, and Microsoft has rewritten a lot of the internals of Microsoft SQL Server to customize it for the Microsoft Windows environment.

■ HOW IS SYBASE SYSTEMS MANAGEMENT STRUCTURED?

This book is for the technology professional who wants to become more knowledgeable about Sybase SQL Server. It's also written for the professional who wants to be more effective at managing a system that includes people as well as technology.

PART I - SYBASE SQL SERVER

We start by exploring Sybase SQL Server in depth for those with an insatiable appetite for details. We cover how SQL Server interacts with disks, memory, CPUs, and the network. Information about SQL Server configuration and data management will help you understand the results of changes you make. Chapters on performance tuning and troubleshooting help you understand when SQL Server isn't working right for you.

PART II - SYSTEMS MANAGEMENT

In this part, *Sybase Systems Management* describes how to get the big picture of an information system. This includes understanding which business problems it is expected to solve, managing the process of making changes, learning which components make up the total system, and learning how much it costs and which benefits it generates for the organization.

REFERENCE INFORMATION

Appendix A contains an overview of Sybase products other tha SQL Server. After that, you'll find an annotated bibliography describing some of my favorite books and an index.

FOUNDATION FOR SYSTEMS DOCUMENTATION

Each chapter of this book is written to assist you in documenting your database system, from vision to implementation. Throughout the text, I advocate the creation of several documents:

- A vision document that describes the purpose and motivations behind the way the information system is set up, overall investment justifications, and the goals for the future. Chapter 11 describes the use of such a document.

- A procedures manual that describes how day-to-day information system operations are to be handled for maximum reliability, performance, usability, efficiency, and for the lowest cost. To make the creation of a procedures manual easier, suggestions are listed at the end of each chapter where we discuss related topics.

- An inventory of your system, which may be in the form of a database, document, or spreadsheet. Chapter 14 helps you determine the relevant elements of a systems inventory.

- Project Proposal documents that describe individual projects that proponents wish to have implemented. See Chapter 12 for a general discussion of information system projects and goals, and Chapter 13 for more information about project leadership.

- An overall cost/benefit analysis for the system that shows what proportion of the overall IS budget is going where and what trends are expected. In Chapter 14 you will find explanations of various forms of cost/benefit analyses.

It may seem inconceivable that you would take the time to create such documents. Some day, when you want to sleep through the night, take a vacation, or leave your present employer on good terms, you will understand.

■ CONVENTIONS

I have used a few conventions to make things less verbose and more readable.

I often refer to the person executing a particular command or managing a particular database as *you*, even though you may not manage all databases at your site or have occasion to issue particular commands. Perhaps if you aren't the *you* to whom I refer, it will at least help you to understand the viewpoint of someone who may report to you or rely on your services.

To illustrate some concepts, this book includes brief descriptions of some commands and Sybase-supplied stored procedures. This book does not replace the Sybase documentation, which should be consulted for full explanations of syntax and functional limitations. Instead of repeating readily available reference information, this book describes the motivations for SQL Server behavior so you can figure things out for yourself.

Examples of SQL and operating system commands appear in many chapters. If you type in the examples and see the results yourself, and perhaps do further experimentation, you will learn far more than if you simply read the chapter. Many of the examples will help you discover the specifics of how your databases are configured. It is assumed that you have a running SQL Server somewhere and that you know the basics of how to access it. It is also hoped that you have sa privileges on an experimentation Server. Except where otherwise specified, the examples of SQL commands in this book are shown as if they were being run with the Sybase ISQL utility. You can run these commands with any SQL utility of your choice. The examples were tested with the first production release of SQL Server 11.0 using ISQL. There is a possibility that something got changed between the final version of the software and the final print of this book, but I did my best to avoid that.

To help you understand what you are reading quickly, the following typographical conventions are used.

Examples of commands you can enter are in this font:

```
> select @@version
```

Descriptive words used to show arguments that you need to supply are shown in italics:

```
> sp_help table_name
```

A ">" introduces SQL commands. Icons that you click on are followed by a colon (:). Commands separated by arrows designate commands selected from a menu.

SQL Server commands and keywords buried in a paragraph, such as DBCC, appear in a fixed pitched font. If it's a SQL Server command, it's in all capital letters. Procedures like sp_help are shown in lowercase letters. Variables that you can supply, column names or other identifiers, such as *filename*, are shown in italics. Where quotes are shown, they must be typed in for the command to be correct. Note that Transact-SQL also needs quotes around character strings that contain nonalphabetic characters, such as spaces or periods. It is assumed that you'll know when to supply quotes in these cases.

Icons in the margins draw attention to features added in Sybase SQL Server versions 10.1 and 11.0, as shown in the following two paragraphs.

Version 10.1 was only released directly to VARs because it implemented features that would simulate row-level locking. This improved how some third-party applications worked because they relied on being able to work with one row at a time without incurring concurrency problems.

Sybase's SQL Server 11.0 brings you unprecedented performance and scalability. It also gives you far more flexibility to configure the Server to match your environment and to design queries that match your applications. SQL Server 11.0 includes all of the 10.1 features. At the time of this writing, System 11 has just been released. I expect it to be quite popular since it adds many features that will make the work of many Systems Managers easier.

I attempt to avoid what can be construed as gender-specific vocabulary. Where singular pronouns make the material more readable, I sometimes use the feminine and sometimes the masculine.

Since all kinds of organizations use Sybase software, the information in this book is intended to be relevant in a business environment, nonprofit organization, or government-supported agency. Where terminology like "business" or "organization" is used, you can infer that the information can be applied to any type of enterprise.

There are a few abbreviations I use that will be familiar to most people who have worked with Sybase on a UNIX environment:

- **$SYBASE** all in caps refers to the directory location of the Sybase software.

- **$DSQUERY or SERVERNAME** all in caps refers to the name of a SQL Server that we are discussing.

- **RUNSERVER** all in caps refers to the command file/script that is run to start a SQL Server that we are discussing. By default it is named *RUNSERVER*, but many people customize it and rename it in the process.

Since *indexes* and *indices* are both acceptable as the plural of *indexes*, I have used the former convention, which is also used by Sybase.

The word *server* has several meanings. To distinguish SQL Server from a server machine, I use *Server* capitalized as an abbreviation for Sybase SQL Server. I qualify other uses of *server* appropriately, using phrases like *server machine* or *HTTP server*.

ACKNOWLEDGMENTS

Many people in my life have contributed to the book you now hold. It would take 700 pages just to explain my respect and gratitude to each of them. So, I shall summarize and hope that autographed napkins or something will allow the unnamed to realize that they too are valued contributors in my life.

First, the book you now hold was made much clearer, more accurate, and more informative in key areas by these fine people who reviewed the manuscript:

- Benjamin von Ullrich, a friend, coworker, confidant, and a guru of things no sane person should know and remember. Ben has spent more hours between 1:00 p.m. and 5:00 a.m. wrestling with SQL Server bits than anyone I know. In addition to always striving to do "the right thing" technically, Ben stands up for the needs of his customers 24 hours a day.

- Robert Garvey, a former Level 3 member, a Sybase employee before there was a Sybase, also a friend, coworker, confidant, and SQL Server guru, especially of technology documented in vain, such as HAVING, segments, floats, and X-Windows variables. Robert wrote the first SQL Server internals manual, coveted by many, which became the foundation for the Sybase Advanced System Administration class.

- Michael Jordan (the world-famous Structural Engineer, not the world-famous basketball star) mentored me throughout my 7 years working at Liftech Consultants, Jordan Woodman Dobson, and related enterprises. If it weren't for Mike, I wouldn't know what quality should be—something you build into the foundation and soul of your company from desk drawers to lunchrooms, from filing systems to software, from swimming pools to container cranes, from employees, to customers, to grandchildren. If it weren't for Mike Jordan, those container cranes that look like horses wouldn't exist. And, well, if they did, they sure wouldn't be the example of world-class, reliable, Real Engineering that shows the world the promise that software should live up to.

- The staff at Prentice Hall, including my editor and morale booster at Prentice Hall, Mark Taub and his very capable assistant Dori Steinhauff. Mark and Dori very efficiently gave me what I needed when I needed it, such as telling me I was doing a good job and to keep working. Joanne Anzalone did a great job managing the book through production, making sure the copyedits got in and taking care of my last-minute worries.

- The anonymous but efficient and knowledgeable editors who found my writing errors, among other things. Their carefully constructed author's guide and templates answered my questions before they came up and then, again, after I had ignored their advice at my own peril and needed to fix things.

If you run into any of these extremely bright, experienced, and wonderful people, you should shower them with money, feed them, or provide them with a social life, as you see fit.

I also acknowledge all of my family, close friends, and my extended family, for encouraging and supporting all of my pursuits. I especially acknowledge my mother for instilling in me a creative spirit. Also, my Aunt Winnie, cousin Stephanie, and late Uncle Verne serve as great models of stability in my life and consistently encourage my intellectual development. For this I am truly grateful.

I am also especially grateful to my writing teachers—friends and mentors all: Puinani Harvey, Kathleen Aldrich, Jeannie Ten Eyck, Gretchen Griswold, Barbara Stebbins, Stanley Cardinet, Michael Goldberg, and Sara McAulay. Many of these teachers are from Magic Mountain Junior High School and Maybeck High School, where all the other teachers and students also created the character behind my words and experience. You can find Sara at California State University Hayward, where she gives you education like it should be.

Without the sound business mentoring and extreme patience with my various youthful extremes from Paul and Bob Stanley of Stanley Enterprises and Michael Jordan of Liftech Consultants, I'd probably still be an underemployed basket case somewhere. I also received guidance from about 50 other coworkers from these companies, and remember them fondly and respectfully.

Then there's Sybase, where, among 6000 people, at least 1000 know me as webmaster, technical support engineer, AnswerBase implementor, and/or general troublemaker. I can't begin to list the people who taught me and who listened to my endless rants about *how things should be done*. In particular, I appreciate Bob Epstein for listening and responding, Mark Hoffman for reading all my fyimarks and making many of the changes suggested, and the many managers that supported me as I hurricaned my way through 3 years of Sybase Life. I am indebted to the members of the defunct Level 3 who got me off to a good start and who were clearly *too good to be true*: Bennet Falk, Robert Garvey, Kathy Saunders, David Eastwood, and Rosemary Allen.

Special thanks to Sandy Emerson, Eric Keibler, Adrian Blakey, Robert Stanley, and the folks in Sybase legal department for helping with this book deal, along with general appreciation for your moral support of my various projects during my time at Sybase.

Then there's my friend, technical mentor, and feeder of humorous bits, David Gould. David not only listened to me rant and rave, he convinced me that I was completely wrong about some of what I was ranting about and illuminated those topics about which I should rant but didn't. He helped me to understand the inexplicable about SQL Server and C and UNIX and our industry and society. Thanks for all the direction.

Finally, my most heartfelt *everything_positive* goes to Bob Ehrlich, my partner, friend, and most staunch supporter during this project, where *everything_positive* includes love, gratitude, respect, and back rubs. Thanks for feeding me, cleaning the house, allowing me to ignore you, listening to me give more detailed status reports than actually requested, not asking me too often if it was Done Yet, and helping me enjoy Hawaii. Harry and Ginger also thank Bob for defleaing, feeding, and playing with them while Mommy was busy.

■ CONTACTING THE AUTHOR

Comments? Questions? Visit **http://www.hogoboom.com**!

SYBASE SQL SERVER

C H A P T E R

1

An External View of SQL Server Structure

SYBASE users perceive databases as several tables, or perhaps as forms and reports. The machines, network, and software that make up the system "see" databases in an entirely different way— as blocks on disk or as electronic signals. SQL Server provides the necessary level of abstraction. Users can manipulate records and fields using the SQL language (or an application) instead of manipulating ones and zeros using electrical current. Today's software can provide enough abstraction to make data understandable, but not enough necessarily to make them meaningful.

We still need humans to step in and do things like supply business rules. We also need people to help to maintain the interface between the users and the hardware—this is where Systems Managers come in. As managers and engineers of data and databases, we are responsible for manipulating the internal arrangement of data so that users can have a simple external view.

The study and application of artificial intelligence may eventually deliver us database systems that do not require as much

3

administration as they do now. They may even assist us by recognizing patterns in our past queries and helping us to arrange our data into more easily accessible sets. However, the ability to predict and shape the future meaning of data will probably remain in the minds of humans, rather than in the electronics of machines.

Today, at least, SQL Server needs help understanding what you find meaningful and what your priorities are. Without your control, it doesn't know whether to optimize on speed, capacity, integrity, or economy. Without you to indicate primary and foreign keys, it can't tell a primary data set from a secondary set. It only knows that three SQL statements are one atomic transaction when a user says they are. SQL Server has increased in complexity, rather than decreased, because SQL Server designers have discovered that the larger the customer base gets, the less possible it is to select preset values that give everyone exactly what they need.

This book, in general, focuses on helping you, as a Systems Manager, to help SQL Server translate between the internal and external view of your data. This chapter gives an external view of SQL Server database structures with that goal in mind. In Chapter 2, we cover the functionality that lets users access meaningful data. Chapters 3 and 4 give you a bottom-up or internal view of these topics. There, we explore how machine-level factors can protect and enhance the value of our data.

As mentioned in the Preface, we will touch on issues related to day to day SQL Server operations, but we will not go into the details. Many thorough texts on database administration already cover these topics. Instead, we focus on *why* rather than *how* SQL Server does its tasks. A lack of understanding about the *why* part results in problems that you must then learn how to correct. Attempting to correct a problem without knowing why it happened results in a black art approach to information systems, which means spending a lot of dark hours at work.

Sybase built its success on the SQL Server RDBMS and the client/server architecture, and so we describe SQL Server in terms of client/server and relational theory in this chapter. Sybase, however, restricts its products to no particular data management philosophy. The company has adopted a strategy of making possible the interconnection of any type of data to any type of user, and its products can access data on all the common data systems that enterprises use. Sybase software can manage data embedded in everything from flat files, to hierarchical databases, to multimedia object stores.

To illustrate concepts throughout this book, we will draw examples from a hypothetical retail store chain called Sandy's Sport Shops. Although most of you work for much larger companies with more intricate management structures, these examples will highlight important considerations.

SANDY'S SPORT SHOP—INTRODUCTION

Sandy's Sport Shops is a chain of four sporting goods stores located in California at popular vacation towns along the coast. Timothy, a Computer Science major at a nearby state college, started working part-time at Sandy's main store during his sophomore year. Tim has concentrated on studying database systems at school. He uses a SQL Server database to store information that he has convinced himself he needs to excel at school. At Sandy's Sport Shops, he soon started playing with the stand-alone PC that Sandy used in the back office to keep track of her company's profits. At first, he set up a menu system so she could get into her favorite applications quickly, then he set up word-processing templates to create flyers and a mailing list. Sandy was impressed at how quickly he completed computer tasks that she never got around to. Tim has assigned himself the task of convincing Sandy that she can't possibly run her business well without installing a computer network for all the stores and setting up what he calls a *Real RDBMS* to keep track of store data. At least once a week he sets up a sample application at school and then brings it in to show Sandy how useful it is. She usually shakes her head and says that *Real Business People* don't need computers to make a profit.

■ CLIENT/SERVER ARCHITECTURE

If we were to approach an information system slowly from far away, as from a spaceship approaching Earth, we would first see its topology. We might see concentrations of resources in big cities like Mexico City, Tokyo, Sao Paulo, New York, and Shanghai. As we came closer, we would see lines of communication between these dense information areas. The nearer we got, the more detail we could see in terms of offices, machines, and disk drives. If we had an instrument that would let us see the movement of data, we would see how the data rush between offices, where they bunch up and where the communication lines see little load at all.

Very likely, the density of data corresponds to the source of revenue for an organization, and the flow of data represents the way goods and services are supplied in exchange for revenue. Our data movement monitoring tool would show us how closely the information systems match the flow of business.

Early information systems concentrated the processing power and data capacity in large, expensive machines. The information system may have been placed in the office closest to where most orders were generated. If the revenue center moved or expanded, the processing center often stayed behind. If there was a significant advantage to a particular location, such as lenient tax laws, a good labor supply, cheap land, or proximity to good transportation routes, the central office went there, and data had to be moved there for processing. In this case, the information system did not match the "business topology" and probably encountered stress along the most commonly used information flow routes.

The advent of personal computers in the 1980s eventually led to the concept of a client/server architecture. In 1987, Sybase delivered the first client/server relational database system. In a client/server environment, the application originating the database query can reside on a different machine than the database server. As long as a client can communicate via a network to a server, it can issue queries and retrieve results without regard to location. Someone in Tokyo can issue a query against a database in Los Angeles to see if a certain movie can be sent to a customer in Sao Paulo. The Shanghai office can find out if there's a good supply of cheap mangoes to be purchased through the Mexico City office that they can have shipped to New York.

As the terms client/server are used to describe machines, typically we envision a client as an inexpensive personal computer and a server as a machine endowed with greater processing power and capacity. For SQL Server, however, this does not have to be the case. One machine may house one or more clients and/or one or more servers. In fact, the distinction between personal computers and minicomputers has blurred recently.

The client/server architecture implemented by Sybase also offers these advantages, which businesses use or not depending on their needs:

- Clients can use the memory and CPU resources on their own machine, rather than vying with other application users and the database software on the server machine.

- Clients and server functions can be distributed among several machines to provide concurrent processing, which increases throughput and response time.

- A machine can be built and optimized specifically for a particular client or server application, rather than needing to provide generic services for all applications relying on centralized resources.

- One database can be shared by many different client systems in use by different offices or divisions within an organization.

- The Open Client/Open Server API that Sybase uses for communication between all of its own products can be built into in-house or third-party applications, providing independence from a particular application vendor, approach, and feature set.

- Disparate data sources, applications, and services can be integrated using the Sybase APIs.

- Versions 10.0 and later of SQL Server comply with ANSI/ISO SQL-89 standard and the entry-level ANSI/ISO SQL-92 criteria, which ensures SQL compatibility with other products.

The business rules and integrity logic that shape the data are independent of location. They may reside in the application or in SQL Server. Storing logic in the Server simplifies management and provides centralized control. Storing logic in local applications can provide the flexibility needed to match quickly changing local conditions or knowledge that is only relevant in a particular locale. The client/server separation of function from geography allows businesses to manipulate the information system to match the business, instead of the opposite.

Relational Database Management Systems

E. F. Codd, a mathematician and database engineer, developed the principles of the relational database model in 1969–1970. C. J. Date has invested a large part of his career in teaching and promoting relational theory to thousands of people since then. The mathematical basis of the model explains the rigor applied by some to defining how data should be represented in a database. The theory, when applied carefully, yields very graceful designs. However, the relative freedom of organizing data in a relational database management system (RDBMS) makes rigid adherence to the theory unnecessary. The ease of data manipulation with SQL means that enthusiastic developers, like our fictional friend Tim, can start setting up a database without training. This low-resistance technology can yield systems based on experience, common sense, or whim. The limitations of hardware and software also mean that resources tend to shape database design as well. Prior investments in nonrelational systems and their associated applications also drive an organization's approach to its data. These forces all contribute to the distance of a database's structure from its theoretical underpinnings. However, total abandonment of the theory generally creates unmanageable results.

A RDBMS such as Sybase SQL Server stores sets of data in tables, organized into rows and columns.[1] (See Table 1-1.) The table stores data of a common format in rows. The columns separate the rows into discrete pieces of information that we can either manipulate as part of a set or individually. Each row typically represents a particular entity, and each column represents a particular aspect of that entity.

---

[1] A table is also called a *relation*. Other terminology for rows is records, n-tuples, or tuples. Columns may also be called *fields* or *attributes*. Like most synonyms in a language, each term has a slightly different shade of meaning. In this book, where we discuss actual practice that sometimes obscures theory, we will use the common terms *row* and *column*.

TABLE 1-1 *An Example of a Table*

Column Heading 1	Column Heading 2	Column Heading 3
I'm	a	row
a		
column		

A row in a table may or may not completely describe an entity. Sometimes a combination of tables describes an entity. Also, one piece of information in one table may serve several roles, just as a person may serve in many capacities. In these common cases, the relationship between tables becomes part of the information value stored in the RDBMS.

Relational operators can access table data at a basic level using one of three operations:

- **Restrict** (Select)   Extract specified rows from a table

- **Project**   Extract specified columns

- **Join**   Merge data vertically from two or more tables on the basis of common values in one or more columns

The result of each of these three operations is another table; this is the property of closure. The output of any operation is the same kind of object as the input. Therefore, the output from one operation can be input to another. With these commands, we operate on data a set at a time, rather than a record at a time. This set processing capability gives relational systems a major distinction among data management systems. We can understand most of the data structure characteristics in a relational system within that context.

The smallest semantic unit of data is a scalar value. These atomic values are logically nondecomposable; if they were decomposed, they would lose their meaning. For example, while 999-88-7777 may be Tim's social security number, the number 999 has no independent meaning as far as Tim's identity goes. At each intersection of a row and a column of a table, we should find one scalar value. In other words, there are no repeating groups. If Tim's *class_requirements* table, instead of having separate columns for *interest*, *relevance*, and *difficulty*, had a *class_quality* column, he might have to resort to adding an entry like "interesting, irrelevant." Such an entry is a repeating group and is discouraged. In such a scheme, you would have to go to greater effort to select values that were interesting and relevant.

Other data storage and management methods include files and hierarchical databases. These preceded the relational model in history and tend to precede it in the implementation of a particular system in an organization as well. The hierarchical system uses a tree structure to completely describe an entity. A file imposes little or no organization on the data at all. The less structure the storage mechanism imposes, the less intrinsic information value it delivers to the user.

A simple ASCII file may contain a to do list in "human format"— that is, organized as the intended reader (usually only one) needs to understand it, such as by priority. An email file has certain headings that identify it to the various mail systems so that the message can be delivered from sender to recipient. A data file might contain fields delimited by commas, tabs, or colons. By adding a consistent structure, more systems can manipulate the data to serve the needs of different users and different applications.

As a Systems Manager, you probably understand at least one reason why the computing world graduated from flat files to database files. A missing comma or a human who doesn't think like everyone else can quickly introduce chaos into an otherwise well-structured file. File systems also don't work well as enterprise data systems because they provide little to fulfill the typical database controls. Combined with the right processing, structured files can offer record-level control. Databases, however, rely on transactional control for integrity purposes and on various forms of object-level control for security.

The hierarchical method imposes a tree structure on data. A tree typically represents an entity or a class of entity. The highest nodes in the tree store more general information about the object. As we move down the tree, we find more specific details. The tree structure implies a particular interpretation of data. Certain queries are easy because the data are already in a desired order. However, the order enforced on the data does not always serve the needs of the user. The overhead of hierarchical systems lies in the effort required to merge new or unusual data into an existing hierarchy or to rearrange hierarchies when reporting needs or the relevance of data attributes change.

Examples of hierarchical and relational storage methods will clarify the design implications of each of these methods.

SANDY'S SPORT SHOPS—DATA STORAGE METHODS

Tim used two different methods to store information about graduate classes he could take if he decided to continue his education. He wasn't exactly sure that a graduate degree would be worth the work, so he spent a lot of time analyzing the possibility—time Sandy thought he should just use studying for the GRE.

Here are Tim's files, stored in hierarchical order in a UNIX file system before he started keeping his data in a database. He used the class number as a file name since he knew he'd want to find classes by number most often. Directories and files are shown first, to the left. Files' contents are indented showing the class name and the class professor on separate lines.

GradClasses
ReqForDegree
200
     "Meta-Abstraction of Information Systems"
     "Om"
291
     "Bit-level Comprehension Mechanisms"
     "Oh"
For_Advisor
273
     "Debugging Advanced Computer Systems"
     "Du Cafe"
255
     "Passion and Loathing in Graduate Research"
     "Yessir"

Interesting
  Relevant
    248
      `"A Discrete Approach to Design by Subtraction"`
      `"Thwir"`
    292
      `"Combinatorial Algorithms for Advanced Pizza Building"`
      `"Parcheezie"`
  Irrelevant
    902
      `"Seminar in Using AI for Cat Feeder Robots"`
      `"Koko"`
PhD_Prerequisites
  Easy
    274
      `"Randomness and Parallel Computation"`
      `"Raceme"`
  Impossible
    300
      `"Concrete Complexity in Arbitrary Symbol Manipulation"`
      `"Poolscrim"`

To get information about a certain type of class, Tim might issue the command:

```
% cat GradClasses/Interesting/Irrelevant/*
```

Table 1-2 illustrates how Tim put part of his information in a relational database table.

TABLE 1-2   *Tim's class_names Table*

class_id	class_name	class_prof
200	Meta-Abstraction of Information Systems	Om
291	Bit-level Comprehension Mechanisms	Oh
273	Debugging Advanced Computer Systems	Du Cafe
255	Passion and Loathing in Graduate Research	Yessir
248	A Discrete Approach to Design by Sub-traction	Thwir

TABLE 1-2   *Tim's class_names Table (Continued)*

class_id	class_name	class_prof
292	Combinatorial Algorithms for Advanced Pizza Building	Parcheezie
902	Seminar in Using AI for Cat Feeder Robots	Koko
274	Randomness and Parallel Computation	Raceme
300	Concrete Complexity in Arbitrary Symbol Manipulation	Poolscrim

Another table, *class_requirements*, contained columns associating each class_id with information about the class, such as requirement met, interest level, and difficulty.

With his relational system, Tim can issue this query:

```
> SELECT *
> from class_names, class_requirements
> where class_names.class_id =
> class_requirements.class_id and
> class_requirements.class_id >= 200 and
> interest = "high" and relevance = "low"
> order by difficulty
> go
```

The structure of the storage mechanism shaped how Tim stored the data. Tim constructed the tree in the first example based on what the data looked like at the time he wanted to store them. Back then, he was only concerned with the relative difficulty of the Ph.D. prerequisites because he wasn't sure that he'd want to go to school that much longer if it was going to be too hard. When he constructed the table representation, he realized it might be useful to add interest, relevance, and difficulty ratings to all classes, not just those in particular branches of the tree.

The relational model allows more flexibility in data storage and introduces complexity in data retrieval. A hierarchical method makes storage complex and data retrieval either easy or complex depending on the type of query. Relational databases require a certain amount of data duplication to maintain key columns, and hierarchical databases generate inefficiencies in the need to traverse deep trees. With tables, those who query the database infer data relationships based on common key elements, such as *class_name*. In contrast, a tree structure implies a particular relationship, and drawing conclusions about other relationships requires significantly more work.

To bring this home, think about whether you would rather access your files in the traditional operating system format—by directory trees—or in that of emerging models where you just select it by attribute, and the particular order of its storage is irrelevant.[2]

Although the industry considers hierarchical database systems dated, we cannot say relational is better in general without looking at the application. Just as technology swings between extremes of centralized control and distributed, organizational methods swing between rigid and flexible. Rather than a persuasive argument, a new vector for the pendulum may make the debate irrelevant. For example, if we could just talk to the computer via a microphone, saying "Please tell me the highest priority item on my to do list," we would stop caring how the data were stored internally. That's because our real concern is "How can I get the data I want," not our ability to micromanage our data. As discussed in Chapter 2, the real answers to intractable problems often come when you take a step back and think about what really provides value.

That said, the perfect data future has not yet arrived, and we must take a hand in helping our computers understand how to "give us the data we really want now." In pursuit of a deeper appreciation for the details of the ultimate solution, we will turn to learning about all the visible and less visible ways that the Sybase SQL Server RDBMS manages your data.

---

[2]WWW, Oberon.

■ DATABASES

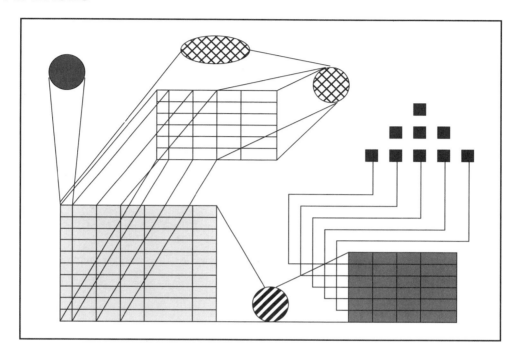

Figure 1.1 Typical database contents: base tables, derived tables, system tables, indexes, and procedural objects.

Databases and SQL Servers exist for the purpose of managing user data. Organizational needs drive the database design depending on the amount and type of activity that the database must support. In this chapter, we will see that the "atomicity" of data values and transactions determine their limits naturally. In contrast, practical rather than theoretical motives tend to set the boundaries of a database.

In theory, a SQL Server database can be anywhere from 2 MB to 256 gigabytes (GB). In practice, we usually see databases from 2 MB to 10 GB. While the nature of the data may indicate a particular database size, administrative concerns usually cap the upper limits. Since transactions may span databases, administrators and designers often split one database into several to simplify backup or minimize downtime.

Databases used for decision support systems (DSS) are typically configured to be *read only* and are periodically updated via mass transfer from an active database. During that mass transfer, the DSS database is unavailable, which might lead the administrators to segment data into separate databases. For online transaction processing, databases may be updated heavily 24 hours a day. In this case, designers and administrators may configure the database in the way that delivers maximum performance and throughput. The primary activity in a database may be to track inventory or to archive the results of research efforts. Each of these leads to different criteria for selecting the size and speed of disk devices and the type of backups to perform, which then influences the database configuration.

Any databases that developers, users, or administrators create with the CREATE DATABASE statement are called user databases. Before you create these, however, the SQL Server installation program creates several system databases used to support SQL Server operations. These are

- **master**   maintains information about SQL Server as a whole
- **model**   used as a template when creating new databases
- **tempdb**   used as scratch space for queries
- **sybsystemprocs**   stores system stored procedures
- **sybsecurity**   stores auditing information (optional)

Chapter 2 gives details about the purpose and operation of each.

In SQL Server, tables designated as *system tables* serve as the data dictionary. The terms *system catalogs* or *data directory* also refer to the function of these tables. Certain system tables describe the content of a database, and each SQL Server database has a set of these tables. The definitions of each of these tables are the same in every database, but the content differs depending on the local objects. Other system tables describe the SQL Server as a whole and reside only in the master database. Chapter 5 is devoted to describing the content and purpose of these tables.

■ Tᴀʙʟᴇs

At their simplest, tables consist of columns and rows of data. A particular data domain defines the valid values for a column. A database designer may or may not explicitly bind the domain restriction to the column, using procedural objects described later, such as constraints or rules. In the absence of explicit domains, users try to determine the domain by looking at the name and datatype of the column. There are several built-in datatypes, and users may create their own.

In mathematics, the term *relation* refers to a table, which gave rise to the description *relational model*. In the model, relations have these properties, to which real-world databases don't always conform:

■ **Uniqueness**   There are no duplicate tuples (rows). This means that no two rows in a table should contain exactly the same values.

■ **Unordered tuples**   Tuples (rows) are unordered from top to bottom. While tables may have a key column based on a sequential number, such a construct is not necessary for the database management system to work.

■ **Unordered attributes**   Attributes (columns) are unordered from left to right. To query a table or add data, the user doesn't need to know the order of the columns, and rearranging the columns should not affect queries.

■ **Atomicity**   All attribute values are atomic. At every row and column position there is always exactly one value, that is, no repeating groups. A relation satisfying this condition is said to be normalized, or in the first normal form.

A consequence of the uniqueness and atomicity properties is that a table always has a primary key. A key is one or more columns that have values that uniquely identify a particular row. In some cases, such a key may consist of all the columns, but usually database designers construct one- or two-column keys. A key makes each row addressable by the user or by a program.

So far, we have described tables at a conceptual level. Different physical types of tables exist in a SQL Server database. The next few sections highlight the distinctions between these types.

BASE TABLES

Tables that store actual data on disk and persist in relatively permanent form are called base tables. Users create them using the CREATE TABLE command, alter them using the ALTER TABLE command, and drop them using the DROP TABLE command. The SELECT INTO command can be used to create a base table from another table. The new table is sometimes called a *snapshot table*.

Every database contains two types of base tables—user tables and system tables.

■ **User tables**   User tables store the data for which the organization needed a database. SQL commands, stored procedures, and applications written using the Open Client API can view and update them. The permissions set by the owner of the table control the ability of users to view, update, and drop user tables.

■ **System tables**   As described earlier, system tables govern the management of the database. The SQL Server installation programs create these tables, and the CREATE DATABASE command adds them to new databases. Users and administrators may query system tables if curious, but the usual manipulation of data does not require users to know about them. Users may not update system tables directly unless the someone having sso_role enabled turned on the allow updates option with sp_configure. Then, by default, only the database owner may update system tables. The only reason someone would need to update system tables would be in an effort to resolve a problem that would otherwise require restoration of a database from backups.

VIEWS (NAMED, DERIVED VIRTUAL TABLES)

The output of relational operations is the same as the input, which is another table. The typical effect of such an operation is called a derived table, which exists at least in memory for the duration of an operation. Using the SELECT INTO command, the derived table can be made into another base table. Using the CRE-ATE VIEW command, the operations that generated the table output can be stored in procedural form and given a regular table name. Subsequent references to that table name cause the procedure to be executed, resulting in the recall of that derived table. A view, which looks like a single table to a user, can actually combine data from many different tables. In fact, it can contain calculated data created by functions such as `avg` or `sum`.

The data in the view change depending on the data in the base table or tables at the time the user references the view. Views can be updated as long as the update falls within the limits on the underlying tables. For example, if a view contains a column derived from a `sum` statement, attempts to update that column will fail since there is no corresponding base table column. Depending on the design of the base tables, users may find that update operations have unexpected results when SQL Server updates the base data as specified. Poorly designed tables or particularly complex view definitions can generate this sort of confusion.

WORK TABLES

SQL Server creates work tables when processing complex queries. For example, the use of `GROUP BY` makes a work table necessary. In these cases, SQL Server creates a work table in the system database `tempdb`. Users cannot access these work tables.

TEMPORARY TABLES

Users can create private scratch tables, called temporary tables in `tempdb` as well. When a user uses a pound sign (#) to prefix a table name in the `CREATE TABLE` or `SELECT INTO` statement, SQL Server automatically creates the table in `tempdb`. For example,

```
> create table #schedule (
> class_id integer not null,
> class_times varchar(30) null)
```

SQL Server modifies the table name by truncating it or extending it with underscores to a 13-character name and then adds a suffix to the table that identifies it as belonging solely to a particular process. Other processes may not access these temporary tables. The tables are automatically destroyed when the process exits. You may have heard people use the phrase "pound sign temporary tables" in speaking. For future reference we will call them *process temporary tables*.

Users can also create regular, shareable temporary tables by changing to `tempdb` and issuing the regular CREATE TABLE statement with a regular table name there. Alternatively, the table can be created from the current database by qualifying the table name with the `tempdb` database name:

```
> create table tempdb..currentgrades
> (class varchar(25) not null,
> grade char(2) not null)
> go
```

Any process can access these tables at any time until SQL Server is next rebooted. SQL Server's reboot process normally includes clearing out `tempdb` entirely.

Database developers sometimes create shareable temporary tables from within stored procedures. The procedure creates tables in `tempdb` using SELECT INTO so that a second stored procedure called by the first can work with previously selected data.

■ Rows

A row in a table is a logical set of data describing some or all aspects of an entity or concept. A row consists of valid values for each column in the table. The number of rows in a table is called its cardinality. The concept of *valid* varies depending on the table definition and the design theory subscribed to. We explore these ideas in the sections about columns and integrity.

SQL Server places no limits on the number of rows possible in a table. Instead, the purpose of the data and the amount and type of space available usually determine this dimension of table size.

KEYS

In our introduction to tables, we described keys as a method for making each row addressable based on the data content of the row. Notice that this description means that a key is primarily conceptual. SQL Server does not require a separate logical method for identifying rows within a table. SQL Server does provide procedures like `sp_primarykey` to make a designer's choice of key columns explicit to users. However, this function is primarily documentary in nature. With System 10 and later releases, SQL Server provides an identity column feature, which can be used to create a column suitable for a primary key, if desired. In other words, a key isn't a particular object in a database. Rather, it is a column or set of columns with a particular designation.

When discussing tables, we noted that the existence of a primary key depended on the principles of atomicity and uniqueness. You can set up SQL Server tables that allow duplicate rows or that store repeating groups, since the system doesn't take it upon itself to force strict adherence to the relational model. All that is necessary to make a column ineligible as a primary key is to allow duplicate values or nulls in that column. It is up to the user and the database developer to ensure that a primary key is available. Table definitions and various features of SQL Server can be used to maintain primary key columns as rigorously as desired.

When there are more than one possible unique keys, those that are not designated primary are called alternate keys. All keys that could be primary or alternate are called *candidate keys*. We call keys based on one column *simple keys* and those involving more than one column *composite keys*. Although unique indexes are often built on candidate keys to enforce uniqueness, do not confuse the concept of an index (discussed later) with the concept of a key. A surrogate, contrived, or artificial key is a column with no business meaning that is added to a table in order to provide a key. It is usually designed for physical optimization purposes, such as improving performance and minimizing contention during key creation.

Foreign keys in a table contain values that are a subset of the values of a candidate key in another table. We call a foreign key value a *reference* to the row containing the matching candidate key value. Maintaining referential integrity means making sure that tables in a database don't contain foreign key values that don't exist in any corresponding primary key. A referential constraint definition on a table (described shortly) rejects any attempted updates to a foreign key column that don't match a previously defined candidate key.

IDENTITY COLUMNS

The problem of creating and maintaining a primary key, in particular, a key that consists of a sequential number identifying each row for business purposes, has occupied database designers since the implementation of the first relational databases. Concurrency control and performance problems make automatic primary key generation somewhat difficult. Sybase added an identity column feature in System 10 to help with the task. Using CREATE TABLE or ALTER TABLE, developers can designate an identity column. Once designated, the column contains a numeric value, starting by default with the number 1 for the first row. For each subsequent row added to the table, a sequential number is automatically assigned as the value to go in the identity column.

The datatype for identity columns is numeric, with a scale of 0, meaning that you can only use integers for this type of column. The sequential number is guaranteed to be unique and (unless identity updates were allowed) the value for each row is guaranteed to be greater than the identity values of the rows added before it. Gaps between identity numbers may occur due to row deletions, SQL Server shutdowns, and transaction roll backs. The primary use of the identity feature is to allow the automatic generation of sequential keys, such as for business transaction numbers.

You can also enable a database-wide auto identity option, which means that every new table created in a particular database automatically contains an identity column. An automatically generated identity column is not visible to the user unless the special identifier SYB_IDENTITY_COL is included in a table query. You can create tables in such databases with explicit identity columns using the identity specifier in the CREATE TABLE command. In this case, the explicit designation overrides the automatic behavior, and the named identity column is visible to users.

Two new options have been added to facilitate the use of isolation level 0 locking in SQL Server versions 10.1 and later. The size of auto identity column configuration variable sets the default size of the column created in a database where the auto identity database option is set to *true*. The identity in nonu-

`nique index` database option tells SQL Server to add the identity column automatically to any index not defined as unique. To use isolation level 0, a table must have a unique index. Turning on the two identity-related database options facilitates isolation level 0 without requiring manual intervention. However, you will probably gain higher performance and better space utilization if you make the effort to replace nonunique indexes with unique indexes where needed. We discuss isolation level 0 more in Chapter 2.

■ COLUMNS

We can conceptualize a column of a table as a vertical slice that contains atomic values of a particular type for each row. The number of columns in a table is called its degree. A more rigorous basis for understanding columns rests on the concept of mathematical domains.

DOMAINS

In mathematics, a domain is a set of valid values that can be used as input to a particular function. An analogy will refresh the concept for those who have been absent from mathematics for a long time. Parking meters in certain Californian cities have a domain consisting of quarters and nickels. Those are the only valid inputs to the meter. Attempts to insert pennies, dimes, or francs will fail to produce the desired result. These latter values are outside the domain.

For a relational database table, a domain for a column is a named set of scalar values all of the same type. The database designers enforce the validity of the values using constructs like database rules and constraints. For example, Sandy's Sport Shops might define a domain for *salaries* as any value from 5000 U.S. dollars to 200,000 U.S. dollars. A particularly restrictive domain for sweatshirt colors might be defined as *{white, yellow, blue, black}*.

Relational database theory specifies that each column must be defined on exactly one underlying domain. The number of underlying domains is called the degree or arity of the relation, starting with unary, binary, and ternary, and ending with *n*-ary.

DATATYPES

SQL Server provides several default datatypes and a facility to create additional named types. You can enforce the concept of domains by employing user-defined types or rules. After reviewing each default type, we will look at how to define new types. Table 1-3 lists the storage requirements for each datatype.

TABLE 1-3   *Storage Requirements for SQL Server Datatypes*

Datatype	Size (bytes)
char (n)	n
varchar (n)	length of the data entered
nchar (n)	n * @@ncharsize[a]
nvarchar (n)	entry length * @@ncharsize[b]
text	0 if NULL or, if not null, 16 bytes plus a multiple of 2 KB up to 2 GB, depending on the amount of data entered (a multiple of 4 KB on Stratus)
binary (n)	n
varbinary (n)	length of the data entered
image	0 if NULL or, if not null, 16 bytes plus a multiple of 2 KB up to 2 GB, depending on the amount of data entered (a multiple of 4 KB on Stratus)
tinyint	1
smallint	2
int	4
numeric (p, s)	2 bytes for precision of 1 or 2, 1 byte for each additional 2 digits of precision to a maximum of 17 bytes
decimal (p, s)	2 bytes for precision of 1 or 2, 1 byte for each additional 2 digits of precision to a maximum of 17 bytes

TABLE 1-3   *Storage Requirements for SQL Server Datatypes (Continued)*

Datatype	Size (bytes)
float (p)	4 for a precision less than 16 and 8 for a precision greater than or equal to 16
double precision	8
real	8
smallmoney	4
money	8
smalldatetime	4
datetime	8
bit	1 byte is used for each 8-bit column in a table. If the number of bit columns is not an even multiple of 8, the remainder uses 1 byte of storage

[a]nchar holds a fixed-length string of national characters, which may be more than 1 byte in size. Use the SQL statement "select @@ncharsize" to see the average character size for the current character set.

[b]nvarchar holds a variable-length string of national characters, which may be more than 1 byte in size. Use the SQL statement "select @@ncharsize" to see the average character size for the current character set; then estimate the average or maximum size of your expected columns.

The various `char` formats store string data. Those prefixed with "var" or "nvar" are variable length, which means that they are null-terminated. The others are fixed length, which means that they are padded with blanks or truncated to the length specified.

The `text` datatype allows you to store long, null-terminated chunks of character data. The `binary`, `varbinary`, and `image` types store raw binary data for which SQL Server has no implicit display or formatting conventions.

Use the `int` datatypes to store numbers that will not need to be represented in decimal format.

The `real`, `float`, and `double precision` types store approximate numeric data. Binary machines cannot represent all decimal numbers accurately in the numeric format used by most operating systems. The precision of decimal numbers increases as room for the number of digits to the right of the decimal point increases. Different operating systems use different representations of numbers, so the precision varies from platform to platform. For these reasons, these types of data formats, using the native operating system representations, are termed approximate. In general, the more precision desired, the longer it takes to access data stored with that precision.

The `numeric` and `decimal` datatypes store exact numeric values, specifying both precision, which is the total number of digits in the number, and scale, which is the number of those digits to the right of the decimal point. These two names for this datatype are synonymous, except that the form "numeric" with scale 0 must be used when defining identity columns. A packed format is used to store these numbers, rather than the native format provided by the operating system. This gives SQL Server consistent control of precision limits.

Values stored using the `money` datatypes are automatically displayed with two digits to the right of the decimal point and a comma after every three digits counting from the left of the decimal point.

The `datetime` datatypes store dates and times in a special internal format, which is accessed using various date conversion functions provided by SQL Server.

The `bit` datatype stores one bit of data as either a *0* or a *1*, which programs typically interpret as *false* or *true*, respectively.

You can create a user-defined type using the system stored procedure `sp_addtype`.

SANDY'S SPORT SHOPS—DATATYPES

While going to college, Tim stored essential information that he learned about professors firsthand or from classmates in a table called *profs*. He rated each professor in a number of quality categories with a value defined from 1 to 10, where 1 indicated a low value for that quality and 10 a high presence of the quality. Since there were several categories, such as friendliness, easiness, and weirdness, he created the following datatype:

```
sp_addtype "rating", "numeric(2,0)"
go
```

Then he created a table using that type as follows:

```
create table profs (
prof_name varchar(30),
prof_subj varchar(10),
yrs_teaching integer,
skill rating,
friendly rating,
easy rating,
weird rating)
go
```

DEFAULTS

You can define a default value by using the CREATE DEFAULT statement. You can then use sp_binddefault to bind that default to a table column or to a user-defined datatype. Whenever a user adds a row to a table with column defaults and does not specify a value for that column, the specified value is inserted into the row.

SANDY'S SPORT SHOPS—DEFAULTS

In his *profs* table, Tim typically did not know the value to fill in for the number of years teaching until he did some research. In fact, he didn't bother to do the research unless he had an imminent opportunity to take a class from a particular professor. He decided to use a value of -1 to indicate an unknown value. He used the following commands to formalize the default.

```
CREATE DEFAULT yr_unknown as "-1"
go
sp_bindefault yr_unknown, "profs.yrs_teaching"
go
```

NULLS

Considerable debate surrounds the concept of NULLs in relational database circles. Allowing a NULL value in a possible key column threatens the usability of that key. It also creates the confusing possibility of almost-duplicate rows.

27

SANDY'S SPORT SHOPS—NULLs:

If Tim's *profs* table allowed nulls in the *prof_subj* field, he might mistakenly add two rows to the table for the same person, especially since spelling is not one of his strong points

TABLE 1-4 Tim's NULL Entry Problem

prof_name	prof_subj	yrs_teaching	skill	friendly	easy	weird
smith	math	15	1	2	1	10
smithe	NULL	15	1	3	1	10

In the case shown in Table 1-4, Tim doesn't really know if there are two entries for the same teacher or whether there are two very similar teachers on campus. Of course, if subject for the second row was also *math*, he still wouldn't know, but he'd be more certain of a duplicate. On the other hand, if it was *psychology*, he might conclude that they were different people.

Tim could get around his NULL problem by defining two tables—one containing all the columns except *prof_subj*, and then creating a second table called *prof_subjects*. The latter table would contain two columns: one for professor name and one for the associated subject. If a professor's subject was unknown, there would be no row in the *prof_subjects* table for that professor. Finding professors about which he did not know enough would be a matter of selecting all professors in the *profs* table that were not also in the *prof_subjects* table.

Another way of handling the problem of unknown values is to define defaults that mean *unknown* but are more specifically related to what is unknown. For example, Tim's *yr_unknown* default represents an unknown year, and a default called *subj_unknown* could represent an unknown subject. In this scenario, uninitiated users would less likely attempt to join tables based on matching unknown values, especially if they were not both represented as -1.

SQL Server lets the table designers define whether to allow nulls. When defining a table with CREATE TABLE, you can indicate NULL or NOT NULL for each column, which means that attempts to insert nulls for the column will be accepted or rejected, respectively.

Some debaters of the null problem have called SQL a language with three-valued logic: *yes*, *no*, and *unknown*, where NULL indicates an unknown value. Some question the value of bothering to store unknown data. Some also say that it leads to confusion, since users attempt to query for values that match NULL. It is not the case that an unknown value in one column is the same as an unknown value in another. For example, it would be invalid to say an unknown professor's subject is the same as an unknown class name, yet users might attempt joins based on such an equality of NULL values. NULL advocates say that, for some cases, all unknowns are equal—you need to find out what's unknown so you can know what research work you have to do.

■ INDEXES

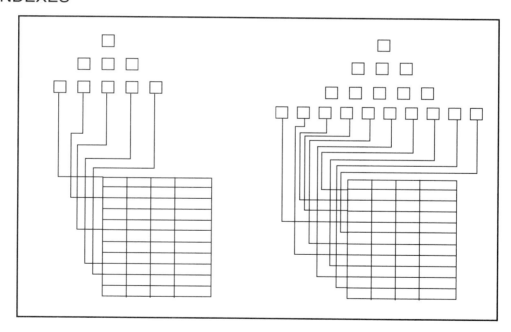

Figure 1.2 A clustered and a nonclustered index.

Indexes are a physical database construct used to facilitate quick access to data locations by index key. We will use the term *index key* to avoid confusion with the concept *candidate key*. You can index noncandidate key columns. While a candidate key gives the address of a specific row in a table, index keys address specific values in the rows and columns of a table.

With the index of this book, you can locate pages where certain information appears by searching an alphabetically ordered word key. Looking up the word *index* in the index at the back of this book should give you the page number of the section you are now reading. Similarly, database indexes let you find data on disk by specifying key information, such as professor name or subject. In the absence of indexes, you would have to scan through a whole table (which could contain several gigabytes of data) in order to find data matching a particular value. That's analogous to needing to read this whole book to find out where the performance impact of indexes, buried somewhere in the middle, is described. Indexes are designed to facilitate data access by providing a faster path to desired data than would be accomplished by a table scan.

Database developers create indexes on user tables. SQL Server creates indexes on system tables at installation time. One or more indexes can be created on one or more columns of a particular table, to facilitate the type of queries commonly used. A table may have zero or more indexes. It can have only one clustered index, but up to 250 nonclustered indexes (though we do not advise pushing the maximum). Indexes facilitate searches, which can be categorized as those seeking all rows meeting a specific qualification and those seeking a specific row. A binary search is done on an index or data page whenever possible.

SQL Server provides two types of indexes—clustered and nonclustered, which we describe in the next sections. For both types, SQL Server stores the index in a tree structure so that data can be found by reading the minimal number of pages. For some read-only queries, the data can be found entirely in the index pages, such that the process never needs to find the actual data page. This type of query is called a covered query, and attempts to increase performance often involve creating such covering indexes.

Recently, Sybase began offering a product called Sybase IQ, which provides five additional types of index. These indexes are based on bitmaps instead of tree structures. The best type of index to use depends on the cardinality of the data and the expected access pattern. Bitmapped indexes primarily facilitate decision support systems so that users can find desired data from any column of any table in a very large database with minimal overhead. Sybase IQ is best suited for databases that are only updated periodically, such as by weekly snapshots of data from an OLTP database.

You can create regular SQL Server indexes either by specifying either a unique or primary key constraint in a CREATE TABLE statement (in SQL Server 10.0 or later versions) or by issuing a CREATE INDEX statement. Using a constraint definition to generate an index automatically further confuses the separate concepts of keys and indexes. However, this syntax was added for SQL 89 compliance. Read the CREATE TABLE entry in the Sybase Commands Reference manuals to understand what each clause of that statement actually does.

Creating an index on a large, existing table takes a considerable amount of time. You can speed up the process by using the WITH SORTED_DATA option on a clustered index if all the data are already in order by the key column of the index to be built. If you can build the index during off hours, you might also find it worthwhile to use sp_configure to shift most of the cache memory to data cache before running create index. This will reduce the amount of I/O necessary and therefore the amount of time required to build the index. You may also find that it helps to use the sp_configure variable extent i/o buffers.

Indexes reside in databases as do tables. In fact, with the exception of the configuration block at the beginning of the master device, SQL Server only stores two basic types of objects on disk: tables and indexes. The underlying representation of all other SQL Server objects consists of rows in system tables. For example, stored procedures get saved as rows in the sysprocedures table.

CLUSTERED INDEXES

A clustered index is one in which the actual data on disk are rearranged so that they are in order by the values in the specified column or columns. Ordering is determined by the default sort order of the SQL Server. For example, the usual binary sort order sorts values in order of the U.S. English alphabet, with uppercase letters preceding corresponding lowercase letters. These indexes generally provide the fastest access to table data when queries are specified in terms of the indexed column.

The lowest level of an index tree is called the leaf level. For a clustered index, the leaf level is the actual data pages. Index page pointers in a clustered index point to data pages, where data can be found in order by value.

NONCLUSTERED INDEXES

Unlike a clustered index, the creation of nonclustered indexes does not rearrange table values. Instead, for each row, the column value is stored with a key value indicating the page on which to find the data.

The leaf pages of a nonclustered index are a level above the actual data pages. Index page pointers in the leaf level of a non-clustered index point to data rows on pages, rather than just to data pages. Consequently, nonclustered indexes require more disk storage space than clustered indexes.

HEAPS

Database developers and engineers call a table with no indexes a heap. To conceptualize a heap, think of a pile of laundry. The ease of access to a particular item in a heap is ranked as follows:

- **Easiest** Something at the top
- **Harder** Something at the bottom
- **Hardest** Something in the middle

Finding something in the middle requires digging through the heap from top to bottom until you find something with an attribute that matches the value you sought.

Besides having typically bad performance for searches, heaps have other qualities. Heap searches tend to fill up data cache and add little or no value to other queries by doing so. Heap updates always go to the end of a table. This causes concurrency problems, since an update means that all subsequent read or update requests on the final page of the table must wait until the original update completes. System 11 has added some features that improve heap performance characteristics, which are described in Chapter 3.

■ SCHEMAS

A schema essentially bundles up related data definition statements. You can envelop one or more table and/or view creation statements and associated permissions statements in one schema. The user defining the schema then owns all objects in it. The CRE-ATE SCHEMA statement was added in System 10 for SQL 89 compliance. Sybase's implementation of it provides a way to document associations between tables and views. Note that there is no *drop schema* statement. Table and view components of a schema are dropped individually. Permissions within a schema are defined in terms of individual objects rather than the whole schema.

Procedure Manual Suggestions

○ Managing User-defined Datatypes

➝ Create a procedure for managing user-defined types that includes documentation of the following:

- All user-defined datatype definitions
- The domain assumptions that led to the type definition
- The objects that depend on each user-defined type
- The person who is responsible for each user-defined type and who should be notified if a change is needed

CHAPTER

An External View of SQL Server Processing

In this chapter, we will continue our survey of SQL Server from the outside looking in. We now turn to the SQL Server activities of data protection and data manipulation. While an RDBMS serves as a storage mechanism for data, the value of the system rests in how users can access the data. A significant part of the value of the RDBMS also lies in protecting the data from inappropriate access.

▦ DATA PROTECTION

The job of protecting data involves guarding against a number of potential threats, represented by these examples:

- **Integrity failure**   Referential integrity is violated by adding a foreign key value that does not match a corresponding primary key value.
- **Hardware failure**   A disk failure causes destruction of part or all of a table or even an entire database.
- **Software failure**   A software bug interferes with normal operation or causes data to be unintentionally added or deleted.

35

■ **User ignorance**   Users might modify data in the wrong tables without realizing their mistakes or realizing them too late.

■ **User maliciousness**   A user could purposely destroy a table or create fake data for personal gain or in response to some emotional pressure.

While SQL Server has features that can help, only concerted, systematic effort can minimize the many risks involved with data storage. Just as the amount of disorder in the universe tends to increase, natural forces tend to work against data safety. Conscious, calm vigilance is the only rational way for a Systems Manager to fight database entropy.

To begin to understand how to maintain control over data, we must understand database integrity. Integrity rules encode real world limits in a database using various mechanisms, including the SQL Server object type called a *rule*. We will refer to the latter object as a SQL Server rule in this section to make the distinction between theory and implementation clear. In other parts of the book, we refer to integrity rules if we mean the rules described here. We have already touched on a few types of integrity without calling them rules as such. Now we will describe the referential integrity, entity integrity, and attribute integrity rules from the relational model.

Referential integrity means that a database must not contain any unmatched foreign key values. For referential integrity, all insertion of new foreign key values must match existing primary key values. If necessary, primary keys may be updated to accommodate a necessary foreign key reference. Similarly, deletion of a primary key means making sure that all rows in other tables with corresponding foreign key values are either dropped or modified to refer to a different key value. Sometimes, we call these operations cascading deletes or updates.

The entity integrity rule requires that no component of the primary key of a base relation may accept NULLs. Our earlier discussions of keys and nulls explained the basis for this rule. The use of default values for missing information helps database designers comply with this rule, while avoiding the overhead associated with enforcing data completeness.

To satisfy the attribute integrity rule, every attribute must draw its values from the relevant domain only. For example, any attempt by Tim to rate a professor with a value over 10 for *friendly* would violate this rule, since the domain only included values from 1 to 10.

To make data conform to defined integrity rules, you have a few options. You can train users very carefully to update all affected tables when updating a key value, to avoid nulls and to stay within domain limits. Such a strategy also involves checking users' work and correcting the data and the users when you encounter rule violations. The more common options in SQL Server databases involve using stored procedures, triggers, constraint definitions, column restrictions, rules, and/or defaults to enforce integrity. The enforcement of integrity rules depends also on an RDBMSs implementation of transactions. Before discussing these, however, we first touch on business rules, which play a large part in a broader definition of integrity.

As a term used to describe people, integrity refers to self-consistency, soundness, completeness, and independence from negative influence. Business rules guide data toward broader integrity goals than simply conforming to certain relational standards. They generally attempt to make the data self-consistent with respect to organizational goals.

For example, going back to the *class_requirements* table, Tim might decide that he should consider no more than five interesting, but irrelevant classes in his school career. Similarly, he realizes he has to take all classes designated as fulfilling the degree requirements in order to graduate from the masters program. He could encode these goals in SQL Server by using the same mechanisms as those used for relational integrity rules.

■ INTEGRITY FEATURES

You can encode and store integrity rules and business rules in SQL Server without relying on users or applications to do the right thing. We have already looked at user-defined types and defaults, which provide a start toward making column domains explicit. The procedural objects described in this section allow you greater integrity control.

By binding SQL Server rules and constraints to tables, you can have SQL Server reject modifications that fail to match defined criteria. With triggers that fire automatically upon row addition, modification, or deletion, you can define cascading action that must also take place. By writing stored procedures for common queries and updates, you can ensure that users follow transaction conventions you establish.

RULES

SQL Server rules define domains by allowing you to specify the limits. After creating a rule, you can bind it to one or more table columns or user-defined datatypes.

SANDY'S SPORT SHOPS—RULES

For example, Tim created one rule for his rating datatype and another for the columns of his class_requirements table:

```
> execute sp_bindrule level_rule,
> "class_requirements.interest"
> execute sp_bindrule level_rule,
> "class_requirements.relevance"
> execute sp_bindrule level_rule,
> "class_requirements.difficulty"
> go
```

When a process attempts to update a column to which a rule is bound, the value to go in the column is passed to the rule as a variable.

TRIGGERS

A trigger is a special form of stored procedure that you attach to a table. When you write it, you determine whether SQL Server should invoke it upon inserts, updates, and/or deletes to the table. Inside the trigger, you can use almost any type of SQL statement. For example, you can check that a foreign key update value matches some primary key value. You can also make it add a value to the table with the primary key. Triggers provide the most flexible mechanism for maintaining database integrity. Client applications are not allowed to bypass triggers.

When you write triggers, you can refer to the values to be added to the table by checking two virtual tables—the *inserted* table and the *deleted* table. Only the triggering process can see these tables, and these tables only contain the information for that instance of the trigger. These tables are actually derived from records in the transaction log. If the logic in the trigger detects an insert, update, or delete that shouldn't have been made, the trigger can issue a ROLLBACK TRANSACTION (or ROLLBACK TRIGGER command in SQL Server versions 10.0 and later).

SANDY'S SPORT SHOPS—TRIGGERS

Tim decided that maximizing the use of good professors at school would help him get through as quickly as possible, so he did this:

```
> create trigger prof_trig on profs
> for insert as
> if
> (select count(*) from inserted
> where inserted.skill > 5
> and inserted.friendly > 5
> and inserted.easy > 5
> and inserted.weird < 5) > 0
> begin
> insert good_profs select prof_name from inserted
> where inserted.skill > 5
> and inserted.friendly > 5
> and inserted.easy > 5
> and inserted.weird < 5
> print "Found a good one!"
> end
> go
```

CONSTRAINTS

Sybase added support for referential constraints in System 10 for compatibility with the SQL database standards. In fact, constraints duplicate functions that you could provide with rules and triggers. You define constraints with the CREATE TABLE statement instead of using CREATE TRIGGER and CREATE RULE.

For clarity, the following list of constraints that can be defined with CREATE TABLE omits the index options. We call Table A the table that you are defining and Table B, the one containing a candidate key that you are referencing.

- **Unique constraint**   Constrains the key column(s) of Table A so that no two rows can have the same nonnull value. This option causes a unique index to be built automatically on the columns. You can specify a fillfactor and whether to make a clustered or nonclustered index.

- **Primary key constraint**   Constrains the key column(s) of Table A so that no two rows can have the same value and so that the value cannot be NULL. This option causes a unique index to be built automatically on the column(s). You can specify a fillfactor and whether to make a clustered or nonclustered index. The difference between this constraint and the unique constraint is that this one does not allow nulls.

- **Foreign key constraint with references clause**   Specifies that the key column(s) of Table A have target keys in the column(s) of Table B listed in the references clause. Any row to be added or modified in a table with a foreign key constraint must exist in Table B in the column referenced. The datatypes of the corresponding columns of Tables A and B must be exactly the same, including the type name. The column(s) in Table B must have a unique index or a primary key constraint.

- **References constraint**   Like the foreign key constraint, a references constraint specifies that the designated column of Table A have values matching those in a designated column of Table B. The datatypes of the corresponding columns of Tables A and B must be exactly the same, including the type name. The column in Table B must have a unique index on it or a primary key constraint on it. The difference between the references constraint and the foreign key constraint is that the foreign key constraint can handle composite keys, while the references constraint may only constrain one column at a time.

- **Check constraint**   The check constraint acts like a rule. With the check clause, you specify a search condition which a new value must satisfy for successful addition to Table A. For the search condition, you supply an IN clause or a LIKE clause, and you may use SQL Server built-in function calls or arithmetic operators. You can also use AND or OR and NOT to string together a series of IN or LIKE clauses.

SANDY'S SPORT SHOPS—CONSTRAINTS

Tim, realizing his data habits would probably be as disorganized as his laundry habits, decided to rebuild his class tables to use constraints:

```
> create table class_names (
> class_id numeric(5,0) constraint class_cnst
> primary key clustered not null,
> class_name varchar(50) not null,
> class_prof varchar(30) null)
> go
> create table class_requirements (
> class_id numeric(5,0)
> references class_names (class_id),
> req_fulfilled varchar(15) default "none" check
> (req_fulfilled in (
> "degree", "advisor", "phd",
> "employment", "none")),
> interest varchar(10),
> relevance varchar(10),
> difficulty varchar(10))
> go
```

STORED PROCEDURES

You can write batches of SQL code and make them into a procedure for later execution. Use the CREATE PROCEDURE command for this purpose. SQL Server parses, optimizes, and compiles the SQL that you supply into internal binary format and then stores it in the sysprocedures table in the database. The Server stores the original SQL commands in the syscomments table of the database.

Subsequent invocation of the stored procedure uses the binary copy, which generally results in faster access than direct

SQL commands.[1] Stored procedures also minimize network traffic, because what would normally be multiple SQL client requests are transmitted as a single request to execute a procedure.

Stored procedures allow you to enforce compliance with business rules. If you create a stored procedure that you own, it can access tables that you own. You can then deny access to your tables from users, but allow access to your stored procedure. Consequently, users may only access your tables by using your stored procedure.

SANDY'S SPORT SHOPS—STORED PROCEDURES

Tim saw a use for stored procedures immediately:

```
> create procedure academic_success as
> begin
> select cn.class_id, class_name,
> class_prof, req_fulfilled,
> interest, relevance, difficulty
> from class_names cn,
> class_requirements cr,
> good_profs gp
> where cn.class_id = cr.class_id and
> cn.class_prof = gp.prof_name and
> req_fulfilled !="none"
> and interest != "low" and
> relevance != "low" and
> difficulty = "low"
> end
> go
```

Sybase provides several system stored procedures for managing SQL Server. A summary of those that Systems Managers use most often follows:

---

[1]In cases where you pass parameters of varying type and number to the stored procedures, these procedures could be slower. Chapter 8 discusses this problem and solutions.

- **sp_addlogin, sp_addgroup, sp_adduser, sp_addalias, sp_addremotelogin, sp_droplogin, sp_locklogin, sp_dropuser, sp_dropgroup**   Define and disable user and group access to SQL Server and databases.

- **sp_addsegment, sp_extendsegment**   Manage segments for customizing device allocation to specific database objects.

- **sp_addserver, sp_dropserver**   Define server names and options for enabling RPCs between different data servers.

- **sp_addthreshold**   Allows you to monitor space usage for segments and trigger events based on the amount of remaining space available.

- **sp_addumpdevice**   Add backup devices (optional with SQL Server version 10 and later).

- **sp_configure**   Set configuration variables for SQL Server as a whole.

- **sp_dboption**   Set options for individual databases.

- **sp_dropdevice**   Used to drop a device. (There is no *sp_addevice* because DISK INIT performs that function. sp_dropdevice exists as a stored procedure rather than a command because it must make certain checks to avoid inadvertently eliminating disk access while objects still reside on it.)

- **sp_help, sp_helpconstraint, sp_helpdb, sp_helpdevice, sp_helpgroup, sp_helpindex, sp_helpjoins, sp_helpkey, sp_helplanguage, sp_helplog, sp_helpremotelogin, sp_helprotect, sp_helpsegment, sp_helpserver, sp_helpsort, sp_helptext, sp_helpthreshold, sp_helpuser, sp_displaylogin**   Get information about various database configuration details.

- **sp_lock**   Used to see which processes are holding locks on which objects. Always check the output of this procedure when users report that their applications appear to be hung.

- **sp_who**   This procedure allows you to see which logins are active in SQL Server at a given time and which database they are using. Use this in conjunction with sp_lock to find out who is blocking whom.

- **sp_spaceused, sp_estspace**   These commands are designed to help you manage space usage in a database. sp_spaceused tells you how much space is currently being used for one or all tables in a database. sp_estspace estimates how much space will be required for a table and its indexes and how long it will take to create the indexes.

Certain idiosyncracies make some commands difficult to find when you need them, so I will draw attention to them here. There is no *sp_helptable*. Instead, you use sp_help tablename to get information about a table. To get a list of all tables in database *db_name*, use the SQL query

```
> select * from db_name..sysobjects where type = "U"

> go
```

People often have trouble finding the `sp_addumpdevice` procedure syntax because the namers did not want to have three d's in a row, but the mind subconsciously supplies the third *d*. Similarly, where a consonant would be duplicated, one instance is removed. For example, in `sp_helprotect`, there is a "p" for "help" and not one for "protect."[2]

If you find these troublesome, you can always make a copy of the `installmaster` script (in the $SYBASE/scripts directory), and then edit the copy to add or duplicate the procedures as you want them to be named. Leave the old commands as well to facilitate references by uninitiated users and by other install scripts.

■ TRANSACTIONS

A database that conforms to all integrity rules defined by the database designers is called consistent. A set of modifications to one or more databases that, treated as a unit, produces a result that leaves the database in a consistent state is a transaction.

After beginning a transaction and issuing some commands, you can either commit or roll back the transaction. During rollback, all data modifications made and all space allocated are undone so that the portion of the database within the scope of the transaction returns to its original state. Because of the possibility of rollback, other transactions are normally not allowed to see modified pages, since those modifications may not persist.

---

[2]You may also find that sp_helpuser isn't as powerful as you might wish.

SANDY'S SPORT SHOPS—TRANSACTIONS

Tim creates two new tables to record information about classes he has taken or intends to take: a *past_classes* table and *future_classes* table. Each table consists of a single *class_id* column. As soon as he finishes a class, Tim moves the row from the second table to the first. He can then see how many classes he has taken or has yet to take using a simple row count. To remove a class from one table and not add to the other would leave the database inconsistent in terms of Tim's goals for the tables. To ensure integrity, Tim makes the modifications in a transaction. For example, after he has finished a psychology class he decided to take, he might make this update:

```
> begin transaction
> declare @cid integer
> select @cid = class_id from class_names
> where class_name like
> "%Comprehension%"
> if @cid != NULL
> begin
> insert into classes_past (class_id)
> values (@cid)
> delete from classes_future
> where class_id = @cid
> end
> select * from classes_past
> go
```

If Tim suddenly realized he had made a mistake, say entering the wrong class name before committing the transaction, he could undo the transaction using the SQL Server ROLLBACK TRANSACTION command. However, since it looks O.K. to him, he commits it:

```
> commit transaction
> go
```

When you commit a transaction, the changes are logged in the last page or pages of the transaction log in the database affected. Transactions that span databases write entries in the log for each database. After updating the log page, the process flushes that page to disk so that there is no chance of losing it in case SQL Server gets shut down for any reason. Next, SQL Server records the changes on the relevant data pages, which may remain in the memory cache from the SELECT command. When the page is flushed to disk during a subsequent checkpoint or memory reclamation process, the new version of the data page from memory overwrites the old version on disk.

Since the commit process records all changes to the transaction log first (called write-ahead logging) and then flushes the log changes to disk, we can consider the transaction complete at commit time. Transaction completion, and therefore database integrity, do not depend on memory management processes for data pages.

The transactional nature of a relational database emerges from the concept of set processing and from the relational integrity rules. Working with sets of tabular input and output means that any operation might modify many rows at a time and that any modification of one table might necessitate a modification in another. Any failure in the middle of a transaction can leave the database in an inconsistent state if there is no ability to roll it back. If you roll back a transaction that caused a trigger to fire, the effects of the trigger are rolled back as well. For greater control, you can use named save points and the ROLLBACK TRIGGER command to roll part of a transaction back, upon encountering a certain condition, and then proceed with an alternative course for the transaction. See the Sybase manuals for more information about programming transactions.

A well-known test for the validity of transactions is called the ACID test:

- **Atomic** A transaction is a single, all or nothing event. There is no possibility for a transaction to be partially committed.

- **Consistent** Consistency must be maintained in the part of the database affected by the transaction. A transaction's output should be the same when given the same input.

- **Isolated** Transactions are isolated from each other; any given transactions are concealed from all the rest until the transaction commits.

- **Durable** Once the transaction commits, that transaction's changes must appear in the database(s) affected, even if the server is rebooted.

The isolation requirement restricts the amount of concurrent activity that may take place, especially for long-running transactions. RDBMSs use one or more locking methods to ensure various levels of transactional consistency. We explore these topics next.

■ LOCKING

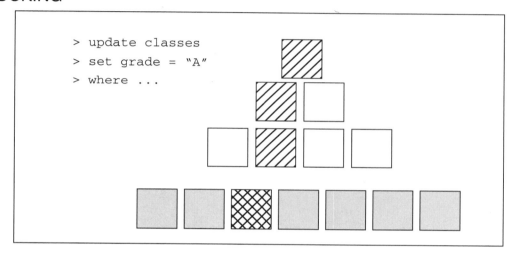

Figure 2.1 An update acquiring table and index locks

SQL Server primarily works with the basic unit of a 2 KB page for reads from disk, writes to disk, memory management, and locking. The SQL Server locking mechanism normally locks a page when a process reads a page, modifies a page, or signals that it intends to modify a page. During modifications, the lock prevents all other processes from writing the page for the duration of the modification. Without locking, if each of two processes wrote a different row on the page, then either copy of the page would be incorrect, since neither would have both changes.

Sybase designers originally made the choice of page-level locking so that SQL Server could provide an optimal mix of performance, concurrency, and consistency for most installations. Since then, four major influences have caused many to advocate the addition of a row-level locking mechanism as well:

47

- The spread of the use of cursors, which provides row-level processing instead of the standard relational set-level processing

- The spread of applications that rely on row-level locking

- The aggressive marketing of row-level locking by competitors that offer it

- The growth of the Sybase customer base from a few installations to thousands and a corresponding increase in "configuration diversity," which makes finding an optimal solution for all customers impossible.

Because there has been so much demand for row-level locking, SQL Server version 10.1 and later includes features that allow you to simulate row-level locking. This was a way to provide the feature some customers want without rewriting a large part of the SQL Server engine to accommodate a new locking mechanism. To create a table that has row-level locking, you can now specify that the maximum number of rows to put on a page is 1. Then, when the Server locks a page, it is only locking one row. This method gives you row-level locking at the cost of space and sometimes of performance. Other more integrated implementations now in the planning stages will provide true row-level locking, but you will need more resources to support it. You will need a great deal of memory and processing overhead to manage the locks. This is expected to reduce performance. In short, only seek row-level locking if you need it.

Database discussions and Sybase documentation usually involve the use of several terms for locking, which we will clarify now:

- **Dirty read**   The ability for one transaction to see the intermediate results of another transaction.

- **Repeatable read**   The ability for transaction A to read the same data at any point in the transaction even if transaction B is in the process of modifying the data.

- **Deadlock**   A situation in which two or more processes each hold some locks and require the locks held by the other processes in order to continue. In other words, one task is waiting on another that cannot continue because it is waiting on the first. When SQL Server detects a deadlock, it chooses a deadlock victim and forces the victim process to release its locks. SQL Server evaluates the amount of CPU time accumulated by each process since login and designates the younger process as the victim.

■ **Spinlock**   A multiprocessor synchronization mechanism to manage the critical sections in the code. This lock restricts a portion of SQL Server execution code so that only one process may execute that portion at one time. Normally, many processes run in parallel on as many CPUs as the system administrator configures, all sharing the SQL Server executable. The short-term spinlocks prevent parallel processing for operations that must happen serially.

■ **Resource lock**   A short-term lock for maintaining consistency in an index page while providing maximum throughput. These locks allow processes to read an index page while another process changes the page. Resource locks lock the page buffer in memory, instead of the actual disk page. A resource lock is only held on an index page until a resource lock on the next level of the index tree is acquired, or until the query is complete.

■ **Shared page lock**   A lock that allows any number of processes to read a page, but prevents any process from modifying it.

■ **Exclusive page lock**   A lock that allows only one process to read or update a page. Only one transaction can lock the page, and no other type of lock can be obtained on that page.

■ **Update lock**   A lock that signals that an exclusive lock may be requested later in the transaction. It allows readers (shared locks) but not writers (exclusive or other update locks) to access the page.[3] A transaction will always have an update lock on a page before it gets an exclusive lock.

■ **Exclusive table lock**   A lock obtained for an entire table. Used when an entire table needs to be locked for the writer, such as when no index is seen as useful for the query during updates and deletes or when a clustered index is being created.

■ **Intent shared table lock**   A lock that indicates at the table level that shared page locks are being acquired. An intent lock doesn't lock the table, but signals the Server so that it knows which other locks are possible without requiring a page by page scan for locks.

■ **Intent exclusive table lock**   Similar to the previous lock, this lock indicates at the table level that exclusive page locks are being acquired.

Four levels of isolation were first defined by Jim Grey. Since then they have been revised and specified in the SQL standard. Here, we will cover the three levels implemented in SQL Server versions 11.0 and later. To facilitate quick comprehension, we will name two processes, A and B, although, in fact, each could repre-

---

[3]Or, as Robert Garvey says, some might translate this to "read, fixin' to write."

sent any number of processes. We will describe these locking levels in the context of SQL Server page locking:

- **Level 0**   Process A, running at isolation level 1 or 3, gets an exclusive lock for each page being changed. Process B, at level 0, can see the change regardless of the exclusive lock. If process A's transaction rolls back, process B still goes forward with the information it first got, not necessarily aware of the rollback. If B calculates something like an average based on its read of A's changed data, and then the change was rolled back, B's average could be wrong. The ability for B to read changed data from A's uncommitted transaction is termed a *dirty read*.

- **Level 1**   Process A gets an exclusive lock for each page it changes and holds the locks until the end of the transaction. An update is consistent, and process B cannot read or change the newly changed pages until the transaction for the first process commits. However, process B can modify pages that A read earlier in the transaction. If A decided to redo its update, different rows might qualify because of B's changes. This is like what might happen if A was standing in the kitchen washing dishes. B could come along and take a dish that A just washed and pour a little milk into it for the cats. When A is done doing what it thought was all the dishes, there is still one dirty dish left—the one that B made while A was busy.

- **Level 3**   Process A gets exclusive locks on pages being changed and gets shared locks on pages it searches during the transaction. Process A holds all locks until the end of the transaction. This approach prevents unrepeatable reads. It ensures that all transactions will be consistent, including those only retrieving data. This level can be achieved in SQL Server by using the HOLDLOCK or READ SERIALIZABLE feature. Until process A commits, process B can neither change data that process A changed nor change the data that process A read while searching for the data it changed. For example, say that process A decided to add 1 to all values greater than 10 at the time it executed. It scans through the table and finds the values that qualify and then proceeds to do the update, holding shared locks on the pages scanned and exclusive locks on the pages updated. Process B would not be able to come along during the process and create more pages with rows containing values greater than 10. To continue with our analogy from level 1, this is comparable to A banning B from coming into the kitchen until A finished washing the dishes.

The ability to specify isolation level 0 in SQL Server was added in version 10.1. Level 0 allows the largest number of processes to work with the same data concurrently, but affords them the least consistent view of the data. Level 3 allows the reverse. At level 0, you can do a table scan without acquiring any transactional table or page locks. Writers will continue to acquire the usual locks, but readers will not have to block on them. Likewise, writers will not have to wait for readers to finish. The downside is that the quality of data that the process at level 0 read may go down because it can see the uncommitted changes of another process that may get rolled back.

With anything but level 3 locking, the effect of running process A and process B concurrently could produce different results than running first A and then B. If we always get the same results whether running the processes in parallel or serially, we would call the transactions serializable. Total concurrency control means that transactions are always serializable. Note that this does not mean that running A and then B would necessarily produce the same results as running B and then A. It means that running A and B interleaved would compare to running either A first or B first. Use HOLDLOCK to enforce serializability.

To use isolation level 0, you need to have a unique index. In version 10.1 and later, you can use the `identity in nonunique index` database option to instruct SQL Server to add an identity column automatically to all indexes not defined as unique. The identity column is added as the last key in the index. This makes nonunique indexes internally unique for use by isolation level 0 scans and by updatable cursor scans. This will increase the density for all indexes, which may degrade performance. Consider an index redesign instead so that you can define appropriate unique indexes manually and help the optimizer choose better plans at the same time.

You can use one of the following new options to specify that you want to use isolation level 0:

- **SET TRANSACTION ISOLATION LEVEL 0**   This sets the isolation level for an entire session.

- **SET TRANSACTION ISOLATION LEVEL READ UNCOMMITTED**   This sets the isolation level for an entire session. (The same as `set transaction isolation level 0`).

- **SELECT...FROM *table*...(AT ISOLATION {READ UNCOMMITTED | READ COMMITTED | SERIALIZABLE})**   This requests a particular isolation level for a single select statement. READ UNCOMMITTED is the same as level 0. READ COMMITTED is the same as level 1, and

51

SERIALIZABLE is the same as level 3 or HOLDLOCK. If there is a UNION operator in the query, the AT ISOLATION clause must be specified after the last SELECT in the statement.

■ **READTEXT table.column text_ptr offset size (AT ISOLATION {READ UNCOMMITTED | READ COMMITTED | SERIALIZABLE})** This sets the isolation level for a single READTEXT command.

Triggers will execute at isolation level 1 or at the session isolation level if more restrictive. Triggers cannot be executed at isolation level 0. Stored procedures always operate at isolation level 1.

The above commands also allow you to specify level 3 locking (HOLDLOCK, SERIALIZABLE) as they have in the past. See the Sybase documentation for more thorough descriptions of the syntax. If a user issues a SELECT statement with HOLDLOCK, but the command is not within an explicit transaction, the process holds the shared locks until the SELECT statement completes. Within a transaction, the process executing a SELECT with HOLDLOCK holds locks until the transaction is committed or rolled back. SQL Server does not lock work tables or process temporary tables since only one process uses them.

Starting with version 10.1, you can configure how many locks a query may acquire before its page locks are upgraded to a table lock. In prior releases, the limit was hard-coded at 200 page locks, which makes sense for small tables, since acquisition of this many locks usually signals that the process intends to update a large portion of the table, and running out of locks could otherwise become a problem. However, for large tables, 200 represents a much smaller percentage of the table and might not indicate an intent to update the whole table at all.

In version 11.0, you can set a high value, a low value, and a percentage for the Server, a database, or a table. The maximum for high and low is the total number of locks that you have configured for the Server. You can use the new procedures sp_setpglockpromote to configure the page locking for a table or a database and sp_dropglockpromote to remove it. You can set the Server-wide values by using sp_configure or sp_setpglockpromote. With sp_configure, you can set these new configuration variables:

■ lock promotion HWM   The high-water mark, or maximum number of page locks that a process may acquire for a single table before SQL Server attempts to escalate to a table lock

■ lock promotion LWM   The low-water mark, or the minimum number of page locks that a process may acquire for a single table before SQL Server considers escalating to a table lock

■ lock promotion PCT   The percentage of a page locks that a process may acquire in comparison to the table size before the Server attempts to escalate to a table lock

The use of three threshold settings adds flexibility not previously available. The Server tries to escalate to a table lock if the number of locks acquired for one pass (scan session) of a query

■ is more than the low-water mark (LWM),

■ is less than the high-water mark (HWM),

■ and the percentage of locks acquired in comparison to the number of rows in the table is greater than lock promotion percent (PCT).

If the number of locks acquired exceeds the HWM, the query attempts to get a table lock without checking the PCT setting. Let's say, for example, that you update a table with 600 rows, and the escalation levels in effect are LWM = 200, HWM = 2000, and PCT = 50. This means that the Server will try to lock the table as soon as a query pass acquires 300 locks, since that's half the table and it's between LWM and HWM. Now, let's say that you have a table with 50,000 rows, and your query updates 300 rows. The query acquires more than 200 locks, but does not escalate to a table lock since this does not constitute 50% of the table.

The syntax for `sp_setpglockpromote` is

```
sp_setpglockpromote {"database" | "table" | "server"}
object_name, lwm, hwm, pct
```

If you are setting the thresholds for the whole server using the server keyword, use NULL for *object_name*. Otherwise, supply the applicable database or table name. If you want to change only one or two of the three threshold settings from a previously set value(s), you can supply the keyword NULL for the remaining value(s). For databases and tables, the lock threshold numbers are stored in the new sysattributes table, so you always need to supply all three values at least once in order to initialize a new row for the system table.

To drop the lock promotion information from `sysattributes` for a table or database, use this procedure:

```
sp_dropglockpromote {"database" | "table"}, object_name
```

The lock promotion settings can be considered as having three levels of granularity: object level, database level, or Server level. The lowest granularity set for a particular object applies. The table setting overrides the database setting, and the database setting overrides the Server setting.

In versions of SQL Server prior to 11.0, a single spinlock is used for managing page locks. Observation led to the conclusion that this limited scalability in multiprocessor systems. In SQL Server 11, multiple spinlocks handle the locking for page locks, table locks, and address locks, for multiprocessor systems.

These new configuration variables affect how locking works, providing that the Server is configured to use more than one engine:

- `address lock spinlock ratio`
- `table lock spinlock ratio`
- `page lock spinlock ratio`
- `freelock transfer block size`
- `max engine freelocks`

The first three of these affect the number of spinlocks per lock hash bucket. A hash bucket is used to manage a lock that is in use. The higher the number of spinlocks is, the more concurrency is provided for this resource. However, more memory is used as well. The last two variables in the list affect how a single engine in a multi-CPU system acquires blocks of locks for its own use. All these variables are described further in Chapter 6. The variables `max online engines`, `max engine freelocks`, `number of locks`, and `freelock transfer block size` are all related. If you change one, be sure to check the others and adjust them as necessary. Another new configuration variable, also described in Chapter 6, is `deadlock checking period`. This sets the amount of time that a process may hold a lock before the Server checks to see if it is involved in a deadlock.

Locking has several performance implications. The first is that a process can be blocked while waiting for another process to complete and release its locks. The more restrictive the locking level is, the more processes get blocked and the longer they have to wait. Next, deadlocking can require that transactions have to be redone occasionally. This causes delays that may be problematic in time-critical systems such as stock trading databases. A lack of indexes can result in more locking and more blocking.[4]

To make it easier to detect performance problems caused by waiting for locks, SQL Server 10.1 introduced trace flag 1213. This enables the monitoring of statistics about lock wait times. After enabling it, you can use the new commands DBCC OBJECT_STATS and DBCC USER_STATS. Output includes the types of locks and the number of milliseconds spent waiting for them. There are many different parameters you can provide to achieve various results, so see the Sybase documentation for details. The use of lock wait monitoring will degrade performance, so only use it for diagnostic purposes and then turn it off.

RECOVERY

When SQL Server is started after a normal shutdown, a power failure, or some other type of crash, it must undergo recovery in order to return the databases to a consistent state. SQL Server also runs recovery after loading a database or transaction log backup. The transaction and trigger roll back routines use the recovery algorithms as well.

Consistency, determined in terms of transactions, means a committed transaction is completely applied, no uncommitted transaction is applied, and no transaction is only partially applied

To go through recovery, SQL Server reads through the transaction log, and uses the log records and timestamp mechanism to

---

[4]Wait to create indexes until off hours, however, since index creation requires table locks.

determine which modifications need to be reapplied and which need to be rolled back. The next two sections describe how the process works.

TIMESTAMPS

Each database maintains a 6-byte integer called a timestamp. SQL Server uses this number to establish the sequence of events in the database. Each database has its own master timestamp, and each page has a timestamp in its page header. Whenever a page is modified, the current master timestamp is copied to the page header and the master timestamp is incremented by 1. When a page is modified, the timestamp from the headers of the pages both before and after the change are recorded in the modification log record(s).

During recovery, SQL server reads through all the transaction records. By comparing the timestamp in each log record with the timestamps on the affected pages, the recovery process can tell whether the modified page had been flushed to disk before the dump or shutdown occurred. The process then rolls transactions forward or back as necessary.

TRANSACTION LOG

The transaction log keeps track of all transactions for the purpose of guaranteeing consistency. It stores the state of database pages before and after any transaction. When an implicit or explicit ROLLBACK TRANSACTION command is issued, that information is used to undo any modifications. After SQL Server is rebooted, the log information allows the SQL Server to recover databases to their previous state.

The transaction log is called a write-ahead log because SQL Server writes log records for a change to disk before changed table or index pages are written. Log pages are flushed to disk whenever a transaction ends, while data or index pages may not be flushed until the checkpoint process completes. In other words, transaction log writes to disk are transactional, but all other writes to disk are not; they wait until a convenient time as determined by SQL Server and various configuration parameters.

The transaction log is stored in the `syslogs` table. `Syslogs` is more special than a regular table and even more special than other system tables for these reasons:

■ Each modification must also be written to the transaction log, which means that `syslogs` is the most heavily modified table in a database.

■ Each modification to `syslogs` must be written upon transaction completion, which means that caching does not do much to mitigate the performance hit of the high disk I/O required for this table.

■ `syslogs` is a table without indexes, which is sometimes referred to as a heap. This means that all new records are written to the end of the table, and that the last page of the table is therefore almost always locked in an active read/write database.

■ Every row of the transaction log is required for the entire database to work. Unlike a data table, where losing a row means losing a single record or table, losing a `syslogs` row generally means you have lost the database.

■ The log is always growing unless you take action to truncate it. This is done with the `DUMP TRANSACTION` command. You can use transaction log dumps as incremental database backups. To monitor log growth and to minimize the possibility of unrecoverable disasters, you must make sure to use the log segment feature and place the log on a separate device from the rest of the database. Any `LOAD TRANSACTION` command will fail if this is not done.

For these reasons, wise Sybase administrators very carefully put `syslogs` on its own segment on the fastest, most reliable device possible for each important database. A transaction log device for which you have responsibility will go bad during your career. Make backups.[5]

A new System 11 memory-only table in the `master` database called `syslogshold` maintains records of the oldest active transaction in each database and the replication server truncation point for each replicated database. You can query the `syslogshold` table to see if a query has left a long-running transaction open that is preventing you from truncating the log. The `syslogshold` table will contain the following information about the oldest active transaction in each database:

[5]Or start preparing for your next career.

■ The server process owning the transaction

■ The date and time that the transaction started

■ The first page number involved in the transaction

■ The log page and row number that serve as the transaction ID

■ The ID of the master transaction for multidatabase transactions

■ DBCC

DBCC stands for Database Consistency Checker, which indicates the original purpose of the command. Over the years, however, it has become a general-purpose diagnostic utility. Sybase has only documented a few of the DBCC commands. Most of the undocumented DBCC commands exist solely to test a particular part of the code. If you report a problem, for example, you may be asked by technical support to use DBCC to enable a certain trace flag. Trace flags usually cause output to be generated and, typically, sent to the errorlog. In a few cases, DBCC flags actually cause other actions to happen as well, such as to disable a task that normally happens automatically.

The commands that do what the DBCC name suggests are used to verify that a database is o.k. before you dump it to disk. These are

■ DBCC CHECKTABLE

■ DBCC CHECKDB

■ DBCC CHECKALLOC

■ DBCC TABLEALLOC

■ DBCC INDEXALLOC

■ DBCC CHECKCATALOG

These commands are not only documented, but strongly recommended in the SQL Server manuals and by technical support. Since SQL Server may allow you to back up an inconsistent database, you may not find corruption until you try to load the dump. A load of an inconsistent database may fail. By running DBCC commands before making the backup, you protect yourself from database disaster.

DBCC TRACEON/TRACEOFF is used to enable or disable a particular trace flag. For example, the two most common trace flags are 3604, which sends DBCC output to your terminal, and 3605, which sends the output to the errorlog. If neither of these traceflags is enabled, the default goes to the console, which is the terminal or window from which you booted SQL Server.

DBCC CHECKTABLE checks the consistency of a base table and its indexes. DBCC CHECKDB checks the consistency of the database by running DBCC CHECKTABLE on every table in it. These utilities check the following:

- All the data page linkages are correct.
- All data rows are correctly placed on the page.
- All index page linkages are correct.
- All index rows are organized on the page in ascending key order.
- All keys on the leaf level of a nonclustered index match the columns of the corresponding data rows.

Since each table and index are checked page by page, and key values are checked row by row, this command can take quite a while to complete. The amount of time required increases with each additional index on the table and with each additional column in a composite index.

DBCC INDEXALLOC checks allocation information for indexes, DBCC TABLEALLOC checks the allocation information for tables, and DBCC CHECKALLOC runs a TABLEALLOC for every table in the database. In general, these commands check that

- The table's data pages are marked for the correct segment usage.
- The object ID in the extent matches the object ID in the sysindexes row.
- The pages recorded as used in the extent allocation structure match those in the page chain.
- The counts in the object allocation structure match the computed counts.

The amount of time taken by DBCC TABLEALLOC and DBCC CHECKALLOC depends on the number and size of objects in the database. One large 100-MB object can be checked more quickly than a hundred 1-MB objects. A useful by-product of these commands is the output, which shows the amount of space allocated in the table or database. Each extent reported as *used* represents 16 KB of disk space.[6]

DBCC CHECKCATALOG checks the consistency of the SQL Server catalogs. It usually runs very quickly.

When DBCC reports an error, it is usually significant and should be resolved as soon as possible. DBCC, if run frequently, protects you from extensive damage caused by failing disks. The sooner you find bad blocks, the sooner you can get your database onto a more stable device.

You can find more information about running DBCC in Chapter 10.

▪ BACKING UP AND LOADING DATABASES

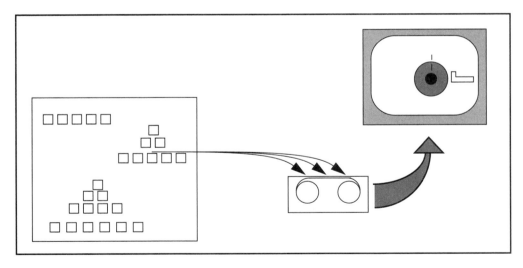

Figure 2.2 Backing up data and keeping it safe

System administrators use the DUMP DATABASE and LOAD DATABASE commands to make and restore backup copies of databases. The DUMP TRANSACTION and LOAD TRANSACTION commands make

---

[6]32 KB on Stratus.

incremental backups. To make backups that truly protect you from data risks, you need to establish a process and use all the discipline at your disposal to carry it out.

1. Decide what to back up and when.

2. Select appropriate backup devices and commands for the backups you plan.

3. Run the DBCC commands described in the last section to check database consistency.

4. Make the backups as planned.

You can write scripts or even programs to automatically make backups on a particular schedule. You can also use Sybase's Enterprise SQL Server Manager product to make scheduled database backups.

Sybase has devoted entire chapters of the System Administration Guide and Troubleshooting Guide to database backups. We use this section to highlight main backup considerations. Chapter 10 covers the task of making a comprehensive backup plan in more detail. Rather than replacing the Sybase documentation, the sections in this book should supplement your understanding of the backup process.

Most sites with large databases make incremental dumps using the DUMP TRANSACTION commands and periodically make full backups using DUMP DATABASE. In some environments, administrators make full database backups nightly using DUMP DATABASE and abandon the logs using DUMP TRANSACTION WITH TRUNCATE_ONLY. In development environments, developers may know that they can rebuild a database entirely from scripts if it gets destroyed. In this case, they don't use DUMP DATABASE at all and routinely abandon the logs using DUMP TRANSACTION WITH TRUNCATE_ONLY. In releases prior to System 10, DUMP DATABASE is a SQL Server process entirely and, in some cases, relies on the use of the Sybase console utility. console basically provides the software with a way of understanding when a tape needs changing.

With System 10, Sybase introduced Backup Server, which also introduced increased performance, increased flexibility, and increased complexity. Backup Server runs as a stand-alone Open Server process and inherently understands about tape changing and a number of other things. As of System 10, `console` is obsolete. When you run `sybinit` to install a SQL Server using versions 10.0 and later, you also have the option to add a Backup Server. This initializes a Backup Server and adds it to the interfaces file.

Backup Server gives you greater control over dump media than the earlier backup mechanisms. For example, with Backup Server you can dump to several backup tapes at once, striping one database across several dump devices working in parallel. You issue the `DUMP` and `LOAD` commands from SQL Server, but Backup Server manages the processes that do the work. A copy of Backup Server must be running on the same machine as the SQL Server, but you can dump and load databases using a Backup Server running on a different machine if you prefer.

You can dump a database while the database is active. However, for versions earlier than 10.0, this causes SQL Server performance to suffer. In 10.0 and later releases, the impact is minimal because of the use of the separate Backup Server process. You may also run more than one dump and load process in parallel, provided each affects a different database and a different dump device. A special locking mechanism prevents you from running more than one dump in a database at a time. The dump process acquires an exclusive table lock on `syslogs`, which only the dump commands may acquire. Although such a lock exists on the `syslogs` table, a special exception allows processes to continue adding records to the end of the log.

DUMP DATABASE

`Dump database` sequentially copies all allocated pages in a database to a dump device, which is either a disk or a tape. The SQL Server or Backup Server process checks that all allocated pages are initialized as they should be. Detection of an allocated but uninitialized page results in a warning. An improperly formatted page header indicates a serious problem and causes the dump process to fail.

Other than those checks, the backup process pays no attention to the database page contents. Specifically, dump makes no checks for data or index consistency. It is assumed that the user has run DBCC CHECKALLOC, DBCC CHECKDB, and DBCC CHECKCATALOG before the dump. If bad spots on a disk have invalidated data, DUMP may blindly write the data to the backup device anyway. A subsequent load of that dump will probably fail during recovery.

DUMP TRANSACTION

In its basic form, DUMP TRANSACTION checkpoints the database, copies log pages to the specified storage medium, and then removes inactive transactions from the log in the database. The inactive portion of the log starts with the beginning of the log and includes all records up to, but not including, the log page on which the oldest active transaction begins. When the oldest active transaction during one dump is still the oldest active transaction during subsequent dumps, no pages are truncated, but additional pages may be copied to the backup device.

SQL Server provides four basic dump transaction options:

■ DUMP TRANSACTION db_name TO device_name Copies the transaction log to a dump device and removes the inactive portion of the log from the database.

■ DUMP TRANSACTION db_name WITH TRUNCATE_ONLY Removes the inactive portion of the transaction log and does not make a backup copy.

■ DUMP TRANSACTION db_name WITH NO_LOG Removes the inactive portion of the transaction log and does not make a backup copy *when there is no other recourse*. Use this command only when the log device is completely out of space and there is not even enough room to add a checkpoint record. Subsequent 813 or 821 errors may occur if continued processing is attempted. Instead, plan on issuing a DUMP DATABASE command next if this situation occurs.

■ DUMP TRANSACTION db_name WITH NO_TRUNCATE Allows recovery of a database that is inaccessible due to failure of a device if the log is still available on another device.

Load Database

LOAD DATABASE reads pages from the backup medium and writes them into the database that you specify. LOAD writes the pages into the same logical locations that they occupied in the original database. SQL Server and Backup Server provide no compression or page reorganization. The destination database needs to be at least as large as the original. Any unallocated pages between the last page restored by the LOAD and the last page allocated for the receiving database are initialized. This means that the load can take a while even if the data in the backup do not take up much space. If you plan to restore a dump into a new copy of a database, use the FOR LOAD option of CREATE DATABASE to avoid initializing the empty pages twice.

After all pages are copied, SQL Server must run recovery on the database. In SQL Server versions before 11.0, LOAD starts recovery automatically when it has finished copying in the backup. In SQL Server 11, you initiate recovery by using the ONLINE DATABASE command. Recovery may take an unexpectedly long time if the transaction log was large and there was a lot of activity in the database since the last load. If you shut down SQL Server during a load for any reason, you can only drop the database or reload it from the beginning. Consequently, do not reboot SQL Server in the middle of the load unless you are sure the process has failed or you have other compelling reasons. If the load does encounter problems, you will find evidence of them in the errorlog. If you have the print recovery information configuration option turned on, the recovery process will report its progress to the errorlog as well. No other processes may run in the database during a load; users who attempt to use the database anyway receive errors.

Load Transaction

LOAD TRANSACTION copies in pages of syslogs, overwriting existing pages. When it finishes the copy, it must go through the recovery process. As with LOAD DATABASE, you initiate recovery in an 11.0 or later Server by using the ONLINE DATABASE command.

No users may use the database during the load or recovery processes. LOAD TRANSACTION recovers the database to its original state at the time the dump transaction started. Recovery rolls back all transactions marked active or aborted. It rolls forward all committed transactions. The work is redone in the order that it was originally done. You must load transaction logs in the same order as they were dumped. SQL Server uses a sequence number to keep track of transaction log dumps. An attempt to load a dump out of order causes the process to fail. An attempt to load a transaction log dump in a database with truncate log on checkpoint or select into/bulk copy set will also fail.

If you reboot SQL Server in the middle of a LOAD TRANSACTION, the recovery process depends on the state of the load at the time of the reboot:

■ If the new log pages had not finished loading, the log is returned to its state prior to the load.

■ If the log pages had finished loading, then recovery is run as it would have done had it not been interrupted.

SQL SERVER 10 TO SQL SERVER 11 DUMP COMPATIBILITY

You can load dumps of any database but master made under SQL Server version 10.0 or later into a version 11.0 SQL Server. When the database undergoes recovery, the upgrade process happens automatically. The upgrade converts log records made under 10.0 to records in the 11.0 format. The log format changed due to other changes in the System 11 code. As a side benefit, the changes that allow this feature to work also make database upgrades independent of each other. This means you do not have to upgrade all the databases for an entire SQL Server at once before any single database will work.[7]

The new concept of an *offline database* has been added. Before recovery and upgrade, a database is offline. After a successful load of a database, you issue the ONLINE DATABASE database_name

---

[7]If you are using Replication Server, there are limitations on using System 10 dumps with SQL Server 11. See the Sybase documentation for Replication Server for more information.

command. This signals to SQL Server that an operator has loaded all the databases and logs required to bring the database to a consistent state. SQL Server then determines whether it needs to perform upgrades to any log records or not. After the upgrade is done, the Server marks the database as *online* by setting a status bit in the `sysdatabases` table. You can use the `sp_helpdb` procedure, which interprets this status bit, to determine whether a given database is online.

The new ONLINE DATABASE command means that you no longer need to use *dbo use only* status when loading a database, since the *offline* status will keep users out. For a database you want to load from a System 10 dump, you will need to turn the *read only* status off if it is set. The upgrade process needs to write to system tables. After the database is online, a user may enter the database and perform normally permitted operations. After upgrading a database, a DUMP DATABASE must be issued before a DUMP TRANSACTION is permitted.

Besides simplifying upgrades, this new functionality is useful if you have an archive procedure that relies on backups made under SQL Server 10.0.

■ SECURITY

SQL Server helps you guard your organization's data by providing mechanisms to authenticate users and to control their access to your information resources. In this section we look at the authentication, access, and auditing features that SQL Server provides.

Sybase added several new security features with System 10, including password expiration, locking of login accounts, encryption of passwords (before that, users could not see each others' passwords, but the `sa` user could see everyone's), and the concept of roles. System 10 also comes with a built-in auditing mechanism. System 10 meets the criteria for the C1 security rating used by the U.S. Government.

SQL SERVER LOGIN ACCOUNT

SQL Server allows you to define two levels of user access.[8] At the SQL Server level, you specify who can log in. A person must have a valid login name and an associated password. SQL Server passwords and logins are independent of the operating system. Typically, however, administrators create SQL Server logins that match the operating system accounts. Users choose their SQL Server passwords, and may opt to duplicate those that they use at the operating system level. A security officer can define a password expiration interval such that users have to change their passwords routinely.

A login account gives individuals access to the SQL Server itself and, in essence, gives them permission to use SQL Server resources. Each time you add a login, the implication is that the other people now have to share SQL Server and machine resources with one more person. In a Server with low utilization, this may not become an issue. However, depending on your machine resources, as soon as you get up to more than a thousand users, your users will encounter contention. The resources that users must share include

- CPU time to run queries and procedures

- Memory to use for buffering data and procedures in cache

- Disk space to store new data, associated index rows, and transaction log records

- Network bandwidth to communicate with the user's client application and with any remote servers involved in transactions

- Object access, which is brokered by means of locks

- User connections, which are configured in SQL Server, but are also limited by the operating system configuration and physical limits

When purchasing a machine to run SQL Server, make sure to purchase enough computing resources to match the number of

---

[8]In this section, we are only discussing the SQL Server authorization method, which is discretionary access control. Readers working with Secure SQL Server systems using MAC are advised to check the documentation for those systems for details about user account management.

users that you expect. For more than a thousand users, you will need multiple CPUs, you will probably require at least 64 megabytes of memory, and you will probably require several gigabytes of disk space, if not several hundred. You will also need to make sure that the operating system can accommodate the number of user connections that you expect to have. For UNIX operating systems, a resource known as a *file descriptor* limits the number of connections in addition to memory. Some versions of UNIX allow 10,000 file descriptors, while others only allow 1024.

DATABASE USER ACCOUNT

In addition to a SQL Server login, each database has an owner and users associated with it. The user names are the same as the login name. You can also alias a login to a different user name. SQL Server only allows access to a database to users listed in that database's `sysusers` table. One SQL Server login can be associated with any number of database user accounts, including none. Each database has its own set of user accounts, which may be the same or different from the sets in other databases.

At minimum, a database user has permission to enter the database. Further access to the database contents depends on permissions assigned by the database or object owners or the people that have been granted the permission to grant permissions. A user account is associated with permissions assigned by the database owner and, with the GRANT option, by other users. Permissions can be granted or denied for almost any operation on any object by using the GRANT and REVOKE commands. (See the Sybase SQL Server Reference Manual for details.) The permissions associated with the user id are stored in the database's `sysprotects` table.

ALIASES

A database alias is a secondary user name associated with a login name. For example, Tim could make a SQL Server login *tim* and a database user *student* in the school database. He could then alias login *tim* to user *student* in the school database. Thereafter, whenever Tim issues a command in the school database, he takes on the identity of *student*.

You can use the aliases feature to create a *group user* for a database. For example, during development you may want to simplify matters by only creating objects owned by the user *developer* in a particular database. Then you could alias all developers to the *developer* user in that database. With this method, you only need to issue desired GRANT and REVOKE commands for the single developer user. Since you could see developer's login names with sp_who, you have more control than if you only had a single SQL Server login named *developer*.

GROUPS

You can create groups to which object access is granted or denied. The use of groups simplifies administration. Typically, users are mapped into groups by department. You could, however, set up a mapping by function such as "secretaries," "engineers," or "managers."

ROLES

Prior to System 10, one privileged user, sa, had power to do anything to any object in a SQL Server. The powers of sa within the scope of a SQL Server resemble those of the operating system special accounts *root, SYSTEM,* or *System Administrator.* Not only were the powers of one user broad; only sa had permission to do certain things that could otherwise be delegated. For example, only sa could allocate or mirror database devices. This led to several people sharing the sa login. Among other things, login sharing makes it difficult to account for who did what. System 10 introduced three roles, shown in Table 2-1, to resolve the problem.

With roles, you can distribute power and responsibility among several people with several roles. Now it is up to the Systems Manager or a system security policy to determine whether one person has total control over SQL Server. Certain operations in SQL Server are protected, such as creating databases, adding logins, and enabling auditing. In SQL Server versions before System 10, certain operations could only be performed by people who have access to the `sa` (System Administrator) account or by the database owner (`dbo`). With System 10, the system administration operations are now associated with roles, so a user does not have to use the `sa` login name to perform these operations. This makes it easier for people to share responsibility for administration and enhances accountability, since `sa` actions can be associated with the different login accounts. The mechanism of roles also provides for a greater level of security than was previously possible. You can set up roles so that a set of people perform `sa` operations, but no one person has permission to perform all privileged operations. In that way, you can ensure that certain critical operations require the cooperation of two or more individuals.

TABLE 2-1   Roles

Role Name	Role Title	Authorized Actions
sa_role	System Adminis-trator	Install SQL Server, grant permissions to other users, create databases, bcp, grant and revoke sa_role to others
sso_role	System Security Officer	Manage SQL Server logins, change passwords, manage the audit system, grant and revoke sso_role and oper_role to others
oper_role	Operator	Backup and restore databases

ACCESS-RELATED COMMANDS

The following commands are used to enable and disable SQL server access.

- ◼ `sp_addlogin` and `sp_droplogin` add and drop login accounts on a SQL Server. You cannot drop a login if there is a corresponding user account in any database managed by the SQL Server, and you cannot drop a user account if that user owns objects in a database. If you need to deny users access but keep their objects, you can use the `sp_locklogin` procedure.

70

- ■ `sp_addremotelogin` and `sp_dropremotelogin` add and drop login mappings that allow local users to perform RPCs on remote servers.

- ■ `sp_addalias` and `sp_dropalias` add and drop database user aliases. A login account is normally mapped to a database user account with a matching name. To map a login to a different database user name, you use `sp_addalias`.

- ■ `sp_addgroup` and `sp_dropgroup` add and drop groups in a database. Use `sp_adduser` to add a user to a group, or use `sp_changegroup` to change a user's membership to a different group.

- ■ `sp_changegroup` changes a user's group. Each user is a member of the group *public* and may also be a member of one additional group. Use `sp_changegroup` to reset the additional group to a different one.

- ■ `sp_modifylogin` changes the default database, language, or full name associated with a login account.

- ■ `sp_password` adds or changes a password associated with a login account.

- ■ `sp_role` grants or revokes roles to a SQL Server login account. This procedure was added in System 10.

- ■ `sp_locklogin` disables a login, but keeps the login record to prevent the objects owned by that login from becoming disowned. This procedure was added in System 10.

- ■ `sp_adduser` and `sp_dropuser` add and drop users of a database. `sp_adduser` is also used to add a user to a group.

In regular usage, you can only issue these commands one at a time in one database and one SQL Server at a time. However, products like Enterprise SQL Server Manager allow you to add multiple users to multiple databases or SQL Servers with one operation.

OBJECT PERMISSIONS

SQL Server manages access by associating users with objects. One user owns a database. The database owner specifies the relationship that the user may have with the object by granting or revoking permissions. You may grant or deny several types of access to a person or group, depending on the object type, as shown in Table 2-2.

TABLE 2-2   *Types of Permissions*

Access type	Entity
create	database, default, procedure, rule, table, view
insert	tables, views
references[a]	tables, views, columns
update	tables, views, columns
delete	tables, views
select	tables, views, columns
execute	stored procedures

[a]In SQL Server 10.0 and later.

A typical way of protecting certain columns of a base table while allowing update access is to create a view. You can revoke all access to the base table, but grant the desired access types to the view.

Managing permissions can become complex. For example, if you create a trigger that does a cascaded update, you must ensure that the user has update permissions on both tables or that the same user who created the trigger also owns the underlying tables. Tools like Enterprise SQL Server Manager let you manage permissions in batches, which can simplify user and object management.

It is possible to give different users different permissions in different databases. For example, user A may be able to create tables in database A, but not drop them, and user B may be able to drop tables in database A but not create them. The roles of A and B could be reversed in database B. Permissions can be good for segmenting work between developers so that their work doesn't conflict, as long as they are working on independent sets of data. Be careful, though, to manage permissions so that if one developer leaves or gets sick, another developer can take over.

A privileged user may use the WITH GRANT OPTION to grant the power to grant others the power to access an object. This type of permission mechanism is the most permissive form of discretionary access control, with the control part being rather loose. One person can grant to 10 other people who may grant to 10 more. Or one person could grant to another who grants all to everyone. Use the WITH GRANT OPTION sparingly or not at all.

AUDIT DATABASE

Sybase introduced an auditing feature in System 10. You can set up an auditing database that records events related to a particular object or to a particular user or both. Administrators with sso_role can review the auditing information periodically to make sure that no unexpected events are occurring. In the event of an incident considered a threat, the login responsible for it can be identified, providing that the right auditing features have been enabled.

Auditing entails extra administrative attention, such as archiving and/or deleting auditing information periodically so that the database doesn't fill up. Also, you need to monitor logins, users, and roles carefully to make sure that users don't share logins. The practice of sharing logins mitigates your ability to tell who really initiated a particular event.

As with any security measures, auditing doesn't make sense unless your organization has a balanced security plan. Ideally, organizations derive security policies from a risk analysis of potential security threats. Chapter 10 includes a discussion of database security concerns to consider.

■ THE TRANSACT-SQL LANGUAGE

Once we have stored data and assured ourselves that we can protect it adequately, we concentrate on manipulating it. Users create their own mental views of data based on the tables they look at, the commands they execute, and the applications they use. As Systems Managers, we usually find ourselves helping users to find ever more efficient ways to access their particular view of the database. The typical Systems Manager's expertise with Transact-SQL tends to cluster around the system administration commands and the commands that generate users' calls for

73

help. Rather than rehash what you can find in the Sybase manuals, we only review the Transact-SQL language here. Those who also develop applications will become familiar with SQL through books devoted to the topic.

Transact-SQL is the Sybase implementation of the SQL language. Two standards influence the current versions of Transact-SQL: SQL 1989 and SQL 1992. System 10 achieved SQL 1989 Level 2 compliance and contains many features that will support SQL 1992 when certification tests for that standard are available.

Since most aspects of RDBMS administration fall outside the scope of the SQL standard, SQL Server includes significant extensions to SQL in that area. Readers new to SQL Server will see many references to system stored procedures, which all start with "sp_". Stored procedures are groups of SQL statements compiled and stored in binary form in the Server. Most SQL Server administration tasks involve executing at least one stored procedure. To see the SQL commands that make up a procedure, use `sp_helptext` in the `master` database for SQL Servers before 10.0 or the `sybsystemprocs` database in 10.0 and subsequent releases:

```
> sp_helptext "sp_help"
> go
```

This example shows you the SQL that generates the `sp_help` output, providing that no one has deleted the text from `syscomments`.

Besides extensions, error messages and keywords distinguish dialects of SQL from one another. Transact-SQL has extensive reporting capabilities for errors and other messages, allowing user-defined messages and allowing for messages in alternate languages as well. In System 10 and later releases, the `sp_checkreswords` displays SQL Server reserved words so that you can avoid using them as identifiers.

Tables 2-3 through 2-8 summarize the Transact-SQL commands, which are grouped by type for quick reference. Duplicates that exist for compliance with SQL 89 appear in parentheses next to the original Sybase command. Abbreviated forms of commands also appear in parentheses. See the Sybase reference manuals for syntax and detailed explanations of these commands.

TABLE 2-3   SQL Server Data Definition Commands[a]

Entity	CREATE	DROP	ALTER	Other
DATABASE	X	X	X	
TABLE	X	X	X	TRUNCATE, DELETE
INDEX	X	X		
DEFAULT	X	X		
PROCEDURE	X	X		
RULE	X	X		
TRIGGER	X	X		
SCHEMA 10.0+	X			
VIEW	X	X		

[a]10.0+ indicates a command available in SQL Server version 10.0 and later.

In Table 2-3, the X's indicate commands that can be made by adding the keyword in the associated column to the word in the row. For example, there is an ALTER DATABASE, but there is no *alter index* command. Table 2-4 summarizes the data manipulation commands. Table 2-5 gives you an idea of the wealth of functions available for transforming data.

TABLE 2-4   Data Manipulation Commands[a]

Command Type	Commands Available
Table Access	SELECT, INSERT, DELETE, UPDATE, READTEXT, WRITETEXT
Program Control	BEGIN...END, BREAK, CONTINUE, DECLARE, EXECUTE, GOTO, IF...ELSE, RETURN, WAITFOR, WHILE, PRINT, RAISERROR, SET
Transactions	BEGIN TRANSACTION (BEGIN TRAN), COMMIT TRANSACTION (COMMIT TRAN, COMMIT WORK 10.0+), PREPARE TRANSACTION, ROLLBACK TRANSACTION (ROLLBACK TRAN, ROLLBACK WORK 10.0+), ROLLBACK TRIGGER 10.0+, SAVE TRANSACTION
Cursor	DECLARE CURSOR, FETCH, CLOSE, DEALLOCATE CURSOR

[a]10.0+ indicates a command available in SQL Server version 10.0 and later.

TABLE 2-5   SQL Server Functions

Function Type	Functions Available
Aggregate	`sum, average, count, max, min`
Datatype Conversion	`convert, hextoint, inttohex`
Date	`getdate, datename, datepart, datediff, dateadd`
Mathematical	`abs, cos, acos, sin, asin, tan, cot, atan, atn2, degrees, radians, sign, ceiling, floor, round, exp, power, log, log10, pi, rand, sqrt`
String	`ascii, char, lower, upper, right, rtrim, ltrim, reverse, replicate, space, stuff, substring, str, char_length, charindex, patindex, difference, soundex`
System	`host_id, host_name, db_id, db_name, suser_id, suser_name, user, user_id, user_name, valid_name, object_id, object_name, col_name, col_length, index_col, datalength, rowcnt, reserved_pgs, curunreservedpgs, data_pgs, used_pgs, isnull, tsequal, lct_admin, proc_role, show_role`
Text and Image	`patindex, textptr, textvalid`

SQL Server has many built-in functions for common transformations that people wish to make to their data. These are shown in Table 2-7. The following built-in functions prove particularly useful for systems management tasks:

- `db_id` (*database_name*)
- `db_name` (*database_id*)
- `object_id` (*object_name*)
- `object_name` (*object_id*)

These allow you to translate between object and database numbers and their corresponding names. For example, when the errorlog refers to a problem in database number 17, you can find the name of the database in question using the command:

```
> select db_name(17)
> go
```

Table 2-6 shows you the commands used to manage SQL Server.

TABLE 2-6   SQL Server Administrative Commands

Command Type	Commands
General	CHECKPOINT, UPDATE STATISTICS, RECONFIG-URE, SHUTDOWN, USE
Device management	DISK INIT, DISK REINIT, DISK REFIT, DISK MIRROR, DISK UNMIRROR, DISK REMIRROR
Backup and recovery	DBCC, DUMP DATABASE, DUMP TRANSACTION, LOAD DATABASE, LOAD TRANSACTION
Users and permis-sions	GRANT, REVOKE, KILL, SETUSER

Transact-SQL allows users to set local variables for use by stored procedures and other applications. In addition, SQL Server sets several global variables that allow users to check the status of SQL Server or of a process. In Transact-SQL, all local variables start with @ and global variables start with @@.

TABLE 2-7   Per-process Variables[a]

Variable	Description
@@rowcount	The maximum number of rows a query should return from the result set
@@char_convert	The character set that should be used
@@client_csname	The client's character set name
@@client_csid	The client's character set ID
@@error	The error code returned by the last command
@@identity	The last value inserted into an identity column
@@isolation	The isolation level in use
@@langid	The language ID in use
@@language	The language in use
@@nestlevel	The level of nesting in the current command; that is, if one procedure calls another, the nesting level is incre-mented
@@procid	The ID of the current procedure executing
@@spid	The current server process id

TABLE 2-7 Per-process Variables[a] (Continued)

Variable	Description
@@sqlstatus	Status from the last `fetch` statement
@@textsize	The amount of the text to read or write
@@tranchained	An indicator of whether transaction chained mode is in use
@@trancount	The nesting level of transactions
@@transtate	The state of a transaction after a statement executes
@@textptr	The pointer to the text or image column that the current process last inserted or updated 10.1+
@@textcolid	The text or image column ID that the current process last inserted or updated 10.1+
@@textdbid	The database ID in which the current process last updated a text or image column 10.1+
@@textobjid	The object ID in which the current process last updated a text or image column 10.1+
@@texttts	The timestamp of the last text or image column that the process updated 10.1+

[a]10.1+ indicates commands available in SQL Server versions 10.1 and later.

10.1

In Version 10.1, five new text information global variables shown at the bottom of Table 2-7 make updates and inserts of TEXT and IMAGE data easier and faster when using the Open Client API. See the Sybase Open Client 10.1 or later documentation for details about how to use these variables.

TABLE 2-8 System-wide Variables

Variable	Description
@@connections	The number of attempted logins since SQL Server was last started
@@cpu_busy	The number of SQL Server ticks that the CPUs have used doing work since the Server was last started
@@idle	The number of SQL Server ticks that the CPUs have been idle since the Server was last started

TABLE 2-8 System-wide Variables (Continued)

Variable	Description
@@io_busy	The number of SQL Server ticks that the Server has used for doing I/O since the Server was last started
@@maxcharlen	The maximum length in bytes of any character in the default SQL Server character set
@@max_connections	The maximum number of connections that the current operating system environment can support
@@ncharsize	The average length in bytes of the SQL Server national character set in use
@@pack_received	The number of network packets received by SQL Server since it was last started
@@pack_sent	The number of network packets sent by SQL Server since it was last started
@@packet_errors	The number of packet errors that have occurred since SQL Server was last started
@@servername	The name of the local SQL Server
@@thresh_hysteresis	The number of pages in the threshold activation zone
@@timeticks	The number of microseconds per SQL Server tick
@@total_errors	The total number of I/O errors that the SQL Server has encountered since it was last started
@@total_read	The total number of pages read from disk since SQL Server was last started
@@total_write	The total number of pages written to disk since SQL Server was last started
@@version	The exact version of the SQL Server binary that is running

SQL Server reserves certain words that you may not use as identifiers for database objects (at least, not without difficulty.) They can, however, be used for naming local variables and stored procedure parameters. The Sybase SQL Server Reference Manuals list these words. Note that client applications may reserve additional keywords that you may also need to avoid.

In System 10 and later releases, you can get a list of keywords by executing the `sp_checkreswords` stored procedure. If you have an earlier release, but have access to System 10 files, you can copy `sp_checkreswords` from the System 10 `installmaster` script and run it in your SQL Server to avoid upgrade difficulties.

Organizations can tailor SQL Server in a number of ways to make it suit the nature of their businesses. To adjust many of the parameters that define how SQL Server functions, system administrators use the `sp_configure` command. `sp_configure` allows you to alter most Server-wide characteristics, such as memory usage, number of simultaneous users, and defaults. Chapters 6 and 7 describe configuration in detail, since customizing the Server for your applications plays such a crucial role in how well your system performs.

Sybase also provides several features for customizing use in a particular locale. These include the

- Ability to use messages in several international languages: You can enable SQL Server to store data and issue messages in several languages in a single database. This entails adding the messages for the language and the supporting character set to SQL Server with the installation program, `sybconfig` or `sybinit`.

- Ability to select a character set that most closely matches the primary language (including multibyte character sets): The Sybase clients and servers provide automatic character conversion. You can store and retrieve data in more than 30 languages. Sybase is a member of the Unicode™ consortium and is implementing Unicode and ISO 10646 support in its key products. Unicode/ISO 10646 is the internationally approved standard for support of multilingual computing. The consortium's goal is to allow you to use data in any modern language on any system worldwide.

- Ability to set date formatting preferences: You can define the way you want to identify day, month, and year and the order in which they appear. You can also define a preference for which day comes first in a week (typically Sunday or Monday).

- Ability to select a sort order that most closely matches the character set and the application. The SQL Server sort order sets the sequence of characters used when arranging data. SQL commands can request that data be returned in ascending or descending alphabetic order. The sort order determines how to treat similar alphabetic characters, such as the uppercase, lowercase, and accented versions of the same letter. You can choose from the following sort orders, which are described in the Sybase SQL Server Manuals: Binary; Dictionary; Dictionary, Case Insensitive; Dictionary, Case Insensitive with Preference; Dictionary, Case and Accent Insensitive.

Character set, sort order, and language are all closely related, since a change in one often requires a corresponding change in another. In Chapter 4, we consider these issues in more detail.

■ SQL SERVER UTILITIES

SQL Server comes with several utilities offered to help you manage SQL Server from the operating system level. You can find descriptions of how these work in Sybase's SQL Server Utility Programs manual for your platform. A brief description of each follows.

■ **backupserver**   `backupserver` starts the Backup Server process, which must be running on your SQL Server in order for you to initiate a `DUMP` or `LOAD` command successfully. Backup Server is a remote server process that communicates with SQL Server using remote procedure calls (RPCs).

■ **console**   `console` is a facility for assisting with SQL Server tape backups before System 10 was released. Console basically makes SQL Server pause when you need to load a new tape and start up again when you've done it. The `console` program is now obsolete

■ **bcp**   The Bulk Copy utility allows you to copy data from tables out to files, with columns delimited as you specify so that the data can be imported back into SQL Server or another database at another time.

■ **buildmaster**   The `buildmaster` program creates a master database device. It is normally run as a transparent part of the install procedure. However, sometimes it becomes necessary to run it to reconfigure SQL Server or rebuild the master device in the event of a serious disk error.

■ **defncopy**   With `defncopy`, you can copy the SQL definitions of views, rules, defaults, triggers, or stored procedures out to disk.

■ **isql**   The Interactive SQL utility, `isql`, is a simple utility for issuing SQL commands to SQL Server.

■ **langinstall**   The `langinstall` utility allows you to add languages to SQL Server. This process copies the language files from disk into the `syslanguages` and `sysmessages` tables.

■ **showserver**   Run the `showserver` utility to determine whether SQL Server is running and to see the command line flags it was started with. This provides the equivalent functionality of the UNIX *ps*, VMS *show process*, or NT *pview* command.

■ **startserver**   `startserver` starts SQL Server from the command line. It runs the `RUNSERVER` script in the SQL Server install directory.

■ SQL SERVER LIMITS

Table 2-9 lists some SQL Server limits that you may find useful to remember. These limits were true for System 11 as of the time this book was published. Some of these may change in later releases. These are the theoretical boundaries. With many, you will discover the practical boundaries of your system and organization to be more restrictive. For example, the amount of data that you can check and back up reliably on the backup media at your disposal is usually less than the SQL Server database size limit.

TABLE 2-9   SQL Server Limits

Maximum Limit	Limit
Number of databases per SQL Server	32,767
Database size	256 GB
Disk fragments for a database (rows in sysusages)[a]	128
Number of databases spanned by one update	8
Number of databases opened by one query	16
Number of tables in a query	16
Number of tables per database	2 billion
Number of columns per table	250
Number of indexes per table	251
Number of rows per table	Limited only by available disk space (unless you have an identity column, for which the maximum row number is limited by the size of the numeric datatype upon which the identity column is built)
Number of columns per composite index	16

TABLE 2-9   SQL Server Limits (Continued)

Maximum Limit	Limit
Number of characters per database object name	30
Number of stored procedure parameters	255
Amount of SQL definition text in a procedure object	16 MB
Number of stored procedures	Limited only by available disk space
Depth of nested transactions	16 levels

[a]This means that the maximum number of times you can extend a database using the ALTER DATABASE command is 127. If you intend to have the largest possible database, you need to create the initial database with a size of 2048 MB and make each additional extension 2048 MB as well, for a total of 2048 MB * 128 = 256 GB.

Procedure Manual Suggestions

○ Starting and Stopping SQL Server

⇒ Write a procedure for shutting down and starting up SQL Server at your site.

⇒ Instructions should include notifying users, normal shutdown, emergency shutdown, start-up instructions, giving users alternate systems for doing work while SQL Server is down, and what to do if recovery fails.

○ Managing Database Objects

⇒ Write a procedure for a method of managing database objects.

⇒ Maintain a list outside SQL Server that lists all objects for each database grouped by type. If objects are created for a particular application, indicate groupings by labels, symbols, or a diagram.

➠ Identify who is responsible for which objects in case they need to be changed or in case a system change is planned that will affect them.

➠ Write a stored procedure or report to update this list frequently. This could be weekly, monthly, or whenever objects are added, modified, or deleted, depending on how dynamic the environment is.

➠ Keep scripts or other methods of re-creating objects handy. Objects tend to get corrupt or inadvertently dropped at the worst possible time.

❍ Backup and Recovery

➠ Write a backup and recovery strategy for both normal operations and disasters. Include scenarios for bad backup drives, bad disk drives, bad media, the primary person responsible for backups leaving the organization, and natural disasters.

➠ Maintain in hard copy, or outside SQL Server for disaster recovery purposes, a list of all dump devices for each database. (When you are trying to load a backup is not the time to try to find out how the backup was made.) The list should include the Server name, the database name, the dump method, and the dump device. Ideally, this information is replicated on labels that are placed on the dump medium.

➠ Maintain a log that records when dumps are made of each database. Write a cron or batch job that periodically checks the log and sends you mail if a dump hasn't been made for a particular database

❍ Avoiding Hard-coded Limits

➠ Establish a design review procedure that ensures a limits check for all database proposals to make sure that a planned database or development effort will not run into any hard-coded SQL Server limits.

○ Managing Stored Procedures

➡ Write a procedure for managing stored procedures.

➡ Keep hard copies of the scripts used to create each stored procedure.

➡ Diagram and publish interdependent procedures so that anyone who changes them will know what effects to expect.

➡ Establish and publish baseline metrics for key procedures. Ask users to notify you when performance has fallen more than 10% below the baseline. Where use of the system varies widely, establish separate baselines for peak periods and off periods.

○ Managing Roles

➡ If you choose to use roles, write a procedure for how they will be used in your SQL Server.

➡ Whenever roles are changed, document the date and time of the change, the reason for the change, and a complete list of roles.

➡ Store the list in hard-copy form or in a safe place outside of SQL Server.

➡ When roles are added, make sure that they reflect the organizational structure of your business.

➡ Make sure that the roles don't conflict in a way that, if one person left the organization, no one would be able to do anything with SQL Server.

○ Managing Object Permissions

➡ Write a procedure for permissions related to object management.

➠ Draw a diagram of all the databases in a SQL Server. Label each database with the person who owns it and is responsible for it when it needs to be changed or fixed.

➠ Label the diagram with any groups that have particular access to each database.

➠ Draw lines around groups of databases to delineate regions that are affected by particular projects.

➠ Post the diagram somewhere visible where it will be viewed frequently so that it is clear who is responsible for what and where cooperation between groups is essential.

➠ Update the diagram as the system and the people change.

CHAPTER

An Internal View of SQL Server Structure

Now that we've seen how SQL Server looks to the user, we will explore how it interacts with machines. Knowing this level of detail will help you prevent common problems or, at least, isolate them quickly when they do occur. Sybase focuses on providing customers with the highest-performance RDBMS system possible for a given hardware architecture. However, most SQL Server systems require tuning before you can get the maximum performance possible for your applications. A SQL Server configuration must make the most of the underlying hardware to deliver optimum results. As you discover how SQL Server uses your system and the kinds of stresses your applications put on the Server, you will better understand whether to spend your budget on memory, on disks, or on a multiprocessor machine. Once you have a good picture of the internals, you can use the configuration commands described in Chapter 6 to tune SQL Server and make the most out of your system resources.

87

We will cover SQL Server's use of the machine it resides on, as shown from top to bottom in Table 3-1. While we won't discuss other uses of the machine than SQL Server, it's good to be aware of those shown in the fourth column, since they sometimes interfere with SQL Server, or vice versa.

TABLE 3-1 *Uses of the Machine Resources*

Machine Resource	SQL Server Use	SQL Server User Use	Other Use
Disks	System databases for managing SQL Server, configuration info, SQL Server files	User databases	Operating system files, user file system, swap, other RDBMSs, or other software
CPU	Server process	User processes within SQL Server process	Operating system, other RDBMSs, or other software
Memory	Server binary, cache, and memory structures to accommodate configuration values set	User processes within SQL Server	Operating system, other RDBMSs, or other software
Network	TDS Packets[a] between client and Server or between two Servers	TDS packets between client and server	Users, other RDBMSs, or other software

[a]The Sybase format for data packets sent over a network is called Tabular Data Stream (TDS).

For the examples in this chapter, we will again observe Tim, who has decided to use his *school* database for experimenting with various SQL Server management options. Of course, he made a backup of the database before doing anything in this chapter.

An RDBMS such as SQL Server devotes most of its activities to storing and managing data. Accordingly, the topics of this book cluster around information, data, and disks. In this section, we look at data storage from several different angles so that you can understand more of the *why's* of SQL Server. By the end, you will have a good idea of how implementation choices affect your ability to manage data. You'll also understand better how well your system copes or fails to cope with the demands placed on it.

■ TERMINOLOGY

Words like server, device, partition, and segment have come to mean many things in our industry. In this chapter, we need to describe some Sybase constructs that use these terms in specific ways. An introduction to each follows:

■ **Server** In industry documentation, a machine can be a server, such as a file server. We also see references to software servers, such as to ftp servers, HTTP servers, or SQL Servers. In this book, we mean *SQL Server* when we use the capitalized word *Server*. We use lowercase and qualifying terms to indicate other types of servers.

■ **SQL Server device** Sybase calls allocations of disk space *devices*. We also call these database devices. Such devices do not correspond exactly to disk drives. We will refer to disk drives as disk devices. To reserve disk space for SQL Server, a portion of a disk is identified by name and size. The disk portion may take the form of a file or an operating system-defined disk partition. Once identified in the Server, this disk portion then becomes known internally as a database device. Sybase also uses the word *devices* to refer to drives used for backups. A backup device might be a tape drive or an operating system file on disk. Each row in the `master` database's `sysdevices` table represents one SQL Server device or a backup device.

■ **Page** SQL Server manipulates disk space in blocks called pages. For all platforms but Stratus, a page occupies 2 KB. For stratus, SQL Server uses 4 KB pages. For this book, 2 KB pages are assumed to keep calculations and explanations simple. Calculations for Stratus pages appear in footnotes.

■ **Extent** SQL Server allocates space for tables and indexes in blocks of eight pages, called extents.

■ **Allocation unit** An allocation unit is a 256-page block of data space in SQL Server.

■ **Disk fragment** We will call a portion of a SQL Server device allocated for use by a database a disk fragment. SQL Server allows you to put one database on many devices, or several databases on one device, or several parts of databases on one device. Each row in the `master` database's `sysusages` table represents one disk fragment.

■ **Disk partition**   A part of a disk device recognized as a partition by the operating system will be called a disk partition in this book.

■ **Table partition**   In SQL Server 11, there is a new option in the ALTER TABLE syntax to divide tables into slices called partitions. We refer to these as table partitions to distinguish them from disk partitions.

■ **Segments**   In SQL Server terminology, segments refer to data allocation mechanisms. Segments are not physical portions of disk. If we were talking about money instead of disk space, a disk fragment would correspond to a wallet full of money, and a segment would correspond to a budget. With one system, our friend Tim might determine that the money in his wallet is devoted to a single books budget and that he would not allow spending on anything else. With another system, Tim would designate the money as shared between the books budget, the tuition budget, and the between-class snack budget. Similarly, you can designate that one disk fragment can be used only for log segment or that it can be used for log, system, and several user segments simultaneously. The syntax for creating tables and indexes includes an ON clause for indicating the segment to use. When SQL Server needs to find a new page, it looks for free pages in the extents already allocated to the table or index that needs more space. If none is found, it searches for a free extent on a device fragment marked with the same segment number as the table or index.

■ **Entities**   We will use the general term *entities* to refer to tables, indexes, and logs and similarly distinct logical structures in SQL Server. These are not technically SQL Server objects, but are discrete sets of specialized SQL Server data that are treated differently from each other on an internal level.

■ DEVICE TYPES AND FEATURES

Hopefully, if you manage a database system backed by significant investment, you have the opportunity to choose the disk devices you use. In established systems or those not considered critical, you may need to use what's already available. Selecting disk devices and deciding which databases to put on which drives involves evaluating several factors. Given a need for, say, 2 GB of database space, we might ask the following questions:

- What are the best devices to buy?
- Which disk features make the most difference?
- Should I use RAID?
- Is it better to store all data on one disk or spread it across many?
- Should data be segregated by device type?
- Does it matter which controller a disk device uses?

In this section we touch on various considerations that will influence how you answer these questions for your site.

At the physical level, most disk devices consist of platters coated with magnetic material. For hard disks, a group of platters is arranged in a stack, attached via a spindle that goes through the center of each platter. A gap between each platter accommodates a moving disk drive access arm. At the end of each arm, a disk head reads and writes data to disk. The head encodes data by applying an electrical charge to tiny portions of the magnetic disk coating, conferring to each portion an "on" or "off" state. (This is a bit of a simplification, but further details don't add much to the understanding of databases.) The operating system (and the human mind) translates on and off to 1 and 0, respectively.

Similar to Morse code, patterns of 1s and 0s can be built upon one another to create bytes, characters, words, sentences, essays, and books. For example, in the ASCII character encoding scheme, the binary number 0100 0001 represents the capital letter A.

Upon bits of magnetic material, a machine imposes order by creating concentric circles called tracks around the disk platters, numbered from 0 to n, where n is one less than the total number of tracks that fit on a platter. Software and hardware separate tracks into sectors and group sectors into clusters. The operating system also groups tracks into cylinders and cylinders into partitions.[1] In the group of platters that make up the disk drive, a

---

[1]Here the terminology breaks down, because C: and D: on your PC can be two partitions on the same drive or two different drives each containing one or more partitions. AIX uses the term partitions to refer to space on a higher logical layer than we are talking about here.

cylinder is a vertical slice of tracks made up of the tracks in the same position on each platter. In other words, cylinder X consists of the track at position X for each platter. A partition is a group of cylinders. The operating system can address each sector of a disk device, so each sector becomes a unit of data storage.

In other words, all the database structures that we examine in this book are essentially nothing to a computer but bits of magnetic dust that are either awake or asleep. When disk drives go bad, it means a bit failed to wake up or fall asleep at the expected moment. It may have even left the room. From this explanation, we become more sympathetic to the otherwise well-behaved computer that becomes unreliable when exposed to extremes of light, heat, humidity, vibration, and sudden losses of power.

▪ DEVICE PERFORMANCE

The slowest piece of the RDBMS system puzzle (besides bottlenecks created by organizational politics) is disk reads and writes (often referred to as disk I/O, or simply I/Os). For this reason, the most frequent goal of performance tuning is to keep the amount of disk I/O as low as possible. The following mechanisms can help you improve SQL Server performance:

- **High performance devices**   Selected by a Systems Manager and provided by the disk manufacturer

- **Controller caching**   Provided as a disk feature by a disk manufacturer

- **SQL Server caching**   Provided by SQL Server and configured by a SQL Server administrator (enhancements in System 11 allow you to bind specific databases, tables, indexes, or logs to their own caches)

- **Dividing data among several controllers**   Managed by a Systems Manager or database administrator

- **Good indexes**   Selected and created by database or table owner or application developer in cooperation with the person or people managing the underlying disk hardware

■ **Optimizer algorithms**   Provided by SQL Server, guided by internal statistics about data distribution and indexes (with System 11, you can also give the optimizer "hints" about which indexes to use)

■ **Intelligent Transact-SQL algorithms**   Designed into applications by developers or used on an ad hoc basis by savvy users

■ **Parallel I/O**   Provided by separating data across several controllers or using RAID technology (we'll look at RAID in the next section)

■ **Optimal I/O sizes**   Provided in System 10 for bulk copy operations by changing network packet sizes and in SQL Server 11 for all data by configuration

Buyers of disk devices usually examine the following factors for evaluating I/O performance:

■ **Sustainable data rate**   The amount of data the disk controller can deliver to the operating system under constant load.

■ **Seek time**   The time it takes the device to find a particular cylinder.

■ **Latency**   The time it takes for the disk to spin around to the desired sector. Latency can be reduced by increasing the rotational speed of the disk. If this is done, however, the number of sectors per track may be limited by how much data the controller can read at once as the disk whizzes by. A reduction in the number of sectors per track translates into an increased number of switches between tracks, which increases response time.

■ **Number of controllers per disk**   One controller may serve one or more disks, which means multiple devices can end up competing with each other for their controller. You can increase database performance by separating user data, indexes, and transaction logs so that each resides on a different controller. Likewise, if you have a choice between several small disks on separate controllers or one large disk, the former will probably yield better performance.

■ **Cache**   Disk controllers usually have onboard memory for caching data. Different caching algorithms may be used, but in general caches try to retain the most frequently or recently requested data. The cache is implemented by adding memory, software for moving data to and from the cache memory, and a main processor to a controller board. For some controllers, a Systems Manager can configure the policies of the cache to maximize the hit rate for their work load. However, caching can sometimes interfere with SQL Server. To troubleshoot, disable controller caching.

■ **I/O size**   The disk or operating system may be optimized for certain disk I/O sizes. SQL Server 4.9.x and 10.0 use 2 KB pages.[2] This means that these versions of SQL Server do not operate optimally under conditions that constrain I/O to a different size. The System 11 SQL Server can adapt to different sizes of I/O by reconfiguration. (See Chapter 6 for configuration information.)

In Chapter 2 we looked at what the SQL Server does to data. Now we can extrapolate how it uses disks. It potentially reads and writes to all data blocks on the portions of disk allocated for database usage. For every access to a table, it potentially uses an index. In fact, indexes are usually created in a way designed to make certain table accesses very fast. Therefore, if certain columns of certain tables are used in a majority of queries, then the portion of the disk containing indexes gets a lot of action. By using SQL Server segments, you can place indexes on specific disks so that you can make sure heavily used indexes are on your faster disk devices. Every data modification command writes a transaction to the transaction log. To improve overall performance for anything but a read-only database, put the transaction log on the fastest, most reliable drive possible.

You can spread a database across several disk partitions by repeatedly[3] using the ALTER DATABASE command to extend it onto additional devices that you have defined on those partitions. If those partitions are on disks with separate controllers and if your applications are such that the access load is evenly balanced across tables, this approach can mean that several controllers can work in parallel to serve all the users' needs.

If you have applications that have an exceptionally high rate of creation of objects, you may want to put object-related system tables (e.g., sysobjects, sysprocedures, and sysindexes) on reliable disks. sysindexes is accessed for virtually every query. sysindexes holds the start and end points of tables and indexes for all objects in a database, so all queries that need to find data or add data to an index or table read sysindexes.

---

[2]4 KB pages on Stratus.

[3]Up to 127 times in SQL Server versions 4.2 through 11.0.

Try to give SQL Server its own disks. In particular, try to keep SQL Server from having to share with any disk used intensively for operating system purposes, such as for swap or temporary files. Also, if the operating system continuously logs audit and performance data, segregate the OS log files on different disks and controllers than SQL Server as well.

Because the log is always written at the end, give `syslogs` its own disk and controller. With this setup, the disk rarely has to seek and can sustain a high I/O rate.

RAID

RAID stands for Redundant Arrays of Independent Disks. With RAID, several disks of the exact same physical size and capacity form an array that looks like a single disk to the operating system. The redundancy can be turned to a cost, performance, or reliability advantage, depending on the RAID level (configuration) you use. However, as with everything else in IT, you cannot optimize on cost, performance, and reliability all at once. The RAID level that you select should match the needs of your applications. RAID has become very popular for database devices. Since RAID devices should look the same to the operating system as other disk devices, Sybase should be able to use these devices as it does any others. However, only some RAID levels pay off for SQL Server versions prior to System 11. In System 11 you can use I/O sizes other than 2 KB, but in earlier releases, every I/O function works in terms of 2 KB pages. Certain levels of RAID rely on other I/O sizes, such as 4 KB. Sybase Technical Support has also handled many cases involving database corruption associated with the use of RAID devices, indicating that in some ways RAID disks are not completely transparent to the operating system and do not behave exactly like regular disks. Test any proposed RAID configurations before implementing them in a production system. Descriptions of each RAID level follow.

Level 0   Data striping, no parity (low cost, high performance, low reliability)

Level 0 yields high I/O performance at a low cost. The failure of a single member of a disk array results in failure of the entire array. Since most RAID 0 implementations use a fixed 4 KB block transfer size, standard SQL Server operations using 2 KB blocks may not benefit from this configuration. The RAID failure possibility exposes SQL Server to more risk. For example, if we put a database on one non-RAID disk, it is subject to the odds of that type of disk failing under a given load in a given time period. Under RAID level 0, if you use n disks, the risk is n times the odds of one of the disks failing.

Level 1   Disk mirroring (high cost, moderate performance, high reliability)

This RAID level provides a mirror for every primary disk in the array. It manages small reads and small writes with a speed equivalent to a single disk. Large reads and writes execute at a speed slower than a single spindle. Compared to SQL Server mirroring, RAID 1 can be faster and more efficient, since mirroring may be contained in disk subsystem firmware instead of software. However, with SQL Server mirroring, physical disk size and type limitation do not constrain the choice of devices. If you have dissimilar disk drives available, Sybase mirroring can use them.

Level 2   Disk striping with error correction bits (high cost, moderate performance, moderate reliability)

Parallel disk arrays are accessed and written concurrently for every access to the virtual disk for both RAID levels 2 and 3. The array management software handles the error detection and correction, relieving the disk firmware of the task. Reliability is improved over a single disk because of the ability to detect and correct data. Again, the complete failure of any disk in the array shuts down the entire array.

Level 3   Disk striping, one parity disk (low cost, variable performance, high reliability)

This level uses fewer parity disks, and implementation does not require special disk hardware. RAID 3 design is optimal for high data transfer capacity for large data objects for noninteractive applications that process sequential files. Small I/O transfers perform poorly. If the array allows a hot-swap of a failed disk, continuous operation may be possible. As with RAID level 0, RAID 3 favors large read, large write environments. For optimal operation, you would need to use the large I/O functionality of System 11. Consider RAID 3 for decision support applications that require large scans and high reliability.

Level 4   One parity disk (low cost, moderate performance, moderate reliability)

All data reside on a single disk of the array, with parity stored on a parity disk. This level of RAID is like level 3, but manages the performance of small transfers for better performance. However, the parity disk becomes a bottleneck for write operations, so the overall performance suffers.

Level 5   Disk striping, parity spread across all disks (low cost, moderate performance, high reliability)

When comparing cost against a mirrored solution (either RAID 1 or Sybase mirroring), RAID 5 is a less expensive solution with generally equal reliability. Read performance is good, but write performance is only moderate. RAID 5 devices would most likely not be a good candidate for a log file where performance is desired and the majority of the activity is writing.

The definitions vary for RAID levels 6 and above, so we will not go into them here.

■ SQL SERVER DEVICES

SQL Server sees disk devices one partition or file at a time. When you install Sybase SQL Server, you specify the size and the location of the master device, the `sybsystemprocs` device, and, optionally, the audit device. The install program uses the build-master utility to initialize the master device and create the master and model databases. The installation program creates the other devices using the DISK INIT command. Thereafter, you initialize new databases devices by executing DISK INIT from within SQL Server. Under some circumstances, you might use the buildmaster utility to re-create a master device to recover from a device failure. A key difference between the master device and other devices lies in the presence of the configuration block. This block of data resides in the first 4 pages of the master device. It contains the defaults for configuration variables, which govern the number of internal server data structures to allocate at boot time.

SANDY'S SPORT SHOPS—DISK DEVICES

Here are examples of each command, as Tim might use them for his school databases on a UNIX System 10 SQL Server:

```
% buildmaster -d master -s 10240
```

In this example, Tim rebuilds a 20-MB master device for his SQL Server. (Buildmaster requires that you specify a size in 2 KB pages.) Next, Tim defined devices for his school databases.

```
> disk init name = "school_dev",
> physname = "/dev/rsd0b",
> vdevno = 2,
> size = 4096
> go
> disk init
> name = "school_log",
> physname = "/dev/rsd2b",
> vdevno = 3,
> size = 1024
> go
```

These commands allocate an 8-MB raw partition for user data and a 2-MB raw partition for transaction logs. Tim put the log device on a second drive, since he knew it was on a separate controller and would yield higher write performance.

■ CONFIGURING DISK DEVICES

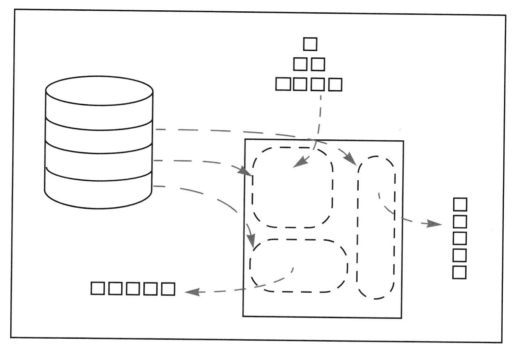

Figure 3.1 Mapping disk devices to segments in a database and then to database objects

With UNIX and DOS devices, you can divide one disk into multiple partitions. You can use different disk partitions for file systems, or database devices or swap as necessary. Each partition consists of a set of cylinders defined by the person formatting the disk.

While the failure of a disk device poses a significant threat to a database, more common disk scenarios related to device configuration threaten your data as well.[4] These include

---

[4]Do not think these things could never happen to you. I have talked very smart people through recovering from backups for each of these scenarios. The problem is that it takes coordination more than intelligence to avoid these causes of failure. Sleep deprivation in Systems Managers also seems to affect the quality of disk management.

- Mistakenly changing the ownership of a disk partition or file so that SQL Server can no longer write to it

- Changing the disk partition or file ownership so that someone other than SQL Server can write to it

- Mistakenly mounting a file system or placing swap on a database device, causing mass destruction of data

- Mistakenly allocating a second SQL Server device or mirror on top of an existing SQL Server device or mirror

- Taking an active disk device off line "for a moment" to add another disk to the controller

- Mistakenly deleting the device file pointer (e.g., */dev/rsd0*)

- Using an automatic disk block swap feature of the operating system or disk device that swaps bad disk blocks with clean ones upon detection of corruption (addressing of disk blocks on raw partitions must be completely transparent to SQL Server for a feature like this to work for database devices)

- Using an operating system backup program on a database device while SQL Server is running

For these reasons, wise Systems Managers make sure that the devices are owned by the `sybase` user and group, and only the `sybase` user and group, at the operating system level. They also restrict access to that user and group to a few well-trained people. Finally, the Systems Manager puts a process in place for documenting all use of all disk devices and partitions so that anyone can tell whether they can use a device.

In the Sybase SQL Server Installation Manuals, the writers encourage you to take certain precautions when allocating disk devices for the Server and your databases. We examine the reasons behind each of those warnings in the next three sections.

USING RAW PARTITIONS INSTEAD OF FILE SYSTEMS ON UNIX PLATFORMS

For UNIX, when you install SQL Server or when you want to allocate more space to it, you are asked to determine a raw partition you can use and warned not to use the file system. We'll now look what a disk partition is and why we call it *raw*. For UNIX, a *non-raw* partition typically has a file system mounted on it. The operating system documentation may refer to raw partitions as *character-oriented devices*, though at least one calls them *block* devices. In any case, look for the ones that allow asynchronous I/O.

In UNIX, devices have multiple file pointers in the devices directory to access a single disk partition. You will find at least one for accessing the partition as a raw device and another for accessing it as a file device. Under BSD UNIX, a raw device file has an `r` prefix, as in `rsd0`. The name `sd0` designates the same device, but for use as in file mode. The naming conventions for SVR4 UNIX are more complex. See the installation guide for your platform for more details about which file pointers to use.

For a raw device, if you ask UNIX to write a block of data, it will do so immediately, bypassing any buffering optimizations that it might otherwise provide. For file systems, if an application makes a request to write a block of data, UNIX adds the data to a write queue in memory. Later, a process can flush the entire write queue to disk, saving time over writes of one block at a time. However, if the machine goes down before the queue gets flushed to disk, several writes may not happen, possibly corrupting the file system (and your databases, if they are on file system devices). For this reason, most UNIX shutdown programs and knowledgeable UNIX Systems Managers issue the `sync` command before shutting down a machine. `sync` flushes data in memory to disk.

Since we try to avoid corruption for mission-critical database systems and since machines tend to go down—whether by user failure, software failure, hardware failure, or power failure— Sybase prefers to take more control over the disk write process. By using a raw device, SQL Server can write straight to disk. SQL Server also optimizes for performance by storing writes in data cache rather than immediately flushing data to disk. However, the transaction-oriented methods of SQL Server provide the recoverability that UNIX doesn't provide. SQL Server writes disk changes first to the transaction log, and then to the database structures. This way, when SQL Server is rebooted after a crash, it can compare the transaction log to what's actually on disk and decide which changes need to be undone or redone.

Fuzzy space availability reporting in BSD UNIX file systems also defeats databases. In BSD UNIX, when you create a file system, you use the m option of the `makefs` or `newfs` command to designate a percentage of free space that the operating system reserves for allocation overhead or for extra room to use when allocation demands force the use of larger blocks than requested. Ten percent is reserved by default. This disk reserve functions much like a fuel reserve. UNIX keeps the reserve somewhat invisible from the user. The `df` command reports file usage in terms of the visible space, so it's possible to receive reports of a file system more than 100% used. While UNIX will let you allocate a file that extends into the extra 10%, it won't let anyone but `root` write beyond that boundary. Therefore, you could (but shouldn't) put a file system on a 1-GB partition and then successfully allocate a 1-GB SQL Server device on it and start using it. However, you would start to receive write errors when SQL Server attempted to use the last 10% of the device. Losing a 90% full 1-GB database creates a great deal of anguish.[5]

AVOIDING CYLINDER ZERO

Some UNIX versions use cylinder 0 of a disk (on the first partition, by default) to record the disk label. If you put a database device on cylinder 0, UNIX will periodically (usually when the machine is rebooted) attempt to read the disk label and find it corrupted. It will then copy the label from duplicate location back on to what it considers to be the appropriate block. If the `master` device is on a partition using cylinder 0, SQL Server will fail to boot because now the block looks inappropriate to it. If the Server does boot in this situation, it will eventually detect data corruption at the beginning of a database device. This occurs frequently among those new to Sybase SQL Server who don't read the

---

[5]Copying out a 90% full 1-GB database device, reformatting a disk, and then doing a logical database rebuild and copying the data back in doesn't make for a great night either.

Sybase Installation Manuals carefully. Sybase Technical Support may ask you to check your disk partitions if you are experiencing these recognizable symptoms.

AVOIDING OVERLAPPING PARTITIONS

If, on a UNIX system, you issue a command that shows you disk partition configuration (such as `dkinfo`), you may notice that by default, the size of the C partition equals the size of all the other partitions added together. This is because UNIX gives you the flexibility (and opportunity for disaster) to address your disk space in more than one way at a time.

To refer to the entire device in the example, you would specify partition C. To refer to the device in pieces, you would use partitions A, B, E, F, and G. You would not refer to partition H unless you wanted F and G grouped together. You could reserve A for the boot partition, mount a file system on B, and use E and F for database partitions. If you later mounted a file system on C or H, you would ruin your databases by overwriting random bits of them. Until you discovered the root of this problem, you might suspect your disk drive of going bad or SQL Server of a database corruption bug.

Sybase Technical Support handles a lot of calls about bad file system devices, overlapping partitions, partition A corruption, and problems resulting from multiple uses of the same disk, as described earlier. When users report corruption, Sybase Technical Support Engineers usually start by suspecting user error, disk problems, and operating system activities in approximately that order, based on the relative frequency of these problems in the customer base.

■ DISK MIRRORING

To guard against the eventuality of disks going bad, SQL Server provides a mirroring function for making secondary copies of database devices. When you create a device mirror, all writes to a primary SQL Server device go to a secondary device as well. If a primary device fails, processing fails over to the mirror device. SQL Server reports the error to the errorlog when this happens. You will also find messages in the errorlog if the mirror stops working.

For providing the best reliability, mirror everything. As a fallback position, at least mirror the `master` device and the transaction logs of your important databases. Corruption of the `master` device makes the entire SQL Server and all databases managed by it unusable until you load the `master` database from backup. Damage to a transaction log corrupts an entire database. With a solid mirroring strategy, you can recover from these errors much more quickly than you could from backups.

To mirror a disk, use the `DISK MIRROR` command. Be sure to select a mirror partition that is the same size as the primary partition. Also, take extra care to ensure that the mirror device is not already in use by another database, by a file system, or by the operating system for swap space. Remarkably often, administrators neglect to check this and corrupt their databases in the act of trying to ensure their safety. This is especially common when two or more people share responsibility for the same disk devices.

SANDY'S SPORT SHOPS—MIRRORING

Tim read about mirroring in the Sybase System Administration Guide and then defined a mirror of his school device:

```
> disk mirror
> name = "school_dev",
> mirror = "/dev/rsd4b"
> go
```

If the same disk controller services both the primary and the mirror partitions, any writes to the secondary device can slow down overall performance of the databases on the primary device. In general, try to mirror onto devices with different controllers.

Most operating systems provide mirroring as well. Sybase does not support operating system mirroring, but it may work as well or better for your system depending on your needs. Some incompatibilities have been discovered from time to time due to implementation of mirroring by operating system vendors. Sybase Technical Support will ask you to disable operating system mirroring in the event of a disk corruption problem to rule that out as a possible cause.

If you determine that you need to use operating system mirroring, check the AnswerBase knowledge base or call Technical Support to find out if there are known conflicts between SQL Server and any relatively new operating system mirroring features provided by your hardware vendor.

■ SYSTEM DATABASES

The SQL Server installation program creates several system databases by default. Versions 4.9.2 of SQL Server and earlier provided the `master`, `model` and `tempdb` databases during installation. System 10 introduced the `sybsecurity` and `sybsystemprocs` databases.

While users may forget about the existence of the system databases, Systems Managers routinely work with `master` and `tempdb`. In the next sections, we look at the specialized purpose of each system database. We'll also cover the administrative attention each requires.

MASTER

The `master` database contains all the information used by SQL Server for managing itself. In addition to the system tables stored in every database, `master` contains several unique system tables. The `master`-only tables contain the names, locations and configurations of all the other databases. They also control which users can log into the SQL Server.

Before System 10, `master` also stored all system stored procedures. In System 10 and later releases, the `sybsystemprocs` database stores most system stored procedures.

Every time you make a SQL Server-wide change, such as adding or dropping a database, device, or login, a row gets modified in a `master`-only system table. Consequently, you need to make backups of the `master` database after each of these changes. If your `master` database gets corrupt and you don't have a current backup, you will not be able to access any of the data in any databases or on any devices added since the backup. Users added since the last backup will not be able to get into the Server. If you attempt to add logins and users back in, but do it in a different order than the first time, users will end up owning the objects of another user and will not own their former objects. There are ways to work around problems like these. However, the workarounds rely on certain information that you previously stored on paper or in a file. In the end, the workarounds require considerably more effort than making a `master` backup and loading it. The size of `master` rarely exceeds a few megabytes, so the backup doesn't take long.

In contrast with other databases, you cannot redefine the segment mapping in the `master` database. The default, data, and log segments are all combined on the `master` device. An important consequence of this is that you cannot dump `master`'s transaction log to a backup device. You can only dump it using the `truncate_only` or `with no_log` options. To back up `master`, you must make a full database dump. If the transaction log in `master` fills up so completely you can't truncate it, your entire SQL Server may fail to operate. Avoid this by making it a habit to truncate the log and then back up the database after making any system-wide change.

To create a new system stored procedure, give it a name starting with "sp_" and place it in the `master` database, if using a pre-10.0 SQL Server, or in the `sybsystemprocs` database, if using SQL Server 10.0 or later. When choosing disk allocation, optimize for reliability. It doesn't make any sense to put `master` on an especially fast disk since users won't access it much.

MODEL

The `model` database serves as a template for all other databases. By default, the `model` database contains all the system tables that must exist in each user database. You can create default objects, such as triggers rules or defaults, by putting them into `model`. When you issue the CREATE DATABASE command, SQL Server copies the entire contents of `model` to the new database. Similarly, any options you set in `model` with `sp_dboption` also carry over to new databases.

Always keep at least one backup of `model`, especially if you have customized it. If someone later rebuilds `model` without knowing about the default objects, databases will stop behaving in ways users or applications may have been taking for granted. Of course, you should document such modifications in your procedures manual.

If you do customize `model`, keep an eye on its size. If it becomes larger than the default database size configured for the Server, you will have a problem when you create a new database if you don't specify an adequate size. Also watch for modifications made to `model` by third-party applications. If they change values in `model`, you might have to be more rigorous about dumping its transaction log and making backups than you would be otherwise.

TEMPDB

The `tempdb` database serves as scratch space for queries. Users may also put temporary tables in `tempdb`. The CREATE TABLE command automatically places any table with a name preceded by a # in `tempdb`. SQL Server rebuilds `tempdb` every time it starts up by copying in the contents of `model`. An application that does a lot of sorting, GROUP BY, aggregates, and similarly complex queries will need a lot of space in `tempdb`. It is also used extensively during index creation. If you have a large number of users, you will need to allocate a lot of disk space to `tempdb`.

By default, `buildmaster` creates `tempdb` on the master device. The first 2 MB must remain on the master device. You can extend it to other devices thereafter. Put `tempdb` on your fastest devices. Some customers have experimented with putting `tempdb` on a RAM drive or solid-state disk. Sometimes they have success with this, and sometimes they experience corruption. If you do use such a device, make sure that it is nonvolatile. It should have battery back up, NVRAM, or integrated failure protection. Before putting such a scheme into production, test it thoroughly. To force use of the faster device, you can drop the `default` and `log` segments from the portion on the master device. Alternatively, you can create a 2-MB dummy table that fills up the first 2 MB in `tempdb` right after booting SQL Server. If you are using System 11, the best alternative is to get a lot of memory and bind all of `tempdb` to RAM.

SYBSYSTEMPROCS

Sybase added the `sybsystemprocs` database with the System 10 release. Since the number of system stored procedures had grown, the size of the default `master` database needed to increase. However, this would have caused customers difficulty since the minimum size of the `master` device needed to be increased. Instead, upgrade creates a new database for stored procedures called `sybsystemprocs`, which resides on its own database device. Only the stored procedures needed for critical operations remain in the `master` database. This new arrangement also serves the needs of those who want to extend system-wide functionality by adding their own stored procedures without filling up `master`.

If your users call a wide variety of system stored procedures frequently, your best performance improvement will come from configuring SQL Server with a large procedure cache, providing that doing so doesn't make the data cache too small. You could also put `sybsystemprocs` on a fast device. Reliability is moderately important since you don't want system procedures to become corrupt. However, in a typical setting, users don't write stored procedures often. Data devices accommodating constant read and write demands contend with far more stress than an infrequently written `sybsystemprocs` device.

SYBSECURITY

In System 10 and later releases, the SQL Server installation program creates the `sybsecurity` database if you choose to enable SQL Server auditing. Besides the system tables present in all databases, `sybsecurity` contains two additional tables, `sysaudits` and `sysauditoptions`. The latter table stores only records for objects and users that you are auditing. The latter holds all the audit records. `Sysaudits` can grow rapidly if you audit common actions.

It's important to purge or archive the `sysaudits` table often so that it doesn't fill up the database. Depending on how much you use it, you may want to put this database on a fast and reliable drive. If you use SQL Server auditing for security purposes, you should also enable any security measures possible to protect this device from unauthorized access. Consider access by software, operating system, network, and physical proximity when determining the precautions to take. We'll review security measures more in Chapter 10.

You could use auditing for reasons other than security. For example, if you have System 11, you might consider binding particular stored procedures or tables to a named cache. By auditing the objects, you can determine if they get used often enough to warrant such special treatment.

USER DATABASES

Sybase refers to all databases other than those described above as user databases. User databases store user data, for which performance, reliability, and cost optimization depend on the applications.

Each user database contains some system tables to keep track of objects in the database. We examine the content of these tables in Chapter 5.

If you are in a position to choose whether to place a mass of data in one big database or to distribute it among several smaller databases, here are some factors to consider:

■ **Segmenting users**   While the careful use of object permissions for users and groups can allow you to control access to data, it can be much simpler to grant or restrict access to segments of data on a database-wide basis, rather than object by object and user by user. Therefore, creating several small databases may allow you to partition data and users easily. For small databases, a Systems Manager may find it easier to delegate responsibility for the database to a database owner (DBO). This DBO then performs all the maintenance necessary for the data. A DBO more familiar with why certain information exists and how it gets processed usually knows better how to manage it.

■ **Segmenting data**   Separating data into small databases may provide advantages for applications that only operate on a logical subset of data. Maintenance and troubleshooting become easier when only one or two applications modify the contents of a database. When ten or more all make their changes in one big database, problems become difficult to sort out. Segmenting data based on processing needs might also assist with administration needs. If an application or users update a logical subset data frequently, it may make sense to buy a particularly reliable and fast disk for that data. While you can also use the SQL Server segment features for this purpose, you might find the basic database mechanism simpler to work with.

■ **Maintainability**   Several maintenance tasks affect one database at a time. These include running DBCC CHECKALLOC, DBCC CHECKDB, DUMP DATABASE, DUMP TRANSACTION, LOAD DATABASE, and LOAD TRANSACTION. If you decide to use several small databases, you can delegate authority for these operations to individual database owners or administrators. On the other hand, if one person is responsible for all of these tasks, you might gain efficiency by doing them on one big database only. These commands tend to slow down or stop operations for the entire database. You may prefer to incur the additional overhead of multiple databases so that maintenance only affects a subset of user operations at any given time.

■ **Recoverability**   When you shut down SQL Server and restart it, each database must go through recovery. This entails reading through the transaction log and making sure that all completed transactions were written to disk and that all incomplete transactions were rolled back. No one may enter a database undergoing recovery. If you store all of your data in one big database, all users will need to wait for recovery to complete before doing any work in the database. If instead, you partition data among several databases, work can begin again as soon as recovery completes in the first database. In the event of a system failure, such as a bad disk or some other error causing corruption, you will need to load data from a backup. LOAD DATABASE also runs the recovery process. While the previous comments about recovery apply, you will also want to take into account the complexity of managing dumps and loads of several databases after a failure. You can only dump or load two databases simultaneously if they are on separate physical devices. In other words, if you need to load several databases after a failure all on one device, you will have to stick around and load each database sequentially. In contrast, for one database, you may be able to start the load and then go get some sleep for a few hours.

Theoretically, one SQL Server can support up to 32,767 user databases. It's hard, however, to imagine anyone managing more than 50 or so. For example, the owner of one database may request a SQL Server shutdown for one reason or another. This would inconvenience all the other database owners. In large systems, Systems Managers may run multiple copies of SQL Server to make it easier to segregate usage and delegate responsibility.

While the advantages appear to weigh heavily in favor of small databases, too many small databases also make maintenance complex. You may find that delegating work to several database owners is a magically freeing experience, but you also lose some control. You must decide to shift your focus to training and mentoring so that your DBOs learn to do what you would do without making the same mistakes that you once made.

■ DATABASE OBJECTS

Each user and system database contains system tables and their indexes, including the transaction log. SQL Server allocates the remaining space to user data and indexes. At the logical level, a database only contains tables and indexes. However, when viewed internally, taking disk interaction into consideration, the distinction between types of tables and indexes becomes apparent. As the next few sections unfold, we'll explore these distinctions.

SQL Server stores data in tables and facilitates access to that data by way of indexes. In addition, a database stores procedural objects: stored procedures, triggers, rules, constraints, defaults, and views. SQL Server stores these objects in the sysprocedures table.

Each object has an object ID which uniquely identifies it within a database. Each base table and index has both an object ID and an index ID. A table and its indexes all share the same object ID but have different index IDs. The combination of object ID and index ID uniquely identifies an index in database. These IDs are transparent to the user, but in some cases they are reported in errors without being referenced by name. Also, errors reference page numbers without reporting a corresponding object ID. In this latter case, you can use the DBCC PAGE command to determine the object ID and then use the object_name() function to determine the name of the object.

▪ SEGMENTS

SQL Server provides Systems Managers with the segment mechanism for associating database objects with particular SQL Server devices. Segments accommodate the different growth rates and the different cost, performance, and reliability requirements for system tables, user tables, indexes, and the log. You can create up to 31 user segments to divide data. For example, Tim could create an index segment for all nonclustered indexes or a *classes* segment for his class-related tables and all of their indexes.

By default, a new database has three segments defined, all sharing the same space:

▪ **default**   All user data automatically get allocated as part of the default segment.

▪ **system**   All system tables must reside on a disk fragment allocated for the system segment.

▪ **log**   The transaction log for each database uses space on a disk fragment allocated for use by the log segment.

For the master database, the system and log segments reside on the same device and cannot be separated. Therefore, when the log fills up, you can no longer make any changes in master, which sometimes makes it unusable.

When defining segments, follow these steps:

▪ Determine relative growth rates of tables and indexes.

- Define a space management strategy (archival, purge, etc.).

- Decide which objects to place on which segments.

- Identify the device fragments to be used, or use DISK INIT to create new devices if necessary.

- Create or extend the databases to use the devices identified if necessary using the ON clause of the CREATE DATABASE or ALTER DATABASE commands.

- Create the necessary segments with sp_addsegment.

- Use the ON clause of the CREATE TABLE or CREATE INDEX commands to designate particular segment usage. For existing objects, you get the best results by creating a new table on the segment that you want and moving the data from the old table to the new using a SELECT statement, other combinations of SQL commands, or bulk copy.

- Set up any threshold procedures with sp_addthreshold.

The leaf pages of a clustered index are the table pages, so normally you would place the clustered index on the same segment as the table. If you move the clustered index to another segment, the table pages eventually move to that segment, but SQL Server reports 2558 errors until all the pages have moved. Similarly, if you use sp_placeobject or drop a segment already in use by an object, you also get 2558 errors. A 2558 error means "something is on the current segment that doesn't belong here."

The segment management functions available in all current versions of SQL Server are

- The ON clause of CREATE DATABASE, ALTER DATABASE, CREATE INDEX, and CREATE TABLE

- sp_addsegment

- sp_dropsegment

- sp_logsegment

In System 10 and later releases, Sybase added functions for supporting segment thresholds. You can specify automatic execution of a particular procedure when the amount of data reaches a particular threshold. Using thresholds to dump the log in the log segment goes a long way toward reducing the effort needed to maintain databases.

Sandy's Sport Shops—Segments

Tim decided to learn about segments, so he decided to experiment with a *school* database. He created it with the command

```
> create database school
> on school_dev = 4
> go
```

This told SQL Server to create a 4 MB database called *school* on a device called `school_dev`. The `default`, `system`, and `log` segments all shared all 4 MB of the database at this point. Once Tim realized that user data, log data, and system tables would intermingle, he decided he wanted to sequester certain data.

Tim figured that the parts of his database where he stores homework get updated frequently, while his class schedules only get updated once a semester. He also remembered that he created a log device *school_log* with the `DISK INIT` command, but he never followed through and allocated log space on that device. Tim started his segment project by allocating a new 4-MB raw disk partition:

```
> disk init
> name = "homework_dev",
> physname = "/dev/rsd0d",
> vdevno = 5,
> size = 2048
> go
```

Then he moved his log to the log segment.

```
> alter database school
> on homework_dev = 2
> log on school_log = 2
> go
```

This `ALTER DATABASE` command extends the size of Tim's school database by 4 MB, putting 2 MB on the new homework device and 2 MB on a previously allocated log device. Tim could have accomplished the designation of the log device by giving the following commands as well:

```
> alter database school
> on school_log = 2
```

114

```
> go
> sp_logdevice school, school_log
> go
```

However, Tim is somewhat lazy and can't understand why anyone would use three different commands rather than one. (He has never needed to rebuild a database from existing scripts after a device failure either.) After the `sp_logdevice` procedure marks a device in a database as a log device, any additional alterations onto that device will be automatically reserved exclusively for the log segment.

Next, Tim made his new *homework* segment:

```
> use master
> go
> alter database school
> on homework_dev = 2
> go
> use school
> go
> sp_addsegment homework, school, homework_dev
> go
```

By default, this combination of commands means that the portion of the school database now residing on *homework_dev* is now allocated for use by the `system`, `default`, and *homework* segments. However, Tim wants the *homework_dev* device to be used exclusively for homework data, so he removes the `default` and `system` segments:

```
> sp_dropsegment "default", school, homework_dev
> go
> sp_dropsegment system, school, homework_dev
> go
```

Now, Tim created homework-related tables to use the new segment.

```
> use school
> go
> create table hw_lisp (
> functions varchar(15) not null,
> arguments varchar(100) null,
> comments varchar(255) null
> )
```

```
> on homework
> go
> create unique clustered index hw_lisp_cl
> on hw_lisp (functions)
> on homework
> go
```

Any data that Tim adds to his new table *hw_lisp* will go automatically onto the *homework_dev* device. In addition, he can see how much space is left on the *homework* segment using the sp_spaceused stored procedure. When all segments are combined on one device, you cannot reserve space for a particular object. For example, the rapid growth of a user table could limit the capacity of the transaction log to an unusably small amount. On the other hand, if Tim runs out of space in the *homework* segment, he will have to create a new device to extend the segment onto, even if there is space elsewhere in the database. Once a table is associated with a particular segment, it can't use the default segment anymore.

As implied in previous discussions about disk usage and performance, people typically use segments to put index and log data on particularly fast and reliable devices. Careful index management plays a key role in getting the best performance from SQL Server.

As with operating system disk quotas, you can use segments to encourage people to purge data at particular points. For example, you could make separate segments for each table in a development environment if testing generates a lot of data. Then those responsible for certain tables will not affect the productivity of others if they do not purge data often enough.

◾ PARTITIONS

By default, the data pages for a table are managed as a single linked list of pages. A table with no clustered index is sometimes referred to as heap storage. In version 11.0 of SQL Server, users can specify that they want to divide pages for heap tables into multiple chains so that they can be accessed in parallel. The data partitioning feature increases performance for some operations on heap tables, such as bulk copy. Operations can perform updates on different points in the table. This means that processes encounter less contention for the last page of the table or the last page of its nonclustered index leaf page.

To divide a table into partitions, use the new syntax for ALTER TABLE. For example, to partition a table called *class_requirements* into four pieces, use this command:

```
> alter table class_requirements partition 4
```

To reunite the table into a single partition, use the command:

```
> alter table class_requirements unpartition
```

The `partition` command allocates new pages for control pages and updates the `syspartitions` table to contain rows for each partition. Neither the PARTITION nor the UNPARTITION command moves existing data; they only change the page pointers in the page chains to separate or join page chain fragments. Unpartitioning a table causes the Server to deallocate control pages, freeing them up for reallocation to data as needed.

A new system table, `syspartitions`, stores information about the partitions defined in each database. It contains

- The object ID
- The partition number
- The partition state
- The logical number of the first page in the partition
- The control page of the partition

Two new configuration variables govern internal SQL Server behavior for partitions:

- Partition groups   The setting for partition groups determines the total number of partitions of tables that the Server can manage. Each partition group contains 16 partition caches for a single table. Each cache manages one partition, storing information such as the last page number of the partition. One table may have several partition groups, but one partition group can only service one table.

- Partition spinlock ratio   A partition spinlock protects a partition cache from being accessed by two processes simultaneously. The setting for partition spinlock ratio determines the number of

117

caches each spinlock protects. Decreasing this ratio improves concurrency at the cost of memory. Each partition spinlock uses 256 bytes of memory.

You can set the number of partitions from two upward; there is no hard-coded upper limit. Instead, the limit is set by the value of `partition groups` that you configure. The partitions are numbered in order, starting with 1. Any pages currently allocated in a table altered into partitions will remain in partition 1. SQL Server will assign subsequent row insertions into other partitions to balance the contention for table pages. If you want to change the number of partitions in a table, first unpartition it, and then repartition it. You also need to unpartition a table before issuing the following commands on a partitioned table: CREATE CLUSTERED INDEX, TRUNCATE TABLE, sp_placeobject.

You cannot partition the following tables:

- System tables

- Work tables

- Temporary tables

- Tables with a clustered index

- Tables with TEXT or IMAGE columns

- Tables that are already partitioned

For partitioned tables, additional pages are added for control purposes, additional rows are added to `sysindexes` for the table, and additional processing is done to determine the partition in which to put the next insert. Therefore, for tables not having heap characteristics (i.e., having nonclustered indexes), the use of partitions may degrade performance.

To see the first page and the control page for each partition of a partitioned table, you can use the new procedure `sp_helpartition`:

```
sp_helpartition table_name
```

The *table_name* that you specify must be that of a table in the current database that is partitioned.

■ ALLOCATION UNITS

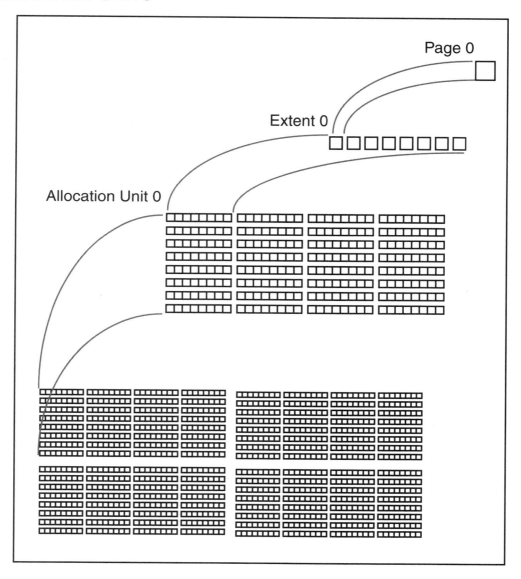

Figure 3.2 A 2 MB database using 2 KB pages has 4 allocation units, each containing 32 extents. Each extent contains 8 pages.

An allocation unit is a group of 256 logically contiguous data pages, which uses one-half of a megabyte of space.[6] You can extend the size of a database by a minimum of one allocation unit at a time.[7] SQL Server reserves the first page of each allocation unit for an allocation page. It uses the allocation page to store data structures that keep track of eight-page extents. Each allocation page can store 32 extent structures. Normally, a user doesn't need to know about allocation units. However, they come to the attention of the administrator by way of the DBCC CHECKALLOC command. This command walks through each allocation unit examining the data structures to make sure that they all agree with each other. The output of DBCC CHECKALLOC reports the status of each allocation unit.

■ EXTENTS

An extent consists of eight logically contiguous pages. It is the smallest amount of space allocated to a table or index. When SQL Server gets new space for a table or index, it allocates one extent at a time. Therefore, when you first create a table or index, the Server always reserves 16 KB of space,[8] even if you only add one page of data to it.

Normally, extents are transparent to the user. In System 10, Sybase introduced the extent i/o buffers configuration option. This allows you to configure a number of extents to prefetch when creating an index. You can improve CREATE INDEX performance significantly if you use this feature.

---

[6]One megabyte for Stratus.

[7]Since CREATE and ALTER DATABASE take a size specification in megabyte units, normally you can't extend or create a database that is not a whole multiple of a megabyte in size. However, if there is only a half a megabyte available on a SQL Server device, the Server will attempt to satisfy your request by using the last half-megabyte and reporting the actual number of pages it allocated. In other words, to get a row in sysusages for half a megabyte, you would need to ALTER or CREATE a database on a device that only had half a megabyte of space left on it. For some disaster recovery scenarios, you need to reproduce the sysusages table exactly, which is why this footnote might someday become relevant to you.

[8]Thirty-two kilobytes for Stratus.

Another way extents come to the attention of a database manager or user indirectly is the output of `sp_spaceused`. This command reports usage in terms of *reserved*, *used*, and *free* space. When the Server allocates space for an object, it allocates one extent at a time. In other words, an extent always belongs to one and only one object, identified by a unique combination of object ID and index ID. When SQL Server allocates an extent, it might only need to write data to one page. In that case, the table has one page *used* and seven pages *reserved* in the new extent. SQL Server refers to extents that are not allocated to any object as *free* space.

■ PAGES

A page is the smallest unit of space SQL Server can use at one time. A SQL Server page consists of 2048 contiguous bytes (or 2 KB) on all platforms except for Stratus, where it is 4096 bytes (4 KB). Different types of pages hold different types of data. Also, SQL Server's page numbering mechanism allows us to distinguish logical pages from virtual pages. We survey page types and numbering in the sections that follow.

PAGE TYPES

Seven page types exist within a SQL Server database. Normally, you do not need to concern yourself with these. However, error messages may reference them, so knowing the page type affected may help you understand the nature of the error.

- ■ **Allocation page** Contains extent data structures, which assist with managing disk space in an allocation unit

- ■ **GAM page** Contains a global allocation map for managing data within a database

- ■ **OAM page** Contains object allocation maps for managing base tables or indexes; each base table and each index has at least one OAM page

- ■ **Table page** Contains data rows for tables (including the transaction log)

- ■ **Index page** Contains key and pointer rows for index entries

- **Text/Image page**   Contains data stored using the text or image datatype

- **Distribution page**   Contains statistical information about an index for use by the query optimizer

In other documentation, you may see references to *data pages* instead of *table page*s. However, to keep things clear, when we later talk about the data cache, we use *data page* as a generic term that refers to either a table page or an index page.

SQL Server maintains each page of a base table in a doubly linked list. A tree structure governs the organization of pages of an index. Pointers on each key row of each index page point to pages or rows below it in the hierarchy. Pointers in the page header link it to neighboring pages on the same level of the tree. For all but the last (leaf) level of an index, the index pointers on a page point to the next index level. The key next to each pointer is the value of the column or columns on which the index is built. Consequently, we refer to indexes built on multiple columns as wide indexes, since each index page must hold more data for each key and therefore holds fewer key rows per page. The advantage of such an index is that it may "cover" frequent queries. This means that all data requested in the query occur in the index pages. In this case, the query can find data without ever reading the actual data pages, which improves performance.

We call the pages at the lowest level of an index the leaf pages. For a clustered index, the leaf level consists of the table pages themselves. Pointers in the next highest layer of index pages point directly to the table pages. In contrast, the leaf pages of a nonclustered index contain pointers to rows instead of to pages. Each pointer associated with a key value points to the row on the page containing that value. For this reason, nonclustered indexes occupy more space than clustered indexes. SQL Server must store a pointer for each row of the table instead of for each page of the table at the leaf level.

SQL Server stores text and image pages in linked lists separately from the list of regular pages for the base table. The table row for a text or image column contains a pointer in the column instead of the table data. The pointer links to the separate page chain for the text or image pages. A sometimes welcome side effect of this organization is that if the disk happens to have a bad spot in a text chain, the damage is isolated from the rest of the table data, and only a row is lost instead of a whole table.

SQL Server allocates pages under these circumstances:

■ **Creating base tables or indexes** CREATE TABLE and CREATE INDEX cause the allocation of an initial extent containing eight pages. For indexing nonempty tables, SQL Server allocates as many extents as are needed for all the key rows of the existing data and for the index tree structure.

■ **Splitting data or index pages** When there is no more room for data on a data or index page, a new page gets allocated and data are moved as needed to accommodate new rows.

■ **Adding overflow pages** When a clustered index page that contains data having the same key value for each row is full, the request to add a new row is accommodated by adding an overflow page.

■ **Creating distribution pages** UPDATE STATISTICS or CREATE INDEX on a nonempty table creates distribution pages.

Allocation of pages implies processing overhead in addition to disk I/O. The overhead includes marking internal global and object allocation structures to indicate that the page is now in use, initializing the page, locking neighboring pages associated with the object to which the page is being added, logging the page allocation, and linking the page into the appropriate page chain.

Page deallocation implies overhead as well. The deallocation overhead involves almost the same steps as allocation, but in reverse. Deallocation adds the step of removing the page from any in-memory caches that refer to it. Deallocation does not involve initialization since it relies on the subsequent page allocation process to do that.

In releases prior to SQL Server 11.0, performance could degrade for large tables that had several OAM pages. For page allocations, the Server used to scan every OAM page. Now it skips over OAM pages considered mostly full. This also reduces contention for each OAM page, improving the performance of page allocations and deallocations. A new configuration variable, page utilization percent, lets you set the level of fullness that will cause the Server to skip OAM page scans. Leave it at the default unless all objects in a database are large. The lower the percent you specify, the more potential you have for wasted space in the database, but the faster large allocation operations will complete. Note that the bulk copy utilities do not check the OAM `page utilization percent`, but instead always allocate new extents until no more are available. This behavior allows time-consuming bulk copy operations to finish as quickly as possible.

PAGE NUMBERING

We count SQL Server pages using two systems:

- **Logical**   A logical page number uniquely identifies each page within a database for SQL Server.

- **Virtual**   A virtual page number uniquely identifies each page on a device for SQL Server.

SQL Server addresses a logical page by its position in a database. Database pages are numbered sequentially from 0 to n, where n is the last page allocated to the database. For example, in a 2-MB database, we find 1024 pages, numbered from 0 to 1023. Since each page uses 2 KB of space, there are 512 pages per megabyte. To convert from megabytes to pages, divide by 512.[9]

For determining a position on a device, SQL Server uses virtual page numbers. A virtual page number looks something like 16777216. The first 4 bytes encode the device number. The remaining bytes store the sequential page number from 0 to n, where n is the last page on the SQL Server device. Note that virtual page numbers don't reflect any database specific information. The *low* and *high* columns in `sysdevices` store the first and last virtual page numbers for the SQL Server device.

To clarify the relationship between virtual and logical pages, let's look at the output from a query of `sysusages`, which reports on every device fragment in use by a database. In the output shown here, we have omitted the last two columns (*pad* and *unreservedpgs*) for simplicity.

---

[9]Divide by 256 for Stratus since each page uses 4 KB of space.

```
> select * from sysusages
> go
dbid    segmap        lstart        size          vstart
------  -----------   -----------   -----------   -----------
     1            7             0          1536             4
     2            7             0          1024          2564
     3            7             0          1024          1540
     4            7             0          6144      16777216
     5            7             0          1024      33554432
(5 rows affected)
```

The *dbid* column identifies the number of the database using each fragment. *segmap* contains a bitmap indicating the segments in use on each device fragment. The *lstart* column contains the first logical page in use on a fragment. *size* shows the number of pages on each fragment. The *vstart* value indicates the first virtual page of the fragment.

The *vstart* of the first row for *dbid 1*, master, is normally 4. The configuration block usually uses pages 0 through 3 of the master device, and the allocation for the master database starts after that. The *vstart* value has a number between *low* and *high* as designated in the sysdevices table.

Every time SQL Server grants a request to allocate space in response to a CREATE DATABASE or ALTER DATABASE command, it adds a row to sysusages. DROP DATABASE removes all rows for the indicated database from sysusages. If you request 5 MB of space with the ALTER or CREATE DATABASE command, but SQL Server only finds 4 MB available, those 4 MB get allocated to the database. The Server displays an informational message to report the number of pages actually allocated after every CREATE or ALTER DATABASE. Always check this message to see if the number of pages matches the number that you expect. (Divide the number of pages by 512 to get the number of megabytes.)

Currently, sysusages can hold no more than 128 rows in sysusages for any database. This can limit your desired expansion of a database if you only alter it a little at a time.

125

The user and administrator normally need not worry about logical or virtual page numbers. However, when error messages refer to page numbers, you can infer the location of the problem on the device if you understand the numbering scheme.

◾ Rows

For tables without any indexes, SQL Server adds rows at the bottom of data pages. No attempt is made to store rows in any particular order, but data are stored contiguously. Rows are consolidated toward the top of the page so that unused space within a page always occurs at the bottom. If a table has a clustered index, rows are stored on the data page in order by the contents of the index column(s).

Adding a row to a table without a clustered index means finding space at the end of a page and appending the data. To add data to a clustered index, SQL Server must make space on the table page at the proper location and shift rows down or onto additional pages as necessary. When updates affect columns with indexed values, the Server must also add entries in the proper key order to the applicable index pages. When a page cannot accommodate a new row, the Server splits the page. A split involves

- ◾ Creating a new data or index page
- ◾ Linking the new page into the appropriate page chains
- ◾ Moving data to the new page

For pages splits in indexes, values are generally divided between the old page and the new one so that the index remains balanced. This practice minimizes locking and improves performance.

Nonclustered indexes in a table result in more overhead for frequently updated tables than tables with only a clustered index or no index at all. For each row that moves to a new page, the nonclustered leaf rows for each nonclustered index pointing to that data must be updated, sometimes requiring index page splits as well. A process encounters similar overhead for deleting data rows from a page. In addition, the process must move data up on a page to make the data contiguous. Knowing this, you will be wise to keep the number of nonclustered indexes as low as possible while still providing adequate paths for frequently accessed data.

In version 10.1, which was optimized for row-level processing, an enhancement was made to the page split algorithm used when inserting into tables with clustered indexes. Now, if sequential inserts are made in the same order as the data pages of a clustered index, not as many pages will be split, resulting in better throughput for such operations.

Starting with version 10.1, you can also specify the number of rows SQL Server should store per table or index leaf page. To change the setting for the data pages of an entire table, use the new stored procedure,

```
sp_chgattribute table_name, "max_rows_per_page", num_rows
```

The *num_rows* value must be an integer from 0 to 256 for data pages. To change the number of rows per page for the leaf pages of an index, use the max_rows_per_page clause in the CREATE TABLE, CREATE INDEX, or ALTER TABLE commands. For example, a relevant portion of the ALTER TABLE command follows:

```
ALTER TABLE table_name
  ADD column_name datatype NOT NULL
  CONSTRAINT constraint_name
  UNIQUE NONCLUSTERED
  WITH MAX_ROWS_PER_PAGE = num_rows
```

For indexes, the acceptable range for *num_rows* is determined by the maximum number of index key rows that will fit on a page. In the relevant database, use this query with the name of the index specified for *index_name* to determine the upper limit:

```
> select
> (select @@pagesize - 32) /
> minlen from sysindexes
> where name = "index_name"
```

Use the rows per page option when you want to use row-level processing or you want to minimize locking contention. Remember that benefits of low values for this variable may be offset by the increased overhead for more frequent page splits. The value that you set for this option does not affect existing pages, but it is maintained during subsequent modifications of the data or index pages. To change `max_rows_per_page` for an entire table, drop and re-create the clustered index.

Procedure Manual Suggestions

○ Managing the Model Database

➠ Create a review process for proposed modifications to `model` so that experienced DBOs and any who may be affected by the change either approve the change or suggest alternate approaches.

➠ Create a procedure that ensures that all modifications to the `model` database are documented.

○ Managing the Sybsecurity Database

➠ Write a procedure for managing the `sybsecurity` database.

➠ List goals of having auditing and establish how much money and time are justified to meet those goals.

➠ Set up a plan for which objects should be audited and why, consistent with the documented goals.

➠ Set up a review procedure and name a person or group responsible for reviewing audit records and when they should be reviewed. (Monthly? Only when a particular event happens? Only when a problem is reported?)

➠ Establish a dump, load, and archive strategy for `sybsecurity`.

➠ Establish how much disk and what sort of backup devices you will need to support your plans.

➠ Make sure that the costs of the plan are within the costs justified.

➠ Publish this procedure in a secure place that is accessible by the appropriate people when necessary.

○ Making Backups of System Databases

➠ Establish a procedure for making a backup of the `master`, `model`, and `sybsystemprocs` databases every time a change is made in these databases.

➠ Make sure that appropriate threshold actions are defined for these databases.

○ Disk Partition Use

➠ Set up a procedure for recording disk partition use that doesn't allow duplicate use of the same partition.

➠ Include a method for assigning consistent names.

➠ Consider creating an electronic log with logic that prohibits people from using disk partitions more than once.

○ Managing Space with Segments and Thresholds

➠ Set up a procedure for managing space, including recommendations or requirements for threshold actions.

➠ Specify that a log file should be kept of all segment additions and deletions.

➠ For each segment, the log file should include the segment name, number, and database(s) that use it and the reason for creation. If the segment is associated with a particular device or type of device, list that too.

➠ Determine the databases and segments where space needs to be managed automatically and where it can be monitored manually.

129

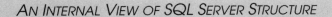

⇒ Establish appropriate thresholds and associated actions.

⇒ Write emergency procedures for what should be done if the normal threshold procedure isn't working for some reason.

⇒ Indicate who is responsible for managing each threshold established.

An Internal View of SQL Server Processing

Having covered the internal structure of SQL Server data, we will turn to aspects of internal processing that affect how your Server responds to user requests.

■ SQL SERVER FILES

As with any major software application, when you install SQL Server, you get a new batch of files to put on your system. SQL Server uses many of these files behind the scenes. If you happen to move them or if they get edited, you may experience strange problems that would be hard to diagnose. So that you might better recognize the symptoms of such a change, we'll highlight a few files and directories that SQL Server relies on.

$SYBASE

Generally, you set the SYBASE environment variable (logical name) to the top of the SQL Server directory tree, although that does not have to be the case. In this directory, you should find the following files by default:

- **The interfaces file**   Defines the network port that the SQL Server listens on for client connections.

- **The servername.krg and servername.srg0 files**   These are files created by SQL Server for managing shared memory on some platforms.

- **The default configuration files, servername.CFG, servername.001, servername.002, etc.**   These files, described in Chapter 6, contain the configuration information for SQL Server versions 11.0 and later.

In the $SYBASE directory, you will find the subdirectories described in the next sections.

install

The `install` directory stores the installation program for SQL Server and the files needed to boot the Server.

- **The installation program**   For System 10 and later, its name is `sybinit`. In previous releases, its name varies for different platforms. `sybinstall` and `sybconfig` are two names from recent history.

- **The errorlog**   This is an operating system file where SQL Server logs informational messages, warnings, and errors.

- **The RUNSERVER file**   A script run at the operating system level for starting SQL Server. Often, people rename this file to be *RUN_myserver*, where *myserver* is the name in the DSQUERY variable used to identify the server.

bin

The `bin` directory stores executable binary files. This directory should be set in the system administrator's search path variable for UNIX and DOS.

- **dataserver**   The SQL Server program.

- **buildmaster**   The utility used to build the master device.

- **backupserver**   The backup server program for versions 10.0 and later.

- **isql**   The ISQL query utility.

■ **console**   The utility for making tape backups in version 4.9.2 and earlier.

■ **startserver**   A script that starts the server. You can also start the server by executing the RUNSERVER file directly from the install directory.

■ **showserver**   A utility for seeing the SQL Server process(es) running on the current machine.

init

The `sybinit` installation program uses the *init* directory to store files for initializing SQL Server.

upgrade

If you use the installation program to upgrade from one release of SQL Server to another, the upgrade process uses files in this directory. It also stores upgrade logs in this directory.

diag

The `diag` directory and subdirectories contain troubleshooting tools Technical Support may use if they dial into your system. If dial-ins are not allowed at your site, you can back up the contents of this directory tree on tape, and then delete it.

scripts

The `scripts` directory contains SQL scripts for populating Server databases. The three most useful scripts are

■ **installmaster**   Creates the system stored procedures in the `master` and `sybsystemprocs` databases

■ **installmodel**   Creates the default database, `model`

■ **installpubs2**   Creates the sample database, `pubs2`

charsets

This directory contains the files that store character set data that SQL Server adds to the server with the install program or the charset utility.

locales

In the `locales` directory, you will find the files that contain SQL Server error messages in various languages and other information pertinent to localization.

termdef

The `termdef` files describe various screen configurations for the APT and DWB utilities. If you don't have APT or DWB, this directory may not exist. Also, if you once had APT or DWB, but traded them in for PowerBuilder, you can delete this directory.

formdef

The files in this directory serve as a default location for forms used by the APT and DWB programs. You may delete this directory if you don't use APT or DWB.

include

The `include` directory contains header files that you may need to include when compiling programs that use the Sybase Open Client or Open Server APIs.

lib

This directory contains the Open Client library files that you must link with any programs you write that make Open Client subroutine calls.

■ CPU USAGE

In Chapter 3, we looked at how SQL Server works with disks. In this section, we'll see how SQL Server uses a machine's CPU resources.

An operating system process is an execution environment that is scheduled onto a physical CPU by the operating system. By default, Sybase SQL Server is one operating system process. If you have multiple CPUs on the machine, you can use sp_configure to tell SQL Server to use additional CPUs. In this case, you can have one SQL Server engine process at the operating system level for each CPU you allow the Server to use.

Sybase uses the word *engine* to refer to the operating system process running on a CPU. Sybase calls the architecture that governs SQL Server's internal management of its engines the Virtual Server Architecture or VSA. The SQL Server engine processes use shared memory to communicate with each other. The Server automatically balances the workload across CPUs (if configured to do so), scheduling and controlling its own processes and using its own threads. Sybase chose this approach to minimize operating system overhead and dependency on system-specific features.

A SQL Server process for a user connection is not the same thing as an operating system process. In this book, the phrases *operating system process* and *engine process* refer to operating system-level processes. The words *user process* or simply *process* refer to processes for a SQL Server user connection unless otherwise qualified.

When a client logs into SQL Server from a different machine via a network, the client process talks to the Server process over the SQL Server query port. (*port* is a TCP/IP term. In DECNet terminology, the VMS documentation refers to network objects instead of ports. For OS/2, named pipes provide network connectivity. Windows NT documentation refers to I/O addresses or ports.) The SQL Server does all the work and returns results by way of the query port. If a user executes a particularly intense SQL Server command, you will not see that user's CPU usage go up by using an operating system CPU monitor. Instead, SQL Server will get credit for the CPU cycles.

The SQL Monitor tool allows you to look "inside" the SQL Server process and see which database user is using which resources. If you don't have SQL Monitor, you can use `sp_monitor` to get a general idea of resource usage by user process.

Each SQL Server engine process keeps track of the registers and file descriptors usable for that CPU. SQL Server schedules tasks onto engines to maximize performance. Engines cooperate such that user processes may run on different engines during their lifetimes, without the user ever knowing. In other words, multiple CPUs look like a single CPU to the user.

When you issue a SQL command, such as

```
> select * from sysobjects where type = "U"

> go
```

SQL Server parses the query, determines the best way to handle the task, and then creates an execution plan. The plan is then executed on a CPU of the machine allocated for use by SQL Server.

Each user connection made to SQL Server starts a process. Such a user process is an execution environment within the Server. SQL Server schedules user processes onto its engine processes when it's necessary to run a command. SQL Server maintains data structures for each process, so execution can be scheduled out and resumed without losing track of where processing stopped.

One user may use several processes by logging in multiple times or by using a front-end application that initiates several connections. Each process counts as a "user connection" when tallying a number to configure with `sp_configure`. For UNIX, the number of file descriptors available at an operating system level determines the upper limit for the number of user connections.

In versions prior to 11.0, SQL Server consistently used engine 0 for network I/O regardless of the number of engines in use. In version 11, each task chooses an engine for network I/O by selecting the engine with the least activity at the time the task begins. This behavior improves scalability for Servers using several CPUs. As a side effect, the number of user connections possible may increase by a multiple of the number of CPUs. This is because you can initiate up to the per-process maximum of connections for each engine process. The overall maximum connection limit for the operating system still applies.

■ MEMORY USAGE

As with processes, SQL Server manages memory on its own, rather than relying on the operating system. Tuning SQL Server's use of memory goes a long way toward improving overall performance. System 11 includes new functionality for the memory manager that allows a great deal more flexibility for improving performance. With the flexibility comes, as you might expect, complexity. The resulting set of options now at the disposal of a System Manger requires careful study in order to achieve the desired results.

SQL Server uses memory for the following:

■ A fixed amount of memory for running the binary (the amount varies depending on the version and platform).

■ A certain amount of memory for each user connection configured. The user process memory is used for structures that store the state of the process and a stack area for processing queries.

■ A certain amount of memory for each of various entities, such as databases, objects, and locks.

■ Memory for additional network I/O beyond the default amount allocated per user connection.

■ A cache for executable images, such as stored procedures and triggers.

■ A cache for table and index data.

Chapter 6, which covers all of the configuration options, describes the options in this list. In this section, we go through the underlying mechanisms of SQL Server memory management so that you can better understand the best changes to make when the time comes.

In general, a cache consists of a block of memory that keeps copies of data that were read from disk at some point. Cache strategies vary, but the basic idea is to store pages that the controlling mechanism (SQL Server in our case) expects to need again sometime. Before going to disk to do I/O for a requested page, the read mechanism checks the cache. Upon finding the requested page in cache, the read process uses it, thus avoiding the overhead of disk I/O. When people refer to cache hit rate, they mean the number of times that processes find data in cache divided by the total number of read requests. Much of SQL Server performance tuning centers around maximizing the cache hit rate.

In the extreme case, in which a process has access to a memory pool as large as the disk area that it accesses, a 100% hit rate could be achieved. Normally, megabytes of disk outnumber megabytes of memory by a large factor. A SQL Server data cache tends to range from a few megabytes to a hundred megabytes. Guessing which data might get reused presents a challenge for the memory manager to address. SQL Server maintains two general-purpose memory caches: one for executable (procedure) objects and one for table and index pages. The size of the memory cache depends on several configuration options. In SQL Server, you specify a total memory size, and you specify certain values for data structures, such as open databases, open objects, and locks. Each of these data structures requires some memory to maintain. The memory left over after you subtract the fixed amount of memory for the Server code and the amount needed for the data structures gets devoted to the memory cache. Using the `procedure cache` configuration variable, you set a percentage of the cache to be devoted to the procedure cache. The remainder becomes the data cache. System 11 memory manager offers a significant increase in functionality. You can subdivide the data cache into named caches, which you can then dedicate to one or more specific entities. We shall explore this feature after discussing the procedure cache.

PROCEDURE CACHE

The procedure cache keeps copies of compiled objects in memory so that future processes may use them as well. If process A calls a stored procedure X and then exits, procedure X stays in memory. If process B then calls stored procedure X, it uses the binary image still in cache. Two processes cannot use the same procedure image at once however. If process C calls stored procedure X while B is still using it, SQL Server loads another copy of procedure X into memory.

Certain actions invalidate procedure images in the cache. These include dropping or altering an underlying table or index, using the `sp_recompile` procedure, or using some of the new System 11 cache binding features on tables accessed by the procedure.

As new procedures are read from disk, older, unused procedures are removed from the cache.

DATA CACHE

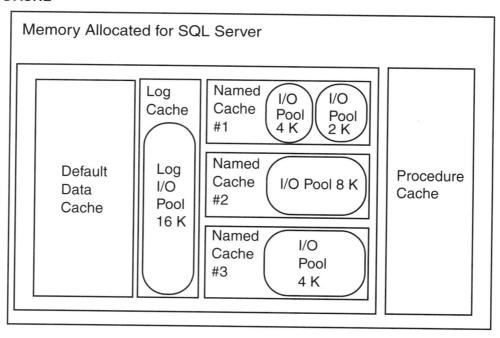

Figure 4.1 A map of memory for a SQL Server with named caches, a log cache, and several I/O pools.

SQL Server engineers refer to the data cache memory manager as the buffer manager, after the name of the relevant code modules. The official name is the *Logical Memory Manager*. How-

139

ever, since the SQL Server errorlog refers to buffers during start-up, and some documentation refers to buffer caches and buffer pools, we will probably see the term creep into everyday use in the greater Sybase community.

The pool of memory devoted to the data cache maintains copies of recently used table and index pages. The data cache is divided into 2-KB chunks for holding page contents and smaller chunks for holding page buffers. One page buffer manages a corresponding page in cache.

By default, disk I/O takes place one page at a time. For each I/O, the disk access arm must move to the appropriate disk track and then wait for the desired page to come under the read head. In SQL Server 10, you can prefetch one or more extents during index creation, which means that I/O is done eight or more pages at a time during that operation. With SQL Server 11, you can enable sequential prefetch for table and index access. This means that when SQL Server reads a requested page it reads the next seven pages on disk as well. Then the disk head only has to wait once—for the starting page of the eight-page chunk. This strategy makes the most sense for tables with clustered indexes.

The System 11 memory manager changes also affect the SQL Server optimizer. The optimizer attempts to guess whether a table is in memory when estimating the cost of disk I/O. To be accurate about comparing access costs, the System 11 optimizer notes whether the object is bound to a cache. You can also give the optimizer "hints" about I/O in System 11. We explore this new functionality in Chapter 8.

In version 11.0, you can create named caches for specific objects, such as selected transaction logs or indexes. If the cache is larger than the objects bound to it, those objects will stay in memory, rather than be swapped out to disk. By carefully analyzing your transactions, you'll be able to use this feature to make significant performance improvements. For example, you can bind `tempdb` to its own cache.

Each cache in System 11 has a unique name, as specified in the configuration file. The default cache is called *default data cache*.

You can configure the size of each cache in terms of pages, kilobytes, megabytes, or gigabytes. The total of the sizes of the named caches will need to fit within the limits of the memory allocated for data cache, as described in Chapter 5. The minimum cache size is 512 KB. Each cache has one of the following types:

- ■ **Default data cache** SQL Server always has a default data cache with the *default data cache* status used by all entities not associated with a named cache. Only the default cache can have the *default data cache* status.

- ■ **Logonly cache** The `logonly` cache contains database pages for log objects only. The only entity you can bind to this type of cache is `syslogs`.

- ■ **Mixed cache** A mixed cache contains both log and nonlog data.

A configuration file entry looks like this for a named cache:

```
[Named Cache:mycache]
     cache size = 512K
     cache status = mixed cache
```

To create a named cache, you can create an entry in the configuration file, as shown above, or you can use the `sp_cacheconfig` stored procedure. The syntax for `sp_cacheconfig` is

```
sp_cacheconfig [cache_name
     [, "cache_size [P | K | M | G]" ]
     [, logonly | mixed ] ]
```

If you execute the procedure with no parameters, you get information about all the caches configured in the Server. If you specify a cache with the *cache_name* parameter, you get or modify information about that cache, depending on the other parameters. You can use any unique 30-character string for *cache_name*, and it can contain spaces and other special characters. If you don't specify a cache size, information about the cache that you specified is reported. Otherwise, to create a new cache, give a new *cache_name* and specify *cache_size* in units indicated by one of the abbreviations shown. The unit abbreviations are P for pages, K for kilobytes, M for megabytes, and G for gigabytes. If you specify a cache type of `logonly` or `mixed`, that type is associated with the cache. Otherwise, it is assumed to be `mixed`. If you specify an existing *cache_name* and a new *cache_size* or type (`logonly` or `mixed`), the cache is changed as specified.

You will need to restart SQL Server after creating or deleting a named cache or changing a named cache size for the change to take effect. However, you can change a named cache status, bind an entity to a cache, or unbind an entity for a cache and have the change take place immediately.

The entities you can bind to named caches are databases, tables, index pages, and transaction logs, with these exceptions:

- The `master` database
- The `master` database system tables
- The `master` database system table index pages
- Entities within `tempdb`

You may bind several entities to one cache, but you cannot bind one entity to multiple caches. Since index pages for an index on a table are considered a separate entity from the rest of the table, you can bind index pages to a different cache than the associated data pages.

To bind an entity to a cache, use the new stored procedure, `sp_bindcache`, which has the following syntax:

```
sp_bindcache cache_name, dbname
[, [owner.]table_name [index_name | "text only"]
```

The *dbname* parameter specifies the database to bind, if there is no entity specified in additional parameters. Otherwise, *dbname* specifies the database that contains the entity. If you use the *index_name* qualifier on the table, then the index pages are bound to the cache. Otherwise, if you just specify the table name, the table's data pages are bound to the cache. Use the *owner* qualifier on the table name if the table is not owned by the same person as the database owner. If you specify the `text only` keyword, the text or image column for the specified table is bound.

To unbind an entity from a named cache, use the procedure

```
sp_unbindcache dbname [, owner.]table_name
[, index_name | "text only" ]
```

Note that for this procedure you don't need to specify a cache name. In fact, if you do, the stored procedure will attempt to interpret the cache name as the database name and return an error. Dropping a table, index, or database also removes all binding information automatically. To unbind all objects from a named cache, use the procedure

```
sp_unbindcache_all cache_name
```

Both of the unbinding procedures flush all dirty pages for affected objects from the cache.

When binding or unbinding a table or an index, `sp_bindcache` acquires an exclusive table lock, so the procedure will need to wait for all other users of the entity to relinquish their locks first.

The new `sp_helpcache` procedure gives you information about particular objects bound to a cache or helps you determine the memory overhead for a cache of a particular size:

```
sp_helpcache [ cache_name | "cache_size[P | K | M |
    G ]" ]
```

If you execute `sp_helpcache` with no parameters, you will get a list of all of the objects bound to caches. Use the *cache_name* parameter to see information about a particular cache. Each cache requires a certain amount of overhead. For example, if you have a 20-MB table cache, the Server will not be able to use all 20 MB for table pages. To see the amount of overhead required for a particular cache size, use the *cache_size* parameter, supplying one of the abbreviations P, K, M, or G to indicate the units pages, kilobytes, megabytes, or gigabytes, respectively.

The SQL Server 11.0 optimizer will take cache bindings into account when building the query plan. If you change the binding of an entity, the `sp_bindcache` procedure marks any stored procedures that reference the entity as needing recompilation. If you bind an entire database to a named cache, all stored procedures that reference entities in the database will require recompilation.

To accommodate some hardware platforms, a `memory alignment boundary` configuration variable has been added in SQL Server 11.0. This variable specifies the memory alignment boundary for caches. It must be a multiple of the default page size, which is 2 KB on all platforms but Stratus, where it is 4 KB. If not set by default, set this variable to the optimal page size for your platform or your disk hardware. All requests for buffers will default to the size specified by this variable. Modifications of this variable affect performance and should not be made unless recommended by Sybase personnel or documentation.

To select appropriate objects to bind to custom-made caches, you will need to know precisely which objects are in most demand, you will need to make sure a useful percentage of these objects will fit in cache, and you will need to be certain that keeping these objects in memory will be worth the expense of depriving other objects of the use of that memory. The performance tuning information in Chapter 8 can help you determine how best to use named caches for your applications.

I/O POOLS (BUFFER POOLS)

With the new cache functionality comes a new concept of buffer pools. A buffer pool is a set of memory buffers that enables a specific I/O size. By default, all buffers are 2 KB, which is the usual size of a page. With System 11, you can create pools with larger buffers. The sizes of the buffers that you can use are 2, 4, 8, or 16 KB.[1] When you define a buffer pool with large buffers and associate an object with that pool, then I/O for that object will be done with the I/O size defined, rather than one page at a time. Carefully used, this also has the potential to increase performance of well-understood transactions dramatically.

After you create a named cache, you can create buffer pools for it. You can either edit the configuration file or use this form of the new `sp_poolconfig` procedure:

```
sp_poolconfig cache_name
[, "mem_size [P | K | M | G]", "buffer_size K"]
```

The *cache_name* is the name of an existing named cache. Indicate the size of the new pool with the *mem_size* parameter, which

---

[1]On Stratus, 4, 8, 16, and 32 KB.

uses the same unit abbreviations as `sp_cacheconfig`. The pool size must be smaller than the size of the cache. Note that each pool requires some overhead memory, so even if the pool size is an even multiple of the I/O size, there will be fewer buffers than that multiple. The *buffer_size* is the size of I/Os, which can be any power of 2 times the page size as noted above. If you execute the `sp_poolconfig` procedure with only the *cache_name* parameter, the current configuration of the cache is displayed.

Each buffer pool has a buffer wash point, which is set by using another form of `sp_poolconfig`:

```
sp_poolconfig cache_name "buffer_sizeK",
"wash=wash_size [P | K | M | G]"
```

With this syntax, *wash_size* is the number of buffer pools to be maintained in a clean state for use by new reads. You can set *wash_size* anywhere from 10 buffers to 80% of the number of buffers in the pool. If you have a low setting for `recovery interval`, you will probably not need to change this value from the defaults. Also, if your CPUs are typically idle and the housekeeper is enabled, you probably will not need to reset this value. Otherwise, you may find that setting it slightly higher improves performance. Note that if you set it too high you can hurt performance due to excessive I/Os. (See the discussion of the housekeeper for more insight into the potential effects.)

You can also use `sp_poolconfig` to change I/O sizes of previously configured pools using this form of the procedure:

```
sp_poolconfig cache_name, "mem_size[P | K | M | G]",
"to_poolK" [, "from_poolK"]]
```

With this syntax, a pool for I/O sizes specified by *"to_poolK"* is expanded to the total size specified by *"mem_size"* by taking memory from the pool for I/O sizes specified in *"from_poolK."* To reduce the size of the I/O pool indicated in *"to_poolK,"* omit the *"from_poolK"* parameter. The memory is returned to the default cache.

To configure the log I/O size, you use the `sp_logiosize` stored procedure. The default I/O size for the transaction log is 4 KB if there is a 4-KB memory pool available. To change the

I/O size for the log, you first need to create a pool of the size needed and then use the sp_logiosize procedure, which has the following syntax:

```
sp_logiosize ["default" | "size" | "all"]
```

Set *size* to the desired size, or use the keyword default to change the log to the default size, which is 4 KB if such a pool exists or 2 KB otherwise. Note that *size* must be entered in quotes but does not include the abbreviation K. The "all" parameter tells the procedure to display the current log I/O size of all databases. If you execute the procedure with no parameters, the Server displays the current I/O size of the log for the current database.

Note that if you have logonly caches all the buffer pools (except the default 2-KB pool) should be matched to logs using sp_bindcache and sp_logiosize. To avoid wasting buffer space, make sure logonly buffer pools with I/O sizes other than those used by logs only exist for the default pool. For example, if you have a 4-KB I/O sized buffer pool in a logonly cache, but have used sp_logiosize to assign all logs to an 8-KB I/O size buffer pool, then the 4-KB I/O size pool will not be used at all and should be deallocated.

Also keep in mind that all pages in a buffer move in and out of cache together, so if you have 8-KB buffers, then 8-KB of data will age out of cache all at once. The large I/Os may not be beneficial in all cases.

There can only be one buffer pool for a particular I/O size per cache. In other words, if you have already defined a pool containing 16-KB buffers in named cache A, you cannot create a second one in that cache.

A configuration file entry for a buffer pool looks like this:

```
[Named Cache:mycache]
    cache size = 1024K
    cache status = mixed cache

[4K I/O Buffer Pool]
    pool size = 512K
    wash size = 120K
```

If you do not specify a buffer pool when you configure a named cache, a default pool of 2-KB buffers is used. If the number of buffers in a pool is less than 512, the default wash size will be 20% of the buffers in the pool. Otherwise, the default wash size is 256 buffers. The size of the default 2-KB pool must be at least 512 KB or some operations on an object bound to the associated cache would fail.

The recovery process will use the SQL Server's default cache only. For this reason, leave adequate room in the default cache. For an active Server, consider increasing the default cache size before rebooting so that recovery completes faster.

You can create and delete buffer pools, change buffer pool sizes, and change buffer wash sizes dynamically without needing to reboot the Server for the change to take effect.

If you want to enable prefetch for tables and indexes in System 11, you first create a buffer pool with the desired I/O size. Each buffer pool handles a different size of I/O. For example, you could have one buffer pool for the 2-KB (single page) I/O size and a second buffer pool with an 8-KB (4 page) I/O size. Once you have an appropriate buffer pool, you configure prefetch for an object. Thereafter, a `set` option controls whether to do prefetch for I/O, if the user determines that a query will benefit from prefetch. Because the system administrator controls the buffer pools and a database owner controls an object, you can prevent users from attempting to do prefetch all the time, which would result in filling up the cache with pages no one needs even the first time. If the nature of certain indexes and the queries tends to result in sequential scans, you may gain a significant performance improvement from using the prefetch feature.

A doubly linked list keeps track of the page buffers in each buffer pool. SQL Server uses a least recently used/most recently used (LRU/MRU) algorithm to manage the cache. The buffer pool list is stored in order from the most recently used pages to the least recently used. When a process wants to access a page, it first checks to see if the page exists in cache. If it doesn't, the Server reads the page from disk into memory, grabs a buffer from the LRU end of the list, updates the buffer to reflect the new page, and then moves the buffer to the MRU end of the list. All other buffers in the list effectively get shifted toward the LRU end. When a process wants to access a page and finds it in cache, it unlinks the buffer from its position in the list and relinks it into the MRU end of the list. Thus, frequently referenced pages tend to stay at the MRU end of the list.

Before it can use a buffer from the LRU end of the list, the process that wants the page must make sure the page is clean. A memory page that contains modifications not yet written to disk is referred to as a dirty page. Instead of making each process wash its own pages one page at a time, SQL Server uses a buffer washing mechanism to clean batches of dirty pages at the LRU end of the list. A fixed area at the end of the buffer list is considered a buffer wash zone. As new pages get added to the MRU end, the other pages move toward the LRU end. When a page enters the wash zone, for example, the last 20% of the chain, these pages are automatically washed as long as they are not active. This way, processes requesting buffers almost always find clean buffers.

When a buffer is modified, it is linked onto a dirty list for the object it belongs to, as well as remaining in the buffer pool list. SQL Server maintains dirty buffer lists so that it can quickly find all dirty buffers at checkpoint time. Cleaning a buffer involves flushing the contents of the page to disk, removing the buffer from the object's dirty list, and then reinitializing the buffer.

In SQL Server 11, system administrators can configure the wash zone using the documented `sp_configure` command or the new configuration file. Prior to System 11, the size of the wash zone is modifiable only by undocumented commands. The wash zone defaults to the smaller of 256 or half of the available buffers in cache. If it is reconfigured to include more buffers, then the effectiveness of the cache is diminished since there are fewer buffers holding pages, resulting in a lower hit rate most of the time. If the wash section is configured to include too few buffers, then performance degrades for individual processes. If a process wants to read a page into memory but cannot find a clean buffer, it must initiate a page wash itself. The process must then wait until the wash completes before it can continue its work.

The performance implications of adjusting this parameter are complex. Trial and error on a test system or careful use of the SQL Server Monitor product may be the best way to figure out the optimal settings for your environment. The best buffer wash configuration will depend on the frequency of cache hits and how useful they are for the areas in which high performance is desired. The size of the cache is also a factor, since a small cache will cause a larger number of cache misses and a need for more processes to clean their own buffers.

The buffer wash mechanism is only one of several SQL Server events that flush dirty pages to disk. Other times that pages get written to disk include the following:

- Any kind of checkpoint flushes all the dirty pages in the database to disk. A checkpoint may be issued by the DBO or someone with sa_role, by the SQL Server, by the normal SHUTDOWN command, or by the DUMP or LOAD commands (except DUMP TRANSACTION WITH NO_LOG).

- When a batch of fast bulk copy or a SELECT INTO completes, the pages for the affected object get flushed to disk.

- When a page gets newly allocated, it gets flushed to disk.

- Right before LOAD DATABASE completes, it flushes all newly loaded pages to disk. Pages not included in the dump being loaded are also initialized and flushed to disk to prevent previous use of the space looking like it belongs to the database.

THE HOUSEKEEPER

SQL Server considers a memory buffer to be *dirty* if it has been used for caching data and the data have changed since last read. Before the Server can use that buffer again, it must clean the buffer. Normally, a percentage of buffers is maintained in the clean state by SQL Server as it runs checkpoint or as new buffers are requested. In System 11, a housekeeper process now cleans buffers if a CPU dedicated to SQL Server is idle. In some environments, this will mean that a process will have a better chance of finding a clean buffer when it needs one, rather than having to initiate the cleaning process during the course of a transaction. In systems where the CPU is idle and the housekeeper finds useful work to do, expect to see better CPU utilization and increased transaction performance. Depending on the recovery interval configured, you may also see reduced checkpoint time and reduced recovery time. The higher the recovery interval, the more of a difference you will see.

At every SQL Server clock tick, the Server looks for new work to do. If it finds none, the housekeeper process will run if enabled. The housekeeper works on one buffer cache at a time. Within each, it cycles through each buffer pool. It does not wash log pages, since they are always written to disk when a transaction completes. The housekeeper yields the CPU often enough so that other SQL Server tasks can use it if new work has arrived.

For SQL Server engines with a lot of idle time, housekeeper may write buffers to disk more often than necessary. For example, a database application may update the same database page repeatedly. If so, the housekeeper may write it after each change, when fewer writes would have been acceptable. Using the new configuration variable `housekeeper free write percent`, you can set an upper limit on the percentage of extra writes by the housekeeper that should be tolerated. The performance effect of the extra writes will be minimal on an inactive machine, but you might want to make this change to minimize disk access. If you set this variable to 0, you disable the housekeeper.

Note that this feature will cause the CPU to accumulate more CPU time than before while idle. Contrary to first impressions, the additional CPU time should indicate less of a performance bottleneck than more. See Chapter 8 for more information about monitoring SQL Server CPU usage.

■ NETWORK USAGE

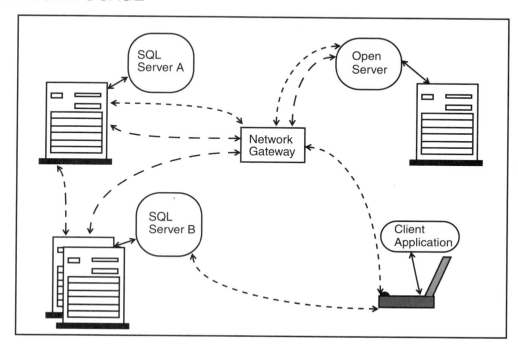

Figure 4.2 RPCs and client/server communications over a network

SQL Server uses the network services provided with the operating system. Because of this, a network administrator or manager usually handles network problems, rather than the Sybase Systems Manager. However, we will cover the basics of SQL Server's interaction with the network so that you and your network administrator can find common ground when discussing problems and possible enhancements.

SQL Server runs over a variety of network protocols, including

■ **TCP/IP** Available for clients and servers on all platforms

■ **DECNet** Available for VMS clients and servers

■ **IPX/SPX** Available for Netware servers and Windows or Windows NT clients

■ **Named Pipes** Available for OS/2 or Windows NT servers and OS/2, Windows, or Windows NT clients.

151

When a user logs into SQL Server, the client application requests a connection from the network to the SQL Server's query port, as designated in the Sybase `interfaces` file. Once the connection is established, SQL Server then exchanges data with the client using a format called Tabular Data Stream, abbreviated TDS. TDS is the Sybase standard protocol between clients and servers. TDS packets are designed to send and receive data structured like database table records and environment descriptors.

The key to a client being able to connect to a SQL Server (or any Open Server for that matter) lies in the proper use of Sybase `interfaces` files. The `interfaces` file is a relatively simple flat file that contains the names of the Servers on the network, their query ports, and their protocols. An `interfaces` file might also contain aliases for Servers so that users can reach them using different names, or different network protocols, or both.

When a user like Tim wants to connect to a Server using the ISQL client application, he either specifies the name of the SQL Server implicitly by having the DSQUERY environment variable set, or explicitly, by a using the -S *servername* command line option (/server_name="*servername*" for OpenVMS). Similarly, he specifies an `interfaces` file either with the SYBASE environment variable or by using the -I *interfaces_file* command line option (/interfaces="*interfaces_file*" for VMS). Internally, ISQL, an Open Client application, looks for the DSQUERY value and then the specified `interfaces` file. Upon finding both, it looks up the network information for the Server using the key provided by the DSQUERY value. If a match is found, the connection is requested from the operating system and, when that request is granted, Tim receives an ISQL prompt that he can now use for issuing queries.

All client applications that access SQL Server directly use the `interfaces` mechanism internally by using certain calls in the API. Instead of using command line options, they may rely on DSQUERY names and `interfaces` file locations provided in other ways, such as by pressing buttons, filling in text forms, using an initialization file, or even by hard-coding locations in the program.

The most common problems with connecting to SQL Server, in approximate order of frequency, are

- Invalid DSQUERY setting or invalid specification of the Server name
- Invalid SYBASE setting or invalid specification of the interfaces file location
- Invalid entry in the interfaces file
- Use of spaces rather than tabs in the interfaces file
- Network refusing connections for the protocol specified
- Network version incompatible with the SQL Server version

To test problems with Open Client applications, make it a habit to test with a script that calls ISQL in a standard way that normally works for you. If this works, you know that the problem exists at the application or the user end. Also, keep online as well as offline backup copies of the interfaces file. Also, various network protocols require various port address specifications, some of which require network addresses padded to certain lengths with zeros. Whenever possible, use the Sybase installation program to create properly formatted interfaces entries.

Protocol problems usually center around new versions of the network software. SQL Server and Open Client make calls to the network software using the network library APIs provided by the network vendor. Sybase uses copies of the network libraries that were current at the time of the SQL Server product release. Version mismatches often cause network connection attempts to fail. The Sybase release notes specify the network version used at the time of release. You can also get current version compatibility information from Technical Support or AnswerBase.

Whenever your network administrators update the version of your network software, keep a close eye on your SQL Server errorlog for unusual messages. Often network errors cause spurious results that users have trouble reporting in any definitive way. The errorlog will help you to correlate user reports with underlying network problems. Try to stay in touch with your network managers so that they let you know about updates ahead of time and so that they are prepared to roll back if you later discover incompatibilities between the new version and SQL Server.

For mission-critical databases, you need to run SQL Server on a part of your network least vulnerable to failures. Avoid installing such a Server on the type of network where, if one node goes down, the whole network goes down. In such a topology, SQL Server functionality and availability depend on the integrity of the network and the skills of the network administrators. Even in a network organized in a more robust manner, you will want SQL Server to exist on a machine that can be accessed via many network routes in case intermediate nodes in the network go down. In other words, if your organization separates network management from SQL Server management, try to influence the arrangement of the network so that the success of SQL Server depends on the people responsible for SQL Server rather than those responsible for the network.

SQL Server uses remote procedure calls (RPCs) for Server to Server communication. This communication may take place between any combination of SQL Servers and Open Server-based applications. By using RPCs from one Server to another in stored procedures, you can often reduce network traffic dramatically, which improves performance for a busy network.

For example, instead of a user first logging into one server and adding data, then logging into a second server and adding the same data, an application could be written so that, upon a user updating a particular table, an RPC sends the update to the second server. You can also use RPCs to divide processing among servers that exist on different machines or to delay processing so that multiple operations are consolidated into a single batch job.

Enabling RPCs between Servers means enabling the following Server-wide configuration variables using `sp_configure`:

- allow remote access
- number of remote connections
- number of remote logins
- number of remote sites

After configuring these parameters for each server that will communicate with other servers, you will need to add the authorized remote sites to each Server's `sysservers` table. In each SQL

Server that is to communicate remotely with another, use the `sp_addserver` command to register the name of each authorized remote site. RPCs will only be allowed to servers that exist in `sysservers`. If you haven't already done so, use the `local` option of `sp_addserver` to inform the SQL Server of its own name. Not only is this needed for remote communications, but it also helps administrators to remember where they are, since it sets the global variable `@@servername`. You will need to reboot SQL Server for the configuration changes and the `sp_addserver` commands to take effect.

Next, you will need to make sure that the `interfaces` file for the Server has entries for all the other servers that it will need to communicate with. Once you have more than two servers, it is extremely wise to institute a policy of keeping master, secondary, and backup interfaces files. The master should have all interfaces entries and should be read only. The secondary interfaces file should be writable by people setting up new servers. Ideally, a batch job will run nightly and merge all new entries from the secondary interfaces file into the master. That way, you will always have one version of each interfaces file entry. Then you can modify secondaries as necessary to allow or deny knowledge of specific remote servers to a local server. Back up all copies of all interfaces files as part of your routine operating system backup. If it is particularly difficult to get a timely restore in your backup scenario, keep shadow copies of your interfaces files online somewhere.

For users to be allowed to initiate RPCs between servers, you will also need to establish a login validation mechanism with `sp_addremotelogin`. If both servers have the same set of login account names, then you can simply add the remote server name with `sp_addremotelogin`. Alternatively, you can use `sp_addremotelogin` to map all local logins to one remote login name or to map each local login name to a different remote login name. Use `sp_adduser` in the remote server to add any necessary database user accounts as well.

In System 10, a server option called `net password encryption` was added that allows passwords to be encrypted as they travel across your network for RPCs between Servers. To use this feature, use `sp_serveroption` to set `net password encryption` to *true*. Then, whenever an RPC is initiated, an encryption key is requested from the remote server, this encryption key is returned to the source server, and the key is used to encrypt the login password that will enable the client to gain access to the remote server via the local server. Note that for non-RPC communication, that is, from a client to a server rather than between servers, you need to indicate that you want password encryption from the client application. For example, in `ISQL` versions released with System 10 and later, you use the `-X` or `/encrypt` option to indicate that you want the password to be transmitted across the network in encrypted form. Client applications must be written to use the Open Client encryption routines in order to make client-side password encryption available to the user.

After testing that everything works, configure your users' environments so that they use the appropriate `interfaces` file.

■ INTERNATIONALIZATION

SQL Server allows you to support operations in multiple languages by providing character sets, sort orders, and language files for messages. We'll look at how each of these work next.

CHARACTER SETS

To understand character sets, let's start at the lowest level and work our way up. As we discussed earlier, a computer ultimately stores electrical signals, which are understood by a layer of abstraction to represent binary numbers, which are understood by another layer of abstraction as decimal numbers. Characters are represented by yet another layer of abstraction on top of that in which each character is encoded as a number. Eventually, this number is translated to a symbol that is recognizable to a human as a character. Machine input and output devices and all the intervening software provide the appropriate translations between layers of abstraction.

At input time, a human usually uses a keyboard to press a key that corresponds to a symbol, such as the capital letter *A*. This symbol is considered a character in some alphabet that the human presumably knows. The workstation hardware reports the key press as a key number to the operating system software, which passes it along to the application software by using some encoding standard.

The three common methods of encoding characters are EBCDIC, ASCII, and Unicode. EBCDIC was created by IBM and is found primarily on their machines. ASCII stands for American Standard Code for Information Interchange and is used by most micro- and minicomputers. Unicode is a new standard created by the Unicode Consortium that can be represented on any machine.

Software, like SQL Server, is perfectly happy to manipulate input information represented as numbers. Eventually, however, hardware needs to output symbols, which it figures out how to display or print by associating a picture of a symbol with a character number. The character number comes from the encoding method. As long as the input device and the output device used the same encoding when matching character symbols to numbers, everything is fine. However, this is frequently not the case. Even when ASCII is used, there are different versions of ASCII.

The ASCII 8-bit encoding method uses 1 byte to store a character of data. This allows it to encode up to 256 characters. The American English alphabet, for which ASCII was designed, conveniently consists of less than 256 characters, so the numerical representation of its upper- and lowercase characters fits in 1 byte and still has room to store additional characters, such as punctuation, control characters, and more. The standard characters, punctuation, and control characters are stored in the first 127 slots, and the "and more" part, which are things like mathematical symbols, are stored in the second 128 slots. In other countries, ASCII is also used. In the other alphabets, however, there are additional important symbols, such as accented versions of upper- and lowercase letters. Most western languages can still fit their characters in 1 byte, but they use the second 128 slots to put in the "nonstandard" symbols.

So, each ASCII-encoded character set contains a different subset of these extended characters. With ASCII encoding, users must choose a character set based on which accented letters, symbols, or other special characters they want. Say, for example, you are representing the French language. In this case, you will need a c with a cedilla. If you want to represent Spanish data, you may also need an inverted question mark. You must either use two character sets, or you must find one character set that has both characters. Once you extend your data processing needs to include more languages, you find that you cannot represent French, Arabic, and Russian in one ASCII-based character set. That's when the software and hardware start having a hard time. After you leave the western European alphabets, you start working with writing systems that are fundamentally different. Some, like Chinese, consist of pen strokes that can be combined in any number of ways to represent different ideas. Trying to break the representation of such languages into characters and then into numbers is more abstraction than most software can handle.

One solution is to use multibyte characters. If a character set uses 2 bytes to store each character, you can store 65,536 different characters. It takes twice as much space to store 2-byte character set data as it does to store character data in a language that uses single-byte character sets. The benefit is that each character of a multibyte character set may convey more meaning with fewer characters or words than a more limited character set.

Some special multibyte character sets have been created for individual alphabets, like Kanji. To use a multibyte character set, you need input devices, operating systems, application software, and output hardware that all use the same multibyte set. Such sets of hardware and software can be collected, and, in fact, Sybase provides a language module that allows you to use multibyte character sets with the standard SQL Server engine.

In response to the complexity, the idea of Unicode was born. Unicode contains a nearly complete superset of all fixed-size and multibyte character standards currently in use and provides symbol sets such as mathematical operators and technical symbols. Sybase is working on supporting Unicode, but that version of the software is not yet available. Meanwhile, we must work with character sets.

For storing data in SQL Server using multiple languages, you will generally need to install all needed character sets and languages in the SQL Server and then use a client in which you can use the SQL SET CHAR_CONVERT CHARSET and SET LANGUAGE commands to change to the needed character set and language for a particular data entry task.

In the *charsets* subdirectory of the main Sybase directory tree, you will find the character set and sort order files. If you look inside these files, you will see comments that show how the characters are encoded and ordered.

Installing a character set involves adding a record to the syscharsets table that tells the SQL Server the codes that make up the character set. You can use the sybinit program to install character sets or you can use the charset utility. Check the SQL Server documentation for details about these operations.

A SQL Server can have several character sets installed. There are three ways in which SQL Server determines which character set to use for a session. First, there is a default Server character set that is configured using sp_configure. This is the format it will use unless a client application makes a different request. Second, a client application written using the Open Client API can call a function that selects the desired character set internally. The client application may or may not give the users of the application a way to override the internal setting. Finally, a user can issue the Transact-SQL SET CHAR_CONVERT CHARSET command.

However, only one sort order can be used. A sort order is the order in which characters are organized in sequence. In dictionaries, we are used to sorting characters in order by their appearance in an alphabet. As you can gather from the preceding discussion, this will not make sense for a Server in which different character sets are in use. To use multiple character sets, the best bet is to use the binary sort order, which organizes characters by their numerical encoding value. This makes the most intrinsic sense to the software and is therefore the fastest.

In a Server using multiple character sets, you will want to retrieve rows with the same character set used during input. For

the expected results, you will need to code a language or character set ID into the record or associate the table with a language in
a record in another table. Then any user or application that
retrieves the data will need to look at the ID of the source data
and set the language and character set appropriately for retrieval.

If a character set is specified by the user or application, but
that character set is not installed in the SQL Server, character set
conversion error messages are generated. You can remedy this by

- Installing the missing character set on the SQL Server and,
  optionally, changing the default SQL Server character set to match
  the client's default
- Change the client's default to match the SQL Server's default
- Use a client SET option to change the character set used for the
  session to one residing on the SQL Server
- Set the no conversion option on

The last option may result in unexpected representations of characters that do not correspond between character sets. For example, it
could be misleading to have the symbol for yen used at input time
and have an accented character returned instead at output time.

It is not wise to try to replace one character set with another
using either the charset utility or sybinit. Doing so may result in
conversion problems and errors indicating data corruption. It is a
better idea to add the character sets you need and leave the
unneeded ones installed.

LANGUAGES

A language, for SQL Server purposes, is the set of status and
error messages expressed in a particular language, such as English,
French, or Japanese. A language may rely on a particular character
set in order to be able to use the accented characters found in the
language. You can use the sybinit program or the langinstall
utility to add a language to SQL Server. When you use the sybinit
program for this purpose, it calls langinstall. langinstall calls
sp_addlanguage. These programs add a row into syslanguages
with the language name, ID, date format, and update version for
the language and then add rows into sysmessages for each error

and status message expressed in the language you are adding. You can install several languages in one SQL Server.

If you intend to use several languages simultaneously, you should also set the SQL Server configuration value for languages in cache appropriately.

As with character sets, there are several options for setting the language to use during a session. You can set a SQL Server default language set with sp_configure, applications can call Open Client routines to select a particular language, and users can use the Transact SQL set language command.

SORT ORDERS

Unlike languages and character sets, you can only have one sort order in a SQL Server. As you might expect, this can present a problem when storing data in different languages with different customs for ordering the alphabet or language symbols. It would not be simple to implement multiple sort orders in SQL Server, since the sort order affects the way data are stored on disk in any index on a column containing a character data type, and it also affects processing of SQL commands, such as the results of an ORDER BY clause.

SQL Server provides the following sort orders:

■ Binary (following the ASCII order of encoding)

■ Dictionary

■ Dictionary, case insensitive

■ Dictionary, case insensitive with preference

■ Case and accent insensitive

See the Sybase SQL Server Reference Manual for descriptions of the differences between these sort orders. Anything but a binary sort order means that the computer has to perform an additional step before knowing the order in which to sort values, so binary is always the fastest.

When we put a set of American English words in alphabetical order, we put the letter A before B and B before C, and so on. We can further define this order to mean ranking uppercase letters before lowercase. For example, *ABbC* rather than *AbBC*. This method of ordering is a convention. For computers, the default convention is to order characters by the numbers used in their ASCII encoding, which is most efficient for the computer. Since ASCII is American in origin, the encoding of the character set was ordered just to provide such efficiencies of sorting things in alphabetical order (for the American English alphabet). However, it did not originally include accented versions of characters or ligatures since American English does not include these. Therefore, if you are representing a non-American language and you are not using multiple character sets, you may want to use a different ordering convention than binary. Also, if you don't want uppercase letters sorted before lowercase, you will need to use a different sort order.

To minimize administration, all SQL Servers in an information system should use one sort order if possible. Joins of data with different sort orders using RPCs could result in misinterpretation. Also, all SQL Servers expected to act as standbys or replicates should have the same sort order. You cannot load a database dump from a SQL Server with one sort order into a SQL Server with a different sort order. Changing sort orders is a long, involved project. You can find the details in the Sybase SQL Server Administration Guide. You will need to make a full backup before starting, and you may have to rebuild many of your indexes. You will also need to drop and re-create any executable objects (stored procedures, triggers, views, etc.) that depend on the changed indexes.

Procedure Manual Suggestions

○ Internationalization

➡ Document the internationalization requirements for your SQL Servers and related applications. Make sure to include standard languages, character sets, sort order, or time zone conventions that must be followed.

CHAPTER

The Sybase SQL Server System Catalogs

The Sybase SQL Server system tables, also known as system catalogs, are how SQL Server manages itself. Understanding how they work is a fast way to become an expert at working through SQL Server problems and proposed changes.

One set of system tables exists only in the `master` database. These tables keep track of the Server as a whole. The second set of tables, found in every database, is used to manage the database. A third set of tables, in the optional `sybsecurity` database, supports the System 10 auditing feature. You can see a list of system tables with the following query:

```
> select name from master..sysobjects where type =
  "S"

> go
```

A few system tables that you will see in the results of this query are not documented in the Sybase manuals and are not documented here either. These tables are memory-only tables used by the Server to manage internal processes.

In this chapter, the tables are organized by function to make the relationships between them clearer. Each table description is accompanied by a SQL query that you can execute to get more familiar with your Server. System table information can also be accessed by stored procedures, but the direct queries will help you better understand how SQL Server works. It is best to log into a test SQL Server as `sa` or someone with `sa_role` when running the examples. Depending on how permissions have been set on your SQL Server, you may not be able to see the results of some of these commands.

The Sybase SQL Server Reference Supplement describes each column of each system table. That information is not duplicated here. Instead, the concepts behind each table are described. After reading this chapter, you will know what the tables are used for, common issues that arise in relation to them, and how they change as your system changes.

■ SERVER MANAGEMENT TABLES

sysservers (master database)

The `sysservers` table lists the remote servers a Server can access over the network. There is one row for the local Server and one row for each remote server that has been enabled with the `sp_addserver` command. Remote servers can include Backup Servers, other SQL Servers, Open Servers, and gateway servers. To look up a remote server by name, the current Server first checks the `sysservers` table for the name and then looks up the address associated with that name in the `interfaces` file.

To see the name and status of each Server,

```
> select srvname, srvnetname, srvstatus
> from master..sysservers
> go
```

There are five `sysconfigures` values that relate to communication with remote Servers: `allow remote access`, `number of remote logins`, `number of remote sites`, `number of remote` connections, and `remote server pre-read packets`. The differences between them are discussed in Chapter 6. `sysservers` is usually small. It grows when the `sp_addserver` procedure is run and shrinks as a result of `sp_dropserver`.

sysdevices (master database)

This table is how SQL Server knows which physical media to write your data to, whether it's in database form or in backup form. To see the database device information, issue this query:

```
> select * from master..sysdevices where cntrltype = 0
> go
```

The values for `low` and `high` are virtual block numbers that relate to blocks on disk. The first byte of `low` in `sysdevices` encodes the device number (`vdevno`) given in the original `DISK INIT` command. You can determine the device number as follows:

```
> select low/(power(2,24))
> from master..sysdevices where cntrltype = 0
> go
```

Phyname is the physical name of the device, such as `/dev/rsd0b` (BSD UNIX), *SYBASE$DISK1:[SQLSVR1]SYBDEV1.DAT* (VMS), or *c:\sqlsrvr1\sybdev1.dat* (MS-DOS). Many databases can reside on one device, or one database can be spread across many devices. See the description of `sysdatabases` for a query that allows you to relate databases to devices.

Rows in `sysdevices` that have non-zero controller types are for predefined backup devices. Issue this query to see the backup media configured in your SQL Server:

```
> select * from master..sysdevices
> where cntrltype != 0
> go
```

The `sysdevices` table is relatively small and changes rarely after initial setup. Rows for disk devices are added to `sysdevices` when the `DISK INIT` command is run and deleted by running `sp_dropdevice`. There is a one to one relationship between the number of rows in `sysdevices` for database devices and the number of physical partitions or files in use. However, the number of rows in `sysdevices` for dump devices only represents different ways to dump. You can have several `sysdevices` rows for one physical dump device on your machine. Rows in `sysdevices` for dump devices are added by using `sp_addumpdevice` and deleted by running `sp_dropdevice`.

sysdatabases (master database)

The `sysdatabases` table keeps track of basic database information. To see which databases a SQL Server manages, execute this query:

```
> select dbid, name, crdate, dumptrdate
> from master..sysdatabases
> order by dbid
> go
```

You will see the database number and name, the date it was created, and the last time the transaction log was dumped.

From `sysdatabases`, `sysusages`, and `sysdevices`, you can get a list of which databases reside on which devices:

```
> select db_name = sd.name,
> logical_dev_name = sdv.name,
> physical_dev_name = sdv.phyname
> from master..sysdatabases sd,
> master..sysusages su,
> master..sysdevices sdv
> where sd.dbid = su.dbid
> and su.vstart between sdv.low and sdv.high
> and cntrltype = 0
> go
```

`sysdatabases` stays relatively small and changes rarely. Rows are added by the CREATE DATABASE command and deleted by the DROP DATABASE command.

sysusages (master database)

The sysusages table keeps track of how database devices are allocated to databases. Each row in sysusages represents a portion of a database residing on a device.

To see the contents of sysusages, issue the query

```
> select * from master..sysusages
> go
```

The *dbid* is the database number. To find the database name associated with a *dbid*, such as *dbid 3*,

```
> select db_name(3)
> go
```

Conversely, to find the *dbid* when you know the database name, such as tempdb,

```
> select db_id("tempdb")
> go
```

The *segmap* column contains a bitmapped status. If you're not familiar with this construct, read the section "Bitmapped Status Values" at the end of this chapter. The *segmap* value represents the type of data that can reside on the device fragment and database of the given row in sysusages. See the description of the sysseg-ments table for more information about the numerical values for each segment.

The *lstart* column is for the logical starting page. A database always starts with page 0.

The *size* column is the number of pages that the given portion of the database contains. A row with an *lstart* of 0 and a size of 1024 means that the row represents a 2-MB portion of a database. The next portion of the database, if there is one, will have an *lstart* of 1024.

The *vstart* column stands for *virtual starting page*. A 4-byte value is used to store the *vstart*, the highest byte of which is used to store the SQL Server device number. The remaining bytes are used to store the virtual page number on the SQL Server device. The *unreservedpgs* column of sysusages was added with System 10 to assist in determining the amount of space left in a database.

To see database names, device numbers, and space in megabytes, try this query:[1]

```
> select dbid, db_name = db_name(dbid),
> device_number = vstart/(power(2,24)),
> free_mb = (unreservedpgs * 2.0) /1024.0
> from master..sysusages
> go
```

The `sysusages` table is generally small and relatively static. It only changes when a CREATE, ALTER, or DROP DATABASE command is issued.

syssegments (all databases)

Segments are more of a concept than a physical entity. They are used to designate where tables may put their data.

Sybase provides three segments automatically: `system`, for system tables; `log`, for the transaction log; and `default`, for user data. Additional segments may be defined with the `sp_addsegment` stored procedure. The CREATE TABLE and ALTER TABLE commands allow you to designate a specific segment to place the table on. If you don't specify a segment, the table is placed on the `default` segment.

If you have a test database, such as *pubs2*, that resides on a device such as *pubsdev*, you can see how segments work using commands like this:

```
> use pubs2
> go
> select * from syssegments
> go
> sp_addsegment "fastdevice", pubs2, pubsdev
> go
> select * from syssegments
> go
```

---

[1]If you are on a Stratus SQL Server, multiply *unreservedpgs* by 4 instead of 2, since Stratus pages are 4 KB each.

The segment numbers from the `syssegments` table are used in the bitmapped *segmap* value in `sysusages`. See the discussion of bitmaps in the section "Bitmapped Status Values" at the end of this chapter.

The `syssegments` table is small and static for the most part. It only changes when `sp_addsegment` and `sp_dropsegment` are run.

If you want to completely restrict creation of objects to specific segments that you have defined in a newly created database, you can drop the `default` segment. Then a segment would have to be specified for each `create table`, `alter table`, or `create index` statement. After data already exist on a default segment in a database, do not drop `default`. Doing so would result in 2558 errors.

Typically, segments are used to manage space or to manage performance. In the first case, you can use segments to effectively set up space quotas for tables and indexes. The System 10 threshold feature can be used to trigger an activity when an "available space is running low" condition is reached. In earlier versions of SQL Server, you can use segments, but you must monitor space on your own.

In the case of performance, segments can be used to put frequently accessed data on particularly fast or reliable devices. Typically, transaction logs and indexes are placed on their own segments. Also, placing a table's data on one segment and its nonclustered indexes on another can increase performance if the segments are associated with different disks on different controllers. In this scenario, the two controllers do less seeking and waiting than one controller would.

systhresholds (all databases)

The concept of thresholds was added in the System 10 SQL Server to help people monitor space. In particular, there has been a great need to avoid running out of transaction log space. In SQL Server, a threshold is a boundary, defined in terms of free space in a segment.

Several thresholds can be defined for one segment. For example, you could define a "warning" threshold, a "preliminary action needed" threshold and an "urgent attention required" threshold. Thresholds are added with the sp_addthreshold procedure and removed with sp_dropthreshold. As well as associating a free space level with the threshold, you specify an action to be taken. The action consists of a stored procedure or remote procedure call that you write. This procedure may write a message to the error log, mail the database owner a message, or execute an automatic DUMP TRANSACTION procedure.

To see if any thresholds have been defined for a database, try this:

```
> select segment, proc_name, free_space
> from systhresholds
> go
```

systhresholds is a small table that only changes with the use of sp_addthreshold or sp_dropthreshold.

syspartitions (all databases)

This table, added in SQL Server 11.0, manages table partitions created with the ALTER TABLE command. See Chapter 3 for a description of table partitions. To see if any partitions have been defined in a database, try the command:

```
> select * from syspartitions
> go
```

The size of syspartitions only changes when partitions are added or removed.

syslogs (all databases)

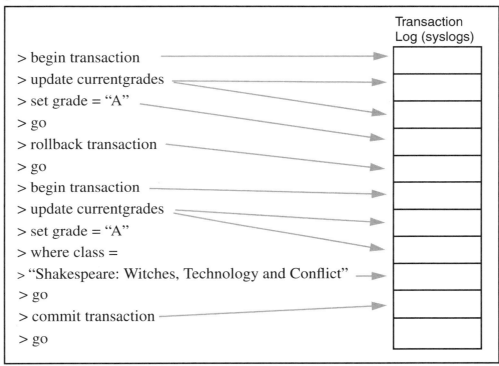

Figure 5.1 All transactions get written to syslogs, the database transaction log.

The syslogs table is also known as the transaction log. Each transaction that modifies data pages on disk is logged in the transaction log. The log for each database is read and replayed during recovery when you boot a SQL Server. It is also read and replayed when you load a database or transaction log dump.

The transaction log is not human readable. It stores its data in binary form so that transactions can be stored and recovered as quickly as possible. The most meaningful information that you can get directly from the syslogs table is a row count. By taking row counts at various discrete intervals, you can estimate how database changes affect the growth of the log.

To experiment, try the following in a test database such as *pubs2* when no one else is using it:

```
> use pubs2
> go
> select count(*) from syslogs
> go
> create table forest (a integer, b char(6))
> go
> insert into forest values (1, "trees")
> go 100
> select count(*) from syslogs
> go
> drop table forest
> go
> dump tran pubs2 with truncate_only
> go
> select count(*) from syslogs
> go
```

The row counting method only gives you an estimate of space usage. DBCC CHECKTABLE gives you the most accurate report of space usage if the log is on its own device (which is recommended). Row counts are quicker, though, and can give you insight into the rate of change.

WARNING: Never try to perform a manual update to syslogs. The Server will attempt to log the fact that it is changing the log. As it does that, it will attempt to log the fact that it's logging the fact that it's changing the log. This recursive behavior ends up filling up the transaction log, which brings all activity in the database to a halt. Furthermore, shutting down and rebooting the SQL Server doesn't help because the recovery process tries to replay the log.

To make backups of a database, you typically dump the log and database at regular intervals. Dumping the database is a full backup, and dumping the log is an incremental backup.

For everything but essentially read-only databases, syslogs should be placed on the fastest, most reliable disks you have.

Consider mirroring these devices as well. The logs are updated so often that the portions of the disks they are on will be the most active of all the database device fragments. If any hardware is going to fail, it will be the transaction log disks or the controllers for those disks. Make sure that DBCC CHECKDB and DBCC CHECKALLOC are run and that backups are made frequently.

sysengines (master database)

This table exists only in memory. It is built dynamically when SQL Server is booted. sysengines keeps track of active CPUs so that threaded processes can be run on multiple CPUs if available. The word engine is used to refer to a CPU process, so if you have a four-CPU system, you could configure SQL Server to use anywhere from one to four engines.

To see the contents of sysengines, issue this query:

```
> select * from master..sysengines
> go
```

The status column of sysengines can be interesting if you are experiencing SQL Server performance problems on multi-CPU machines. Check the value of affinitied from time to time. If most processes seem to be affinitied to one engine, check the status values to see if the other engines are offline.

Since sysengines is built automatically and not stored on disk, no disk space issues are associated with it.

sysconfigures (master database)

sysconfigures is a memory-only table that is built every time SQL Server is booted. The default configuration area is the first 4 KB of disk space on the partition allocated for your master device. The master database, which is the first database on the master device, has a *vstart* value of 4 in sysusages. This is because logical pages 0 through 3 are reserved for the configuration area. If you are using SQL Server 11.0 or a later version, configuration values to use are taken from the configuration file, if found. Otherwise, the configuration block values are used. In earlier releases, the configuration block holds the most recent configuration settings written as a result of the `reconfigure` command.

The `sysconfigures` table stores all the values you can set with `sp_configure`, and a few more. Examples of configuration variables you can set are the number of pages of memory allocated for SQL Server and the maximum number of user connections allowed. When you reset a value with `sp_configure`, the new value is written to the `sysconfigures` table. The old value is retained in the `syscurconfigs` table. After running `sp_configure`, in a pre-11.0 Server, you are prompted to give the `reconfigure` command. Reconfigure causes the new value to be written to `syscurconfigs` and to the configuration area on disk. In version 11.0 and later, you use the `WRITE` option of `sp_configure` to save a configuration change to a file. For some configuration values, SQL Server must be rebooted for the change to take effect.

When you run `sp_configure` with no parameters, a table containing each configuration value is displayed. The *Config Value* column shows the value from `sysconfigures`, and the *Run Value* column shows the value from `syscurconfigs`.

Chapter 6 explains each configuration value in detail.

syscurconfigs (master database)

This memory-only table is like `sysconfigures`, but shows the values that were set as of the last time `reconfigure` or the `WRITE` option of `sp_configure` was run.

To see the current configuration values in effect, use

```
> select * from master..syscurconfigs
> go
```

sysattributes (all databases)

System 11 uses a new system table called `sysattributes`, which stores special configuration information for entities such as tables, databases, and engines. An entity is any item addressable by SQL Server, such as engines and table partitions. The System

11 release primarily stores information about bindings of objects to named buffer caches in sysattributes. The storage of information in sysattributes is optional, so not every SQL Server entity has sysattributes rows.

In general, the table stores the object name, the attribute name, and the attribute value. Database object attributes are stored in the copy of sysattributes in the relevant database. Entries for database attributes are in the sysattributes table in master. The sysattributes in master contains rows for each valid attribute class and attribute name for the SQL Server. This new functionality facilitates the storage of metadata about entities that applications may wish to store in SQL Server.

The columns in sysattributes are shown in Table 5-1.

TABLE 5-1   Sysattributes Columns

Column Name	Description
class	Attribute class ID
attribute	Attribute ID
object_type	Table, index, etc.
object	Object ID, user ID, database ID, or other identifier
object_info1, object_info2, object_info3	Any integer information needed to further identify an object
object_cinfo	Any character information needed to further identify an object
int_value, char_value, text_value, image_value	Attribute value, using the appropriate datatype
comments	Used for comments or additional necessary information

sp_help, sp_helpdb, and sp_helpindex report any sysattributes rows specific to the entity for which help is requested, if they exist. Part of the process of dropping an object is now to drop the related rows from `sysattributes`. (If you have ever needed to drop an object using a manual procedure from Technical Support, you will now need to remember to drop any relevant rows from `sysattributes` as well.)

Many operations, such as binding objects to cache, update `sysattributes` automatically. The new stored procedure `sp_chgattribute` is provided as a mechanism for changing attributes not otherwise updated. With the initial release of SQL Server 11, this procedure only allows you to change the `max_rows_per_page` value for a table or index. When an entity is dropped, the corresponding rows in `sysattributes` are deleted. The `sp_chgattribute` syntax is

```
sp_chgattribute object_name, option_name,
  option_value
```

For example, to set the maximum number of rows per page for the classes table, Tim might use this command:

```
> sp_chgattribute class_names, "max_rows_per_page", 4
```

See   for more information about the `max_rows_per_page` option.

sysmessages (master database)

SQL Server uses two primary methods to communicate with the user. The first is query results, that is, answering whatever question the user asked via a SQL command. The second is runtime messages and error codes. These messages are written to the standard output device and sometimes to the error log as well. These inform the user of the status of an operation or of a problem. The SQL Server messages and error codes that are operating system-independent are stored in `sysmessages`.

The messages in `sysmessages` range from informative ("New user added.") to confusing ("Can't find a range table entry for range %d."). Each also has an error number. Some of these error numbers are so frequently encountered or indicate particularly bad problems that experienced Sybase users refer to them solely by number (e.g., 2525, 605, and 821). Normally, when users encounter an error, the error number and message are given. Variables that have values for specific details of the error context, such as database ID, are embedded in the message.

A direct select from sysmessages will show you the generic form of the message, with format strings serving as placeholders for the context variables. To find the error messages that go with the error codes cited above, issue this query:

```
> select error, severity, dlevel, langid, description
> from master..sysmessages
> where error in (605, 821, 2525)
> go
```

To see all the messages that contain a particular word, such as sysindexes,

```
> select error, description from master..sysmessages
> where description like "%sysindexes%"
> go
```

Some SQL Server error messages don't appear in sysmessages. These are the ones that appear only in the errorlog, starting with indicators such as *kdconfig*. They are most often related to hardware and are operating system specific.

If your system has a language other than English installed, sysmessages will contain error messages in that language. If you have more than one language installed, there will be one set of rows in sysmessages for each language. In other words, the addition of each language increases the size of sysmessages by the number of rows needed for one language. In SQL Server 11.0, there are approximately 3250 rows in sysmessages for English.

sysusermessages (all databases)

sysusermessages is like sysmessages, but it is used to maintain customized messages developed specifically for your system. For example, developers may add user-defined messages for indicating status for a particular stored procedure.

To see the first five custom messages added to a database, try this command:

```
> use master
> go
> set rowcount 5
> select error, description from sysusermessages
> set rowcount 0
> go
```

The size of this table only changes when messages are added with the `sp_addmessage` or `sp_dropmessage` stored procedures. Also, third-party applications may take advantage of the custom message facility offered by SQL Server. In this case, `sysusermessages` may grow a substantial amount when you install the application.

It is wise to ask an application vendor whether customized messages are added to this table. Custom messages add some complexity to the investigative work of the people who support your system. To get appropriate technical support, they will need to determine whether they are working with an application error message or with a SQL Server error message. Since there are so many third-party applications, Sybase technical support engineers may not be aware of the meaning of a particular third-party vendor's error messages. However, a vendor or developer who has taken care to write very informative messages that are easily distinguishable as part of the application can make the troubleshooter's job much easier.

Custom messages are helpful during debugging for reporting errors that occur when a specific stored procedure is run. Also, informational messages can be added to stored procedures that remind the user to perform a specific action that is not related to data in the SQL Server. Another example of capitalizing on custom messages is to trigger a message when a particular value of a variable is reached. For example, when a telesales representative makes his or her one-hundredth sale, you could print a "Good Job!" message.

syslanguages (master database)

In the 4.2 release of SQL Server, Sybase added support for internationalization. Since then Sybase has continued to enhance products to make them usable globally. `syslanguages` is one of the tables associated with this effort. Each row in `syslanguages` identifies a language and the date format associated with that language. When selecting languages to configure, the installation program populates this table. You can add languages later by running the installation program again, but this time only selecting the additional languages option.

You can configure SQL Server to use several languages at once. You establish the default language by using `sp_configure`. Any user may specify a preferred language among those installed by using the SET LANGUAGE command. Note that the data in your database are only available in the language the data were input in. Besides dates and user messages, SQL Server does not provide general data translation services.

To see if your SQL Server is currently configured for any languages and how these languages refer to dates, issue this query:

```
> select name, dateformat, months, shortmonths, days
> from master..syslanguages
> go
```

In a newly installed SQL Server configured only for the English language, this table is empty.

`syslanguages` is a small table, which only grows when a language is added to SQL Server. There are no significant disk usage requirements for it. There are space implications of the other language support tables (`sysmessages`, `syscharsets`) in the master database though, so language installation should be thought through carefully.

syscharsets (master database)

SQL Server uses `syscharsets` to keep track of all the ways that character data may be stored in your database. A character set is a table of values software uses to represent character symbols internally. Rather than manipulate an image of an A, for example, the standard ASCII character set represents it as the decimal value 65.

179

This query shows you which character sets and sort orders have been installed on your SQL Server:

```
> select id, name, description from master..syscharsets

> go
```

ASCII or extended ASCII encoding is the standard method for languages such as English, French, and German. The alphabets for these languages only need a single byte to represent a character. A byte can represent 256 distinct numbers (0 through 255 or -128 through +127), which means that it can represent 256 distinct characters. The first 128 characters of all the character sets are usually the same, containing the usual upper- and lowercase letters, punctuation, and control characters. The remaining 128 characters differentiate the various character sets.

Different computer vendors have implemented different extensions of the basic ASCII character set. SQL Server supports IBM's Code Page 850 (cp850) and Code Page 437 (cp437), Apple's Macintosh (mac), and generic ASCII for English-language text. SQL Server also supports the ISO-8859-1 (iso_1) character set, which is used for many European languages.

Languages such as Japanese have a much more complex character set and require more than 256 values to store all the characters. For this reason, the 4.2 SQL Server International release introduced the multibyte character set. Since computer programs have traditionally relied on single-byte character encoding, they often do not cope well with multibyte characters. If your system is to be used for international business, it is wise to ensure that any application you use with SQL Server was designed to handle multibyte characters. Extra testing is recommended.

Occasionally, SQL Server will report errors about character sets being incompatible. This happens when a client application requests a character set not installed on the SQL Server. The easiest way to work around this problem is to add the application's character set to the SQL Server. In pre-4.9.1 SQL Servers, you can do this with the `charset` utility, and in System 10 and later releases, you can use the `sybinit` installation program.

The `syscharsets` table serves two purposes. In addition to managing character representation, it manages sort orders. A sort order is the alphabetical ranking of characters. Since this ranking is dependent on the set of characters, character sets and sort orders are closely linked. When the SQL Server builds an index, for example, it uses the sort order to determine whether to put all words beginning with uppercase letters first or whether to disregard case. The sort order is also used to determine whether o with a circumflex comes before or after an o with an umlaut.

The contents of `syscharsets` are relatively static. They normally only change when a character set is added.

■ OBJECT MANAGEMENT TABLES

systypes (all databases)

`systypes` stores the properties of system and user-defined datatypes. These properties include physical properties, such as whether the datatype has a variable or fixed length, whether it allows nulls, and how many bits of storage it consumes. `systypes` also maintains logical properties of each type, such as whether a default is bound to the type.

Run this query to see some of the type information in the `master` database:

```
> select name, type, length, allownulls, tdefault,
  domain
> from master..systypes
> go
```

This table grows slowly. It undergoes the most change during development, and only then if the developers choose to make extensive use of user-defined datatypes. `sp_addtype` and `sp_droptype` add and remove rows from this table, respectively.

User-defined datatypes help most when developing a database that consistently uses a particular type definition, such as *char(30) not null*. User-defined datatypes can also be associated with stored procedures used to generate defaults and perform integrity checks. These techniques can be much easier to implement than associating the default or integrity check to each column of each table using the same datatype.

An overabundance of user-defined datatypes, however, makes it difficult for system maintainers to know the original decisions made by the developers and to make intelligent changes. Also, the SQL Server must do extra work for each non-system type, so performance may be affected.

sysobjects (all databases)

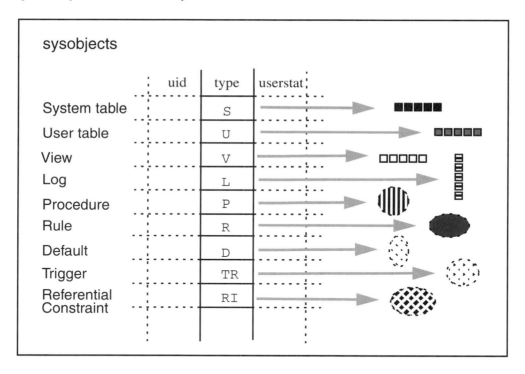

Figure 5.2 Each database object has a record in the sysobjects table.

The sysobjects table keeps track of the tables, views, procedures, rules, defaults, triggers, and constraints in a database. The ID column seen so frequently in system tables is the unique ID for each object in the database. The character value in the type column signals the object type. For example, type "U" stands for user table and type "S" stands for system table.

The following queries result in the names, ids, and creation dates of all the user tables and views in the *pubs2* sample database:

```
> use pubs2
> go
> select name, type, id, crdate
> from sysobjects where type in ("U", "V")
> go
```

This query will tell you how many views, rules, defaults, triggers, and constraints are defined in *pubs2*:

```
> select count(*) from sysobjects
> where type in ("V", "R", "D", "TR", "RI")
> go
```

The growth of this table is high during development. It fluctuates rapidly as views, rules, defaults, triggers, and constraints are tested. During production, the growth typically levels off in user databases. In `tempdb` and some types of user databases, the creation and deletion of objects is part of the day to day activity in the database.

For a discussion of each type of object and how it is used, see Chapter 1. Like `sysindexes`, the data in this table are referenced more frequently than most other system tables.

syslocks (master database)

`syslocks` is a dynamic table populated by processes as they acquire locks. Locking is the method by which SQL Server maintains data integrity at the page and transaction levels. For example, if a process intends to update a row on a data page, it acquires a lock for that page before performing the update. During the time the lock is held, no other process can update data on that page.

To see the first 10 rows of information about locks currently held in your SQL Server, give this query:

```
> set rowcount 10
> select * from master..syslocks
> set rowcount 0
> go
```

Select from `syslocks` or issue `sp_lock` if you suspect that your system is experiencing excessive locking.

sysprocedures (all databases)

`sysprocedures` maintains binary parse trees of the procedural objects used in your database. When you create stored procedures, views, defaults, rules, triggers, procedures, defaults, and check constraints, SQL Server parses them and places them in `sysprocedures`.

To get an idea of how much space these objects use in the *pubs2* sample database, issue these commands:

```
> use pubs2
> go
> dbcc checktable ("sysprocedures")
> go
```

The output of DBCC CHECKTABLE is the number of data pages allocated to that table. Many Sybase users monitor the rate of growth of this table by counting the rows in `sysprocedures`, since DBCC CHECKTABLE often takes a long time to run:

```
> select count (*) from sysprocedures
> go
```

As is common with binary images, objects in `sysprocedures` can use a large amount of space in a database.

The growth rate of this table is steep during development. During production, it grows incrementally due to reresolution and recompilation, even when new objects aren't being added. This problem is typically managed by periodically dropping and re-creating stored procedures. See Chapter 8 for more information about this issue and other performance issues related to stored procedures.

syscolumns (all databases)

syscolumns maintains physical and logical information about every column of every table and view in a database. It also contains a row for each parameter of a procedure. Procedure parameters, like table columns, are associated with their data types and sizes. The *colid* value is used by tables such as sysdepends and sysconstraints to keep track of column-related actions.

For some observations about the columns in a database, try these queries:

```
> select distinct name, type
> from syscolumns
> select count(*) from syscolumns
> go
```

The relationship between the row counts from the two select statements is a measure of the duplication of column names in the database, where the columns do not have the same types. A database can be very confusing if many of the columns with the same names contain different types of data. Well-planned naming conventions can enable more efficient and reliable maintenance. Another naming-related problem is accidentally choosing column names that are reserved words in SQL Server. To help you avoid this, System 10 provides the sp_checkreswords stored procedure:

```
> sp_checkreswords
> go
```

This procedure will report back any reserved words in use by your SQL Server for user objects.

This query allows you to see the widest columns in the database:

```
> select name, type, length
> from syscolumns
> go
```

185

When wide columns, such as long, fixed-length character columns, are used in indexes, the indexes take up more space than those for integer columns. In extreme cases, wide indexes require many more pages to store and thus require a deeper index tree and more reads during retrieval by that index. Thus, performance is affected. Variable-length columns and those that allow nulls can be poor choices for indexes as well. Indexing issues are discussed in Chapter 8. As with other object-related tables, growth in syscolumns increases rapidly during development, and then levels off in production. If many stored procedures with parameters are added and dropped during development, the contents of syscolumns could fluctuate widely.

syskeys (all databases)

A key in a database is a column that is used to relate one table with another. The ID columns in many of the system tables are good examples of keys. A key is more of a concept than a separate physical entity in SQL Server, although qualities of keys, such as uniqueness, are enforced using indexes. You can document keys using the sp_primarykey and sp_foreignkey stored procedures. This lets people know which columns are designed to match related columns between tables when they run sp_help on a table. Each table can have up to eight key columns defined in SQL Server. Each may also have eight dependent keys.

To see the keys for the *titles* table in the *pubs2* sample database, try

```
> use pubs2
> go
> select id, type, depid, keycnt, size
> from syskeys
> where id = object_id("titles")
> go
```

Often, clustered indexes are placed on key columns, since the key values are frequently used in complex queries. Sometimes it doesn't make sense to always put the clustered index, which can yield the best performance, on the primary key column. In some applications, the column users specify for selecting data, such as *last name*, is not the same as the key column, such as *customer ID*.

The size of syskeys changes as sp_primarykey, sp_foreignkey, and sp_dropkey are used, which is relatively infrequent in the typical production system.

sysindexes (all databases)

sysindexes maintains information about the physical locations of table data and indexes. There is one row for each table's data, one row for each nonclustered index of a table, and one row for each text and image column of a table. Information about clustered indexes is maintained in the table data row.

For example, to see the information maintained about syscharsets in the master database, issue this query:

```
> select si.name, indid, first, root, segment
> from master..sysindexes si, master..sysobjects so
> where si.id = so.id and so.name = "syscharsets"
> go
```

The *indid* value is the index ID. A value of 255 is used for text and image data. A value of 0 indicates the row for information about the data stored in the table. Clustered indexes are designated by an indid of 1, and nonclustered indexes may have any value from 2 to 250.

The sysindexes table is one of the most active system tables. It usually doesn't increase as much as syslogs or sysprocedures, but it is accessed very frequently. If you have fast devices to spare, this table is a good candidate for placing on such devices. Every time you access a table, SQL Server uses sysindexes to find that table. The value in the *first* column of sysindexes for the data or clustered index row (indid 0 or 1) of a table is the logical page number on the segment. The value of the *root* column for the index rows is the logical page number of the root page of the index.

sysdepends (all databases)

sysdepends keeps track of the interrelationships of procedures, views, and triggers. There is a row for each trigger, procedure, or view that references another trigger, procedure, or view in the same database. This table is used by the sp_depends stored procedure, which allows you to see what other objects will be affected if you change a given object.

To see the contents of the sysdepends table in a database, issue this query:

```
> select * from sysdepends
> go
```

This table often grows quickly during development, especially if lots of procedures, views, and triggers are used to maintain integrity. The changes usually level out during production.

The existence of the sysdepends table does not guarantee that you will be notified if you change something that something else depends on. It does give you a method by which you can check your work and the work of others. It can be indispensable when a large group of developers is working on the same database. Communication methods such as diagrams and design documents are the best methods of keeping dependencies between database objects clear. The sp_depends stored procedure is no replacement for good design, but it can help with design and maintenance.

sysconstraints (all databases)

The concept of constraints was introduced in SQL Server with System 10 to maintain compliance with the ANSI SQL standard. Constraints enable objects to maintain referential integrity. You can also use triggers, rules, and stored procedures for this purpose. Each method has its own benefits and shortcomings, so it's best to determine system requirements first and then match requirements to methods.

A table or a column may have a REFERENCES or CHECK constraint that is declared when using the CREATE TABLE or ALTER

TABLE statement. The following query will show you all the tables that have constraints declared in the current database:

```
> select distinct tableid, so.name
> from sysconstraints sc, sysobjects so
> where sc.tableid = so.id
> go
```

Since constraints typically enforce business rules, there is a strong relationship between this table and the business side of your system. For example, a constraint could be used to ensure that each row in an airline ticket table was associated with a row in the tables for planes and seats. Changes in business rules may result in required changes to the constraints you define. Similarly, the wise addition of constraints can greatly enhance data quality. The unwise addition of constraints can make users more frustrated or slow the system down.

When business rules change relatively frequently or errors in data entry are relatively rare, it might not make sense to use constraints. Instead, you may want to make a stored procedure that checks data periodically and prints an exception report for any discrepancies it finds. The discrepancies can then be adjusted by hand.

The size of this table changes as constraints are added and removed with the CREATE TABLE, ALTER TABLE, and DROP TABLE commands. Since this type of activity is most common during development, the changes in the size of this table typically become minimal as the system goes into production.

sysreferences (all databases)

sysreferences was added in the System 10 SQL Server to support referential integrity constraints. It is analogous to sysdepends, although it provides support for more strongly bound relationships between tables and columns than sysdepends.

As with all objects in SQL Server, constraints have object IDs. In addition, the object that has the constraint has an object ID, the object that the constraint references has an object ID, and the index on the constraint column has an ID. These IDs are maintained in the `sysreferences` table in the *constrid, tableid, reftabid,* and *indexid* columns, respectively.

To see the constrained and referenced tables for each constraint in the table, try this query:

```
> select table_with_constraint =
> (select so.name from sysreferences sr, sysobjects so
> where sr.tableid = so.id),
> table_referenced =
> (select so.name from sysreferences sr, sysobjects so
> where sr.reftabid = so.id)
> go
```

Like `sysconstraints`, the size of this table changes as references and constraints are declared or dropped. The system aspects of `sysreferences` are similar to those for `sysconstraints`.

syscomments (all databases)

`syscomments` stores the text of SQL definition statements for each compiled object. For example, for a stored procedure, the text column contains the complete text of the SQL commands that make up the stored procedure. Compiled objects include views, rules, defaults, triggers, and procedures. The text column of `syscomments` holds up to 255 characters. If an object needs more than 255 characters, rows are added for the additional text. The *colid* and *colid2* tables are used to keep track of the text sequences.

To see the text of the `sp_configure` stored procedure, issue the query

```
> select so.name, text
> from master..syscomments sc, master..sysobjects so
> where sc.id = so.id and so.name = "sp_configure"
> go
```

Normally, you would use `sp_helptext` procedure or `defncopy` utility to see the information given by this command.

The `sysprocedures` table description above includes a procedure for managing stored procedures. If you want to put that procedure in place, you may want to use the contents of this table. You can use `bcp` or `defncopy` to copy its contents if you don't have the original scripts used to create the procedures.

This table exists purely for informational purposes. It is used by the `sp_helptext` procedure. For security or space purposes, some or all of the rows may be deleted. Make sure that you have a backup, perhaps in both `bcp` and `defncopy` format, before you take this step.

This table expands quickly and changes frequently during development. Objects like stored procedures and triggers are typically created, tested, dropped, and re-created many times. As a system moves into production, the growth rate slows.

■ SECURITY AND USER MANAGEMENT TABLES

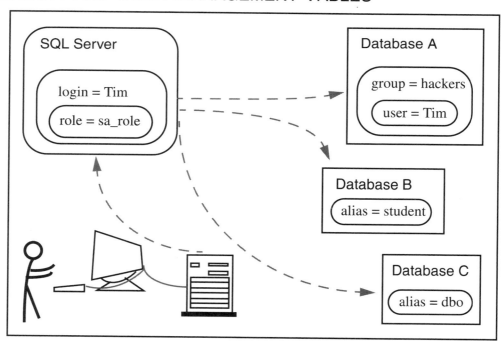

Figure 5.3 One person can have several identities. Here, Tim has sa_role, belongs to a group *hackers* in one database, is aliased to *student* in another database, and owns a third database, therefore becoming aliased to *dbo*.

The system relationships and disk usage implications are primarily the same for all the system tables in this section. Basically, these tables maintain processes run by people who use SQL Server to perform a task. Changes to SQL Server data access can affect how your organization runs, and changes in the organization may necessitate changes to object permissions.

The system issues for all of these tables center around how people behave and the business tasks that they are empowered to carry out. Several different security methods are provided by SQL Server, especially in System 10 and later. The choice of methods will depend strongly on the security needs and organizational structure of your company or institution.

The 4.9.x and earlier Servers provided security by methods such as object ownership and access by logins, users, and groups. The concept of roles was added in System 10 to support ANSI compliance and to enhance security. Like groups, roles allow a class of users to be granted or denied access to database objects and commands.

The tables related to security represent organizational decisions. Can a person have both `sa_role` and `sso_role`? The `sso_role` is the System Security Officer role, which is invested with the power to add logins to the Server. It is possible to create a system with checks and balances using roles such that, if the person with `sa_role` leaves, the system security officer can log in and prevent the former `sa` from logging in again. Beware, however, of creating a maze of roles and permissions that you can never get out of. It is possible to make your SQL Server try to represent more organization than your business actually has. In that case, you will probably be creating inconvenience and only an illusion of security. For example, if several people have *root*, *SYSTEM*, or *System Administrator* privileges on the machine, they can change the permission or even remove the disk device on which an otherwise secured database resides.

Except where noted otherwise in each description, these tables tend to grow quickly at the end of development and beginning of deployment. After that, they grow as the number of system users grows. The disk space usage tends not to be as much of a critical issue as other user-related resources, such as the memory and network bandwidth required to support additional user connections.

syslogins (master database)

Each user who is allowed to log into SQL Server does so using a login name and password. Logins, which are SQL Server-wide access mechanisms, are often confused with users, which are database-wide access mechanisms. A login name and password do not have to be the same as the operating system login and password, although administration of the system is simplified if they are.

To see the logins defined for the Server and the default database for each, issue this query:

```
> select name, dbname from master..syslogins

> go
```

Since the password is encrypted, you will not be able to select the password column from `syslogins`. The `syslogins` table in System 10 has several more columns than the one for earlier Servers. The System 10 `syslogins` includes information used to maintain and show system usage statistics.

By selecting from the System 10 `syslogins` table, you can determine relative levels of activity by different logins:

```
> select name, totcpu, accdate from master..syslogins

> having totcpu = max(totcpu)

> select name, totio, accdate from syslogins

> go
```

These numbers are reset at an interval that is set using `sp_configure`. The *accdate* column stores the date the login was added or the last date the statistics were cleared. Use the `sp_clearstats` command to zero the statistics.

sysusers (all databases)

The `sysusers` table contains one row for each user and one row for each group that can access the database. Each row contains an *suid* (Server login ID), a *uid* (user ID), and a *gid* (group ID). When the *gid* and the *uid* are the same in one row, that row is for the group. When they are different, it means that the user is a member of the group identified by `gid`. A special group, called *public*, encompasses all valid logins to the SQL Server and has an *suid* of -2. Other groups have a Server user ID that is the same as the group ID, but negative.

To see the names of every user and group for the `master` database,

```
> select su.suid, user_name = su.name, su.gid,
> login_name = sl.name
> from master..sysusers su, master..syslogins sl
> where su.suid = sl.suid
> go
```

Use this query to see what groups are defined in the `master` database:

```
> select suid, uid, gid, name from master..sysusers
> where uid = gid
> go
```

sysalternates (all databases)

The `sysalternates` table allows you to create aliases for users. For example, you might decide to use project names when identifying database owners instead of people. In that case, you could have a database called *payrolldb* owned by *payroll*. However, you would still want to keep track of people who log into SQL Server by login ID. To do this, you would create an alias with the `sp_addalias` stored procedure. Two people, such as Olivia and Vladimir, would both take on the identity of the user *payroll* when in the *payrolldb* database. With System 10, the concept of roles was added to provide another method of managing this type of scenario. The role's implementation also supports security.

To see how `sysalternates` works, try this query:

```
> select sa.suid, altsuid, sl.name
> from sysalternates sa, master..syslogins sl
> where sa.altsuid = sl.suid
> go
```

The relationship between `sysalternates` and the rest of the system is organizational. If your business shares a SQL Server for several independent projects or departments, it may make sense to use the aliasing feature provided via the `sysalternates` table.

sysloginroles (master database)

To be compliant with the ANSI SQL Standard and to provide more robust security, the concept of roles was added to System 10 SQL Server. Several new tables, such as `sysloginroles`, were added to support this functionality. `sysloginroles` maintains roles that each login can play.

On development Servers, several users often log in under the same login and share the same password. By default, a user name that is the same as the login is associated with the login, and everyone has all the permissions to access objects owned by that user. While this is convenient for the programmers, it makes it difficult for a system administrator to find out exactly who is logged into a SQL Server at a given time or who might be blocking whom when excessive locking occurs.

Using roles, all developers could have different logins but the same role. Anyone with that role would be allowed to access the objects, as defined by the permissions granted to that role. This concept is analogous to the concept of groups at the operating system level. A great deal of control can be exercised via roles. Role management can also get complicated quickly.

To see who has which roles in your SQL Server,

```
> select slr.suid, sl.name, slr.srid, ssr.name
> from master..sysloginroles slr,
> master..syslogins sl,
> master..syssrvroles ssr
> where slr.suid = sl.suid
> and slr.srid = ssr.srid
> go
```

syssrvroles (master database)

syssrvroles, like sysloginroles, supports the System 10 roles functionality. This table maintains a list of all the Server-wide role names and IDs. An example role is sa_role, which is allowed to perform Sybase system administration tasks, such as making a database backup.

This table is simple and usually small, so you can look at it in its entirety:

```
> select * from master..syssrvroles
> go
```

sysroles (all databases)

The sysroles table is like syssrvroles, but it is used to track roles for individual databases.

To see the roles in the *pubs2* sample database, issue this query:

```
> select id, lrid from pubs2..sysroles
> go
```

Like syssrvroles, sysroles was added in System 10.

sysprotects (all databases)

sysprotects keeps track of who can use which object by having a row for each GRANT and REVOKE statement that has been issued in the database.

For example, to allow a user to update the *titles* table in *pubs2*, you can give these commands:

```
> use pubs2
> go
> sp_adduser tim
> go
> sp_addgroup hackers
> go
> grant update, insert on titles to tim
> revoke update on titles to hackers
> revoke delete on titles from public
> go
> sp_helprotect titles
> go
```

The first grant allows Tim to modify or add rows to titles. The first revoke prevents a group called *hackers* from modifying the titles table. The last revoke prevents anyone from deleting rows from titles. See the Sybase System Administration guide for more information about the grant and revoke commands.

For a look at how the sysprotects table works, issue this query:

```
> select object = object_name(sp.id),
> grantor = user_name(grantor),
> receiver = user_name(sp.uid)
> from master..sysprotects sp
> where sp.uid != user_id("dbo")
> go
```

This shows you the permissions granted to and denied from all the users who are not dbo in the master database.

For more complete information about protections on objects, use the sp_helprotect procedure.

The growth of sysprotects depends on how access to objects by people is managed in your SQL Server. How you populate it depends a lot on your site and mode of operation. If there are a lot of objects with restricted or specially granted permissions, there will be many rows in sysprotects. Except for highly sensitive systems, the `sysprotects` table is usually pretty small while development is in progress. When a system is ready to be put into production, it is likely to become heavily populated toward the end of the project. Plan on leaving enough room on disk for last-minute surges of space usage in tables like this one.

syslabels (all databases, Secure SQL Server only)

The `syslabels` table exists to enforce Mandatory Access Control (MAC) in Secure SQL Server. Labels are used to code levels of access for objects and users.

sysremotelogins (master database)

The `sysremotelogins` table is how SQL Server knows which users on the local Server are associated with other user names on remote Servers. Servers that can generate RPCs include other SQL Servers, Open Servers, or gateway Servers.

To see the first five rows of this table, issue this query:

```
> set rowcount 5
> select * from master..sysremotelogins
> set rowcount 0
> go
```

The growth of the `sysremotelogins` table depends highly on the number of remote Servers that you have and their degree of interconnection. One row is added to `sysremotelogins` every time you issue `sp_addremotelogin` to add a user, and one row is deleted every time you run `sp_dropremotelogin`.

The effect of changes to remote logins on your system will be related to network bandwidth and to organizational style. If you have 10 Servers on 10 different machines and you have 100 users, adding a remote login to every Server for every user results in the most open system. It also means that you are not attempting to restrict network usage in any way as it relates to the Servers.

In contrast, if you store a lot of sensitive data in a Server, such as payroll information, you can keep the number of users who have access down by only giving a few people remote log-ins on the payroll Server. On a development Server, you may want to keep network usage down until you are ready to completely deploy the system or until you get higher-capacity network connections in place. You can also change the sp_configure value of remote connections, which restricts the number of remote processes that are allowed to and from the Server at any given time.

sysprocesses (master database)

sysprocesses is a memory-only table that SQL Server uses to tell who is doing what, when, and how. For an example of what sysprocesses can tell you about your system, try this query:

```
> select sp.suid, sl.name, sp.status, hostname,
> program_name, cmd, cpu, physical_io,
> memusage, dbid
> from master..sysprocesses sp, master..syslogins sl
> where sp.suid = sl.suid order by cpu
> go
```

This query tells you who has used the most CPU time since the statistics were last cleared.

The *cpu* column shows the number of SQL Server ticks. The physical I/O is measured in the number of data pages that have been read from or written to disk. The *memusage* column reports memory usage in bytes.

Since this is a memory-only table, it uses space in memory, but not on disk. The amount of memory it requires is directly related to the number of active processes.

The sysprocesses table is key to managing the relationship of your SQL Server to the rest of your computer system and user community. Along with seeing who is blocking whom, you can see who is using the most and the least CPU, physical I/O, and memory. If you monitor usage on a regular basis, you will be able to tell how the system is being used. For those using the most of the system resources, find out what they are doing. Perhaps the application they are using could be rewritten to use fewer processes, less memory, less CPU time, or fewer disk accesses. They may be pleased that you are asking, because processes that use these resources are sometimes are slow due to suboptimal design. For those that use the system least, find out why they are not using it. Are they relying too heavily on an old system or a manual process?

sysaudits (sybsecurity database only)

The `sybsecurity` database was added with System 10. It is used to store auditing information.

Auditing is typically used as a security measure. Events designated by the person responsible for system security are recorded for databases where security needs to be tracked. The `sysaudits` table contains a row for each event logged. The columns store the time, user login, `dbid`, and `objectid` affected.

Another use for auditing is as a troubleshooting or systems analysis tool. For example, you could write two versions of a particular stored procedure that runs a report and use `sysaudits` to see which the users prefer.

If you have permission to select from `sysaudits`, try this query:

```
> select event, eventtime, dbname, loginname,
> objname, objowner
> from sybsecurity..sysaudits
> go
```

The values corresponding to event numbers are given in the Sybase SQL Server Reference manuals.

Depending on which objects, users, or databases are chosen for auditing, the growth of this table can be quite high. Its nature is also to be constantly increasing. If a frequent event is chosen for logging, plan for storage management and system performance impact carefully. Placing the database on a fast disk on a separate controller from other database devices will keep audit logging from getting backed up and affecting performance in user databases. Since auditing is usually undertaken for security purposes, make sure you have a complete security plan that restricts users from accessing the `sysaudits` table. Finally, don't enable auditing before you figure out an archive plan. Depending on the events you audit, you may run out of space frequently.

sysauditoptions

The `sysauditoptions` table defines all system-wide audit options that can be used.

For an overview of audit options, issue this query, if you have permissions to do so:

```
> select num, sval, comment
> from sybsecurity..sysauditoptions
> go
```

■ DIRECT UPDATES OF SYSTEM TABLES

Sometimes, if you call Sybase Technical Support, they can help you fix a problem by walking you through a direct update of a system table. The easiest way to break a SQL Server is also by directly updating a system table. Therefore, it's important to be careful.

If you want to experiment and have a good environment for it, a good way to learn how all this works is to set up a test SQL Server and play with it after reading this chapter. Make sure that the devices on your test SQL Server are not the same as those on any production Server. Also, set your SQL Server up on a different CPU than any production Server, or, if you must share a CPU, do your experiments during a time when your production Server is not in use. I strongly request that you do not call technical support with questions or problems about your experimentation Server. The experts that know how to get you out of trouble are in high demand, and your call would take them away from helping someone with a production Server problem.

If you cause SQL Server to "spin out," use up all the CPU, or hang, you will need to issue a command to kill the process at the operating system level from the machine running the SQL Server process.

For UNIX and VMS, first get the process ID using the `showserver` command. Then unconditionally kill the process.

For UNIX, use the `kill` command:

```
% kill -9 <process_id>
```

For VMS, use the `stop` command:

```
$ STOP PROCESS/ID = <process_id>
```

For the PC operating systems, if you cannot stop the process with the usual shutdown methods, you usually need to reboot the machine on which the SQL Server is running.

Since direct updates to system tables can be destructive, Sybase officially recommends that you do not update system tables directly. Instead, stored procedures, such as `sp_dropuser`, are provided that allow you to make system changes safely. There are two ways to see what system tables are changed with which system procedures and how.

If you want to see what a particular stored procedure updates or queries, you can give the `sp_helptext` command followed by the name of the stored procedure. For versions earlier than 10.0, execute this query in the `master` database. Otherwise, run it in `sybsystemprocs` for most procedures. For example,

```
> sp_helptext sp_dropuser

> go
```

From the query results, you can see that, if you were to try to drop a user manually and missed one of the steps in the above procedure, your system would be off balance and errors would result. On the other hand, if `sp_dropuser` fails to drop a user because of some problem, you can follow the script and carefully do everything manually.

If you want to see how stored procedures access a particular table, such as `sysindexes`, you can look at the `installmaster` file, which is a simple ASCII script for loading system stored procedures into the `master` or `sybsystemprocs` database. When you install a new Server, `sybconfig` (4.9.x) or `sybinit` (System 10) runs this script. If you ever have to recover from a disaster, the Sybase Troubleshooting Guide or Technical Support will often direct you to run `installmaster` directly. The script is located in the `scripts` subdirectory.

■ BITMAPPED STATUS VALUES

Many of the system tables have bitmapped status values. What follows is an explanation of bit mapping that will help you understand these values. Computer science texts discuss representation of numbers in computers with much greater detail, if you are interested in finding out more.

Bitmapping is a nonintuitive but compact way of indicating a status. One byte of computer storage consists of a string of 8 bits. A bit is simply a spot that can store two values. Electronically, the two values are usually *on* and *off* or *high* and *low*. The abstraction used by computer languages is 1 and 0, with 1 usually meaning *on* or *true* and 0 meaning *off* or *false*. So a string of 8 bits to represent *on again, off again* repeatedly is

```
1010 1010
```

In print, bit strings are usually grouped in fours for readability. Any integer between 0 and 255, that is, 256 unsigned integers, can be represented in an 8-bit-long byte. Each position in the byte represents 2 to the *nth* power, where n is the bit string position starting with zero and counting from right to left. (Computers don't necessarily store numbers from right to left, but this abstraction for explaining this concept is the most common.) The integer value of the byte is the sum of the powers of 2 represented by the bits holding a 1.

For example, in the string given above, we can calculate the following, with the rightmost bit shown at the top and the left at the bottom:

$$0 \times 2^0 = 0 \times 1 = 0$$
$$1 \times 2^1 = 1 \times 2 = 2$$
$$0 \times 2^2 = 0 \times 4 = 0$$
$$1 \times 2^3 = 1 \times 8 = 8$$

$$0 \times 2^4 = 0 \times 16 = 0$$
$$1 \times 2^5 = 1 \times 32 = 32$$
$$0 \times 2^6 = 0 \times 64 = 0$$
$$1 \times 2^7 = 1 \times 128 = 128$$

To get a numeric value for the byte, we add up the power of 2 value for each bit position with a 1 in it:

$$2 + 8 + 32 + 128 = 170$$

To make things slightly more complicated, sometimes negative integers need to be stored in a byte. In this case, what is commonly called the high-order bit, the left most in our example, is used to indicate the sign of a number. If it's a 1, the number is negative. The two's complement is used to represent the value, a concept that we won't discuss here. After 1 bit is reserved for the sign, 7 bits remain for storing an integer in a byte.

Thus, in signed, 1-byte integers, you can store numbers between −128 and +127, which is still a total of 256 values.

In SQL Server, when you see a value like 170 in the status value of a system table, what it means is bit 0 off, bit 1 on, bit 2 off, and so on. Each bit represents a different state independent of the other bits. For example, in sysusages, the *segmap* value is a bitmap. Bit 0 *on* means "this part of the database is used for system tables." Bit 1 *on* means "this part of the database is the default place to store user data." Bit 2 on means "this part of the database is for syslogs." If the *segmap* value is 7 (1 + 2 + 4), this means that portion of the database can be used for system tables ($2^0 = 1$), user data ($2^1 = 2$), or the transaction log ($2^2 = 4$). A *segmap* of 4 means that it can only be used for the transaction log. A *segmap* value higher than 7 indicates that a user-defined segment is in use.

Procedure Manual Suggestions

○ Managing User-defined Messages

⇒ Document whether your system uses the user message feature. If it does, maintain a list of the messages associated with each application.

⇒ Establish and publish a list of who is responsible for handling a particular group of messages when questions or problems are encountered

⇒ Update your lists when the `sysusermessages` table changes.

CHAPTER

SQL Server System-wide Configuration

When you install SQL Server, a default configuration determines the software's initial behavior and performance. Most customers reconfigure SQL Server thereafter to suit their resources, data, and applications. You can configure almost all areas of system resource usage and many facets of data organization within SQL Server. Typically, administrators reconfigure SQL Server with the goal of increasing performance. A need for increased user or data capacity also tends to motivate reconfiguration.

Configuration of SQL Server falls into the three main categories shown in Table 6-1.

TABLE 6-1 *Configuration Categories*

Category	Primary Commands	Who Issues Commands
Configuring behavior for the entire server	Configuration file or `sp_configure` and `buildmaster`	sa
Configuring database behavior	`sp_dboption`	sa or dbo
Configuring user environment	`Set` options	User or application developer

This chapter takes up the Server-wide configuration category, describing the general process of Server configuration and then exploring how each configuration option affects SQL Server processing. Chapter 7 describes database and session-level configuration.

In many cases, such as with the memory and networking parameters, the purposes and effects of changing many different variables are intertwined. In this chapter, you will find the variables grouped broadly by function. Many variables belong in more than one group no matter how we organize them. As with many elements of complex systems, you can't change one element without changing a set of elements, and you can't understand one without understanding the set. In System 11, the new configuration interface reports these parameters in several smaller groups and shows some parameters more than one group.

In releases prior to System 11, administrators primarily configure SQL Server by using the `sp_configure` system stored procedure. However, in a few instances you might need to perform additional tuning with `buildmaster` or DBCC commands. With the System 11 release, configuration commands are now stored in a configuration file, which is a human-readable file formatted so that the Server can also understand it. With System 11, you can configure SQL Server by modifying the file and reloading it or rebooting, or by issuing a `sp_configure` command for a particular configuration variable.

■ CONFIGURATION BLOCK

SQL Server's default configuration values are stored on disk in a special area called the configuration block. This block occupies the first four pages on the `master` device. It is normally invisible to the administrator and the user.

Sometimes, in SQL Server releases earlier than 11.0, you may need to view or modify the configuration variables using the `buildmaster` command to recover from a problem or to accommodate last-minute changes in new operating system versions. Since this configuration area uses the first blocks of a partition, a mistaken attempt by a root user to mount a file system on top of the partition can destroy the configuration area, resulting in an unbootable SQL Server. This happens under operating systems that write the disk label in the first block of a partition. Sometimes, you can use the `buildmaster` command to fix this problem, depending on how soon you discover the error.

The `buildmaster` command is a low-level access utility for the configuration block. You can write values directly to the configuration block using `buildmaster,` although this is usually not advised. Most `buildmaster` values have corresponding `sp_configure` parameters. In fact, `sp_configure` does more than just change the given variable. It also recalculates other internal values in some cases. The `buildmaster` options that have no corresponding `sp_configure` options in releases before 11.0 were used for internal structures that customers were not expected to need to change. For these reasons, only a few of the `buildmaster` options were documented and supported. While it doesn't take much imagination to figure out the undocumented variables and methods for changing them, it takes expertise to fix the consequences. You should only use `buildmaster` in documented ways or at the direction of a technical support engineer. You can cause SQL Server to crash at unexpected times if you change undocumented values with `buildmaster`. In version 11, SQL Server makes the buildmaster values viewable and settable by using `sp_configure`.

In releases before 11.0, the `buildmaster` -d *master_device* -y (UNIX and DOS) or `buildmaster /disk="master_device" /alter="all"`

(VMS) command lists out all the configuration block names and values.

■ SP_CONFIGURE COMMAND

For most server-wide configuration, you use the `sp_configure` command. The general form for the `sp_configure` command is

```
> sp_configure configuration_name, value
```

You only need to specify enough of the name to make it unique. For example, you could issue either of the following two commands to achieve the same results:

```
> sp_configure audit, 100
> go
> sp_configure "audit queue size", 100
> go
```

If a parameter includes blanks (as in the second example) or reserved words, you must enclose it in quotation marks.

The general process for determining and setting configuration values follows:

1. Execute `sp_configure` with no parameters to review the current configuration values.

2. Save the current settings in an operating system file or in hard-copy form.

3. Determine the new values for the configuration variables that you want to change.

4. Make the changes using `sp_configure` (or by editing and loading the configuration data file for System 11).

5. Execute `sp_configure` with no parameters to verify that you made the changes you intended to make.

6. If the changes are to dynamic variables that can be reset without rebooting SQL Server, test the new functionality.

7. If using a version before 11.0, issue the `reconfigure` command, which writes the new values to disk in the configuration area and updates the `sysconfigures` and `syscurconfigs` tables. If using 11.0 or later, use the `write`

option of `sp_configure` to save a copy of the current configuration to a configuration file.

8. If the changes are static variables, reboot SQL Server and test the new functionality.

9. Issue `sp_configure` with no parameters and save the output in an archive area, preferably in hard-copy form, for future reference.

Systems Managers can make things worse when they reconfigure SQL Server, especially in the areas that affect memory usage. Save hard copies of output from `sp_configure` before and after making changes. Normally, avoiding hard copy simplifies desk management, but for this purpose, hard copy will save you time in case of an unanticipated error. It is much harder to accidentally overwrite a piece of paper that you carefully file away than it is to overwrite a file that you save to disk when caught up in the enthusiasm of reconfiguration.

11.0 ▷ SYSTEM 11 CONFIGURATION CHANGES

    Before System 11, some variables stored in the configuration block, such as `ctimemax`, were neither visible nor modifiable unless you used semi-documented, semi-supported commands. Now, most of the configuration block variables are fully supported, and you can access them using `sp_configure`. Also, the modifiable variables now appear in a configuration file, which is a regular ASCII file. Administrators may reconfigure the Server by editing the configuration file or by continuing to use the `sp_configure` stored procedure. In the configuration file, variables are configured using the following syntax:

```
variable_name={value | default}
```

    If you use the keyword `default`, the internal, hard-coded value for the variable is used.

    The configuration block variables now accessible through the new configuration interface appear in Table 6-2.

TABLE 6-2 *Renamed Configuration Block Variables*

Configuration Block Variable Name in Versions Prior to 11.0	Configuration Variable Name in SQL Server 11.0
calignment	memory alignment boundary
cbufwashsize	None—modified for each I/O size pool in a buffer cache using sp_poolconfig
cclkrate	sql server clock tick length
cfgcprot	permission cache entries
cguardsz	stack guard size
cindextrips	number of index trips
cmaxnetworks	max number network listeners
cmaxscheds	i/o polling process count
cnalarm	number of alarms
cnblkio	disk i/o structures
cnlanginfo	number of languages in cache
cnmaxaio_engine	max async i/os per engine
cnmaxaio_server	max async i/os per server
cnmbox	number of mailboxes
cnmsg	number of messages
coamtrips	number of oam trips
cpreallocext	number of pre-allocated extents
cschedspins	runnable process search count
csortbufsize	number of sort buffers
csortpgcount	sort page count
ctimemax	cpu grace time
cmrstart	shared memory starting address

Some of the configuration variables available through sp_configure also have new names. These are listed in Table 6-3.

TABLE 6-3 *Configuration Variable Name Changes*

Pre-System 11 Configuration Variable Name	System 11 Configuration Variable Name
cpu flush	cpu accounting flush interval
database size	default database size
default language	default language id
devices	number of devices
extent i/o buffers	number of extent i/o buffers
fillfactor	default fill factor percent
i/o flush	i/o accounting flush interval
locks	number of locks
maximum network packet size	max network packet size
memory	total memory
open databases	number of open databases
open objects	number of open objects
password expiration interval	systemwide password expiration
pre-read packets	remote server pre-read packets
procedure cache	procedure cache size
recovery flags	print recovery information
recovery interval	recovery interval in minutes
remote access	allow remote access
remote connections	number of remote connections
remote logins	number of remote logins
remote sites	number of remote sites
tape retention	tape retention in days
user connections	number of user connections

Finally, certain common trace flags have transcended their initial purpose as diagnostic aids and have become full-fledged configuration variables, as shown in Table 6-4.

213

TABLE 6-4 *Traceflags Replaced by Configuration Variables*

Trace Flag before Version 11.0	SQL Server 11.0 Configuration Variable
1204	print deadlock information
1603	allow sql server async i/o
1610	tcp no delay
1611	lock shared memory

When SQL Server 11.0 or a later release is booted, the system table, `syscurconfigs`, is built from the configuration file or from hard-coded defaults if the Server can't find a valid configuration file. A command line flag (-c on most systems) now indicates the location of the desired configuration file. If the configuration flag is not supplied at start-up, the Server looks for the configuration file in the `SYBASE` directory tree. It looks for a file named *SERVER-NAME*.cfg, where *SERVERNAME* is the name of the Server as specified in the RUNSERVER file. If you specify a file name on the `dataserver` command line for a configuration file that does not exist, the Server will not boot. If a configuration file is missing an option, SQL Server will use the default value for that option. When the Server finds a statement in a configuration file that it doesn't recognize, it will continue to boot and report an error to the errorlog. If it finds an illegal value for a configuration variable, the Server will report the error and will continue to boot using the default value.

Because the `sp_configure` procedure makes the output fit the screen, you may not be able to see the full path of the configuration file used in its output. Use a query like this to find the exact configuration file the Server is using:

```
> select cc.value2
> from master..syscurconfigs cc, master..sysconfig-
  ures cf
> where cc.config = cf.config
> and cf.name = "configuration file"
> go
```

Use caution when editing the configuration file to avoid introducing invalid values. Also, use the operating system file protection mechanisms to keep unauthorized users from changing or moving the file. Note that when you create a configuration file at the operating system level you own the file with the default permissions for your account. Be sure to change the permissions so that the sybase account can subsequently access the file if necessary. If SQL Server writes the file, the ownership and permissions default to those for the sybase account.

While booting, the Server writes a copy of the configuration values from the sysconfigures table to a file named *SERVER-NAME*.bak in the SYBASE directory tree. When you use sp_configure to update a variable, the Server updates the configuration file, renames the old version, and reports a message about the change to the error log.

Configuration variables now have expertise levels associated with them. Only users with a particular display level can see all of the settings. Other users see more limited views. This mechanism essentially hides variables that don't require changes often and that require significant expertise to set correctly. The sp_displaylevel procedure allows you to view or set the display level for sp_configure output:

```
sp_displaylevel user_name
      [, basic | intermediate | comprehensive ]
```

If you execute this procedure with only *user_name* as a parameter, you will see the display level defined for that user. The basic, intermediate, and comprehensive keywords determine how much information the user sees. All users may see basic options. Users who set their display level to intermediate will see basic and intermediate options. Expert users who want to fine tune the Server can see all variables if they set the display level to comprehensive.

The Server now groups configuration variables into families. For example, if you only want to see the network-related variables, you can issue sp_configure with the parameter *Network*. All family names begin with the initial letter capitalized, so you can distinguish them from other contents of the sysconfigures table. The family names are

- Backup/Recovery
- Cache Manager
- Configuration Options
- Disk I/O
- General Information
- Languages
- Lock Manager
- Memory Use
- Network Communication
- O/S Resources
- Physical Memory
- Physical Resources
- Processors
- SQL Server Administration
- User Environment

To make it easier for system administrators to tell when they are reaching the limits of their physical memory, the `sp_configure` output now shows the memory usage associated with various configuration variables.

Associated with all these changes, the `sp_configure` procedure has new syntax. To set a configuration value online, use this form of the procedure:

```
sp_configure
    [ unique_config_name_string, value |
    group_name |
    config_name_string ]
```

Executing `sp_configure` without any arguments tells SQL Server to display all configuration values at the display level set for the current user. If you specify a configuration name for *config_name_string*, but no value, the values for all configuration variables matching the string that you give are displayed. If you specify a name string for *unique_config_name_string* that uniquely identifies a variable along with a *value*, the specified value is set for the variable. If you give the name of a variable group *group_name* as the only parameter to sp_configure, the Server displays all configuration variables and values in the group.

A new, second form of sp_configure gives you a way to read and write configuration files online. The syntax for this form is

```
sp_configure configuration_file, 0,
    { "write" | "read" | "verify" | "restore" },
    "filename"
```

If only the keyword configuration_file is given, sp_configure displays the contents of the currently loaded configuration file. If you use the read option, the Server reads the configuration file specified by the *filename* parameter that you supplied. The verify option checks to make sure that the values in the specified *filename* are valid. Use write to save the current configuration settings to *filename*.

To set a configuration variable to its default, use this form of sp_configure:

```
sp_configure unique_config_name_string, 0, "default"
```

The keyword default tells the procedure to use the internal, hard-coded value for the variable.

As with earlier versions, some configuration values are static, meaning that you must reboot SQL Server for the changes to take effect. If you attempt to read a configuration file that contains changes to static variables, SQL Server will report an error and the read will fail. To enable such changes, you will need to boot with the new configuration file instead.

If you write to a *filename* matching a file that already exists, the existing file will be renamed. The new name will follow the convention *filename.nnn,* where *nnn* is a sequential number between 001 and 999 greater than the last value used for the file.

The reconfigure command is obsolete, but has been retained temporarily to give administrators time to change their scripts. Since all settable configuration variables have been made visible and modifiable with the new configuration routines, buildmaster -y is obsolete as well.

■ SERVER MANAGEMENT CONFIGURATION VALUES

total memory

The value you set for `total memory` determines the total amount of physical memory that SQL Server requests from the operating system. Specify the `total memory` setting in 2-KB units. SQL Server allocates a portion of this memory for internal data structures and for the executable code for it to run. Some of the values set with `sp_configure` also allocate space from the memory pool. These include `number of user connections`, `stack size`, `number of remote connections`, `number of devices`, `number of open databases`, `number of open objects`, `number of locks`, `language in cache`, `number of extent I/O buffers`, and `default network packet size`. After satisfying these needs, SQL Server dedicates the remaining memory to data and procedure cache. You specify the split between these two cache types by using `sp_configure` to set the `procedure cache` percentage. System 11 introduces additional user control by allowing you to divide the buffer caches into several different named caches to which you can bind specific entities.

While you may configure SQL Server to use the maximum physical memory available on the host computer, this may affect the ability of the operating system or any other applications to run on the machine.

Systems Managers typically change the value of the `memory` configuration variable when

■ Adding or removing physical memory on the computer system

■ Adapting the Server to match changes in the computer system

■ Allocating memory for extent I/O buffers or additional network memory

■ Tuning overall SQL Server performance

executable code size

The value for this variable is fixed and is meant for informative purposes only. By looking at this value, you can tell how much memory you need to reserve for use by the SQL Server binary.

shared memory starting address

The value of this variable determines the virtual starting address of SQL Server's shared memory region. Normally, you should not need to reset this unless instructed to do so by the Sybase documentation or Sybase Technical Support.

procedure cache percent (and data cache)

SQL Server uses the memory pool allocated with the `memory` option for four general purposes:

■ Maintaining SQL Server executable in memory

■ Storing process data in structures allocated by various configuration options (such as open databases and open objects)

■ Compiling and executing queries

■ Caching database objects

The cache for the last of these purposes is divided into procedure cache and data cache. The `procedure cache size` option sets the percentage of the cache to devote to retaining copies of procedure objects in memory. The remainder of the cache is dedicated to maintaining copies of table and index pages in memory.

When you create a stored procedure, you define it as a series of SQL statements. SQL Server then parses these statements into an intermediate binary form and stores them in the `sysprocedures` system table. When you run a stored procedure for the first time, SQL Server compiles the procedure in memory and executes it. The compiled image stays in the procedure cache until more commonly used procedures take its place.

The data cache is used to store data pages in memory. By default, it holds most recently used data and index pages. Older pages are copied to disk (flushed) as space is needed for new pages. By default, SQL Server uses the LRU/MRU strategy to manage both caches.

max online engines

The `maximum online engines` parameter sets the number of processors to use for a multiprocessor system. For example, if you have a six-CPU machine and want SQL Server to use three, set `maximum online engines` to 3. In some cases, you would not want to set this to the maximum number of processors available, since SQL Server then ends up competing with the operating system. Since SQL Server relies on the operating system for some functions, such as I/O, it is important to leave enough processing power for base-level functions. Also plan on reserving more than one CPU for non-SQL Server use if you rely on the machine for other tasks, such as ftp, NFS, WWW, or a heavily updated file system. If a CPU devoted to SQL Server fails for some reason, SQL Server runs with one less CPU; it does not attempt to gain use of another that may exist on the system.

min online engines

SQL Server does not currently use the setting of this parameter. Leave it set to the default of 1.

cpu accounting flush interval

The *totcpu* column of the `syslogins` table stores the amount of CPU time used by each SQL Server login account. The `cpu flush interval` setting determines how often `cpu` usage data are added to the `syslogins` table. Specify the interval in terms of the number of machine clock ticks. The time value of a machine tick varies depending on the hardware.

i/o accounting flush interval

Like `cpu flush interval`, `i/o flush interval` is used to determine how often the accounting variables are updated in `syslogins`. For I/O flush interval, set the number of I/Os that a user process should initiate before the *totio* column of `syslogins` is updated. A larger interval means that SQL Server doesn't have to stop and update statistics as often.

default database size

When someone issues a CREATE DATABASE command without specifying a size, SQL Server uses the default size specified by this setting. By default, this is set to 2 MB. Rather than rely on this setting, people should always think through the anticipated storage capacity of a database before creating it. Constantly using ALTER DATABASE to accommodate growth leads to a highly complicated mapping of database space to physical disk and becomes unmanageable as soon as you have a few large databases. (Without archive discipline on the part of the administrators, databases grow without bound.) Also, if you store scripts of the CREATE DATABASE session, reusing these scripts could have unexpected results if they rely on a default that has since been reset.

number of devices

This devices parameter controls the maximum database device number that SQL Server may address. The value you use for devices does not affect the number of predefined dump devices. The design of this parameter assumes that you will number your devices sequentially, beginning with 0, the master device. If the number for devices is N, then you cannot have a device numbered higher than N – 1. If you number your devices as expected, N is the total number of devices you may have. On the other hand, if you set devices to 10, but you have only even-numbered devices, you will only be able to use devices 0, 2, 4, 6 and 8, or half the number of devices you might expect.

Since the default is 10, you must increase this number if you intend to use a lot of devices. Each device uses approximately 1/2 KB of memory. If you happen to reset your configuration values to the defaults using buildmaster when you have more than 10 devices, those devices will remain inactive next time you boot SQL Server. This means the databases on them will be marked *suspect*. See the Sybase SQL Server Troubleshooting Guide for information about getting around this problem.

Be very careful when reconfiguring this value downward. If you have more than 10 devices in a pre-System 11 SQL Server and you use `buildmaster` -r (UNIX) or `buildmaster /reconfigure` (Open-VMS) to reset the defaults, be sure to set the number of devices back up to the number you need before rebooting SQL Server. You can set the number of devices with `buildmaster -d device_name -y devices=N` (UNIX) or `buildmaster /disk=device_name /alter="devices=N` (OpenVMS) where *N* is at least one more than the highest device number you have before rebooting SQL Server.

The `sp_helpdevice` command reports the device numbers for each database device in use by SQL Server. You can also see just device numbers and names using this SQL query:

```
> select name, low/power(2,24)
> from master..sysdevices
> where cntrltype = 0
> go
```

recovery interval in minutes

Some aspects of SQL Server's memory manager were changed in System 11, which changes the meaning of this parameter. First, we will look at how the previous versions of SQL Server operated so that we can understand the subsequent design choices.

The `recovery interval` parameter roughly controls how often the `checkpoint` process runs. A small number, such as *1*, means that it runs more often, while a larger number, such as *10*, means it runs less frequently. The `checkpoint` process goes through the data cache and flushes any data pages that have been modified to disk. (Data pages in memory that have been modified are also called dirty pages or dirty buffers.) The net effect of running `checkpoint` frequently is that when the database next goes through recovery (either during a database load or a SQL Server reboot), less of the transaction log needs to be reapplied, thus speeding up the recovery process.

The number you specify was originally intended to correspond to minutes of recovery work. A very rough estimate of the time required to apply a log record is used to calculate how often `checkpoint` needs to run to keep the recovery time within the specified interval. In practice, the amount of work a log record represents varies, so the time to recover varies also.

When `checkpoint` runs, it puts a certain load on the SQL Server to read through all the memory and write it all to disk. Sometimes `checkpoint` degrades performance noticeably while it is running. The effect of a higher number means that more and more I/Os are saved up, which means that `checkpoint` has more work to do when it eventually does run. If SQL Server must be rebooted for some reason, it will take longer to recover. To minimize recovery time then, keep the `recovery interval` at the minimum.

System 11 alleviates the performance effect of the `checkpoint` process in SQL Servers where the workload varies frequently between high and low extremes. In System 11, a new process called the HouseKeeper wakes up at regular intervals and checks the CPU utilization. Upon detecting an idle CPU, the house-keeper process moves through each buffer pool in each buffer cache, writing out dirty pages. When CPU utilization starts to rise again, the housekeeper function stops.

If the `trunc log on chkpt` option is set in a database, `checkpoint` may also cause the log to be truncated every time the `recovery interval` is reached. This may also cause a noticeable delay each time `checkpoint` runs. If `checkpoint` runs frequently, however, the amount of truncation work will remain small as well. Increasing the `recovery interval` will cause lower performance for a longer period of time while more truncation work is done, but the slow times will be spread out more.

print recovery information

If you set `print recovery information` to 1 (interpreted as *true*), SQL Server writes the status (either *rolled forward* or *rolled back*) of named transactions to the error log during recovery. The information can help you find out what went wrong if the Server encounters any problems during recovery. Turning on this feature has some impact on recovery performance, but can save you critical diagnostic time in the event of trouble. Consider leaving it turned on all the time if you can afford the extra time for recovery and if you tend to have trouble booting. Also, if recovery takes a long time, you might find that the status information serves as a good progress indicator. If you are using SQL Server 11, you can just modify this variable in the configuration file before reboot if you anticipate needing the status information.

allow updates to system tables

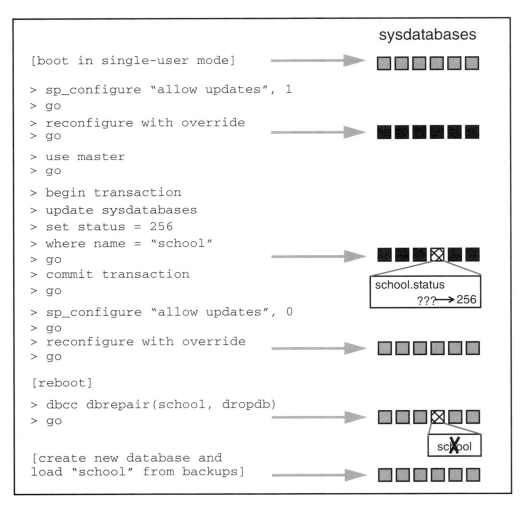

```
sysdatabases

[boot in single-user mode]      ➤  ⬜⬜⬜⬜⬜⬜

> sp_configure "allow updates", 1
> go
> reconfigure with override      ➤  ⬛⬛⬛⬛⬛⬛
> go

> use master
> go

> begin transaction
> update sysdatabases
> set status = 256
> where name = "school"
> go                             ➤  ⬛⬛⬛⊠⬛⬛
> commit transaction
> go                                 school.status
                                        ???➤256

> sp_configure "allow updates", 0
> go
> reconfigure with override      ➤  ⬜⬜⬜⬜⬜⬜
> go

[reboot]

> dbcc dbrepair(school, dropdb)
> go                             ➤  ⬜⬜⬜⊠⬜⬜
                                        school

[create new database and
load "school" from backups]      ➤  ⬜⬜⬜⬜⬜⬜
```

Figure 6.1 One of the few procedures requiring updates to system catalogs: dropping a database that can't otherwise be dropped. (From the Sybase SQL Server Troubleshooting Guide.)

Normally, you should never need to update system catalogs directly. SQL Server protects you from doing so inadvertently by rejecting any system table updates unless you have taken certain actions. Sometimes, however, the only way to recover from a problem is to update certain values in system tables, based on instructions from Technical Support. Setting `allow updates` to 1 (*true*) allows you to update system tables directly using SQL commands. You must have `sso_role` to set this option. After you set `allow updates` to 1, you must issue the command RECONFIGURE WITH OVERRIDE to signal to SQL Server that you know what you're doing (or think you do).

Remember to turn it back off when you're done. When `allow updates` is on, any person with `sa_role` permissions may update system catalogs. This access level is similar to being logged in as *root* (UNIX), *Administrator* (NT), or *SYSTEM* (VMS). An unplanned update to a system catalog can make SQL Server unbootable or databases inaccessible. If you create a stored procedure while `allow updates` is enabled, that procedure "inherits" allow update permission and may modify system tables even after you turn off `allow updates` later. This is much like the `set uid` feature in UNIX. As with that feature, it leaves a significant opening for security breaches, so you should be very careful when you set `allow updates`. If you must enable `allow updates` to repair a serious problem, you would normally boot the server in single-user mode to prevent access during this time. Making such a practice routine will keep the window of vulnerability to a minimum.

Note, there are a few hidden system tables that are not treated like all the others and are not guarded by the `allow updates` parameter. These have names that begin with "*spt_*". Do not modify these tables under any circumstances unless a technical support engineer instructs you to do so for some reason. Dropping these causes the entire Server to become unusable.

tape retention in days

Sybase provides the `tape retention period` setting as a safeguard for you to keep yourself from unintentionally overwrit-

225

ing a recent backup tape. The retention period is the number of days that you want a backup tape to remain unwriteable. If someone attempts to make another SQL Server backup on this tape before the retention period has expired, a warning message is issued. The operator may override this warning if desired. The System 10 and later versions of the DUMP DATABASE and DUMP TRANSACTION commands allow you to provide a retaindays option, which overrides the default tape retention value configured. Note that the operating system will not recognize the retention period written on tape by SQL Server, so it would still be possible for someone to overwrite the tape for another purpose. For more protection, your backup strategy should include a consistent method of using human-readable labels stuck to the tape casing.

upgrade version

The SQL Server installation program modifies the upgrade version variable when it completes an installation or upgrade. If an upgrade fails, leaving SQL Server in some intermediate but runnable state, you will be able to tell because the upgrade version variable will remain at the old setting. You should not change this setting.

event buffers per engine

This variable determines the maximum number of recorded events to store for analysis by the SQL Monitor program. As monitorable events happen, SQL Server stores them in the event queue, which is comprised of event buffers. If SQL Monitor does not read events fast enough, the oldest events are lost and replaced by new events. If you find that you are losing events, set this value higher. The SQL Monitor documentation describes how to determine the best size for this variable. If you do not monitor events using SQL Monitor, set this variable to 1. Each event buffer uses 100 bytes of memory.

number of alarms

The WAITFOR command uses an internal construct known as an alarm to alert SQL Server to the need to resume a task. SQL Server also uses alarms for other operations. You should not decrease this value below the default. Set it higher if you use WAITFOR frequently. Each `alarm` uses 20 bytes of memory.

number of mailboxes

SQL Server stores communications between internal service processes in storage structures called mail boxes. This variable determines the number of mailbox structures allocated.

number of messages

This variable sets the maximum number of message structures allocated for communication between internal service processes.

allow sql server async i/o

Asynchronous disk I/O allows SQL Server to initiate a disk operation and then to continue processing other data while the disk operation is completed. This can improve performance and recoverability when using raw disk partitions. In some cases, you will need to configure asynchronous I/O at the operating system level as well. You will find information and instructions in the SQL Server installation guide and release notes for your platform. Set this variable to 1 to enable or 0 to disable asynchronous I/O for SQL Server. Enable async I/O if you are using raw devices.

o/s async i/o enabled

This variable indicates whether async I/O has been enabled at the operating system level. This value is not meant to be modified directly, but to be used to signal whether async I/O can be set at the SQL Server level. To use asynchronous I/O, it must be enabled at both the operating system and SQL Server levels.

disk i/o structures

To initiate an I/O request, a SQL Server task uses a disk I/O structure. The number of I/O structures SQL Server allocates at start-up is controlled by this variable. Normally, the default value should be adequate. If it is less than the maximum number of asynchronous I/Os configured for your operating system, you can increase it up to that maximum. Don't set it any higher than that, or performance may suffer rather than improve.

If the setting of this or any of the asynchronous I/O values described next exceeds the operating system settings, you will see messages in the errorlog that start like *dstartio: i/o request repeatedly delayed....* If operating system performance monitors indicate high values for disk I/O wait times or queue lengths on the partitions used for SQL Server, you may need to reset the asynchronous I/O settings at the SQL Server or operating system level.

max async i/os per server

SQL Server can queue I/Os at a particular rate, and the operating system can service these I/O requests at a particular rate. If SQL Server queues them faster than the operating system can service them, a queue is used to buffer outstanding I/Os. The max async i/os per server variable sets the number of asynchronous I/O requests that may be outstanding at one time for SQL Server. The setting of this variable should match the corresponding setting for maximum asynchronous I/Os in the operating system. See the Sybase installation guide and your operating system manuals for more information about configuring your operating system. If SQL Server is configured for a higher rate of concurrent asynchronous I/O requests than the operating system is configured for, SQL Server performance will degrade while it repeatedly requeues I/Os.

11.0 max async i/os per engine

This is the number of outstanding asynchronous I/O requests per SQL Server engine. The setting of this variable should match the corresponding setting for per-process asynchronous I/Os in the operating system. If you have a single-CPU machine, make sure that `max async i/os per engine` and `max async i/os per server` (`cnmaxio_engine` and `cnmaxio_server`) are set to the same value.

11.0 o/s file descriptors

This read-only variable lets you know the number of per-process file descriptors that have been configured at the operating system level. To change this value, you will need to reconfigure the operating system as described in the vendor's documentation.

11.0 lock shared memory

The value of this variable indicates whether the operating system is allowed to swap SQL Server memory pages to disk. Generally, you want to disallow swapping by setting this variable to *true*. However, not all platforms support lockable memory. Check the Sybase installation manuals to verify. If it is supported, you will also need to set operating system permissions so that the `sybase` account can do the locking. You must also have sufficient physical memory to accommodate the amount of memory the Server needs to lock.

11.0 number of index trips

A page is removed from data cache when it reaches the wash marker at the LRU area of the buffer chain, which indicates that it is no longer a recently used page. In environments with high OLTP demands, it is often beneficial to keep index pages in cache longer. To allow for this possibility, SQL Server allows an index to take multiple passes through the wash section without being purged from memory. The number of passes is set with the `index trips` variable.

number of oam trips

Similarly to index pages, keeping OAM pages in cache, even when less recently used than some data pages, can result in performance benefits. This is especially the case with operations that do a great deal of page allocation and deallocation, such as bulk copy or large-scale deletes. The `number of oam trips` setting tells SQL Server how many passes through the wash section an OAM page may take before being flushed from memory. Do not set this variable higher than 2 or 3 or the cache will fill up with OAM pages, not leaving adequate room for regular data.

page utilization percent

A large table may use more than one OAM page. To allocate or deallocate a page, SQL Server scans the object's OAM pages, in order, to find free extents. To have the Server skip over OAM pages considered mostly full, set `page utilization percent` to a number less than 100. For example, if an OAM page for a large object is 90% full, and you have set `page utilization percent` to *85*, then the Server won't waste time searching that OAM page and will look for one with more space instead. This also reduces contention for each OAM page, improving the performance of page allocations and deallocations. Leave this value at the default unless all objects in a database are large. The lower the percent you specify, the more potential you have for wasted space in the database, but the faster large allocation operations will complete. Note that the bulk copy utilities do not check `page utilization percent`, but instead always allocate new extents in order until no more are available.

total data cache size

This value is not configurable, but is calculated from the value of total memory and procedure cache percentage. It is now included in the `sp_configure` output to make the amount of data cache space easier to see at a glance.

number of pre-allocated extents

An extent is a set of eight contiguous pages. By default, SQL Server allocates one extent one at a time when initializing new space for an object. You can set `number of pre-allocated extent` to any number up to 31 to tell the Server to allocate that many extents at a time for bulk copy operations. This can minimize the internal overhead of processing the allocations and reduce logging for large BCP batches. If the Server preallocates more extents than necessary for a BCP batch, it deallocates them upon completion. Use benchmarking and testing to determine the optimal settings for the batch sizes you use.

number of sort buffers

Sorting operations use page-sized buffers to hold intermediate results. These buffers are taken from data cache. If you are creating indexes, set the `number of sort buffers` to eight times the number of extent I/O buffers for optimal results. If you create an index with this value set above the default and then dump the transaction log, the Server attempts to re-create the index during load. This process will require the same settings for `number of sort buffers` as those set during the original index creation process. To avoid the need to make this change, always dump the database after creating an index.

sort page count

In addition to page buffers, a sort operation requires about 50 bytes of memory for processing each row. The `sort page count` setting specifies the total memory for this overhead that the sort can use from data cache. For optimal results, set this value to

```
number of sort buffers × rows per data page / 50
```

This process will require the same settings for number of sort buffers as those set during the original index creation process. To avoid the need to make this change, always dump the database after creating an index.

runnable process search count

11.0

This variable sets the number of times an engine will check for a runnable task before relinquishing the CPU. You should not need to change this value from the default. For single-processor environments, you may see a benefit to dropping this variable to 1 if there is significant load on the system. For some situations, a special value 0 is used to force the SQL Server engines to check for tasks continuously, which causes the engines to use 100% of the CPU. This is typically only used in real-time systems.

i/o polling process count

11.0

The SQL Server scheduler checks for the completion of previously queued disk and network I/O after every SQL Server clock tick and after the number of processes specified by `i/o polling process count` have run. Due to the small size of a SQL Server clock tick, changing this variable may not have much of an effect on your system. If you have a very fast machine, high transaction rates, and high I/O demands, however, you may be able to improve performance by increasing the value of this variable. A higher setting means that there is less overhead for checking I/O and that, collectively, processes get more CPU time before having to stop while the Server looks for I/O status. Note that other variables—`time slice` and `cpu grace time`—affect the CPU time of individual processes. Processes may also depend on I/O for continuing their work, so adjusting this variable may be more hindrance than help. Careful performance analysis and tuning should guide any changes.

sql server clock tick length

This variable sets the SQL Server clock tick length in microseconds. Note that this value may be different from the clock tick length of the machine on which SQL Server is running. SQL Server suspends runnable tasks to check for network and disk I/O at each tick. Environments with relatively high CPU demands in relationship to I/O demands may benefit from setting this value higher, because the Server will spend less time checking for I/O, depending on the setting of `i/o polling process count`. Note that you will need to increase `cpu grace time` to compensate for any change in clock tick length. For example, if you double clock tick length, you should halve `cpu grace time`.

housekeeper free write percent

For SQL Server engines with a lot of idle time, the housekeeper may write buffers to disk more often than necessary. For example, a database application may update the same database page repeatedly. If so, the housekeeper may write it after each change, when fewer writes would have been acceptable. Using the new configuration variable, `housekeeper free write percent`, you can set an upper limit on the percentage of extra writes by the housekeeper that should be tolerated. Set this variable to 0 to disable the housekeeper. See Chapter 4 for more information about the housekeeper.

memory alignment boundary

To accommodate some hardware platforms, a `memory alignment boundary` configuration variable has been added in SQL Server 11.0. This variable specifies the memory alignment boundary for caches. It must be a multiple of the default page size, which is 2 KB.[1] If not set adequately by default, set this variable

---

[1] Four kilobytes on Stratus.

to the optimal page size for your platform or your disk hardware. All requests for buffers will default to the size specified by this variable. Modifications of this variable affect performance and should not be made unless recommended by Sybase personnel or documentation.

configuration file

The setting for `configuration file` specifies the name of the configuration file most recently loaded using `sp_configure` or during SQL Server start-up.

■ OBJECT AND DATA MANAGEMENT CONFIGURATION VALUES

number of open databases

The `number of open databases` parameter controls how many databases may be in use simultaneously. Internally, the variable determines how many database descriptors SQL Server allocates in memory at boot time. Each open database requires approximately 33 KB of additional memory for SQL Server 11. The system databases `master`, `model`, `tempdb`, and `sybsystemprocs` should be included in your count of databases that the Server may open simultaneously. Every user could use `tempdb` for some queries. When you execute system stored procedures, the `master` and `sybsystemprocs` databases get opened. The Server opens the `model` database at boot time and when creating new databases. If you have installed auditing, assume that the `sybsecurity` database will remain open most of the time as well.

number of open objects

The `number of open objects` parameter controls how many database objects, such as tables, and stored procedures may be in use simultaneously and how many may be involved in a single transaction. Internally, it sets the number of object descriptors allocated in memory. Each open object requires approximately 315 bytes of memory. Judging demand for open objects provides a particular challenge, so system administrators usually find it better to sacrifice a little memory by overestimating than to limit the ability of users to do their work.

number of locks

The number of locks variable sets the number of locks that can be active at one time. As a general rule, expect each process to use 20 locks. Use a higher number if your SQL Server gets used by poorly designed applications or by queries that access tables with insufficient indexes. Each lock you set uses an additional 80 bytes of memory.

11.0 ▷ deadlock retries

The setting of this variable tells SQL Server how many times to allow a transaction to attempt to get a lock after it fails as the victim of a deadlock. After this many tries, the transaction is aborted. For a well-designed application, you shouldn't need to set this variable any higher than 3. If you find you need to set it higher to avoid frequent transaction rollbacks, you probably need to rework the application anyway for optimum results.

11.0 ▷ deadlock checking period

Before version 11.0, SQL Server checked for possible deadlocks as soon as any process began to wait for a lock. This creates unnecessary overhead for processes not in danger of encountering deadlocks. With the new lock functionality, a service task called DEADLOCK TUNE runs periodically, checking for deadlocks after the delay specified by the value of the deadlock checking period variable. Setting the period to a value near 0 means that processes encountering deadlocks are notified sooner, while those not in a deadlock are sometimes delayed unnecessarily. Setting the checking period higher means deadlocks take longer to detect, but the processes that get their locks before the checking period don't incur extra overhead.

address lock spinlock ratio

This variable sets the number of address lock hash buckets managed by a single spinlock. A hash bucket is an internal structure for managing lists of outstanding locks. The default value of 100 means that there are 10 locks per spinlock, which proved adequate in Sybase internal benchmarks. If you configure more spinlocks than the total number of hash buckets (currently 1031), one spinlock will be used per hash bucket. Each `address lock spinlock` you configure consumes up to 256 bytes of memory. Normally, you should not need to change this value unless instructed to do so by Sybase.

table lock spinlock ratio

This sets the number of table lock hash buckets managed by a single spinlock. The default value of 20 means that there are 5 locks per spinlock, which proved adequate in Sybase internal benchmarks. If you configure more spinlocks than the total number of hash buckets (currently 101), one spinlock will be used per hash bucket. Each `table lock spinlock` you configure consumes up to 512 bytes of memory.

11.0 ▷ ***page lock spinlock ratio***

This sets the number of page lock hash buckets managed by a single spinlock. The default value of 100 means that there are 10 locks per spinlock, which proved adequate in Sybase internal benchmarks. If you configure more spinlocks than the total number of hash buckets (currently 1031), one spinlock will be used per hash bucket. Each `page lock spinlock` you configure consumes up to 512 bytes of memory.

11.0 ▷ ***freelock transfer block size***

A special cache known as an *engine freelock cache* keeps a subset of locks available for a SQL Server engine to use. When the engine runs out of locks, a block of locks is moved from a global freelock list to the engine freelock cache. The `freelock transfer block size` variable sets the number of locks to transfer at once. You can change this value without needing to reboot the Server. The value you set cannot exceed more than half the number of locks available in an engine's freelock list, which is determined as follows:

```
max engine freelocks percent * number of locks /
max online engines / 2
```

11.0 ▷ ***max engine freelocks***

This variable determines the number of freelocks available in each engine freelock cache, specified as a percentage of the total number of locks available on the Server. You can set to any value from 1 to 50 percent. You can change this value without needing to reboot the Server.

default fill factor percent

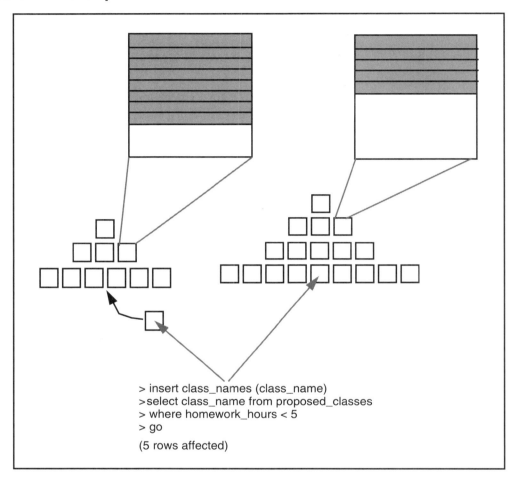

Figure 6.2 A lower fill factor setting results in a larger index. However, since there is less need for page splits during subsequent inserts, indexes with a lower fill factor can yield better performance.

The `fill factor` setting determines how full SQL Server makes index pages when you create an index. If you set the value to zero, the default is used, which is 100% full leaf pages (which is the data pages in the case of a clustered index). Room is left for growth in the index pages at higher levels of the index. For space considerations, you might think of setting `fill factor` to 100%. However, each time you add data to a table with one or more indexes, it must insert a row into the index. If inserting the row requires the addition of an index page, you incur the overhead of a page split when adding it to the index.

Not only do page splits demand I/O, but they also acquire locks on other index pages while adding the new page to the index tree. These locks can conflict with other index accesses, delaying processing on all sides. Removing data from an index page can sometimes also incur this overhead. To avoid frequent page splits, use a `fill factor` setting that gives indexes room to expand. Using a minimal `fill factor` only makes sense for read-only databases.

The optimum value for this parameter depends on how fast processes add and remove data from the table and whether modifications affect indexed columns. The smaller the value you use for `fill factor` (other than 0, which indicates a default setting), the more space each index takes.

You can override the Server-wide `fill factor` value by using the FILLFACTOR clause of the CREATE INDEX command.

Note that this parameter only affects page utilization at index creation time. SQL Server currently makes no effort to maintain the `fill factor` in pages thereafter. In fact, it attempts to divide rows evenly between pages during index splits in order to avoid further splits. For this reason, some Sybase administrators periodically rebuild the indexes to return them to a particular `fill factor`. Note that rebuilding an index invalidates any related stored procedures and other compiled objects that may be in cache. These objects will need to be reresolved and recompiled before their next use. The process of reresolution is discussed in Chapter 8.

identity burning set factor

System 10 SQL Server allows users to create tables with identity columns. When a user adds a row to such a table, the Server automatically assigns a unique sequential key value to the row and inserts it in the identity column. The numbers used for key values come from a pool stored in memory. When SQL Server assigns a new column value, it reads the current maximum value from memory and adds 1. After a block of values has been used, SQL Server reads the next block from disk. In the event of an emergency shutdown, unused numbers in a block are discarded, leaving gaps in the IDENTITY column value. The identity burning set factor changes the percentage of potential column values available in each block. The need for performance should be weighed for the inconvenience of number gaps when setting this value.

The range of the burning set factor in SQL Server is a percentage between 0.00001% and 99.99999%. To convert the percentage you want to a value that sp_configure can manage, you must multiply it by 100,000 (10^5) so that you end up with a number between 1 and 9,999,999. For example, for a setting of 0.05%, use the value 5000.

identity grab size

This variable allows you to specify the number of identity column values to reserve for each table in cache.

size of auto identity column

The size of auto identity column configuration variable sets the default size of the column created in a database where the auto identity database option is set to *true*.

allow nested triggers

The nested triggers flag indicates whether triggers may call other triggers. A value of *0* disallows nesting, and a setting of *1* (the default) allows nesting.

Most frequently, you would need nested triggers if you have a trigger that causes data to be updated in a column also bound to a trigger. Database designers usually use triggers to enforce integrity and business rules. Triggers maintain data integrity when human procedures do not provide sufficient control.

number of extent I/O buffers

When creating indexes, SQL Server normally reads and writes intermediate sort results and index pages to disk one page at a time. By configuring extent I/O buffers, you can configure SQL Server to behave more efficiently, working with one or more extents at a time instead. Each SQL Server extent contains eight pages, so setting extent i/o buffers to 3 means that create index would manipulate 24 pages at a time. For a table containing hundreds of thousands of rows, setting extent I/O buffers to *100* or so can allow you to build a clustered index in minutes instead of hours. For each extent I/O buffer configured, the server allocates eight data pages from the memory pool configured using the total memory parameter.

When you set a nonzero value for this parameter, the first create index process uses all extent I/O buffers. While that index process runs, subsequent index requests will use single page I/O. For the best performance, create indexes one at a time and schedule this task for the times of lowest demand for SQL Server resources.

■ LANGUAGE AND LOCALIZATION CONFIGURATION VALUES

default sortorder id

The sort order value indicates the sort order in effect for a SQL Server. You cannot change the sort order by changing sort order id with sp_configure since other processing is also required. Reconfiguration of sort order affects how the Server writes data on disk. You can only set it using the SQL Server installation program. Changing all your data to use a new sort order involves quite a lot of work, so plan the appropriate sort order carefully and try to set it correctly at installation time.

default language id

The `default language` setting indicates the language for displaying SQL server messages if the user has not set it otherwise. A user or client application may specify an alternate language by using the `set language` command.

By default, `default language` is set to U.S. English, which always has a language ID of 0. The Server assigns other languages unique numbers sequentially as they are added.

number of languages in cache

The setting for `language cache` indicates how many languages can be retained in memory at once. Each additional language requires about 877 bytes of additional memory. Set this parameter to the number of languages you expect users to request simultaneously. Setting this to *1* when more than one language is in use may adversely affect the speed with which SQL Server returns messages, warnings, and errors to users.

default character set id

SQL Server uses the default character set specified by the configured `default character set ID`. You can only change this value to an ID that corresponds to a character set already installed in SQL Server. You can use the SQL Server installation program or the `langinstall` utility to install character sets.

■ CONNECTION AND PROCESS MANAGEMENT CONFIGURATION VALUES

time slice

The `time slice` variable sets the maximum number of milliseconds during which a process can use a CPU before giving it up to another process. You should not need to change `time slice` under normal circumstances. Normally, a process should finish well within the default limit. If you set `time slice` too low, SQL Server may spend too much time switching processes. If you set it too high, users may experience longer response times.

The default value for `time slice` varies from platform to platform since clock speeds vary. Normally, only runaway processes result in a time slice error at the default setting. Sometimes, processes that get time sliced cause the SQL Server to become unrunnable or unusable because the process doesn't exit gracefully and doesn't release all locks and memory resources used. Setting this value too low could cause time-slice errors, which will be reported in the log. Setting this value too high can also cause problems, since it affects the ability for other processes to get resources as they need them. A significant difference in CPU speed between your system and the system SQL Server was optimized on may justify a higher or lower setting.

number of user connections

The setting for `user connections` determines the number of simultaneous users SQL Server can accommodate. Specifically, the internal resources for a `user connection` include a memory structure for storing details about the user, such as the status of the various set options, as well as a stack area in memory for processing. Each SQL Server user connection requires a file descriptor (network I/O channel) provided by the operating system. Given sufficient memory, the maximum for `user connection` setting depends on the operating system file descriptor limit. Use the command

```
> select @@max_connections
> go
```

to see the file descriptor limit for your system. If you have the opportunity to evaluate the operating system you will use for a planned application, and you anticipate the need for lots of users, ask the vendor about the file descriptor limit. After the number of simultaneous users has reached the number specified with this setting, additional users cannot log in. If one user logs out, the next attempt at a user connection will succeed.

Each `user connection` requires 50-100 KB (platform dependent) of memory plus the size of the stack set with the `stack size` configuration variable. Increasing the `stack size` or `default packet size` variables increases the amount of memory required for each user. Set the number of user connections high enough to accommodate your users, but don't set it so high that you leave insufficient memory for data and procedure cache.

The number of user connections does not necessarily correspond to the number of users. Many client applications open several connections at once, reserving some for read or browse processes and others for write commands. Client applications that allow multiple windows may use additional connections for each window. When purchasing a client application, ask about the number of user connections made and how they are used. Find out if you have any means of controlling the number used.

Keep in mind that SQL Server uses some file descriptors, so users do not have access to the total specified in the `@@max_connections` variable. SQL Server uses

- One for each configured network listener (i.e., one for every "master" line in the interfaces file entry for the server

- One for standard output

- One for the error log file

- On VMS, one for internal use

- One for each SQL Server disk device

- One for each SQL Server mirror device

- One for each remote server (including Backup Server) active at a given time

To determine the number of user connections that you need to accommodate the number of users accessing SQL Server simultaneously, periodically issue an `sp_who` command and record the results. If you run a `cron` or batch job to do this once every half-hour for a representative month, you should be able to determine the usage patterns and peak times of day.

stack size

The stack size variable sets the amount of stack space reserved for each user connection. The amount of stack space a user requires depends heavily on the type of queries the user executes. A complex query may require more memory than the default stack area provides. Such a condition causes the user's query to fail. SQL Server prints a message and rolls back the transaction. If many queries fail this way, increase the stack size or rewrite the query. Doing so directly increases the memory allocation, which reduces the size of the memory pool for procedure and data cache.

Increasing stack size increases the memory usage for each user connection, diverting memory from the procedure or data cache. If only one user runs into the upper limit on stack size once a month, ask the user or developer to rewrite the query rather than reset the default size for each user. SQL Server requires a stack size that is an even multiple of SQL Server's page size. If you specify a value not evenly divisible by 2 KB,[2] SQL Server rounds the value up to the nearest multiple when you issue the RECONFIGURE command or use the verify or write options of sp_configure. Upon rounding stack size, SQL Server displays an informational message containing the recomputed value.

▶ 11.0 stack guard size

The stack guard area is the last region of a process stack. By default, it is 4 KB. If a process is allowed to use more memory than its stack will allow, it will corrupt the memory area of another process, causing serious problems. The guard area stores a consistent, known pattern. If the Server detects that this pattern has been corrupted, it knows that the process has overflowed its stack and the Server terminates the process. A process that uses a lot of stack space may not only overwrite the guard area, but overwrite memory beyond it before the Server detects

---

[2]Four kilobytes for Stratus.

the problem. Thus, the memory for other processes or even SQL Server can get corrupted, which causes all sorts of otherwise inexplicable but severe problems. Increasing stack guard size may help to avoid this disaster. Under normal circumstances, you avoid stack overflow by setting stack size adequately, rather than resizing the guard area. If this is still not adequate, try breaking up queries that use a lot of stack space. As with `stack size`, increases to the `stack guard size` variable increase the overall amount of memory required for each user connection. So, for example, if you increase the `guard size` by 2 KB and you have 500 users, user connections will consume an additional megabyte of memory.

cpu grace time

This is the maximum amount of time in milliseconds that a user process is allowed to run without voluntarily yielding the CPU. Normally, a process should stop itself at intervals less than the value of the `time slice` variable to yield the CPU to other processes. If it does not do so and runs longer than the value of `cpu grace time`, the Server will terminate it with a time-slice error.

allow remote access

A value of *0* for `remote access` disables remote procedure calls (RPCs) between Servers, and a value of *1* enables them. In SQL Server 10.0 and later releases, only someone with `sso_role` permission set can reset the `allow remote access` variable. Backup Server uses RPCs to communicate with the SQL Server for which it is dumping or restoring data, so you must enable this feature when using Backup Server. Also, enable `remote access` if the SQL Server you are configuring will need to communicate with an Open Server or another middleware application. If you enable remote access while `remote logins`, `remote sites`, `remote connections`, and `pre-read packets` are set to *0*, the Server will automatically set defaults for these variables. All of these variables must be set properly for RPCs to work as expected.

number of remote connections

`Remote connections` is the number of incoming and outgoing connections that can be active at any one time for the SQL Server you are configuring. Frequently, administrators confuse this parameter with `number of remote logins`, which affect outbound connections only. Add the expected number of remote and local connections when configuring `number of user connections`.

number of remote logins

The value for `remote logins` determines the number of outbound user connections that may be active at one time in the SQL Server. This setting does not limit the number of RPCs that may come in to the SQL Server.

number of remote sites

The `remote sites` setting determines the number of simultaneous RPC generating programs that can access SQL Server. For example, each Backup Server and Open Server application counts as a `remote site`. Set the `remote sites` parameter to the number of simultaneous remote sites that you expect the SQL Server to connect to at any given time. For example, if you have one Open Server program and one Backup Server, but you never use both at the same time, you only need to configure one remote site. The number of remote sites corresponds to what is called a site handler. This handler is an area of memory used to store status information about the connection with the remote server.

remote server pre-read packets

SQL Server operates more efficiently for large data transfers when it reads more than one network packet at a time. The `pre-read packets` variable allows you to specify the number of TDS packets to read at a time when receiving RPCs. The optimal setting will depend on the default size of your network packets and the average size of network transfers with the RPCs that you issue. If your applications instead generate a large number of small transfers, leave `number of pre-read packets` at the default of 3.

default network packet size

The `default network packet size` variable establishes the size of network packets used when client applications communicate with SQL Server without specifying a packet size. By default, SQL Server uses 512 bytes for its packets. A large `default packet size` can increase performance for applications that generate large amounts of I/O in a single operation. In other cases, you will want to use a small default, since increasing the packet size also requires that you make a corresponding increase in the amount of memory devoted to network connections. You can set `default network packet size` to any multiple of 512 bytes up to a maximum of 524,288. SQL Server rounds down values that are uneven multiples of 512.

The memory required to support the `default packet size` is taken from the main memory pool set with the `total memory` configuration parameter. When you increase `default packet size`, make sure to leave enough memory for data and procedure caches.

Each SQL Server user connection uses

- One read buffer
- One read overflow buffer
- One write buffer

Each of these buffers requires the number of bytes specified as the `default packet size`. Therefore, to determine the total amount of memory allocated for network packets, multiply the number of user connections by 3 and then by the default network packet size.

If you increase this setting, you must also increase the `maximum network packet size` to at least the same value.

maximum network packet size

If programmed to do so, a client can request any network packet size up to the maximum you specify with the `maximum network packet size` variable. Performance can be increased for applications reading or writing large text or image values by increasing the maximum. For short queries, keep the `default packet size` small, but set the maximum large enough to accommodate bulk reads and writes when necessary.

Set the maximum in conjunction with setting `additional network memory` (described next) so the Server can provide the maximum requested by the client. SQL Server guarantees that every user connection can log in at the default packet size. If you increase `maximum network packet size`, but leave `additional network memory` at 0, clients will only be able to use the default packet sizes. Clients requesting larger packet sizes will receive warnings indicating that they have to use the default size.

Both the `bcp` and `isql` programs allow users to request large packet sizes. Application developers can write Open Client programs such that they provide an option to request variable packet sizes as well.

For best network performance, choose a `default packet size` that is compatible with the underlying packet size on the network. Doing so can reduce the number of reads and writes to the network and can minimize unused space in network packets. By following this recommendation you can increase throughput for a network that services a significant volume of communication between SQL Servers and client applications.

additional network memory

SQL Server reserves the amount of memory needed for each network connection based on the `default packet size`. For clients that generate large I/Os, such as `bcp`, you can increase performance by providing a larger maximum packet size and configuring `additional network memory`. `additional network memory` is allocated above and beyond the value specified by the total memory variable. For example, if you set the total memory configuration to 32 MB, and you set additional network memory to 8 MB, SQL Server will request 40 MB from the operating system at boot time. If the machine only has 32 MB of physical memory, SQL Server may fail to boot, depending on the operating system you are using and on the swap space configuration.

max number network listeners

This variable specifies the number of master ports on which SQL Server listens for requests. Normally, you only need one port per network protocol. For example, if you are running the SQL Server under both TCP and DECNet, set this value to 2. For a single network type, a value of 1 is sufficient.

tcp no delay

If you are using TCP/IP for your client/server communications, you may be able to improve performance by disabling a TCP behavior known as *packet batching.* By default, TCP delays small logical packets so that it can batch them into larger physical packets and conserve on the number of packets transmitted. In some environments, you may see a performance improvement by enabling tcp no delay. This tells TCP to send all packets as soon as possible regardless of their size. This option increases network traffic. Be sure to monitor performance before and after trying this change to make sure that you see an improvement. For already congested networks, you may see performance degradation. To enable this option in SQL Servers earlier than version 11.0, boot with trace flag 1610.

user log cache size

In System 11, processes now have a private log cache that helps them avoid contention for the last page of the transaction log. Each process uses its own cache for the log records it generates. Instead of flushing the log page after each log record is written, the log cache is flushed when the transaction commits or when the log cache fills up. The `user log cache size` establishes the size of each user's log cache in bytes. The default size is one page and the maximum is 2 GB. Try to set this to a size no larger than the maximum size needed to store the log information for a large transaction and slightly more than the size of the log records for an average transaction. One way to determine the size of log records for a transaction is to do the following on a test database in single-user mode:

- Truncate the transaction log to make it as small as possible.
- Use `DBCC CHECKTABLE(syslogs)` in the database to determine the current size of `syslogs`.
- Issue the transaction.
- Use `DBCC CHECKTABLE` to determine the new size of `syslogs`.
- Subtract the original `syslogs` size from the new size to determine the change caused by the transaction.

You will need to do this process for all of your typical transactions to determine the average size of log records for your mix of transactions. Then you can set the `user log cache size` variable accordingly. Alternatively, you could use trial and error; slowly change this variable in isolation and measure the performance impact after each change.

11.0 user log cache spinlock ratio

The `user log cache spinlock ratio` variable essentially sets the number of spinlocks that can be used for managing user log caches for Servers using more than one CPU. This configuration value can have a high impact on performance, so you will need to experiment to determine the optimal setting. Each user log cache spinlock that you use consumes 256 bytes of memory. For example, a ratio of 3 tells SQL Server to use one log cache spinlock for every three log caches. If you have 1200 users configured, you will have 400 log cache spinlocks, which use a total of approximately 100 KB of memory. You only need one spinlock for a single-CPU Server, so set `user log cache spinlock ratio` to 1 in this case.

■ SECURITY MANAGEMENT CONFIGURATION VALUES

system-wide password expiration

By specifying a nonzero `password expiration interval`, you can control how often users must change their passwords. Specify this value in days. For example, to force users to change their passwords approximately every 3 months, set this value to 90. The default setting of zero means that passwords never expire. Only a login with the `sso_role` set may change this interval.

When users log in, SQL Server notifies them if their passwords are about to expire. When the number of days remaining before expiration is less than 7 days or 25% of the value of the expiration interval, users are warned about the number of days remaining before expiration. After passwords expire, users can log into SQL Server, but cannot successfully execute any commands until they change their passwords. A login with the `sso_role` set can reset user passwords. Users who are logged in when their passwords expire are not affected until the next time they log in.

Note that nothing in SQL Server prevents a user from setting his or her password to a new value and then immediately changing it back to an old value. To enforce reasonable password precautions, establish and promote a written policy as well as providing programmatic solutions.

audit queue size

This variable determines the number of audit records that the in-memory audit queue can hold. This queue holds audit records generated by users until the records can be processed and written to the audit trail. Only a login with `sso_role` enabled can change this value. If the queue is large, records may remain in memory a long time before getting flushed to disk. If the system happens to undergo an emergency shutdown, these records, which could contain clues about the shutdown, will not be written to disk.

A single audit record requires 424 bytes in memory, although it might only occupy 22 bytes when written to a data page. The memory requirement for the `default audit queue size` of *100* is approximately 42 KB. The *extrainfo* field and *name* fields in `sysaudits` hold variable-length data, so if audit records contain values for these fields, the audit record takes more space. If the Server crashes, it can lose the number of records specified as the audit queue size plus 20. After leaving the audit queue, audit records may remain on a page in memory until they are written to `sysaudits` on disk. `Sysaudits` pages are flushed to disk at most every 20 records. A data page can accommodate from 4 to 80 audit records.

11.0 ▶ *permission cache entries*

The `permission cache entries` variable determines the number of permission records that can be cached in memory. The permission cache stores portions of the `sysprotects` table in memory to make permission checking faster. If your SQL Server operations check permissions frequently, you may see a performance improvement if you raise this value. However, since the entire permissions cache is flushed every time permissions are granted or revoked on an object, it usually doesn't make sense to set this value high during development. Each cache entry consumes 28 bytes of memory.

Procedure Manual Suggestions

○ Documenting a Standard Configuration

➡ Document a standard, baseline configuration for
- SQL Server machines, including recommended processor type, amount of RAM, number of CPUs, and OS configuration parameters

- •SQL Server, including all configuration values for the standard SQL Server machine with a typical number of users and amount of processing

- •Databases, including the use of segments and database partitions

- •Sessions, including any variables that users or applications will need to set to make a particular function work correctly

➡ This standard configuration will serve as a template for people who do not yet know what the complete application will look like, but need to acquire hardware and software before the details will be determined.

➡ Document why certain settings are the way they are for those setting up a Server in your environment for the first time.

○ Managing Server Configuration

➡ Write a procedure that outlines methods for reconfiguring SQL Server when necessary.

➡ Ensure that system administrators calculate memory usage for all changes and consider any performance effect that the changes may have. If the effect of the change on performance is unknown, specify that testing occur on a nonproduction system.

➡ Specify that system administrators save hard copies of `sp_configure` output before and after any changes.

➡ Designate a specific central location for filing the output.

➡ Make note of the vulnerability of having `allow updates` turned on, and include a way of avoiding problems

C H A P T E R

Database and User Environment Configuration

W hile `sp_configure` shapes SQL Server processing as a whole, a database owner can affect the behavior of specific databases by setting database options. Furthermore, users can influence how SQL Server behaves for them by setting session-level options. The extensive customization possible makes SQL Server flexible enough to suit any type of data processing environment.

■ DATABASE OPTIONS

The system administrator or database owner can set options such as `single user` mode or `read only` access by using the `sp_dboption` command. The general form of this command is

> `sp_dboption [db_name, option_name, {true | false}]`

Executing the command with no parameters instructs SQL Server to display all possible settings. When setting an option, as

255

with `sp_configure` configuration names, you need only specify a unique portion of the option name. To specify an option name that includes embedded blanks, punctuation, or keywords, you must surround the option by quotes.

For example, the commands

```
> use master
> go
> sp_dboption school, "read only", true
> go
> use school
> go
> checkpoint
> go
```

disallow updates in the *school* database.

The `sp_dboption` command must be issued from the `master` database, but then you must use the database that was changed and issue a `checkpoint` in it. After `checkpoint` completes, the option takes effect. You cannot set options for the `master` database. Using `sp_dboption` in the `model` database causes all new databases to have the same settings as `model` by default.

Only the database owner or someone with `sa_role` permission may reset database options using `sp_dboption`.

The general process for setting database options is as follows:

- Determine the settings necessary after evaluating goals and possible consequences.
- Issue the USE `master` command if you are not currently in the master database.
- Execute one or more `sp_dboption` commands for a selected database.
- Issue the USE *database* command for the database affected.
- Issue the `checkpoint` command.
- Use `sp_helpdb` to verify your results.

In the following sections, we explore the options available for customizing aspects of individual databases. Sybase added many of these options in System 10 in order to comply with the ANSI SQL 89 standard. Since many default aspects of SQL Server didn't comply, yet many customers were already using and relying on the default behaviors, options were added to provide compliance and maximum flexibility at the same time.

abort tran on log full

If a transaction will cause the transaction log to be full (as determined by the `last chance threshold`), SQL Server releases 10.0 and later will abort the transaction if you set `abort tran on log full` to *true*. If you set it to *false*, the transaction will be suspended until the transaction log is freed up. The *true* setting is recommended since it can be very difficult to free up log space otherwise.

allow nulls by default

When creating a table, for each column you define, you can specify whether the column allows NULL values. If you do not specify how to handle NULLs in the database, the SQL Server default determines the behavior. The default is to not allow NULLs. To make it easier to rebuild or rearrange databases and tables, save scripts of any CREATE TABLE commands you issue. If you do this, explicitly specify NULL or NOT NULL for each column, since the setting for the database may not be the same next time you execute the script.

auto identity

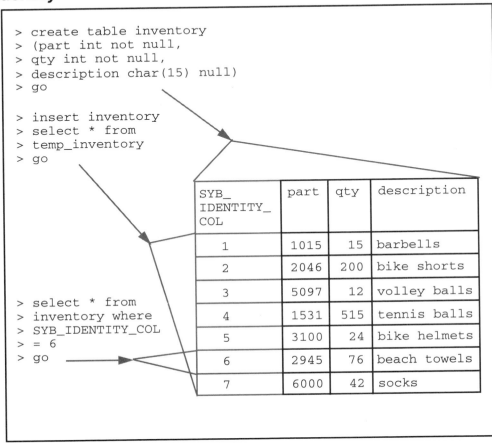

Figure 7.1 When you create a table, an identity column is added to it automatically if `auto identity` is *true*. You can reference the identity column by using the name *SYB_IDENTITY_COL*.

When you set `auto identity` to *true* in a System 10 or 10.1 database, every `CREATE TABLE` command implicitly adds a 10-digit identity column to the table, so you don't have to include the `IDENTITY` keyword. With System 11, you can set the size of the auto identity column using a configuration variable, as described in Chapter 6. An `IDENTITY` column is a column in which SQL Server automatically inserts a sequential value for each row added to the table. This column is typically used as a key. The values in an automatic identity column cannot be seen unless the value SYB_IDENTITY_COL is specified in the column name part of the SELECT command. Specifying a primary key, unique constraint, or IDENTITY column in a create table statement overrides the automatic identity behavior. The SYB_IDENTITY_COL name is not used with explicit identity columns, since they are visible to users.

identity in nonunique index

This database option tells SQL Server to add an identity column automatically to any index not defined as unique. To use isolation level 0, a table must have a unique index. Turning on the identity-related configuration variables and database options facilitates isolation level 0 without requiring manual intervention. However, you will probably gain higher performance and better space utilization if you make the effort to replace nonunique indexes with unique indexes where needed.

dbo use only

When you set dbo use only to *true*, only the database owner (DBO) or someone with sa_role enabled (since sa takes on the dbo identity when using a database) can use the database. You can only finish setting this option by using the checkpoint command when no one besides dbo is in the database. Set dbo use only to *true* when reorganizing a database or recovering from some sort of database failure that requires you to rebuild or modify tables.

ddl in tran

By default, SQL Server does not allow you to use certain commands, categorized as data definition language (DDL) commands, within transactions. The SQL Server ddl in tran option allows you to override this behavior in versions 10.0 and later. When you set this option to *true*, users may issue the following commands within transactions:

- CREATE/DROP/ALTER TABLE
- CREATE/DROP DEFAULT
- CREATE/DROP INDEX
- CREATE/DROP PROCEDURE
- CREATE/DROP RULE
- CREATE SCHEMA
- CREATE/DROP TRIGGER
- CREATE/DROP VIEW
- GRANT/REVOKE

You may not issue these commands in transactions regardless of the setting of `ddl in tran`:

- ALTER/LOAD/CREATE/DROP DATABASE
- DISK INIT
- LOAD TRANSACTION
- RECONFIGURE
- SELECT INTO
- TRUNCATE TABLE
- UPDATE STATISTICS

Also, system procedures that change the master database, such as `sp_dboption` and `sp_configure`, cannot be used inside user-defined transactions even with `ddl in tran` set.

For system tables, which play a part in almost any SQL query, keeping a high level of concurrent access enhances overall SQL Server performance. However, the DDL commands hold locks on system tables. If you set `ddl in tran` to *true*, it increases the likelihood that someone will start a transaction, issue a DDL command, then fail to commit the transaction, or continue with a very long transaction. This blocks all other users. For the best performance, only set `ddl in tran` to *true* for short periods of time or in environments where everyone understands the consequences.

Since setting a database option in the model database causes all new databases to have the option set by default, do not set `ddl in tran` to *true* in `model`. Always leave `ddl in tran` set to *false* in `tempdb`.

no chkpt on recovery

The `no chkpt on recovery` option helps you maintain warm backups of your databases. A warm backup, briefly, is a copy of a database you maintain on a separate SQL Server in case your primary Server or database encounters trouble. You make a warm backup by taking dumps of a running database and its transaction logs and loading them immediately into the duplicate database.

A sequential integer value called a *timestamp* marks the sequence of each transaction log dump. When you load the transaction logs in the second database, you may only load them in order from earliest to latest, as indicated by the timestamp. Normally, when a database or transaction log load completes, SQL Server issues a `checkpoint` that writes a record to the transaction log. Since the sequence number of the `checkpoint` record exceeds that of all the transaction log backups, the Server disallows all attempts to load earlier transaction logs. When you turn on `no chckpt on recovery`, the `checkpoint` record does not get written to the log, so subsequent loads of the transaction log can succeed.

no free space acctg

By setting `no free space acctg` to *true* in a 10.0 or later SQL Server, you disable accounting of free space. Since execution of threshold actions defined for nonlog segments relies on free space accounting, setting this option to *true* disables the threshold action. When free space accounting is disabled, recovery finishes more quickly because it doesn't need to calculate free space for each segment.

read only

By setting `read only` to *true*, you can disallow any data modification commands in the database. Since you must use the database and perform a `checkpoint` for the option to take effect, you will need to be the only user at that point. Some people set archive or standby databases `read only`. Since the execution of views, triggers, and stored procedures causes query plans to be generated, and the process of generating a query plan requires a write to the `sysprocedures` system table, it's usually not practical to protect a reporting database by setting it to `read only`.

select into/bulkcopy

Certain operations are not logged because they cause a large set of data to be modified. These are `SELECT INTO`, fast bulk copy and `writetext`. After performing these operations, you cannot make or load transaction log dumps, since the transaction log loses meaning when unlogged actions take place. When you set `select into/bulkcopy`, keep in mind that you're making it possible for someone to execute commands that will disable the recovery benefits of transaction log dumps.

If you want to be able to make and load transaction logs after unlogged actions, perform the following steps:

- Enable `select into/bulk copy`.
- Execute the unlogged commands.
- Disable `select into/bulk copy`.
- Make a database dump.

After all of these steps, you may make transaction log dumps again. Slow `bcp`, which involves tables with indexes or triggers, does not require that you set `select into/bulk copy` to *true*. Slow `bcp` is logged. If you do not use the transaction dump or load features at all, you could leave `select into/bulk copy` turned *on* in a database. This is sometimes done during database development.

single user

Set `single user` to *true* if you want to make sure that only one user can use the database at a time. Normally, you would only set this when you are setting up a database or performing maintenance procedures. Since you must use the database and issue a checkpoint for the option to take effect, you will need to be the only user in the database at that time.

trunc log on chkpt

This command signals the automatic checkpoint command to truncate the transaction log at checkpoint time. Use this when you either don't care about dumping and loading your database (for scratch databases or development) or when you use full database dumps only. Note that when a user issues checkpoint explicitly the log is not truncated automatically even if this option is set to *true*.

■ USER ENVIRONMENT CONFIGURATION

Several set commands allow users to customize how SQL Server behaves under certain situations on a session by session basis. When a user connection is initiated in SQL Server, a session is begun. Any of the options set as described in this section remain set until reset or until the connection terminates. Using these commands, each process can create its own environment.

The values in braces ({ }) indicate the value or values that you may set. A vertical bar (|) separates values that you may choose among. Brackets ([ ]) indicate optional clauses, parameters, or keywords. In some cases, the same option with different clauses is explained under separate headings to simplify explanations. For this reason, the representation of the syntax here may vary from the Sybase documentation.

ansinull {on | off}

The setting of ansinull controls whether SQL Server warns the user when a comparison (= or !=) or an aggregate (e.g., sum, avg, or count) involves a NULL value. With ansinull *on*, the user gets a warning; otherwise, SQL Server silently processes the query. If you think of NULL as *unknown*, ignoring an unknown value could affect the validity of conclusions based on queries involving NULLS, especially in the cases of sums and averages.

ansi_permissions {on | off}

The SQL standard specifies that permissions checking for update and delete statements should include both the appropriate update/delete permissions on the columns to modify, as well as select permissions on the columns used in the WHERE or SET clauses used to qualify the scope of the modification. With ansi_permissions *on*, SQL Server conforms to the ANSI specified behavior. Otherwise, SQL Server only checks for update and delete permissions on the columns to be modified.

fipsflagger {on | off}

With fipsflagger set *on*, SQL Server warns users each time their queries involve Transact-SQL extensions to entry-level SQL92 standard. Otherwise, SQL server doesn't provide an alert upon use of nonstandard SQL.

arithabort arith_overflow {on | off}

An arithmetic overflow error is one in which a statement attempts to divide by zero, or when the datatype for a variable is too small to hold the results of an arithmetic or conversion operation. With the arithabort arith_overflow set off, the statement causing the error gets aborted. Turned *on*, this option causes both the statement to get aborted and the associated transaction or batch to get rolled back.

arithabort numeric_truncation {on | off}

If a datatype conversion involving a numeric datatype variable causes a loss of precision, the statement causing the error gets aborted if you have arithabort numeric_truncation set *on*.

Otherwise, the results get truncated and statement processing continues.

arithignore [arith_overflow] {on | off}

Setting this option to *on* causes SQL Server to issue a warning when a statement causes an arithmetic overflow error.

chained {on | off}

If you set SQL Server to operate in `chained` mode, it automatically executes a `BEGIN TRANSACTION` before any `SELECT`, `INSERT`, `UPDATE`, `DELETE`, `OPEN,` or `FETCH` command.

close on endtran {on | off}

With `close on endtran` set, SQL Server automatically closes all cursors opened within a transaction at the end of that transaction. Otherwise, users must issue close statements explicitly.

transaction isolation level {0 | 1 | 3} or transaction isolation level {read uncommitted | read committed | serializable}

With `transaction isolation` set to 3 or `SERIALIZABLE`, SQL Server enforces isolation level 3 as specified in the SQL 1989 specification. At level 3, SQL Server effectively applies a `HOLDLOCK` to all `SELECT` operations in a transaction. This means that during a transaction all select operations get an exclusive lock on selected items, blocking access to those objects by any other process. If users also set the `transaction chained` mode on, all implicit transactions execute at isolation level 3 as well. Setting the `transaction isolation level` to 1 or `READ COMMITTED` returns SQL Server to its default locking behavior, which allows more concurrent access than isolation level 3. Setting isolation level 0 or `READ UNCOMMITTED` allows "dirty reads." This last option was added in SQL Server version 10.1. See Chapter 2 for a more thorough discussion of isolation levels.

noexec {on | off}

Set `noexec` to on if you want to compile a query, but not execute it. Usually, users set this option in conjunction with `set showplan` to see how the optimizer will utilize indexes for the query. After you set `noexec`, the only other command that SQL Server will execute is `set noexec off`. Therefore, set `showplan` to *on* before setting `noexec` to *on* if you intend to use both options.

parseonly {on | off}

When `parseonly` is *on*, SQL Server parses queries but does not compile or execute them. Use `parseonly` to determine whether a query will raise any errors. This can be especially useful in an Open Client program where you process unpredictable user queries or in a statement that you suspect will raise an arithmetic error condition.

procid {on | off}

Setting `procid` *on* in an Open Client DB-Library program signals SQL Server to send the ID of the stored procedure being executed to the program before the stored procedure returns any results.

showplan {on | off}

With `showplan` set to *on*, SQL Server displays the query plan generated by the optimizer before executing the query. The query plan shows any indexes that the query will use and the order in which tables accessed by the query will be processed. Typically, users set the `showplan` and `noexec` options to determine whether query is using the expected indexes. This information helps application developers determine what indexes are useful or where indexes may improve query performance.

flushmessage {on | off}

By default, SQL Server waits to return messages to the user until the associated query completes or until the message buffer fills up, whichever comes first. Users can set `flushmessage` *on* if they want to see messages as soon as their process encounters the condition generating the message.

forceplan {on | off}

A significant performance factor in queries with joins is the order in which tables are scanned to find matches between corresponding rows. By default, the optimizer uses a cost-estimating method to determine the optimum join order. With the `set forceplan on` feature, you can specify exactly which join order to use. After you execute the `set forceplan on` command, SQL Server uses the order of the tables in the FROM clause of any subsequent query as the join order. Use `set forceplan off` to tell the optimizer to resume the use of normal costing methods. This `set` option existed in previous versions, but was unsupported.

prefetch {on | off}

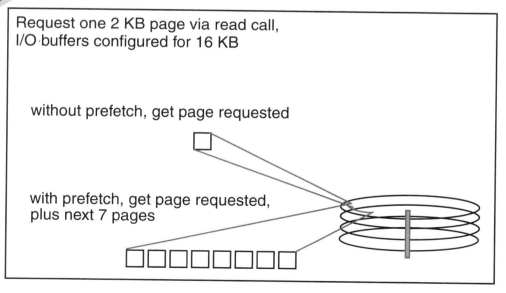

Figure 7.2 When prefetch is enabled, you leverage the time it took to position the disk during a read.

267

Prefetching means that if a single page is requested SQL Server will also fetch additional pages that it anticipates needing to finish processing the query. In SQL Server 11.0, the optimizer considers prefetching automatically for certain queries, but this behavior is also modifiable by the user. The number of pages that the Server should prefetch while executing the query when prefetch is *on* is determined by the memory I/O pools configured for the objects queried. See Chapter 8 for more detailed information about how prefetch works.

statistics io {on | off}

When you set statistics io *on*, SQL Server displays the number of scans and logical and physical I/Os for a query. Use this option for query performance tuning to determine why a particular query executes particularly quickly or slowly. An unusually high number of I/Os often indicates the failure to use an optimal index or join order. Application developers and those that troubleshoot applications typically set this option in conjunction with showplan to determine the cause of a query performance problem.

statistics subquerycache {on | off}

A new session-level command, set statistics subquerycache on, outputs the number of cache hits and misses and the number of rows in the subquery cache for each subquery during execution. Similar to the other set statistics commands, this option is designed to help you diagnose query performance.

statistics time {on | off}

By setting statistics time *on*, users can find out the number of machine clock ticks it takes SQL Server to parse and compile a command. A clock tick is machine dependent. Users can derive the most benefit by comparing time values relative to time values for other queries to see what types of processing take the longest. Note that execution time is not reported; that depends primarily on the I/O required to process the query.

rowcount {number_of_rows}

Normally, SQL Server returns all rows that satisfy a query. When you set `rowcount` to a nonzero number of rows, the Server returns a maximum of the number of rows specified. To turn off a `rowcount` setting, set `rowcount` to *0*. If you are new to a database, you might find it helpful to set `rowcount` to *5* or less to browse a table schema and the type data it contains all on one screen.

cursor rows {number_of_rows} for {cursor name}

When users work with cursors, they can set `cursor rows` to the number of rows that they want returned for each `FETCH` command that does not have an `INTO` clause for the designated cursor.

dup_in_subquery {on | off}

If you issue a query involving a subquery, such as

```
> select *
> from profs
> where prof_name in
> (select class_prof from class_names)
> go
```

The subquery (the one in parentheses) could return duplicate values if the *class_names* table contained two rows with the same professor name. The SQL standard specifies that duplicate result rows such as this be eliminated so that the subquery returns a list of unique values. Versions of SQL Server prior to System 10 did not eliminate duplicates. In System 10, Sybase introduced the `dup_in_subquery` option to allow users to choose between the SQL standard behavior or the Sybase behavior. In future releases, Sybase plans to remove this option and enforce only the SQL standard behavior. This option was provided in System 10 to give customers time to make any necessary adjustments in their applications.

nocount {on | off}

By default, after SQL Server returns the results for a query, it displays the number of rows returned. Set nocount *on* if you don't want the number of result rows returned. Developers typically use this option in stored procedures and client applications when the information is superfluous. A user or application can always check the value of @@rowcount to determine the number of rows returned, whether nocount is *on* or *off*.

quoted_identifier {on | off}

Users may use an identifier for a table, view, or column name that doesn't follow the rules for identifiers if they enclose the identifier in double quotes and set quoted_identifier *on*. (See the Sybase Manuals for the rules for identifiers.) When this option is *on*, users can only enclose character and binary strings in single quotes to distinguish them from identifiers. With this option off, users can use single or double quotes to delimit strings, and invalid identifiers aren't allowed. Sybase provided this option in System 10 because so many new keywords were added.

textsize {number_of_KB} {on | off}

When you issue a SELECT statement to retrieve the value from a text or image variable, SQL Server only returns the first 32 KB of data by default. You can set textsize to a value in bytes to make SQL Server return the specified amount instead. Setting textsize to 0 returns the setting to the 32 KB default.

self-recursion {on | off}

By default, SQL Server does not allow a trigger to call itself. To allow this behavior, set self-recursion *on* in the session that causes the trigger to fire. If a trigger causes a trigger besides itself to fire, the self-recursion setting turns off automatically.

string_rtruncation {on | off}

When a statement inserts or updates a character string, the value supplied may not fit in the datatype to receive the value. In this case, if users have set `string_rtruncation` to *on*, SQL Server will issue a warning and will not truncate the string. Otherwise, with it set to *off*, SQL Server silently truncates the right end of string to fit and continues processing.[1]

offsets {select | from | order | compute | table | procedure | statement | param | execute} {on | off}

Developers can use the offsets option in an Open Client program to get the position of specified keywords in a query. If an offset of -1 is returned, then the program can tell that the keyword is not used in the query. For example, the presence or absence of the procedure keyword might signal the program to follow differing branches of logic.

table count {1-8}

By default, the optimizer considers tables in sets of four when permuting join orders and evaluating costs. In SQL Server 11, you can use this session-level option to tell the optimizer to consider anywhere from one to eight tables at once. Setting this value higher than 4 may improve throughput, but will delay response time.

char_convert {off | on [with {error | no_error}]}

By default, SQL Server automatically converts characters between the character sets used between the client application and the Server. When a SQL Server character cannot be translated to the client's character set, a warning is issued and the affected characters are replaced by question marks (?). To suspend charac-

---

[1]This may seem opposite of what you'd expect. If you think of it as the warning being on or off, rather than the truncation, it makes more sense.

ter conversion, users can set `char_convert` to *off*. Each ASCII character is represented by a number between 0 and 254. With two different character sets, character number 142 might be represented as a letter with a different accent in each. With conversion *on*, SQL Server attempts to change the numbers so that the representations match. Turning off conversion causes the same character code numbers to be transmitted back and forth, which could result in differing representations between client and server. Users can set `char_convert` *on* to start conversion after they have explicitly turned it off. If users supply the `with no_error` clause, they won't be warned about characters that can't be converted. These characters will still be replaced by question marks.

char_convert charset {[with {error | no_error}]

If users set `char_convert` and supply a `charset` parameter, the conversion changes to that client character set. The `charset` parameter can be a character set ID or name from `syscharsets`.

datefirst {1 | 2 | 3 | 4 | 5 | 6 | 7}

Users may set `datefirst` to a number from 1 to 7 to indicate the day of the week that they consider to be the start of the week. A value of 1 indicates Sunday, 2 Monday, and so on. This option is provided for internationalization. In the United States, Sunday is generally considered the first day of the week, while other countries consider Monday to be first. This setting affects the results of the `datepart` and `datename` functions.

dateformat {mdy | dmy | ymd | ydm | myd | dym}

Users can set `dateformat` to specify the order in which they will enter date values for `datetime` or `smalldatetime` data types. In the possible values for the setting, the *m* indicates month, *d* indicates day, and *y* indicates year.

language {language name}

By setting the language option to the name of a language from the syslanguages table, users specify the language in which they want to see SQL Server messages.

identity_insert {[[database.[owner.]]table name} {on | off}

Normally, you cannot insert a value directly into the identity column of a table. However, sometimes this may become necessary if you have gaps to fill in due to a system failure or due to deleted records that you need to reinsert. Set identity_insert to *on* for a table to allow insertion of values into the identity column of a table. Only if you have a unique index on the identity column does SQL Server check to make sure that the value you insert is unique. You can never issue an update for an identity column. For the effect of an update, you would have to turn on identity_insert, save the row values, delete the row, and then reinsert the row with the desired identity value.

role {"sa_role" | "sso_role" | "oper_role"} {on | off}

If the sa_role, sso_role, or oper_role is associated with your SQL Server login account, the role is turned on automatically when you log in to SQL Server. You can turn off the special privileges associated with the role by setting the applicable role to *off*. You might want to do this to test what people without that role can and cannot do, or you might turn it off to protect yourself from inadvertently executing a privileged command.

Procedure Manual Suggestions

○ Managing Database Configuration

➠ Write a procedure that describes procedures for setting database options with sp_dboption.

➡ Include warnings about the possible effects of each option on database integrity, space usage, and SQL Server performance.

➡ Describe the effects of making changes in `model`, and establish a method for database administrators to coordinate any defaults that they want to set.

Performance Analysis and Tuning

"Sybase Technical Support, this is Lucky, may I help you?"

"Yeah. My name is Victor, and you better be able to help. Our queries are suddenly running too slow and we're losing a million dollars a minute. I need you to ftp us The Performance Bug Fix by noon."

"Well, I'm not sure what you mean. There's no one bug and no one solution that impacts performance across the board. I'll need to ask you for more details about the problem, such as when it started."

"I don't have time for that. Uh oh...here comes my manager, Buck,...Here, try to explain this to him!"

"This is Buck...we've been a customer of Sybase's for 43 years and I'm going to call Mark Hoffman if you don't fix your problem in the next hour."

"Buck, I appreciate your concern. I'd like you to talk to my manager to make sure we can devote our best efforts to the problem."

"Good."

The call is transferred. Escalations happen. Two hours later, Lucky calls Victor. "Hi, Victor, it's Lucky from technical support. My manager has asked me to work with you around the clock to resolve this issue. I'll need to ask you for more details about your problem, such as when it started."

"Well, we just cut over from development using a 4.2 SQL Server on a PC to production 11.0 SQL Server on a 6 processor Foobox X42 and our application stopped working...since the second machine is 20 times faster, we expected it to handle 12-way joins on tables that are 20 times bigger without choking."

The preceding scenario is fictitious, but it could be converted to a real account of any number of Sybase technical support cases by changing only a few details. Occasionally, a bug in a new SQL Server version does affect performance in certain cases. However, the resolution of the vast majority of performance problems lies in performance tuning and application redesign. In this chapter, we'll discuss the factors that most affect the performance of SQL Server. Perhaps the ideal RDBMS would have less complexity yielding fewer bugs and would tune itself. However, since that RDBMS doesn't exist yet, we'll address performance issues that exist in the real world today. As with most aspects of SQL Server, your applications will determine which types of performance tuning will help. However, we can say that System 11 provides the best opportunities to improve performance over all other releases. A complete understanding of page and index types serves as a foundation for understanding this chapter. Chapter 1 lays that foundation, so if you aren't already familiar with that material, you may want to go back and read it.

Poor performance stems from two types of bottlenecks. The first is the time it takes to use a particular resource, such as reading a page from disk. The second is waiting for a resource that is already in use, such as waiting to acquire a lock on a page. In many cases, the user running the slow process will not be able to distinguish between a processing delay and a queueing delay. For example, a user may not realize how many data pages a particular query has to read from disk or how many other users require access to a specific object at a given time. Systems Managers, however, quickly get used to the differences and may succeed in training their users to make the distinctions as well.

A Systems Manager usually has slightly more control over processing bottlenecks than over queueing bottlenecks. You probably request additional hardware or reconfigure SQL Server to take advantage of it on a routine basis. In contrast, the resolution of a queueing problem often lies in application design over which Systems Managers have limited control. Also, unfortunately, systems people are usually brought in to resolve such a problem after it has been discovered, rather than during the design phase.

Finally, with performance, as with any other focus of optimization, trade-offs apply. Remember that increasing performance may come at the cost of hardware, system analysis time, or security. For example, when setting the audit queue size, a larger audit queue improves performance, but leaves the system at greater risk because it could lose more records if the Server process terminates unexpectedly. Do your best to educate decision makers and developers about these trade-offs to avoid unpleasant surprises.

In this chapter, we use the following terms that you may find unfamiliar:

- **optimizer** The optimizer is a portion of SQL Server that tries to determine the most efficient way to process a query, given all the information at its disposal.

- **distribution page** A distribution page is a special page associated with each index that keeps track of two types of statistics about the index, which are the distribution of key values and the table's density.

- **density** The average number of duplicate keys in a table is represented by a value known as its density.

- **index selectivity**   The precision with which a table row can be found, given the key columns of the index, is called the selectivity of the index. If there are duplicate values in a key, then the index isn't as selective as a unique index.

- **composite key**   A composite key is an index key composed of more than one column.

- **covered queries and covering indexes**   Covered queries are those that involve values existing in the key of a nonclustered index, such that the query can be resolved solely by reading the index pages, thus avoiding the I/O of reading table pages. Covering indexes are those that involve a number of columns such that one or more typical queries are covered. All contents of the query (e.g., select list, qualifications, and order by columns) need to be resolvable by the index pages for the nonclustered index to be considered "covering" for a particular query.

- **short circuiting**   When evaluating an expression that can be true if only one of its components is true, such as an OR or IN clause, a program can stop evaluating the expression as soon as it finds the first true component. This method of avoiding excess evaluation is called short circuiting. For example, consider Tim talking to himself while looking through the schedule of classes. "I hate all English classes, but I have to take one upper division English class to fulfill requirements. It's all the same to me as long as I can take a 10:00 a.m. class on Tuesdays." As soon as Tim finds the first upper division English class at 10:00 a.m. on Tuesday, he can stop looking for additional matches.

SQL SERVER PERFORMANCE FACTORS

The corollary of Murphy's law that applies to SQL Server performance is, "Anything that can make SQL Server perform faster than any other RDBMS can make SQL Server perform slower than any other RDBMS." Every performance aspect that you can tune is like a dial on a stereo system. If you turn the volume all the way up, you not only lose fidelity, but you blow out your speakers. If you turn the volume all the way down, you hear neither the fidelity nor the music. Getting the audio experience you want means adjusting your expectations to fit your budget, acquiring the appropriate hardware to play your choice of music, and then finding an appropriate balance between all the aspects of the system that you can tune. Often, with especially high expectations, you need to do a lot of research to know which hardware is best; then you have to read the manuals to find out which settings you can tune. SQL Server requires a similar level of attention for optimal tuning. Since it takes in-depth knowledge of your application and hardware to do tuning, this book can't tell you exactly which values to set. You'll need to use the information presented, your experience, and your knowledge of your system to make educated guesses. Then you'll need to test your results and adjust your guesses accordingly.

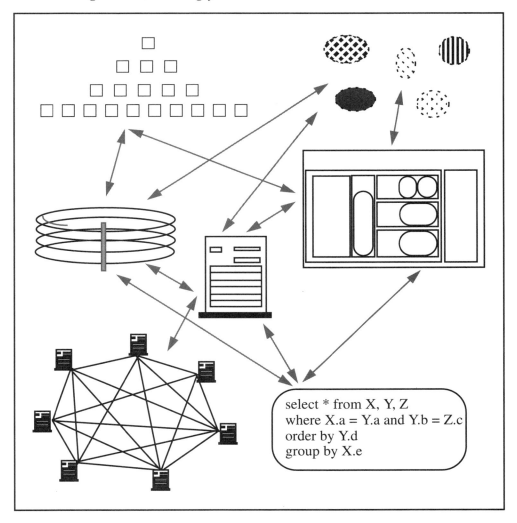

Figure 8.1 Performance depends on the interrelationships of all system elements.

279

The following list outlines the aspects of SQL Server that affect performance and that add to the complexity of identifying performance problems:

- Index usage, including number of indexes, placement on tables, type (clustered or nonclustered, bitwise), use of keys, use of fill factor, uniqueness, use of constraints, index page utilization, accuracy of distribution and density statistics, and applicability to queries

- Query formation, including selection criteria, operators, functions, expressions, and especially subqueries, aggregates, sorting, and grouping

- Procedural object usage, such as rules, triggers, and stored procedures, including such factors such as object sizes, modularity, interaction between objects, and maintenance

- Memory usage, including physical amount available, SQL Server configuration and allocation for particular tasks, and use by other applications

- Disk usage, including number of disks and controllers, I/O rate, controller cache usage, disk sizes, disk partitioning, configuration of asynchronous I/O, page utilization, transaction log placement, index placement, tempdb size, tempdb placement, consistency of allocation, access patterns, mirroring, auditing, and use by other applications

- CPU usage, including number of CPUs, operating system support and configuration, SQL Server configuration, and use by other applications

- Network usage, including network protocol, bandwidth, software, network configuration, database client and server configuration, RPC design, and usage patterns by all applications

- Database and application design, including number of tables, table design, degree of normalization, transaction design, locking behavior, use of identity features, use of cursors, number and types of applications, and table sizes

- SQL Server version, including availability of optimal processing strategies, Server and database configuration options, correction of problems, and interaction with operating system version, operating system utilities, hardware version, and network version

- SQL Server activities, such as database and transaction log dumps and loads, changes to objects, checkpoints, use of SQL Server Monitor, use of DBCC, use of auditing, and use of third-party utilities

We have discussed a number of these issues in previous chapters. Before discussing the rest, we'll first consider the process of setting performance goals and measures.

■ SETTING PERFORMANCE GOALS AND MEASURING RESULTS

There are three general goals for performance tuning:

1. To get the performance of critical operations within acceptable limits. The acceptable limits are set by business constraints, such as the amount of time your customers are willing to stay on hold or the amount of time you have to perform maintenance operations.

2. To find the perfect balance that yields the most optimum performance possible for your use of the system. This goal takes a lot longer and a lot more money to achieve than goal 1. Yet this goal remains popular since the competitive advantage of some businesses lies in the speed with which they can complete transactions.

3. To get a certain person or group of people to stop bothering you about a certain problem. Many systems professionals find themselves embarking on a performance tuning path because of this immediate need. Pursuing this goal blindly can lead to ongoing problems, since you can usually tune the response of one operation at the expense of others.

To achieve either of the first two goals, you will need to know the performance level you are starting at, and you will need to measure the performance results of each tuning operation you perform. For the third goal, you will first need to understand the problem. The analysis process described in Chapter 10 may help.

PERFORMANCE TUNING PROCESS

The general steps that people use when tuning SQL Server performance follow. For best results, document each of these steps as you undertake them. Especially take care to record *before* and *after* results from each tuning change.

- Identify your performance goals.
- Identify the key transactions or operations requiring optimum performance.
- Inventory the current hardware, software, and network resources available.
- Identify the current utilization percentage of resources during periods of highest and lowest usage.
- Determine the conditions under which the system is at minimum, average, and maximum load, for example, at a particular time of day, when a particular batch job runs, or when external conditions such as stock market activity reach their peak.
- Measure current baseline performance of the key transactions or operations under current minimum, average, and maximum load conditions.
- Set a target result for each key transaction or operation for each condition.
- Set up a way of monitoring resource utilization and transaction or operation performance with one or more monitoring tools.
- Make incremental, isolated changes to components suspected of contributing to the current performance bottleneck.
- Monitor the results for each change under each operational condition.
- Continue making changes as follows:
  - If improvement is seen after a change, continue to adjust the identified component in the same direction as the last change unless you have reached the physical limits of the system.
  - If no change in performance is seen, set the component back to starting position and try another component.
  - If decreased performance is seen, adjust the component in the opposite direction from that chosen originally unless you have reached the physical limits of the system.
- Iteratively adjust each aspect of the system until all desired results are achieved.

For many configuration changes, you will need to make the change and then shut down the system and reboot it. Ideally, you will be able to perform this tuning process on a special test system that models the production system so that you don't affect other users' work. However, if you must use the production system for tuning, perform this process for the minimum load condition first. Then, when you believe you have found the most optimal aspects to tune and the most optimal settings, you can try your results on the system under average and maximum loads. Peak periods are, of course, the last time you want to make a mistake that significantly downgrades performance. You should do the final set of modifications and testing on the production system when you are fresh and alert. The end of a long day of performance tuning and testing iterations is not the time to try implementing a big change on a mission-critical system.

The benefit of isolating and testing one system aspect at a time is that you understand exactly what makes which differences. If you subsequently change system conditions, you will be in a better position to retune the system quickly. In some cases, you will not be able to make isolated changes. For example, by increasing the SQL Server procedure cache percentage, you decrease the data cache percentage. With components that cannot be isolated, learn all you can about their interaction so that you understand the trade-off relationships within the interdependent group. You can then use this knowledge, combined with a solid understanding of the change in conditions, to guide your tuning efforts.

Pay particular attention to the physical limits of your system when tuning. In some cases, such as with memory-related parameters, SQL Server will let you set a configuration higher than the underlying hardware will support. Subsequently, the Server will not boot or will not operate correctly. You must then bring the system back to a stable state, which can take a considerable amount of time.

IDENTIFYING KEY TRANSACTIONS OR OPERATIONS

A system can attempt to do all processes for all users equally well, or it can optimize some operations at the expense of others. Usually, certain transactions or operations represent key factors in the effectiveness of an information system. You can usually enjoy visible, quick success if you identify and optimize these key activities instead of trying to optimize everything at once. The key activities may be those that

- Are most frequent
- Affect the most data
- Affect the largest number of database objects
- Require the most CPU time
- Are considered mission critical
- Provide the highest business value
- Are performed by key personnel

DETERMINING *CPU*, *MEMORY*, *AND* *NETWORK* *CAPACITY*

For a systematic, controlled approach to performance tuning, you will need to discover the physical limits of the machine and network supporting SQL Server. We will refer to the machine as the Server machine to distinguish it from client machines, file servers, or other entities. When we consider the network, we mean all parts of the network that affect SQL Server operations. Find out the following as completely as possible:

- The amount of memory on the Server machine in megabytes
- The amount of swap space configured on the Server machine
- The number of CPUs on the Server machine
- The theoretical maximum speed of the network, given the protocols and transmission media
- The number of client and server machines on the network (roughly)
- The topology of the network (i.e., the number of subnets and how they are interconnected)
- The amount of disk space on the Server machine
- The I/O rate of all disks attached to the Server machine
- The number of disk controllers and how they are attached to which disks on the Server machine

- ■ Special performance features of disk devices, such as whether they are RAID devices

- ■ The current use of all disk space attached to the Server machine, either by direct connection or distributed file systems, such as NFS.

To determine the baseline performance of your system, start by taking samples of key statistics at regular intervals throughout the day. By monitoring the system, you will find out the time or conditions under which your system experiences its maximum, minimum, and average loads. Take care to measure the system when it is handling a normal transaction mix.

There are various software tools available for gathering this information. Many of these come with the operating system, and others are available in the public domain. UNIX systems come with `vmstat`, `iostat`, and `netstat`, Open VMS comes with `MONITOR`, and Windows NT comes with `perfmon`. Each operating system has its own way of collecting and reporting statistics, so you will need to consult the vendor-supplied manuals or knowledgeable people in your organization to find out which statistics best represent your system. Find monitoring tools that will give you these resource usage statistics at the operating system level:

- ■ Disk space

- ■ I/O rates

- ■ I/O queuing behavior

- ■ Memory utilization

- ■ Memory paging and swapping activity

- ■ Network throughput

- ■ Network response time

You can either analyze the statistics manually or find a program that will help you analyze them. Many tools help you see usage patterns by graphing the measurements over time.

To monitor CPU usage, you will need to use SQL Monitor or `sp_monitor` because the OS level measures will be misleading. Since SQL Server does is own scheduling, it routinely performs a task to check if there is work to do. This checking is viewed by the operating system as the execution of an instruction and, consequently, the CPU is reported as busy. In System 11, the housekeeper function also takes advantage of idle CPUs to do work that saves transaction time later. SQL Server can actually be 90% idle when the OS thinks its 90% busy. SQL Monitor and `sp_monitor` are described in the section "SQL Server Performance-related Commands" on page 329.

For monitoring SQL Server use internally, you can use the `sp_monitor` system stored procedure or the SQL Monitor product. There are also third-party applications that help you simulate workloads so that you can gauge the effect of performance tuning without having to practice on your production server.

Keep your performance measurements in a file so that you can later compare results of system changes with your original baseline performance. Once you improve the system performance, that becomes the new baseline. Users will soon forget that it was any slower and will complain if the system happens to go back to its old behavior. Do your best to manage expectations. When you need to ask for money to buy new disks or memory in order to continue meeting expectations, you can use previous analyses and documentation to support your request. If you were once able to improve performance without capital improvements, management will always hope that you can do it again.

If there are any other applications that run on the machine besides SQL Server, you should know what they are. Also, identify the operating system functions that need to run at all times. Operating system functions and other applications vie for the same resources that SQL Server uses. You will also need to know the percentage of each Server machine and network resource that each application uses. Find out the incremental load that any resource-intensive operations have on the system.

MEASURING PERFORMANCE

To make accurate measurements, you need to keep all variables but the one you are testing equal if possible. For example, don't compare the results of a memory reallocation for an index build at midnight to an index build at 10:00 a.m. unless the processing load is comparable at those two times of day.

The performance variables you choose to measure may include any of the following:

■ **Transaction response time**   The time it takes critical transaction types to start returning results at times of minimum, average, and maximum load on the system. To measure this, you will need to identify the transactions that the business considers critical and then time them in a way that isolates them from other fluctuations of the system.

■ **Time for a given operation**   The time it takes to complete a key operation, such as making backups, rebuilding indexes, or running DBCCs.

■ **Transaction throughput**   The rate at which transactions are submitted and completed, usually measured in transactions per minute or per second for RDBMSs.

■ **Processing delay**   The time elapsed between the submission of a task and its completion.

■ **Load**   The number of simultaneous active tasks performing a known set of operations.

■ **Capacity**   The maximum load that can be accommodated with a given set of hardware and software.

BENCHMARKS

In the press, you will see benchmarks published for various software and hardware. Benchmarks are an attempt to compare similar products in similar ways in order to distinguish the performance aspects of each. For RDBMS OLTP systems, the benchmark considered most relevant at the time of this writing is the TPC-C. It attempts to simulate a typical workload and measure performance under scenarios that might be found in the real world. Previous RDBMS benchmarks, such as the TPC-A and TPC-B, primarily stressed one aspect of a system that usually doesn't represent the workload of an organization. As such, they weren't entirely useful for predicting whether the system with the highest benchmark rating would have the best performance in a real-world environment.

TPC-C uses a set of five transactions and executes them against a database defined with nine row types. The mix of applications is represented by these transactions: heavy OLTP, light OLTP, mid-weight batch, light query, and heavy query. To simulate the mix of a standard workload, these transactions are executed with a particular, stated frequency.

When TPC-C results are released, a disclosure report is published that explains the exact conditions under which the rating was attained. By examining the details, customers have a better chance of determining whether the system tested has any relevance to their goals. The disclosure report includes descriptions of configurations, response time metrics, performance on specified tests, actual queries, and the programs used.

While good performance on a TPC-C test indicates potential success for an OLTP environment, it may not predict performance in a decision support system (DSS) environment well. The Transaction Processing Performance Council is currently working on a TPC-D benchmark that will help to compare DSS performance. A TPC-E benchmark, also in progress, will be used to compare very large enterprise or mainframe systems.

The TPC benchmarks and procedures are managed by the Transaction Processing Performance Council.[1]

---

[1]More information about TPC can be found at http://www.tpc.org or by writing to The Transaction Processing Performance Council at 777 N. First Street, Suite 600, San Jose, CA, 95112, USA.

■ UNDERSTANDING THE SQL SERVER QUERY PROCESS

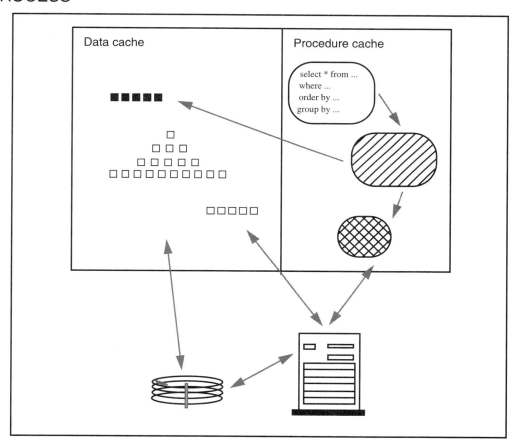

select * from ...
where ...
order by ...
group by ...

Data cache

Procedure cache

Figure 8.2 A query is parsed, resulting in a parse tree, which is resolved and written to disk in sysprocedures, then optimized to create a query plan. Upon execution, indexes and tables are read as per the query plan in order to return the desired results as quickly as possible.

To understand why tuning different aspects of SQL Server has certain effects, we will consider the work of a SQL Server query after a user has issued a typical select, insert, update, or delete operation.

PARSING

First, SQL Server has to translate human-readable SQL into steps recognized by the query processing routines. This is called parsing. Parsing results in a database-independent parse tree.

NORMALIZATION (RESOLUTION)

The next step is normalization (sometimes called resolution). In this step, names are translated to object IDs, view references are translated to base table references, and object permissions are checked. This process creates a database-dependent structure called a query tree. If a stored procedure is being defined, the query tree is stored in binary form in the `sysprocedures` table.

COMPILATION AND OPTIMIZATION

Next comes compilation and optimization. In this step, SQL Server creates a query plan. The optimizer looks at the query and determines the most efficient way to find and return the desired results. It needs to know which indexes to try and which order to check for matches in the case of joins. The number of I/Os, which is the principal component in query performance, will differ for each strategy depending on the indexes on the tables and whether either of the tables will fit into data cache. The optimizer looks at both physical I/O, which is the access of a physical page on disk, and logical I/O, which is the access of a page in memory.

In general, the optimizer's strategy is to minimize the number of logical page accesses altogether and to minimize physical I/Os by making use of data cache. For each search condition, join clause, and OR clause in the query, the optimizer chooses the cheapest index and evaluates it against no index at all. The optimizer evaluates its options in the following steps:

- **Look for search arguments (SARGs)** A SARG is an expression in the qualifications that can be resolved using an index in the form of *column operator constant*, such as *class_id = 200*. It cannot involve a function or an OR clause. In addition, the operator cannot be !=. It can be =, >, <, >=, or <=.

■ **Find qualifications with ORs** Resolving an OR query requires finding matches after two sets of comparisons and then eliminating any duplicate results. Because there are two sets of comparisons, two useful indexes may be used if both are selective enough.

■ **Match indexes to search arguments** The optimizer looks for indexes that match the search clauses. Useful indexes are those in which at least the first key column of the index has the information necessary to serve a SARG. The more consecutive columns in the index that match the SARGs, the more useful the index is.

■ **Rank useful indexes** The optimizer ranks indexes and compares their costs to a table scan, taking into account the number of rows likely to satisfy the clause and the number of pages that would need to be accessed to find the qualifying rows. Index selectivity is evaluated to estimate the number of rows that will satisfy the query. To estimate selectivity, the optimizer uses special index statistics stored on the distribution page for the index, providing that the distribution page exists. If statistics are not available, the optimizer guesses about the selectivity using magic numbers. For equality comparisons, the magic number is 10%. For closed interval comparisons, 25% is used. For inequality or open interval comparisons, 33% is used. Equality on a unique index is an exception and is always considered the most selective since it identifies a single row. The more rows that qualify, the less selective the index is considered to be. If the datatype in the SARG does not match the datatype of a key column in an index, or if the value of the SARG is not known at compile time, the distribution statistics cannot be used, and the fixed percentage is used instead. Several methods are used to estimate the number of logical I/Os depending on the SARG and the type of index:

- For a table scan, the optimizer uses information in the internal OAM page to estimate the number of data pages in the table.

- For a clustered, nonunique index, the optimizer adds the number of the levels in the index to the number of data pages. It calculates logical I/Os by dividing the number of qualifying rows by the number of rows per data page.

- For a nonclustered, nonunique index that does not cover the query, the optimizer adds the number of levels in the index plus the number of leaf pages plus the number of qualifying rows. It assumes that each row is on a separate page, since that is the worst-case scenario for nonclustered indexes.

- For a unique index where the query is searching for equality on all parts of the key, the logical I/O count is 1 plus the number of index levels.

- For a covering nonclustered index, the logical I/Os are calculated as if the index were clustered. That is, it doesn't add in the number of qualifying rows.

■ **Find indexes for join clauses** A join clause has the form *column operator column* and involves two tables. For example, *class_names.class_id = class_requirements.class_id*. Given two tables X and Y, join selectivity estimates how many rows from Table X will join with a single row from Table Y. If there is no distribution page for the index, selectivity is considered to be 1 divided by the number of rows in the smaller table. If statistics are available, the join selectivity is based on the density value stored on the distribution page, which represents the average percentage of duplicate rows in the table. An index with a large number of duplicates has low selectivity.

■ **Evaluate join order** When selecting the join order, the best index for the join clauses is evaluated. Permutations of table orders and join indexes are compared based on I/O and CPU cost, and the best plan is chosen. Each clause has a best index, and only one index will be used per table reference. The performance is based on how many times the query on the innermost table will be done. The processing order is determined by the restrictions on the rows that can be applied to each table from the WHERE clause. Choices are made using the index rankings calculated above. When evaluating the costs of join order, the optimizer also checks if the tables will fit in cache. If so, physical I/O is not included in the cost of the plan. Otherwise, physical I/O, estimated at 18 milliseconds per I/O, is added to logical I/O, estimated at 2 milliseconds per I/O.

■ **Evaluate reformatting** A strategy known as *reformatting* is used when there are no indexes or no useful indexes. This means that SQL Server will create a worktable, sort it, and create an index on it at run time. If there is an ORDER BY and no index, the optimizer will create a worktable. If there is an ORDER BY and a clause that specifies a nonclustered index, the reformatting strategy will be avoided. The existence of a GROUP BY will cause a worktable to be created whether there is an index or not. However, if a clustered index is specified in the WHERE clause of a query with a GROUP BY, the index will be used to help create the worktable, even if the index isn't particularly selective.

In SQL Server 10.1 and later, the optimizer considers the cost of sorting when evaluating query plans, which should result in fewer sorts and better performance for ORDER BY queries. The indexes of tables lead a query to return data that are sorted by the order of the indexes. In some cases, a particular choice of indexes for a query containing an ORDER BY clause could return a result set that is already in order, thereby eliminating the need for a sort. Starting in version 10.1, the optimizer will take this possibility into account when evaluating query plans. It will now calculate an estimated sort cost when selecting a query plan. In addition to counting the index density and selectivity for counting logical page I/O, the optimizer will determine if a particular index selection avoids a sort.

Once it figures out what to do in what order, the optimizer creates a command tree known as a query plan. At this point, the query is compiled.

To see how the optimizer processes a query and calculates estimates, you can use the commands set showplan on, set statistics i/o on, and set statistics time on. You may also find the trace flags 302 and 310 useful. These are all described at the end of this chapter.

EXECUTION

Finally, we reach the execution stage. Once a compiled plan exists, it can be scheduled and run. The query is executed following the query plan. Execution may involve any of the following:

■ **Index search**   Looking up the starting location of an index in sysindexes and then finding the relevant data pages by following the index pointers associated with the key values specified in the query

■ **Table scan**   Looking up the disk location of the starting or ending point of a table and then following page pointers until the target values are found

■ **Data cache search**   Searching the data cache for any table and index pages that the Server might be able to find in memory and thereby avoid reading from disk

■ **Procedure cache search**   Searching the procedure cache for any stored procedures, triggers, or views related to the query that we may be able to avoid reading from disk

■ **Disk I/O**   Reading from disk any pages not found in cache

■ **Data retrieval from page**   Having found a target page, locating and reading the desired row or rows from the page

■ **Data page locking**   Depending on the isolation level of the query, acquiring locks from a lock pool and recording the use of these locks in a lock chain in order to prevent other processes from specific types of access to the table pages

■ **Index page locking**   If updating a page, acquiring a resource lock on index pages for adding or removing index rows or for splitting or combining index pages

■ **Code locking** Depending on the nature of the query, acquiring what SQL Server calls a spinlock to prevent other processes from accessing a particular part of the execution code that must always be run serially, rather than in parallel with other processes

■ **Logging** Recording any intended changes of table pages, index pages, extents, or allocation maps to the transaction log

■ **Page allocation or deallocation** Allocating or deallocating pages for use by a table or index. This process involves modifying global and object allocation maps and logging such changes. This may also involve the creation or destruction of extents and allocation maps.

■ **Writing table changes** Making all requested changes on the relevant table pages and rewriting index pages as necessary to keep them in sync with the data

■ **Integrity checking** Checking whether intended modifications fall within the boundaries set by rules, column definitions, index specifications, and integrity constraints, and rejecting the update if the modifications or access requested fall outside the boundaries protected

■ **Trigger firing** Executing trigger actions associated with tables being accessed, which may further involve any of the actions described in this list

■ **Default substitution** Supplying any defaults necessary on inserts or modifications to tables containing columns with specified defaults

■ **Auditing** Writing an audit record to the audit queue and ultimately to the `sysaudits` table in the `sybsecurity` database if auditing has been enabled for the activity, object, or user associated with the query

Now that we've looked at the general query process, we can turn to specific actions that you can take to tune SQL Server performance.

■ OPTIMIZING INDEXES

An index attempts to tell the SQL Server optimizer the most efficient way to get to a particular data item depending on the value of that data item. The clues that the index gives are the data in the key columns of the index, the datatypes in the key columns, whether the index is unique, whether the index allows NULLs, the number of duplicate values in the key, and whether the index is clustered or nonclustered.

294

Adding the right types of indexes in the right places and removing suboptimal indexes from the wrong places usually go a long way toward optimizing a poorly performing SQL Server application. In this section, we'll explore the aspects of SQL Server indexes that most affect performance.

UPDATE STATISTICS

Each index has a distribution page that maintains statistics about the index. The optimizer uses this page to determine whether the index is useful for a particular query. The statistics are calculated when the index is created on a table containing data and when the UPDATE STATISTICS command is run on the table or index. The statistics are not dynamically recalculated. This means that, as the table data change, the statistics can get out of date, leading the optimizer to pursue suboptimal plans. Until UPDATE STATISTICS is run, a table does not have a statistics page if the index was built when the table was empty or if the table was truncated. If an index has no statistics page, the optimizer will not plan on using that index at all, and if faced with searching that table, it will resort to a table scan. This should be avoided, of course, both because of the inefficiency of the scan, but also because all the effort that goes into maintaining the useless index during index, deletes, and updates never pays off.

Run update statistics routinely if your tables undergo frequent change. The statistics attempt to characterize the table in two ways. The first way is by storing data distribution information. The second is by storing an average index density, described at the beginning of this chapter.

The distribution information is like a bar chart, but instead of the relative height of each bar being different and the widths the same, in the distribution statistics the height is the same and the widths are different. In practice, the Server creates distribution statistics as follows. First, the available space on the page for distribution statistics is divided by the number of bytes in the leading column of the index. This gives us the number of storage cells for distribution information. Then the number of rows in the table is divided by the number of cells to give us the number of rows per cell, which we'll call n. The distribution cells are populated with the value of the leading index column every n rows. For example, let's say that the optimizer is evaluating a query that requests rows for years 1929 to 1959, and there is an index on a year column of the table. The optimizer can read the distribution page and find out approximately how many rows there are between 1929 and 1959. It looks for the first cell that contains 1929 and the last cell that contains 1959, adds up the intervening number of cells, and then multiplies that by the number of rows per cell. This gives the optimizer an estimate of the number of rows of the table it will need to read if it uses that index.

As you can see, missing or outdated statistics can make the optimizer very inaccurate. With no distribution page to work with, the optimizer uses "magic numbers" to estimate qualified row counts, and it uses 1 divided by the number of rows of the smaller table to estimate join selectivity.

To look for indexes that have no statistics pages, write a query that looks for rows in `sysindexes` with a value of 0 in the *distribution* column and a value between 1 and 250 in the *indid* column. If a distribution page has been created, its logical page number is stored in the *distribution* column of *sysindexes* in the row representing the index. You can use the `object_name` function to convert object IDs from *sysindexes* into index names, or you can do a join with *sysobjects.id* to get the corresponding value of *sysobjects.name*.

Run `sp_recompile` on a table after running update statistics to mark procedures as requiring recompilation and therefore reoptimization.

USING UNIQUE INDEXES

When you have a unique index on a table, this means each row is uniquely identified in the table by the keys of the index. A query specifying a value used as the first key column of a unique index will find the desired rows with a minimal number of I/Os. In contrast, if there are a lot of duplicate values in the columns used for an index key, then a query may need to access several pages of a table before finding the desired row or rows. In this case, SQL Server must also use additional aspects of the query to determine which of the rows containing duplicates to return. If you know that all the values of an index key will be unique, be sure to define the index as unique so that the optimizer knows it can take advantage of the high selectivity.

SELECTING INDEX KEYS

Try to select key columns that use short datatypes so that you can pack as many index keys and pointers into an index page as possible. By doing so, you keep the number of index pages a query must traverse to a minimum. Furthermore, use integers as key values whenever you can, since they provide faster access than any other datatype.[2] In general, numeric types will be more efficient than character string types. Small key values also allow the distribution page to track more index steps, which helps the optimizer choose the best access path more reliably.

An index is useful when the query specifies a search argument that matches the first column of the index. The distribution statistics on the distribution page for each index tell the optimizer about the first columns of a composite index. Try to make the first columns of the index the most selective, and try to get users and applications to use those columns as a search argument in their queries.

USING CLUSTERED INDEXES

Clustered indexes offer more advantages than nonclustered indexes. The lowest level of the clustered index—the leaf level—is the table pages themselves, rather than an index layer that points to the table pages, as in a clustered index. Because the key values of the leaf level are the data rows, the data rows are in

---

[2]Someone might claim that datetime is just as fast since it's based on an integer, but then you incur processing when that datatype is interpreted into date format. Also, datetime may not provide a unique value.

order physically. Queries that involve range checking (BETWEEN, less than, greater than, etc.) or those that use GROUP BY or ORDER BY can take great advantage of the preordered data, sometimes avoiding the cost of a sort. Also, for these queries and for joins, several rows can be accessed from one logical I/O. In contrast, queries using a nonclustered index usually incur at least one I/O per row rather than one per page at the leaf level. In addition, given the same keys and the same table size, queries using a clustered index require at least one less I/O than a nonclustered index because there is one less level of pages in the index.

You do not need to create the clustered index on the primary key of a table. In fact, in many cases this wastes the value of the index since the primary key column is used less frequently in search clauses than other columns. To optimize performance in a database, make sure every table has a clustered index on the columns that queries most often reference.

USING COVERING INDEXES

As described at the start of this chapter, a nonclustered index with a large number of key columns may become a covering index for queries that reference those columns, and this will improve the performance of those queries. This saves at least the I/O for traversing an additional page chain and may save several more if the index values are in the order needed by a query requesting several rows. In this case, the behavior is like a clustered index in that there's only one I/O needed per page, rather than one per row at the leaf level. If a large number of queries or significant queries could take advantage of covering, it may be worthwhile to create the additional indexes. Also, since index pages are more likely to stay in cache (depending on the setting of the `index trips` configuration variable), covered queries will encounter less physical I/O.

However, if the potentially covered queries are not common or are not considered critical, the addition of a covering index may make performance worse. With covering indexes, you tend to have keys consisting of several columns, which we refer to as "wide" keys. Consequently, it takes several bytes to store each key and fewer key values can fit on one index page. Therefore, the index requires more index pages to represent all the key values, and the index must become deeper (i.e., have more levels). The addition of an index level means that every query that is not covered has to incur the cost of at least one more I/O to traverse the index. Also, the addition of each index adds to the total disk space used by indexes and subtracts from the capacity you have for tables and the transaction log. Otherwise unneeded indexes also make updates slower for the affected table, since the addition, modification, or deletion of a table row will require more corresponding index changes at the same time. Also keep in mind that a wide key means that the index is larger and so, by default, more pages end up in data cache when you reference the index pages. If the index is not very useful to other queries, this uses data cache inefficiently, and extra overhead must be incurred to clear it out. In SQL Server 11, you can mitigate this effect by using the MRU buffer replacement strategy (See "Query Hints," later.) and by using named caches (See Chapter 4).

DETERMINING THE OPTIMAL NUMBER OF INDEXES

The best columns for an index are those that match the following criteria for common and critical queries:

- Those likely to be used in WHERE clauses
- Those likely to be used for joins
- Those used for aggregates
- Those used in GROUP BY clauses
- Those used in ORDER BY clauses
- Those needed to enforce uniqueness
- Those that will cover queries
- Those that will help to distribute data across the physical media in a way that improves I/O performance

Since the columns that users need vary, developers often create several indexes to suit as many types of queries as possible. We've already discussed one disadvantage of this approach.

Another downside is that the optimizer ends up with too many permutations and combinations of indexes and tables to consider. With too many options, the optimizer figures that it will spend more time figuring out what to do than just doing it. In this case, it may never get around to analyzing the best index. The forceindex and forceplan features, documented in System 11 but available in undocumented form earlier, can be used to give the optimizer hints in this situation. These features are described in the section "SQL Server Performance-related Commands" on page 329.

Yet another ill effect of too many indexes is that it increases the amount of time needed to run DBCC CHECKDB, CHECKTABLE, and CHECKINDEX commands. These commands are used to make sure that indexes are not corrupt. To do this, these DBCC commands check each index page. The more indexes you have, the longer it takes to run DBCCs.

BITWISE INDEXES

So far, the performance tuning we have been discussing concerns predictable queries. However, applications such as DSSs need to respond to unpredictable queries on very large sets of data. In this case, you may find that the new Sybase IQ product improves your performance dramatically. Contact Sybase for more detailed information about this product.

■ OPTIMIZING QUERIES

Most database activities involve accessing table or index pages for user or system objects. The faster SQL Server can access pages, the better it performs. Accessing a page in memory takes a fraction of the time that it takes to read it from disk.[3] A great deal of performance tuning effort goes into eliminating page accesses altogether or getting pages from memory instead of disk. Because of the strategies the SQL Server optimizer chooses, some queries

---

[3]SQL Server assumes that the fraction is approximately 1/9. The relative performance on your hardware may be different.

end up using more I/O than necessary or going to disk instead of going to memory. This section describes a few of the finer points of query design that make a significant difference for large tables and for very complex queries.

LIKE

When using the LIKE predicate, SQL Server can't make use of the indexes and distribution pages if you begin with a wild card search character such as % or _. For example, avoid

```
> select * from profs where prof_name like "%son"
```
and prefer the form
```
> select * from profs where prof_name like "s%"
```

To understand why this is, think about how you would search the index. When you start with a %, you need to look for the ends of keys, which aren't stored in any order at all. This means that you would have to read all key pages in the lowest level of a non-clustered index or you would just go to the data pages and do a table scan for a clustered index. To do this effectively, you would essentially need a reverse index.[4]

RELATIONAL OPERATORS AND BETWEEN

Because the B-tree traversal methods are not applicable to the not equals (!=) comparison, these cannot be optimized for index selection. Again, to understand this behavior, think about which pointers you follow in the index. Similar to the case of a leading wildcard operator, you would need to scan the entire leaf level of the index to find applicable values.

For the remaining relational operators, avoid extra I/Os by using those that make use of equal to, such as >=, <=, or =. The others, > and <, require that you read pages that you may never use. For example, avoid queries like

---

[4]You could conceivably create your own by indexing a derived column created with the `reverse` function, but it might not be worth the effort to keep in sync. You would also need the front end to be intelligent enough to reverse queries that start with %.

```
> select * from profs where yrs_teaching > 2
```

and prefer queries like

```
> select * from profs where yrs_teaching >= 3
```

In the first example, you end up reading all index pages where the value equals 2 just to find where the value of 3 starts. In the second example, you start directly at the right place.

A BETWEEN is the same as a combination of a >= and a <= comparison. That is, the following two queries are the same internally:

```
> select * from profs
> where yrs_teaching between 1 and 5
> select * from profs
> where yrs_teaching >= 1 and yrs_teaching <=5
```

Note, however, that SQL standard requires that the following return no result rows:

```
> select * from profs
> where yrs_teaching between 5 and 1
```

So that form does not have the same results as

```
> select * from profs
> where yrs_teaching <= 5 and yrs_teaching >=1
```

NOT EXISTS AND NOT IN

Similarly to !=, we also want to avoid the negative forms of existence queries (NOT EXISTS and NOT IN). Also avoid COUNT. Try to use EXISTS if possible. The latter approach proves faster since the query knows to stop looking as soon as it finds the first matching row. Some programmers try to use COUNT and have the process pursue an alternate path of logic if the total is greater than 0. However, this requires the most I/O of all, which is not necessary unless you need the count for something else.

IN AND OR

To process an IN or OR statement, SQL Server pursues one of two strategies. It can use a table scan and compare each row to all selection criteria, or it can use indexes to find qualifying rows, put them into a worktable, sort the table to remove duplicates, and then use worktable to find and get each row from real table. The latter is called a dynamic index in `showplan` output. To use the worktable strategy, there must be a highly selective index on each column that defines the search criteria. Otherwise, a table scan is used.

In System 11 subqueries, `IN` and `OR` can be short-circuited, resulting in better response time. In some cases, you can use a UNION instead, which also results in better performance.

SUBQUERIES

Subqueries are those that appear as a separate select statement whose results are used to qualify the results of the main query. Some subqueries can be rewritten (flattened) as joins, and some cannot. For example,

```
> select * from profs where prof_name in
> (select class_prof from class_names)
```

can be flattened to

```
> select * from profs p, class_names c
> where p.prof_name = c.class_prof
```

However, the following subquery cannot:

```
> select * from profs where yrs_teaching >=
> (select sum(yrs_teaching) from profs where
> weird >= 5)
```

In version 11, the portion of the SQL Server that generates subquery plans has been rewritten for two reasons. In earlier releases, subqueries that could not be flattened were sometimes optimized poorly. Also, in certain cases of NULLs and duplicate values, they produced results that were defined as incorrect in the ANSI SQL Standard.

Response time is improved for almost all subqueries that cannot be flattened to joins. In particular, `NOT IN`, `NOT EXISTS`, `ALL`, and subqueries in `OR` clauses are handled much more efficiently.

In versions prior to System 11, SQL Server processed subqueries inside-out, meaning that the results of the subquery were determined before evaluating the main query. The nested loop strategy means that the subquery expression is evaluated once for every outer row at most. In some cases, short circuiting prevents a process from ever needing to evaluate the subquery. A special cache stores results of previous executions of the subquery. The internal JOIN and GROUP BY previously used in the worktables are also no longer necessary. Also, a join for a subquery in an OR clause is no longer unoptimizable. Subqueries using the DISTINCT keyword are also more efficient since a sort step is no longer needed. Instead, a special aggregate is used to stop evaluation after a duplicate value is encountered for a result. Overall, the nested loop strategy improves response time because the process doesn't have to wait while the subquery is materialized.

If you are using System 10 or an earlier version, you can find various whitepapers and presentations discussing ways to get around the shortcomings of the optimizer's handling of subqueries. Since System 11's performance is better in so many ways, we won't dwell here on these tricks, since you might as well put your energy into upgrading to System 11. You will get much more performance benefit per hour spent.

As a side effect of rewriting the subquery routines, views containing aggregates work more efficiently. Also, the SQL Server 11 subquery changes made it easier to correct certain behaviors considered incorrect in the SQL Standard. A correlation column is a column specified in the FROM clause of the outer query, which is also referenced in the subquery. The table containing the correlation column is known as the correlation variable. Several restrictions on subqueries, including those related to correlation variables, are now removed. In version 11 of SQL Server, you can reference a correlated variable in any part of the subquery, including expressions and comparisons. You can also use DISTINCT in a subquery that also has a GROUP BY clause.

Two new subquery restrictions have been added. In SQL Server 11, you may have no more than 16 subqueries on the single side of a union, and you may not use subqueries in updatable cursors.

The SQL Server 11 upgrade process does not automatically upgrade procedures to use the new processing algorithm. You will need to drop and re-create compiled objects to use this feature. The new `sp_procqmode` procedure allows you to see the subquery processing mode for an object:

```
sp_procqmode [ object_name [, detail]]
```

Used with only the *object_name* parameter, `sp_procqmode` will tell you the type of the object and whether it was compiled with pre-System 11 subquery behavior, or with the new behavior. If you supply the parameter `detail,` the output also shows you whether the object has subqueries and whether text used to parse the object is in `syscomments`. If you want to drop and re-create the object to use the new System 11 behavior and if you don't have the original scripts, you may be able to use the text in `syscomments` to rebuild it. However, it is possible for system administrators to remove rows from `syscomments`, so the existence of text in `syscomments` does not guarantee success. Saving scripts provides the best recoverability, so you should plan for doing so in the future if it is within your scope of control.

In SQL Server 10, a temporary command, `set dup_in_subquery`, was added to give developers time to change programs that relied on a SQL Server subquery behavior considered incorrect by the SQL standard. This command is no longer available in version 11.0 of the Server.

Another incorrect behavior has been fixed for subqueries as well. If the correlated expression subquery in the SET clause of an UPDATE returns no matching rows, NULL is returned and an error is raised. In prior releases, the subquery returned 0, which could lead to inserting values of 0. Now procedures can recognize the attempt to update with a NULL value.

DATATYPE MISMATCHES

One of the most subtle problems with queries is the attempt to compare columns with different datatypes in a WHERE clause.

For example, float and integer are different datatypes. In this query, where *gpa* is defined as a float column with a nonunique index, the index is not used:

```
> select name, gpa from students where gpa = 4
```

That's because the search is for a number interpreted as an integer. For this query to take advantage of the index, use

```
> select name, gpa from students where gpa = 4.0
```

This problem becomes especially apparent with stored procedure parameters, where the caller of the procedure may not have any idea of the indexes on an underlying table. The following similar datatypes are incompatible for the purposes of WHERE clause comparisons:

- float and integer
- char and varchar
- binary and varbinary

The difference between the variable-length types is the presence of a NULL at the end. Note, however, that the comparison of an integer field disallowing nulls and one allowing nulls can be optimized.

When there is a datatype mismatch, the datatype lower in the type hierarchy is converted to the higher type. This conversion can be especially costly for joins. Performance may improve if you force conversion of the other type by using the convert function in the WHERE clause. Because of implicit conversion, comparing a numeric against a constant larger than the definition of the column can create a problem as well. To see the type hierarchy, do a SELECT from the systypes table.

You may find that you can avoid this problem by using user-defined datatypes for columns frequently used in WHERE clauses and join clauses. Then, encourage developers to write applications that use those datatypes in search arguments.

JOINS

By default, joins of more than four tables are evaluated four tables at a time. In SQL Server 11, you can change this to any number between 1 and 8 using the `set table count` option. For each set of tables, the best outer table is found and saved, and the remaining combinations are evaluated to determine the next outermost table until done. Sometimes you can give the optimizer choices it wouldn't otherwise consider by adding redundant predicates. For example, these two queries are the same, but the latter query provides more flexibility:

```
> select * from A where a = b and b = c
> select * from A where a = b and b = c and a = c
```

In the first query, the optimizer doesn't consider joining a to c, leaving out several possible join orders.

Joins are slower and more CPU intensive with large character strings. Also, avoid joins with columns containing any NULL values.

FUNCTIONS AND LOCAL VARIABLES

Avoid using functions in a search argument. Since the value of the function will not be known until run time, the optimizer can't use the distribution statistics to evaluate costs. The same is true for local variables. In these cases, the optimizer may try to guess the selectivity. For example, if the query involves an equality comparison, the optimizer will use the density statistic. Otherwise, magic numbers (gross estimates) are used.

EXPRESSIONS

The optimizer also can't use the distribution statistics when there is an algebraic expression in the WHERE clause. For example, avoid the following:

```
> select prof_name from profs
> where yrs_teaching * .2 > 4
```

You could rearrange this to

```
> select prof_name from profs
> where yrs_teaching > 4/2
```

which yields a better plan. It can be optimized, given sufficient indexes, because the part of the expression to the left of the relational operator is a column that can match an index. The part of the expression to the right is a constant. However, it still takes time to perform the calculation. Issue the query as follows for optimum results:

```
> select prof_name from profs
> where yrs_teaching > 2
```

AGGREGATES

When calculating aggregates on a column, include a search clause even if it specifies all of the rows. For example,

```
> select avg(income) from students where gpa >= .1
```

uses the index on *gpa*, while this query uses no index because it has to scan the table anyway:

```
> select avg(income) from students
```

The `min` and `max` aggregates are specially optimized exceptions. Evaluation of these can stop as soon as the first qualifying row is found if the aggregate is on the first column of an index, if there is no other aggregate or GROUP BY in the query, and, in the case of MAX, if there is no WHERE clause.

QUERY HINTS

The SQL Server 11.0 optimizer has been modified to take advantage of the performance benefits expected to accompany named caches and large I/Os. In addition, you can now "help" the optimizer by giving it documented and supported hints. Hints include

■ **Prefetch** Prefetching means that if a single page is requested SQL Server will also fetch additional pages that it anticipates needing to finish processing the query. In SQL Server 11.0, the optimizer considers prefetching automatically for certain queries, but this behavior is modifiable by the user. The user can also specify the number of pages the Server should prefetch while executing the query.

■ **Buffer replacement strategy**   The Server's buffer manager (logical memory manager) attempts to determine the most optimal pages to store in cache in order to maximize cache hit rate. In versions before 11.0, the LRU buffer replacement strategy is always used to this end. The LRU strategy replaces the least recently used pages when new buffers are needed. The use-and-discard strategy, or MRU replacement strategy, means that the most recently read pages will be replaced immediately after they have been used.

■ **Join order**   A significant performance factor in queries with joins is the order in which tables are scanned to find matches between corresponding rows. By default, the optimizer uses a cost estimating method to determine the optimum join order. With the `set forceplan on` feature, you can specify exactly which join order to use. After you execute the `set forceplan on` command, SQL Server uses the order of the tables in the FROM clause of any subsequent query as the join order. Use `set forceplan off` to tell the optimizer to resume the use of normal costing methods. This `set` option existed in previous versions, but was unsupported.

■ **Size of table groups in join evaluations**   By default, the optimizer considers tables in sets of four when permuting join orders and evaluating costs. In SQL Server 11, you can use a session-level option to set the number of groups. With the new `set table count` option, you tell the SQL Server optimizer to consider anywhere from 1 to 8 tables at once. Setting this value higher than 4 may improve throughput, but will delay response time.

■ **Indexes to use**   Normally, the optimizer uses various methods to determine the best indexes to use for processing a query. With new SELECT syntax, you can tell the optimizer which index to use for each table in a FROM clause. The new functionality replaces the unsupported `forceindex` feature from previous releases.

The new hint functionality is supported by various modifications to default behavior and by new commands and options you can use to enforce a particular strategy. For prefetch, the 11.0 optimizer recognizes if a prefetch strategy will benefit the query and builds such a plan, providing that several conditions are met. First, the optimizer assumes that the data pages of a clustered index and the leaf pages of a nonclustered index can be prefetched. If the optimizer determines that a query plan may involve a sequential scan of such pages and buffer pools of larger than 2 KB I/O are available, it will consider a prefetch strategy. Next, each index and table will have a status bit in sysindexes that indicates whether it should be used for the prefetch and MRU strategies when the optimizer deems them worthwhile. By default, the MRU strategy is enabled for table scans and index scans. You can turn the status values off and on by using the new `sp_cachestrategy` procedure, which has this syntax:

```
sp_cachestrategy [owner.]tablename[.index_name]
        [, { prefetch | mru } [, { "off" | "on" } ]]
```

If you use `sp_cachestrategy` with only a database and object name specified, you will get a report of the current settings for the object. To specify the `text` datatype pages only for a strategy, use the name of the table with the text column prefixed with the letter *t* as the *index_name*.

For objects with the prefetch status bit set to *on*, you can also use the command `set prefetch [off | on]` to disable or enable prefetch for a session. This allows different users to use different prefetch strategies for the same object. For example, an OLTP user may decide that prefetch is unnecessary, while a DSS user would find it highly desirable. With prefetch and appropriate I/O memory pools enabled, you can perform I/Os that read up to eight data pages at a time.

Modifications to the SELECT, UPDATE, and DELETE statements allow you to tell the optimizer how to process a query at execution time. For example, the relevant subset of the new SELECT syntax follows:

```
SELECT ...
[FROM table_name
    [(indid | INDEX index_name [PREFETCH size]
    [LRU | MRU])
    [, table_name...]
[WHERE ...]
```

The corresponding portions of UPDATE and DELETE that specify query strategy have the same syntax. Use the INDEX keyword and *index_name* parameter to make index selection explicit for each table. The old `forceindex` method of using only the *indid* will be supported at first to enable the transition to the new method. It will eventually become obsolete. Use the table name for the *index_name* parameter if you want to specify a table scan. The *size* for `prefetch` should be specified in kilobytes, and it should be a size that matches an I/O pool in the object's cache. The use of a prefetch size of 2 KB tells the Server not to use prefetch and overrides behavior specified by the `set prefetch` command.

There are also a few miscellaneous changes that improve query behavior.

■ The optimizer now uses double-precision datatypes when considering cost calculations since the integer arithmetic in previous releases sometimes resulted in datatype overflows.

■ A new session-level command, `set statistics subquerycache on`, outputs the number of cache hits and misses and the number of rows in the subquery cache for each subquery during execution. Like the other `set statistics` commands, this option is designed to help you diagnose query performance.

For those of you upgrading applications from older releases, note that the optimizer will start to make new choices about whether to keep pages in cache. For example, if a query requires a scan of a large table, the optimizer may decide automatically to use the MRU replacement strategy. If the inner table of a join is small, the optimizer will probably use the LRU replacement strategy for the table. As usual, we hope the optimizer will do the right thing. However, when preparing for your upgrade, consider these changes. If your applications start behaving differently than you expect, try different combinations of the prefetch, MRU, join, and index selection optimizer hints to see if they improve the situation.

■ OPTIMIZING STORED PROCEDURES

A way to optimize a system for compute-intensive operations is to minimize the use of ad hoc queries. Create stored procedures to do the most commonly requested tasks. Since procedures are partially processed ahead of time, they take less time to execute. They also improve productivity for users unfamiliar with SQL. This approach may also reduce support calls that might otherwise result from poorly written queries. Stored procedures, however, can also have poor performance if not designed to avoid some inherent limitations.

MULTIPLE COPIES IN CACHE

Stored procedures, when created, go through the same states as queries—parsing, resolution, and compilation—but the intermediate forms are stored on disk. The SQL statements are stored in `syscomments` and can be accessed subsequently with `sp_helptext`. The parsed and resolved form is stored in `sysprocedures`. When a new stored procedure is run for the first time, the query tree is read from `sysprocedures` and compiled to create a query plan. The query plan is the optimized data access path that will be used to execute the procedure. A query plan resides only in procedure cache memory.

SQL Server determines the optimal data access path based on

- The SQL stored in the query tree

- Statistics for each table and index referenced in the procedure

- The values of any parameters passed to the procedure on the first execution

After the process that first executed the procedure finishes, the compiled query plan stays in memory. Any other process can reuse a query plan in cache as long as no other process is currently using it. If a process wants to execute a procedure, but the existing query plan is in use, then a new copy of the query plan is created and loaded into procedure cache.

Note that the optimization only takes into account the initial conditions under which the plan was compiled. If the composition of the table changes dramatically such that the statistics are no longer valid, the query plan may become suboptimal. Also, if the procedure is executed with different parameters, and these parameters are used in a WHERE clause, the original optimization may not serve the current execution well.

Users have no control over which version of an existing query plan they will get for a given execution. Two different users might get different execution times for the same procedure, given the same data and parameters. To avoid this problem, you can recompile the procedure as described at the end of the next section.

RERESOLUTION AND RECOMPILATION

If you change an object referred to by a stored procedure, such as dropping and re-creating an underlying table, the procedure needs to be reresolved and recompiled. As you may recall, a normalized query only knows about an object by its object ID, and the ID changes when you drop and re-create the object. The reresolution and recompilation process happens automatically, but it delays execution. Reresolution also causes the size of the procedure to grow a bit. This is because, for various reasons, the new ID of the changed object is added to the resolved form of the procedure, rather than replacing the old ID. Other accommodations in the query tree must also be made. Before System 10, the growth of the query tree caused problems because it would exceed the 64-KB limit for these trees and would use up more procedure cache space. In subsequent releases, you can boot SQL Server with trace flag 241 to enable an automatic compression process that reclaims unused space in resolved procedures. The use of this trace flag can affect performance though, since the compression will take additional time when generating a query plan.

Automatic reresolution and recompilation can be triggered by any of the following activities:

- Loading the database containing the procedure from a dump (all executable objects are reresolved after LOAD DATABASE)

- Dropping, creating, or altering a table referenced by the procedure

- Dropping and re-creating the database containing a table referenced by the procedure

- Binding or unbinding a rule to a table referenced by the procedure

- Binding or unbinding a default to a table referenced by the procedure

- Dropping and re-creating (or just dropping) an index referenced by the procedure

The addition of a new index to a table referenced by a procedure will have no effect on the versions of the procedure already in memory. Running UPDATE STATISTICS will not affect existing query plans either. To realize the benefits of adding an index, you can force recompilation of related procedures. There are several ways to force recompilation of a stored procedure:

- To ensure that you always get your own plan, you can use the `with recompile` option of the `exec` command.

- To ensure that all users get their own plans with each execution, you can use the `with recompile` option of the `create procedure` command.

- You can drop and re-create the stored procedure, which flushes all existing plans from the cache.

- You can use the `sp_recompile` procedure on underlying tables, which flushes all plans from cache but does not create a new query tree.

PARAMETERS AND VARIABLES

If you need to use dynamic values in a WHERE clause in a stored procedure, try to use parameters rather than local variables to supply them. The optimizer can't predict the value of a declared variable at compile time, but it does know at least one value of a parameter at compile time. You also can use two procedures to mitigate this problem. In the first procedure, derive the value of the variable and then call the second procedure with that value.

The datatypes of the stored procedure parameters are established at compilation time and are reflected in the query plan as it exists in cache. Since SQL Server char(10) is considered a different datatype than varchar(10), this means that execution of a cached stored procedure will have suboptimal performance if called with a similar looking parameter that is actually a different datatype. Multiple simultaneous executions of a stored procedure may mean that one copy of the plan is optimized for a varchar(10) and another is optimized for a char(15). There is no guarantee that a user will get the copy most suited to his query.

TEMPORARY TABLES

As with local variables, the optimizer has no information about tables that are created within a stored procedure. Rather than give up entirely, the optimizer assumes that these tables have 10 data pages and 100 rows. If you expect a dynamically created table to have a different size, try creating the table outside the stored procedure in which it is used. The use of two stored procedures can help here, too. Write one that creates the table and calls the second procedure. Have the second procedure issue the query.

■ OPTIMIZING OPERATING ENVIRONMENT

Besides getting fast hardware and a lot of it, you can influence SQL Server performance by paying attention to the operating environment. This section raises a few points that may help you tune the greater system of which SQL Server is a part.

SQL SERVER PRIORITY

Many operating systems dynamically adjust process priority depending on CPU usage. In addition, privileged users can change the priority of a process. Be careful not to let the priority of the SQL Server processes get lowered by the operating system or by other users. If SQL Server's priority is lowered, performance will degrade. If you can issue an OS command to fix the priority of the SQL Server process at a constant high value, do so. However, make sure that you don't set the SQL Server priority so high that the operating system performance suffers. SQL Server relies on the operating system running well also.

CPU AFFINITY

SQL Server automatically associates SQL Server engines to CPUs. This is called binding or affinitying. By setting a binding once at boot time, the Server avoids the overhead associated with moving process information between CPUs. The binding only changes if a CPU goes offline. SQL Server schedules tasks onto engines as needed, and one task may run on different engines during its lifetime.

In System 10 and previous versions, all network I/O occurred on one CPU—the one bound to engine 0—regardless

315

of the number of CPUs available. In System 11, this restriction was eliminated, which may result in a performance improvement for systems with multiple CPUs. At login time, the Server assigns a task to an engine for network I/O by choosing the CPU with the least amount of activity at that time. The network I/O for the task stays affinitied to the engine selected unless the CPU goes offline.

TRACE FLAGS 5101 AND 5102

Some operating systems implement asynchronous I/O through threads. This can interfere with SQL Server if the threads are bound to the same CPU as a SQL Server engine. Excessive context switches between engines and threads can result in lower performance. In this case, if you are using three or more CPUs, booting SQL Server with trace flags 5101 and 5102 may help.

Normally, each engine manages its own disk I/O. This behavior provides maximum I/O throughput in completely symmetric operating systems. In non-fully symmetric systems, however, SQL Server contends with the operating system kernel. If you boot SQL Server with trace flag 5101, I/O is affinitied to engine 0. Tasks will still request disk I/O from any engine, but engine 0 will service the request. Do not use this trace flag with fully symmetric operating systems since it will degrade performance.

If you use trace flag 5101, you may also need to use trace flag 5102 to avoid a performance bottleneck on engine 0. Trace flag 5102 forces non-I/O tasks off engine 0. As with trace flag 5101, this will only result in performance improvement for non-fully symmetric systems running a SQL Server that performs all network I/O on engine 0.

REDUCING NETWORK TRAFFIC

Often the best overall improvement you can make to improve network performance is to reduce the number of packets you send. Sometimes queries are not formed optimally and thus bring back more data than the user really wanted. By designing your application carefully, you can allow client applications to preview the results of their data. For example, if a query gets issued that could potentially bring back 1000 rows, the application might be able to anticipate this by looking at the query and the target tables. Instead of bringing back the whole result set, it could bring back a few rows as a preview. Alternatively, the application could have a preview mode in which it initially always sets `rowcount` to 20, and then users are asked to click another button if they want to bring back all results. In this case, users would only have to do extra waiting when requesting more than 20 rows. By setting the default number of rows returned to a value somewhat higher than the average number requested, users only have to wait for the extreme cases.

NETWORK CONFIGURATION

Consult your sources of network hardware and software configuration information to make sure your network is optimized for SQL Server traffic. The choice of network protocols, the number of routers, gateways, and bridges that must be negotiated, and configuration parameters such as network buffers and `keepalive` can all make a difference in the performance of client/server communication. In many cases, you will have little control over the network. However, you might find that by relocating SQL Server to a different subnetwork you can provide clients a more direct route to the data they need.

If you can influence the choice of network transport stacks for PCs, choose a stack that supports attention signals, also referred to as out-of-band data. Attention signals allow an Open Client application to use the `dbcancel()` routine to interrupt SQL Server while it is sending back results. If such a mechanism isn't available, there is only a one-way path between client and server, and the results of a query occupy that path. PC users, after determining that they no longer want to see the results of a large query, are not able to cancel, and often resort to rebooting their workstations. This typically results in a SQL Server process that is unusable and unkillable until you reboot the Server.[5]

OPTIMIZING DESIGN

The key requirement for designing applications for many concurrent users is to design tables and queries such that users don't get in each others' way. For database applications, this comes down to applying a practical amount of normalization, using simple, modular queries and avoiding excessive locking. Depending on the form of a query, a transaction may lock one page of a table or the entire table, one page of an index, or a significant portion of the index.

There is a well-understood process for altering a logical database design so that you end up with a design that takes into account physical constraints. Another book in the PTR reference series, *Physical Database Design for Sybase SQL Server*,[6] does a good job of describing this process. In many cases, you don't start with a logical or a physical design, but with a database that someone untrained in database theory set up or with a database configured to work with exceptional requirements of a primary application. In these situations, you may find yourself using trial and error to resolve problems based on your best guesses about what will yield improvement. In this section, we'll provide some tips that may lead you to the right modifications.

APPLICATION DESIGN

In some cases, moving processing from SQL Server to a client application can result in performance improvements over stored procedures or ad hoc queries. If access is only allowed through the application, you can prevent users from issuing poorly formed queries that use excessive resources. Also, mov-

---

[5]These are commonly known as *zombie* processes.

[6]Dean Muench, Rob Gillette, and Jean Tabaka, *Physical Database Design for Sybase SQL Server* (Upper Saddle River, N.J.: Prentice Hall, 1994).

ing calculations, sorting, and datatype manipulations can often provide a better balance of CPU resources between client workstations and the Server machine. If you can use arrays in client application to store intermediate results instead of SQL Server temporary tables, you can also take advantage of the client workstation's memory, rather than relying on the caching behavior of the Server.

On the client side, you can also influence the design of transactions to minimize Server activity. For example, for tables that are heaps, such as `syslogs,` contention for last page of the table can be high. If you are implementing multiple statements as a single transaction, you can minimize the number of times the last page needs to be locked. Similarly, if modifying several columns of a table, compile all the changes into one statement, rather than updating one column at a time.

Choose third-party applications carefully. Try to use those that provide enough flexibility so that you can tune them to use the Server efficiently. For those that work with many different RDBMSs, you will want to make sure you can configure the application to use features only available on SQL Server. Also make sure you can find out the SQL that it is sending to the Server in case you need to analyze performance or correct errors.

The process of key generation tends to cause concurrency problems, since many methods result in table hot spots and excessive locking. In System 10 and later servers, the identity feature may provide the functionality you need. If you are using System 11, consider using a named cache to keep tables containing the values used to generate keys in memory. Several whitepapers have been written on the topic of generating sequential and random keys. Some assumptions in these papers change with System 11. Check AnswerBase, the Sybase WWW site, and ISUG Conference Proceedings for the most current developments in this area.

TABLE DESIGN

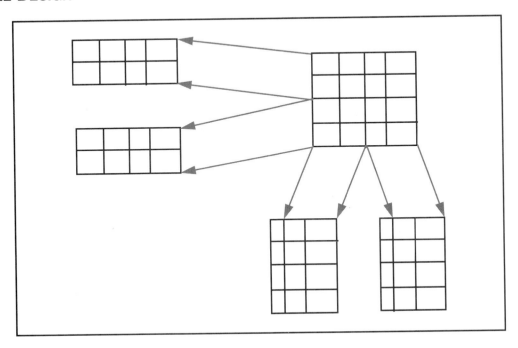

Figure 8.3 Two ways to split a table for a possible performance increase. A vertical split often requires the addition of a key upon which the two sides can be joined when necessary.

During logical database design, the process of normalization is used to minimize duplicate information and maximize data integrity. In some cases, selective denormalization may be needed to improve performance based on physical constraints. Table 8-1 shows the possible advantages and disadvantages of some modifications that you might find useful.

TABLE 8-1   *Denormalization Trade-offs for Performance Improvement*

Modification	Possible Advantages	Possible Disadvantages
Adding redundant columns	Reduced number of joins, reduced locking	Increased space usage, fewer rows per page, more processing required to synchronize duplicate columns
Adding derived columns, such as aggregated or calculated data that would otherwise be derived in transactions	Reduced number of joins with detail tables, reduced CPU usage for calculations	Increased space usage, more I/Os for all queries accessing the table due to the additional column width, more processing required to synchronize table when detail data changes
Adding tables containing derived data	Reduced number or cost of joins, reduced CPU usage for calculations	Increased space usage, more processing required to synchronize table when detail data changes
Combining two or more tables into one, usually by duplicating values in a column	Reduced number of joins	Increased space usage, more I/Os for all queries accessing the table due to the additional table width, more processing required to synchronize changes
Splitting tables horizontally or vertically	Reduced I/O for queries needing a logical subset of data, reduced size of indexes (fewer levels and/or more key rows per page), distribution of data across physical media, reduced size of data rows resulting in more rows per page and less wasted space	Increased number of joins, more locking, may need to add redundant key and synchronize changes
Duplicating a subset of a table for use by certain queries that don't need the whole table.	Reduced index size, reduced number of I/Os for queries on the duplicated subset, reduced locking on main table	Increased space usage, more processing required to synchronize changes

321

Making changes such as those listed does not always have the intended results, so plan on experimenting on a development server before putting such a scheme into production use. Also make a plan to roll back to the previous design if necessary. Sometimes test cases work better than the full-scale implementation does.

IN-PLACE UPDATES

When you update a row in a table, you essentially delete the old copy of the data and insert the new copy. In general, this can be done either by deleting the entire row and adding a new row that reflects the change or by editing the old row itself, leaving it where it is. The latter is referred to as an in-place update. SQL Server selects one of these options depending on how much work it thinks will be needed. Because the values being changed exist on data and index pages that are "packed" (i.e., that have no free space between them), an update might have the following effects:

- Incorporating the changed data makes the row wider or narrower, so all the other data on the page would have to be shifted up or down to accommodate.

- Shifting data up or down may incur a page split or merge.

- The changed data are in a column that is part of a key in one or more indexes, and so the indexes have to be updated as well.

- The index being changed might be the index that was required to find the row to be updated. If so, the change might mean a cursor could get confused, say by making a row requalify farther down in the result set.

In versions of SQL Server before 11.0, update methods that handled these effects were characterized in two ways—*direct* versus *deferred* and *in-place* versus *non-in-place*. A deferred operation takes place in two phases. In the first, the affected pages are read and the anticipated changes to these pages are logged. In the second phase, the log records are reread and the pages are reread, and then the object's pages are modified. In direct mode, there is only one phase. For each change to the row of an object, the change is logged and the row is modified on the data page. An in-place operation is a type of direct operation that means the data do not move on the data page. In this case, the change is implemented as a direct replacement of the row on the page, rather than as a row delete followed by a row insert. Because there is less logging and lower chances of lock contention and page splitting, in-place updates are faster by an order of magnitude. In-place operations have the best performance because they use fewer log records and require fewer I/Os. Direct updates require less time than deferred since they require fewer I/Os as well. The gain in performance depends on the number of indexes.

For an in-place operation, SQL Servers earlier than 11.0 require that the following can be determined at compile time:

- ■ The columns to be updated cannot be in the index used to locate the row to update.
- ■ Only one row may be affected and a unique index must be used to access the row.
- ■ The columns to be updated cannot allow nulls or be defined to use a variable-length datatype.
- ■ There must be no update trigger on the table and the table must not be replicated.

While these requirements are quite restrictive, you may find that you can tune critical transactions to fit within these boundaries, yielding important throughput improvements.

In System 11, new methods are used and many restrictions removed, resulting in higher query performance overall. The new algorithms reduce the amount of locking and traffic in indexes as well.

Two new direct-update methods are characterized as *expensive* or *cheap*. A *cheap* direct update means that the modified data row is replaced in its original row position because the modified row fits on the existing page. If the row length changes, any rows following the modified row on the page are shifted. If the modified row will not fit on the existing page, the *expensive update* mode is used. The data row must be deleted along with all its associated index entries, and then the new data row must be inserted by traversing the clustered index, if available, and inserting the corresponding index entries.

The deferred update mode will always be done in the abnormal case when duplicate rows are not allowed, but there is no unique nonclustered index and there is a nonunique clustered index on the table.[7] Otherwise, in-place updates will be done under any of the following conditions:

- The index used to find the row to modify (the search index) is nonclustered and does not need to be modified, no variable-length columns are modified, and no other indexes need to be modified.

- The search index is nonclustered and unique, the search index does not need to be modified, no variable-length columns are modified, a clustered index elsewhere in the query does not need to be modified, but other nonclustered indexes do not need to be modified.

- The search index is a clustered index, the index pages will not need to be changed, and only fixed-length columns are being modified.

- A table scan is used to find the rows to modify, and only fixed-length columns are being modified.

Note that the restrictions on the number of rows to be modified is lifted, as are the restrictions for tables that have triggers or are replicated.

All deletes are now done in expensive direct mode. For a non-in-place update, the delete portion is done in direct mode, and the insert part is done in direct or deferred mode for the data rows or the index rows as applicable. In general, the Server will try to do as much of the updates in direct mode as possible. It needs to use the deferred mode if a nonunique search index is used and variable-length columns are being updated. It also uses deferred mode if the search index is not unique and a clustered index is being modified.

CURSORS

Cursors allow you to perform row-level processing instead of the traditional set-level processing of a relational system. While set processing is the natural method for relational databases,

[7]In other words, if no duplicates are allowed, you should define a unique index.

applications are often written using programming languages, which are record oriented. Record-level processing sometimes matches the operations users need to perform as well. Using cursors, a query still returns a set of results, but applications can address individual rows within the set. Users can change row position within a result set using a process called scrolling or browsing.

Cursors have been implemented with SQL Server in a variety of ways. With System 10 and later releases, you can use Server cursors. These use the standard SQL Server locking methods unless you use a command to change the transaction isolation level or specify the type of locks to acquire. The cursor position and type affect the pages locked. The cursor position moves as a result of the `fetch` command, which retrieves a subset of rows from a result set. By default, shared locks are acquired for read-only cursors, and update and exclusive locks are used as needed for update cursors. If the cursor includes a construct such as ORDER BY that requires creation of a temporary worktable, all locks are released on the base table, allowing others to update it without restriction.

The cursor result set is generated as the FETCH command is used to retrieve rows, rather than being generated all at once ahead of time. Locks are acquired during the FETCH, rather than when the cursor is declared. This is more efficient in cases where not all rows are fetched from the cursor. For example, the application may decide to stop fetching when a desired row is found or when too many rows were returned and the query needs to be rephrased. Using cursors, the first results are often returned more quickly than a normal SELECT, since results are returned as soon as the first qualifying page of data is found. Response time for cursors may not improve, however, if processing must be done on intermediate results. For example, ORDER BY, GROUP BY, and aggregates involve finding the entire result set and rearranging it before starting to return it.

Tables accessed using cursors should have at least one unique index, and the values in that index should not be updated by the cursor. Otherwise, if the update causes the location of the value in an index column to move, the cursor might see the associated data row more than once. Server cursors are not updatable in SELECT statements involving DISTINCT, GROUP BY, ORDER BY, UNION, or aggregate functions.

You can also use client-side cursors in Open Client applications. CT-Lib and DB-Lib have different cursor mechanisms. In general, the CT-Lib functionality provides better concurrency and performance. In DB-Lib, the client maintains a snapshot of data, performing row-level processing on that snapshot. Before writing results back to the server, the application must compare time-stamps between the snapshot and the Server data to make sure the data have not changed. This takes time and results in redoing the operation when data have changed.

You can also write programs that simulate cursor behavior by storing query results in arrays. For example, SQR provides a simple mechanism for bringing query results into arrays. In these cases, however, you must write checks to maintain concurrency yourself.

With all types of cursors, but especially client side, pay careful attention to locking. If an application process selects more rows than it really needs, but doesn't release the lock, it can prevent other copies of the application from functioning. This is exacerbated by the use of networking protocols that don't allow attention signals for cancelling large queries. (See "Network Configuration" on page 317 for more information about this problem.)

■ MINIMIZING LOCKING

Locking can cause delays that appear to users as if the Server or the client application is hung. Usually, if a poor design results in excessive locking, no amount of performance tuning will help. In many situations, you may not be involved in the original design, but you will be pulled into redesign discussions when problems need to be fixed. Sometimes all it takes to resolve a problem is the addition of an index or the rewrite of the most common query.

To improve locking behavior, consider some of these modifications.

■ To minimize contention for pages, keep transactions as small and short as possible. This approach also makes it easier to truncate the log when necessary.

■ Consider alternatives to updates and deletes that affect large portions of a table. One method for periodic mass updates is (1) use SELECT INTO to copy the rows to keep into a new table; (2) sp_rename the old table to a temporary name, and sp_rename the new table to the original name of the old table; (3) verify that all went as planned; and (4) drop the old table. This can be much more efficient than a large delete, provided that you do not need to use transaction log dumps. This method operates more quickly by avoiding logging and thereby shortens the processing window that blocks out other users. The trade-off is that related stored procedures will need to be reresolved and recompiled.

■ Never include any user interaction or other communications between client and server in the middle of transactions.

■ If you use chained transactions, make sure that applications don't hold long-term locks in the middle of transactions, especially if using HOLDLOCK.

■ Use temporary tables to avoid deadlocks.

■ Reduce the stringency of locking where it isn't needed. Avoid HOLDLOCK if possible or enable dirty reads if compatible with the application's purpose. See Chapter 2 for more information about locking levels.

■ In SQL Server 10.1, you can boot with trace flag 1214 to tell the Server to place shared locks instead of update locks on pages at the leaf level of nonclustered indexes if update cursors are used. This only improves performance for in-place updates. If non-in-place updates occur and the base row moves, this trace flag may introduce deadlocking in index pages.

■ If using 10.1 or later, reset the lock escalation threshold (described in Chapter 2) to avoid table locks on large tables where you are updating more then 200 rows.

The process for troubleshooting a locking problem usually consists of the following steps:

■ Use sp_lock to see what locks are being held on which objects by which processes.

■ Use sp_who to see who is being blocked by whom and to get information about what processes users are running.

■ Use DBCC TRACEON(3604) followed by DBCC PAGE(*database*, *page_number*) to see the header of the page appearing in the sp_lock output. The page header identifies the index level of the object being locked. In the DBCC PAGE output, look for the values of *level* and *indid* to see whether the leaf level of the index is consistently involved, indicating a possible hot spot or a problem that fill factor might resolve. A hot spot is a page that several transactions need to access and update. It is usually the last page of the table or the leaf page of the index that points to the last page of the table.

The types of locks are summarized in Table 8-2.

TABLE 8-2   Default Lock Types and Blocking

SQL Statement	Table Lock	Page Lock	Will Block Table Lock of Type	Will Block Page Lock of Type
Insert	Intent exclusive	Exclusive	Shared, exclusive	All
Select	Intent shared	Shared	Exclusive	Exclusive
Update, with index	Intent exclusive	Update, exclusive	Shared, exclusive	All
Update, without index	Exclusive	n/a	All	All
Delete, with index	Intent exclusive	Update, exclusive	Shared, exclusive	All
Delete, without index	Exclusive	n/a	All	All
Create clustered index	Exclusive	n/a	All	All
Create nonclustered index	Shared	n/a	Intent exclusive	None

By default, SQL Server only holds shared page or table locks for the amount of time it takes to retrieve the data. If HOLDLOCK or transaction isolation level 3 is used, the Server holds the shared locks until the transaction completes. SQL Server always holds an exclusive page or table lock until the enclosing transaction commits or aborts. If you send a single SQL statement without a BEGIN TRANSACTION and without chained mode on, the Server will hold the lock until it has satisfied the query. Intent and update locks are also held for the duration of the transaction.

Normally, SQL Server tries to acquire page locks. However, when it has acquired enough page locks during a transaction to cross the lock escalation threshold, the Server escalates to the use of table locks. It does so in an effort to avoid the overhead of acquiring each of several single locks and to avoid using up all available locks. In versions prior to 10.1, the lock escalation threshold is set at 200 locks. In 10.1 and later releases, you can set the threshold using configuration parameters and the `sp_setpglockpromote` stored procedure. Regardless of the SQL Server version, it is still desirable to avoid reaching the maximum lock threshold. A selective index, as described in earlier sections of this chapter, is often enough to avoid locking more pages than necessary.

SQL SERVER PERFORMANCE-RELATED COMMANDS

In this chapter we have referred to several diagnostic commands that may help with SQL Server performance tuning. A brief description of each follows. These commands are each documented in Sybase manuals and whitepapers as well. All these commands are only intended for helping with troubleshooting. As such, they will slow down performance in order to provide the information you request. Therefore, use them as conservatively as you can. Certain commands, such as `buildmaster` (for SQL Server versions prior to 11.0) and DBCC MEMUSAGE, are only marginally documented in Sybase whitepapers and the troubleshooting guides and generally are not supported. These commands can be useful for troubleshooting but can also be dangerous. Because of their unsupported and thus unreliable nature, these commands are not documented here. Check the Sybase troubleshooting guides and AnswerBase for current details and cautions.

USING TRACE FLAGS

In general, you either boot the Server using a trace flag as a command line option, or you enable the trace flag while the Server is running by using the DBCC TRACEON command.

To boot SQL Server with a trace flag for UNIX or VMS, edit the RUNSERVER file and add the trace flag to the command line that executes the dataserver binary. For UNIX systems, use -T*trace_number*. For VMS, use /trace=*trace_number*. For NOVELL systems, use the -T*trace_number* in the LOAD command for SQL Server. For Windows NT and OS/2, use /T*trace_number* in the command line used to start the Server.

To enable a trace flag using DBCC, you execute the command DBCC TRACEON(*trace_number*). For DBCC commands that yield output, you will need to first enable trace flag 3604, which tells SQL Server to direct trace output to the window you are using.

TRACE FLAG 302

Use the command DBCC TRACEON(3604, 302) command; then issue a query for insight into how the optimizer calculates costs for alternative search arguments and join clauses. Check the output to make sure that it includes all the WHERE clauses you supplied. If an expected clause is not evaluated, this means that the optimizer didn't consider it to be a relevant search argument or join clause. It may be that there was a datatype mismatch, an OR type of clause, or that no distribution statistics exist for the index. Also check the trace flag output to find out if the optimizer is using accurate row counts. If, based on distribution statistics, the optimizer thinks it may need to access a large percentage of the rows, it will choose a table scan over indexed access. If the total row counts look wrong, use DBCC CHECKTABLE to update them on the OAM page. Next, check the trace flag output for the assumptions about logical I/O costs. The unexpected use of a table scan may indicate that the statistics distribution page needs to be updated. Also notice the join order. If the join order doesn't make sense to you, you may want to try the forceplan feature described in this section to see the results of a different join order.

TRACE FLAG 310

This trace flag works similarly to trace flag 302 in that it shows you information that the optimizer uses to generate a query plan. In this case, you will see output of the optimizer's cost analyses for permutations of indexes and join orders. If you see the phrase "query connected" in the output, this means that the optimizer considers the join optimizable. A join order is the order in which tables will be considered. The optimizer gives each table in the query a number, numbering the first table appearing in the FROM clause as 0, the second as 1, and so on. In the trace flag output, notation like "0-2-1" indicates the join order under consideration. The time estimate used for comparison by the optimizer is based on the following formula: 2 milliseconds per logical page I/O (lp) plus 18 milliseconds per physical page I/O (pp). Note that this number is a relative value assigned by the SQL Server and is not the actual amount of time.

SQL MONITOR

SQL Monitor is a Sybase product that complements SQL Server but is not necessary for its operation. SQL Monitor consists of a Monitor Server and a Monitor Client. The Monitor Server attaches to SQL Server shared memory and helps you analyze performance by continuously monitoring several internal counters. The SQL Monitor Client displays the data gathered in graphic and ASCII format. By obtaining information from shared memory, SQL Monitor does not increase the load on SQL Server. SQL Monitor Server uses SQL Server internal global variables and a memory area known as an event buffer internal to record data. The global variables keep a running total of server-level statistics, such as the total number of device I/Os. The event buffer keeps track of atomic events.

sp_monitor

The SQL Server sp_monitor procedure checks global variables used for tracking SQL Server performance. The spt_monitor table in the master database contains a row that stores the last measurements made by sp_monitor. With each execution of sp_monitor, the spt_monitor row is compared with the current values of the global variables. See the Sybase Commands Reference manual for a description of the sp_monitor output. For multiple-CPU systems, the sp_monitor statistics represent the average performance of all the CPUs.

Execute the sp_monitor stored procedure at regular intervals, say every 10 seconds. Watch for significant changes between the values or for lack of change. To monitor trends, you can save sp_monitor output into a history table, which you can later analyze.

set statistics io on/off

The statistics I/O option allows you to see the number of physical and logical I/Os. Use SET STATISTICS IO ON to turn it on, and SET STATISTICS IO OFF to turn it off. If you see relatively large physical and logical I/Os for common queries, use the index and query tuning hints described in this chapter to try to reduce I/O. The ratio of physical reads to logical reads will indicate how much the data cache is being used for the query. If you are using a System 11 server, a high ratio may lead you to bind a table or index to a named cache or to determine that using the MRU buffer replacement strategy will use data cache more efficiently.

set statistics time on/off

To see the amount of CPU time SQL Server took to parse, compile, and execute a statement, use the SET STATISTICS TIME ON command. The output displays CPU times in machine-dependent ticks. Even if you don't know the number of ticks per second for your machine, comparing the output of different queries will tell you which operate most and least efficiently. A large difference between elapsed time and execution time may also indicate a blocking or network problem.

set showplan on/off

The showplan utility (also known as *Explain* in some client applications) lets you see exactly how the optimizer processes the query, including the indexes and any worktable strategies used. Use this tool if you suspect that the optimizer is not choosing the best query plan. You can also use it to test your understanding of the query process. Try to predict what plan the optimizer will generate for a query; then use showplan to verify your results.

forceindex

The forceindex feature of SQL Server allows you to identify the index you want used for a table in query plan. To use the forceindex feature in SQL Server versions before System 11, put the ID of index in parentheses after table name in the FROM clause. In later versions, put the keyword INDEX followed by the index name in parentheses after the table name in the FROM clause. When using forceindex, you are basically taking on the optimizer's job. Keep in mind that your results may or may not be better than the optimizer's in various cases, depending on other circumstances in the context of the query. Be sure to use the SET SHOWPLAN and STATISTICS commands on to verify that your version of optimization really does work better for the common case. This command is documented and supported in SQL Server 11.0 and later releases. It was available in previous releases, but unsupported.

set forceplan on/off

The forceplan option allows you to determine the join order for a query. To use it, use the SET FORCEPLAN ON command. Thereafter, queries will use tables in the order that they appear in FROM clauses until you issue SET FORCEPLAN OFF. This command is documented and supported in SQL Server 11.0 and later releases. It was available in previous releases, but unsupported.

DBCC OBJECT_STATS AND *DBCC USER_STATS*

In SQL Server version 10.1, two new DBCC commands were created for monitoring the use of locks. These are DBCC OBJECT_STATS and DBCC USER_STATS. These commands are used to see the total amount of time spent waiting for shared, update, and exclusive page locks on a table by table or on a process by process basis; respectively. To enable the lock monitoring for these DBCC commands, enable trace flag 1213. In the output, the time spent waiting is measured in microseconds.

CHAPTER

Enterprise Data Strategies

As soon as you have more than a few databases serving
more than a few departments in an organization, you have an
enterprise database system. With such systems come more complex data problems and more complex solutions. In this chapter
we start to look at enterprise-wide information system strategies.
Rather than providing step by step guides for each, which would
take several books, we touch on the most common issues people
face when designing these solutions. SQL Server-specific information is given where it applies. You are urged to read the relevant manuals for other technology involved in these types of
projects. In some cases, the discussions in this chapter may lead
you to discover that a small, handcrafted solution will do the job
you need better than an expensive, leading-edge solution. If you
are looking into the future of your career, the overviews presented here may help you decide which paths of information systems management to follow next.

▪ Determining a Storage Management Strategy

The ideal system delivers everyone exactly the information they need exactly when they need it. If an organization could somehow keep all its data online indefinitely in one format, it could always have consistent access to its data. However, the search and retrieval time (not to mention maintenance time) would become unmanageable. In practice, no software is infinitely scalable, so this solution is not possible anyway. Similarly, if only a small amount of data are stored online, they can be accessed quickly and inexpensively, but they would not serve most user's needs most of the time. When data are needed in several formats, several languages, or on several platforms, the complexity of the ideal system increases. Understanding this, a Systems Manager relentlessly pursues the question of how much data to keep online and in which formats. As we have seen before, the practical solution pursues the ideal, but balances the benefits of easy, timely access against the costs of keeping it that way.

Systems Managers usually pursue several solutions simultaneously. One is to try to identify data they can eliminate altogether. Such data might include accounting data older than the law requires an organization to keep, or data that are stored on an obsolete medium, such as 8" floppy disks. Another solution, for the vast majority of data that organizations are unwilling to discard, is to set up an archive strategy. For data proven to have significant value when kept online, another storage strategy might call for distributing databases among database servers running on various machines. When managers consider it imperative to keep massive amounts of data online, using parallel database technology such as Sybase MPP (Navigation Server) becomes an option.

To choose well among these options, however, a Systems Manager needs to find out what value the organization perceives the data to have.

DATA ROLES AND DATA VALUE OVER TIME

The value of data depends on its business roles in the organization. Typical roles include

- ■ Recording business transactions that make up an organization's revenue stream. This is usually called operations data. The related information processing strategy is often characterized as online transaction processing (OLTP).

- ■ Supporting business transactions, such as providing reference information to answer customer presales questions. This type of information need may be served by knowledge base systems.

- ■ Supporting information transfer between departments in order to synchronize operations. The industry tends to characterize this information processing need as distributed computing.

- ■ Supporting decision making, either in the form of reports or ad hoc queries. For example, historical sales data can be used to project future trends and predict the success rate of various marketing campaigns. Systems devoted to such analysis and decision making are coming to be known as decision support systems (DSS) and online analytical processing (OLAP) systems.

- ■ Disseminating information from a few people to many, such as publishing new information or distributing procedural documents. This information challenge usually falls under the categories of document management and electronic publishing.

- ■ Providing reference material for research activities that contribute to future products and services. This type of information need may be served by knowledge base systems or by distributed information libraries, which is one way of thinking of the WWW and other Internet-based repositories.

- ■ Providing customer service. This usually comes from analysis of historical transaction data, as stored in the original OLTP system or in a secondary reference repository.

- ■ Reporting recent results and measuring performance against goals. Copies of OLTP data made for reporting databases often serve this need.

Whether you are in a position to initiate new database projects or not, try to determine the roles that you and others expect your data to play. Identify the most critical information and determine whether management would consider it part of general overhead or as a cost of sales. For example, if having information available enables sales, determine how much of the cost of the sale can be invested in sales support and still yield adequate profit. If the information primarily serves a general business support role, such as accounting, determine the portion of overhead that can be invested in systems for keeping business support efficient. Identify where value could be derived from keeping the data online, and estimate the corresponding amount of cost savings or revenue generation.

Once you determine the information essential to the organization's functions, investigate the value of that information over time. As information loses value, plan to move it to systems that are less expensive to maintain. Ideally, you archive information as soon as the cost of keeping it online outweighs the value of having it easily accessible. In some cases, you can supplement archiving with summarizing, so the value of the data is compressed into a smaller database or into reports.

To analyze data's time value, identify how the data are used for the purposes listed above. See if you can correlate the frequency of access and the age of data to determine when archiving makes sense.

When considering a storage management strategy, the users' arguments for and against archiving will help to illuminate the value of the information. The most persuasive arguments will compare the cost of maintaining data online to the benefits of investing that money into another needed business improvement. For example, with fewer SQL databases or 30% less data to manage, you might be able to shift IS staff from data maintenance to application development. Opposing arguments may highlight uses for the data that were not immediately apparent. For example, someone may propose providing a new service for a distributor's customers by allowing them access to historical data about their ordering patterns. The charge for the service may support the cost of keeping the data online for other purposes as well.

Also consider the time it will take to unarchive data. If you only receive one request a month for an archived document, users may consider a 2-hour retrieval time reasonable. However, if the request frequency climbs to once a day, then investing some time and money into improving the archive procedures will make sense.

MATCHING INFORMATION TO INFORMATION SYSTEMS

You may not need to keep all online data in a primary relational database for it to provide value to users. Consider transferring data from the source that generated it to a secondary archive or processing location. For example, the primary machine for recording business transactions may be optimized for processing by having several CPUs and several megabytes of memory. There may also be significant investment made in keeping downtime on that system to an absolute minimum By moving historical data for reporting and analysis to a different SQL Server on a different machine, you can reduce the load on the primary machine. You may also find that you can configure the secondary machine with less memory and CPU power than the primary machine.

For another example, we can imagine a business in which mainframes are used for the primary data store, but users use PC workstations for 90% of their work tasks. In this case, it may make sense to maintain a SQL Server on a PC in the PC LAN and to use a gateway process to download local copies of data from the mainframe. The PC server can then be used to perform certain processing best done on a PC and return reformatted data to the mainframe. Or, a day's worth of data can be "cached" on the PC network server so that users only need to go to the mainframe on the rare occasions when they need older data.

Interviews with users and monitoring system resources will help you determine where division of labor between systems may pay off.

For some data, you may be able to store reports in a document storage and retrieval system, rather than maintaining all the source data in a database. You might also find that text information may be just as well indexed if you use text search and retrieval technology. Information in this form might provide sufficient value if kept on an HSC or on a CD-ROM at a significantly lower cost than a relational database. The advantages of document systems usually include lower maintenance requirements and lower hardware resource requirements.

To match access requirements with storage systems, look at

■ The business and processing rules involved for data access and validation

■ The user involvement and processing required for quickly finding needed information

■ The amount of control required to make sure users only access and change data they are authorized to access and change

■ The amount of time a user can afford to wait before receiving the information requested

■ The differences between the requirements for initial information storage and subsequent retrieval, for example, the difference in needs between information as recording a business transaction and information as reference material

■ The total amount of data to be kept online

Once you've identified the roles and the time value of your data, think about where your data fit among the requirements above. This analysis will help you explore appropriate technology for online storage and for archiving.

Rather than the time value of data, the sheer volume may drive you to consider archive strategies. For example, one SQL Server can theoretically store more than a terabyte of data. However, backing up a terabyte of data or doing joins across gigabyte-sized tables takes the practical limit down considerably. Given that disks fail, having that much data under the control of one database server also exposes the system to the risk of significant downtime. If you expect this to become a problem, you will need to perform a capacity analysis. In the next section, we'll look at estimating the storage capacity you need for SQL Server data.

ESTIMATING STORAGE REQUIREMENTS FOR SQL SERVER

By estimating data growth rates and the storage capacity of your current or planned system, you will be able to tell whether your information storage plan is technically feasible. Capacity planning will also tell you how much hardware and software you will need to plan on purchasing. In this section, we look at how to estimate space usage for SQL Server data. For other data, use what you know about the data and the storage technology for making similar estimates. In Chapter 8, where we looked at performance issues, you will find information to help you determine the CPU, network, and memory capacity required for SQL Server-based systems.

For determining SQL Server database size, you will need to estimate the sizes of the tables and the indexes. You will also need to determine how much transaction log space to reserve. Depending on the precision you need, you can use one of two different methods to estimate future storage requirements for index and table space. For a rough estimate, you can measure current storage space used and prorate that usage by the percentage of growth or shrinkage you expect in the amount of data. Good historical records of the storage growth or shrinkage leading up to the size of the current system will improve the accuracy of this method. For a more precise estimate or for situations where there are no existing data, you can create dummy tables and indexes and then use sp_estspace to calculate the expected space usage. We will look at both of these methods in the following sections. We will also look at ways to determine the amount of log space you will need.

Estimating Table and Index Space Based on Current Usage

1. Measure the amount of data in use now for tables. For an active database, you can use DBCC CHECKALLOC to get an accurate picture of space used for each table and index. Include the system tables. (See Chapter 5 for a discussion of each system table and how it grows.) For now, exclude the space used for the transaction log and indexes. When projecting growth rate, remember to include the possibility of business changes, such as opening or closing offices, adding or dropping products or services, and adding or reducing the number of employees. Such changes may affect both table size and the number of tables in the database.

2. Subtract the space used by any data you intend to archive.

3. Estimate index space as a percentage of the space used by the underlying tables. Factors that affect index space are the number of indexes per table, the number of columns in the

indexes, the size of the key data for each index column, the number of rows in the table, and the cardinality of the data (for clustered indexes). For each relevant table, determine the ratio of the current index space used and the total space used. Apply that ratio to the expected future table size to project an index growth rate. Modify your estimate or create estimates for various scenarios for any assumptions that you don't have high confidence about, such as number of indexes per table or the composition of key columns.

4. Determine the amount of time it took to build up the data that must be retained online.

5. Use the results of the previous steps to determine the growth rate of the data, for example, 15 MB per month.

6. Determine the archive rate you expect to sustain, for example, 5 MB per month.

7. The difference between the growth rate and the archive rate will help you establish the net gain or loss in the amount of data each month.

8. Calculate the total data storage requirements at the end of the current planning horizon, such as at the end of the current year, the fiscal year, or the end of 3 years. Adjust for any events that would change the data storage rates in the time period selected.

9. Compare the expected data storage requirements with the capacity of your current system, taking into account physical, practical, and theoretical limits. Take into account such things as maintenance time and hard-drive space.

The result of performing this analysis will tell you how long you will be able to work your current system in its current configuration. You'll better understand whether to proceed as planned, reexamine archive criteria, change the design to reduce growth, or start planning for resizing the system.

Estimating Table and Index Space by Calculation

With System 10, Sybase introduced the `sp_estspace` stored procedure to help database administrators predict how much space they will need and how much time it will take to create an index on the full table. To use `sp_estspace`, you will need to do the following for each table:

1. Create a dummy version of the table if it doesn't already exist. The columns do not have to be in any particular order, and you do not have to create the rules, defaults, triggers, and so on. (We will look at the space used by those later.)

2. Create dummy indexes for the table if they do not already exist. These should be the type of indexes that will appear on the real table and should include all the columns you expect to use in the index.

3. Estimate the number of rows for the table.

4. If you want to estimate the maximum space usage, identify the variable-length columns. Otherwise, `sp_estspace` will calculate an average length, which is defined to be half of the length of these columns.

5. Estimate the maximum or average length (depending on your needs) for all the text and image columns per row of the table.

6. Determine the index fill factor you will use when creating the index.

7. If you want to know how long the index would take to be created, supply the I/O rate for the target machine in terms of I/Os per second.

8. Run `sp_estspace`, supplying the expected parameters as determined in steps 1 through 7. The output will show you the expected size of the table and its indexes in SQL Server pages in kilobytes and in megabytes.

If you read the text of `sp_estspace`, which you can find in the `installmaster` file under the scripts directory, you will see that it calculates size by using the *length* columns in `syscolumns`. The length column is determined by the datatype of the column. Table 1-3 showed storage requirements for each datatype. SQL Server requires a certain amount of overhead to track data in the database. This overhead is included in the `sp_estspace` calculations. If you want to refine the way `sp_estspace` calculates the average length for variable-length columns, you can make a copy of the script, modify the script appropriately, and then install it in your SQL Server. Give it a different name than `sp_estspace` so that users will understand that it doesn't conform to the description in the reference manuals.

Estimate System Table Space

The size for system tables in a database can be estimated with `sp_estspace` as well. However, to determine row count, you will need to have a good understanding of the expected objects in the database and the number of system table rows required for each. Table 9-1 shows how system table rows correspond to objects and database activities.

The space required for system tables depends on the objects that you have in your database.

TABLE 9-1   System Table Storage

System Table	A row is added for each:
sysusermessages	user message
sysalternates	database user alias
sysroles	user for which a role is enabled
sysusers	database user
sysprotects	instance of access permissions granted or revoked
sysprocedures	stored procedure, trigger, rule, default, view, constraint
syscolumns	column in a table or parameter in a procedure
systypes	datatype
syskeys	key defined with `sp_primarykey`, `sp_commonkey`, or `sp_foreignkey`
sysobjects	system table, user table, view, procedure, rule, default, trigger, and constraint
syscomments	stored procedure, view, rule, default, trigger, and constraint line of text
sysdepends	procedure, view, or table referenced by a procedure, view, or trigger
syssegments	segment defined with `sp_addsegment`
sysindexes	table (or table partition for System 11), index on a table, text column, image column
systhresholds	threshold defined with `sp_addthreshold`
sysreferences	constraint defined on a table or column
sysconstraints	constraint defined on a table or column

Estimating Log Space

Each SQL Server database, including each system database, has one transaction log. The function of the log is to store transaction information for recovery purposes, as described in Chapter 2. It is not possible to turn off transaction logging without corrupting the database. The transaction log for a database records all data modifications made by all transactions that affect data in that database. Transactions that modify data in more than one database have transaction log records in each database affected. As transactions occur, data are added to the log and the log grows in size. When you dump a database and truncate a transaction log, the inactive part of the log is removed and the transaction log length shrinks.

Ideally, when you establish a disaster recovery strategy, you determine how often you intend to truncate the transaction log data based on how much data you could afford to lose if you lost the transaction log device. In practice, many system administrators base this decision on the time of day they can reserve for maintenance, the amount of space they have available for the log, and their level of motivation for making backups. In any case, you will need to learn the minimum and maximum amount of transaction log space you need for the database to function efficiently between log truncation times. You will also need to learn how quickly the logs grow for your databases.

The growth rate of the log varies depending on database activity. The size and mix of database transactions vary depending on usage, so you may find it difficult to estimate transaction log space and growth precisely. You may be able to get an estimate by setting up a test database that mimics the layout of your real database. Use test cases to determine the amount of log growth for each of your typical transactions, and multiply that by the number of transactions per day.

The following activities cause rows to be added to the transaction log:

■ Beginning and committing transactions (explicitly or implicitly)

■ Adding rows to tables

- Deleting rows from tables
- Updating (modifying) rows in tables
- Allocating pages and extents to accommodate more table or index data
- Deallocating pages or extents when data are removed from tables or indexes
- Dumping or truncating the transaction log
- Checkpointing the database
- Creating tables, indexes, or other database objects
- Dropping tables, indexes, or other database objects
- Most system administration tasks, such as setting a database option or adding a user, cause rows in system tables to be added, deleted, or modified. These changes are recorded in the transaction log like any other update.

In many cases, determining the mix and number of transactions is difficult. In practice, most Sybase administrators estimate log growth by trial and error. A typical rule of thumb is to start by allowing 10% to 25% of the of database size for log. If the log tends to fill up between database and transaction log dumps, then you will need to increase the size of the log or increase the frequency of dumps.

The transaction log will grow significantly and unpredictably during development, since objects, indexes, and users will be added, dropped, and modified frequently. During production, fluctuations tend to fall into more routine patterns. Watch the rate of transaction log growth to determine if it hovers around a constant or if it tends to fluctuate in ways that you can predict by looking at business activity.

MAINTAINING POINTERS TO DOCUMENTS INSTEAD OF COPIES

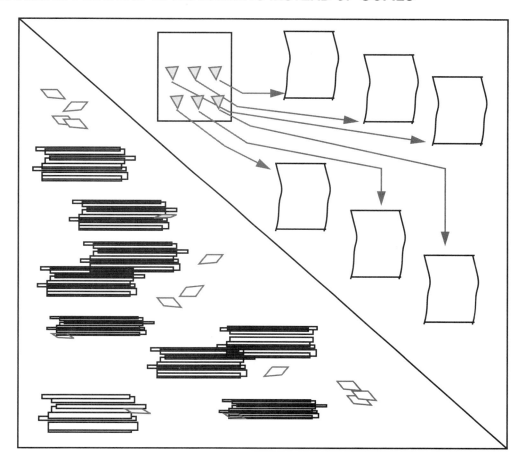

Figure 9.1 One way to clear desk space is to designate centralized sources for documents, and just keep indexes of the contents of each repository. The WWW is an ideal mechanism for this.

Sometimes through growth or lack of attention, a great deal of collective organizational energy will be invested in maintaining multiple copies of data. This includes informative mail messages, presentations, reports, and product documentation. By setting up a centralized, electronic information distribution model in an organization, you can save everyone time, including your own staff. Since redundancy usually means there are several obsolete and incorrect copies of documents around, you can improve information reliability by creating a system in which the most current information is in a single, predictable place. Set up a central, searchable document system or a WWW server that contains relatively static reference information. Let everyone who generates information know that, instead of distributing multiple copies, they can just distribute one, in electronic form, to the information repository maintainers. That done, all that gets distributed in the ideal organization are information locations, or pointers, rather than copies.

THE MYTH OF TOTAL INTEGRATION

If we take eliminating redundancy to the extreme, we run into another problem. There is a great attraction to the idea of saving all similar data in a single format. For example, we might dream of saving all documents in SGML so that they can be put in one big searchable SGML archive. In reality, lots of software that produces organizational documents don't export to SGML. Spreadsheet, presentation data, and reports may be stored in binary or even SQL format. We find we can't omit non-SGML data from a central repository because it often yields as much value as a word processing generated document. This problem leads some organizations to try to mandate the use of a particular protocol and supporting programs so that all files are interchangeable. This approach runs into problems as well. Someone will always have a word processing program they like better, and they will resent attempts to force them to use a product they consider inferior. Also, the standard program may become obsolete if the vendor goes out of business, sells off a key division, or fails to keep up with the leading edge.

We may end up spending more energy, time and money in pursuit of integration and standardization than we would by maintaining different systems for diverse data. In our industry, which thrives on change, you may need to accept that you will not be able to enforce an information format standard. Having reached this conclusion, you'll find it won't make sense to archive all data in the same way. There is some data that you will naturally keep as SQL Server data. Other data may stay as word processing files in a file system.

The latest trend in the industry for grappling with this problem is the concept of storing data and their associated programs in object-oriented information systems. In summary, this consists of storing each data item along with the name and the version of the software needed to present and possibly manipulate it. The data presentation software is either stored in the database or is pointed to by the database, such that function calls allow you to retrieve the data and automatically bring them up in the relevant application. (This will not seem particularly new to Macintosh users.) It remains to be seen whether it will solve the problem efficiently with a reasonable amount of investment in open systems. It will require good integration between the database and the application to manage the problem of incompatible file formats between versions of applications. Keeping multiple versions of applications around won't necessarily work because of the trend toward dynamically loaded library modules, which don't like to have multiple versions of themselves in memory.

As with most system problems, you can avoid making a bad investment in a total-integration solution by going through a formal proposal process and performing a cost/benefit analysis. No one technology approach is superior for all applications.

ARCHIVING

After you have gone through the analysis from the previous sections, you will have an idea of the information to keep online. Before committing to removing information based on your analysis, publish a report of your assumptions and your conclusions. Give all groups that may be affected a chance to review and confirm your results. Overlooking an undocumented but frequent use for the information could create operational problems. The people that generate information tend to get upset if the results of their work suddenly disappear without notice.

Options for archiving include single-stage archiving, in which online data are moved directly to backup media or multiple-stage archiving where data are first migrated to secondary systems and then eventually moved to offline backup media.

Sybase provides several ways to automate archiving. Some people use SQL Server segments and SQL Server thresholds (in version 10.0 and later). By setting up thresholds, you can automatically receive notification when a table reaches a certain size and determine whether it is growing faster than expected. You can also set up a threshold procedure that automatically takes certain action when the threshold is reached. Typically, this means dumping the transaction log for the log segment. It could also mean something as complex as launching an Open Client or Open Server program that uses BCP routines to copy out data, migrates the data to a HSC, and then deletes the data from the original table. You can achieve similar results with operating system batch jobs or Enterprise SQL Server Manager. Thresholds can be somewhat unreliable for several reasons difficult to avoid, so the best strategy might be to combine a few approaches. For example, you could use several thresholds on a segment to notify you of table growth and then use the data you collect about growth rates to establish cron jobs that automatically manage data.

Once you have copied data to a safe archive, you can again use various strategies for deleting it from the original database. For removing outdated data, the table design may either lead you to truncate the entire table at regular intervals or to delete rows based on certain criteria. If deleting selected records, you may find it worthwhile to write stored procedures that carefully select the rows to delete, rather than relying on manual procedures by specific people. Third-party applications such as SQL Backtrack™ from DataTools can also be used to back up data on an object by object basis. Chapter 10 discusses setting up a backup and recovery plan, much of which is also relevant to the task of data archival.

■ SYSTEM MIGRATION

In information systems with a mainframe or other centralized, proprietary system, you will probably find yourself analyzing the cost or process of migrating at least some of your processing to client/server applications. A plan of phased migration rather than sudden wholesale replacement often works best.

■ The organization can adapt to the change slowly over time.

■ You can address migration issues slowly rather than all at once.

■ You can reduce the risk of unanticipated failures and roll back if necessary.

■ You can improve the way you do each migration phase by building on the experience from the previous one.

Regardless of how you arrange it, the process requires the usual project planning steps before you start the mass movement of data. Many of the issues discussed in the "Data Warehouses" section, such as data compatibility, are also relevant under this topic. In addition, plan for:

■ Analyzing data

■ Redesigning organizational processes as well as applications

■ Moving data considered important

■ Replacing applications by purchasing third-party software or by rewriting them

■ Resolving data and programming incompatibilities, such as record formats and versions of compilers

■ Retraining both users and systems personnel

■ Testing

■ Debugging

■ Setting up new information processing policies and procedures

■ Synchronizing data between systems during the migration

■ Maintaining both the old and new systems during migration

During data migration or a data reorganization project, you may have a need to rearrange and reformat SQL Server data. A few methods for accomplishing this appear in the following list.

Be sure to test your method to make sure that no data or precision is lost when moving data between columns with different formats.

- For copying some or all rows of data from one or more columns of a table into another table or database, you can use the SELECT INTO command.

- For copying of data from all columns of a table into another table or database, you can use the bulk copy utility or API.

- To move a subset of the rows and columns to another table based on specific criteria, you can use an INSERT command with a SELECT clause using any conversion functions necessary.

- To move a subset of rows and columns or to transform data in some way before the copy, you can first create a view that contains the columns and/or rows that you want and then do a SELECT INTO from the view. This gives you the opportunity to preview the effect of changes before you commit yourself to the results. You may even find that the view fulfills the original request and that you don't need to completely reorganize data at all.

- To put indexes on new segments, you will have the most reliable results if you drop the index and re-create it using the ON clause of the CREATE INDEX command.

- To put tables on new segments, you can first use the sp_rename procedure to rename the old table to another name and then use SELECT INTO or BCP to transfer all the data from the old table into a new one with the original name in the new segment. By renaming the tables, existing applications will continue to work. However, stored procedures and other procedural objects based on the affected table will be automatically recompiled. This will cause them to grow slightly in size.

- To move tables from one database to another, you can use SQL Server Manager or third-party tools that backup and restore individual database objects.

- To move a large set of tables from one database and SQL Server to another database and Server, you can use DUMP and LOAD to create a new copy of the source database in a second SQL Server. Then you can modify the copy to contain only the contents that you need and use sp_renamedb to give it an appropriate name.

- To migrate a small amount of data between databases, you can use stored procedures. However, keep in mind that a large number of cross-database transactions can complicate recovery. It is wise to dump any databases affected by such transactions immediately after the migration operation.

■ For moving databases to new SQL Servers, BCP or DUMP and LOAD DATABASE will have the best results depending on the size of the database. It is also possible to create RPCs to do this, but this method will only be worth the effort if you only plan to migrate a subset of data identified by specific attributes or values.

■ For moving relatively small amounts of data across heterogenous systems, you can use BCP in character mode.

■ For moving large amounts of data across heterogenous systems, you can use OmniSQL or InfoPump, depending on the systems to be bridged.

■ DATA CONVERSION

A common task in data management is converting data between formats. Four common situations that necessitate conversion are

■ Using the same data with a different application.

■ Upgrade of a software application requires conversion of its data files.

■ Change of hardware requires that data be moved and converted.

■ Certain data are to be stored in a particular format for uniform access.

There are several ways to handle conversion:

■ Convert only recent data

■ Convert all data at once

■ Convert data as needed

■ Always save data in two formats simultaneously

In each situation, the time and cost must be weighed to determine which solution makes the most sense. There are several Sybase solutions for all these problems, and there are also third-party solutions and applications that you can develop yourself.

■ In SQL Server, there are implicit conversions between some datatypes, and there are functions you can use to convert other datatypes. (See the discussion of datatype conversion functions in the Sybase Commands Reference Manuals.) You can perform ad hoc conversions using Transact-SQL, or you can write a stored procedure or trigger for routine conversions.

■ If you need to convert between SQL Server data and another format, you can use the BCP utility or API.

■ For continuous conversion of SQL Server data for use in another type of Server, you may find that you can use the Replication Server APIs or a product built on them.

■ You can use Open Client or Open Server applications for almost any type of data conversion at any time. Open Client may be especially useful when the conversion requires programmatic bounds checking. Open Server may be the right solution for you if you need to distribute the results of conversions to several different locations or if you need to collect data to be converted from several different locations.

■ With the InformationCONNECT middleware, you can convert between data on heterogenous systems.

For converting data between heterogenous systems, remember that the conversion may involve the following activities to address typical incompatibilities between systems:

■ Translating from EBCDIC to ASCII or Unicode character encoding

■ Converting between float and packed decimal datatypes without losing precision, which is often determined by the underlying precision and formats provided by the operating system

■ Converting records to lengths within the boundaries of SQL Server's row size (1962 bytes, excluding `text` and `image` data)

■ Converting money and date datatypes to SQL Server equivalents

When upgrading software or hardware, either make a copy of all data to convert or only convert a small amount at first to verify that the upgrade works as expected. When upgrading applications, you will also need to choose whether to upgrade every user simultaneously or to perform a staged upgrade that allows you more time and less pressure to resolve any problems associated with the upgrade.

■ DATA REPLICATION

Setting up enterprise-wide systems often involves replication technology. It may take the form of databases dumped and loaded into secondary systems, or it may involve using products like Sybase's Replication Server.

Often, replication is used to extract data from operational sources and copy relevant portions or summaries to reporting databases. A replicated system can be protected from network or system outages that affect a centralized system. Also, users of replicate systems are likely to experience increased query performance both because they are competing with fewer users for resources and because they do not need to traverse the network as far to get their data. There is also less contention due to locking if the replicate is read only.

Replication can also be used for global operations to do a smooth hand off between time zones. This scenario could involve transferring all a database's data at once to the next time zone or constantly replicating it to other sites and allowing the concept of "primary" transfer from one site to the next during the day.

If the number of users of one set of data exceeds the resources of a single SQL Server, you can use the replication approach to spread the load across multiple copies of the data. This works best if only one set of users primarily writes the data, and the others primarily read the data. If all sets of users need to write data, then you will need to apply logic—often very complex—to synchronize the data sets periodically.

REPLICATION METHODS

Replication has become a popular term to characterize a data strategy. However, the basic idea, data copying, has always existed. Replication is not new, but we have new ways to do it. Depending on the complexity of what you need to do, you may need a product like Replication Server, or you may just need to learn Perl. The differentiation between replication methods lies in these factors:

- Latency, which is the time to copy a specific set of data from source to target

- Flexibility, analyzed in terms of the granularity of data that can be replicated and the types of transformations that can be performed on it during the copy process

- Transactional integrity, which a copy mechanism may or may not support

- Volume of data that can be handled by the replication method

- Complexity of replication system operation and maintenance

■ Resource usage, which determines how much supporting software and hardware must be purchased to make the system meet the goals set for it

■ Risk of failure, that is, how likely is it that a failure of one part of the system disables the entire system

A list of common replication methods and related considerations follows:

■ **SQL server dumps and loads** You can copy data from one SQL Server database to another using the SQL Server DUMP and LOAD commands. The replicate data may not become available in a timely manner, however, since users cannot access replicate data until the load completes. Also, with DUMP and LOAD, you get an entire database in its complete, detailed state, rather than being able to subscribe to a subset that you define or being able to transform data using SQL statements. You must also configure the replicate database to match the configuration of the original in terms of disk and segment usage.

■ **Operating system dumps and loads** While not supported for Sybase databases, you may find OS copying utilities useful for other data formats. For example, you could use the bulk copy routines or SQL to copy data out of a database and then use dd, cpio, tar, or backup software to copy it to another system.

■ **Table snapshots** A table snapshot is a copy of all or part of a table at a particular point in time. You can use SQL commands like an INSERT with a SELECT or SELECT INTO to create table snapshots. You can also use BCP Open Client programs or operating system commands to copy tables. The main disadvantages of this approach are that you do not get a consistent, transactional view, and making snapshots of very large tables or of more than a few tables becomes unwieldy.

■ **Stored procedures, triggers, and rules** You can use SQL Server procedures, triggers, and rules to set up a system in which selected data are replicated when initially entered into the table or when modified or removed. This works for small data sets or for derived data. For complex replication or large amounts of data, however, this approach can result in high administrative and performance overhead. Maintaining a transactional view of data with this method can require significant programming. If this is your goal, take care to write the logic such that you undo the secondary copy of the transaction if the primary is rolled back.

■ **InfoPump** InfoPump is a Sybase middleware product that allows you to copy data from various mainframe sources and formats. During the copy process, you can define transformations on a replicate data set such as summarizing it or denormalizing it. InfoPump is designed to work with high volumes of data.

356

■ **InformationCONNECT**   InformationCONNECT is a set of Sybase middleware products that allows you to access data in various database formats residing on various machines and operating systems. Many people use it to enable applications that can access data in heterogenous systems and to do things like perform SQL joins across Oracle and Sybase tables. However, you could also use this product to collect data from various sources and copy it into one summary database periodically. For example, sales, accounts receivable, and shipping data could be summarized into a product distribution database on a weekly basis for decision support. As with other programmatic solutions, getting a transactional view of data may take significant design and coding work.

■ **Front-end applications**   You can do replication up front by writing data entry applications that write the same transactions to two databases. This scenario requires employing methods to ensure that data remain synchronized if one of the databases fails. This uses more network overhead than other solutions, but may be the most reliable for a subset of transactions that you want to make sure to duplicate.

■ **Replication server**   Replication Server allows transactions to be replicated to different SQL Servers or other database systems as the transactions happen. Data are replicated by subscription. A remote site can subscribe to selected tables as needed. This method is designed to be fast, it keeps the replicate data current, transformations can be performed on the data during the replication process, and users can continue to use the replicate database as updates occur. A disadvantage of Replication Server is that, in the event of a failure of a primary system, some transactions will be lost, depending on the volume and latency of replication. Replication Server can handle large volumes of data, but also requires significant administration.

■ **Two-phase commit**   Two-phase commit can be a method of synchronized data distribution, while the other replication methods are asynchronous. With a two-phase commit algorithm, a transaction is committed only if all the interconnected distributed sites are up and accept the transaction. The price of syncronization is administrative complexity, heavy use of the network, and increased downtime, since a failure of any one site brings all sites to a halt.

Goals for your replication solution and the limitations of your information system will lead you to select a strategy from those listed above or maybe even to create a new system.

REPLICATION TOPOGRAPHY

We can typify replication schemes as master/slave or as peer to peer. The relationships can be seen in the three types of replication sites possible. From a primary or master site, data are replicated to other systems. Secondary or slave sites receive data from one or more primary sites. Peer sites serve both as a source and a target for replicate data. In peer sites, care must be taken to avoid update conflicts. This can be done by making certain sets of data read only, by avoiding updates to some sets of data based on source logic, by using a two-phase commit model, or by designing a conflict resolution mechanism into the replication application that uses flags or time stamps to determine the most recent data.

A disadvantage of the master/slave schema is that it introduces a single point of failure at the primary site. This can be a problem if the secondary system relies on continuous, real-time updates. In other situations, the master/slave scheme works well in failure mode because, if the primary goes down, the secondary sites have at least some of the data needed to continue processing. In a two-phase commit model, which is peer to peer in nature, the failure of one site brings all sites down. In this case, there are multiple points of failure, each of which brings the whole system down.

If you plan to use Replication Server for a peer to peer type of system, you will need to set up a data source tracking mechanism so that you can track updates reliably. Specifically, a set of data should have a primary site and replicate sites and should only be updated at its primary site. You can build such mechanisms into SQL Server data by adding source columns to tables and coding control mechanisms to only allow updates if the source column matches some value set in the Server considered primary. Set up a source transfer or proxy mechanism for handling the case in which the primary source for a set of data fails, and the replicate sites must be able to continue processing. You will also need to set up a procedure for resynchronizing data and returning the source designation to the original site once it has recovered.

A replication system in which one database can contain a mix of primary and replicate data can also introduce complexity into your backup procedures. To have a set of backups that can return an enterprise data system to a consistent state, you will need to have a complete set of backups made at the same time from all sites containing primary data.

We can also characterize replication methods as fitting into one of two different models—push and pull. With the push model, all replicate data are sent to the target sites as they are modified. With the pull model, each target solicits data when it needs them. The push model is good for continuous, nearly real time propagation. The pull model works best for systems with less immediate concurrency requirements and when you need to keep network traffic to a minimum.

While we typically think of replication distributing data from a central site out to remote sites, it can also function as a way to collect information from several remote sites and send it to a central site for consolidation.

When replicating data, it is often possible to replicate all or part of a set of data. In some cases, replicate data are summarized, transformed, or denormalized. While this works for decision support, you might not find this beneficial for regular operations. In particular, it may be hard to reconcile data between sites when they have been manipulated. For example, if every site calculates total sales based on its replicate set of data, but only subtotals were replicated, it could be hard to find the basic problem if the totals don't agree between sites. The processing necessary to undo replication transformations may be difficult or impossible to discover.

When replicating data across heterogenous systems, also take care with translations between datatypes. In particular, representation of float data is different on different machines and precision may be lost. You may also lose precision when converting between datatypes with different internal representations, such as between EBCDIC and ASCII or between packed decimal and float. Check the limits and mapping of each datatype that you intend to replicate before going into production.

When determining administration resources needed to set up and maintain a replication system, be sure to account for a thorough design and analysis phase, hardware and software resources, testing, replication system maintenance, careful monitoring of latency, and recovery planning. When planning recovery systems, consider the possible failure of each element of the replication system in turn and then consider the failure of likely combinations of system elements.

■ DATA WAREHOUSES

A data warehouse, as usually described, stores large amounts of data to support decision making. The data are usually refreshed on a periodic basis by making copies from OLTP sources. Data warehouses are often coupled with simple or complex decision support applications used to help users analyze the large volumes of data. In this book, we do not consider the concept of a *data warehouse* as synonymous with *Decision Support Systems* (DSS) or *Online Analytical Processing* (OLAP). A data warehouse serves as a repository for a large amount of data. DSS and OLAP systems are application-enabled systems for analyzing business data. DSS and OLAP may use a data warehouse as a source of useful information, but it takes more than data to support the decision making necessary to run a business. We discuss DSS and OLAP in the section after this one.

A data warehouse usually involves more than a gigabyte of data and is expected to support unpredictable queries. When making configuration decisions, data warehouse managers usually strive for ease of use, ease of maintenance, and high performance. As a repository for enterprise information, the data warehouse information is expected to be accurate and current within published guidelines.

The contents of a data warehouse usually start as operational data that custom-built applications summarize, filter, aggregate, or reformat to suit the purpose of the system. Information may also get sorted into groups and merged with external data, such as economic indicators, demographic data, stock prices, market trend metrics, credit histories, or suppliers' product catalog data.

Some enterprises envision a data warehouse as a repository for a variety of information stored in various formats. This could include tabular data, reports, documents, photographs, videos, graphs, drawings, audio recordings, schedules, presentations, and other specialized output from applications used for daily operations.

Organizations may use centralized or distributed data warehouses. Distributed warehouses allow remote offices to customize the data and applications to suit local conditions. A distributed model can also reduce the load on the network.

If your organization seeks economies by consolidating all operations into a centralized data system, your requirements will include the need to share data or applications between different departments. It will probably also need to support updates from diverse client applications. When the number of source departments becomes large, beware of too much centralization.

Overcentralization can result in problems of unsupportable requirements, loss of data quality, and interdepartmental conflicts. For example, an operational database for product sales information may need to be accessed and manipulated by sales, marketing, order fulfillment, management, accounting, and information systems. By the time you combine requirements from each department, your database may serve everyone's needs adequately, but do nothing exceptionally well. You can also end up with a database with stringent requirements set by one department that keep all other departments from utilizing the data effectively. Different levels of commitment to data quality can affect the data for all departments negatively since, whatever the results, they won't be reliable. In a centralized scenario, the time at which each department reaches its peak usage of the data or applications can create conflicts. For example, at the end of a sales period, like the end of the month, there may be especially high input of sales information. At the same time, the accounting personnel may be preparing tax reports. These may conflict, resulting in high tension because each group feels that it is essential that they get their work done first.

In addition to the usual project planning steps, setting up a data warehouse[1] involves

- Defining the objectives for the warehouse that justify the expense of setting it up

- Identifying the user base

- Identifying the sources of the data, both internal and external to the organization

- Investigating any quality improvements needed in the source data

- Defining the transformations of source data to target to ensure that data of the necessary quality can be imported into the warehouse

- Determining the ultimate volume of data to be stored in the warehouse, the amount of data to be added during each update cycle, and the rate at which new data must be added

- Determining how current information must be to be useful and how long it must be kept

- Identifying the business rules for maintaining the data

- Determining whether additional information needs to be generated to serve the warehouse objectives, such as adding dates and times to all records in order to enable historical trend analysis

- Planning and implementing useful prototypes if needed

- Developing conceptual, logical, and physical models of the data warehouse

- Defining the physical requirements for data movement, especially from external sources, including a network usage and capacity analysis

- Defining the requirements for refreshing and purging warehouse data

- Defining the hardware, network, and applications needed to support the data warehouse

- Creating a maintenance, backup, and recovery plan

[1]Or more than one, if you expect contention for the new resource among users and applications.

■ Implementing the applications for extracting, transforming, and loading source data, such as stored procedures, client applications, customized programs, Replication Server, InformationCONNECT products, or InfoPump

■ Developing and testing the data extract, transformation, and loading processes

■ Defining source tables and any necessary data manipulation programs to reside at the source

■ Loading the initial data set

■ Testing the ability of the system to meet objectives

■ Testing a complete refresh cycle, including purging old data and loading new data

■ Tuning query performance, possibly by server reconfiguration modifications to the database design

■ Implementing and testing the maintenance, backup, and recovery plan

■ Providing training for system administrators and for users, including information about tools, data, and processes needed to ensure the integrity of the system

This list is not necessarily in order, since the objectives and sources for your data will determine which tasks depend on others. For example, it may be necessary to develop a conceptual model or prototype before knowing whether the expense to set up the full system is justified.

Before embarking on such a major project, make sure that the data warehouse will serve business needs that cannot be met more efficiently in other ways. A strong desire to impose order on chaos is not, in itself, an economically justifiable goal.[2] If you are sure of the economic justification, but have not yet convinced everyone you need to involve, plan to implement small pilots that solve current business problems and that you may be able to incorporate in the final solution. In this way, you can build up credibility for the idea with demonstrable results. Pilots also help you demonstrate your implementation abilities.

---

[2]Such projects always create a strong emotional pull, but they tend to be really expensive to do right.

When designing or acquiring applications, select software that can handle large amounts of data efficiently. In particular, pay close attention to how applications use indexes and to the amount of concurrency they allow. An application primarily designed for transaction processing may have weaknesses that keep it from being a good choice for a data warehouse. Watch out for excessive locking, excessive use of user connections, and complex database design requirements that will make common queries nonintuitive.

Some warehouse designs provide summary data and then give users the opportunity to drill down into operations systems for detailed analysis. In some of these cases, you can use products like Sybase's InformationCONNECT middleware to provide the transparent access to the systems managing the detail information. Users shouldn't have to figure out how to merge information from multiple sources if the middleware can do it as well or better.

A particularly difficult and typical problem in creating a data warehouse is bringing all data input to a consistent quality level. Quality problems can happen when the department responsible for inputting the data has no direct connection to the department that requires the data input for analysis. For example, in a telesales order application, those inputting the data may be concerned primarily with making the sale. They may not care if they misspell the orderer's name or company. This can result in a duplicate record for the same entity. Those that analyze the market will find that the duplicate entries bias their results.

When building the warehouse, you will need to make choices about how to clean up missing or incorrect data. Design your processes so that you preserve the meaning of the data most needed for supporting the way the warehouse will be used. Approaches to solving data quality problems include

- Coding validation rules into the source systems or into the data warehouse transformation procedures

- Using data analysis techniques or utilities

- Applying correction programs

■ Rejecting suspect data sources or specific data items that can be determined to be incorrect programmatically

■ Establishing procedures to prevent poor data at the source

■ Establishing programs and procedures to monitor data quality throughout the life of the system

Other data problems that you may need to resolve when implementing a warehouse system include

■ Reconciling inconsistent data formats

■ Decoding data that uses lookup tables in the source system

■ Reconciling similar looking data fields that have different meanings in different systems

■ Deriving data where the information needed does not exist in any source

■ Setting up a unique identification system if current identification systems in distributed databases will conflict when combined

■ Integrating data in various formats from external sources that may require licensing and specialized software or hardware

After setting up your system, your most pressing problem may become query performance. With large volumes of data and requirements for decision support, you will need to index the tables and configure the underlying hardware for maximum performance. Sybase IQ is designed to boost performance for unpredictable queries in DSSs. Also read Chapter 8, which describes performance tuning, so that you can identify and eliminate design- and configuration-related bottlenecks ahead of time.

■ DECISION SUPPORT SYSTEMS AND ONLINE ANALYTICAL PROCESSING

A decision support system (DSS) consists of databases and applications designed to help managers answer questions about running their organization. The decision support system should provide information in a way that will improve the chances of the organization's success beyond what can already be achieved by knowledgable, well-trained managers. With particularly well designed decision support systems, the ability of poorly trained managers to analyze data and predict trends may be enhanced.[3] Questions that decision support systems answer are typically those for

- Selecting effective marketing strategies
- Predicting sales trends
- Monitoring and improving services
- Controlling costs
- Analyzing risks
- Forecasting growth

Some examples of questions that managers want answers for are

- If, for our credit card services, we decide to reduce our direct mail efforts by 10% in favor of telemarketing, what would the cost and revenue impact be?
- How much more or less revenue would we earn if we change the pricing structure of our science fiction action/adventure toys?
- If we are able to take advantage of the emerging produce exports of Peru, which of our customers would be most willing to buy them and at what price?

A related information system approach, online analytical processing (OLAP), is the ability for managers to use an interactive system for investigating multiple dimensions of data and performing complex analysis. OLAP tools allow users to interactively drill into and explore consistently formatted data, analyze trends, and find statistical relationships.

The concept of data dimensionality gaining recent attention is the characterization of various data aspects as if they were vectors along various axes of a coordinate system. Dimensions might include time, location, or level of detail. For example, let's say that we are studying why some college students do better than others. We could represent all students as rows in a table. The columns would represent aspects of an entity of type *student*. These could include high school, year of graduation from high school,

---

[3]One should not count on this as sole justification for the system without first finding out the exact managerial shortcomings that are hampering the business. Sometimes it takes more than better information to solve the problem.

location of high school, college, location of college, combined family income, IQ, preparative class work, grades, test-taking ability, learning style, preferred subject matter, extracurricular activities, parental or mentor support during academic career, and psychological profile. The dimension of each aspect could represent changes over time or changes in levels of detail.

To perform an interactive analysis to sort this information out, we might start with a table representing one student with columns containing school years and rows containing subject matter, as shown in Table 9-2.

TABLE 9-2   *Two Dimensions of Academic Performance for Student X*

Student X	HS 9th	HS 10th	HS 11th	HS 12th	UG Fresh	UG Soph	UG Jr	UG Sr
Math	A	A	A-	B	B	B-	B	D
History	B-	B+	B+	B+	A	A	A	A
English	C	A	A	B-	A-	B+	A	A
Science	A-	A	B	B	C	C	C-	D
Art	C	A	C	B+	B+	B+	A	A

By looking at these data, we might start to speculate about this student. When he did well in math, he did well in science as well. Later, when he did well in the arts, he also did well in history and English. We also notice trends in time. The student appears to have lost focus in the twelfth grade of high school and then found it again, but only for specific subjects, in his senior year of undergraduate work at college. It appears this student can do well in any topic when he applies himself, but that he doesn't always choose to do so. Now, perhaps we want to explore the trend of association between subjects. We would look at another few students one at a time to see if there's a trend and then at several students at a broader level, say summarizing the grades of all graduates of a particular college.

We might also want to look at semesters instead of years, or at classes in the subjects, or at all students from a particular income level. These different levels of detail would require different tables or a different way of storing the data.

Once you attempt to correlate a third aspect with two others, however, such as geographical region and clustering of math and science, you end up with a need to represent data in another row and column table, while it might be better stored in a conventional program array and envisioned as a cube. OLAP applications specialize in enabling this type of analysis in database systems.

Typically, businesses without OLAP systems prepare multiple reports that only show one or two dimensions of data in aggregate form. From these data, a knowledgeable manager notices trends and forecasts future performance and mentally constructs the third dimension or makes lucky guesses based on hunches.

While a decision support system may or may not be considered an OLAP system, the implementation issues for both are similar. Therefore, we discuss them together for the rest of this section. Like data warehouse systems, DSS and OLAP applications require ongoing data extraction, data movement, data transformation, process management, and metadata management. Most of the considerations discussed under data warehousing apply here as well.

For decision support, the configuration and applications used to access the data depend on the way decision makers want to see the information. Questions to ask the potential users during the design phase include

- Do you want to see statistical summaries, such as in the form of percentages? Do you want to be able to drill down to the supporting detail?

- Do you want to see graphs that show trends?

- Do you want to see all the data in a summarized or graphical "big picture" format?

- Do you want to follow a particular data element through an organizational process or through time?

- Do you want to attempt to correlate data, such as associating trends in business with buyer profiles, with market changes, or with the activities of the competition?

- Do you want to analyze trends over time?

- Are the data you want to see predictable? Do you want to see certain statistics month after month?

- Do you want to see your past decisions and the results of those decisions?

- Do you need to see data at some starting point before knowing what to look at next?

- Are you looking at the information system to guide your thinking? To interact with you and lead you to new conclusions?

- Do you already know exactly what's important and just want to get to particular data quickly?

- Do you want information to lend structure to your decision making or to inspire new, innovative ideas?

Once you know this information, you can determine whether you need to organize the information in a particular way so that the query results can be returned with adequate performance. You also begin to understand the form that the querying application should take.

A decision support system can manipulate information in several ways to help a decision maker who wants more than data summaries. These include

- Trade-off analysis, in which advantages and disadvantages of a particular approach are listed, along with a weighting that indicates the relative importance of each item in the lists.

- Weighting, which can be used when comparing two or more alternative products or solutions to a problem. Each alternative is rated on a scale for a number of attributes that constitute the relevant features of the product or solution. The most highly rated item is selected.

- Goal programming, in which a set of goals is prioritized, and a solution that provides the most optimal path to the goals is selected. This may involve modeling the situation as a mathematical equation with several variables and then solving it. A simpler trial and error, what-if approach may also be used.

- Sequential elimination, in which desired features for a product or solution are listed in order from most to least important, along with constraints that define how well a solution must fit a desired model in order to be considered. Available solutions are compared against these features and are eliminated as they fail to meet the important criteria, as well as the competing alternatives.

■ Risk analysis, in which the possible success of alternative solutions to a problem are presented as a point along a continuum from complete certainty to complete uncertainty. Usually, a percentage is used to represent the probability of a particular outcome.

Generally, decision makers will not want to learn complex programming languages to perform analyses such as these. Instead, they will prefer choosing menu options or clicking on icons. It should be intuitive how to go from the current set of data presented to the next set of data desired. The user interface can be designed to support any or all of these methods. While a less sophisticated system helps improve decision making by presenting accurate information, a true DSS will improve decision making by helping the user to think about the right things.

For OLAP, some technological approaches have already been taken toward creating suitable systems. These include multidimensional databases, middleware, and query environments.

■ Multidimensional databases store information along predefined dimensions and precompute aggregates. This solution is best for systems where the dimensions of interest are known, the data set size is limited, the number of dimensions is small, there is sufficient time to refresh the database and calculate the aggregates, and it is acceptable to duplicate data to conform to the specialized environment of the database.

■ Multidimensional middleware stands between relational back-end and front-end client tools to provide multidimensional services. Multidimensional middleware works best when scalability, sharing analytical definitions between users, access to detail data, and use of an existing relational infrastructure are important.

■ Multidimensional query environments provide local dimension definitions and download detail data into the local workstation. These solutions work well when the data set size is small, end users want analytical flexibility, an existing data warehouse is in production, and use of an existing relational infrastructure is important.

■ DISTRIBUTED, INTEROPERABLE SYSTEMS

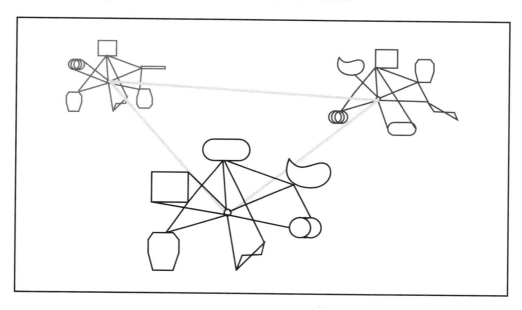

Figure 9.2 The more innovative our technology and the more successful our enterprises, the more complex and challenging we find the task of integration.

There's nothing new or leading-edge about distributed information systems. We have all had them since the day our organizations started business. Some information is distributed into our desk drawers, some on our desktops, some on our counter tops at home, some in our garages, attics, and basements, and a lot on various computers from mainframes to notebook PCs. The promise of the next wave of enterprise information system technology is not more of this, but the integration and interoperability of distributed systems. Perhaps you will never be able to have a desk drawer full of scraps of paper interoperate with your workstation, but interoperability between a palmtop and your workstation could discourage you from filling desk drawers with paper scraps in the first place. In various publications, a variety of different solutions can be called distributed processing, so be sure to understand what anyone who tries to sell you on a *distributed processing system* will really deliver for your money, time, or effort.

Most of the electronic information systems we find in enterprises today lie somewhere along a continuum from centralized to distributed. In fact, the history of an organization's IS solutions may be characterized by swings from one extreme to the other. Centralization and distribution each have different appeal for different people. Many IS professionals would prefer centralized rather than distributed systems. A centralized system gives us the easiest type of environment to manage—one in which there is a single operating system and a single type of machine upon which an entire business is run. A strategy for minimizing costs by minimizing complexity might be to force everyone to stay on one architecture. However, users tend to want distributed systems. A business has many information and computing needs, and different computer architectures are best suited for different needs. PCs may be good for spreadsheet users, but we might prefer to have a mainframe handle our bank's automatic teller network.

In previous chapters, we have looked at some of the factors in deciding whether to keep data in one large database or in several smaller ones. For larger data systems, we find ourselves choosing between one large Server or several smaller ones. In general, the issues are the same: maintainability, performance, practical capacity, and fitness for a purpose. Segregating data among servers generally increases the complexity of maintenance, but makes recovering from problems easier, since damage is usually limited by the boundaries of one Server. Performance and network usage can be better with distributed systems if a well-designed process is put in place for recombining data when a centralized view is needed. The existence of multiple servers multiplies the complexity of the system. In situations where it makes sense not to distribute data, the physical limits of a single RDBMS server may drive you to divide data among servers when you would otherwise leave them combined.

In addition, the following conditions in your current system may drive you to distribute processing:

■ Certain source data can only be created or stored on a particular type of machine.

- Certain data can only be manipulated by a particular application on a particular type of machine.

- High-volume operations require dividing data processing among regions or time zones.

- Different regions require different data sets and applications to accommodate localized operations.

- SQL Servers need to be kept close to applications used in a particular region, department, or subset of the customer base.

- Different SQL Servers are required for different operating systems.

- Growth or change in business operations necessitates additional systems or systems with a fundamentally different design.

- Business units need to develop applications independently of business-wide information system initiatives.

- Data need to be controlled near their origin.

- Network traffic needs to be reduced by having users perform retrieval and update operations locally, or the WAN is too slow to allow remote retrieval and update.

- Processing needs to continue if the network or a central site goes down.

- Management wants to spend less money on large-scale centralized hardware and software.

Meanwhile, these conditions of a system that has become distributed may lead you to try to centralize processing:

- Access to information needed for decision making is slow, especially when methods for extracting the data have not been previously defined.

- Datatypes in one system may not match datatypes of other systems and may introduce inaccuracy when compared without careful analysis.

- Effort is duplicated when developing new reports since the source of the existing reports may not be accessible to all users.

- Because of multitudes of reports existing in a wide variety of formats duplicating each others' contents, it's never clear which report presents data most accurately.

- A great deal of effort is expended to combine information from reports generated by separate systems.

- Data quality is extremely inconsistent.

- Data duplication is uncontrolled.

■ One logical transaction is divided into multiple transactions processed at different locations, and integrity control is vested in manual processes that often fail because people have varying levels of training and experience.

■ Differing localization conventions may make it extremely difficult to compare data from different systems (e.g., comparing data entered in different time zones but without date and time stamps).

■ Finding people trained to support all types of hardware and operating systems is difficult.

■ More systems mean that you have more system administrators and the amount of coordination required between them increases.

At any stage of life, most systems consist of some centralized technology and some distributed. Some systems may be very old, with islands of newer technology filling in the gaps. Usually, the older technology is retained since it works, it is essential to the workings of the current business, and it cannot be replaced without substantial investment. However, the older systems often bring us data in fixed files that are only understandable in conjunction with an application program to which we may or may not have the source code. The draw of newer technology, like RDBMSs, is that you can solve problems by simply writing a SQL query, instead of writing an entire program to extract and format the proper fields from data files. Seeking a balance between old and new while solving problems with distribution and centralization will lead you to choose a strategy of evolutionary interoperability. You can retain the parts of your system that work and still be able to take advantage of leaps in technology that provide your business with a competitive advantage.

With persistence, any program can be interoperable with any other. For example, mainframe data can be downloaded to a UNIX machine, analyzed, converted to a graphical representation, and distributed and displayed on a Macintosh. However, this doesn't mean that the new age of distributed computing has completely arrived. The process just described may involve ten programs and three network protocols. When one element goes wrong, it can be very difficult to discover which it is. While this solution is interoperable and distributed, it is still not what we really want. It is not enough to stop the swing between centralization and distribution, and it is not enough to keep us from wanting to replace our systems every 3 years.

An ideal distributed, interoperable, and integrated system would be flexible, expandable, and modular and would provide security and allow communication without respect to network, hardware, or software boundaries. It would introduce consistency and efficiency and simplify user access to the data they need. Output from one program would serve as input to another without the need for the user to reformat the data. Each element of the system would have an error detection and reporting mechanism that would make it easy to isolate and resolve problems. APIs would be forward and backward compatible. You will not find technology solutions today that meet all these goals. However, don't let that stop you from evaluating proposed solutions as leading toward these goals.

For today, our overall challenge is to enable distributed processing for operations enhanced by distribution and to enforce the design discipline that will provide users with the reliability and consistency of centralized systems. Initiatives like creating a data warehouse may stem from a reaction to too much undisciplined distribution. Similarly, a mandate to support heterogenous, networked systems may come as a reaction to the stifling effect of being forced to work within the limits of one architecture. As usual, cost/benefit analyses and careful comparisons between expected and actual results will help you determine where to strike a balance between distribution and control.

The requirements for the type of interoperable systems we want tends to expand client/server from a two-tier to a three-tier architecture:

- Clients, which handle presentation services and some or all application logic. Examples include PCs or workstations running a windowing-system-based application, a character-based mail reader, or a cash register.

- Middleware, which provides services such as interoperability, networking, and message management. Examples are gateways, replication servers, message queuing systems, and transaction monitors. In DCE, the middleware layer also handles security measures such as authentication and encryption.

■ Servers, which provide direct service management to multiple service requestors (clients). Examples are database servers such as Sybase SQL Server, mail servers, or HTTP (WWW) servers.

In the Sybase architecture, data and processing can be distributed and made interoperable by various combinations of

■ SQL Servers using RPCs to communicate

■ Custom Open Client programs

■ Custom Open Server programs

■ Sybase or third-party client applications

■ Sybase or third-party middleware applications

■ Replication technology

■ Sybase or third-party management tools

In general, managing a distributed, interoperable system includes distributing the software, configuration files, and knowledge necessary to all users requiring that interoperability. It also includes enabling security mechanisms to keep users from using resources they don't need or are not authorized to use.

Areas requiring increased attention in a distributed processing environment include

■ Performance

■ System availability and reliability

■ Problem resolution when any of multiple components may be at fault

■ Capacity planning

■ Monitoring and meeting service and support expectations

■ Inventory management

■ License management

■ Software distribution

■ Change management

■ Security

■ Accounting and charge back

The complexity of distributed systems comes from the number of connections between components. The number of connections between components increases more rapidly than does the number of components. Furthermore, each protocol transformation that data encounter along their path between source and target increases the number of things that can go wrong.

For illustration, let's imagine a server environment in which each server can interoperate with every other server via a direct connection. If there are n servers, then there are $n(n-1)/2$ possible connections. This means, for three servers, that you have only 3 connections. As soon as you get to five servers, the number of connections doubles to 10. When you add two more servers, the number of connections has tripled to 21. At 100 servers, you have 4950 connections, or 49.5 times the number of connections as servers. When you think about adding clients into the mix of connections, you start to realize how much complexity a distributed system introduces, especially if you are responsible for troubleshooting.

In practice, you can only afford to pay attention to a subset of connections. To monitor interconnections carefully, you can group similar connections, say all those from a particular operating system to another, and closely watch best case, worst case, typical, and random cases. Testing of new services requires testing each of these sets of interconnections, in addition to general load testing and verification of algorithms.

The next step in client/server computing for anyone who has done the math is to somehow standardize these routes to minimize the differences between them. One solution is to keep the vendor environment as homogenous as possible and hope that the vendor keeps its services self-consistent while staying on the leading edge. Another is to set up standards for interconnection in distributed environments. This leads us to the DCE standard.

THE DISTRIBUTED COMPUTING ENVIRONMENT STANDARD

Industry professionals and various vendors have anticipated the complexity that comes with distributed systems and have joined forces to propose distributed computing environment (DCE) standards. The purpose of DCE is to provide a layer of abstraction between applications and the underlying host system hardware and software. This means that applications shouldn't need to worry how to make a particular kernel call on a particular operating system. Instead, they should just be able to ask for the same service on every host machine, and the DCE service implementation should provide the translation between the service name and the appropriate kernel calls. The promise of DCE is to facilitate distributed computing by providing transparency and control while minimizing the risks. In this section, we'll look at the services and Sybase's plans to support them.[4]

The work on DCE has been done under the auspices of the Open Software Foundation (OSF), a nonprofit company founded in 1988. OSF is dedicated to the goal of creating a vendor-neutral computing environment. Its membership includes systems vendors, independent software vendors, end users, government agencies, research centers, and universities. Sybase is a member of OSF.

Sybase support of the standards primarily means that the Sybase Open Client and Open Server APIs will allow developers to take advantage of DCE services. Developers will need to use CT-Library rather than DB-Library to take advantage of DCE. You will be able to choose whether to write applications using DCE depending on your environment. For operating systems not providing a DCE implementation, such as Microsoft Windows NT, you will also be able to use the vendor-supplied alternatives to DCE. For example, Sybase will support the directory and authentication services provided with Banyan StreetTalk, Microsoft Windows NT, and Novell Netware. The Open Client/Open Server APIs will provide access to the Directory Services, Security Services, DCE RPCs, DCE Threads, and the Time Service.

The DCE Directory Service will allow applications to look up Servers based on criteria defined in a resource directory. Users will not have to know the names of Servers and the location of

---

[4]Things change rapidly in the information industry, so although I have read information about Sybase's plans in this area it is possible that the plans will change before implementation. This book then should not be construed as promising anything about current or future Sybase software.

interfaces files. Instead, users will be able to use a directory browse feature to pick from a list or to search for a variety of Server attributes. The directory service also describes security services used by entities in the directory. Open Server routines will be able to register their status and their supported security mechanisms. Client applications will be able to select among the security options available.

The DCE security services include

■ Authentication, which verifies the identity of users

■ Encryption, which protects data from unauthorized interpretation

■ Authorization, which controls access to resources

Sybase will initially support DCE encryption and authentication in Open Client and Open Server applications. User names, passwords, data, and check sums will be protected by encryption as they travel between clients and servers. Servers will continue to provide internal authorization services by using the Sybase object protection mechanisms that already exist. The DCE encryption mechanism for U.S. systems will be the Data Encryption Standard (DES). Application developers can also choose to use another encryption mechanism or none at all. All the host machines in a specific DCE environment, however, must use compatible encryption methods for communicating with each other. The DCE authentication service is based on Kerberos Version 5 network authentication.

DCE RPCs are remote procedure calls for distributed applications. The database transaction RPCs already implemented by Sybase applications will execute through a DCE pipe, which is a transport mechanism provided by DCE RPCs. DCE RPCs are protected by the security services. DCE RPCs provide network and protocol transparency, reliable distribution recovery, independent directory services, and security within the DCE environment.

DCE threads are POSIX threads, which will be supported by Open Server. Each client connection will use a thread, and each internal task will use a thread as well. Open Server will offer both preemptive and nonpreemptive modes on DCE platforms. Open Server 10.0 on NT, Netware, and OS/2 already use the native threads provided by these operating systems. Client-Library will be DCE threadsafe since the Open Server applications will be able to use preemptive mode.

A thread can be thought of as a unit of execution for use by a task. A multithreaded application is one that can execute several tasks simultaneously, regardless of how many CPUs are available. If there is only one CPU and there are 10 threads, then each thread vies with the others for use of the CPU. A key difference between a threaded and a nonthreaded program is that the non-threaded program runs from start to end without interruption within the context of that program. A threaded program allows multiple tasks to be interrupted and restarted dynamically so that the program can make the best use of the resources available to it. For example, if one thread is waiting for user input, another thread could use the CPU to calculate a sum. In a nonthreaded environment, the program would not be able to do anything while waiting for the user. A preemptive thread is one that can interrupt another thread to use a resource if the preempting thread is considered by the program to have higher priority. In contrast, a nonpreemptive thread must wait until another thread completes before being able to take its turn to use system resources. Preemptive threads require more programming care because they must be able to pick up at any point where they might have left off. In a nonpreemptive system, threads only interrupt themselves when they are at a good stopping place.

The DCE distributed time service will be integrated with the existing time API in Open Client CT-Lib and Open Server. When called, this routine will return the time from the DCE time service instead of from the native operating system.

■ THE STANDARDS STRATEGY

When selecting technology, you can pick unique, innovative technology that solves an old problem in a new way, or you can adopt technology that adheres to standards in order to avoid dependence on a particular vendor. While new technology can help a business attain a competitive edge, the standards-based approach will provide the most flexible, maintainable system for day to day use. When deciding between these two divergent approaches, a cost/benefit analysis will help you make a decision. In particular, analyze the expected lifetime of the proposed system. In this section, we explore the known benefits of the standards-based approach.

There are a few types of standards:

■ Official (de jure) standards published by a national or international standards bodies. These bodies operate under procedures designed to guarantee that the standards they produce are open and unbiased.

■ Standards developed and adopted by consortia, usually of interested vendors. These standards tend to be somewhat biased toward the common interests of the members of the consortium. They tend to be open to the extent that the members represent a broad base of the user population.

■ De facto standards, developed by a dominant technology vendor. These standards tend to be biased toward the vendor that developed the standard.

■ De facto standards developed by a community of dedicated users. These standards tend to be biased toward a particular technology. These standards usually come about because a group of highly enthusiastic users gathered around a promising technology and wrote software to support a community standard. In particular, the Internet programmer community has developed some of the most workable, open, ad hoc standards we have.

The primary benefit of sticking to standards is to avoid the costs of being bound up with the limitations of a particular platform or vendor. If a vendor of a proprietary system goes out of business and your IS strategy depends on its system, then you either go out of business, too, or you must absorb a large reengineering cost. By adopting open standards and biasing your acquisition decisions toward technology providers that adhere to them, you can extend the life of your system choices. You can also avoid the need to constantly retrain programmers to learn new programming languages and interfaces. For popular standards, you can hire employees that already know the standard, rather than having to train them. By adopting popular standards, you also become part of a larger user community that can be tapped for solutions to common problems. A broad-based user community also becomes a more powerful force than a single-vendor user community when lobbying for advances in the state of the art. You can have some feeling of comfort in knowing that, if there is a flaw in the design behind the standard, others have found it and a fix is being researched. If you run into a flaw in one vendor's implementation of the standard, you are also in a better position to swap out components until you discover the one causing problems.

In some cases, there are no reliable standards. This can happen for several reasons:

- For a new technology, putting boundaries around it at an early stage would limit the innovations that might otherwise emerge from it.

- When two powerful but conflicting approaches could be taken to solving a problem, the marketplace becomes divided and is unwilling to bet on one of them.

- When one vendor dominates a market, it becomes the definer of the de facto standard. A vendor that attempts to create an alternative standard in this situation is taking a huge risk. It would be difficult to gather the critical mass in the marketplace needed to both take over the market and force abandonment of a working standard. The cases in which such an approach might work are if the de facto standard is fatally flawed, if the popularity of the market leader is on the decline, if the popularity of the market leader could be put on the decline by a superior product, or if a sudden shift in the market alters perceived needs and thus opens the need for a new standard.

- There may be too many proposed standards. In this case, the diversity of offerings divides the market, making it impossible for one approach to gather a significant margin of support. The significance of the margin required depends on the vendors that are needed to support the standard. For example, a standard to be implemented in hardware must gain the buy-in of the major hardware vendors in the selected market, which is rarely comprised of more than 10 dominant players. These vendors will find it expensive to support more than one or two of a set of competing standards.

- A standard that finally comes out of committee after years of laborious work may not be widely adopted because it is too complicated, lacks advantage over the existing de facto solution, or has become too distant from current needs of users.

Because there are so many cases in which standards fail, you cannot reasonably expect to implement a 100% standards-based system. Your organization may be well enough served by innovative or efficient nonstandard solutions that you determine to be worth the risk of departing from the common path.

At any time, your technology solution is only as strong as its weakest link. When reading trade magazines, news groups, and marketing material and when listening to sales pitches, form a mental picture of the components of your system. Think about which technology could be substituted if one of the links of your chain failed. The most vulnerable parts of your system will be the nonstandard parts. Evaluate the percentage of your system that is exposed to this type of risk.

A summary of protocols becoming standard that you may find of interest follows:

- DCE—Distributed Computing Environment, a standard championed by the Open Software Foundation (OSF). DCE provides distributed operation with a common services environment across platforms. DCE is described elsewhere in this chapter.

- POSIX—from OSF, originally proposed by IEEE. POSIX is a series of standards for operating system interfaces and utilities to facilitate making applications portable across a range of POSIX compliant operating systems.

- SQL—Standard Query Language, from the International Organization for Standardization (ISO) and the American National Standards Institute (ANSI) supplemented by the efforts of the SQL/Access group under X/Open. All these groups are international in representation, and seek to contribute to the de jure SQL standards. SQL originated at IBM.

- HTTP—Hypertext Transport Protocol, which originated at CERN. This is the protocol that is used to deliver information via the WWW. It is not yet standardized, but the Internet Engineering Task Force (IETF) is working on it.

- MIME—Multipurpose Internet Mail Extensions, standardized by IETF. The MIME specification allows a file type to be associated with an external application that understands the file type. This is used by mail systems and WWW servers to automatically respond to requests for data in a special format by calling the program that understands that format.

- SGML—Standard Generalized Markup Language, standardized by ISO. This is a document markup language that originated at IBM in the 1970s. Its purpose is to provide a way of marking documents logically, rather than physically, so that the information can be represented on a variety of output devices.

- HTML—Hypertext Markup Language is a subset of SGML, which originated at CERN. A standard for it is being worked on by the IETF. It is the default data format supported by HTTP, the foundation of the WWW.

- CGI—Common Gateway Interface. This is the protocol that defines the default way for WWW servers to call external programs that perform specialized processing to clients via the WWW.

- CORBA—Common Object Request Broker Architecture, produced by Object Management Group (OMG). With CORBA, clients send requests to an object request broker, which locates the target object implementation (a server), forwards the request, receives the reply, and returns it to the client. Every object's public interface is defined in a system- and language-independent way using the OMG's Interface Definition Language (IDL). CORBA takes an object-oriented approach that encourages inheritance. The Object Request Broker specifies the interface that must be used and the information that must be presented when one object communicates with another.

- SNMP—The Simple Network Management Protocol. Created and released by the Internet Engineering Task Force (IETF), SNMP is a way of managing multivendor TCP/IP networks. The SNMP architecture comprises several components, including the manager, the agent, and the management information base (MIB) and the protocol used to communicate management information between these components.

When managing an environment that involves several machine architectures and/or several operating systems, you become more and more interested in standards and protocols that let you perform similar operations in similar ways on all platforms. However, you will never perform all operations in the same way on all platforms— the ability to do so would imply that you don't need a heterogenous environment at all. In fact, until the perfect machine, operating system, and technology company arrive, each platform and each operating system will do a particular thing particularly well. Ideally, your environment should try to maximize the ability for users to use the right tool for each job, yet keep from detracting from their productivity by making them perform the same job on every platform in a different way. Then the information system design goals become a combination of maximizing how you enable unique operations on particular environments and minimizing the differences between environments for the common operations.

If you pursue this goal, your standards strategy will include

■ Following the development of standards in all the areas that involve mundane operations on each platform and implementing those that fit your business best.

■ Following the unique, breakthrough advances on each platform and implementing those where you can afford the risk of the technology being abandoned at some point in the future. A new technology usually starts to become standardized or gets abandoned within 2 years after the mainstream technology market becomes aware of it.

■ Influencing the development and ongoing support of standards in the areas that most affect your organization.

■ BEYOND ORGANIZATIONAL SYSTEMS

Most database applications serve the employees of the organization that maintains the database, and these employees serve the customers of the organization. In a few cases, organizations provide customers direct or mediated access to databases as part of their product and service offerings. This frees up employees to do truly value-added work.

Many industry forecasters have predicted business trends that will make boundaries between organizations more permeable. More and more functions will be handled by outsourcing firms, consultants, and contractors, especially in the areas of information processing. In addition, companies will share more and more information with their strategic partners. For example, many foundation software vendors like Sybase provide VARs with early releases of new software to facilitate the building and testing of third-party applications ahead of time. In addition, the parties of these alliances may realize that they can leverage their marketing efforts by analyzing their aggregated customer data together.

We are beginning to see more and more companies provide customers information on the WWW. While the information offered via WWW servers primarily consists of marketing materials, we are starting to see offerings of demonstration programs and technical support information. These materials were previously distributed in paper or magnetic tape form. The next step from flat WWW pages is to store this information in a database server accessed via a WWW gateway. In essence, companies are extending their databases beyond their own borders and bypassing intermediate forms of paper, magnetic tape, and telephone calls.

To make a database available beyond corporate boundaries, you will need to do a number of things in addition to the usual project planning steps:

- Determine the data and applications to be placed on the WWW site.

- Perform a network security analysis to determine if your organization is truly ready to risk the insecurity of interfacing with the Internet. There are several books on this subject, and there are new, relevant whitepapers being published on the WWW as well.

- Establish Internet access to your organization.

- Set up a firewall system to protect your internal network from the security risks of the Internet.

- Set up a SQL Server inside or outside the firewall.

- Set up an HTTP (WWW) server outside the firewall.

- Set up a gateway program so that the database server serves WWW pages or use an HTTP server product that has built-in database system calls.

- If data are to be received from users, code the gateway program to send the information through the firewall, or code it to dump it to an intermediate file and use a second, more trusted program to transfer the data through the firewall.

- Set up an operations procedure and a mechanism for refreshing the data in the SQL Server outside the firewall. Prepare both for a routine refresh and for a refresh needed in case the data get corrupted.

- Set up a customer service and support function to help users with any problems or questions they may have.

- Coordinate your plans with any other departments that may be affected. For example, if you intend to ship product via the WWW, you will probably need to involve your lawyers, your current shipping department, your marketing department, your sales department, your accountants, and your customer service department.

- Write documentation for publication in WWW format and in print that describes the operation of the system for customers. The printed copies should be prepared for distribution to the customer base by direct mail or the sales force. The WWW copies should explain the site for random visitors and for customers that find the site on their own.

Procedure Manual Suggestions

○ Archiving Data

⇒ Document the archive strategy for each database and for the input and output data associated with applications.

⇒ Describe expectations of the short- and long-term value of data.

○ Managing Communication between Servers

⇒ Write a procedure for maintaining systems with interconnected data servers.

⇒ Draw a diagram of each SQL Server, Open Server, and gateway Server in your system. Draw arrows between them representing the direction in which RPCs can be issued. Label the incoming arrow with the number of logins and connections that are allowed in the receiving Server. Label each Server with its name and its machine name, model, network address, operating system name, and operating system version.

⇒ Update this drawing whenever you make changes and especially when you add a Server.

 If you ever have problems requiring troubleshooting, you will speed up the process greatly by providing this diagram to the troubleshooter. Being familiar with the diagram will also make you intuitively aware how adding or subtracting another subnetwork or another Server will significantly change how well the system performs.

CHAPTER

Preventing and Resolving Problems

Systems managers may spend anywhere from 5% to 100% of their days solving problems reactively. In most of this book, we have concentrated on understanding how SQL Server works so you can derive specialized solutions to specialized problems quickly. This means reserving time to read and experiment proactively. If you are using 100% of your time for troubleshooting, try to find a way to invest the first or last half-hour to hour of your day learning how to get control of your system. The information in this chapter may help you work toward that goal. However, this chapter is no substitute for the Sybase Troubleshooting Guides and Error Manuals, which are indispensable reference manuals for any Systems Manager.

■ BACKUP AND RECOVERY

In Chapter 2, we got an idea of how the DUMP and LOAD commands work. In this section, we'll look at when and how to do backups so that you are protected against disaster. We'll start by looking at the reasons database corruption happens:

- The disk goes bad.
- The disk controller mechanism or memory goes bad.
- The controller or disk array firmware has bugs.
- The information system software has bugs.
- The operating system tries to use database device for swap.
- Another application or system administrator tries to use database device for another database, mirror, or file system.

The Systems Manager possibly has direct control over the last two and has only a little influence over the rest. In the case of bugs, the Systems Manager can attempt to influence the developers directly through user lobbies or through direct intervention through one high-level manager calling another. In the case of hardware going bad, Systems Managers can influence their fate as far as they are willing to research reliability data and refuse to use prototype hardware for production systems.

Given that much of data integrity is out of control, your strategy turns toward protecting yourself *when* disaster strikes. This takes the form of the following:

- **Backups**   You can make backups at the SQL Server or operating system level. Sybase only supports SQL Server backups. SQL Server backups can be made while the SQL Server is running. Operating system backups tend to corrupt the database if made while SQL Server is running. There are also third-party applications that make SQL Server backups safely.

- **Standby systems**   You can use backups to create hot and warm standby systems on nearby machines or machines at remote sites.

- **Mirroring**   You can use hardware, operating system, or SQL Server mirroring. Sybase only supports SQL Server mirroring. Hardware mirroring is provided in the form of RAID or other fault-tolerant hardware schemes. In this case, a whole drive subsystem is mirrored, perhaps even providing error correction features. At the operating system level, you can usually only mirror an entire disk drive. SQL Server allows you to mirror database devices, which may represent only a portion of a disk drive.

- **Arrangements for off-site disaster systems**   Some businesses provide disaster services by which an entire off-site computer site can be rented for the period of the disaster.

Throughout this book, we have referred to performance advantages of distributing databases across devices. Given that your disk devices will go bad at some point, we next need to look at the recovery implications.

Sandy's Sport Shops—Backup Scenarios

During his lunch break at work, Tim started thinking of how he would set up a backup system for the shop if he could ever get Sandy to approve it. As a test, he started to experiment with backup scenarios for his school data. In all cases, he planned to keep `master`, `model`, and `tempdb` on the master device and `sybsystemprocs` on the `sybsystemprocs` device. He had never installed auditing and didn't plan to.

During this process, he decided to divide up the school database into one database for *homework*, one for *classes*, and one for *instructors*. He figured he could probably use three partitions on three different disks with three different controllers. These scenarios cover the possibilities Tim considered. He labeled his partitions A, B, and C. Being somewhat lazy, Tim decided that making incremental transaction log backups would be too much trouble, so he planned to make full database backups every week.

Scenario 1   Put one database on each partition - Put the *homework* database on partition 1, *classes* on 2, and *instructors* on 3.

Scenario 2   Put one type of data on each partition - Put the data and clustered indexes for all databases on partition 1, nonclustered indexes for all databases on 2, and logs for all databases on partition 3.

Scenario 3   Stripe each type of data for each database "diagonally" across partitions - For the *homework* database, put the data and clustered indexes on partition 1, put the nonclustered indexes on partition 2, and the logs on partition 3. For *classes*, put the data and clustered indexes on partition 2, put the nonclustered indexes on partition 3, and the logs on partition 1. For *instructors*, put the data and clustered indexes on partition 3, put the nonclustered indexes on partition 1, and the logs on partition 2.

391

Let's see how a disaster would affect the databases in each of Tim's three scenarios. In scenario 1, if any raw partition goes bad, the other two databases keep functioning. As soon as the bad drive is replaced, Tim can load the affected database from backup. If Tim found space on another working drive, he could move the database to that drive immediately, rather than waiting for the replacement of the original bad drive. If Tim spreads his data across multiple disks as in scenario 2 and partition 3 goes bad, all three databases are down and will need to be reloaded once the drive is replaced. Scenario 3 suffers the same fate as 2. No matter what, different pieces of each database will be offline until the bad device is replaced. In addition, the confusing distribution of databases across devices provides extra opportunity for human error.

For recoverability, Tim decided that scenario 1 provided the best results among the three. However, for performance, scenario 2 might work better if fast devices were chosen for partitions 2 and 3. Tim realized that if he planned on making dumps of his transaction logs, he could achieve higher reliability for scenario 2 as well.

Sandy happened to wander by while Tim was doing his analysis, muttering to himself. After he explained the situation and she studied his paper for a moment, she asked, "What if you repartition your three partitions into nine partitions? Wouldn't that isolate the bad portion of disk long enough for you to rescue the data in the other databases before they became unusable?"

Tim started to protest and then realized that she was right. This scenario provided the most protection of all. He thanked her, and then mentally told himself that by getting her to participate it would be easier to get her support for buying the disks later on.

Database backups protect you from three types of failure. The first is a system failure that destroys data, such as disk failure. The second is user error that destroys data, such as deleting all rows in a table by accident. The third is deliberate maliciousness in which an employee or outsider destroys data, such as by infecting your software with a virus. In any case, you will need to recover the data from backup copies you have saved. The age of your backups will determine their value for recovery purposes. A backup you made last week doesn't reflect any of the processing you have done this week. A backup you made a minute ago saves you from re-creating any more than a few transactions. The older your backups are, the more work you lose.

METHODS

In addition to time of backup, method of backup affects how quickly you can return to normal processing after a failure. As usual, your methods will depend on your business, the highest risks of failure, and the amount of time and money you can devote to protecting your data. Here are the most common backup methods people use:

■ **Backup Server (System 10 and later) or DUMP, LOAD, and console (releases earlier than 10.0)** These are the Sybase-supplied backup facilities. Backup Server is an Open Server application that runs as a separate process outside SQL Server. Backup Server is called automatically via RPCs when you issue the DUMP and LOAD commands in a System 10 or later generation SQL Server. The predecessors to Backup Server are versions of the DUMP and LOAD commands that run as part of SQL Server processing. These earlier commands are used in conjunction with the console utility when making multitape dumps. Many consider the speed, independent processing, and convenience of Backup Server a major motivation to upgrade from pre-System 10 releases. Backup Server does fast backups while the database is online with minimal degradation of other processing. It also handles large databases well, interfaces with a variety of backup devices, and can make dumps in parallel stripes if you have multiple tape devices available. If you are running a pre-System 10 Server, you use the DUMP and LOAD commands to make backups after you use sp_addumpdevice to configure the location that you will dump to (a file or backup device). If you use this method and need several tapes to hold a dump, you also use the console utility, which manages the tape-changing process.

■ **Bulk Copy** You can backup selected data by using Bulk Copy. If weekly backups are sufficient for most of your data needs, but you have a particular table that you want to back up on a daily basis, this might be feasible. You could use bcp or a program written using the Open Client bcp routines to copy the table.

■ **Replication** You can use replication technology to make backups for warm standby purposes. See Chapter 9 for a discussion of various replication methods. The replication delay or lag time will determine how much data you could lose if your primary system goes down. Because Replication Server copies transactions in real time, replication is no replacement for offline storage. For example, if someone deletes all the rows in a table by accident, a replicated copy of that event will not help you.

- **Operating system backups**   Operating system backups are not supported by Sybase, but they may serve your needs for client application files or for data that you have bulk copied into files. Sybase does not support operating system backup programs because they sometimes cause database corruption, especially if SQL Server is running during the backup. This is due to the lack of transaction-oriented concurrency control of operating system copy utilities.

- **Third-party applications**   Third-party applications, such as SQL Backtrack, can also be used to make SQL Server backups and object-level backups. These are supported by their vendors rather than by Sybase. However, since such vendors have a vested interest in keeping their product viable, they are usually Sybase VARs and will work with Sybase to make the product work correctly. Likewise, Sybase wants its VARs to be successful since application-related sales benefit Sybase as well.

PLAN AND PROCEDURES

A good, well-documented backup strategy will include measures to ensure that

- The maximum limit on the amount of data you might lose in the case of the disaster is replaceable by regenerating the transactions.

- Recovering from disaster will happen quickly enough that it won't seriously affect the organization's profitability.

- You take all precautions possible to avoid losing data, including performing routine preventive maintenance.

- You make sure that the database is in good condition when you dump it.

- You protect the backup media from all possible failures.

- You set a maximum limit on how long you can afford to be offline while recovering from a disaster.

- You provide alternative backup and restore options for certain items, such as by keeping scripts of stored procedures and by keeping bcp or hard copies of system tables that you might need to rebuild the master database (syslogins, sysusers, sysusages, sysdatabases, sysdevices).

- You anticipate as many high-risk failure scenarios as possible and guard against each as necessary.

To help with the last item, consider these possible disasters and evaluate the relative risk to your organization:

- A disk for one or more user databases goes bad.
- The disk for the master device goes bad.
- Database corruption happens for any of a number of reasons.
- The network goes down for any reason.
- The Server machine goes down for a short period of time (e.g., due to a power outage).
- The Server machine goes down for a long period of time because of hardware problems.
- The operating system version is bad and must be upgraded or rolled back.
- The operating system must be reconfigured.
- Someone inadvertently or maliciously destroys data in a way that you immediately detect.
- Someone inadvertently or maliciously destroys data in a way that goes undetected for weeks.
- The file system containing the errorlog goes down or runs out of room, or the ownership gets changed so that you can't write to it.
- While dumping to a file, the file system runs out of space.
- While loading from a file, the file system disk goes offline or goes bad.
- The tape drive that you dump to fails while dumping or loading.
- The ownership of the dump file changes so that you can't load it.
- Someone inadvertently or maliciously deletes the dump files.
- Someone inadvertently or maliciously overwrites your backup tapes.
- Your backup tapes get stolen or lost.
- The ownership of the disk devices get changed such that SQL Server can't write to them or, sometimes worse, such that someone else can write to them.
- The applications you normally use for data input stop working.
- The applications you normally use for data output stop working.
- The middleware you normally use stops working.
- The location where you store your backup tapes gets destroyed by fire, flood, leaks in the roof, vandals, or pests.

- Your primary or secondary mirror device fails.

- Both sides of your mirror fail at once.

- A new version of hardware or software (application, server, disk, network, etc.) fails under unexpected or untested conditions, destroying data in the process.

To guard against situations in which a fire or other disaster destroys the building where you store your computers and tapes, store backups and recovery scripts in a safe off-site location, such as a bank deposit box. Some system administrators have been known to use their houses or cars as a secondary location. This only provides protection if the system administrator doesn't become incapacitated by the same disaster as the backups. You can alternate between two different administrators. For organizations with remote sites, you can send duplicates of backup files or tapes to a secondary site for safekeeping. In some areas, data archival companies provide the service of storing your data safely off site for time periods that you choose.

In addition to dumping databases and transaction logs on a schedule you set with the above things in mind, you should also make backups under these conditions:

- Dump the master database after any change, such as adding databases, users, or any system stored procedure that modifies the state of the system. If your system goes down after such a change, but before you make a backup, those accounts or other changes will be lost. If you lose the master database and don't have a backup after the execution of CREATE or ALTER DATABASE commands, you're really in trouble because there will be no record of the device allocations made to the database. In other words, if you load the old copy of master and run with it, someone could CREATE or ALTER a different DATABASE on the same part of disk, making the previous databases unrecoverable.[1]

---

[1] There are sometimes creative ways of getting out of these messes by following directions in the Troubleshooting Guides, but they're always risky and time consuming. In contrast, backing up master is usually quick and painless. To put it another way, its usually faster to back up master than it is to explain to your boss why you didn't back it up. I know I've made this point several times, but you'd be surprised at how often master is allowed to slip through the cracks.

■ Dump all databases after changing the sort order, since you will not be able to load previously made dumps.

■ Dump databases after any unlogged operations, since you will not be able to load transaction logs. Unlogged activities are SELECT INTO, fast bulk copy, TRUNCATE TABLE, and writetext in unlogged mode. Except for TRUNCATE TABLE, these unlogged activities may only happen when the SELECT INTO/BULK COPY database option is set to *true*.

■ Dump databases after creating an index. This is not entirely necessary as long as you checkpoint the database after index creation. However, keep in mind that when you create an index the fact that you created an index is logged, and the allocation necessary is logged, but not the details of inserting index rows onto index pages. If for some reason a checkpoint is not performed before the next boot of the SQL Server, the log is replayed during recovery and the entire CREATE INDEX is done again, taking as long as it took the first time.

■ Dump databases after the log has been truncated.

STANDBY ENVIRONMENTS

If you determine that you cannot afford to have your system down as long as it would take to load a backup, you may decide to create a standby system. A standby system is a secondary copy of all necessary databases that you switch to in the event of failure of the primary copies.

People speak of hot and warm standby systems. The difference in "temperature" of a standby is how closely it matches the state of the primary system in time. For example, if switching to a standby system means you would only lose 2 minutes' worth of data, you may consider it a hot standby. If the standby is made such that you would lose an hour's or a day's worth of data in the event of the failure of the primary, then you would have a warm standby. If you need to set up a new machine and SQL Server after several days and nights of trying to restore a primary, beware of frostbite.

To set up a standby environment, you will need to set up the system as you would a primary. In addition, before loading any dumps of the primary into the standby system, do the following:

■ Set `no chkpt on recovery` to *true* using `sp_dboption` if you are using transaction log dumps to maintain the standby.

■ Set `read only` to *true* using `sp_dboption`. Optionally, you can also set `dbo use only` to *true*, although this limits the standby's possible additional value as a reporting database.[2]

■ Set up methods and procedures for avoiding logged activity in the standby Server if you are using transaction log dumps to maintain the standby. Leaving read-only status set to *true* may accomplish this as long as DBOs and those with `sa_role` take care not to make changes.[3]

■ Set up methods and procedures for avoiding nonlogged activity in the production Server if you plan to use transaction log dumps to maintain the standby.

■ Set login and user policies for when the secondary system is not active.

■ Set policies for maintaining the secondary Server and keeping all reconfigurations of the primary in sync with the standby.

■ Create and maintain scripts (or other mechanisms) for creating all objects (tables, indexes, stored procedures, triggers, etc.) created in the primary that will also need to be created in the standby.

■ Determine the limit on the maximum downtime that can be tolerated, and set up procedures to keep the downtime within that boundary.

■ Set a goal for the amount of downtime for a variety of possible recovery scenarios that is somewhat less than the maximum.

■ Create and test a plan for backup and recovery such that the downtime goals can be met for a variety of different disasters.

■ Identify a person who agrees to take responsibility for maintaining the Server and its databases in a way that provides maximum protection against disaster.

■ Establish methods and policies to prevent anyone from pressing the system into use without authorization.

■ Establish methods and procedures for handling the conditions that may precipitate use of the standby.

---

[2]Read-only status also imposes some limits on this possibility since procedural objects in that database couldn't be recompiled.

[3]With SQL Server 11, keep in mind that `read only` will need to be turned off if, for some reason, you intend to load pre-11.0 dumps. Normally, standby databases should be managed by the same version of SQL Server as the primary.

■ Set limits on the use of the standby to make sure that the primary gets fixed as soon as possible so that the standby may return to its previous role.

■ Create an alternative plan that takes effect if the primary is down and the standby fails as well.

■ Create a periodic testing plan to make sure the standby is functional when needed.

■ Check the results of automated dump procedures from time to time to make sure they haven't failed.

■ Create scripts and procedures that allow the failover to happen as smoothly as possible.

■ Run DBCCs periodically to ensure that a quiet failure of a disk on a disk for the standby system doesn't keep your failover scheme from working as expected.

Keep in mind that you must do as much as possible to isolate the standby system from the primary so that you can isolate it from the problems that may affect the primary. This means using a different machine, a different SQL Server (but the same version), and, if possible, even a different subnetwork. Use exactly the same operating system and networking type, versions, and patch levels for the standby system. Failing over to a backup is not the time that you want to discover incompatibilities in system software.

Since maintaining a standby can involve considerable expense, some people make additional use of their standby systems as reporting databases. If you create a standby using dumps and loads of transaction logs, use the `read only` database option to make sure that no one modifies the standby system. Such a modification would invalidate the log dumps and you would not be able to load them. Instead, you would need to resynchronize the primary and secondary using full database backups or similar measures.

Methods for creating and maintaining standby systems include the use of

■ Dumps and loads to disk and then using remote mounting of file systems or operating system utilities (e.g., ftp, cpio) to transfer files

■ Fault-tolerant hardware that automatically fails over to standby components upon detecting failure

■ Operating system or Sybase mirroring

■ Replication

To switch over to a standby, you will usually need to do the following:

■ If using transaction log dumps for creating the standby and if the transaction log device is intact on the primary, use DUMP TRANSACTION WITH NO_TRUNCATE to capture the final transaction log and then load it into the standby.

■ Ensure that your standby has current versions of syslogins from the primary master database and sysusers from all primary user databases included in the standby system.

■ Reconfigure the secondary as necessary for use. This includes setting Server-wide configuration such as increasing memory, locks, open objects, and so on, to match the primary and resetting any database options that were used to maintain the standby status, such as turning off the read only option.

■ Alert users to log into the standby system or switch the names of the primary and standby in the RUNSERVER and interfaces files.

■ Work feverishly to get the primary working again. Consider appointing a deputy to answer user and management questions while you do this.

PROTECTING THE MASTER DATABASE

For a SQL Server to function, its master database must not have any data problems. Take extra care to protect it from harm, check it periodically using DBCC, and back it up. The normal procedure for recovering from a failure of the master database is to use buildmaster to create the database and then load a current dump of master. If you don't have a current dump, you will have to re-create master exactly as it existed before the problem. For this purpose, you will need the following:

■ All the scripts that you would need to rebuild the database. This includes scripts of all tables, indexes, rules, defaults, triggers, constraints, and views defined in master.

■ Make bcp copies of the following system tables in the master database: syslogins, sysusers, sysdatabases, sysdevices, sysusages.

■ Hard copies of all of the above (as an extra measure of protection).

400

Make it a policy not to allow user objects in the master database and not to allow user databases in the master device. Otherwise, such objects may be unrecoverable if you need to rebuild the master device or the master database.

If an application over which you have no control stores objects in the `master` database, you will need to reinstall that application if you didn't have a valid `master` database dump.

MANAGING THE TRANSACTION LOG

The transaction log records transactions before they are committed to the disk pages for the affected tables. A transaction log dump is like an incremental backup. It records transactions starting where the last dump database or dump transaction command left off. Depending on the applications and environments, SQL Server administrators usually use some combination of database and transaction log dumps. A large cause of technical support calls is not understanding the conditions under which a transaction log dump is not valid. The conditions in the following list invalidate backup schemes that rely on the logs because they mean that the logs can't be dumped or loaded:

- Activity occurs between the load of a database or transaction log and the load of the next log in the sequence. The log dump is detected to be out of order because SQL Server compares the highest timestamp for the database to the timestamp of the log and finds that the log is older than the database. Therefore, it will not allow the log to be loaded because it can't restore the database to a previous state known to be consistent.

- Since the last database dump, a `dump transaction` command is used the `WITH NO_LOG` or `WITH TRUNCATE_ONLY` clause. In this case, the log records are permanently lost, so they can't be backed up subsequently.

- There has been a `SELECT INTO`, fast bulk copy, `TRUNCATE TABLE`, or unlogged `WRITETEXT` operation in the database since the last dump database or dump transaction command. Since these actions don't write the results of their actions to the log, the log would be unable to re-create the state of the database as it existed after these operations. It simply doesn't know what data were there. Replaying transactions that were based on database transformations by these actions wouldn't make any sense.

401

■ Truncate log on checkpoint is set to *true* in the source database. If checkpoint truncates the log, SQL Server knows it will not have log records to replay. The recovery process relies on a checkpoint that was performed without a truncation.

■ The transaction log for which a LOAD is being attempted is from a different version of SQL server than the previous database dump loaded, or it is from a different platform.

Many users ask about reading the transaction log records. There are no Sybase-supplied methods for doing this.[4] The transaction log stores data in binary form for compactness and for security. However, you can learn various things about the transaction log using other methods:

■ `select count(*) from syslogs` will tell you how many log records there are in the transaction log.

■ `select name, dumptrdate, logptr from sysdatabases` will tell you the database names, the date of the last transaction log dump, and, when the database is closed, the first data page of the transaction log for each database.

■ `DBCC CHECKTABLE (syslogs)` and `DBCC TABLEALLOC (syslogs)` will tell you of any integrity problems with the log and the space used by the log.

■ `sp_helpdb` *dbname* will tell you the database options that affect how the log is managed internally.

---

[4]I understand there is now a third-party product that allows you to read the transaction log. In System 11, the format of log records changed, so verify version compatibility when considering such a tool.

THRESHOLDS

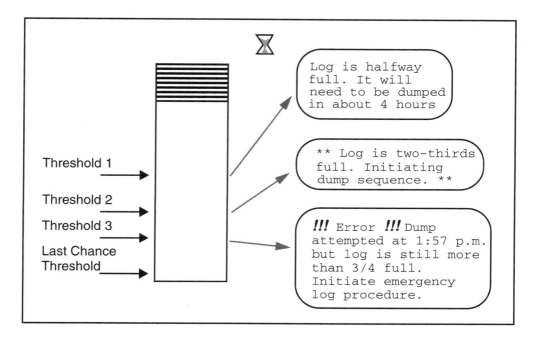

Threshold 1

Threshold 2

Threshold 3

Last Chance
Threshold

Log is halfway full. It will need to be dumped in about 4 hours

** Log is two-thirds full. Initiating dump sequence. **

!!! Error *!!!* Dump attempted at 1:57 p.m. but log is still more than 3/4 full. Initiate emergency log procedure.

Figure 10.1 Almost all functions are disabled when the log reaches its last chance threshold (LCT). You can set up threshold procedures at points before the LCT to protect yourself against log emergencies.

The transaction log grows as quickly as transactions happen in user databases. A log-full condition can compromise the integrity of a database. A set of functions for monitoring and managing space thresholds was introduced in System 10 to help avoid this problem. Thresholds are limits that you set on the use of database segments such that, when the use of the segment crosses the threshold, some action is triggered. With SQL Server thresholds, the trigger action is a stored procedure that you write. The stored procedure can be an RPC if you like. The most typical use for thresholds is to make automatic dumps of the transaction log. However, you can also use them to monitor space usage by other tables and by indexes.

Each database has its own set of thresholds. You can define as many as 256 in a database. There is one required threshold, called the *last chance threshold* for the transaction log. Once the transaction log space usage crosses the last chance threshold, a system administrator must dump the log before any more transactions can take place in the database.

Threshold information is maintained in system tables when the database is closed and is maintained in memory when the database is open.[5] While the database is open, you can extract the current space used in a threshold by using the `curunreservedpgs()` function, described in the Sybase SQL Server Reference manuals. You can retrieve space usage information from `systhresholds` and `sysdatabases` in `master` when the database is closed.

If a threshold is full, you will see the value *LOG SUSPEND* in the `sysprocesses` table for user processes that have been suspended because the database has encountered the last chance threshold. If you want user transactions to be aborted rather than suspended when the log is full, you can set the database option `abort xact when log is full` to *true* using `sp_dboption`. The `lct_admin` function, described in the Sybase Commands Reference manual, manages the log's last chance threshold. You cannot issue a DUMP DATABASE or CHECKPOINT command once you have reached last chance threshold in the log. If the `select into/bulk copy` option is enabled for a database that has reached the last chance threshold, you won't be able to dump the log either. Your only option will be to use `lct_admin` to unsuspend the log and then immediately dump it. If other users try to commit their work, they will fill up the log before you get a chance to dump it. If a database has reached the last chance threshold and you shut the Server down, recovery will not run on that database when you reboot the Server. To keep a database from getting in this state, make every effort to dump the log before reaching the last chance threshold and turn on the `abort xact` option for additional protection.

---

[5] A database is *open* when someone is using it. Select the `spid` and `dbid` columns from `master..sysprocesses` to see which databases have been opened by whom at any point in time.

Space usage in a segment can fluctuate around the threshold value without repeatedly triggering the threshold because there is an internal setting called a *hysteresis cutoff*. The global variable, @@thresh_hysteresis, holds this value, currently set at 256 pages. To trigger the threshold action, the space usage has to decrease to within the number of pages specified by @@thresh_hysteresis. To retrigger the threshold, the space has to be restored to more than @@thresh_hysteresis pages above the threshold and then fall below the hysteresis cutoff again. Without this control, the successive allocation and deallocation of extents near the threshold by various processes would force the threshold action to trigger excessively often. No threshold can be closer than two times @@thresh_hysteresis to any other threshold.

When a threshold is crossed in a way that triggers the threshold action, the following happens:

- SQL Server finds the threshold action by reading the systhresholds table.

- The Server creates a limited login as the last user who created or modified the threshold, using permissions that are the lesser of the login's permissions and the roles mask stored with the threshold.

- The threshold process does a use database.

- The stored procedure or RPC defined as the threshold action is executed.

- If this is the last chance threshold for the log segment, the database is marked as *almost full*, which means that the only actions possible are to dump the log or unsuspend the database using lct_admin.

If any of these actions fails, the threshold action terminates and an error is reported to the error log. Error messages and any output from PRINT or RAISERROR statements are printed to the log. Other output, such as the results of SELECT statements, are not sent anywhere since the login is a limited user.

It is possible to hit more than one threshold simultaneously since one piece of disk can have allocations for multiple segments, each with its own thresholds.

If you do not want to use thresholds, you can tell SQL Server not to track free space by setting the database option `disable free space acctg` to *true*. Setting this option also speeds up fast bulk copy operations.

Threshold procedures can fail under a number of circumstances that you should be aware of:

- The threshold procedure might get deleted.
- Someone could drop and re-create a different procedure with the same name if they have access to the same login as the original owner.
- The stored procedure could encounter problems, such as not being able to fit in procedure cache.
- SQL Server may not be able to find a spare user connection for the threshold process.
- The threshold procedure may not have permissions to do all that it is programmed to do.
- The threshold procedure might try to perform a logged action in a database that is full and get put to sleep like any other user.
- Someone could turn on the `disable free space accounting` option.
- The commands specified in the threshold action might fail for a number of reasons, such as Backup Server being unavailable, a device going offline, a tape missing, or a full or busy dump device.

SYBASE DISK MIRRORING

One common precaution you can take that will allow you to recover from disk problems quickly is to mirror your most important database devices. If you don't have enough disk resources to mirror everything, start by mirroring the master device and the transaction logs for key databases.

Mirroring becomes disabled whenever a write to either disk in a mirrored pair fails. SQL Server will not always detect the first failure of a device since that section of the disk may not encounter much database activity. When the Server does detect an error on the primary device of a mirror pair, processing fails over to the functioning disk. If the Server detects failure on the secondary device, the mirror is simply disabled. In both cases, an error is reported to the errorlog. Since you my not be checking your errorlog when this happens, it is wise to set up a batch job that periodically checks for mirror-related errors in the Sybase errorlog and notifies you by mail when it finds something. While you are at it, make the procedure check operating system logs as well, since disk corruption may get reported there first.

To reactivate mirroring, you will need to replace the disk if it failed or turn it back on if it simply went offline temporarily. If your replace the disk, prepare it for use as you did when initially setting it up. This involves partitioning, changing partition ownership to sybase where necessary, and setting disk permissions so that the sybase user can read and write it. Then you will need to issue the DISK REMIRROR command. This command will take awhile to complete since the entire working half of the mirror needs to be copied to the new half. Check the errorlog and the status in sysdevices to verify that the remirroring completed successfully.

DBCC

An issue that becomes particularly problematic for large databases is the challenge of maintaining integrity. Sybase provides several DBCC routines that verify integrity of data storage on disk and strongly recommends that these checks be performed before making backups. However, these checks take a long time to run. For many sites, running DBCCs as often as recommended would take over a day or a week. Many of these sites require 24-hour access to their databases, making it even more difficult to find time to perform maintenance operations.

Aside from the unacceptable "solution" of not running DBCC checks at all, Sybase Systems Managers usually resolve this problem in one of the following ways:

- Dumping the database during the system maintenance window, loading it into a secondary system, and running checks on the secondary system

- Using replication technology to transfer data to a secondary system and running the checks there

407

■ Using an object-level checking mechanism and cycling through checks of a subset of objects each day such that the total set is checked weekly or monthly

■ Using front-end applications that write transactions to a primary and a secondary system simultaneously and then using the secondary to run checks and make backups

In all these scenarios, there is risk that the data corruption will not be detected before backups are made. A backup may complete successfully, but it will not be loadable. In the first two scenarios, serious corruption may prevent the completion of the copy operation.

Because there is such a high risk of a hardware failure, or other problems that result in data corruption, mirror your most important data on secondary disks. The cost of doing so is usually much less than recovering from data lost as a result of failure.

For most accuracy, DBCC needs to be run with the database in single-user mode. In versions after 4.9.1, DBCC includes a fix option that the Server uses to correct minor errors that it can correct accurately. Use that option to avoid seeing errors related to allocation, in particular. If DBCC reports warnings and errors, look up any unfamiliar problems in the Sybase Error Manuals. DBCC has the best chance of detecting disk corruption in a database at an early stage if you run it regularly. DBCC prints out diagnostic information as well as errors. Since the diagnostic output can be lengthy for large databases, many people write operating system batch jobs that run the DBCCs on all target databases or objects, search for errors, and mail any anomalies found to the database administrators. Make sure to mail the output to more than one person so that the effect of someone going on vacation isn't a loss of a database.

DBCC is the most famous SQL Server utility and is both the most revered and most distrusted. DBCC stands for database consistency checker. While this is its most important function, its use has expanded. The way that DBCC is implemented provides Sybase support engineers a way to debug SQL Server when it is experiencing problems. In addition to the documented DBCC commands, several documented and undocumented diagnostic commands are built into the code for identifying and resolving problems. Chapter 2 described the DBCC commands that check database consistency. The following documented DBCC commands are used to diagnose or resolve specific problems:

- ■ **DBCC DBREPAIR (DROPDB, *db_name*)**   This command allows you to drop a database that has been marked suspect by recovery so that you can then re-create it and reload it from backups. When a database has been marked *suspect*, it is not possible to drop it with the normal DROP DATABASE command. See the Sybase SQL Server Troubleshooting Guide for more information about this type of problem.

- ■ **DBCC REINDEX**   This command checks indexes for errors and then drops and re-creates suspect indexes. In particular, it is used after changing the SQL Server sort order.

- ■ **DBCC FIX_TEXT**   This command upgrades text values after changing SQL Server's character set to a multibyte character set.

- ■ **DBCC PAGE**   This command gives information about a data page header and is used for troubleshooting purposes. This is supported only for the uses described in the Sybase Troubleshooting Guide.

- ■ **DBCC MEMUSAGE**   This command gives information about memory usage and is used to learn which procedures are in cache. It should only be used in single-user mode. In multiprocessing systems, it can result in time-slice errors. In single-processor systems, all other activity will be blocked while it is running. This is supported only for the uses described in the Sybase Troubleshooting Guide.

Sybase has traditionally decided that documentation serves as the boundary between bugs and supported features. Except for obvious documentation bugs, if an operation does not work as documented, it is considered a bug and is queued to engineering for a fix. Anything that is undocumented is not considered a feature of the software and is therefore not guaranteed to work. Therefore, undocumented, unsupported DBCC commands are unreliable. Undocumented DBCC commands may not work the same way from one version to the next. Since undocumented DBCC commands are unsupported, they are not tested extensively, and bugs reported on them are given low priority. A bug with DBCC is considered a lower priority than customer-requested bug fixes for documented commands.

If you need functionality that you think undocumented DBCC commands provide, log a feature request for that functionality, rather than requesting documentation. This approach has a better chance of leading to a more robust solution. The International Sybase User Group (ISUG) has also been very successful at helping Sybase set priorities for feature improvements. They publish an enhancements report every conference that contains a list of enhancements that the ISUG membership has ranked and voted on. Sybase does act on this report. The ISUG conferences also give you an opportunity to talk to Sybase executives and engineers and make your case in person. I've seen both of these methods result in visible changes within a year or less of the initial problem report.[6]

It would be irresponsible to commit undocumented DBCC commands to print here since they are unsupported, undocumented, and dangerous. However, many of them have been discovered and published unofficially on the Internet. If you use them, be aware of the risks.

RECOVERING FROM DATA CORRUPTION

In general, recovering from data corruption means identifying the cause, correcting the problem, and then restoring from backups. Among these steps, determining the cause of corruption proves most difficult.

Any of the following can cause database corruption:

■ **Inadvertent device sharing** Either random or regular corruption shows up when one disk partition gets used for two different purposes. For example, the Server machine uses partition *d* for swap, but SQL Server also uses partition *d* for a database. Each process thinks it has exclusive use of partition *d*. Another common occurrence is that one Server machine is used to run two SQL

---

[6]Why, yes, this is a plug for ISUG. The organization has been quite effective at helping Sybase set priorities and address quality problems. For example, the Sybase Errors Manual would not exist in its current complete state if it weren't for ISUG. Several new whitepapers and presentations are generated for each ISUG conference, so if you become a member and go to conferences, you are bound to increase your knowledge about Sybase software.

Servers. The DBA of one SQL Server uses partition *d* for a database, the DBA for the other Server uses partition *d* for a mirror of another database. Many variations occur on this theme.

Hardware failure Disks go bad. Sometimes disks have hot swap features. These are not always compatible with SQL Server. Check the Sybase Release Bulletins and Installation Guides for reports of known problems of this sort. New releases of controller firmware sometimes have problems with their cache implementations. These bugs tend to show up in particular with transaction log devices since they receive extremely high volume, high frequency writes. For ongoing corruption problems like log and index errors that Technical Support cannot easily diagnose after prolonged analysis, consider asking the hardware vendor to temporarily swap out the disk controller. This is not a frequent enough problem that you should never consider a new controller model, but you should always suspect hardware as well as software with corruption problems.

Operating system problems The operating system may have an error that causes it to panic or to terminate abnormally. This usually doesn't corrupt SQL Server databases, but if disk addressing mechanisms suffer, the data may suffer, too.

Network problems The network could fail to deliver packets, or it could use bad calls, or someone could change the routing in small but important ways. Upgrades to the protocol stacks often make changes to calls that affect SQL Server and incompatibilities arise. Always monitor the SQL Server errorlog closely for network-related errors and always stay in close contact with your network administrators. Seemingly minor changes in network routing information broadcast from routers can sever or impair connectivity between a SQL Server and its clients or other Servers. (While this generally doesn't cause corruption, it can cause hangs, which are sometimes just as damaging to operations.) If your system encompasses many subnets, routers, and protocols, you would be wise to learn enough network-related vocabulary to be able to ask your network administrators "exactly what they did last night" and go deeper into any vague responses that they might give.

Running out of space Running out of log space can make it impossible to recover a database in some circumstances. If you are running SQL Server 10.0 or later, make use of the threshold functions to help avoid this situation.

Application bugs Applications may write the wrong data to a table, causing integrity problems.

Server bugs Although corruption is not caused by SQL Server bugs as much as people think, it does happen. Be sure to rule out other possibilities first; then check with Sybase Technical Support if you suspect this. Be prepared for the engineers to ask you to reproduce the conditions of the corruption. In most cases, there have to be certain, repeatable conditions in which the problem occurs in order for an engineer to be able to find and fix a bug. You cannot generalize from an error, such as 605, to a bug, since one error can be the symptom of many different problems.

■ **Using undocumented DBCC commands**   Undocumented DBCC commands can be dangerous, as mentioned in several places. People with the privileges needed to use these commands have the power to corrupt a database.

■ **Hex editors**   It is fairly trivial to write a C program to read and write a block on disk as it pleases if you can log into the operating system as *root, SYSTEM, System Administrator,* or *sybase.* Someone who was ignorant or who had malicious intent could destroy data this way.

Once you identify the source of the problem, determining how to protect against its recurrence is fairly straightforward. If, however, you just restore from backups and never investigate the problem, it will probably happen again. In many cases, it recurs immediately. Even if it doesn't happen again, this problem-solving approach tends to lead Systems Managers to lose control of their time and their systems.

When you are ready to restore your data, your recovery process may mean

■ Recovering all the databases and logs that were on the affected device

■ Reloading the databases and replaying the logs (if the logs were on a separate device from the rest of the database)

■ Recovering all the data and the logs for one database

■ Dropping a corrupt object and recovering it or rebuilding it from scripts or object-level backups

■ Updating system tables

■ Rebooting SQL Server

The Sybase SQL Server Troubleshooting Guide describes all these processes in detail, so we won't repeat that discussion here.

■ IMPROVING MAINTAINABILITY

You can do certain activities that will go a long way toward keeping your production environment running well.

■ **Reboot periodically even if not needed**.   Clearing out memory can do wonders for cached stored procedures that are unusable and for other in-memory structures that get fragmented at the SQL

Server level and at the Operating System level due to virtual memory management. Rebooting also gets rid of zombie processes. A little downtime at an off-peak time can save a lot of downtime during peak processing.

- **Get an appropriate support contract**   Sybase sells a support contract at several pricing levels depending on the amount of support you need. If you're running a 24-hour shop, someday you will want to call Technical Support in the middle of the night or on a weekend. If you tend to do your upgrades and maintenance on weekends, this is also when you will run into problems and want to call for support. Do a cost/benefit analysis to determine the appropriate level of support.

- **Don't look for and install every Sybase EBF or SWR** The acronym EBF originally stood for Emergency Bug Fix. It was a one-off fix designed to resolve a particular problem that happened under particular identifiable conditions. If several people reported similar symptoms under the same conditions, they would get sent the EBF as well. Now, in response to customer demand, anyone with a support contract can get almost any EBF, and there's not as much diagnosis happening to make sure that the EBF will really solve a given problem. Unfortunately, not all EBFs are regression tested because the original problem was, after all, an emergency, and the customer who encountered the problem was simply using it until the next version with the real, tested fix was available. Today, these patches have been renamed to Software Releases, or SWRs. Some of them are one-offs and some are rollups. The rollups are fully regression tested. The one-offs are not. The rollups are based on the stable codeline at the time of the rollup. This means that, if a hardware vendor has since upgraded the operating system, Sybase will release the SWR on the new version of the OS. Sybase does not always regression test old SQL Server releases against new OS releases or old OS releases against new SQL Server releases, since the OS forward and backward compatibility is the responsibility of the OS vendor. In short, Sybase customers that aggressively pursue every SQL Server patch find this strategy also commits them to upgrading their OS at the same time or possibly running into compatibility problems.

- **Configure recovery interval to a low number, such as 1**   This affects performance slightly while running SQL server, but makes reboots faster.[7] You will need to decide whether routine performance or restart performance is more important.

- **Configure print recovery information (recovery flags) to 1 (*true*)** This flag tells SQL Server to report the number of transactions rolled forward and back in the errorlog during recovery. This helps you to

---

[7]The amount of impact depends on the release of SQL Server you run under. Under 11, the impact is much less than under 4.9.2.

monitor the recovery process. This flag can slow recovery slightly for the I/O required to report progress, but it is generally worthwhile.

■ **Disallow users from creating objects in the master database**   Users who create tables and procedures in the `master` database may inadvertently fill up the database and prevent logging. This keeps the entire Server from functioning.

■ **Make each user's default database something other than master**   The master database is the default value for the default database. This can lead to the problem just described. If you don't know where the user will need to work most often, set the user's default to `tempdb`. If new users don't know the effects of their actions, at least they only affect a scratch database.

■ **Keep scripts of all user objects**   While this may be impossible for someone in your position, try to encourage this practice. It not only improves recoverability of individual objects, but it can also be used as documentation. As external documentation, users won't put an additional query load on the Server trying to discover the nature of its contents. You can also use such scripts as samples that other developers can copy and modify for their own purposes.

■ **Know where the errorlogs are and monitor them closely**   Make it a habit to check SQL Server, operating system, network, and application errorlogs routinely. By detecting signs of trouble early, you can prevent total disaster. Also try to select third-party applications that have errorlogs, or at least some way of capturing the error messages and exact SQL generated by the application.

■ **Keep enough space on hand for all errorlogs**   Nothing fills up a file system faster than an errorlog that only needs to be purged at the desire of the System Administrator. It usually fills up when the one person whose job it is to track it is on vacation.

MONITORING AND ELIMINATING CAUSES OF FAILURE

Creating careful database procedures and then following them will minimize the number of repeated mistakes.

Have all DBAs and Systems Managers record major system changes in a log of some sort. In particular, configuration changes and disk partition usage should be recorded. Also, the failure of components should be recorded and analyzed from time to time. If a particular model of disk fails more often than others, for example, the log will tell you and you can investigate another sort of disk.

Also report metrics on how well the system is functioning. Manage the expectations of management by describing the metrics and the factors that affect positive and negative changes. For example, if you can prove that a lack of disk space causes SQL Server to go down more often, management may approve disk purchases more readily.

Also institute a program to encourage users to report all problems. When users encounter errors that are not immediately understood, they should record the full error messages, including the values of the variables giving the error context. The full errors should then be reported to the person responsible for handling database problems and questions. In practice, errors don't get reported for four main reasons:

■ **Users don't take the time to write down the full error.** Try explaining to users that the failure to report the context of the message, such as database ID or table name, often makes the solution difficult to determine or causes the problem to remain hidden until it becomes much more serious.

■ **The error scrolls off the screen.** Teach users about how to use scroll lock, cut and paste, or print screen features of their workstations.

■ **The error is buried by the application.** Speak to the application developer or vendor and strongly suggest that they provide a function to pass through SQL Server errors.

■ **Users think that they were the ones malfunctioning rather than the system.** Users often don't report the error at all because they don't want to be perceived as ignorant or they don't want to waste someone's time. Unfortunately, this behavior breaks the feedback loop that might otherwise signal the designer to make the system more intuitive. It also tends to create an antagonistic relationship between the user and "the system," such that the user rebels and reverts to using pencil and paper. Publicize known problems so that everyone knows exactly how to avoid them. Help users understand that computers are supposed to serve users, and not the other way around. Let them know that their insight can help designers to improve the computer's social skills. It may help to have a test environment around so that users can feel safe about experimenting without the worry that they will break the system.

SETTING UP MULTIPLE SQL SERVER ENVIRONMENTS

Setting up test and training environments can help you encourage users not to practice with production environments. Consider setting up one or more development environments for the following uses:

- Developing new applications
- Developing new database designs
- Testing new SQL Server configurations
- Testing new versions of Server software
- Testing new versions of applications
- Serving as a general testing environment
- Serving as a training environment for employees
- Serving as a prototype for gathering feedback

To maintain a development environment, you need

- Database space usage policies
- Login and user policies
- Policies for maintaining a particular test configuration, if necessary
- Scripts to rebuild the environment when needed
- A backup plan for the test environment (or a clearly communicated policy of not backing it up)
- Someone to take responsibility for maintaining the environment in a way that is suitable for its intended purposes

COMMUNICATING ABOUT DOWNTIME

As the number of SQL Server users increases, the demands to reduce downtime go up and the number of problems requiring downtime go up. To manage the results of this paradox, you must focus on communication with users. In your communications, you will need to convince users that maintenance downtime now will save unanticipated emergency downtime later.

Tell users ahead of time when you will be bringing the system down. Users who are surprised by sudden, unannounced downtime will wish to complain to you and your manager about it at length, and their complaints will not necessarily stop once the system is back up. Your internal argument for not announcing it might be that people will request that you delay the shutdown. In this case, you should attempt to justify the reason for the shutdown in the notice. Explain that requests for delay would have to cite exceptional circumstances. This will, hopefully, prevent people from wasting your time attempting to justify trivial requests. If users have a legitimate reason for delay, such as the need to do something that will have a significant revenue impact, then you should succumb to their wishes. Otherwise, they will take extreme measures to discredit you after the fact. If they do not have a legitimate reason, use the discussion to enhance your diplomatic expertise and educate them about what it takes to provide them with a system that runs reliably. This is one of those situations in which you need to invest now to reap rewards that will last your entire career.

You may find it helpful to provide a small application internally that is always available to report status. For example, Sybase, Inc., uses one for its own operations which is a simple script available to users from the operating system prompt. To see whether a particular public server is having problems or will be shut down in the near future, you can issue the command name qualified by the server name. The program simply outputs a text file that explains whether it's running normally or if there are shutdowns planned in the near future. If running normally, the file tells you who to call to report problems. If the system is experiencing problems, the file reports the expected time for recovery. If shutdowns are planned, the file explains why and when and who to call to discuss related issues. The DBAs are trained to modify the status message as soon as problems that can't be fixed immediately are encountered. This approach prevents hundreds of users from calling the support center to report a problem, which could further delay resolution. Users are trained to look at the status report first and only report the problem if they don't see the problem described in the status report.

■ AUTOMATING LOGINS

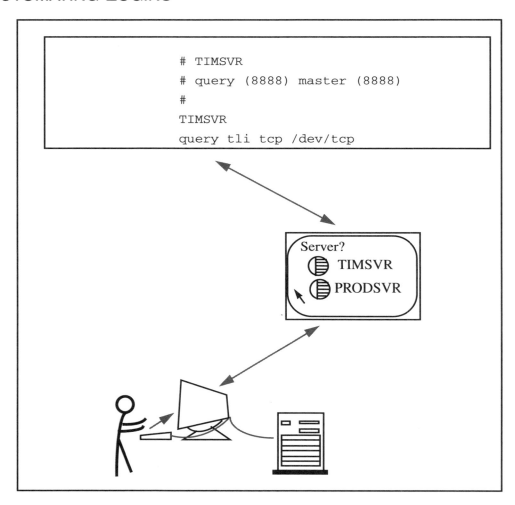

```
# TIMSVR
# query (8888) master (8888)
#
TIMSVR
query tli tcp /dev/tcp
```

Server?
TIMSVR
PRODSVR

Figure 10.2 With several Servers, users find it easier to log in using a GUI than having to remember and type server names and interfaces file locations.

To successfully log into a SQL Server, you need a server name, an interfaces file (or directory service) that maps the server name to a specific machine and network service, a login account on the SQL Server, and a user account in a database. The server name is established when a SQL Server is installed, and you can set a

418

default using the DSQUERY environment variable. The location of the interfaces file is referred to by the SYBASE environment variable. The login and user accounts exist in each SQL Server and database that the user needs access to.

Once you have more than one SQL Server, you will need to set up ways of allowing everyone to log into the systems that they need and to prevent people from logging into systems that they don't need. This usually includes setting up

- Multiple interfaces files
- Controls on who can log in on the machine housing the SQL Server
- SQL Server login accounts
- Database user accounts
- Automated methods for logging into different servers so that users don't always have to type interfaces file locations and Server names

An interfaces file maps the name of a SQL Server, such as *SYB_PROD*, to a point addressable in the network, which generally consists of a network protocol, a machine name, and a port or socket number. For a completely open environment, you can put all Server names in one interfaces file and distribute it to all machines in the network. Alternatively, you can have several interfaces files in several locations that each include a subset of Server entries.

Hiding an interfaces file is not enough to prevent someone from accessing a Server, since interfaces files can be created with a text editor. However, if you hide an interfaces file and hide the name of the machine with the SQL Server, people will find it harder to learn where a Server that you wish to protect is located. You may want to do this if you want people to be able to connect to the server, but not necessarily have access to the configuration files, master interfaces file, and similar files associated with the server location. In such a case you should also protect the files at the operating system level.

For providing access to multiple SQL Servers, you can set up command files that automatically supply the correct values for DSQUERY and SYBASE depending on the name of the command file or its arguments. You could also write a menu system that allows people to select a server at login time or to click on a named icon in a window.

In an in-house or third-party application, the DSQUERY and SYBASE variables may be hard coded or derived from other application variables. As such, they may be hidden from the user.

Beyond setting the basic SQL Server location, users or applications may want to use any of the SET commands to further modify the client connection with the SQL Server. In applications that provide access to Transact-SQL, users can simply give the SET command, such as SET ROWCOUNT 5. With an Open Client application, you set the SET options using library routines. A third-party application writer may give users the options to reset these or may hard code the values needed.

■ MANAGING CONNECTIONS

The maximum number of SQL Server user connections varies from operating system to operating system. In SQL Server, a global variable, @@max_connections, tells you the maximum number of connections you have to work with, assuming that only one SQL Server is running on the machine and that no other applications are running on the machine that will require connection resources.

One user may use several connections, especially if using a sophisticated client application. Such tools commonly use at least two connections, one for selects and one for updates. It is possible to establish more login accounts than the number of user connections that you have because not everyone will necessarily use the SQL Server at the same time. If you are adding active logins at a steadily increasing rate and not dropping any, you will eventually find that users can't get in the SQL Server because there are no free connections.

You can use sp_who to monitor the number of connections in use at any time. A sample of the output from a System 11 SQL Server is shown in Table 10-1.

TABLE 10-1   *sp_who output*

spid	status	loginame	hostname	blk	dbname	cmd
1	running	sa	graduate	0	master	SELECT
2	sleeping	NULL		0	master	NETWORK HANDLER
3	sleeping	NULL		0	master	DEADLOCK TUNE
4	sleeping	NULL		0	master	MIRROR HANDLER
5	sleeping	NULL		0	master	HOUSEKEEPER
6	sleeping	NULL		0	master	CHECKPOINT SLEEP
7	running	tim	graduate	0	school	SELECT

The *spid* column tells you the server process ID. The *status* column shows the state of the connection. *loginame* shows the login account name. The *blk* column gives you the *spid* of a process blocking, if there is one, or 0 if the given process is not blocked. The *dbname* column indicates the database the user is logged into. The *cmd* column tells you roughly what the login is doing.

One key to accommodating a large number of users is to get them to log out when they are not active in the database. There are a few ways to do this. One is to write some sort of stored procedure, RPC program, ESSM script, or cron job that notifies you when a login has been inactive for a certain period of time. You can direct the procedure to look at the status column of syspro-cesses to determine the activity level.

The possible status values in System 10 are

■ infected

■ background

■ recv sleep

■ send sleep

■ alarm sleep

■ lock sleep

■ sleeping

■ runnable

■ running

■ stopped

■ bad status

■ log suspend

Continuously inactive logins indicate the possibility that a user has gone home, is on vacation, or is out to lunch. At that point you may be tempted to use the KILL command from SQL Server or from the operating system. This does not always work for various reasons. Basically, in SQL Server, a sleeping process cannot be killed until it wakes up. If you do manage to kill it, it may not be able to clean up properly after itself. Getting a sleeping process to wake up is difficult, especially if it is asleep on network I/O. You can have the network wake up processes that have been sleeping on network I/O too long by changing the network keepalive configuration variable. See the SQL Server installation and release documents for pointers about keepalive for your platform. See your network and/or Operating System documentation for more guidance about setting such options. In general, it is best to try to get the user to exit gracefully. However, for networks with PCs for client workstations, users tend to reboot frequently, and the keepalive functionality of the network is sometimes the only practical option for cleaning up the dropped connections.

One way to make sure that users exit is to write applications that initiate a new user connection, perform an operation, and then log back out. Of course, this only makes sense for infrequent operations where performance is not important and interaction between the client and the server is minimal. Another, more workable method is to set a timer in the application that automatically logs the user out after no activity has been done for more than a certain number of minutes.

After you have reached the maximum number of user connections that one machine can support, you must determine whether it is worthwhile to set up a second SQL Server on a second machine for particular databases or operations. The method you use to divide operations and databases depends on the applications. Sometimes you can divide operations along regional lines, for example, having one server for each country or state in which you do business. The nice thing about this approach is that it also allows you to map system maintenance downtime to the non-business hours for that region. You might also divide up SQL Servers by department so that, for example, accounting works against one SQL Server and Human Resources against another.

When you do divide operations between SQL Servers, you have new problems. These include having twice as many Servers to maintain and keeping data in sync between databases. See the discussions of replication and distributed systems in Chapter 9 for ideas about managing these issues.

If you have enabled communication between Servers via RPCs, it will also be wise to monitor remote connections. Doing so will help you track network demand and will also help you learn what improvements are needed to make the right data accessible to the right people. The `sysprocesses` table can help you monitor remote users, since the *program_name* column tells you the application that initiated the connection. You can set up a batch job at the operating system level or with a stored procedure that saves the current contents of `sysprocesses` at regular intervals. You can use this information to determine the maximum number of remote connections and remote logins to set. A lot of RPC activity by different logins may indicate a need to combine or replicate databases. You might be able to reduce the amount of overhead associated with these connections by saving up transactions in an Open Server application and then running them as a batch. Such a batch might be run once an hour or once a day, depending on the urgency of the transactions. If it only needs to run once a day, you can save it for non-peak processing times. Be sure, however, not to expect to run it during the same time that you reserve for maintenance, since the two operations may conflict with each other.

■ INCREASING SECURITY

Good security is provided as much by organizational process as by technology. For example, the poor choice of passwords presents the number one security risk for most organizations. Correcting this problem requires policies and documentation above all.

It is strongly recommended that you hire a security expert or consultant to establish a complete plan for your organization. If your security system is out of balance, you have no security. For example, if you have a maze of interdependent roles, rules, and permissions in SQL Server to prevent unauthorized data access, but you have no paper shredders, your data are not protected. Similarly, if you store backup tapes in a location accessible by anyone, anyone could take your data.

A security inventory should identify both the data that must be secured and the threats that are possible. The types of threats that you should consider fall into three categories: people reading data they shouldn't be allowed to read, people writing incorrect data considered misleading (misinformation), and people destroying data the organization requires in order to do its work. These threats may happen as a result of honest mistakes, technology failures, or malicious intent.

A security plan should consider threats from the following angles, evaluate relative risks, and determine the protective measures needed.

- System failure
- Power failure
- Natural disaster
- Loss of key personnel
- Malicious attack
- Ignorant attack
- Insider attack
- Outsider attack
- Attack by one or more people
- Attack via software

- ■ Attack via hardware
- ■ Attack via network
- ■ Attack on facilities

Protection against malicious activities should include preventative measures based on anticipated motives for various types of attack. Such motives may include

- ■ Profit or some type of gain
- ■ Desire to protect someone in particular
- ■ Desire to hurt someone in particular
- ■ Desire to help someone in particular
- ■ Desire to harm the organization's ability to play in the marketplace
- ■ Desire to get revenge on the organization for some perceived wrong
- ■ Desire to damage the organization's ability to achieve a particular objective, such as using bad press to stop a business transaction

Implementing a security system will involve trade-offs since there's no perfect security, and nearly perfect security is extremely expensive. Design your security system to give priority to protecting those things that the organization considers most valuable. After creating a security plan, the processes you might put in place to enhance security might include

- ■ Documentation and approval of the security plan
- ■ Random and targeted security audits
- ■ Random and routine security reports
- ■ A well-defined process for closing security loopholes that includes the identification of persons who take responsibility for this task
- ■ Investment in people to stay on top of security-related trends, threats, and technology
- ■ Coherent implementation of security features provided by various software components in a system
- ■ Password selection criteria that you document and enforce consistently[8]

---

[8]This can be automated so that common passwords are rejected, reused passwords are not possible, and so on, but you will also need to build a "wrapper" around sp_password such that your mechanism with the additional checks must be called instead of allowing direct execution of sp_password.

425

■ Methods used to protect the physical media and equipment

■ Promotion of a teamwork-based environment committed to continual self-improvement so that problems are addressed rather than ignored

When working with Sybase software, you may want to do the following to take advantage of the security features provided in System 10 and later:

■ Use client-side encryption provided by the Open Client API.

■ Enable the `net password encryption` option for RPCs between Servers.

■ Use the DCE services if supported by your system, using the most applicable security protocols for your organization.

■ Guard access to database objects and procedures by using the `GRANT` and `REVOKE` commands consistently and carefully.

■ Use roles to set up database administration so that the cooperation of two or more people is required in order to take action that would be hard to undo.

■ Use the SQL Server 10.0 and later auditing features.

■ Force people to log in with traceable names rather than with anonymous department names or with the `sa` account. (You might consider tying the SQL Server login names to the operating system account names.) Also, after assigning sa_role, lock the sa account. Also lock any other "generic" accounts created during development.

■ Use views. You can give update permission on a view, while disallowing access on the underlying base table(s). This allows you to protect users from seeing and updating certain columns or rows, depending on the definition of the view.

■ Use stored procedures. You can disallow all access to objects except by use of specific stored procedures that you write. This also provides better security because it protects against users inadvertently affecting more than one row of a table at a time or from inputting data that your stored procedure determines to be incorrect.

■ Use the Sybase Secure SQL Server, the Audit Server, and a secure operating system.

Also be careful of SQL Server operations that can affect security. For example, if you create scripts that automatically log into SQL Server, do not use the `isql` or `BCP` command line option to supply the password. On many operating systems, the command to list active processes will show the password. The most common way to handle this problem on UNIX is to supply the password in a read-protected file that is redirected into the `isql` command line as a *here* document. For example,

```
#!/bin/csh
setenv DSQUERY SCHOOL
setenv SYBASE /sybase/SQLServer/
isql -U sandy >! /work/out.dat << ENDOFSCRIPT
beaches
select * from school..profs
go
exit
ENDOFSCRIPT
```

Be sure to keep any standby systems inaccessible until activated.

If you implement the SQL Server auditing feature, you will need to take care to maintain the following aspects of the system:

- Set the `audit queue` configuration variable appropriately.
- Run DBCCs on the audit database routinely and fix any problems found immediately.
- Protect access to the audit database.
- Truncate the log in the audit database.
- Periodically review and report on the audit records stored.
- Archive audit information if considered necessary.
- Truncate the audit records periodically so that the database doesn't fill up.

If the `sysaudits` table fills up, the audit process will terminate as soon as it tries to insert the records and fails. Thereafter, until the problem is fixed, user processes will terminate if they perform actions that trigger auditing. When this condition is reached, a user with the `sso_role` enabled can still perform auditable tasks, which should include immediately freeing up some space in the `sybsecurity` database. At that point, a user with `sa_role` enabled should shut down and restart SQL Server. Note that when the

427

audit process has terminated abnormally a user with `sso_role` but without `sa_role` does not have permission to shut down SQL Server.

The extent to which you implement auditing depends on the types of threats that you want to protect against and the amount of effort that you expect to put into reviewing the audit records. You can limit the amount of information that you need to sift through by selectively auditing certain actions, people, or objects about which you have particular concern or by writing stored procedures or other programs to analyze audit data for patterns and for deviations from those patterns.

Although we pay attention to the information systems, people are still the source of information most of the time and, as such, represent a threat in that they can simply tell someone what they know and that person can tell someone else. The way to guard against this threat is to focus on procedures that improve the security consciousness and the accountability of your people. Efforts to promote this may include

- Establishing and publishing very clear policies in which the boundaries between O.K. and not O.K. are very clear
- Writing or presenting case studies that highlight the ways in which security can be violated
- Holding contests internally for trusted employees to see if they can get around security measures
- Hiring crackers to attempt to crack into your own system
- Running background checks on employees before hiring them
- Periodically reevaluating who establishes and measures the sensitivity of the data in the database
- Keeping a list of security standards against which you judge new software before purchase

■ UPGRADING SQL SERVER

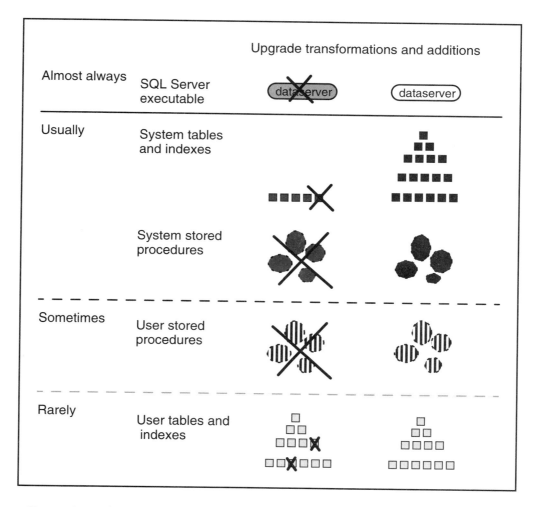

Figure 10.3 SQL Server upgrades typically consist of rebooting under a new version of the executable, adding and/or modifying system tables, and adding and/or modifying system procedures. For some upgrades, user stored procedures are recompiled. On rare occasions, an upgrade requires modifying the format of data pages on disk for user tables and indexes.

Periodically, Sybase releases new versions of SQL Server. The new versions you might receive include

- One-off SWRs to fix a particular, serious problem
- Rollup SWRs that fix a number of problems reported by customers
- Major releases that include new functionality, as well as incorporating the bug fixes from prior SWRs

New releases may offer additional functionality that you need, but they may also contain changes that affect the behavior of something that you have come to rely on, such as duplicates in subqueries. New versions may make some operations easier, faster, or more secure. However, you should always set up a new SQL Server in a test or development environment before pressing it into production.

When you are upgrading any part of a system, planning ahead will save you from having to roll back or deal with sudden unexpected failures. A successful upgrade process includes

- Getting authorization to upgrade
- Reading upgrade documentation
- Determining whether scripts and applications associated with the component being upgraded need to be modified
- Letting users know in advance about the upgrade and associated changes and the expected timing of upgrade events
- Setting up a test version of the new system
- Testing critical functionality required for daily operations
- Testing new functionality
- Upgrading a copy of the data files for the test system if necessary
- Running both versions in parallel and benchmarking performance
- Testing all normal and critical business operations
- Addressing any concerns that users have about the upgrade
- Comparing the results of processing run on both versions
- Making the new version the main version
- Testing the new production system
- Handling trouble reports
- Purging the old version

These tasks are listed roughly in order, although they may be rearranged to suit the type of component being upgraded. Steps may be added or deleted based on existing procedures at your site, except for the testing!

In some upgrade cases there is a choice between a phased implementation of the upgrade and a quick cut-over. A phased approach is easier to roll back, provides for more flexible training schedules, and presents lower risk. If a rollback is necessary, only a portion of processing is affected by the attempted implementation. A phased approach also gives developers more time to modify all existing applications. Of course, this approach also has disadvantages. You need to maintain and support parallel systems, and both systems will consume valuable resources. There are also significant data synchronization needs that come up, which may not be simple to solve, especially if the current system involves replication and distribution. At the end of a phased approach, it may also become necessary to merge the data input to the old system with the input to the new system.

■ TROUBLESHOOTING

Any IS professional's job includes a large amount of problem solving. This section includes suggestions that have proved successful in at least one troubleshooter's career. To solve a technical problem, you often need to solve human problems first. To get to the bottom of a problem, you will need to get the user reporting the problem to give you all the relevant details. There are a few emotional forces that work against you. By working with your users and keeping these responses in mind, you can adopt an attitude that counteracts the user's failings and makes problem resolution faster. You may also find that you get less frustrated and enjoy your job more.

■ **Panic** You cannot get relevant details out of people who are panicking. The first thing you need to do is to calm them down. Being calm and methodical yourself will help. If necessary, tell users about your credentials and your experience and the number of other similar problems that you have solved. This should help them gain confidence in your ability to stop whatever is making them panic. Panic is an extreme form of fear that may or may not be directly related to the actual conditions that triggered it. Greater than the fear of breaking the system is the fear of not surviving the results, such as by getting fired. A person who is panicking feels unsafe, so you need to do whatever you can to at least restore the illusion of safety. Panic may turn into anger, or anger may be the first response, which is a defense against fear. Treat the situation the same. Stay calm and convince them that their full cooperation will lead to the best resolution.

■ **Fear**   Users who are afraid of technology will be afraid that they broke the system. They may want to avoid being blamed for doing something terribly wrong, so they may cover their tracks by not telling you everything that you need to know. You can help put such users at ease by saying things like, "Everyone does that" or "Well, that program interface isn't very intuitive, is it?" Once users realize that they all do similar things and are no worse than anyone else, they're more likely to give you the facts you need.

■ **Pessimism**   People who fundamentally don't like computers (or who have worked with them a lot) know that computers are very fallible. Such people may be amazed that anything ever does work. This attitude leads some users to give up on seeking solutions, to lump all error messages into a single category that translates roughly into "You're doomed," or even to actively use features that make the technology fail so that they can prove that the computer shouldn't be relied on as heavily as it is. The motives behind this are varied and may be centered in job security fears. In this situation, empathy and even joining in with sarcastic remarks about the computer will help the user know that you are not ignorant of the problems that they see. If you are "on their side," they are much more likely to give you the information you need. In some cases, you can completely turn the situation around by saying to a naysayer, "Well, what would you do if you were in my place?" or "What do you think the company should do instead of using the computers?" or even "Would you be willing to head up a task force to study the problem and recommend alternatives?" Surprisingly often, such approaches can turn the most rigorous opposition into the most positive support. The pessimistic attitude may stem from a feeling of powerlessness, so if the person can become an agent of change, they may feel more power over what otherwise feels oppressive.

■ **Ego**   Ego is the system administrator's worst enemy. Your ego will prevent you from wanting to let users get off the hook easily if they did something stupid. Your users' egos will prevent them from admitting ignorance. Do your best to create an environment of humble truth seeking, at least while trying to resolve system problems. If ego is still getting in the way, convince your ego or the user's that the system is already broken, so the joint resolution of the problem between you will demonstrate a superior ability to work as a team to solve a difficult problem.

Once you accommodate human vulnerabilities, you can get to the technical problem by asking questions. You can take two approaches to asking the questions in the following list. You can ask those that you think will result in the most revealing answers first, solve problems that you think may exist based on those answers, and then stop asking questions and fixing things as soon as you get back to a resolution considered acceptable. Or you can ask all these questions, form a composite picture of the situation based on all the answers, and the pursue an approach of fixing all the problems, starting with what appears to be the biggest problem first. Your style will depend on your own personality and the amount of time you have. The more experienced you are, the more likely it is that the first question you ask is the right one, and you can resolve the problem based on that answer. If you're really, really experienced, you can stand behind the user and watch them perform the activity in question, and then the problem will stop happening.[9] If you have to ask questions, they will fall into the familiar pattern of what, when, who, where, how, and why. The following list describes some of the most revealing questions.

■ **Can you tell me everything you noticed about what happened?**   The answer to this will vary depending on how much the user was paying attention to the problem process and how much the user doesn't want to admit to doing. Try to present yourself as understanding, yet inquisitive as possible. This allows you to extract the information you need from the user in a way that doesn't encourage evasion. Write down all the key facts and consider them to be clues or parameters that your hypothesis of the solution must match.

■ **Were there any error messages?**   In the beginning, the answer is usually no. However, the more users get used to you asking, the more they will start watching. Suggesting possible error messages may trigger the user's memory, but avoid "leading the witness." Concentrate on getting the specific messages. For example, a report of a 605 tells you some information, but the associated page numbers, object number, and database ID reported in the 605 message tell you a lot more.

---

[9]This is because, as a former co-worker, Tom Ward, explained to me long ago, every electronic device has an ADC and an IDC. The ADC is the Anxiety Detection Circuit and the IDC is the Idiot Detection Circut. When a calm or knowledgeable person stands or sits in front of the device, the applicable circuit closes and the problem stops.

■ **Who did it happen to? Everyone, some set of people, or just you?** The answer to this will tell you if it was a generalized system problem, a problem that a certain set of people encounter because of some aspect that they share in common, or a problem localized to the activities of just one person.

■ **How familiar are you with the system?** You can't always ask this straight out, but you can listen for the answer in the way the user talks to you. You need to know if they know enough to avoid common pitfalls. Sometimes a person who doesn't know much does run into a complex problem, but nine times out of ten, a new person hits the same old problem that almost every other new person does. If you realize that the person is a new user, see if you can narrow the problem down to your top ten or so problem-causing scenarios. (Surely you have such a list of frequently asked questions! If not, start making it now and then publish it for all your users to access. This will prevent several trouble calls.)

■ **When did the problem start? Does it happen every time? How often does it happen? Can you make it happen again?** The answers to these questions will go a long way toward isolating the problem. If the operation in question had been working fine for some time for this person and then suddenly stopped, you can look for things like software version changes, configuration changes, and hardware changes. If the problem happens every time for this person, but never for another person, establish the order in which the sequence of operations is performed and compare software and hardware configurations.

■ **Did you try turning the problem component off and on?** Experienced system administrators know that restarting anything—a printer, a modem, a machine, a window manager, a login, or a SQL Server—tends to resolve a lot of problems. It takes a little more talent to find out why. In general, turning something off and on resets it to an initial, known state. Multiuser software like SQL Server tends to get confused when something doesn't go as planned, and it can't find its way back to a known state. All software is generated by programmers, and a large majority of programmers always make the same two mistakes that lead to problems you can fix by resets—forgetting to initialize variables and forgetting to check boundary conditions.

■ **What has changed that you know about?** The first answer to this is usually "nothing." If so, don't patronize the user by asking, "Really? Are you sure?" Instead, give examples of things that typically change. For example, say, "Oh, that's strange because usually I see this problem when there's a configuration file change or a new version of a DLL." This approach both aids the user's memory and paves the way for the user to report what really changed without having to admit that they forgot to tell you everything in the first place.

434

■ **Where exactly does the problem seem to be?**   Ultimately, you need to isolate the problem. If the problem is in an application, this may mean somehow finding out what SQL statement the application delivers to the Server for execution. If you can get the query to execute correctly through a simple tool like ISQL, but it doesn't work in the application, then you know the problem is not in the Server's response to the query itself, but in some other aspect of the application. For example, it could be a SET command issued by the application or by the user. The problem of isolation tends to be one of sequential elimination. That is, you need to take away one complicating factor at a time until the operation works, or you need to start with a simple form of the operation that does work and build up to the actual implementation until something stops working. This process is slow, but tends to be the most illuminating. One way to find out how a toaster works is to unplug it, take it apart, and then put it back together again. Of course, the risk of this approach is that you forget how to put it back together, someone wants to use the toaster while you have it in pieces, or someone wants you to do something else.

■ **What is the difference between your beta testing and the production environment? How many users were there and how big were the tables? Were the versions of the Server and the network exactly the same?**   Ask developers these questions when they put a system into development and it doesn't work as expected. (Reread the section on *panic.*)

■ **Why were you trying to do it that way?**   This is generally a question you ask when you're busy and you know another way to do it that does work. This is a workaround type of question. The user may or may not be satisfied with a workaround. At minimum though, a workaround gives you more time to resolve the original problem under less pressure. Depending on whether you work well under pressure, this may or may not be an option you want to pursue.

■ **How important is it?**   If you are like most Systems Managers, you simply don't have time to fix every problem that gets discovered. If a problem is relatively minor, you may need to ask yourself and the user a philosophical question. Is it better to work on this small problem or to use the time to work on a more essential task that will have a much bigger impact on the technical quality of life in your organization? Some problems require an extraordinary amount of effort to resolve that is far out of proportion to the possible benefit received.

■ **How's the hardware? How's the network? How's the operating system?** Your user may not know the answer to this question, but if it looks like you have a large-scale SQL Server problem, you will need to find out if any problems are being reported at the hardware level. Check the operating system error reporting facilities, check with other administrators, and ask around to find out if any other users are experiencing similar problems.

■ **What configuration of hardware, operating systems, Server, network, application, and middleware are you using?** The user never knows the answer to these questions, but by the time you get to the bottom of this list, you may be dealing with a software bug nestled between layers and layers of software complexity. If you can't isolate a problem, you can try a known combination of versions that works and incrementally swap in the versions that match the problem environment until the problem is discovered. Once you find the problem element, you can more easily determine if the problem is a bug or a configuration problem.

Once you've asked all the relevant questions from the user that reports the problem, you may want to further investigate the details by asking other users or administrators if they have run into the same problem. Go back through the list above and try to fill in any major gaps.

■ THE SQL SERVER ERRORLOG

You can get a great deal of information from the SQL Server errorlog, which is located in the `install` subdirectory of the Sybase directory tree by default. Table 10-2 shows how to interpret various elements of the errorlog.

TABLE 10-2   SQL Server Errorlog[a]

Record in Errorlog	Information
00:95/11/13 16:09:45.50 kernel Using config area from primary master device.	The first two fields of an errorlog entry show you the date and time of the message.
00:95/11/13 16:09:46.67 kernel Configuration Error: Configuration file, '/dbms/sybase/REL11B2_SSM.cfg', does not exist.	Pay attention to any messages that start with "Error" or "Warning." They indicate situations you should be aware of. In this case, it could not find a configuration file that matched the SQL Server name.
00:95/11/13 16:09:46.95 kernel Warning: A configuration file was not specified and the default file '/dbms/sybase/REL11B2_SSM.cfg' does not exist. SQL Server creates the default file with the default configuration.	Since SQL Server couldn't find a configuration file in the right place, it created a default file during installation.
00:95/11/13 16:09:47.18 kernel Using 1024 file descriptors.	This UNIX system has 1024 file descriptors available for use by SQL Server.

TABLE 10-2   SQL Server Errorlog[a] (Continued)

Record in Errorlog	Information
00:95/11/13 16:09:47.20 kernel SQL Server/11.0/B/Sun_svr4/OS 5.4/2/OPT/Sat Oct 7 14:27:58 PDT 1995	This is the exact identification of the binary. It is an 11.0 Beta 2 version of SQL Server that was built on a Sun machine running Solaris 5.4 on October 7, 1995. It is the OPTimized version, rather than a diagnostic version.
00:95/11/13 16:09:47.20 kernel Confidential property of Sybase, Inc....	Several messages identifying the legal ownership and uses of the binary follow this one.
00:95/11/13 16:09:47.21 kernel Logging SQL Server messages in file '/dbms/sybase/REL11B2_SSM_errorlog'	This is the location of this errorlog. Since errors get reported to the start-up window as well as the errorlog, this message might help someone with a view of that window to find the error log quickly.
00:95/11/13 16:09:47.32 kernel Network and device connection limit is 1016.	SQL Server has subtracted 8 file descriptors for its own use, leaving 1016 for actual user connections.
00:95/11/13 16:09:47.76 server Number of proc buffers allocated: 495.	In theory, the procedure cache can hold 495 procedures.
00:95/11/13 16:09:47.77 server Number of blocks left for proc headers: 559.	There are 559 pages of memory available for procedures in procedure cache.
00:95/11/13 16:09:48.63 server Memory allocated for the default data cache: 3756 Kb	The data cache can hold approximately 3.7 MB of data.
00:95/11/13 16:09:48.65 server Size of the 2K memory pool: 3756 Kb	All of the memory for data cache is in the default memory pool, which consists of 2-KB buffers.
00:95/11/13 16:09:48.82 kernel Initializing virtual device 0, '/dbms/sybase/devices/master.dat'	The master database is being opened at the following location. This location is set in the dataserver command line.
00:95/11/13 16:09:48.84 kernel Virtual device 0 started using standard unix i/o.	The master device for this example is running on a file system (not recommended for production use!).
00:95/11/13 16:09:50.54 server Opening Master Database ...	SQL Server is opening the database. If it fails for any reason, such as not having permissions to read the underlying device, errors to that effect will follow this message.
00:95/11/13 16:09:53.70 server Loading SQL Server's default sort order and character set	SQL Server loads the default sort order and character set into memory.

PREVENTING AND RESOLVING PROBLEMS

TABLE 10-2   SQL Server Errorlog[a] (Continued)

Record in Errorlog	Information
00:95/11/13 16:09:53.85 kernel ninit:0: listener type: master	The networking is started for the "master" port.
00:95/11/13 16:09:53.85 kernel ninit:0: listener endpoint: /dev/tcp	SQL Server is using TCP for networking.
00:95/11/13 16:09:53.85 kernel ninit:0: listener raw address: \x00021b5882d63c900000000000000000	The port address for SQL Server is stored in binary form for SVR4 platforms.
00:95/11/13 16:09:53.85 kernel ninit:0: transport provider: T_COTS_ORD	Networking initialized successfully using a mode known as "Connection service with orderly release."
00:95/11/13 16:09:54.10 server Recovering database 'master'	SQL Server opens the master database and runs recovery on it.
00:95/11/13 16:09:54.35 server Recovery dbid 1 ckpt (1460,26)	Recovery is running on database ID 1 (master), where the checkpoint record was on logical page 1460, row 26.
00:95/11/13 16:09:54.35 server Recovery no active transactions before ckpt.	There are no active transactions before checkpoint, so there is nothing to reconstruct by reconciling the log and the disk records.
00:95/11/13 16:09:55.17 server Database 'master' is now online.	The master database has recovered successfully. If it hadn't, then error messages would follow and the Server would shut down.
00:95/11/13 16:09:55.25 server The transaction log in the database 'master' will use I/O size of 2 Kb.	The transaction log for master has not been bound to a named cache with larger I/O size than the default of 2 KB.
00:95/11/13 16:09:55.37 server server is unnamed	The SQL Server has not been named by using the local option of sp_addserver.
00:95/11/13 16:09:55.43 server Warning: The 'sysconfigures' table is not updated since the SQL Server is started with the default configuration.	Since we're using the defaults, there's no need to use the configuration file to construct the sysconfigures table.
00:95/11/13 17:03:56.17 server Recovering database 'model'.	Now we'll recover the model database.
00:95/11/13 17:03:56.27 server Recovery dbid 3 ckpt (391,30) oldest tran=(391,29)	DBID 3, which is model, had a checkpoint record on page 391, row 30, and the oldest active transaction is on page 391, row 29.
00:95/11/13 17:03:56.28 server 1 transactions rolled forward.	The open transaction is rolled forward.

TABLE 10-2   SQL Server Errorlog[a] (Continued)

Record in Errorlog	Information
00:95/11/13 17:03:56.93 server The transaction log in the database 'model' will use I/O size of 2 Kb.	The transaction log for `model` has not been bound to a named cache with larger I/O size than the default of 2 KB.
00:95/11/13 17:03:56.94 server Database 'model' is now online.	The `model` database recovered successfully.
00:95/11/13 16:09:55.95 server Clearing temp db	The `tempdb` database is reinitialized.
00:95/11/13 16:09:57.37 server Recovery complete.	Recovery of all databases has completed, so all the data is safely online.
00:95/11/13 16:09:57.37 server SQL Server's default sort order is: 00:95/11/13 16:09:57.37 server 'bin_iso_1' (ID = 50) 00:95/11/13 16:09:57.38 server on top of default character set 00:95/11/13 16:09:57.38 server 'iso_1' (ID = 1)	SQL Server is using the default sort order of binary for the ISO_1, character set. The sort order id 50 (syscharsets.id) and the character set ID (syscharsets.csid) 1.
00:95/11/13 16:16:17.84 server The configuration option 'allow updates to system tables' has been changed by 'sa' from '0' to '1'.	Someone has configured "Allow Updates" to true, meaning that system tables could be updated directly using SQL.

[a]Observant readers will notice that this errorlog has been doctored for explanation purposes.

SQL Server writes information to the errorlog as it starts up and as it detects conditions that it considers noteworthy. Every time you start up SQL Server, the new errorlog information is appended to the old. Therefore, to eliminate old errorlog information, you will need to shut down SQL Server, remove lines from the old errorlog or move the entire file, and then restart SQL Server. You can either delete the old errorlogs, or you can archive them on tape or on paper, perhaps as part of an automated start-up procedure. If any errors are reported in the log, you should keep it until all the problems generating the errors are resolved. After that, you may still want to keep it as a debugging aid for the next time such a problem occurs. Technical Support cases regarding SQL Server are resolved in large part by looking at the errorlog. Even if you don't see anything unusual, a trained technical support person may see subtleties that provide insight into the problem, so don't throw away logs that may contain evidence.

However, do remove or prune your errorlog from time to time since it may end up growing enough to fill up your file system. Using a combination of operating system utilities, you can set up batch jobs that search the errorlog for signs of problems periodically and alert you by sending you mail or printing an error report somewhere.

Procedure Manual Suggestions

○ Notifying Users about Downtime

⇒ Establish a procedure for letting users know when the system is or will be down for planned maintenance and for emergencies.

○ Reporting Errors

⇒ Include a training plan that encourages proper error message reporting as a feedback mechanism.

⇒ Provide error reporting forms or applications that encourage users to report exact error messages and conditions

⇒ Make sure that the error reporting system provides some immediate feedback to the users so that they know their report wasn't ignored and that it will continue to be worthwhile to report problems.

○ Disaster Recovery

⇒ If your master database gets corrupt or cannot be loaded from backup, you can rebuild it without losing the data in the rest of the SQL Server. To rebuild, however, you must know the previous contents of `sysdatabases`, `sysusages`, and `sysdevices`. Write a procedure for keeping track of all changes to these tables.

➠ Plan to make hard copies or files stored outside SQL Server of the contents of each of these tables each time a database or device is added, dropped, or altered.

➠ In case you ever have to logically rebuild an entire SQL Server, save scripts of every session in which you issue one of the following commands: CREATE DATABASE; ALTER DATABASE; DROP DATABASE; DISK INIT; sp_dropdevice.

○ **Contacting Vendors**

➠ Write a procedure for calling hardware and software vendors when there are problems.

➠ Include the names and titles of people authorized to call the vendors.

➠ Document vendor phone numbers and your account numbers.

➠ Provide a format for gathering information before making the phone call, such as the make and model of the machine, any errors reported, and the hours during which the machine may be brought down for routine service.

➠ Document who is authorized to approve charges for emergency service.

○ **Passwords**

➠ Write a procedure that sets standards for choosing and changing passwords.

➠ Discourage the use of login and password sharing, and make clear other ways to achieve the same benefits, such as the use of roles, groups, or aliases.

○ **Upgrades**

➠ Write an upgrade policy that describes the minimum time that an upgrade should be run in parallel with the old version.

➠ Describe conditions for accepting or rejecting an upgrade.

SYSTEMS MANAGEMENT

CHAPTER

11

Establishing System Goals

The vision that guides an information system determines its quality and its ability to meet organizational goals. Similarly, a lack of vision translates to poor return on the information system investment. To the extent that your system vision coincides with the organizational vision, you will be able to justify ongoing investment in your system. To the extent that you keep this vision clear and well publicized, you will receive support while carrying out your goals. To the extent that you deliver results consistent with your vision, you will enhance your own career. A well-chosen vision allows you to help your organization meet its goals while helping you have a fulfilling career, stay out of trouble, and keep users happy.

Perhaps this ideal seems beyond your reach for you or for your organization. In this chapter, we'll explore goals, vision, and systems from many angles, from the corporate to the personal. We'll start by looking at exactly what an information system is and how an organization hopes it will work. Then we'll look at information systems people and see how they participate in the broader organizational system. From that foundation, we can discuss goals and vision while keeping an eye on the practical limits of a technology professional's life.

■ THE INFORMATION SYSTEM

We could think of information systems as collections of computer hardware and software, possibly networked together. We could extend this concept to include the people needed to run and maintain the computing resources. However, this description still wouldn't be complete. In this book, we describe an information system as an interdependent combination of computing resources, data, and people that create value by supporting organizational goals.

This book describes Sybase software as one or more components of a system and suggests that you set your work goals with a similar understanding of the interdependent nature of systems. In the technological landscape of the 1990s, we are discovering that system complexity often makes the net effect of interdependent changes unpredictable. By creating a vision that serves as a framework for your goals, you can continuously improve your information system so that employees and owners alike think of it as an organizational asset, rather than as a set of hurdles they must always jump. When solving a mathematical system of equations, we choose which variables to solve for. Similarly, the vision for an information system tells us which business solutions the system is supposed to provide. By consistently taking directed action to support that vision, and objectively evaluating and refining the results, Systems Managers create value for the organization and its customers.

On a personal level, interdependence means that as the person responsible for a particular component, such as Sybase SQL Server, your work affects the system, and changes in other parts of the system affect you. For example, if you configure SQL Server to use so much memory that it causes other applications to swap out, you can slow down key operations to unacceptable levels. If users accidently unleash poorly formed SQL queries, they can lock out all other users trying to use the Server. If your network administrator upgrades your TCP/IP software without telling you, you may be surprised by errors in the SQL Server errorlog. If upper management changes organizational structure, the frequency or quality of database backups might be affected, and you might be saddled with the blame if these data are lost for any reason. This might seem like a burdensome state of affairs. On the other hand, if you realize that you can think ahead and avert such disasters, you become an agent of improvement in the system. No one else—not users, not managers, not network gurus—is in a better position than you to be a pivot point of positive system changes. Once you see the organization's dependence on the information system, you realize you can be a pivot point of organizational improvement as well.

■ THE SYSTEMS MANAGER'S JOB

Some of you might completely reject the idea that your job has or should have anything to do with anything that "goes on at the top" of the organization. A constant exposure to urgent problems tends to turn systems people into pessimists. If you're a typical computer systems person, you may not feel that you have much power to make a difference in your organization. You may not want to. You may perceive that there is not enough of an investment in the information system for it to be managed well, that the organization is already too poorly managed for you to make it successful, or that the overall market for the business is declining despite everyone's best efforts. Pretend for now that this chapter is fiction then and try to suspend disbelief. Form a mental picture of the organization that you'd like to work for and try on the ideas in this chapter in that context. An imaginary step back from the organization or up the organization chart may help you see how your actions could make a difference if you could change one or two elements of your current situation. If you once felt ownership of your work and have since lost it, the section "Personal Goals" might help you reawaken the passion for your craft without forgetting the lessons of original experience that caused the change in your outlook.

As a reader of this book and a user of Sybase products, you could be part of an information technology (IT) department implementing a client/server architecture, you could be a database consultant, you could be an end user who wants your company to start "right sizing," or you could be anywhere in between. You might be starting a new business built around distributed computing from the outset. Perhaps as LAN administrator, you have taken your PC network as far as you can and now realize that you need to advance to the next level of computing.

Regardless of the details, if you are responsible for Sybase products in an organization, this book will refer to your work as *systems management*. As discussed in the preface, it may not seem as if the title of *Systems Manager* fits you. Even if your job is to know technical details and act on them when necessary, your choice of priorities will affect how well the information system helps your organization stay successful. Even if you are only one member of a large information technology organization, you will benefit from approaching your job as managing information rather than manipulating technology. Viewing your work in the context of a system will give you the perspective necessary to manage client/server software effectively.

We also refer to the organization's computing resources as *your system*. For the database consultants and developers among you, you may not wish to see yourself as having that much responsibility, but much of the information will still apply. If you take your work seriously, you will feel ownership of the part of the system you worked on. A sense of ownership also drives you to produce your best results.

■ THE SYSTEM VISION

While a technical issue like "improving performance" may be one of your goals, deciding how to best achieve that goal depends on your system vision. Is improving performance worth the cost of faster disks? Whose performance is suffering? If trade-offs have to be made, what can be sacrificed? You could answer these questions in the short term by doing whatever seems easiest and fastest. Or you could take a step back to think about the best solution. Organizational goals and constraints, technology, and your own experience shape your concept of "best." A vision unites these elements, giving you the ability to choose goals and priorities.

Even if the ideal system is unreachable, aim for it anyway. Aiming high helps you to admit to your real potential and live up to it. A commitment to consistently pursuing incremental, positive change can result in greater accomplishments than you would have foreseen. A habit of identifying the adverse changes that unexpected events bring and turning them around before they do too much damage also yields great rewards.

Here is one vision of an ideal database system environment:

- A corporate information architecture has been defined.
- Each information system person's roles and responsibilities are known.
- Changes to the system are planned well in advance.
- Changes are implemented carefully and flawlessly.
- All the users are happy with the system.
- The system costs are well under control.
- The system contributes to the organization's profitability and competitiveness.
- When the organization changes, it is easy to change the system.

The 1990s computing environment rarely lives up to this vision. Technology and markets change too fast for our information systems to keep up. The demand for system functionality usually exceeds the resources allocated. For many, the Systems Manager's vision reduces to having the appreciation of system improvements consistently outweigh the dissatisfaction at its shortcomings. Our thoughts take the shape of trade-offs, like "If we can write a new reports that users like, perhaps we won't suffer too much grief from users who have been barred from making ad hoc SQL queries."

Choosing which tasks to do at any given moment can constantly challenge your peace of mind. By deciding what to do each day, month, or year, you effectively decide which tasks will remain undone during that time. You may have given up on attempting to manage your time because it is too disheartening to confront what you won't be able to do.

The executives of an organization presumably agreed to invest in the information system for a reason. Perhaps reaching only a few significant goals will make that investment pay off. Some possible executive expectations for systems follow:

- Get expected return on investment
- Help to expand market share
- Support innovation in the organization's market
- Improve worker productivity
- Improve worker satisfaction and reduce turnover
- Develop employee potential
- Improve organizational profitability or cash flow
- Supply needed information faster
- Increase system reliability
- Reduce the cost of doing business
- Make system maintenance less disruptive to the business
- Contribute to the organization's ability to make the difference it wants to make in the industry

The top priority among these items would depend on the organization's primary business goals for the month, quarter, or year.

When asked independently about departmental goals, task-oriented Systems Managers might make a far different list:

- Maintain and update hardware and/or software
- Monitor and analyze network usage
- Answer questions
- Write reports
- Manage users

■ Train users

■ Manage data

■ Maintain security

How Systems Managers typically rank their tasks varies with the performance of the system and the demands of the day:

■ Stay out of trouble

■ Handling crisis-generating problems

■ Keeping the boss happy

■ Learn technology of most interest

■ Desire to keep users happy

■ Desire to help the organization to meet its goals

By comparing the lists of Systems Managers and executive managers, you can start to see how conflict might arise between them. Ideally, there is a match between executive's management's priorities and the Systems Manager's priorities. A lack of such a match corresponds to an inability to achieve consistent results.

After creating a system vision, the next most important task is to document it. All system investors and users should know what services to expect from it. They should also know what isn't among your goals so they don't have expectations that you have no plans of meeting. A written description of how the system works now, how it should work next month, next year, in 5 years, and in 10 years will help the Systems Manager stay focused on priorities from moment to moment. A vision gives you the clarity to say no to the trivial and yes to the essential.

For example, perhaps your system vision, signed off by the highest levels of management, documents that the business needs to process transactions at a certain minimum rate to function profitably. Later, if someone proposes saving money by leasing slower telecommunications facilities, all you have to do is show them the analysis in your vision document. You will be able to reject their proposal without being accused of political malice. Any assumptions made in the analysis will also be documented so that it's clear which changes in technology would justify a review.

Another advantage of creating and making such documentation is to help you delegate work to others. When you go on vacation or get promoted, you should feel confident that all you worked for will not be lost.

This remainder of this chapter will help you start thinking about and documenting the elements of your system vision. Your vision document is different from a procedures manual. The vision document describes how the system should look and behave in the future. A procedures manual describes policies for system use and how your system should function today. You will find suggestions for a procedures manual throughout this book. Creating a manual to guide daily operations will help you eventually reach the goals described in your vision document.

ORGANIZATIONAL GOALS

The type of business the organization focuses on shapes the management of its information. For example, depending on where a company is trying to make or save money, the primary goal of implementing Sybase software could be to improve work flow, to improve inventory tracking, or to facilitate decision making. The first goal might call for using PowerBuilder to provide better user interfaces. The second might strive to automate every operation from purchasing to delivery by using Open Server to link disparate systems. The third might concentrate on using SQL Server to create a central information repository.

To begin creating your system vision, first look at opportunities. This chapter helps you to look at typical organizational goals, technology-driven goals, and personal goals. Later, you can refine your vision to determine which opportunities deserve your attention most. Chapter 12 discusses how to choose objectives for maximum success.

If a company or organization needs to accomplish specific objectives to stay viable, management will consider tasks supporting this goal essential. Technical people who wish to be rewarded by management will propose and implement the information system changes that can help with the organization's current challenges. A well-run IS department also anticipates changes in the business and makes corresponding information system proposals as necessary. To plan for this, you must understand the business of your company or organization now and which business it intends to be in for the next 10 years.

For example, the general business goals of a bicycle shop might be

■ To sell more bicycles than any other bicycle shop in town.

■ After reaching yearly revenue goals, expand to sell sporting goods.

The corresponding system will need to go from handling a few highly popular models and makes of bicycles to handling a much larger, more diverse inventory. The information system, which starts by handling a high volume of similar transactions against a small inventory table, may now require complex procedures to combine elements from many different inventory tables efficiently. At the same time, the hardware may need a memory upgrade to handle the increased processing load.

The business needs of a multinational, rapidly expanding manufacturing conglomerate will take on much more complexity. In this case, the system vision may reflect the nature of the revenue stream. The system will need to be global, easily modifiable, and capable of integration with almost any other system that might be merged into the corporation. The technology choices will center around sharing data among everything from PCs to mainframes. The databases may need to support data entered across 10 time zones and in twice as many languages.

Analyzing the organization and its markets may seem like an inappropriate task for someone in your position. However, many managers and executives do not undertake this type of planning at the systems level. They may underestimate how difficult it is to make system changes. Their exposure to technical details may only go as far as reading product advertisements. They may assume that lower levels of management should be able to do whatever it takes to make the system work for the business. Rather than being surprised by unreasonable system requests from such sources, you can learn to think like an executive.

Stay aware of planned business changes, and think about the corresponding system changes that will be needed to support them. Document your analysis and supply it to your boss. Even if you don't get credit for your ideas, you will stand a better chance of getting an appropriate budget for the changes. In most cases, you will earn a reputation as someone who has the organization's best interests at heart.

The next few sections discuss typical organizational concerns.

PROFITABILITY

Let's imagine two entrepreneurs debating about the point of running a business. One claims that a business exists to make money. If you can make 10% on investment by putting it in a fund, why would you expend effort to create a business that earns less than 10% profit? The other claims that making money is boring. He says that you shouldn't spend most of your waking life just making money. According to him, a business exists to create things and provide services for people. Applying your unique talents to create something new or to help someone should be the ultimate goal of any worker.

In reality, businesses cannot survive if they are not profitable, and they cannot make a profit if they don't provide a product or service that people are willing to trade money for. Both people were right. The key fact is that executive management rarely cares as much about keeping internal computer system users happy as it does about making a profit or helping external customers. While this may seem dismaying at first, think about how happy your users would be if they were unemployed. Your customers are your users. One of your goals can be to find solutions that increase profitability and keep users happy at the same time.

When thinking about how your information system supports the business, evaluate how it makes its money and what products and services it provides. Then think about where your system supports these activities. Are there system weaknesses that hinder profitability?

For example, say that a controller has demanded that you make it easier to import and export accounting data between his spreadsheet and SQL Server, an accounting manager wants you to write a new payroll program that she claims will help her avoid needing to hire another accountant, and another manager wants you to take on the quality goal of reducing downtime to no more than 2 hours a month. Your priorities, if profit directed, would depend on what cost savings or revenue generation would result from each improvement. In a system that only processes orders 10 hours a day, the goal of reducing downtime doesn't make as much sense as working toward keeping downtime to off hours. Unless the system consistently fails during peak periods, avoiding hiring a new person would have a higher payoff and deserve a higher priority. The accounting problem probably needs reformulating before you can analyze it. It's possible that the spreadsheet isn't even the right tool for the job if profitability truly rests on the solution.

MARKETS AND COMPETITION

Competition shapes the amount of profits that you make and how you make them. Businesses that compete with yours may claim to provide faster, cheaper, or better service or goods. Their computer system may make the difference between your abilities and theirs, or their lack of investment may even make their operations cheaper. Stay aware of your competition, and think about what changes to your system would make your business more competitive. Many businesses use investment in information system improvements as part of a marketing campaign that underscores their claims of commitment to service or quality. Think over the priorities that you pursued in the last year and how they may have affected your business's strategic standing in its marketplace. Consider where a change in priorities could make a difference for next year. If you were in marketing, how would you play up the differences between your system and the competition's? What system functions are visible to your customers or future customers?

If service quality would draw customers, perhaps you can write stored procedures or triggers that will allow errors during order processing to be caught before the customer gets off the phone. Maybe your high-end customers would be more willing to give you lucrative contracts if you could provide customized billing.

In a not-for-profit organization, a small improvement in system efficiency could make a large difference in conserving hard-won donations or grants or in lessening the requirements for volunteer help. Small programs could search for and eliminate duplicate entries on mailing lists or allow you to analyze donation patterns of contributors by zip code or time of year.

While a new market may be a new geographical area, it may also be a new product area or a new consumer group for an existing product. As companies attempt to serve new markets, their information systems often need to adapt. For example, companies may expand into markets that require unanticipated changes in billing systems. Instead of getting the majority of their income from a few large billings to key clients, they start earning a high percentage of income from many small sales to many people. Where the overhead of a custom billing system may be adequate for a few large invoices, it can break down under the strain of hundreds of single line-item bills. This type of change could motivate the migration from spreadsheets on a few PCs to a multiuser client/server database system.

If you stay in touch with those in charge of business development at your company, you can help guide the investment decisions required to make market changes profitable.

GLOBALIZATION

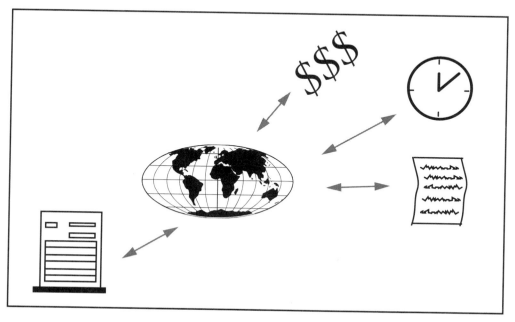

Figure 11.1 In a global information system, time data, money data, and documents are translated for each locale.

The economy and social systems of the world are shifting from national to global. An organization that is just starting to do business outside the borders of its own country may benefit from expanding its reach. Organizations that have remote offices, but are just now investing in a global information system, will reduce delays and expenses caused by miscommunication and misunderstanding.

The worldwide marketplace can deliver great profit for those that enter it carefully. Allowing professionals to share ideas and experience between different cultural and geographical frames of reference often results in innovation. Offices in multiple time zones linked by a WAN can operate worldwide 24 hours a day without having to employ three shifts of workers at each location. However, high risks, especially a lack of international business laws, cultural misunderstanding, and currency fluctuations, can ruin an organization that did not appropriately assess the adaptations they would need to make. Almost every business adaptation for global markets implies a system adaptation to help minimize the risk. Table 11-1 shows typical challenges and possible system changes.

TABLE 11-1   Possible Adaptations for Global Organizations

Business Adaptation	Possible System Adaptation
Handle multiple currencies that constantly fluctuate	Provide immediate access to currency updates
	Create built-in currency conversion and comparison utilities
	Create built-in procedures to revalue any important business quantity in any currency upon demand
	Create programs to analyze currency trends
	Ensure adequate precision in money datatypes and calculation
Work with diverse systems of commerce and law	Generate standard alternate contracts based on locale
	Set up and use a document control system for contracts and other standard documents
	Add methods for tracking products or services subject to export laws and regulations.
	Add order management processing to dynamically calculate quotes and orders based on local currency, laws, taxes, and tariffs
	Design flexible programs for tax and tariff calculation, reporting, and payment
Conform to international technology standards, or set standards where none exist	Document standards used or needed to get business
	Document requirements and methods for conversions between nonstandard formats and protocols
Work with differences in services and service levels available	Set up service contracts with local service vendors or other multinationals, especially for telecommunication

TABLE 11-1   *Possible Adaptations for Global Organizations (Continued)*

Business Adaptation	Possible System Adaptation
	Maintain online documentation of all contracts
	Set up redundant communication links for handling node failures
Provide products and services in multiple languages	Allow for data entry and storage in other languages
	Allow for multibyte character sets
Work in multiple time zones	Plan for storing data in one time, e.g., Universal Coordinated Time, and provide conversion utilities at the client side
	Determine which parts of the system will be in use 24 hours per day and ensure that they can withstand constant load
	Plan for providing 24-hour, localized support for crucial system components
	Plan for handling downtime both for routine maintenance and for emergencies
Work with different cultures and cultural tensions	Provide personnel with training in languages and cultural conventions
	Make alliances with local businesses and universities
	Donate old computer equipment, software, or books to local schools or businesses
	Adjust employment policies to accommodate shorter or more flexible hours to suit local standards
	Adjust employment practices to comply with local employment laws
Increase coordination and cooperation between offices	Prepare for increased WAN usage
	Prepare disaster recovery plan for local telecommunications crises
	Set up video conferencing facilities

The wide variation in the communications media and services available in each country create a particular challenge for most information systems designed for the United States. In the United States there are approximately 20 times as many phones per person as there are in China or Brazil or Russia. A business that only does business in the United States can contact most of its customers by telephone. Businesses in other countries must rely on the postal system or travel. In countries without the telecommunications service that the United States enjoys, you can measure business transactions in days rather than in seconds.

Besides preparing for differing electronic services, include plans for adapting to local personnel conditions, such as longer vacation time in Europe or a need for training in locales where opportunities for technical education are scarce. Local workers should be employed to assist with cultural differences, while headquarters personnel should be relocated to establish corporate expectations. Budget for travel at many layers of management, since time zone differences and patriotism create departmental difficulties best resolved by face to face meetings. Travel also broadens the perspective of headquarters employees, making them more aware of the challenges and opportunities abroad.

Managers of companies that want to expand operations globally must evaluate the potential market, determine the percent of income that they hope to receive from beyond their current borders, and then determine the costs and risks associated with earning that income. As an information Systems Manager, you can help management prepare a realistic systems cost estimate. Your projections should reflect all adaptations needed to cope with special conditions.

MANAGING OPERATIONAL COMPLEXITY

Rapidly growing organizations find that an informal infrastructure that worked for 100 employees breaks down after the one-thousandth employee is hired. Similarly, large organizations that cut costs by eliminating employees compromise their operational abilities. Their infrastructure may have relied on controls provided by personnel with specialized roles. Beyond resizing, organizations experience operational complexity due to the conditions of the 1990s economic climate. External and internal changes that businesses must adapt to include

- Mergers
- Acquisitions
- Separation into divisions
- Outsourcing of major business segments
- Alliances with other organizations
- Deregulation
- Privatization
- Transition to public stock
- Rapid growth
- Change in market due to government changes
- Change in market due to breakthrough technology
- New laws or regulations
- Routine changes, such as yearly tax revisions
- Change in growth rate or size of business
- Change in executive or strategic management
- Corporate or departmental reorganization
- Geographic expansion or shifting
- Renewed focus on profitability or cost reduction

Upon seeing an operational problem caused by these changes, management often calls for an investment in the information system to help manage the change. Forward thinking managers continuously reevaluate their information processing needs and decide whether to change, extend, integrate, or replace their systems to respond to current conditions. Quickly growing companies must assess the capacity of their system and create new strategies for keeping up with expected growth. Businesses alliances require integration of objectives, strategies, and policies, which often translates to information sharing and creation of new data pipelines.

For those managing Sybase software, these changes often mean purchasing and installing new systems management tools, creating or merging databases, and setting up Open Server applications to send data between different systems. You may find yourself writing procedures to convert between datatypes or creating a bulk transfer of records to a new database systems.

Changes made under the pressure of an operational problem rarely succeed as quickly as necessary. Executive management may not involve information Systems Managers when planning a merger, takeover, layoff, or reorganization. For best results, a Systems Manager thinks ahead and prepares solutions for several what-if scenarios. Unfortunately for executive management, Systems Managers are rarely motivated to think of the type of business changes that have unfortunate consequences for employees. Effective executives will ask their corporate information officers to prepare and update plans for typical scenarios annually or semiannually.

PRODUCTIVITY

The proliferation of relatively inexpensive desktop computers and software has introduced complexity in the task of understanding work and accounting for employee time. When a system primarily consisted of a large, expensive computer in an air-conditioned room with dedicated operators, defining the system boundaries was simple. It was easy to provide accounting of exactly which staff time could be thought of as computer overhead and which was properly charged to profit making activities of the business.

In many organizations, you can now find a PC on each employee's desk. Computer programs and data come from people distributed throughout the organization or even throughout the world on the Internet. Employees find it difficult to specify which parts of their day were spent supporting computer functions and which were devoted to revenue-generating activities. The concept of worker productivity has become blurred as job descriptions have expanded to include interaction with computers. It becomes difficult to decide between adding a technical employee or adding a computer administrator to increase total output.

The boundaries between system components are also becoming fuzzier. One application and its associated databases could be classified as decision support by managerial users. The same data coupled with a different application might be considered a data processing system by someone else in the organization. On a managerial level, the accounting for such a system needs to shift away from the specifics of the hardware or software and onto the kind of work it facilitates.

Instead of delineating systems or subsystems by the computer hardware or applications used, we need to understand systems in terms of the ways in which they support the organization. An system engineer's job description needs to shift from "keeping the computers up," or even "keeping the costs down" to "continually improving how an organization functions by turning data into informational assets."

A Systems Manager can help the organization understand its informational assets, liabilities, and expenses by maintaining clear documentation about the system services and costs as advocated in this book. Chapter 14 describes how to inventory your system and evaluate costs and benefits. Documenting your findings and making them available to upper management at any time will clarify how the system supports revenue generation. A good analysis will let management know where to focus system investments for increased productivity.

■ Tᴇᴄʜɴᴏʟᴏɢʏ-ᴅʀɪᴠᴇɴ Gᴏᴀʟꜱ

Along with organizational needs, technology drives its own goals. A new approach to a computing problem can make a business's operations much cheaper or more efficient. At the same time, the use of technology introduces new levels of complexity in a business. Technology-inspired goals should still be evaluated in the context of helping a business to profit by offering products and services. This section describes some recent technology challenges and some guidelines for managing them.

MANAGING ACCELERATING PRODUCT CYCLES

Computer information systems exist within a constantly accelerating industry. When we once could expect an upgrade in CPU speed to be available every 2 years, we can now upgrade every 3 months. Similarly, software product cycles have shortened. Between our hardware, networks, and software, we can upgrade something at least once a month. In the computer trade journals, we see new products come out every week. New protocols and new vocabulary are created daily. Upon reading about new offerings, our users frequently demand that we incorporate the new technology into our systems immediately.

Computer professionals both appreciate and abhor software upgrades. While introducing new features, upgrades also require data conversion, introduce new bugs, and cause compatibility conflicts. Software companies usually allow customers to stay on a prior version long enough to plan and perform the upgrade. After awhile, however, it becomes expensive for the software vendor to support old versions. While it may seem unfriendly to require consumers to upgrade constantly, upgrades are market driven. Existing customers demand to have bugs fixed and features improved. New customers compare features and may make their choice based on whether the software under consideration has as many features as its competition. Finally, software upgrades become necessary as hardware improves.

The situation will not improve until poor quality and excessive complexity make it extremely clear to consumers and vendors that more features do not necessarily mean better software. A Systems Manager can start to bring rationality back into the market by becoming a responsible consumer. Evaluate each new upgrade to determine if it has any features or bug fixes that make it worth your time to upgrade. If it doesn't, notify the software company of your findings. At some point, the software industry must realize that the market will go to those that can produce the most reliable and most useful software, not just software that has more features and looks more exciting. Lasting software companies must first be profitable and second produce software. Consequently, their first priority is always to go where the market is. As long as a vendor's competition wins business by having more features, it will continue to create feature-laden upgrades.

Even without upgrades, short product cycles constantly create work. After you have evaluated a new product or standard and decided whether to adopt it, others within your company will ask you to justify your decision. If you look at all the products available, you could spend all your time evaluating and justifying. Writing and publishing a long-term information strategy will help you to communicate your constraints and goals to users. If you also publish your technology evaluations, your user base will learn your expectations and requirements. Their demands will be tempered by knowing ahead of time whether there is any precedent for acceptance of their request. Such a strategy may place the burden of evaluation back on the requestors. You can ask those interested in new technology to perform an evaluation that meets published criteria before you will consider it.

Another cost of constantly changing technology is the constant requirement to learn new things. The information industry is as research intensive as being a doctor or a lawyer. When hiring computer professionals, be sure to include interview questions that help you to discover how a person learns and adapts to new technology. One of the biggest complaints about IT departments is that they are mired in the past. This may stem from a lack of acceptance of change in the nature of the industry since the mid 1980s.

For the first 40 years of computing, industry knowledge was concentrated in a few minds. No one could make decisions about the system without consulting these experts. With the introduction of compilers like FORTRAN and smaller computers, anyone who had access to a computer and was willing to read a few books and experiment could become knowledgeable. In the innovation-hungry information systems environment today, the demand and rewards have gone from those with mastery of specific deep, knowledge to those that have mastery of change and broad, varied knowledge. While there is still a need for deep expertise, it is risky to acquire it in a particular language or architecture, since innovation could make that technology obsolete tomorrow.

Yet another result of the constant demand for features is the increase in code complexity. As soon as the amount of source code in a general-pu1rpose program such as SQL Server increases beyond a certain point, it becomes more difficult to test. It also becomes impossible to make sure the software will perform correctly at all extremes of use by a diverse customer base. In particular, parallel processing on multiple CPUs presents special concurrency problems that are extremely hard to debug. Sybase is in the process of reengineering its whole test system so that the quality of the software can be better evaluated and improved. Instead of testing the behavior of a particular command, the premises and the state of the system will be evaluated at each processing step. The entire industry will need to evolve toward new testing methodologies to increase quality significantly.

One way to deal with the problems generated by programming complexity is to perform your own testing of upgrades and new products. Some companies test all Sybase upgrades by running them through a custom test suite that represents most of the work that they do. If the upgrade fails to perform properly under these conditions, customer support and engineering management are notified. Whether you choose this route or not, you should always run an upgrade concurrently with the current version for a week to a month or more to make sure that no unexpected changes in the software will affect your operations. In cases where it would not be worth the evaluation time to test a new version with a bug fix, it's better to work around the problem than to demand the fix.

In some cases, you can turn short product cycles to your advantage. Software vendors typically fix problems in new releases. If you are a large enough customer or belong to a large group of influence, such as a user group, a standards body, or the government, you can often drive a software company to change its products in particularly important ways.

Next, if a software company has done its market research, new features solve old problems and make information processing easier or more efficient. When you get an upgrade, you can determine whether it's worth implementing by looking at the problems that have been solved, estimating the resulting time or money savings, and then comparing that with an estimate of the cost of implementation. If the investment appears worth it, upgrade. Otherwise, let the company know that the market segment you represent may reject the change.

The job of Systems Manager can be frustrating due to the amount and rate of change in the industry. If you decide that you're committed to becoming an expert Systems Manager, the most important thing to learn is how to learn. By taking every day's experiences as feedback, you can refine your approach for the next day. In this industry, the excitement of new technology is reduced to an experience of constant frustration if learning to learn is not one of your daily priorities. On the positive side, the constant influx of new technology makes information processing an exciting industry for those who love to learn or are easily bored. If your computing strategy is to stay near the leading edge, you should be able to attract and retain the brightest and most innovative employees. This payoff can make dealing with all the complexity worth your attention.

RIGHT SIZING

The desire to "right size" computing motivates many corporations to reshape their system vision. Ideally, the right-sized computer system matches the needs and rate of change of the departments that they serve with maximum flexibility and responsiveness. The usual stated goals of technology right sizing are

- For employees to be able to use the best computing resources for the task at hand

- For the computing resources to be closest to those responsible for the task

- To reduce computing costs by moving toward the previous two goals

Ultimately, the real motivation is to "right budget." An organization may choose to start right sizing when it decides to confront the change in technology over the last 10 years. In the previous era of computing, computers were much more expensive than people. The mainframe and the software licenses for it could cost 10 to 20 times a person's salary. Energy that went into minimizing how much CPU time had to be used to complete a given task was well justified. Now CPU power has come down in cost, and the value of people who understand technology has increased. Today, several powerful computers and a large selection of software can be acquired for the price of one person's salary for a year. The focus of efforts during the current information revolution is on shifting as much work to the computer as possible. Right sizing effectively redistributes resources in two ways and, as many IS professionals have discovered, redistributes political power at the same time.

First, right sizing redistributes processing power, shifting both hardware and software. Typically, the right sizing investment moves CPU power away from mainframes toward personal computers. In a growing company, it can also move from a small peer to peer network of personal computers toward a centralized network.

Second, right sizing redistributes information power and responsibility among users. When leaving the mainframe environment and going to PCs, users will no longer rely on a central IT department to produce specific, difficult to change reports. They will achieve greater independence from centralized authority. Departments will often take on new responsibility for data processing, creating their own reports and developing their own software. Users going from a small, peer to peer PC LAN to a centralized network are freed to concentrate on information content instead of information management. This shift often results in compromised security.

Because of these changes, many believe that any right sizing project should be accompanied by business process reengineering. In any case, careful planning must precede a successful transition. The arguments for right sizing may rest on the advantage of the change in hardware or the change in processing alternatives for users. To be successful, the analysis and execution of such a plan should include the hardware, software, and human components. It should also examine the quality and efficiency of the inputs and outputs. For example, you can use tools like PowerBuilder to create input screens that are much more understandable, making input more reliable. Similarly, report-writing tools can make it easier to design output to facilitate quick comprehension of processing results. Without such analysis, unexpected challenges can eat away at the promise of improved productivity.

When processing power is distributed to desktops, Systems Managers have more desktop problems to solve. The organization faces more demand by users to purchase software and needs to decide how such purchases are managed. In some cases the central IT department can lower organizational costs by arranging site licenses for popular desktop programs. If users are free to acquire software on their own, the IT department needs to decide whether to support that software or make the users responsible. IT managers need to decide whether all PC software purchases must go through them to simplify accounting of licenses and inventory or whether it's more cost effective to distribute that record keeping as well.

When going from mainframes to minicomputers or to PCs, data control and data quality often suffer. While flexible, accessible systems bring resources closer to the user, they also put the responsibility for data accuracy in the user's hands. IT departments may consider it part of their charter to check their output. Users for whom data processing is a minor component of their job description may not approach this task with as much expertise or rigor.

Downsizing makes it easier for departments to undertake their own software development, rather than relying on a central IT department. Often when the machines are downsized, so is the IT department. This adds impetus to the trend of distributing development backlogs to the departments that requested them. With centralized control before right sizing, development requests are often queued with all other organizational requests. Priority for completion is less often analyzed in terms of business needs than given to those with most political power. After right sizing, departments can take on computing changes within the context of their own budgets and priorities. This allows users to be more involved in the technology selection and development. The resulting solutions more closely match user and business needs.

A disadvantage of redistributing information generation is that departmental developers often lack the experience and training acquired by the IT staff. Results will need to go through more thorough testing and analysis to verify accuracy. Another disadvantage is that departments may now produce inconsistent reports and analysis. If several departments report up through one vice-president, she may now receive three or four differently prepared of reports instead of one.

To make the transition smooth, the IT department can take on a consultative role for departmental developers. It can also develop written guidelines, based on experience, that describe success factors for application development and information presentation within the organization. The former IT center may be best utilized if tasked with helping different groups to achieve consistent results when performing similar tasks.

Beyond the difficulties of changing roles in an organization, right sizing increases the challenge of supporting the complex interrelationships of multiple protocols, applications, networks, and hardware. The new system will lack the stability and reliability of the old one. However, unlike centralized systems, when a portion of the system does fail, other parts of it usually remain functioning. Including software for distributed systems management in a right sizing project's requirements and budgets will alleviate this problem. Support of standards, implementation of controls, interoperability testing, and rigorous documentation of specifications also minimize instability in distributed systems.

SCALABILITY

Another factor that determines an organization's computing requirements is scalability. Scalability means that, if the volume of data to be processed goes up or down significantly, then the system should be able to handle the change, providing that resources, such as memory and disk space, are adjusted. In nonscalable systems, for example, the performance starts leveling off unacceptably at a certain high point, or the overhead is excessive at a low point. Systems not designed for scaling up might suffer reliability problems under unanticipated load. In reality, almost any system is unscalable past certain points. Try to estimate your current capacity and growth rate, and project your data processing requirements for the next 5 years. If your organization expects high growth or rapid fluctuations, it either needs a system that can scale to projected levels, or it needs to accept that the entire system will need replacement at some point.

Projecting past 5 years rarely makes sense because technology changes so rapidly. A breakthrough in the speed of disk storage or network bandwidth might mean that your company would be willing to invest in a new system to take advantage of these improvements. On the other hand, a small, quickly growing company should think about the next 5 years carefully. If, for example, a start-up company is running on a network of a few PCs, it should plan on upgrading the system if the company eventually expects to have a thousand employees. At that time, it will probably have the resources necessary to make a larger system investment. However, if making significant investment in custom development for the system, it may be worthwhile to for Systems Managers to seek a loan or lease that will allow the company to start out on the system that it will eventually need.

CONFORMANCE TO STANDARDS

One way that a consumer can influence the computer industry is by embracing or rejecting standards. Standards proposed by independent international bodies, such as the OSI standards for networking, take a long time to develop, but solve the technical problem addressed for a broad set of consumers.

Standards developed by consortia representing vendors and consumers act more quickly and still generate widely applicable technical solutions, although perhaps biased toward the member organizations and their markets.

Open, ad hoc standards are those that gain widespread popularity because of ease of use or because the vendor that created them dominates the market. These standards are usually licensed so that vendors other than the originator can offer products based on them. In this case, a narrower set of engineering viewpoints goes into creating the standard, but it can still be implemented under a wide variety of conditions. Products based on open ad hoc standards can be integrated widely in a network of heterogeneous platforms.

Finally, proprietary ad hoc standards create the most work for Systems Managers. They usually mean that one product can only run on a subset of the popular architectures or is only compatible with one vendor's products. Organizations with such products find that their output cannot be used as is on other platforms or with other products. They must invest energy, time, and money in data conversion. Another down side of using products that do not support open protocols means that if the vendor goes out of business or stops supporting the product you must convert your data store to another format. In such cases, you may even find yourself converting your archives if the product will no longer run on subsequent upgrades of the underlying hardware platform.

Systems Managers concerned about these issues can subscribe to trade magazines that discuss various standards. Companies may also choose to participate in standards-creating bodies. Choosing and documenting standards requirements will serve to simplify selecting and implementing new products, especially in organizations with widely distributed information systems. Training and supporting users also becomes easier for standards-based systems.

MANAGING SUPPORT COMPLEXITY

At one time, IT departments supported one version of a product on one platform under one operating system. As they transition to supporting three versions of products on three platforms and three operating systems, the time and money needed more than triples. The number of people that have all the relevant technical expertise to support the system drops dramatically. While the number of applications can be daunting, the real support complexity stems from the combinations of all these items. Networks provide a clear example. Between the network protocol, the transport media (twisted pair, coax cable, fiber, satellite), the gateways, bridges, routers and repeaters, and the software and hardware, it's often difficult to tell where a problem lies.

Organizations with centralized system support may encounter problems if they let users purchase and use the software and hardware of their choice. One strategy for avoiding trouble is to pick a corporate standard for each application area and only offer central support for that package. Users may purchase other packages, but they would be asked to provide support within their own departments. Another strategy is to select the top three most popular packages and allow users to select their favorite among the choices. Departmental cross charges may be used for support of unpopular but highly specialized applications. In some cases, support can be outsourced less expensively than providing it in house. For mission-critical software, you may find that you can better meet your requirements for quick access to technical expertise with special vendor programs like the Sybase Alliance program than by hiring full-time specialists.

ELIMINATING BOTTLENECKS

Perfectly balanced systems are rare. Most systems have bottlenecks—a critical portion of the system that does not have enough capacity. A slow disk controller on a key database device, a lack of memory on a server, or a network connection that repeatedly fails can slow down an otherwise responsive system. When you fix a problem that eliminates a bottleneck, the system either becomes perfectly balanced or the bottleneck shifts to another piece of the system. Strive for the former, but don't count on it.

Whenever you make a change to the system, think about whether you will be creating a bottleneck somewhere. Will increasing the performance of the disks cause a higher demand for memory? Will increasing the capacity of the network mean that more people use the system, thus increasing the level of database administration required? Will improved CPU performance in a new machine cause users to process more data and therefore make more demand for disk space? In many cases, you may choose to go ahead with the task. However, by thinking about the impact the change of the system will have, you will be able to plan ahead for acquiring more resources.

Besides capacity bottlenecks, you can also look for points of vulnerability in your system. These include weak spots where, if key components failed, the whole system would halt, or security holes through which unauthorized personnel could gain access to sensitive information would appear.

Under the best conditions, you should attempt to provide system balance by increasing capacity, adding redundancy or backup for weak components, and filling or monitoring security holes. If you do not have the resources or time needed to take these measures, at least document the sensitive spots for management. If the system does become compromised, your forethought will keep your professional competence from coming under attack.

■ PERSONAL GOALS

If you are a technical person, at first glance, management goals may not seem to match your goals. You may find it worthwhile to examine the gaps and narrow them if possible. Management is responsible for keeping the business or organization profitable, ultimately ensuring the continuing distribution of your paycheck and advancement of the organization's cause. Aligning your personal goals with system and management goals, if possible, will result in a more fulfilling career.

DOING THE RIGHT THING

Systems engineers often have different opinions about what should be done than their managers. While engineering opinions are shaped by working with technology, managers often get their information from marketing and form opinions based on corporate goals that you may not know about. Consider a task where your opinion differs from management's. If you put yourself in a manager's shoes, think about their goals, and the priority level still seems wrong, bringing the issue to management's attention may benefit everyone. Management styles vary, of course, and your perception of organizational openness should guide you. However, if you approach management with an attitude of thinking that there must be a misunderstanding and that you want to help with the company's mission, managers will most likely treat you with respect. If this seems like a risky approach, you may try it with a small matter first. When you cannot narrow the gap, document your concerns. Keep in mind that you will need to defend claims that you were negligent if the problems you predicted do arise. If you've reached total burn out, it may be time for you to change jobs.

CAREER ADVANCEMENT

A mismatch between responsibility and personal interests creates priority gaps. What is good for the organization is not always technically interesting. Sometimes a task becomes a priority for you because you want to learn something new, gain a marketable skill, or get the attention of key people. If these tasks also serve an organizational goal, it is worthwhile to make them a priority. Otherwise, if they only serve you, consider doing them on your own time. You may need company equipment to accomplish your objectives. You can leverage your interests by asking your management's permission to use the equipment or facility. In many cases, they will be happy to comply and will appreciate your initiative. Managers appreciate "self-starters." If you accomplish your goals, they will also appreciate being part of your success. If you make sure to thank them and give them credit, they will support you in the future as well. Currently, there is a large market for experienced Sybase professionals. Most managers will want to retain proven talent such as you and will do what they can to keep you happy with your job.

If you expect to move out of the job you currently hold, start training one of your subordinates to take over. If you have no subordinates, start creating documentation of all that you do so that someone could take over with minimal training. Once management is confident that losing you won't create serious problems, it becomes easier to promote you. If you plan to leave the company, it always pays off to leave on good terms. They will refer you work if you become a consultant, co-workers will supply references for later job moves, and disgruntled managers won't spread discouraging stories about you to potential employers.

Some people feel that by making themselves indispensable they are creating job security for themselves. This is rarely the case. Actually, such people are often considered troublesome to their managers. In reality, you can be fired or laid off at any time, and someone can always be hired to fulfill your role. The new person may not do your job as well, or as fast, or with the same level of commitment, but he or she will probably try harder to please your managers—something managers usually like. Instead of making yourself indispensable, make yourself replicable. Seek general skills that you can apply anywhere. This means that you can leave at any time and find another job doing similar work. The "indispensable" route usually leads you to mold yourself to fit a particular organization. Ultimately, you end up at a loss because you are trapped in the position that you create.

CRISIS AVOIDANCE

It's easy to get caught up in handling and avoiding crisis situations. Working in this mode is rarely rewarding and rarely advances organizational goals. If you only have time for crises, then people must turn things into a crisis to get your attention. Rather than encourage this behavior, you must take time for addressing issues proactively and for preventive maintenance. You may fear that people will get upset if you turn your attention away from their critical task. However, people are probably already upset that your system and department are always in crisis.

There is a counterproductive psychological reward to constantly handling crisis. When you resolve the crisis, you and others may feel that you are a hero or heroine for resolving their problem in such a crucial time. You may also find you work better or smarter under pressure or with less sleep. It is important to step back and accept the realization that many such crises could have been prevented had you been more conscientious ahead of time. Your work habits could be causing the company to lose money or miss opportunities that would otherwise be available. A journal of what you do every day, the causes and results of your actions, may be revealing. You may find the section on time management in Chapter 13 helpful as well.

Sometimes avoiding crisis is impossible. Disk drives go bad, new software fails, people suddenly leave the company or get placed in new positions, and nature delivers earthquakes, floods, and fire. How can you be most effective under these circumstances?

Stay calm and think positively. It is difficult to emphasize how important these two simple habits are. Staying calm simply helps you to be able to continue thinking clearly. It is well documented that adrenaline is the result of the fight or flight syndrome. You will rarely resolve a crisis most effectively with the instinctual first response. In fact, resolving a crisis usually involves getting information from other people about what happened or encouraging them to take specific actions to help you to resolve the crisis. If you are calm, you will be much more likely to get what you need from people.

Thinking positively allows you to solve problems creatively. If you are pessimistic (as many Systems Managers in constant crisis are), if you think that the solution to the current problem is impossible for you to bring about, you will not be motivated enough to do the type of thinking necessary. If, on the other hand, you assure yourself that problems like this have occurred and been resolved before, then such a solution is possible in this case.

If you think of yourself as someone capable of having break-through ideas, you will have them. You will also earn a great deal of praise in the process. The computer industry thrives on innovation. Try thinking of problem solving as innovation for awhile, and see if you are more able to keep crisis away. Instead of leaping immediately to the conclusion that you can't do something when a surprise comes up, assume that you can do it and see where your thoughts lead you.

■ THE RIGHT SYSTEM FOR THE ORGANIZATION

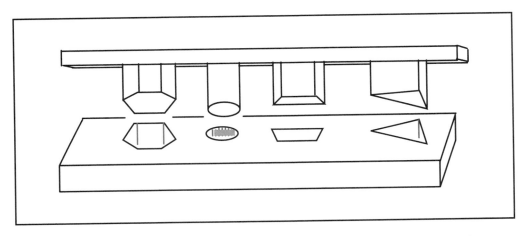

Figure 11.2 Fitting an information system to an organization usually involves more than simply finding square pegs for square holes.

Having considered the possible goals for the system, Systems Managers should next analyze the organizations that they work for. Organizational style will set the parameters for a successful system.

INFORMATION AND ORGANIZATIONAL STYLE

A computer system should support the style of information flow through the corporation for effective use of resources. It doesn't make sense to have information that is freely available when decision-making power isn't widely distributed. Similarly, distributed decision-making power can be disastrous if good information is only available to the highest layers of the organization.

The system should also match the level of structure in the organization, imposing no more or no fewer rules than those that guide other employee actions. In a highly structured organization, top-level managers create the rules, and rules are only broken or bent at their discretion. In a semistructured organization, employees at all levels decide how rules are enforced, but an overall philosophy guides when to apply the rules and when to relax them. In unstructured organizations, rules either don't exist or are created and disposed of for the task at hand. The implementation of business rules in the information system should be as flexible or as rigid as the culture that guides the employees who input and use the data. An unstructured information system in a structured business will be perceived as posing security hazards. A highly structured system in an unstructured organization will probably go unused, as people will use "back doors" to get their data more easily.

The management structure of an organization should also determine the shape of the information system. A strict hierarchical organization of authority may mean that the system needs to provide extensive security and authentication. For example, information used at the executive levels of the organization would not be modifiable or even visible to those at lower levels of the organizational chart. Companies with matrix-style management will need a very flexible system. It should be easy to set up new projects, add new users, transfer user information between projects, and reconfigure the system.

Management structure will also contribute to determining priorities for the information system. If management is primarily top down, then getting information up to people at the top layers is the most important. There will be less focus on enabling many users to use the system and more on making more information available for a selected group of users. If the managerial style is predominantly bottom up, and decision making is delegated as far as possible to operational experts, then the information strategy should focus on coordinating, distributing, and sharing information widely and swiftly. Emphasis should also be placed on making sure that people are well trained in using the system effectively so that input and output are as accurate as possible.

An example of setting up Sybase to match organizational style is to control the visibility of SQL Servers in the interfaces files and remote hosts tables. In the case of hierarchical management, you might configure several SQL Servers, one for each layer of management, with interfaces files that are not visible to each other. You could set up each server so that a user could not log into the SQL server machine or even know the name of the server used at the highest levels of management. Inside SQL Server, no remote hosts would be listed, thereby disabling remote procedure call (RPC) access between servers. In the case of the matrix-managed company, it might make sense to have one SQL Server for each project, with all the servers listed as remote hosts in each interfaces file. RPCs would be enabled between all machines so that common project data could be shared and information could be easily transferred between projects.

Sometimes an organizational change will necessitate a change in information systems. A small organization where all information is shared relatively freely may change its information policies as the company grows. At that point, security requirements may make it necessary to reengineer the information system. A company may spin off into divisions, with the result that information processing and reporting need to be distributed to lower levels of management and perhaps to a broader audience. The acquisition of one company by another may mean a blending of the two companies' information resources and requirements. A demand for closer cost tracking may motivate requests to separate data into databases by department. When organizations undergo structural change, the cultural influences on the information systems should be reexamined. Plan and document any recommended changes that should be made to reflect the new conditions.

SYSTEM-DRIVEN ORGANIZATIONAL CHANGES

While it is usually true that a business change will necessitate a system change, the opposite also occurs. Right sizing can mean redeploying people and expertise from a central IS department to business units or product divisions. Computers may eliminate routine work, meaning that employees either lose jobs or are retrained. When this becomes a trend, the average employee hired is more technical and must be payed more. The salary percentage of the company expenses change.

Changes to systems can also make it harder or easier for groups to work together. For example, data sources used by many departments can be integrated, or data to be guarded can be partitioned off from interdepartmental use. Telecommunications systems can make it easier to work away from the office.

When preparing a System Vision document, think about the effects that the system that you envision would have on business functions. Consider which activities could be facilitated by a system and which would be hindered.

While organizational style can change as a result of promoting or replacing key leaders, it takes much more to change a corporation's culture. Likewise, system changes will affect organizational culture, but a new system won't fundamentally and immediately change the culture. A company that functions largely because people have key relationships that they use to get what they need will not suddenly become procedure oriented when a new database system that enforces business rules is put in place. Similarly, an overly rigid company will not become innovative and creative if manuals are thrown out or PCs replace mainframes. Traditions and management priorities must be reshaped—a change that typically takes longer than a computer system modification.

SELECTING GOALS AND OBJECTIVES

Responsibility for a computer system, in whole or in part, demands constant assessment of priorities to achieve a variety of objectives that lead up to organizational goals. Documenting a vision of your expectations for the system will help you to stay focused on your priorities. It can also serve to ensure that your goals and those of your organization's management stay synchronized.

Having read this chapter to this point and having considered organizational goals, technology-driven goals, and your personal goals, now select one major goal in each area for the current year. Then pick one goal from each area for the next 5 years. Forget for the moment that you don't have time, that you don't have budget, and that you don't have energy. Select the goals that seem most profitable for everyone concerned. Pretend that you are your manager, then a subordinate, and then a user. From each of these perspectives, decide whether you would support the goals you picked. Make adjustments as necessary. As you read the next chapter, you will find ways to select the right projects and objectives that lead up to these goals. When you form a concrete picture that specifies a particular result you intend to achieve by a particular date, you lend a focus to your work that makes it more possible to do what you say you want to do.

While a goal is typically a broad picture of a desired result, a set of objectives describes the tactical steps you intend to use to achieve that result. A project is a way of binding objectives into a framework that you can sell and implement in a specified amount of time. To break down a goal into a set of objectives, think about how your system will look and behave when you've reached your goal. Then work backward to make a list of the intermediate milestones that much be reached in order for that goal to become real. Finally, consider the projects that you could initiate that would get you to each milestone. Start with projects that fit within your current budget and scope of influence. The accomplishment of these projects should build your credibility so that you can then carry off the next level of project needed.

As you work with the system, read the rest of this book, and talk with others, you will be able to refine your list of objectives, describing them with more and more technical accuracy. You will also start choosing projects based on effective and practical strategies. In the next chapter, we'll look at the elements of successful projects.

Procedure Manual Suggestions

○ Document System Goals

➡ Write a few paragraphs about each of the technological motives behind the current information system.

➡ Write paragraphs describing future technology directions for the system and the supporting reasons.

➡ Include any requirements that have been determined for

• Right sizing

• Standards

• Scalability

○ Information System Solutions

➡ Write a short paragraph about each of the business problems that the current information system is meant to solve in the areas of

• Profitability

• Markets and competitiveness

• Globalization

• Operations

• Productivity

➡ Include any business limits that must be met by the system, such as

• Transaction rate

• System availability time

• Quality assurance metrics

➡ Also describe business metrics that determine system investment, such as percentage of revenue cost per transaction

○ Organizational Structure

➡ As an introduction to your procedures manual, write a brief description of the informational and organizational style of your organization. Include an overview of the management structure.

CHAPTER

Implementing the Right Projects

Once you have a vision, accomplishing what you envision relies on consistently choosing and accomplishing the right projects to lead you in the right direction. These choices require clarity, focus, and discipline. A project may be large or small, and its duration may range anywhere from hours to months. In any case, while driving it through implementation, you will face many challenges. This chapter discusses general strategies for managing the changes that you make to your system in pursuit of your vision. It also gives practical tips for avoiding influences that distract you from your goals.

■ CHOOSING WHAT TO CHANGE

Computer systems constantly require changes that aren't on your list of objectives. They may be as small as fixing a problem in a script or as large as replacing several disk drives. With all the changes required and the usual urgency with which they are expected, many Systems Managers find themselves losing focus and instead becoming "interrupt driven." They go from task to task based on who asked for something most urgently and most recently.

This work style leads to burnout and frustration, both among those who practice it and their managers. Users also become weary of uncertainty about the completion of their request. They find ways to go around procedures or to turn routine requests into emergencies warranting immediate attention.

While it's tempting to just jump in and do what needs to be done, what needs to be done is not always obvious. The possible side effects of a change made under pressure may not be seen either and frequently result in unforeseen system disasters. Planning ahead will save you from having to make ten new changes to fix the results of one unplanned change.

To get out of interrupt mode, analyze your system following the suggestions in these last four chapters of this book. You will build a framework of understanding and of priorities. As new information and new requests arise, you will be able to integrate them into the framework. If you attempt to manage a database or a whole computer system without having this framework, each new request just stacks up as if in a huge pile. Like searching for something in an unindexed heap, systems management without an organizing principle is only randomly successful and rarely efficient.

It may seem that any problem could be overanalyzed and that, with all you have to do, you don't have time to plan everything, let alone read about planning. It is certainly true that you need to associate different levels of planning with projects of different scope. However, even the small projects can benefit from being planned in advance. In many cases, the planning doesn't have to be written down—only thought through. If you plan effectively, you can turn the request into a way of serving another of your objectives.

PROJECT IDEAS

A project starts as an idea. It may come to you while sitting in a meeting or just before you fall asleep. It may appear as a solution to a problem, or it may be someone else's idea that gets assigned to you. Remember this key point about ideas: *Not all ideas should be implemented.* Write down your ideas and examine them a day or two later using the criteria described in this section. If you are a project leader, you will devote a significant portion of your life implementing ideas. For the best results, you must "own" each project. By the time you finish, each project reflects your abilities, your dedication, and your management philosophy. Ultimately, you will judge yourself by your results, and so will your peers. Pick projects that you can stand behind 100%.

That said, also remember that some of your projects will fail. If all your projects succeed, you're not trying enough important projects. Breakthrough innovation usually requires repeated, failed attempts at a solution to a difficult problem. The key is to learn to meet failure with the enthusiasm to try again with a different approach. Otherwise, a habit of giving up after your failures will lead you to choose less and less rewarding goals. So, stand behind your projects 100%, but if they fail, get up and stand behind a different version of the project 100% all over again. Avoid the trap of moving your target just because you failed. Only switch your goals if you become convinced that you chose the original goal for the wrong reasons.

Now let's examine which ideas tend to become information systems projects and why. To become an effective information systems project, an idea usually matches a general management objective for the organization:

- ■ Adapt to changes in the market
- ■ Increase profitability
- ■ Solve a serious problem
- ■ Explore new technology
- ■ Take advantage of a strategic opportunity
- ■ Enter a new market

When you wonder why an idea got "sold" to management, examine which objectives it met for the person or people who "bought" it. That person will judge the results of the project on those merits. The people with jobs affected by the project—users and other managers—usually like to see new systems deliver improvements in the specific areas of

- Efficiency
- Accuracy
- Security
- Output quality
- Integration between systems
- Worker satisfaction
- User satisfaction
- Company reputation
- Current technology
- New products

A failure to address any of the concerns in the previous two lists indicates a project conceived for the wrong reasons. For the sake of your own career and the success of your department, avoid undertaking a systems project without

- Broad or significant management support
- Appropriate timing for expected completion
- A clearly defined problem to be solved
- Assurance that the proposed project provides the best solution to the problem
- Clearly defined goals and measurements of success
- A reasonable chance of project success, given the time, money, organizational processes, and existing resources allotted
- Assurance that the project is technically, operationally, and economically feasible

BALANCING COSTS AND BENEFITS

At a high level, a vision will guide how your system looks. Analyzing the costs and benefits of each component of your system develops your understanding of the system's interaction with the business. While your vision is only bounded by your imagination, your implementation will be limited by the amount of time and money that the organization is willing to invest. Even after selecting goals and objectives, you will still need to set priorities among options that appear to be equally important.

A guideline for choosing which tasks to put first is to evaluate the level of benefit received for the effort expended. One method is to prepare a simple estimate of the cost and/or the number of person-hours it would take to make each change. Next, prepare a quantitative estimate of the benefits of each change. For example, if you expect the primary benefit to be productivity, list the number of person-hours that would be saved if the change was made. If the benefit would be money saved or market share increase, list the savings or percentage increase expected. Group tasks by the type of benefit. Finally, prepare a ratio for each item of the benefits expected over the investment. The ratios for each item should make clear which tasks will yield the best results.

Table 12-1 gives an example of a list of SQL Server tasks analyzed as described. With this example, you can see that tasks that seemed similar in duration have dramatically different effects on the system as a whole. This example also shows a danger of such analysis. It neglects to show that the reconfiguration of packet size will also have a detrimental affect on small transactions. In fact, the first ratio should be recalculated. The "intangibles" in the backup automation project merit quite a bit of attention, yet, since quantifying them proves difficult, an analysis such as this discounts them. The errorlog program may also have additional costs due to data loss. Consequently, this method of analysis should only be used for small, short projects where the side effects are well known and where you can quantify the benefits in terms of a single variable, such as time. More complex projects benefit from more thorough weighing of costs and benefits, as described in Chapter 14. While imperfect, you can still learn from lists like the above. If you make them frequently, you will soon internalize the relative merits of each system change when proposed. Showing your analysis to your manager or users periodically will make your reasoning about the order in which you do things clearer.

TABLE 12-1   *Example of Simple Cost/Benefit Ratio for Time Investment*

Task	Description of Benefit	Cost in Hours	Savings (total time for all affected)	Ratio (savings/cost in hours per week)
Reconfigure packet size	Makes image transactions faster	2	10 seconds/transaction * 100 users * 50 transactions/day = 70 hours/week	35
Automate back-ups	Saves effort, prevents "forgetting" and mistakes	3	1/2 hour/week + intangibles	.2
Write errorlog scanning program	Allows preventive maintenance	2	1 hour/month downtime * 100 users = 23 hours/week	11.5
Analyze locking behavior and fix underlying problem	Reduce user phone calls and delays	4	1 1/2 hr/week * 4 users = 6 hours/week	1.5

After this exercise, consider looking back over the goals and objectives you selected as part of your system vision. You may want to modify them based on the impact and efficiency yielded by estimating the cost/benefit ratios. You may decide to include a cost/benefit analysis in your system vision document. While preparing the analysis will be time consuming, it may help you shape the budget for information system resources.

EFFICIENCY VERSUS PRODUCTIVITY

Before deciding to use technology to making an inefficient task faster, you can often profit by taking a step back to decide whether another project might make the task completely unnecessary. For example, say that one of your projects involves evaluating Enterprise SQL Server Manager (ESSM) and another involves writing a program to scan the errorlog and send you mail when there are errors. The second becomes unnecessary if you do decide to purchase ESSM. Management guru Peter Drucker addresses the need for increasing productivity:

> ...The first question in increasing productivity in knowledge and service work has to be: What is the task? What do we try to accomplish? Why do it at all? The easiest—but perhaps also the greatest—increases in productivity in such work come from redefining the task, and especially from eliminating what needs not be done.

> ...To do this requires that we ask in respect to every knowledge and service job: "What do we pay for?" "What value is this job supposed to add?"[1]

He also points out a distinction in marketing that could apply just as well to programming. Instead of asking what the market is for a product, he advocates asking what is the market for what the program does. When applied to programming, you might take another look at your priority list.

Instead of deciding how many people would want a particular program, ask yourself what people would use the output or effect of that program for and how much they would value it. Upon analysis, you may discover that you could provide the same amount of value using an entirely different method, such as purchasing a data analysis program rather than writing your own. Unless you work for a software company, your users will typically have less knowledge about ways to approach technical problems than you do. You best serve your users by always probing beyond their initial application requests to find out the real functionality sought.

---

[1]From MANAGING FOR THE FUTURE by Peter Drucker. Copyright (c) 1992 by Peter Drucker. A Truman Talley Book. Used by permission of Dutton Signet, a division of Penguin Books USA Inc., pp. 98, 102

MANAGING THE SCOPE OF CHANGES

The proper amount of planning effort to devote to a system change depends on the scope of the change. If you resist planning, you may find yourself giving priority to small tasks that require little analysis. Besides an immediate sense of accomplishment, completing small tasks also gives you the benefit of pleasing the person that asked for the change. The frequent reward of happy users can lure Systems Managers away from keeping their management happy. At the end of a year managed this way, you will have few significant system improvements to your credit. It may be hard to get funding for new hardware, software, or system help as a result. Many Systems Managers never realize that their funding comes from making the system help an organization to maximize profits and market share. Unfortunately, information systems investments are rarely inspired by a desire to make users happy.

Another poor strategy is to concentrate so fully on a large project that small, routine tasks are ignored. When large projects fall behind schedule, these small tasks usually suffer. However, the schedule and budget for large projects usually involve the assumption that everyday tasks will receive the usual level of attention. When these tasks fall behind, the system infrastructure may start to unravel, causing further delays to the large project.

Big projects often require the investment of a significant amount of time and money before results are seen. During this time, uninformed users may perceive a lack of progress. Such "invisible investments" can lead to crisis situations during the budget cycle or during cost-cutting efforts. More than one project has lost its budget halfway through in such tough times. Large projects—those that will take more than 2 or 3 months to complete—should be planned so that intermediate results are visible and well publicized. Follow the well-proven methods of project planning, including the creation and routine updates of a project schedule. Intersperse small projects with large ones so that your users will be satisfied with constant, small improvements while they are waiting for the big ones.

Finally, manage your changes so that small projects don't turn into large ones. Perfectionists typically use the task of fixing one problem as an opportunity to fix others. The size of the project then balloons, and results are not delivered within the expected time frame. Another problem with expanding scope can be infatuation with a particular technology or image. A misguided focus like this can lead you to pick the solution that most matches a marketing picture, rather than the one that makes most sense functionally. A large project, analyzed and planned carefully, always delays the delivery of results to users. While the total solution seems the most attractive from an engineering standpoint, users typically appreciate solutions that you can give them today. Don't undertake a large project when a small one will suffice.

■ CHOOSING WHAT NOT TO CHANGE

While information system modifications solve many organizational problems, they won't solve all of them. Resist the tendency to apply programming to all situations. Sometimes the appropriate approach to a situation seems so unpleasant that an information system solution is tried first. In practice, solving the wrong problems wastes a great deal of money, time, and human effort. The next few sections describe common mistakes of this type.

IMPROVEMENT IS NOT ALWAYS NECESSARY

Even if there are no problems to fix, improvements can always be made. There are databases to back up, user-requested modifications to make, and new database features to test. When you find yourself doing an inefficient or boring task, you may think of ways to automate it. You may even start to write the program to automate the task and forget your original task. Rather than tackling the most urgent tasks, identify the most essential, and plan when, where, and how to accomplish them. A Systems Manager that does this well will earn the respect necessary to acquire more resources to do more of the work.

Sometimes, the best solution to a problem is to make no changes at all. Doing a 15-minute task manually every week may not make sense to you if you could write a program in an hour that would do the same thing. But evaluating the time trade-off isn't enough. Step back and decide whether speeding up that task is as important as some other goal that might even make the task unnecessary.

MAINTAIN PERSPECTIVE

A disproportionate mental picture of your system has an unfortunate influence on your selection of objectives and judgment of priorities.

One emergency can shift your priorities dramatically. Or it may keep its proper place in your list, but take up a disproportionate amount of your boss's attention. One bad experience with a particular piece of software or hardware can cause you or others to discount using it again, even if the chances of the problem being repeated are slim. Your experience may have also been rare among all the other users of the item.

Recent events may also take on more weight in your perspective than older events. This can bias you to forget the goals you made at the beginning of the month or the year. Given a series of presentations from vendors, this phenomenon can lead you to prefer the last product described.

To avoid losing perspective, stay aware of any tendencies you have toward bias. Also, maintain a system vision in which you know the costs, benefits, and behavior of all major elements of your system over time. Refer to it often, or even post it on your office wall.

Many people benefit from giving their manager a weekly report of objectives on the first day of every week. In the report, objectives for the previous week and the current week are listed. The report also indicates which of last week's objectives weren't completed and why. The manager's reaction to the report doesn't matter as much as the submitter's. The benefit of this method lies primarily in the reporters' reactions to their ability to predict what they can accomplish in a week. Eventually, people using this method learn to focus on tasks more clearly and to estimate their abilities more accurately.

DON'T TRY PROGRAMMING WHAT YOU CAN'T DESCRIBE

Much of the joy of programming, like that of writing, is spontaneously following a line of thought to see where it ends. Sometimes this results in a work of true elegance, innovation, and brilliance. Sometimes it ends at a brick wall. Usually, it ends after a great deal of time seems to have passed far more quickly than usual. Allowing programmers to indulge in "free programming" occasionally stimulates creativity and innovation. However, this approach fails for most day to day needs. When there are specific goals and deadlines to meet, coding should only start after the problem to be solved is described in words.

If a person can't describe what the program does in conversation, the program can't be written. A high-level description of program flow meets this requirement. A tendency to treat logic as "technical details" should be avoided. For example, "Please write me a program that, for each employee, lists the person's name and their average length of service." is sufficient, providing that the data exist. On the other hand, "I want an application that tells me the 100 most important employees in the company" is insufficient. At a minimum, you would need to know the criteria for judging "important" and the time frame from which "importance" data are to be sampled. There needs to be human logic before you can turn it into computer logic.

AVOID CHANGING A SYSTEM TO AVOID A CONFRONTATION

Attempts at programs to handle personnel problems result in particularly poorly designed system elements. In particular, one incident often drives mandates to change procedures for everyone, rather than confronting the person involved.

For example, let's say that at one time an employee got extremely angry and ran a program incorrectly just for spite. One solution would be to deny access to that program to all but a select few. However, this problem will cause many other people to become less productive and may cause their morale to suffer as well.

In this type of situation, evaluate the risks. Compare how much damage is done when advantage is taken of an open system and how much benefit is received by keeping the system open? Also, look at the other weaknesses revealed by the situation. A person motivated to be this destructive probably did not suddenly become that way and probably will not reform overnight. Next time, the angry employee may find a different system weakness to exploit. More appropriate than changing the computer system would be to work with the angry person at the first sign of distress. Either resolve the underlying issue or move the person to a position where risk is minimized. While computers need systems maintenance, humans need human care and attention. Fixing human problems with computer solutions is misguided at best.

Whenever software attempts to solve human problems, it becomes very complex. Software becomes excessively complicated when organizations attempt to resolve management issues through software instead of by direct negotiation. In the ways that people are hardest to manage, the software used is also hardest to manage. For example, security features like roles, alternates, and permissions can be seen as ways to distribute power and territory within a SQL Server. They can become very complex as the number and diversity of people working with the system increase.

ATTEMPTING TO SOLVE ALL PROBLEMS WITH ONE METHOD

Different technical philosophies underlie information processing strategy. One philosophy guides developers to provide complete, interdependent solutions. Another advocates giving users modules that can be mixed and matched. The industry pendulum swings between these extremes.

The early versions of operating systems provide one example. The designers of UNIX believed in the principle of flexibility, giving users the power of many small interchangeable parts. If you had a problem to solve, you picked the utilities that comprised each step of the solution and you chained them together. In contrast, each VMS program has a large number of command options that essentially provide the same type of processing that you can get from UNIX. Instead of having one print program, each program has its own print option. Some programmers use shared library routines and some build in their own version of print functionality. UNIX typically runs faster, is more customizable, and can be extended more easily. OpenVMS is more reliable and requires less technical expertise for the average function, and users can typically decide how to accomplish system tasks more quickly.

A problem with the preprogrammed approach can be that the lack of specialization often results in a lack of brilliance. A number of required tasks are performed adequately, rather than exceptionally. The benefit is that typical solutions require less planning and organizational skill by users. Right now, the industry is embracing the concept of objects, which are essentially small interchangeable parts, each having built-in methods of performing all expected functions. Objects mix the interchangeable approach with the preprogrammed consistency approach. So far, however, objects require a great deal of time to implement well, and poor predictions about desired functionality may affect all programs dependent on the object.

The key is to remember that no approach is fundamentally right. Think through problems to decide when providing packaged solution makes sense and when to attack problems one element at a time. Beware when someone requests an approach rather than a function. They may have succumbed to a marketing vision of a particular application vendor. Alternatively, they may feel inadequate to deal with the task of training their staff to plan and organize their work. While these may be valid concerns, large, multifunctional programs are much harder to test and debug than smaller ones, take much longer to implement, require large, long-term investments, and are less flexible when business changes are needed. Whenever such an approach is requested, make sure that the effort required will not outweigh the effort of providing alternative solutions.

AVOID CHANGING THE SYSTEM TO PLEASE ONE PERSON

Sometimes one person in an organization makes a disproportionate amount of demands about how the information system should behave. The person may speak to anyone who will listen about perceived failings in the current system. It is not uncommon to see systems that are significantly biased toward a single user's desires, especially when that person is in a position with a high level of authority. Designing a multiuser system around one person eventually leads to significant problems. That person may leave the company or may lose political favor. When a system only reflects one person's desires, it unfairly keeps necessary functionality out of reach of other users.

Cases like this often involve deeper personal issues. The person may want more recognition or power within the company or may want your job. Try to discover the underlying problem. Depending on the culture of your organization, a direct confrontation may give you the best results. Perhaps such people are like children, who will challenge the limits until they will stretch no further. The extent that you allow them to stretch the limits will be the extent to which they manage your time instead of you. In some cases, you will need to agree to disagree with them. In extreme cases, you may need to ask your manager to inform the demanding person that it's not in the organization's best interest to undertake the requested changes.

AVOID USING NEW TECHNOLOGY WITHOUT A SUPPORTING BUSINESS NEED

Too often, optimistic managers or engineers make investments in new technology simply because it's reached widespread popularity. While small projects in new areas may be necessary to be informed or stay competitive, all large projects should be justified as supporting a business need. Make sure that all proposals contain supporting evidence to prove that a new solution will serve business needs better than existing alternatives. The rewards of new technology often fail to pay off because the bugs haven't been worked out yet. Also, at the beginning of penetration into the market, there are not enough test cases to prove the technology to be as valuable as initially presumed.

■ CHOOSING WHEN TO MAKE CHANGES

After you've chosen which changes to make, you will need to plan when to make them. Learning the patterns of organizational timing and user timing will help you take advantage of the slow times and avoid crisis during the peak periods. Learning your personal patterns of working with time will help you stay productive when you need to and still have time to relax.

ORGANIZATIONAL TIMING

Organizations typically have business cycles that put stress on information systems. The wise Systems Manager will try to avoid making big changes during these times.

The close of accounting periods generate heavy activity for the financial portions of the system. These include end of month, end of quarter, end of fiscal year, and other tax deadlines. Introduce yourself to your controller or accountant and find out when these times are. You may be rewarded by extra leniency next time you request their services, such as processing a rush purchase order.

Many businesses find that sales peak during particular seasons, either due to the nature of the product or service or during times of year when consumer spending increases throughout most markets.

Besides helping you avoid implementation problems, noticing these patterns will help you plan for introducing changes when users will most appreciate them.

USER TIMING

Another pattern to notice is fluctuations in user load on your system. In summer and winter, vacations and holidays may cause particularly light usage. You can use these times to test new programs or bring the system down for extended maintenance. If you know that a particular group of users will be in training for a week, you can plan work on their part of the system. Alternatively, during these times when user demands will be lighter than usual, you can plan to undertake projects that demand long stretches of concentration.

PERSONAL TIMING

Finally, become aware of your personal peaks and valleys. The week before vacation typically becomes a hectic race to take care of things that no one else can do. Planning large projects during this time doesn't make sense. Similarly, the month before getting married or having a child is rarely productive. Time of day can also affect personal productivity. The adjustment to short daylight hours in winter typically causes a loss of enthusiasm. Similarly, the onset of spring shortens attention spans and increases desires to leave work early. Naturally, the expectations upon you will not necessarily change during these times. However, temper your expectations of yourself and avoid making promises you'll regret.

■ INITIATING PROJECTS

Your project management expertise will affect the funding for your projects, the quality with which they are delivered, and the enthusiasm by which they are received by users. Your vision for the project provides the foundation for its success. In Chapter 11 we looked at your vision for the entire information system. The system vision will shape each of your projects. Create a project vision that fits into the overall vision for your system.

For significant projects, everyone you talk to will ask you to describe your work. Soon, after having explained it to several people—your friends, your peers, your co-workers, your managers, and those you supervise—you will know how to summarize the project in ways that anyone can understand. Your description will probably include an overview of how the system behaves now, what changes you will make, and how the new system will behave. To gather the most support for your project, prepare a concise explanation ahead of time. Otherwise, your first attempts at summaries may leave the listener wondering. People may not believe that you know what you're doing.

Make it a goal to have listeners walk away having an accurate picture of what you are undertaking, what is and is not part of the project, and why it's needed. With a good description, they may even offer to help. Ideally, the picture you have painted for your listeners will be so clear and memorable that they will be able to describe the project to someone else in a way that gains that person's support as well. Try not to waste a single opportunity to share your project vision clearly with anyone who asks. You know you have successfully "sold" a project in this way when, someday, you hear someone explaining or justifying something using the same language that you used to promote your project.

When creating your project vision, ask yourself whether it is focused, memorable, and repeatable and whether it awakens in people a desire to support your goal. If you were an executive making budget decisions and you had to choose between your vision and that of another manager, would you choose your own? Think about the project team members. If they get other job offers, would they think of your project vision and decide to stay a part of it? Can even your detractors state your vision accurately? Does your vision make you want to wake up in the morning[2] to make it become a reality?

---

[2]O.K. Before noon then.

THE ROLE OF PROJECT DOCUMENTS

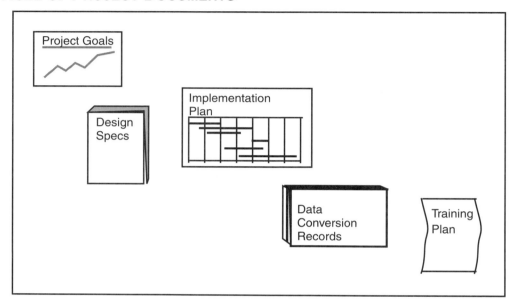

Figure 12.1 A few of the documents you might create during the course of a project.

Documents guide a project from brainstorming through implementation. The written word can help you promote your system and help users accept it when implemented. As with training and maintenance, think of documentation as an ongoing task.

Write down your project vision first. After you have tested it on a few people, "publish it" within the organization. Publishing your project ideas may involve making a presentation, writing a whitepaper, or putting electronic documents up on a WWW site. Writing project documents for a wide audience does a few things. First, it helps you to clarify your vision—it helps you to think through details and anticipate questions. Next, it makes your ideas concrete in other people's minds. If you make the documents short, but well written and compelling, readers will help you to create the project that you envision. People who agree with your ideas will copy your documents and give them to others. This serves as a powerful promotional mechanism, since you don't have to meet with each person personally to sell your ideas.

Project documents that you may write include

- The project proposal
- The project plan
- Research papers (whitepapers)
- Reference manuals
- Answers to frequently asked questions
- Procedure manuals
- Training manuals
- Help documents

As well as representing a project, documentation can also shape the way that an organization works. For example, documentation of a software system can enable people to become more productive or can confuse them into thinking that the system is too difficult to understand. It should be easier to read and refer to documentation than to find and ask the people with the answers.

There is a tendency to put documentation last, but such a tendency ultimately results in an organization with a weak infrastructure. Without documents describing ideal and practical processes, people must rely on their own sense of how things should be done. This may have very inconsistent results when someone leaves his job or goes on vacation or the organization grows such that there are now a team of people to do a particular function, rather than one person. Furthermore, security is weakened, since what was once left to one person's integrity is now left to many people's sense of right and wrong. In an organization with high turnover, this is disastrous. After a certain point, the vision and knowledge of the founding employees of a company go when they go. If this vision and sense of history are gone, the foundations of a company can be shaken. Mistakes get repeated, and a group of people new to the company may not have as unified a direction as the "old guard." You can avoid this fate by making documentation your cornerstone.

When preparing documentation, as with all writing, think about your potential readers and your intended results. You might want to

- Convey information
- Communicate corporate culture
- Establish authority
- Maintain control
- Motivate support for an idea

An organization with too many documents used for control purposes can be rigid and inflexible. Control documents vest authority in the documents and in those who wrote them. In contrast, an organization with too few documented procedures can be disorganized and inefficient. An organization that relies instead on recommendations, procedures, and guidelines will create a flexible culture that stresses informed authority.

Some organizations rely on experts rather than documents. In these cases, information is controlled by the self-imposed standards of the experts. Such a culture cultivates gurus and confers authority on those who have a lot of information. This type of organization may provide the most flexibility. If, however, the organization undergoes rapid growth, it may run out of experts. Also, experts may tire of repeatedly answering the same questions. To avoid such problems, establish a mentoring program in which you encourage experts to write papers, give classes, and otherwise distribute their expertise throughout the organization.

In an organization that uses documents to guide the organization's culture and results, you can change the organization by changing the documents. The documents that new employees receive can set their expectations as much or more than their managers can. Documents that define an organization include

- Corporate reports
- Decision-making reports
- Performance reports (actual versus expected results)
- Forms
- Policy manuals
- Letters, memos, and email
- WWW documents
- Technical documentation

When creating new documents, pay attention to their form just as you would when designing new software. For example, a sales report may consist of tables listing highs, lows, averages, and projected performance. You could present the same information by replacing or augmenting the tables with pie charts and bar graphs. Different users viewing the different forms of the report could form vastly different impressions of the output. Like a data entry screen, document design influences productivity. It also affects reader opinion about the writers and the system that generated the information.

Make sure to store documents carefully. If you create a centralized repository, everyone in the organization can find reference information with little assistance from a specific person. If, however, people keep their own stashes in their offices, more effort is required to distribute documents among people and to bring new people up to speed. If no one trusts that reports are being stored properly, everyone will hoard data. This approach leads to rapidly increasing demand for desk space, disk space, data administration, and support services.

THE PROPOSAL

A project leader uses a written proposal to make a case for investing an organization's time, energy, and resources into a project. If successful, the proposal persuades investors to let you spend their money. The proposal also convinces potential team members to invest themselves in creating high-quality results. The proposal makes the vision for the project both vivid and concrete.

Get all key players to contribute to and review the proposal and then to sign off on it formally when it's done. The resulting document serves as a commitment by the team that created it. It also provides a point of reference for new team members and for those who will maintain the system later.

A written proposal typically provides readers with

■ A description of the problem to be solved by the project

■ The expected benefits of the project

- A description of the business and technical requirements that the project must meet
- A description of the business and technical strategy for solving the problem in a way that meets the requirements
- Arguments describing why the project provides the best solution to the problem
- The qualifications of the key players to carry out the plan.
- An estimated schedule and budget
- A cost/benefit analysis
- A set of deliverables and limits that clearly define the scope of the project
- An analysis of any exposure to risk either by implementing the plan or failing to implement it correctly
- Proposed metrics that will be used to verify the project's success

Optionally, you can incorporate other elements to enhance the proposal's chance of success, such as

- Suggestions for financing the project
- The proposed project team
- A marketing plan
- A transition plan
- A training plan
- Issues that need to be resolved for the project to move forward

Write the proposal carefully. It makes an impression on readers' minds about the communication and organizational abilities of the writer. It also forms their first impressions about the project.

GETTING APPROVALS AND SUPPORT

The process for getting approval and budget to implement a project depends heavily on organizational style and the organization's business model. Your ability to get your project funded will depend on how much people agree that your vision fits with the organization's goals.

To get project support, you must sell the value of the project. We will refer to those who will invest resources in the project as the buyers. There are basically two ways to sell an idea. You can scare buyers into thinking that if they don't take your advice to buy they will suffer some fate that they wish to avoid. Alternatively, you can lead buyers to the belief that if they take your advice they will experience something that they wish to experience. Most sales involve some of each type of selling.

The extent to which a sale succeeds is the extent to which the buyers trust the seller's message about either of these outcomes. Gaining that trust, is of course, the hard part. Trust is based on many personal factors, which require talent to control. Buyers also base their trust on believing whether you have presented all the facts about the deal and nothing but the facts. If you have prepared for the sale by the methods described in this book—preparing a vision, a project plan, and a cost/benefit analysis—you will have the facts. If the buyers have any doubts, they may ask, directly or indirectly, for verification of your facts.

If you think about the buyers' viewpoint and present your analysis in the way that they will think about it, you will also gain trust and respect. If you make clear that you're proposing a business plan, that it fits into the vision for the organization, and that you understand it's an investment that must pay off like any other, the buyer will know you are more than a "hacker." By demonstrating to them that you can think as they do, you are also demonstrating that you have at least the basic skills and understanding that it takes to implement a project.

This approach may not seem applicable to your situation. If you work for the government, for example, you can't just go directly to the president and ask for the money to implement a decision support system. However, you could conceivably create a vision statement that's powerful enough to get passed along to people who can act on it. Similarly, in a not-for-profit organization, you could write a position paper and release it to the press. This in turn may result in donations toward your organization.

One of the worst things that can happen to a project is for it to fail to meet its goals after the investment has been made. The project may remain uncompleted or unable to make the expected return on investment. This happens often, so plan for it, watch for it, and react early. One cause might be that the objectives of the project are not the same in the minds of the project leaders, project team members, investors, and managers. Another cause could be that one or more key leaders may take full and exclusive responsibility for project objectives and then leave the organization or get promoted. Subsequently, new players brought in fail to support the project as enthusiastically as the originators. A large part of project leadership involves "keeping people in the loop" to avoid these types of problems. Project documents can help with this task as well.

Another type of problem is that certain managers or team members may not agree with the objectives defined on paper. They may not agree because someone failed to consult with them before the project was started, and they felt that they should have been involved. If experts are not given real roles in projects in their areas of expertise, they often refuse to support the project. Experts or interested parties may also block a project because they perceive it as threatening a project that they wanted implemented instead. People resistant to a project might also feel that the completion of the project will endanger their employment or status in the company. A common way to avoid these reactions is to get informal approval from all key players who feel that they should be involved. Such approval can be gained by talking to them about the project ahead of time and asking for their input, requesting their participation, or explaining how the project can benefit them.

DOCUMENTING REQUIREMENTS

You can solve an information systems problem with various combinations of hardware, software, and methods. To choose the optimal solutions, a project leader compares how all the proposed solutions meet project requirements. For example, if a requirement is high throughput for data entry, you might consider having two different SQL Servers for data input and writing an application to combine and report results. On the other hand, if a requirement is that the system provide optimal performance for decision support (a large amount of data that may be queried any number of ways at any time), the above solution wouldn't work because there would be constant RPCs between the two SQL Servers. In this case, you might put your money into a high-end machine with especially fast disks, plentiful memory, and a copy of Sybase IQ.

For best results, systems analysts use both analytic and empirical methods. With theoretical analysis, we try to compare alternatives fairly and objectively based on critical measures. Our observation and experience help us select the critical factors to compare.

Remember that requirements differ from desires and features. Guard against comparing features that meet implicit, unstated project objectives. Compare only the essential—factors that, if missing, would cause the project to fail to meet its goals.

Document all requirements. Requirements allow you to weed out options that should not be considered and give you something by which to measure the success of the project. When you publish project requirements, you also help rank the work of the project team. Contracts for hardware, software, and especially services may include a clause that specifies key requirements to be met for the contract to be valid. (Remember to check with your legal counsel before adding such clauses.)

Once you have documented your requirements, ask at least one other person to review and approve them. Ask your reviewer to verify that you haven't omitted anything important and that you have interpreted organizational standards correctly.

The remainder of this section describes possible requirements for SQL Server projects. As you consider requirements, you may decide to rewrite project goals and revise the project proposal.

Solve the Problem

A project must solve one or more problems that it promises to solve. Surprisingly often, technology becomes so alluring that people forget about solving problems and instead look for ways to use features. Specifically, a project should solve a business problem. A focus on solving a technical problem often leads to losing sight of the purpose of the information system. People adept at solving technical puzzles often forget to step back and make sure they are solving the right problem. Some business problems that indicate the need for information system solutions follow:

- Increase in the number of errors in data input or output
- Data processing too slow
- Important data processing inadvertently omitted
- Data processed incorrectly
- User complaints
- Loss of customer sales
- Increase in customer complaints
- Vendor/supplier complaints

Besides looking at obvious problems, these questions will help you take a step back and make sure you are approaching the business problem:

- Do data flow to the right people?
- Do data flow to any of the wrong people?
- Where are there bottlenecks in data processing?
- Is work duplicated?
- How much processing do data need as they flow through the organization?
- Where do most errors get introduced?
- Will a new technology approach really solve the problem better than a new management approach?

Performance

A common requirement for SQL Server includes the ability to support certain performance needs. Depending on your goals, this may mean a certain number of transactions per second, the completion of a key batch procedure within a certain time period, or the maximum amount of time that should elapse before receiving the result of a typical query at peak load. The best way to evaluate systems for a particular performance requirement is to simulate a typical workload and compare results for different software and hardware combinations, using your current system as a benchmark. Set performance goals for each stage of the development process if possible. The later in the implementation process that you try to improve performance, the more it will cost.

Architecture and Interoperability

Consider whether you require particular hardware, operating system, network, or protocol support for the project technology. An existing system usually determines this requirement. For example, your organization might want to protect previous investments in training, in the existing architecture, or in compatible software. Alternatively, your organization might want to get rid of an obscure or obsolete architecture because it's too hard to find supporting hardware and software or because it's too expensive to hire people experienced with using it.

Reliability

All software and hardware fail under some conditions. A reliability requirement sets expectations for how much failure your organization can tolerate. Some technology is more reliable than others, and some has been specially designed for fault tolerance. You will also need to build processes and methods into your system such that recovery can be swift and reliable if failure does occur. A business that does business 24 hours a day, 7 days a week, will be able to tolerate failure less than one that only uses the system Monday through Friday, 10 to 12 hours a day. However, under the increased load, the former business will encounter more failure. For exceptional reliability requirements, consider the exceptional measures that you will need to take.

A common metric used for reliability, especially for hardware, is mean time between failure (MTBF). In other words, if your main UNIX server had a hardware failure three times in the last year, the MTBF is 4 months (12 months per year divided by 3 times per year). It is a little more complex to measure software this way because we need to define failure. We do not typically consider user error as a failure for determining software reliability. However the user-interface design of software can still be a factor of reliability, since it can designed in such a way that it minimizes user error. Another problem with measuring MTBF for information systems is determining the scope of failure that constitutes a measurable amount. For example, is a problem that only affects one user counted with equal weight as a failure that affects all users on a machine or all users on a network?

Determine your requirements for how reliable the system must be to succeed. Also think about requirements for recovery time and reliability in the event of a failure.

Scalability

In a quickly growing business, a system must be scalable. You should be able to incrementally add resources, such as memory, disks, or CPUs, and increase processing power. You should also be able to add more users, more machines, or more transactions up to a specified load without requiring a system redesign.

The ability to scale down may also be a requirement. Consider the minimum configuration for the system if you need to create portable applications. For example, field employees may need a system that allows them to input data through a laptop PC or Mac and then upload the data to a central location for processing.

Finally, scalability also implies a level of tolerance for change. A business or organization that experiences seasonal swings or one that is new and has unpredictable growth may need to be able to add and subtract from the system processing and cost on a month's notice.

Distributed Processing

In addition to scalability, you can judge a system solution based on how well it tolerates distribution across an organization. Providing a system that can share all data between two or three sites around a country is a different problem then sharing all data between ten or more sites. Increasing the number of sites can cause the amount of data to be kept in sync to become unwieldy or can result in intolerable network delays. Consider how much of the organization any new system components must serve. Must the project application run on all platforms at all home offices and in the field or just in one location on one platform?

Communications and Networking Integration

If one or more networks are already in place, evaluate whether the project will require any new connections. Establish whether the proposed software must run on one network protocol or on many. Are there requirements of the network system itself, such as needing an upgrade in bandwidth to handle the new load?

If no network is in place, document whether the project includes adding one or whether that is covered in a separate proposal. Document requirements for certain protocols if necessary. Specify which machines must be able to connect to the new system. Consider whether employees, customers, or contractors will need to access the system by modem or by other remote connection technology.

Systems Management

Systems management requirements include such things as being able to make backups while the system is running, monitor performance remotely, mirror databases, perform multiple operations with a single command, and perform unattended maintenance operations. Think about the features most necessary to maintain your ability to meet reliability requirements. To achieve the highest reliability, you will need to invest in systems management processes.

Service and Support

Determine the level of service and technical support essential for the system to meet its goals. If the system is expected to run for 24 hours a day, 7 days a week, you may need to obtain a 24-

hour support contract. Most companies sell different support contracts based on your needs. If most of the weekend failures that you can imagine would be able to wait until Monday morning, then your requirements in this area will be much lower. For hardware, on-site service almost always makes sense. Packing equipment and taking it to and from a service center involves time and money and increases the risk of damage during transport.

Competitive Differentiation

If your system will be visible to your customers, document any requirements necessary for performing particular operations better than your competition.

Security

Security requirements fall into two broad categories. The first is how well you must protect against attacks to your system from people outside the organization. The second is how easily someone from inside your company can access data they aren't authorized to access. The former garners a great deal of media attention, but the latter often proves to be a more significant risk. An organization that is serious about security should document a security policy and various levels of risk that range from *tolerable with corrective action* to *must be avoided at all costs*.

Typical RDBMS requirements include whether transactions need to be encrypted or authenticated, whether the length of passwords is controlled, whether password expiration can be enforced, and whether access permissions can be granted and denied on an object by object and user by user basis.

Profit Improvement

If the system must operate less expensively than the current system to be worthwhile, document the level of improvement required. If necessary, document whether the requirement is to be met by facilitating increased revenues or by reducing costs.

Standards

Document any standards that the system must adhere to for business or technical reasons. These might include the FIPS government standard, the SQL 89 standard, or standards associated with a particular operating system.

■ DESIGN

Database design usually involves mapping data to databases and examining the processes used for getting information into and out of the system. Several database texts describe the process of logical and physical database design. Logical design concerns organizing data such that you can ensure integrity and support business rules. Physical database design involves organizing data so that you can maximize performance and reliability.

Project design means establishing the set of all the puzzle pieces that will fit together and creating a strategy for putting them together in the right order. Many textbooks and consulting organizations describe various project design methods. In the absence of a formal framework, a project design may mix up logical, physical, and political desires into one loosely bounded package. Naturally, the more loose you allow the boundaries to be, the more loose your schedule will be and the more money you will spend in not entirely productive ways.

Do not confuse "an architecture" with a design. In our industry, the word *architecture* has come to mean any number of things. Often, it's used as a way to knit together a company's product offerings in a way that's easy to describe. While interfaces and structure are a valid part of a design, they are not the only parts. The next few sections describe elements of design that you may want to think about using to lend structure to your project.

DERIVING DESIGN FROM REQUIREMENTS

After defining requirements, systems engineering involves designing a solution that fits. With some requirements, such as standards support, a vendor of a particular component will let you know whether the product conforms. With others, like performance, you will need to examine both the documented claims of the vendor and the configuration in place at your site.

When evaluating possible system changes, examine your inventory of the existing hardware and software. Decide whether any of it can be put to better use in the new system. In some cases, hardware can be upgraded or expanded more cheaply than it can be replaced. Be careful, however, not to include a component just because it has never been used to its potential. Sometimes such a component requires concessions in other areas, such as special types of software or disks that will not be compatible with future extensions of the system.

When considering alternative designs, ask questions like the following to determine which will best serve the organization:

- What is the expected transaction volume?
- What is the expected storage growth?
- How and where is information currently stored? How will that change?
- How much effort will be expended to manipulate data?
- What communication takes place between business sites?

As a way of understanding how data flows in an organization, software engineers and systems analysts use various database and system design tools, such as data flow diagrams and entity-relationship diagrams. Most database texts cover these in detail. Such diagrams help project designers to develop an understanding both of the system in place and how it will change.

HUMAN-CENTERED SOFTWARE

Teachers of writing, sales, public speaking, and politics advise their students to know their audience before trying to tell them something. Unfortunately, such advice has taken lower priority among teachers of computer science. Instead, programmers are revered for knowing their hardware, software, and algorithms. In our industry, we have placed the focus on the machine. If, as a leader, you want to provide an exceptionally successful business solution through an information system, you must temporarily forget the technology and start thinking like a user.

Some programmers, often described as "hardcore," will take a stated problem and deliver a very technical solution. They are very interested in topics such as performance, minimizing disk space, efficient memory use, or algorithms that cause a leap in technology. As a designer of a data input or delivery system, however, you will need to understand the human side of the human/computer interaction as much as the computer side. If the average user will stare at a screen for 2 minutes to figure out which menu option to choose, it will not be as important that a clever algorithm saved 30 seconds of run time. If the design of the interface causes data input errors, the resulting inaccuracy will outweigh any gains in efficient storage. If a decision support program allows sloppy queries that waste system resources, then conservative memory use will not have any visible payoffs.

Someone who doesn't understand how people behave in relation to the system might be tempted to solve data entry problems by extensive use of input checking and popup windows. While judicious use of these is helpful in general, they don't address the fundamental problem. Focus instead on designing the system such that the human's initial responses to the computer will result in success. A designer may try to aim for artificial intelligence by giving the human a long string of options to which he must respond, but the brilliance of the program will fail to impress the user if the miskeying of one response requires him to abort the whole program and start over again. Undo and redo options go a long way toward bridging the gap between the average human and the average program. So does automatic file save, where the user can set the number of backup copies to keep around. Make the default at least 3.

As well as making input and query screens intuitive, incorporate instant feedback into the interface to assist users as well:

- Echo all user input to the screen.

- Ask the user to confirm any action that is difficult to undo.

- Display a progress indicator whenever the program will take more than 5 seconds to complete an operation.

- Display an estimated completion time whenever the program will take more than 5 minutes to complete an operation.

You can also gain insight by examining the context in which users work. For example, if working on a stock trading system, users are under time pressure and may not want to think through too much before hitting a key. An application suited to such needs will only put a few buttons on each screen, make the most common actions the quickest, and hide the options that are hardest to undo. You can get a good idea of context from

- Samples of current input and output data
- Interviews of users
- Interviews of management
- Employee or customer questionnaire responses
- Observation of the organization
- Feedback from prototypes
- Market analysis

After having formed your own impressions, often limited to the context of your own relationship with computers, you will need to talk to your users. The greater your capacity for empathy with a diverse set of people is, the more usable your software can become.

INVOLVING END USERS IN DESIGN

Solicit and incorporate user input at all stages of a project. Users of the current system, who must live with its failings every day, will have a lot of ideas on how the system can be improved. Introducing a new system without their input is risky. They will be frustrated if you carry the worst problems of the old system over to the new.

By talking to users, you not only start to understand their needs, but you help them to feel comfortable with the idea of a new system. No matter how much better the new system may make their jobs, users will undergo stress as they adapt. You can minimize the stress by making it a system that they look forward to. Besides human stress that results in illness and low morale, a bad system transition creates organizational stress by temporarily slowing information processing, increasing employee turnover, and increasing the chance that important processes get overlooked.

You can get user input during the design process by

- Interviewing users
- Soliciting free-form comments
- Administering anonymous or signed questionnaires
- Providing prototypes for users to respond to
- Observing users of the current system

By observation, find out

- The time to execute each operation
- The frequency of performing the most common operation
- The relative frequencies of different operations
- The overall effort expended on reformatting or re-creating data as they flow from one human being through the system and to another human being
- How many employees work with the most commonly used information

For useful direct information, ask users for

- Opinions about the old system
- Expectations for the new system
- Wish lists for the new system
- Problems frequently encountered with the old system
- The information formats considered most useful
- The information sources considered most useful
- Experience with how the system supports or hampers decision making
- The consequences of bad or missing data on their work

The opportunity to respond to your inquiries will also help people think ahead to the time when they won't be using the old system. They may start to ask questions about how the new system will fit with the patterns that they have established. This type of feedback can be extremely valuable, because the questions can illuminate needs that had not been stated earlier during the formal requirements-gathering stage. If you also allow users to review your designs as they progress, you may also learn how the proposed operation will support or conflict with current operational procedures.

View all user interaction as information exchange, rather than as one-way flow toward the designers. When interviewing users about their needs, you are implicitly selling them on the idea that you can provide them with the system they want. Users who feel that they helped with the design will have less motivation to criticize it. Beware, however, of asking for comments and then not responding to them. Consider reporting on all suggestions, noting which will and will not be implemented and why. It's O.K. to admit that you don't have unlimited resources for the project as long as you make some important improvements. It's less well received if the organization invested significantly in a project that did nothing to make the lives of users better.

When analyzing user input, especially for large user or customer bases, consult with references about how to create statistically valid questionnaires and analysis. Watch for these common influences that skew responses:

- Users perceive the project as a threat to their jobs.
- Answers reflect users' emotional responses to recent actions by the organization.
- Users forgot the facts in question.
- Users may be unwilling to report unpleasant incidents or facts.
- Users may have negative life circumstances that influence their opinions of everything.
- Users may make incorrect assumptions to fill gaps in their knowledge.
- Users may compromise the accuracy and depth of answers because they don't perceive giving input as a high-priority task.
- Users may lie about events or facts under pressure from peers or superiors or because of their own role in them.
- The project may appear to be self-serving, especially when proposed and run by a consultant.

Give users an opportunity to feel that they have a significant impact on the quality of the hours they spend at work if they provide you input objectively and in a timely manner.

DESIGNING INTUITIVE INTERFACES

Computer users recognize intuitive design. Someone who does not inherently love computer hacking will reach for a Macintosh before they reach for a UNIX workstation. Designing intuitive programs entails getting an understanding of people such that you know what most people see when they look at a computer screen. Recognize that, since you are a computer expert, you are in a terrible position to know what is intuitive to the average person.

For insight into designing intuitive interfaces, read *The Design of Everyday Things*.[3] This book is only about 200 pages long, is fun to read, and is highly informative. Reading Norman's book will ultimately pay off in time, money, and your professional well-being. If enough professors, managers, and individual contributors read it all at once, the software industry might advance more in 18 months than it has in the last 10 years.

The amount of effort you put into designing an intuitive user interface will pay off in several ways:

- More productive users
- Lower training requirements
- Lower support requirements
- Fewer mistakes
- Less job frustration among users
- Better reputation for the organization, project team, and project leader

The key to intuitive design is building on what people already know. If you have something that looks like a push button on the screen, then users infer that they can click on that button to perform an action. By the same token, a button-shaped icon that does not perform an action when clicked on makes your program confusing. The location of the button can lead users to form correct or incorrect assumptions. For example, you could put a "next screen" button in the top left of a window and a "previous screen" button right below it. As a programmer you might think

---

[3]Donald A. Norman, *The Design of Everyday Things* (New York, N.Y.: Doubleday, 1988).

this is intuitive because you are used to stacks, where the most current thing is pushed on top and the old stuff is buried below. However, the average user is much more likely to associate traversing windows with reading books than with manipulating stack pointers. Therefore, a much more intuitive design, at least for people who read left to right, is to put the previous screen button in the upper- or lower-left corner and the next-screen button in the upper or lower right. The choice of the top or bottom of the window will depend on window size. To make the program most friendly for diverse users, you could even make buttons repositionable so that users can put them wherever they want.

Your potential users can be a great help in designing intuitive user interfaces. You can test your assumptions about intuitive designs by creating prototypes of your screens. Give different screens to different sets of users. Watch them attempt to perform the action required, and see which group achieves the best results.

Another element of user friendly design is fault tolerance. For example, it is typical for programs to ask twice if users are sure when they are about to delete a whole directory full of files or reformat a hard disk. OpenVMS does a good job of this. First, it saves an unlimited number of previous versions of files by default. Second, it lets you give program options in any order. You never have to retype a command line because you didn't put the option in the right place. Third, OpenVMS is case insensitive so that you never get unexpected results from using a lowercase option instead of an uppercase option.

DESIGNING IN QUALITY

Another criterion for good design is reliability. A good systems design will minimize the need for attention by systems personnel. It will also minimize support calls from users.

You can increase a program's quality by anticipating and working to avoid the problems in the following list. For error conditions that you can't control, at least try to make diagnosis easy and strive for graceful recovery. Watch for

- ■ Failure when integrating program modules written by different programmers
- ■ Failure when installing the program
- ■ Failure when upgrading the program
- ■ Failure when users configure the program incorrectly
- ■ Internal failure due to encountering an internal limit or an external system limit
- ■ Internal failure due to incorrect use of the programming language
- ■ Internal failure due to incorrect subroutine or function call
- ■ Failure to call the operating system or other external library routines correctly
- ■ Failure to handle incorrect user input well
- ■ Failure to terminate gracefully upon request
- ■ Failure on hardware and software configurations that you never tested
- ■ Failure to interoperate with various versions of other hardware, software, or networks
- ■ Failure under peak loads
- ■ Failure to scale up well
- ■ Failure when hardware fails
- ■ Failure when operating system fails
- ■ Failure when network fails
- ■ Failure when power goes off
- ■ Failure to interface correctly with input and output devices
- ■ Failure to coordinate concurrent processes for multitasking systems

As you determine each feature of the application that you are building, create a test plan for that functionality. As you think about testing the ways that the program or users could go wrong, you may think of ways to improve the design up front.

For maintainability, think about the people who will eventually fix and upgrade the program as problems are discovered and as needs change. Make sure programs conform to well-documented programming style standards.

Some actions that you can take *at the beginning* to build quality into the information system infrastructure are the following:

■ Create input applications rather than relying on users to generate optimal SQL

■ Use integrity features and stored procedures

■ Make prompts for input information clear

■ Provide defaults for the most common input values

■ Use pull-down menus instead of data-entry boxes

■ Use error checking code liberally

■ Code the application to give feedback about what each operation did after execution

■ Provide an undo option in the application

■ Code in the ability to produce variance reports that users can use to validate input that looks unusual

■ Write SQL code that checks SQL Server global variables such as @@error, @@rowcount, and @@transtate to make sure that transactions completed as expected

■ Use SQL Server features such as transaction save points and the `rollback trigger` command to isolate commands into manageable chunks and roll them back when necessary

■ Use a source-code control program to manage stored procedures and other SQL objects, as well as other application code

■ Provide prewritten reports so that users don't block others with suboptimal SQL

■ Provide built-in ways to check the results of processing

■ Anticipate and provide recovery actions for various failure scenarios, such as user input error, output device failure, and exceeding limits

Designing in Flexibility

Because the computer industry moves so quickly, the viability of a fixed, long-term computing strategy has declined. Few experienced IS professionals have confidence that such a strategy will ever come to fruition as projected. Make any software project flexible enough that you can remove any element without causing the whole system to fail. If an element fails to meet this test, document the process for ensuring its availability.

Software companies routinely go out of business, change management, grow spectacularly, and take precipitous dives. As companies become more dependent on software for competitive differentiation, their success and failure ride the same curves as their technology. Anticipate how the organization will adapt to technology change and how the technology will adapt to organizational change. Imagine the possibility of each key vendor's change in fortune or lack of foresight. Either take responsibility for helping the vendor succeed or lay the foundation for alternative strategies, or both.

ENCOURAGING INNOVATIVE SOLUTIONS

Innovation drives the software industry. Organizations want to distinguish themselves from their competitors, consultants want to distinguish their work, customers want new features but less complexity, and everyone wants to remove old barriers. Innovation results from solving an old problem in a new way or designing a system that bypasses the source of the problem altogether.

The quickest route to innovation comes from questioning assumptions. Does the program have to be command oriented or can it be made to be graphic? Do users really need to be prompted for value X—can it just be the default? Is there a library of routines that can be used to draw all the buttons rather than designing them yourself? Can input be scanned rather than typed? Do you really need to implement only one of two choices instead of both?

Creativity can be fostered on a project by providing times for sharing ideas freely. Set up design sessions in which you encourage all project team members to brainstorm ideas. If working in an environment where change is rare, try having an off-site meeting to inspire innovative thinking. If you take the programming team to another location, like a hotel suite or a ranch house, the design work may improve dramatically.

A habit of reading widely in many fields also yields innovative approaches. Subscribe to magazines that describe other systems solutions, read books about design techniques, and read the newspaper to learn of business trends. Sometimes reading in an unrelated area, such as science, can lead to breakthroughs in programming as well.

■ VALIDATION AND VERIFICATION

A professional experienced with the implementation of a particular technology may be able to see ahead accurately enough to create a design on paper that works just as described. More often, people find that technology provides too many variables to predict reliably. In these cases, consider employing one the techniques described in this section to give your project the best probability of success.

PROTOTYPING

Figure 12.2 Prototyping allows you to try out ideas and prevent expensive mistakes.

Prototyping helps you to verify a program's ability to meet complex requirements such as those related to performance, networking, and security. A prototype is a model of an application that you build for test purposes only. By building prototypes at the beginning of the schedule, developers can also test and refine proposed methods of team interaction.

A prototype often tests only one aspect of a systems solution—the one most in question. Strive to build prototypes in less than a month, make them easily modifiable, and prepare yourself to throw them away if they prove unworkable. Your temporary system can serve the following purposes:

- Demonstrate feasibility of project to users and managers.
- Provide feedback about the features that will make the system most easy to sell.
- Get user and management suggestions about the best and worst features of a proposed system.
- Learn which parts of a system should be completed first for maximum user benefit.
- Allow designers to work through solutions when methods are unfamiliar and might produce unpredictable results.
- Test software or hardware features that the vendor supports, but that aren't used by much of its installed base.

For large projects, a traditional design approach may take so long that managers and end users see no sign of progress for months or years after the proposal is accepted. In rapidly changing organizations, such a project may not be responsive enough to changing user requirements. In 18 months, the initial project supporters can quit or be reorganized, the market can shift, or the business can change. Also, project members may concentrate so fully on delivering the project that they isolate themselves from the eventual users of the system. Meanwhile, the users feel alienated and like they invested time in providing user requirements that no one paid attention to. Prototyping can help you avoid these problems.

If you design prototypes to be easily revised, you can set up an evolutionary system model that serves as a constant proof of concept for management. You will also have a constant way to solicit and incorporate relevant user feedback and gauge user acceptance.

There is a temptation when building a prototype to let it expand to become the project itself. You might end up short-circuiting the requirements analysis or design phase in this case and creating a system that fails to live up to the proposal. To avoid this, set limits on the budget and time frame for implementing the prototype.

FEASIBILITY STUDIES

To convince yourself and others that a new method or new technology will work, perform a feasibility study. For example, a feasibility study might include a study of network throughput. Such an analysis might take into account the number of transactions to be performed per day, the rate at which transactions must be performed, the amount of data transmitted per transaction, and any work flow peaks and valleys. From this information and an analysis of current network throughput, an analyst could determine whether the current network can support the expected increase in load. If additional throughput will be required, the analyst can use the study results to justify additional budget allocations.

Besides determining whether a proposed solution meets requirements, you may also need to answer feasibility questions in the following areas:

- Does the proposed schedule solve the problem in the right time frame?
- Does adequate technology exist to solve the problem?
- Will the new system allow users to work more productively than the old one?
- Will the system be maintainable with existing or proposed IT staffing levels?
- Will new demands on existing systems be well within current bandwidth and capacity limits?
- Will users adopt the new system?
- Will departments need to be reorganized to deploy the new system properly? Are management and workers sufficiently prepared for such a move?
- Will the organization require more highly skilled workers to operate the new system?
- Will management need to rearrange budgeting categories and allocations to accommodate a new business model imposed by the system?

Strive to evaluate feasibility objectively. Check your assumptions and your conclusions with selected users and members of the management team. If the answer to only a few of these questions is no, then brainstorm with the project team or selected users about what could be done to make the project feasible. Ask yourself which of the project assumptions you are making are causing it to fail to meet feasibility criteria. Determine if your assumptions are wrong or if you must change the project proposal.

If the answers to most of these questions indicate feasibility problems, then the motivation behind the project probably fails to meet criteria given earlier in this chapter. In this case, if you can, reject the proposal or give it low priority until significant changes in the plan, technology, budgets, or organization merit another evaluation. You can either write a report about the failure of the project to meet feasibility criteria, talk to project supporters about such problems, or discuss alternative ways that the project supporter's needs could be addressed.

REVIEW AND TESTING

Many talk about quality improvement and testing as if they happen at the same time—at the end of the project. It's too late at that point. Perhaps the roots of this also lie in computer science education, where we focus on exploring new methods more than creating software to serve human needs. As we implied in the sections on design, the work that you do at the beginning of the project makes the most difference in the number of errors that you encounter at the end. Fortunately, our relatively young industry has discovered this as well, and most modern books on program design advocate modular programing. Complete and test one module at a time instead of writing the entire application and testing it all at the end.

The other source of quality loss is denial. Programmers don't admit to themselves that they are not self-sufficient and that they need help making programs robust. Programmers also "forget" that it takes them three times longer to write a program than they think. Project leaders don't admit that they didn't estimate the schedule properly and that they need to extend the end date rather than cut testing short.

As a programmer finishes coding a module, have it reviewed by at least one other person. For each module, make sure that the programmer, another programmer, and a user each test the program. Reviewers should double-check for the most common programming errors:

- Failing to initialize variables

- Failing to check boundary conditions

- Calling routines or functions with improper arguments—the wrong values, the wrong types, the wrong number, or in the wrong order

- Loops that require a specific exit value in a variable that is either not incremented or can acquire values outside the termination range (e.g., negative)

- Arithmetic overflow or underflow, especially in loop variables

- Dependence on global variables that may be unreliable due to being reset by other routines

- Not checking to make sure that user input is within expected values or is in expected format

- Not anticipating simultaneous events properly in a multiuser system

- Depending on external library routines that behave differently from version to version

Also involve users in testing. During testing, users can and will test all the parts of the program that you are least likely to test. If the system has a weakness in the area of data input, the users will find it, since they will be less aware of the restrictions of the program. They also may carry over assumptions about the old system that no longer hold with the new. In some cases, it may be worthwhile to provide duplicate functionality so that users can do things in both the old and new ways. The designers and programmers should watch these tests so that they can see where users most often make mistakes. Problem areas indicate a failure of the program to be clear about its expectations.

Some programmers are only familiar with working on projects over which they have sole control as the designer, author, tester, and maintainer of the program. When the size of a project becomes more than one person can handle, the programmers will need to transition to a team work model. In a programming project team, design decisions, code, files, and responsibility must be shared in ways that minimize conflict. Unfortunately, when a project is perceived to be small, and team members or managers don't realize how much complexity is involved, there is often little focus placed on process and much on delivery date. In these situations, problems arise with controlling code. Several versions of a program may be lying around. The original programmer may know which version of the main program gets linked with which library and which versions of the header files, but if that programmer is replaced or joined by others, confusion abounds. Get in the habit of instituting a file and version control mechanism for any and all projects once they start. Consider using a source code control system.

■ IMPLEMENTATION

Once you've decided what to do, your ability to execute the right tasks in the right order comes into play. The smaller the project is and the fewer people on the project team, the easier this process is. For the rest of the project universe, however, implementation stirs up all sorts of unanticipated challenges. The on-time, on-budget software project is highly prized and rarely accomplished. The next few segments of this chapter describe ways to avoid the most common disasters.

CREATING A PROJECT PLAN

A project plan helps ensure that the project delivered matches the proposed project. Essentially, it consists of a strategy for meeting goals in the form of tasks and an implementation schedule. Some people only include a schedule of milestones—events that delimit phases of the project—in the proposal. This can work provided that you create a more complete version before implementation and before you commit to the finish date.

To create a plan, break the project down into tasks. For a small, well-defined project that involves technology that you are familiar with, you might be able to list all the tasks in sufficient detail yourself. Otherwise, create the task list using input from the team members and discussions with other experts. Avoid the temptation to list a vague task that you can't describe or one that relies on "magic" that the task implementor doesn't know how to research or invent. Succumbing to the desire to leave key details for later weakens the possibility of meeting the planned completion date. First, the person assigned to execute a vague task may not interpret it correctly. Second, since you don't understand what is involved, you may not allow enough time or budget for it. Third, without understanding the task, you may not understand the dependencies correctly, throwing the whole schedule into doubt.

Combine short tasks into a larger unit if each will take a team member less than a day to complete. Leave a short task separate, however, if it has strategic dependencies before and after it. Break into subtasks any large task that would take one person more than 2 weeks to accomplish. The reason for these guidelines is practical. People who perceive that they have too many tasks may feel too daunted to begin any. People who perceive that they have more than 2 weeks to accomplish their work may think that they have plenty of time ahead of them and consequently waste time or procrastinate.

Another factor for determining the scope of a task is the level of team interaction required to complete it. Usually, one or more team members is assigned one task, and where one task depends on another, the team members for the two tasks must communicate. If small interdependent tasks are assigned to ten different people to accomplish in parallel, then ten people will need to coordinate with each other. Instead, if five tasks are given to each of two people, then interaction is only required between two team members. The latter approach will be much simpler and less time consuming. A book that explores this problem with great insight is *The Mythical Man-Month*.[4] It's under 200 pages long and it's easy reading. After you're done, you'll understand why the industry finds it so difficult to produce reliable software on time. Even better, if you take its wisdom to heart, you'll bring our profession closer toward improving this situation.

Include team coordination activities, such as meetings, interviews, and user feedback sessions, as separate tasks. Forgetting these time-consuming activities can ruin a schedule. Building

---

[4]Frederick P. Brooks, Jr., *The Mythical Man-Month, Essays on Software Engineering* (Philippines: Addison-Wesley Publishing Company, Inc., 1975).

them into other tasks such as programming and research can result in miscommunication. Also, since each activity has a different purpose, you will have problems if you decide to drop a compound task but don't remember that one part of it is still essential.

After listing the essential project tasks, estimate the time required for each. The duration of a task will vary depending on the size and abilities of the team. Estimating how long it takes someone to do something proves quite challenging. If you're in complete control of a project and thoroughly familiar with what needs to be done, your estimates may only be off by a factor of 2. If you don't know what needs to be done, multiply by 3. If significant coordination with others is involved, multiply by 4 or more. Interruptions do the most damage to estimates—phone calls, email messages, unplanned meetings, and general problems such as computer breakdowns. When calculating task durations, document any assumptions that the estimates rely on. If background conditions change, you or someone will need to know what to include when recalculating your schedule. Documented assumptions also make it clear which project changes could affect the critical path.

Once you have a list of tasks and corresponding time estimates, order the list by dependency. Determine which tasks can be started right away and which tasks rely on others before they can be begun. There are several methods of creating project schedules, also called project plans. The two most common are to use Gantt and PERT charts. You can use these methods to graph a project plan on paper, on a spreadsheet, or with specialized software. Project planning software becomes especially helpful when creating what-if scenarios to determine whether adding more people could shorten the schedule or estimating how long the project will take with minimal resources.

A Gantt chart shows the timeline along the chart horizontally and lists short task descriptions vertically along the left side. For each task, a horizontal bar is shown to the right of the task description, arranged along the timeline to indicate the start and end times. The length of the bar represents the task duration. The tasks are typically grouped from top to bottom by project module in the order of expected completion. Symbols can be used to distinguish the bars such that you can see the current week, uncompleted tasks, completed tasks, and partially completed tasks at a glance. Gantt charts are good for communicating with end users and members of management.

A PERT chart represents a project by a network of nodes and arrows. Activities are represented as arrows. Nodes are events that indicate the completion of the task. The length of the lines do not represent duration. Instead, each path has a numerical length value that is either indicated on the chart or in an accompanying table. You can use several tables to show how the total project time varies depending on the resources allotted to the task. Nodes are arranged such that dependencies are shown. No path can be taken to a node that doesn't go through all other nodes that it depends on. PERT charts are good for determining task precedence, the critical path, and slack time.

The critical path is the longest path from the start to end of the project with all dependencies taken into account and no gaps between interdependent tasks. The length of this path, as measured in the time to complete each task on the path, is the expected duration of the project. The completion date of the last task on the critical path task is the completion date of the project. Tasks that are not on the critical path are still necessary, but can be completed in parallel with others. Slack time is the time that a task can slide before affecting the critical path. The object of project scheduling is to determine the critical path and arrange tasks and resources such that this path is as short as possible. Any delay on a task on the critical path will cause a delay in the entire project.

Have the project plan reviewed and approved by all team members and your manager. Distribute copies to key supporters of the project.

MAKING THE BUILD VERSUS BUY DECISION

Near the beginning of the project, you will need to evaluate whether to build a customized system or buy off-the-shelf applications that meet your needs.

Your ability to use packaged systems will depend on the uniqueness of your requirements. Packaged systems tend to work well for the most common configurations found in the vendor's customer base and to underperform for the exceptions. If an application vendor claims interoperability on a number of different platforms, products, operating systems, or database systems, it may only use a subset of the features available on each. If you have a heterogeneous environment in which such interoperability is required, this type of package may be optimal. However, if an extension of standard behavior, such as SQL Server stored procedures, will make a significant difference in the performance of the proposed system, a customized or extensible solution may be better.

The build versus buy decision comes down to differences between how the proposed systems would conform to requirements and to the differences in the cost. For comparing costs, perform a cost/benefit analysis as described in Chapter 14.

DECIDING WHETHER TO USE CONSULTANTS

Closely related to the previous question is the question of whether to use consultants to develop and implement all or part of the project. Information Systems consultants are usually seasoned professionals who have been in the software industry for several years and bring a level of diverse experience. Organizations usually hire consultants to implement information system projects when the work needs to be finished quickly, when in-house developers are not available for the project, or when necessary expertise does not exist in the organization.

Management considerations also influence the decision to use consultants. Consultants usually do not require as much supervision as regular employees do. Consultants also work on a fee basis and do not require all the benefits provided to employees. Sometimes, if there are concerns about unexpected swings in cash flow, companies bring in consultants since they can be brought in and let go quickly.

One disadvantage of using consultants is that they are not as likely as regular employees to share the organizational vision. They are not as likely to be influenced by management issues either positively or negatively. (This can be an asset in an organization undergoing a lot of change.) Consultants tend to focus on the project and avoid distraction by the day to day activities that define the current organizational culture.

Although consultants usually do not require as much direction as full-time employees, it is still important to recognize the need to manage consultants. Use a formal agreement that clearly delineates responsibility. When consultants are responsible for managing projects, they should not be solely responsible for managing employees of your organization. To stay motivated, employees need a company representative to guide their careers and human needs. Organizational loyalty is also maintained by keeping the link between managers and employees in-house.

Document any assumptions about the work that you expect consultants to do. Also ask consultants to document any of their assumptions in advance so that you can verify that the assumptions are correct.

Consider the following questions:

- Does the consultant keep the source code and all copyrights to programs and documents developed under the contract?

- Is the consultant responsible for documentation?

- Is the consultant responsible for training?

- When are program or documentation errors corrected by the consultant? Is the consultant paid for time spent correcting errors? How soon must you report the errors for the consultant to be responsible for fixing them?

- Is the consultant responsible for errors of omission if you didn't inform him or her of the full requirements?

- If consultants require specialized software for the project, do they pay for the license or does the organization? Who keeps the license?

Answer these questions in your contract with the consultant. Make sure that your organization's legal counsel reviews any contracts before you sign them.

In addition to the considerations outlined above, you can also perform a cost/benefit analysis to decide how much of an advantage consultants provide in terms of the budget and schedule.

A unique benefit that outside consultants provide is the ability to do zero-based analysis. In other words, they are detached from the historical, personal, and political perspectives that sometimes limit the objectivity of long-time employees. Consultants can say to themselves, "If I were starting from ground zero, how would I reach the project goals?" Then they can select from the current organization any existing elements that support the goal and bring in the resources and direction to create what's missing. For the same reasons, employees often resent outsiders. The consultant may be seen as dispassionate about the qualities that make an organization unique. In fact, some of the things that create a particular corporate culture may be in the way of the organization reaching its stated goals. A responsible consultant will point this out so that managers can determine whether they are willing to give up that aspect of the culture or whether their goals were not stated accurately.

The disadvantage of freedom of an organization's history is ignorance of it. As often said, the penalty of being ignorant of history is being doomed to repeat it. A responsible consultant, after performing a zero-based assessment, will also do enough research on the organization to learn about past attempts to solve the problem. If the analyst finds results that indicate his or her conclusions had been reached and acted on before, he or she should find out why the intended result was never achieved. When experienced managers are hired into an organization, they often say, "The past is the past, let's move on." However, they must listen to people to learn why the past still lives on in the corporate memory. Was a lesson learned from the past by the organization, or are its employees afraid the lesson was not learned well enough? At the same time, employees should not cling to the past. It should not be an excuse to give up on solutions and tolerate mediocrity.

ESTABLISHING METRICS

If a project requires the investment of a significant portion of organizational resources, you will be asked to justify the expense. This will occur both when asking for project approval initially and later while the organization pays off the investment. To keep the number of unexpected inquiries to a minimum, regularly publish a report showing measurements that indicate how well the goals of the project are being met.

As anyone who has studied statistics knows, numbers can be misleading. Select meaningful events to measure, and ensure that you are measuring what you intend to measure. When measuring human productivity, be particularly careful to include both quality and quantity measurements. For example, someone running an organization that receives orders by phone may decide to measure productivity by the number of orders taken per hour per person. Then a simple average could be calculated, and order takers might be compared to the average. However, there are problems with this approach. The first is that certain people may perform so much above or below the average that it becomes misleading. The person who has only been taking orders one week shouldn't be expected to be as productive as one who has been taking them for 17 years. A second problem is that an order taker might be able to increase numbers of orders taken by taking less time to make the customer feel comfortable or by not being as careful about details. In this case, a worker who appears highly productive could be causing an increase in items returned for refund or a loss of repeat sales.

Used carefully, statistics can be valuable. For example, it makes sense to monitor the performance of computers. Numbers are also useful indicators if a particular average hovers around a constant when measured week after week, but then suddenly jumps or drops.

The best choice of metrics will be those that measure specific targets mentioned as part of requirements documentation and in the project goals. The most important measurement of a project to upper levels of management will be return on investment. The calculation ROI is discussed in Chapter 14. To facilitate this calculation, keep good records of the money spent and build in methods of measuring productivity or revenue gained. Assure management, with the support of good numbers, that a certain amount of money or time was saved as a result of the project. Providing these numbers before they are demanded can result in more confidence in the project.

In addition to measuring the success of a project after completion, you can use metrics to monitor the progress of project implementation. Progress is best measured by whether milestones are completed on time. You can also monitor project quality by watching how many problems come up during testing, providing that you have put a thorough testing mechanism in place and that you use it.

DESIGNING A TRAINING PROGRAM

Good training for information systems users reduces the time spent correcting errors, the time wasted on suboptimal ways of doing things, and the time spent searching for solutions when problems arise. It also enhances the chances for your organization to achieve a competitive advantage through staff expertise. As with quality systems, the closer to the beginning of a project that you design a training plan, the less expensive and more effective it will be.

Highly technical people who keep up to date in their fields by constantly reading manuals, books, magazines, and electronic documents tend to discount the need for training. Training also tends to take the back seat in the minds of managers who spend little time in their day to day life in front of a computer. However, people who are not technology specialists—who use the computer as a means to some other goal—are not likely to read computer magazines in their spare time and will not be easily persuaded to do so. Technologists often fail to realize why everyone isn't as excited about the specifics of computer systems as they are. To avoid bias introduced by such experts, have a range of users observed, surveyed, or interviewed to determine how they use the system and to identify key areas where they could be more productive with training. While the results should be shared with those implementing the technology, an impartial person or stratified team should conduct the analysis to avoid a bias toward or away from the average user's needs.

It is common to expect some people to be trained on specific hardware or software before they join a company. In fact, they may be hired on the strength of this experience. To stay up with current breakthroughs in the field, they may need ongoing training, documentation, or other training support. On the other hand, some technology that you have may be so specialized that it would be unlikely to find someone with this experience. Also, for such skills, people will be less willing to learn on their own time or under their own motivation because there is little hope for that skill to be useful if they need to change jobs.

Short-sighted managers may fear that by providing extensive training they are making it easier for employees to enhance their résumés and leave the company. This is always a possibility. However, the other side of this risk is that employees will become even more loyal, be more productive, and contribute more expertise to share around the organization. Some would argue that a strategy for retaining employees is to provide them better opportunities than your competitors do. Ongoing training can be seen as a benefit, along with health care, profit sharing, and stock options. If employees do not receive the training that they feel they need to excel at their jobs, they may leave anyway. Employees may feel that it is not worth staying at a company that doesn't invite excellence.

There are usually two types of training programs. The first comes with the introduction of a new technology. In this case, all users must be trained on the new system. They will need information about the differences and similarities between the old and new systems. Special attention will need to be paid to those who may be resistant to the change, especially if they think the system will change the quality of their job for the worse.

The second type of training program is ongoing or cyclical. It is used to introduce people to new features of the system as it is improved. Ongoing training can also highlight underutilized features that the original training didn't cover. You will also need to train new employees as they join the organization and employees who were on leave, vacation, or business trips during the original training. Having a training center and staff will help you stay on top of such training needs.

Training can come in several forms and can be delivered by a variety of methods. An in-house training staff can provide ongoing training for all key technology used in an organization. Such an department will be responsive to all levels of users. Permanent staff will be able to keep current with trends and features of particular interest to an organization's users. Give permanent training staff time to research developments. Also give them the ability to influence the curriculum based on technological advances and student feedback.

Technology vendors usually provide classes for helping people learn their products. The vendor either designs and offers the classes or outsources them to firms that specialize in education. Individuals from your firm that need the training can be sent off site for the class. This may involve travel costs and the cost of displacing or delaying the work that the person usually does. If a large population of your users need training, many computer vendors offer on-site classes or provide train-the-trainer training. If train-the-trainer options are not provided, you can identify one or a few people with good communication skills to take a class and take copious notes so that they can come back and train the people at your site. This also allows you to customize the training and strip out unneeded information.

Keep in mind that one advantage of training at a vendor's training center is that, if there are exercises, each student usually gets the use of a computer for completing them. Unless you already have an on-site training facility, setting up a room with 10 or more computers and software for exercises requires advance planning and a few days of at least one person's time.

For giving specialized training to one or two people who will be responsible for a system, you can often hire a consultant who is an expert in the field. This proves most efficient if the people to be trained already have some of the information or skills needed and just need to have the gaps filled in. Also, this is a common option when a consultant has also provided a customized solution, such as a specialized network installation. In such cases, negotiate the training arrangement when you write the original contract. Otherwise, you are at the consultant's mercy if he delivers a system that you don't understand. Specify in the contract if you are to receive all information necessary to be able to offer such training to others in your organization. Avoid an unexpected need to pay the consultant for additional training materials. A consultant deserves to be paid for creating such materials, but you should always know the full costs ahead of time.

Users who want to further their careers may want to take classes at nearby universities, colleges, and training institutions. You can pay for the tuition and book costs either fully or partially, depending on how much your organization is interested in investing in the expertise of its people. Some organizations require that students get a certain grade in the class in order to receive reimbursement. Be careful when providing such arrangements. If sudden overtime demands cause an employee to fall behind in his classwork, he or she will resent the imposition. To create a supportive environment for continuing education, management should take care to shelter students from such interruptions.

Finally, computer system knowledge can come in other forms than classroom delivery. Many vendors, including Sybase, make software tutorials available for customers. These allow you to provide consistent training regardless of student locations and time constraints. Also, as mentioned before, many people learn better from books or self-study materials than from classes. Experienced people and quick learners often prefer books because they are not slowed down by material presented at the pace required by the average student. Creating a book and magazine budget as an alternative to training can prove cost effective. If you are concerned whether the employee is really staying up to date, you can build a testing mechanism into your education program.

TRANSITION SUPPORT

All the above arguments for good training may cause you to overlook another portion of your user base—those who would rather things stayed the same. For these people, you need to provide transition support, both psychologically and technologically. You may encounter reluctance to adopt the new system for various reasons:

- Employees resistant to change may avoid classes and the need to learn.

- Employees may consider their job a temporary occupation rather than a career, or they may be more concerned with child-rearing or a second job.

- Employees may fear that they or their friends will lose their jobs as a result of the system change.

- Employees may have had a personal investment in a different solution from the one developed.

- Employees may succumb to the general human fear of the unknown.

- Employees who find it hard to get their work done on time already may resist further demands on their time to switch systems.

- Employees may fear that the new system will be less efficient than the old one, especially if they have developed efficient working patterns around the old one.

- Employees may think that the new system is a good idea, but may procrastinate learning its features, thinking it's too big or too hard a task.

- Experienced long-term employees may avoid a system introduced to help productivity if they feel that their experience already makes them more productive than most.

As we discussed earlier, getting user input and preparing people for change during project implementation can go a long way toward minimizing these risks. Discuss concerns about employment issues with your organization's human resources department, and work with any employee associations to keep communications channels clear. You might be able to provide special transition benefits such as bonuses, parties, or extra time off to encourage employees to adapt. While it is the employer's prerogative to define the work it wants its employees to do, happier employees will produce higher-quality results. Recovering from making employees unhappy can be quite expensive due to potential productivity losses, quality loss, high turnover costs, litigation, and bad publicity.

Creating and introducing a new system can also create a lot of stress for systems engineers. A transition usually requires that systems personnel have to support both the old system and a new one at once. Furthermore, if they have highly specialized knowledge about older systems that will no longer be necessary, they will worry about how the organization perceives their value. Make an effort to communicate new expectations and to help people adapt to new roles that they might want to take on.

TECHNICAL SUPPORT

Technical support comes in as many forms as training. You can use any of the methods in this section during the transition to the new system and afterward. Trying a variety of support options during the transition can help you determine those most useful for ongoing use.

"ASK THE EXPERTS" SESSIONS

During the transition, you can help people use the new system and explore its features by holding "Ask the Experts" sessions. Snack food, beverages, and an informal setting can create an environment in which users feel more comfortable about asking "dumb" questions or experimenting without feeling that they are wasting time. During this time, the designers or expert users of the system can explain key features or perhaps focus on a new feature each week in a series of sessions. After a few regular sessions, users may start sharing tips and techniques among themselves, which helps the overall level of expertise in the group rise.

TECHNICAL SUPPORT HOT LINE

During the transition, you can expect a flood of questions about how to use the new system. People may forget the proper methods from their training. Or they may not have paid much attention during training because they didn't think that they'd need that feature or that it would be in the documentation. Hopefully, online help and documentation will assist people. Also be sure to provide especially responsive technical support to avoid the possibility of outright rejection of the system.

If the organizational environment already involves high stress and constrictive time pressures, then any system problem can create a crisis requiring immediate attention. Consider setting up a special telephone line or email address for people to use when they have urgent questions and problems.

After a few days of operation, those staffing the hot lines can compile lists of frequently asked questions (FAQs) and their answers for broad distribution. If your in-house support staff encounters a large number of repeat questions or notices an area of particular difficulty, it may be worth the investment to set up a WWW site, fax-back system, or automated voicemail system.

If you continue using the hot line for ongoing support, you will need to set up a priority system and time commitments so that you respond to the most critical issues first. If you let users know that it will take a day to get back to them about low-priority questions, users will often find the answers themselves using other means. Avoid making calls low priority when there are no alternative sources of help for users and when they consider the call important. This encourages escalations and support policy abuses.

HELP DESKS

A help desk is like a hot line, but those staffing it generally help people on a first come, first served basis. Unlike a hot line, there should be more time for information services staff to help users think through problems. The main advantage of a help desk is that it increases the overall system knowledge in a department by information exchange. Help desks are usually staffed by systems experts. They are either entirely responsible for the help desk function, or they share it with others so that each person rotates through systems work and help desk work. An advantage of rotation is that it allows the experts to alternate experience using the system with experience helping people. One disadvantage is that hard-core systems people may lack people skills and end up unintentionally alienating people. The advantage of full-time help desk staff is that they become very efficient at handling certain types of problems, and can be chosen for their people skills. However, if help desk staff spend all day every day with people, they lose the opportunity to work with the technology themselves and may lose their technical edge. One solution to this problem is to hire enough help desk people so that they can alternate between the help function and working with the technology. Hire people that have a good blend of customer service skills and technical knowledge.

If you do set up a help desk, also set up a hot line so that you still have a priority system for problems. Otherwise, the help desk will function like a hot line and will not elevate the overall competence of the group.

ONLINE FORUMS

Online forums include electronic mailing lists, newsgroups, and chat areas in internal networks or in public networks like the Internet. By using these methods, users can share problems and solutions among themselves without burdening your support organization.

INTERNAL HELP DOCUMENTS

UNIX, VMS, and MS-Windows all have built-in help systems that provide online documentation about the operating system functionality. Furthermore, all these can be extended by Systems Managers to include their own documents. On UNIX, the mechanism is `man` pages; on OpenVMS, you can set up a hierarchical help system; and on Microsoft's Windows systems, you can compile online help libraries as separate programs. You can also create your own help system using a platform-independent technology like a WWW server. You might find online knowledge-base tools useful as well.

Any system you choose will require an initial investment to set up. You will need to create the documentation, convert it to the format used by the distribution system, make the viewing software and documentation available for all users, and provide system support and maintenance. For large repositories, you will also need to set up some sort of search mechanism. The variety and formats of your documents, your network configuration, your operating systems, and the level of sophistication of your users should guide the system that you choose and implement.

USER GROUPS AND CONFERENCES

In addition to documents and network resources, most popular technology products have associated user groups. User groups are consortia of users that gather to discuss the technical details of the technology around which they are organized. Sometimes these forums are funded partially by the vendor of the products. In most cases, user groups provide periodic meetings, newsletters, networks of consultants, a mechanism for sharing technical information, and an opportunity to lobby the product vendor.

BOOKS, MAGAZINES, CD-ROMS, AND THE WWW

Books, magazines, CD-ROMs, and WWW documentation are essential for technology experts to stay current in their fields. As the information revolution continues to outpace itself, the amount of technical information grows rapidly. If your company strives to stay on the leading edge, provide a library, a publication purchasing mechanism, and Internet access for technical personnel. Electronic sources can hold much more information and are much easier to search than printed media.

OUTSOURCING SUPPORT

In some cases, your organization may find it worthwhile to outsource support. Some companies offer transparent support systems. A small organization may also contract with a consulting firm to provide support with a particular technology or for a particular time period. If your organization is undergoing rapid fluctuation in size, one of these may be an attractive alternative to staffing up and later laying off support personnel. Also, a company that is geographically dispersed might be able to take advantage of a large company's global support organization, rather than needing to hire technical specialists for support in each major city.

■ JUST DO IT

The suggestions in this chapter advocate a reasoned approach to projects, implying that projects lacking careful planning risk failure. For each suggestion, we have looked at the types of failure that ignoring the suggestion can bring about. All that said, sometimes you have a project that you must do immediately. The risk of not doing it far outweighs the risk of not doing it right, for example, a response to an emergency such as an earthquake. Don't let all these suggestions stop you from taking action. If you make one important improvement in each project that you do, you will eventually develop your own, highly effective work habits.

In Chapter 13 we look at the human element of project implementation—project leadership. When it comes to software projects, how you work with people has at least a great impact on the project as how you work with technology.

Procedure Manual Suggestions

○ Requests for Information Systems Changes

⇒ Document a procedure for submitting requests for information systems change.

⇒ Direct requestors to include a description of the problem to be solved as well as the proposed solution. Have them discuss also why a problem should be solved, including an assessment of the estimated value to be received when the project is completed.

○ System Timing Considerations

➡ Document all business and user cycles you know of that stress the information system.

➡ Write a procedure for system maintenance that takes advantage of the slower times.

○ Creating Proposals

➡ Create a recommended format for IT project proposals.

➡ List all elements considered essential for executives to make a decision.

➡ Set a standard for accountability—make sure that proposals include documentation of the metrics to be used to report project progress and success.

➡ Describe the review and sign-off process for the proposal.

➡ Describe who must be contacted and how if the project gets approved. Include the source of information about accounting requirements and procedures, hiring policies, contract policies, and any other support functions that must be involved.

○ Information System Project Standards

➡ Write a procedure that outlines the organization's standards for a successful information systems project.

➡ Include standard design criteria and requirements.

➡ Include any corporate standards for measuring quality and project success.

➡ Document the required elements of a training plan.

➡ Document the required elements of a support plan.

○ Consultant Arrangements

➠ Document organizational procedures for selecting and retaining consultants.

➠ Describe which other departments must be involved, such as legal, accounting, or human resources.

➠ Describe any organizational standards for evaluating consultants, such as a minimum number of alternative consultants that must be allowed to bid on a project.

➠ List any standard clauses that a contract must include, or describe who to contact for that information.

➠ Document who has signing authority for consultant contracts.

➠ Describe how to make arrangements to maximize the consultants' productivity, such as providing them a phone, a phone list, and a workstation.

➠ Describe the procedures for submitting invoices for payment. Include any standard format required for invoices.

○ Programming Standards

➠ Document programming standards that you want to be applied throughout development. Set up a mechanism for enforcing them, such as by including checks during a formal review or acceptance testing. The standards should cover

- Stored procedure and trigger calling conventions and parameter passing conventions; that is, is nesting O.K., in what order are parameters passed, how is rollback to be handled?

- Techniques to be used to optimize performance, including tips and metrics

- Table design conventions, such as data types, rules, index types, and the use of NULLs

- Standards for use of locking isolation levels to avoid contention, yet provide adequate consistency

○ Naming Conventions

➠ Establish naming conventions for application entities to be stored in SQL Server:

- Choose names that make maintenance easy.
- Choose names that make object misuse hard.
- Choose database names that make role and responsibility clear.
- Choose table names that make the table's purpose obvious.
- Choose column names that make the domain clear.
- Choose index names that make the association with the underlying table clear.
- Choose constraint names that make table and domain clear.
- Choose default names that make the purpose of the value clear.
- Choose rule names that make the purpose of the restriction clear.
- Choose segment names that make allocation rules clear.

CHAPTER

Project Leadership

This chapter gives you several suggestions about project leadership. You can think of it more like a building supply store than a blueprint. The way you choose and employ these ideas depends on your style, your organization, the people you work with, the goals for the project, and the overall constraints of your environment. The information presented comes from books, tapes, training, mentoring, observation, and experience and from correcting mistakes. Because we are always growing—as people, as organizations, as participants in a world economy—there are always new challenges. Define leadership for yourself every day by creating breakthrough solutions to difficult problems.

■ LEADERSHIP, MANAGEMENT, AND COORDINATION

Projects succeed under unlikely conditions and fail under good conditions. For a project to live up to its promise, it needs strong leadership. The words *manage* and *management* connote working within a framework to overcome obstacles or take advantage of localized opportunities. A project often involves creating new frameworks where none existed or replacing structures that fail to meet user needs. In this case, management skill—ability to work within existing frameworks—often ends up being a detriment rather than an asset.

People responsible for a project, regardless of what they call themselves, may act in the role of leader, manager, or coordinator. Each role is different, and some are more comfortable than others. Individuals with a great deal of psychological flexibility can change to the most effective work style for each situation. Identifying your predominate work style and that of your co-workers will allow you to make the best matches between people and responsibilities.

People who act as coordinators typically view their responsibility as making sure that everything happens as planned so that the results fit together properly. Coordinators concern themselves with making sure that employees have everything needed to complete a task as promised. In interacting with others, coordinators concentrate on facilitating particular tasks. They rarely see themselves as agents of significant change. They often don't feel that they have the power to persuade upper management to change direction if goals seem misguided. Sudden changes in plan or a failure of a piece of a plan outside his level of responsibility can hinder a coordinator's effectiveness.

In the role we'll call *manager*, people see their job as ensuring that they deliver whatever their superiors ask for. In contrast with coordinators, they focus more on people and results than tasks and processes. Managers see themselves as go-betweens, making sure that subordinates produce results that superiors expect. A change in plans is viewed as a temporary setback requiring a different strategy for meeting the expectations of superiors. People accustomed to acting in this capacity are likely to be weakest if they encounter a change in management structure such that previous superiors leave the company or get promoted. Unless this type of person follows their old superior to a new job, her focus changes to discovering the goals and expectations of the new superiors.

Managers that you might find in the above category include people who are or were once in positions of authority in rigidly hierarchical organizations. Their background can give them the discipline and strength of character to reject excuses and demand success. They can encourage loyalty to the organization and maintain a clear focus on goals. In some organizations where you might find these managers, there is little room for questioning superiors or making excuses for failure. Leadership and respect are won by successive years of service and accomplishment of goals. However, some elements of this model don't work well in a technology business. In technology, the vision must be re-created daily, and those closer to the bottom of the organization often understand it better than those at the top. The technological playing field changes often due to rapid breakthroughs. One year's nobody can become next year's celebrity by innovating. In a company growing quickly, it is common for someone to skip the experience of working on several layers of management and go straight to the top. Managers cannot assume that subordinates will automatically follow orders. By adapting to a style of mentoring and listening, rather than ordering, and to facilitating vertical communication, managers with a more disciplined background can bring formidable power and guidance to an organization in flux.

People in the role of *leader* see themselves as creators. They look into the future, the marketplace, and the organizational context and then envision what they will create to meet tomorrow's needs. In leadership roles, people react to changes as different or new variables in an equation and change other variables as necessary to achieve the right result. If their organization needs to change direction or seems to be getting off course, leaders will drive the new vision through the organization or persuade management to stay focused. Leaders concentrate on empowering subordinates and rarely understand a "can't do" attitude. Managers of this type are most vulnerable to high expectations of themselves and others, rather than to external changes. They will expect subordinates to create or discern direction for themselves, rather than waiting for it to come down from above.

Typically, those most comfortable with the leadership role will end up at the top layer of an organization. In the lower layers we find more people who tend to act as managers and coordinators. In a poorly managed project or company that's failing, someone often knows the solution to the organization's ills. However, a mismatch between responsibilities and management style prevents people from acting on their knowledge. If the person who can tell what needs to be done doesn't have the motivation or the authority to take responsibility for doing it, the organization fails just as much as if the insight never existed.

Think about whether you typically fall into a particular role. Evaluate whether you are in the right position for the type of manager that you are. If you are not, decide whether you need to change positions or learn another management style. If you also recognize the style of other managers that you work with, you can learn to talk to them in the language that best motivates them to action. You will get best results from a coordinator by stressing logistics. A manager will be persuaded by arguments that certain things need to happen in order for stated organizational goals to be met. You will impress a leader most with your ability to create innovative, timely solutions.

So far, we have looked at how management style shapes choices made within an organization. Responsibilities within a management hierarchy also affect the type of leadership a person provides. Those at the bottom layers of an organization tend to make tactical decisions. Leaders at the top establish strategies. Middle management ensures that goals set by the top can be accomplished by those at the bottom. In a small company or department, one person might have responsibility at two or more levels. Ideally, a person in this position understands which decisions to make under which roles. A strategic manager who attempts to make technical decisions may let a desired profit strategy bias his technical evaluation. A person used to making technical decisions may try to solve all business problems by throwing technology at them. Similar problems arise when someone is promoted into a new level of responsibility. It is more comfortable to make decisions at the previous level than to break new ground and become effective in the new position.

■ SELECTING A PROJECT LEADER

The selection process for a project leader varies depending on the project and the organization. In some cases, the person that has an idea for a project becomes its de facto leader. Larger projects may get assigned to full-time project managers. Project leaders may have the opportunity to write proposals and participate in design, or they may be selected after a schedule and budget are approved. Organizations may also hire consultants to lead a project, transfer managers to different department for the duration of a project, or transfer the project to another department or even to another company for implementation. A person's job responsibilities may include project management as well as information systems management. In any case, the project leader needs the qualifications, commitment, and enthusiasm necessary for taking on the following responsibilities:

■ Articulate the goals and strategy to "sell" the project to all affected parts of the organization

■ Prepare a project proposal if not already prepared and "sold"

■ Plan project tasks

■ Create a schedule for completing the tasks within established time and resource constraints

■ Select team members

■ Assign tasks to team members

■ Build and maintain team focus, commitment, and morale

■ Maintain communication between team members and other key players in the organization

■ Monitor project, comparing planned time, tasks, and budget against actual performance

■ Adjust the plan where feedback necessitates change

■ Ensure that project members accomplish assigned tasks on or ahead of time and within budget

While this list may seem short, it takes a talented leader to bring a project in on time and have it meet all its requirements. A project succeeds or fails depending on the commitment of the team members. The leader needs to stay committed to the project and to motivate all team members to share that commitment.

The adjustment step requires particular attention. Something always happens to derail project plans, so the project succeeds based on the project team's ability to recover from setbacks. We can summarize one leadership style popular in companies willing to take high risks for high rewards as Ready, Fire, Aim. In other words, getting mired in analysis can be as dangerous as firing the wrong way in some situations. However, it must be noted that, after an unaimed shot that fails to reach its target, you must correct your aim. The point is still to hit the target. Upon missing after the first shot, some managers will move the target. This tendency stems from fear of looking bad to peers and superiors and from someone's ego preventing her from seeing that she missed the target. Beyond the failure to live up to expectations, hitting such a cheapened target is just less rewarding. Allow enough tolerance for error in your leadership style so that you can ultimately reach a goal worth attaining.

COMMUNICATION

Good communication builds teamwork. Regular project-related communication typically includes

- Organization vision
- Project vision
- Project goals
- Project schedule
- Feedback between team members
- Feedback between users and team members
- Articulation of strategy to key players in the rest of the organization

Many stressful situations challenge a team during project implementation. For example, the budget may change, organizational changes may cause the schedule to slip, estimates may have been wrong, interpersonal conflicts may affect team interaction, or business strategies might change.

To keep the team focused, continuously make the project vision, goals, and strategy clear, verbally and in writing. To help protect the team from outside demands on their time, you can use project bulletin boards, newsletters, and electronic communications to inform interested nonteam members. Whenever a change occurs in the business, team, or project, clearly describe the associated adaptations that you will make in the project strategy. Follow the maxim: praise in public, criticize in private. If you must confront someone about doing a task poorly, do it in private to avoid undermining team coherency. At the same time, pointing out the successes of the team in public motivates everyone to continue living up to your good expectations.

Also seek communication from team members so that you can gain rapport and support. Team members may wish to tell you about

- Personal goals
- Career aspirations
- Doubts about the project technology
- Concerns about meeting the schedule
- Challenges to key assumptions held by one or more key players

A consultant from outside the organization who is acting as project lead will also benefit from receiving the following additional messages:

- Warnings about political conflicts
- Industry trends
- Impending organizational changes that may affect the project

Create an atmosphere of open communication, rather than one in which everyone quietly goes along with you and then blames you when things go wrong. People who feel that they can't talk to you directly often communicate indirectly, such as by complaints, gossip, and subtle project sabotage.

Another key to deploying a project successfully is to share information with the ultimate users of the technology under development. Users may look upon a highly motivated team suspiciously unless the team's mission is very clear. Help users to envision how the project will make the organization better. Provide feedback mechanisms. Most information systems projects also need cooperation from other departments, such as legal, marketing, shipping, or customer service. Keep the affected departments informed as the project progresses so that they can support you when the time comes.

■ TEAM BUILDING

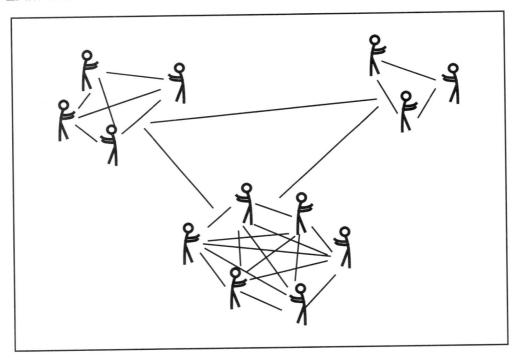

Figure 13.1 Coordinating a large project team can prove challenging. Dividing into subgroups can reduce the number of communications paths and thereby minimize miscommunication.

A project leader typically takes responsibility for facilitating team interaction. Tensions that can derail a project can arise due to personality conflicts, miscommunication, disagreements with project approach, personal issues, time pressure, or organizational stresses. Such issues need to be addressed as if they were on the project plan. During project start-up, establish communication processes as a scheduled project task. Such an approach can help minimize unexpected delays for resolving team problems.

On an effective team, each member will be capable of more than one task. Inevitably, at least one team member will go on vacation, get sick, get called for jury duty, go to training, leave the company, or get called out on a personal emergency. In these situations, other team members need to be willing and able to pick up the work. Ideally, the whole team accepts responsibility for the team's results. Everyone should realize that if one team member can't deliver the expected results and no one else picks them up, then the whole team and the whole project fails.

The project manager is responsible for seeing that things get done on time. Questions project managers ask to keep unexpected delays to a minimum include

■ Are relationship frictions causing a slowdown in communication?

■ Are corporate politics causing delay or miscommunication?

■ Are personal problems distracting a team member?

■ Are resources such as computer equipment and productivity tools available when needed?

■ Are team members working within their areas of expertise?

■ Are goals attainable?

The last point takes on particular importance for high-profile projects. If goals seem too difficult, a sense of being overwhelmed can paralyze the team members. Rather than discussions about overcoming obstacles, conversations can become pessimistic discussions of the project failing or team member faults.

Another purpose of goals is to set expectations between the project leader and the team members. If the leader's expectations are too high, team members may reject the goals altogether. If expectations seem low, team members may feel that the project leader doesn't respect their expertise. Ideally, you can set project goals slightly higher than team members' current skill levels will allow them to reach. Discuss expectations with the team so everyone agrees on worthwhile, achievable, and challenging goals.

Team members often complain if they don't feel valued, if they feel that they are underpaid, if they have been asked to do something that they feel underqualified for, if they personally object to the task, or if another manager's desires conflicts with a request. In these cases, try to get to the underlying issue. Training, increased benefits, more formal or informal recognition, time off to handle personal crises, or an anonymous way of documenting complaints may help you to resolve the true issue.

Some team members are naturally quiet. Take special care to solicit their input. If they listen and think more than they talk, they probably have something important to say when they do speak.

To avoid losing team members to other organizations, help everyone to feel that their full participation is needed in order to complete the project with the quality that they helped to envision. Let them know how the project will benefit themselves, their careers, and the organization.

Finally, take care of every person on the team. There is a tendency to "grease the squeaky wheel," that is, to pay extra attention to the person who complains the most. Make sure you grease all the wheels. You especially want to reward those who do a good job without a lot of excuses. However, don't avoid greasing a squeaky wheel, or you'll end up silencing the person who serves as your feedback mechanism. A management culture that rewards only silence tends to go off track as much as one that rewards crisis.

■ MOTIVATION

Most employees will be motivated to complete attainable goals whose results simultaneously further their personal vision, the project vision, and the organizational vision. On a personal level, team members want to take pride in the project when they tell their friends and family what they worked to create. They will want to work on projects that they consider career enhancing. If the project is innovative, they will want to feel that the project somehow furthered the state of the art, either in terms of technology or in terms of the organization's industry. Some people do their best when they know that their work will make the lives of co-workers or customers better.

Team leaders driven by a particular motivation, such as to earn respect, may assume that other people are motivated by the same things. Such an assumption proves false. For example, some people enjoy the feeling of success that comes from overcoming a challenge, while others do everything they can to avoid challenge. At any time, a team member may quit the organization or transfer into another department. Never assume that organizational inertia will be strong enough to resist other pulls in a person's life. Even if a team member has skills in plentiful supply, the cost of training a new person can strain a tight budget or schedule. Such transitions also create tension in relationships between team members. In prosperous locales, beware of assuming that salary alone provides enough motivation. Employees typically spend half of their waking lives at work, commuting to and from work, and studying for work during their healthiest years. Those who take a careful look at their lives will want work that they find fulfilling in areas other than compensation.

You can provide deeper motivation by getting to know your team members. Learn what would make them want to go to work in the morning. Everyone has at least one valuable asset. Find it.

Needs that people feel motivated to fulfill in their work and elsewhere include

- Belonging to an organization or team
- Desire for recognition and respect
- Desire for companionship
- Desire to help people
- Security and stability
- Career enhancement
- Opportunity to learn new things
- Desire to gain personal power

- Desire to work with respected peers or leaders
- Mobility and control over work environment
- Independence from authority
- Ability to express ideas
- Ability to express creativity
- Desire to innovate
- Desire to contribute to leading-edge developments in the industry
- Need to support a family
- Desire for a more luxurious life-style

Observing patterns in team member conversations may give you hints for determining their motivations. Ask yourself questions like these:

- Who are the person's heroes? Does the person refer often to his family? To people who are rich or powerful? To people who are famous?
- Does the person get excited about technological advances? about cars or artwork she has or wants to acquire?
- How does the person discuss activities—as a process or as an accomplishment? Would he more enjoy doing his own home improvements or designing them for a contractor to carry out?
- How does the person talk about politics—as a means for accomplishing societal goals or as an oppressive force?

If you intend to create a leading-edge system, make sure that your people know that they have the opportunity to create something new and unique. They may be interested in opportunities to write about the experience for a trade journal or to make a presentation at a company meeting or a conference. Where this would not jeopardize proprietary information, help team members to discover such opportunities and participate in them.

■ SUCCESSFUL MEETINGS

Meetings can either be a valuable communication opportunity or a phenomenal waste of time. To improve the odds of the former, request that anyone in your department or organization who calls a meeting follow these guidelines:

■ Define the purpose of the meeting and all desired outcomes. Whether published or kept private, this will allow you to know when conversation is off track and whether the meeting was successful. If you find the purpose hard to define, you may not need a meeting.

■ Create an agenda in advance and estimate the time needed for each item. Important discussions may require more time than planned, but this will help you keep the meeting on track. It will also help you know whether one meeting is enough or too many.

■ Do not expect to achieve more than two or three outcomes per hour of meeting. Typically, the effectiveness of a meeting declines as its length increases. Any 1-hour meeting with an agenda more than five items long will probably not only fail to accomplish its goals, but attendees will see that the agenda is unrealistic and might abandon it altogether.

■ Plan for meetings that last less than an hour and a half. If you need more time, schedule more meetings, or plan for a 5 to 10 minute break after each hour. People's attention spans wander after about 45 minutes. Beware of people checking their voice mail or visiting their offices during long breaks. Distractions like these tend to destroy focus and to make people late returning to the meeting.

■ Publish the meeting agenda, location, and duration ahead of time. Don't give people an excuse for tardiness because they didn't know where and when the meeting was. When you give people a chance to prepare for the meeting topic, you encourage informed opinions rather than on the spot reactions.

■ Make sure all attendees know why they were invited, what they are expected to contribute, and, sometimes more importantly, what they are not expected to contribute. They should know what will be considered off topic.

■ Start the meeting on time and end early. People who arrive late to meetings effectively punish those who showed up on time. Toleration of lateness can lead to an entire organization that is routinely late. Often, the people who arrive on time start discussing the topic and then must waste time rehashing the discussion for latecomers. In debates, the early people may side against the latecomers because of a point that was well made before the latecomers arrived. End early so that people have time to get to subsequent appointments and meetings on time. Short meetings can be most effective, since people know there is no room for side-talk and chatter.

- For long meetings, do not let the length of the meeting lull people into believing that they can afford to waste time. The agenda should make it clear that the subject requires careful use of every minute allotted for the meeting. Do your best to maintain a sense of urgency.

- If there is flexibility in the agenda, allow people to suggest additional topics or remove proposed topics at the start of the meeting. People who feel coerced into following an agenda that they don't agree with will not contribute as much as they are capable of. If necessary, write down proposed agenda items and schedule a follow-up meeting for addressing them fully.

- Arrange for all equipment and information to be ready and in the meeting room 10 minutes early. Remember to arrange for a conference phone, phone numbers, overhead projectors, computers, microphones, or reference materials if necessary. When reserving the room, include the setup time and any tear-down time.

- Establish a leader, notetaker, and timekeeper for the meeting ahead of time. Let all attendees know who is filling which roles.

- Have the notetaker write down each action item, the name of the person who agrees to "own" the action item, and the date that the owner commits to deliver the action. Select a person to make sure each action item is completed by the agreed time.

- The notetaker should also document all decisions. People who don't agree with decisions made have a way of remembering them incorrectly or forgetting them altogether. Similarly, those who agreed tend to enhance their recall of the decision. If a key person later leaves the organization or is missing at a critical time, others who assumed that someone else had the information will be left in the dark. If attendees agree, you can also tape the meeting so that all ideas are retained as presented.

- Have the notes distributed as soon as possible after the meeting. Make sure you store a separate file copy in case organizational changes disperse the original decision makers.

- The timekeeper makes sure the discussion doesn't stray off topic and suggests taking tangential discussions offline. The timekeeper also lets people know when discussion time is up. Optionally, if all agree, the timekeeper can be tasked with keeping people from interrupting each other and from unjustly dominating the meeting.

- If brainstorming, do not allow people to criticize brainstormed ideas. The brainstorming process relies on freedom of thought. Innovation rarely occurs in an environment of negative thinking.

566

■ If necessary, schedule the next meeting while still in the current meeting. Not all meetings require follow-up. For those that do, the enthusiasm for scheduling another meeting will be highest at the end of a productive meeting.

■ TIME MANAGEMENT

Project managers must manage their own time and help their subordinates to manage theirs. If you find yourself routinely unable to meet important obligations in your personal and work life, study time management. An introductory time management exercise is given later. If you can't keep a commitment to yourself, you will find it difficult to help your project team members to meet their commitments.

For project management, the first time management skill requiring mastery is the ability to list all the essential steps needed to achieve a particular result. You may find it helpful to envision the completed project and work backward through the critical steps for making the project a reality.

When making commitments, multiply your estimates by some factor. Try to get the task done earlier than estimated, but don't guarantee it. To learn what your "optimism factors" are, keep a time log. When sitting down to do a task, estimate how long you think it will take, then write down the times that you begin and end the task. To some extent, you can subtract time for breaks and interruptions, but remember that you are rarely in a position to subtract them from a project schedule. After making this a practice for a few days, you will learn to be more realistic about your abilities or to work more efficiently.

Another critical aspect of time management to master is convincing yourself and others that you have set the right priorities. In any organization, people will try to give you work that you (or your managers) don't consider critical to your job or project. This happens at home as well. Those of us that like making others happy are especially vulnerable to requests to do one little favor or to help on something that's not in our responsibility, but is for the broader good of the organization. Try to deflect these tasks toward the person or department that would be

<

PROJECT LEADERSHIP

responsible ideally. It ultimately strengthens an organization if people can get the same results "going through channels" as attempting to go through a back door, especially if you help to put the channels in the right places.[1] As another approach, try to delegate the task to someone who has more time or whose career would be enhanced by learning to do it. In any case, keep these types of charitable, but project-derailing tasks to a minimum. If you find you particularly enjoy certain work, or you discover that no one in the organization is responsible but that the task is important, consider changing your department's charter and budget to include such things. Learning to say no to nonpriorities means that you can say yes to the essential tasks and people in your life.

A QUICK TIME MANAGEMENT LESSON

If you repeatedly have too much to do and no energy to do it all, you may benefit from learning a little (or a lot) about time management. If you set yourself particularly high goals while reading this chapter and the last, you will need to manage your time carefully to be successful. Here's a short overview for those who wonder whether it's worthwhile to spend time learning how to manage time. It will also serve as a refresher for those who once knew.

Most time management and success formulas in book, tape, or seminar form can be summarized as follows:

1. Discover what you really want to accomplish during your lifetime in your personal, family, and career life.

2. Start with a goal in each area and work backward to determine the steps necessary to accomplish each goal.

---

[1] A large part of a manager's job is "channel design." Treat it like the design of your kitchen—something usable no matter how many you must cook for or how hot it gets. If your organization's channels don't work under stress, you encourage the use of back doors, which tends to waste resources and produce poorer-quality results.

3. Work toward your goals every day, giving the most time and best attention to the highest-priority items.

4. Stay determined and stay physically, emotionally, and spiritually healthy.

At the same time that you schedule time for important things, save time for unimportant things and for unexpected opportunities. A schedule that is full of nothing but the next achievement becomes too tough to live by and ultimately gets abandoned.

If you have never tried to manage your time, here is an exercise to try. It should only take you about 10 minutes a day.

First, divide your daily work into four or five categories. They may be similar to those given in the preface. Put these in order of priority. Next, determine the percentage of time that you think you would ideally spend on each task. In other words, giving a task a higher than average percentage indicates that it is that much more important than the rest. Table 13-1 is an example.

TABLE 13-1   Sample Priority Allocation

Percent of Time	Task Category
30%	Change the system to make improvements that support business goals
25%	Change the system to eliminate or minimize recurring problems
15%	Answer questions about the system for users and management
15%	Fix reported problems with the current system
15%	Find time, money, and people to do all the above

For five goals, the average is 20%. Since we assigned the first two goals with an above average ranking, we have determined that these deserve proportionately more of our effort than the remaining three.

Next, make a grid like the one shown in Table 13-2, which has a row for each task category. Make a column for each day of the week. Add rows for noting the time of day that each day's work began and ended, the duration of each day, and any comments.

TABLE 13-2   *Sample Time Log*

Time Log	Monday	Tuesday	Wednesday	Thursday	Friday
Work toward system goals				.	
Resolve recurring issues					
Answer questions					
Fix problems					
Acquire resources					
Total hours recorded					
Time work started					
Time work ended					
Total hours at work					
Notes					

Each day, put a tick mark in each category for each half-hour worked under the column for that day. Round up anything that took 15 minutes or more, and leave off anything that took less time. Record the time you began and ended work. Use the time work started and ended each day to calculate the total hours at work. Add up the tick marks to calculate how much time you spent working on each category. Make notes on the bottom of the page about specific difficulties or successes that you had with tasks or any tasks you did that you could not categorize. This is a good place to note whether you are more or less productive at certain times of the day, working with certain people, or working on specific activities.

Do *not* spend 2 or more hours writing a program to record your hours each day. Just make this chart on a piece of scrap paper and use a pen to fill it in. If it is useful beyond the first week, then you can take a little time to automate the process.

You will learn several things from this exercise. First, you will probably learn that a half-hour goes by faster than you think. You may also find it difficult to account for large chunks of every day. Usually, people discover that they need to leave more time for reacting to unexpected failures and taking advantage of rare opportunities. Finally, and most importantly, you will find out what your priorities really are. If you spend half (50%) of your day on problems, on some level you have perceived that your real priority is to fix problems.

The roots of the discrepancy between stated and actual priorities are diverse. In some cases, you may feel that your company's expectations of you are incompatible with your priorities. In other cases, you may not have faith that the benefits of concentrating on your priority activities outweigh the consequences of letting nonpriority activities slide. Insecurity about your ability to accomplish a priority task may lead you to spend your time on tasks that you feel more confident about instead.

After a week or two, you may choose to change your stated priorities to match what you are really able to accomplish each day. Alternatively, you can start taking action to talk yourself, your boss, and your co-workers into helping you to support your real priorities. Spending a day or a week in a time management seminar will help you to learn more about goal setting and self-discipline. If you commute, consider acquiring a time management program on cassette tapes that you can listen to on your way to work.

■ PREVENTING AND RECOVERING FROM DELAYS

Figure 13.2 It takes more effort to push the clock back after hitting obstacles than it does to plan ahead to avoid obstacles.

To prevent project delays, make sure that all team members always know the number of weeks remaining in the schedule, which tasks are on the critical path, the target completion date, the exact consequences of being late, and the rewards of being on time or early.

At the beginning of each task, look ahead and evaluate any risks to the schedule. Think about technology discoveries that might change the plan. Also plan for any time off that team members may require. Anticipate vacations, illness, and corporate events. Find ways to help people so that they don't leave when they are most needed.

Keep an eye on the tasks that team members work on, and keep them from working on other projects without your approval. Also watch out for creeping scope—the problem of including more and more in the project without adjusting the schedule and budget. One way to stay focused is to concentrate on project deliverables. Agree with the project team on a list of deliverables and associated dates. When a deliverable is complete, make sure that work on that phase of the project stops. Help team members to avoid the temptation to continue improving the results after the due date. Encourage them to complete core functionality ahead of schedule so that they have the time to refine the design at the end.

As the project progresses, let team members know when their tasks are on the critical path and help them to do everything within their power to complete the task on time or earlier with the highest quality possible. Communicate to the team when certain team members are "on the path," and ask everyone to help to keep the interruptions of those people to a minimum.

When a project falls behind or if the organization's political or economic climate suddenly changes, it may become necessary to complete the project sooner than the current schedule projects. Ideally, this means doing whatever is possible to finish ahead of time while keeping the quality loss and additional costs as minimal as possible. Doing so requires that you examine all tasks on the critical path. Common ways of shortening a project schedule follow, with some providing better results than others:

- Delaying tasks that aren't really necessary until after roll out

- Cutting tasks or features determined to be nonessential

- Reducing the number or length of tests

- Reducing the time for user feedback or management sign off

- Lowering quality standards

- Adding more people to the project

- Asking people to work longer hours and rewarding them for doing so

- Adding more or faster hardware to the project, often by renting or borrowing it

- Using productivity-enhancing software, tools, or techniques

573

You can also gather team members to consider the situation and brainstorm other innovative solutions. When a project schedule becomes compressed, the tension often rises, so even more attention must be paid to keeping the team together. Team members should be encouraged to participate in the solution, rather than being blamed for the problem.

Sometimes these measures result in the critical path switching to other tasks or results in multiple critical paths. Be sure to reevaluate the project plan to make sure that you know the new critical path or paths.

■ MANAGING EXPECTATIONS

When you make an improvement to the computer system, your users will be happy for awhile. And then, eventually, they will want another improvement as good as the last. When you make changes, you raise the expectations of you and of the system. Once a 30-second transaction only takes 15 seconds, any subsequent return to the old performance will make formerly accepting users irate. Changes that deliver only sporadic improvement may be worse than no change at all.

You can turn this tendency of human nature to your advantage. Plan your changes so that you deliver results slightly ahead of the time it takes people to get weary of the old system. However, when users need to adapt their behavior for a change, take care to balance your timing so that you don't introduce change too often. Requiring people to constantly learn new things to get their work done will also frustrate them. Predictability will serve you well in this situation. If you release changes on a reliable schedule, such as once a quarter or on Friday afternoons, users will be more patient in the interim. Those who like to feel in control will learn to plan ahead for making routine adjustments to their work habits.

Another way to manage user opinion of the system is to make it as self-regulating as possible. You can write cron or batch jobs that check for common problems or exceptionally high resource usage and email you a report when limits are exceeded. This allows you to detect and fix problems before users need to complain to you. The system will appear to operate more smoothly simply because users don't have to stop their work to help you to do yours.

Finally, you can attempt to stay ahead of your users by thinking about the problem after next. After you make one task easier, does the computing bottleneck shift to another task? If you make it easier to create reports, do you then need to create a system for helping users to keep their reports organized? Thinking ahead to the future "market" for your services will help you to anticipate needs before they become crises.

■ MANAGING RESISTANCE TO CHANGE

People have a natural resistance to change stemming from fear of the unknown. If you are making a large change to a computer system in wide use for everyday work, you will need an extensive plan for introducing the changes. If you publicize your plans and vision widely and in enough detail, the new system will feel familiar by the time it arrives. More extraordinary resistance, discussed in the following paragraphs, has roots in other causes.

If you are in an organization to which new technology is rarely introduced, you are likely to encounter people who don't trust computers at all. They will stick to familiar tools that they have confidence about—pens, paper, typewriters, or old applications. No matter how much you try to convince them that their productivity will increase with the improved system, they will resist it. Most workers don't care as much about their productivity as they do about the quality of their work lives. To confront this problem, you will need to see the system through users' eyes before you implement the changes.

Interview the people whose jobs will be most affected by the change. What would they like the new system to do? What do they dislike most about their job? What do they wish they could do? By providing answers that help people to get things that they have always wanted, they are much more likely to feel that you are on their side.

If potential users of the new system believe that increased productivity will eliminate their jobs, either assure them that this isn't the case or explain what plans the company has for retraining workers. Technology tends to eliminate repetitive jobs that don't require creativity. Rather than seeing this as a threat, people can see it as an opportunity to do work that uses their human creativity and intelligence. Help users to find where they want to create value in the world, rather than clinging to the work that once provided a sense of security.

If you can, commit to helping users to find other work more interesting to them if they do gain so much productivity that jobs could be eliminated. It will be in the business's best interest to find out the maximum productivity this way, rather than having the system fail to deliver promised results because of employee resistance.

▪ COMMUNICATION

People often react to change negatively, even if the net result of the change benefits them. This is particularly true when people are asked to learn to work differently because the computer system has changed. Whenever you accomplish a task, big or small, you change the system. In most cases, it will affect one or more people who didn't request the change. If you don't notify them ahead of time, they may either be upset at a resulting disruption of their work or that you chose to make a change other than one that they requested. Although many people may not notice, the one or two that do may be your boss or your customer. If you spend a lot of time making changes that are not perceptible, people may question exactly how you spend your valuable time.

To minimize user resistance to change, you can employ two common methods. The first is to include the users in all phases of the project, from soliciting requirements to evaluation and acceptance testing. Second, clearly communicate ahead of time any system changes. This allows people to prepare for the change mentally. It also gives users a chance to warn you of any planned activities that will either be delayed because of your change or any activities that may cause your plans to fail.

If you announce the changes that you expect to have positive results ahead of time, people will give you credit for doing the right thing at the right time. It is also essential to announce the changes that will have a negative effect on some people. Otherwise, users may feel like you made things difficult with no warning and have little respect for their needs. That sort of impression is never forgotten. People who are affected by your actions in this way will often make things more difficult for you later.

Any change to the system will probably change the whole system in some small or large way. It is always wise to think about the expected state of the new system and what business impact it may have. Your predictions may be wrong, but the thought process will be valuable. The more times you think through changes, the better you will become. You will gain credibility as you tell people what to expect and your predictions come true.

To make changes efficiently and keep control of your time, be sure to communicate with users of the system. Significant changes can be broadcast in email. Small changes could be posted where people can look if interested, such as an internal news group, bulletin board, or WWW server. Changes should be announced twice. State the task and the reasons for it ahead of time. After making the change, report on how the implementation went and whether the goals were accomplished. A public history of successful implementations will serve your career and your reputation well. If there is a high chance of the implementation failing to meet its goals, note this in the initial announcement. At worst, people will fault the requirements for taking such a risk rather than your competence. At best, users may think of ways to help you to reduce the risks. You may even consider writing a stored procedure, such as `sp_whatsnew`, that any user can execute at any time to learn what upgrades or changes you've made lately and any that you are planning next.

Procedure Manual Suggestions

○ Notifying Users of System Changes

⇒ Write a procedure for letting users know about system changes ahead of time and after implementation.

⇒ Ahead of time, the time, date, purpose, and scope of the change should be communicated to anyone who might be affected. Users should also learn ahead of time about anything they may need to do differently after the change is made.

⇒ After the change, users should receive a report of how well the implementation of the change went and a reminder of any adjustments that they may need to make.

○ Recommended Communication Methods

⇒ Establish a recommended procedure for project communications.

⇒ Document the preferred media and formats for communicating with team members, executive management, the users, other members of the organization, customers, and, if applicable, the press.

⇒ Document methods for providing project feedback.

⇒ Establish a procedure for escalating an issue when normal communication channels don't work.

○ Project Document Storage

⇒ Establish a filing system for storing project records (memos, letters, meeting notes, invoices, contracts, proposals, vendor literature, reports, etc.).

⇒ Include an archival method and schedule.

⇒ Describe who can get access to the project documents and how.

Identifying the Costs, Benefits, and Functions of System Components

To create a map that will guide you to the system you envision, you need to start with a picture of your current location. A thorough cost/benefit analysis based on a complete system inventory will create that picture for you. The techniques of cost/benefit analysis also help you analyze a proposal in order to see if the proposed change accurately reflects the terrain that you need to cover. A solid understanding of your system components—from both a technical standpoint and a cost/benefit standpoint—will help to guide your intuition about the major interactions between system elements. In exchange for your effort to create an exhaustive system analysis, you will reap the benefits of a high credibility rating by your higher ups, favorable budget decisions, and great time savings. In contrast, Systems Managers at the extremes of ignorance about the costs, components, and requirements of their systems tend to lose their budgets and their jobs during hard times. You can probably get along O.K. if you're somewhere between these extremes, as long as you know where you are in that range and why you are there.

The best time to learn the cost of your system is when you aren't considering any major changes. Otherwise, you may bias results toward or away from a plan that you agree or disagree with. Starting with an impartial baseline gives you a more accurate foundation for evaluating results of subsequent changes. A thorough analysis of the costs of your system could take anywhere from a day to a month of your time. The thought of tackling almost any other task will appeal to you more than discovering exactly how much money your system costs. Perhaps you wish to keep these costs hidden so that no one will know how much is going into computers instead of into their paychecks. However, you will receive several benefits in exchange for your efforts.

First, the process of analysis will help you form more educated opinions. You will know the components that had to be purchased to create the system now in place, and you will have a good idea about the cost of replacing elements when they break. If, for example, someone claimed that you could save a lot of money if your small PC LAN was peer to peer instead of client/server, you could argue that the cost of the servers is more than made up by the savings in centralized administration. You might also cite the savings in maintenance and support costs.

By backing up your opinions with accurate cost estimates, you will achieve credibility. The reputation will serve you well when your boss next considers giving out raises and promotions. Another benefit of credibility is gaining influence in decision making. When someone less knowledgeable than you makes a proposal, management will ask you to review it for accuracy. You will then have the power to shape such investments before they are made instead of cleaning up afterward.

Knowing your costs enables you to answer small system investment questions easily. For example, while reading trade magazines, you will notice how much the new printers are and you will be able to compare these costs to the cost of maintaining one of your current printers. If someone asks you whether it would be worth it to buy a second printer for the front office or to sell the current printer and buy a faster one, you can have an immediate answer. Depending on the printer usage, you might convince them that, for the cost of time now spent waiting for printer jobs, the department could donate the current printer to a local high school and buy two faster ones.

When you know the costs of your system, you can make decisions more quickly. Most businesses and organizations go through cycles. At a certain point in the cycle, things become hectic and crises strike. Use the noncrisis times to prepare your thorough cost/benefit analysis. Then, later, when you are under pressure, you will be able to consider alternatives and recommend a reasonable course of action (that you won't have to fix up later) much more quickly. Keep the key figures of your cost analyses available where you can find them quickly. Remember the approximate costs of the most expensive system components, so when someone asks, you won't have to stop and look them up.

Think about which data will most serve you during a crisis, and make plans for preparing it in advance. Also think about times when you will be on vacation and important dates for your friends and family. Prepare to have things run smoothly during those times so you won't be paged or called into the office.

In the rest of this chapter, we will discuss an idealized cost/benefit analysis that incorporates an ideal inventory. Practical matters will force you to cut corners. However, knowing the ideals will help you to communicate persuasively with those who can help you to pursue your system goals.

We will start by looking at general techniques of financial analysis and then move into exploring the system that you will be analyzing.

■ TECHNIQUES OF COST/BENEFIT ANALYSIS

A costs/benefit analysis for a proposed system entails

■ Inventorying the elements of the system under consideration and of any system or part of a system to be replaced by a new system.

■ Selecting a system time horizon for analysis purposes, such as 10 years

- Estimating the cost of the current system over the selected period
- Estimating the cost of the proposed system over the selected period
- Estimating the cost of the change
- Evaluating the benefits of the proposed change
- Assigning a quantitative value to the benefits
- Using accurate methods to compare the costs and benefits

For small changes, the experienced professional can complete a sufficient analysis in a few minutes. Where the risks are greater and the project larger, Systems Managers should make a thorough analysis that they submit for review to other managers and technical experts for validation.

A business can also profit from making a baseline analysis of a current system when it has been a long time since the last review. Even a coarse baseline estimate of the costs and benefits will serve Systems Managers who must take care of more crucial tasks before analyzing the system in detail.

Systems Managers new to a company may also develop a full analysis to get the financial perspective needed to decide which changes to make first. An ability to deliver the right results from the start will assure management that they hired the right person for the job.

Amazingly often in large and small businesses alike, someone proposes a change to a system so compellingly, no one performs an analysis at all. Either the costs and risks of the project are considered insignificant, the benefits are described in an attractive way, or unfounded assumptions are made about the actual costs, benefits, and affected system elements. This practice ultimately results in the organization wasting money and time. Such projects rarely meet the required deadlines. Projects also fail to live up to expectations when planners perform an incomplete cost/benefit analysis. They may leave out crucial costs of labor, the cost of money, or the cost of a delay during the transition from the old system to the new.

A hidden benefit of undertaking a thorough analysis of your system in the near future is that you may find several costs that you can minimize right away. For example, you might find that you can save money by switching from a 5 day a week service contract to a 24 hour week contract or go from a regular contract to a charge by call contract. You could discover that a proposed system change that you had a bad feeling about truly did suffer from incorrect analysis. By explaining the faults of the suggested implementation, you may save substantial amounts of time and money for your organization.

When you create an inventory of your system, consider putting the information in a simple database or spreadsheet so that you can use it as the basis for subsequent cost/benefit analysis, to perform what-if analyses, or to make it available to others. Your accountant or controller may have already compiled some of the information you need. If such information is accessible to you, find out if you can get a copy. Financial professionals usually appreciate attempts to see things their way and may also appreciate any system improvements that help them. If the inventory records are created manually, you may be able to help them by supplying the information you compile. Such cooperation makes later contract negotiations and purchases go more smoothly since such interactions require close work between the financial people and the systems people.

In this chapter, we will again use our fictional characters, Tim and Sandy, to illustrate some of the techniques of systems analysis. We start with the following scenario.

SANDY'S SPORT SHOPS—TIM'S COST/BENEFIT ANALYSIS

Shortly after he started working full time, Sandy asked Tim to reprogram the three cash registers since taxes went up a quarter of a percent and since she also wanted to implement some special discounting.

After spending an afternoon figuring out how to do it, Tim implemented the change the next day and it worked perfectly. They briefly considered Tim trying to explain the update process over the phone to the clerks or the managers at the other stores. Sandy decided instead to take him on a road trip to reprogram the rest of the cash registers in the other shops the following week. She decided it would be less risky and wouldn't waste her managers' time. Besides, she wanted to verify the results herself and take the opportunity to see how the other managers and stores were doing.

During the long hours in the car, Tim started thinking about all the things they could do if they used networked PCs with bar code scanners instead of programmable cash registers, if they used a networked database system, and if they used modems to transmit each store's data at the end of every day. He started talking to Sandy about the benefits of automatic inventorying, automatic price scanning, daily detailed knowledge about each store's sales, and the ability for him to manage the store's computers without having to take long road trips. Being a smart, knowledgeable business woman with several more years of experience in the business world than Tim, she was skeptical. "Sure Tim, that all sounds great, but it's going to cost a fortune."

"Yeah, but it will pay itself off in no time. Think about the money you'll save on inventories alone—you won't have to pay people overtime to stay late and count stuff each month and you won't have to close the store once every quarter for the full inventory."

"O.K., Tim. You do a cost/benefit analysis for me and I'll think about it."

Tim scribbled on a piece of paper for a few minutes while Sandy drove. In 10 minutes, he read it to her.

"O.K. Sandy. Listen to this—I was right. Let's say we make about $500 profit a day per store on days we're open, so if we can stay open for the four days a year we usually close for inventory, we'll save $8000 for all the stores. On top of that, we usually pay two clerks per store overtime to count stuff all day, which adds up to another $2500. I figure it will cost us about $750 each for eight computers—they don't have to be that fancy, and I can put them together from parts. It will cost another, say, $2000 for the scanners and modems, and no more than $2000 for the database software. So if we spend $10,000 we'll save $10,500 this year alone, and start saving even more after that. What do you think now?"

"I think it's going to be a long drive, Tim. There are just a few things they didn't teach you in your programming classes."

In the initial example given of Sandy's sport shops, Tim's analysis overlooked many of the variables used in calculating the cost of a system. While he concluded that the system would pay for itself, he didn't perform enough of an analysis of benefits to convince Sandy that she might not gain even more by a different investment altogether, such as in increased advertising. Also, his analysis neglected system lifetime, training, the cost of money, the expenses of the change such as rewiring, and the ongoing costs, such as maintenance and support. Since he's used to receiving his paycheck on time, it also never occurred to him that Sandy might encounter cash flow problems if she made such a significant investment. In the next few sections, we will review the factors to consider when evaluating system changes.

EXPECTED LIFETIME OF A NEW SYSTEM

Experienced managers know that the expense of a system extends far beyond its initial purchase. To capture a system's total cost, evaluate the system over the course of its expected lifetime. Estimates of how long a system will last vary from person to person. Organizational factors also influence expectations.

If a system will take 2 years to build before its ready to deliver any benefits, it will take at least 2 years, if not 3 or 4, for the system to start paying for itself in savings over the old system. In this case, one hopes for a life span of over 5 years. On the other hand, a technologist may look at the pace of the computing industry and estimate that no system is really as efficient as it could be after 3 years. It only takes 2 or 3 years for old software and equipment to be supplanted by newer, cheaper, and more advanced technology.

An accountant views the lifetime of an investment quite differently. Instead of function and customer satisfaction, the accountant sees a system in terms of initial cost, depreciation, and taxation. Generally, businesses depreciate computer equipment over 5 years. The accountant will resist the idea of abandoning computer equipment before taking the full depreciation. In some cases, arranging trade-ins or donating the equipment to charity may offset the concern.

Renting or leasing equipment can also mitigate the problems with short computer life span. For new software systems, try separating projects into self-contained segments so that you can put modules into use as soon as they are completed. Parts of the system can then start paying for themselves before project completion.

When preparing a baseline cost analysis, pick a time period that starts now and ends when you expect to need to replace major system components or at the end of the management planning window, such as 5 years. For analyzing proposals, select a time period consistent with organizational expectations.

ANALYZING COST VARIATIONS OVER TIME

An accurate analysis also takes into account variance in costs over a system's lifetime. Maintenance and support may be included with the first year of a new hardware purchase. Thereafter, the vendor might require that you pay a monthly, quarterly, or yearly fee for continuing service. The older equipment gets, the more often it needs repair, so charge-by-call support becomes more expensive. Also, old equipment tends to be demoralizing. People who work with obsolete equipment may lose productivity or allow their work quality to fail, believing that their efforts don't make a difference anyway. Such costs may go unaccounted for if you don't watch for them. Other types of changes in usage may affect costs as well. Software licenses fees often vary depending on the number of users. If you expect system usage to grow or fall dramatically, adjust the relevant estimates as well. Keep in mind that maintenance costs also rise rapidly with a rapid increase in the user base.

To find the variations in costs over time, examine historical records of system costs. Try to find maintenance records for representative components so that you can calculate the average number of repair and maintenance calls made per year based on the component's age. Also look at the rate of purchases of software updates so that you can estimate their equivalent of maintenance costs.

To simplify later calculations, separate the system component costs into one-time charges and ongoing charges. Then estimate the total costs of keeping each item running for the selected system lifetime.

SANDY'S SPORT SHOPS—MAINTENANCE

Two hours later, Tim conceded that the computers might break down in a way that he could not fix or that they might need parts. Tim and Sandy agreed to add 10% to the estimated computer cost for maintenance. Tim also realized that it would make sense to spend a little more money up front and buy new computers that would come with first-year maintenance contracts free. Although he would enjoy putting the machines together himself, new computers would be more reliable. Purchasing the latest equipment would also mean that they would stay technologically current longer. They estimated that the eight new computers would be $1500 each, since they wouldn't need to be particularly fancy, and that the maintenance cost for 3 years would be $150 each per year. Finally, Sandy convinced Tim that being open the days that they used to be closed for inventory wouldn't necessarily boost sales. However, since she planned to do advertising to boost sales anyway, she conceded that he could use his original hopes for increased income.

A computer's nominal value is the amount paid for it on the purchase date. Since the value of currency changes due to inflation, $100 will buy you more today than it will in 5 years. Also, the time value of a certain sum of money is analyzed by figuring out what its purchase power would be after a period of time earning interest. Using the invoice price to compare a computer bought 10 years ago and one bought today would give you misleading results. Instead, various cost analysis methods, described later, have emerged for accurately comparing expenditures and income over a long period of time.

USING COST ANALYSIS METHODS

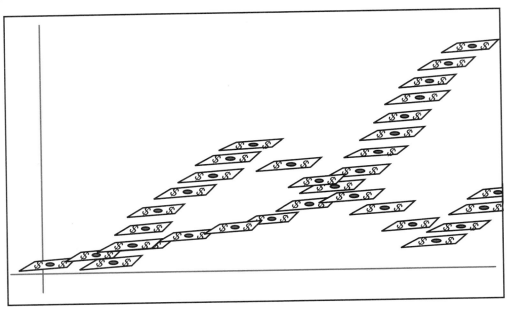

Figure 14.1 It's not always obvious at first glance which of two courses of action will result in better overall returns. Financial analysis helps you understand long-term risks and rewards.

Knowing each of the common ways to evaluate investments will help you to explain proposed changes to the people that manage your organization using concepts they will understand and be willing to act on.

■ **Net present value** When making a major system investment, you spend today's currency to enhance profits at some later date. Because you can earn a return on the investment of your money, for example, 10% in a money market fund, a current liquid asset is more valuable than the same amount of tomorrow's profits. You would have to increase the value by 10% per year to end up with a future value equivalent to the current sum. When evaluating capital expenditures such as system upgrades, the rate of return for investments is called the cost of money or the opportunity cost. For a system change to pay off, it needs to overcome both the initial cost of the investment and the cost of money. The net present value method assesses the total investment and the total benefits over the life of the system. Given a discount (interest) rate of i and a number of periods n, we can calculate a discount multiplier using the following formula: $1/(1 + i)^n$. Most spreadsheets have built-in present value functions. The discount rate that you choose will depend on the size and duration of your investment's payback period (described next) and the amount of risk that you are counting on. As with all investments, the higher the risk that you assume is, the higher your possible returns (and losses) are. If you know you are taking on a high-risk project, choose a high discount rate accordingly. For that project to be worth it, it will have to pay off better than more conservative, more sure investments. The accounting department of your organization may have particular rates used for all analysis or may help you to choose a reasonable number based on its knowledge of the current financial market.

■ **Payback analysis**   Companies use payback analysis to evaluate the timing of their investments. The payback period is the time it takes for a system investment to start to realize a profit. To evaluate the payback period, determine the number of years in operation that the information system needs to have to pay for the cost of investing in it. By graphing the cumulative costs against the cumulative benefits of the proposed system, you can tell when the investment starts to pay off. Businesses often have a set time period for payback assessments, since the ability to accurately project the usefulness of the system and the real savings diminishes after 3 to 5 years. For the most accurate results, use the net present value of the cumulative costs and benefits.

■ **Return on investment**   The return on investment (ROI) is the ratio of total benefits divided by total costs for the duration of the project. Managers use this as a quick way to compare investments with similar time periods. However, since it does not take into account the cost of money, the internal rate of return ratio is more accurate.

■ **Internal rate of return**   The internal rate of return (IRR) method, like ROI, uses the ratio of total benefits by total costs for the project duration, but uses the net present value of the costs and benefits in the calculation. When comparing investments with different return periods and different initial investments, the IRR calculation produces more accurate results than the simple ROI ratio.

■ **Cash flow**   A cash flow analysis evaluates the pattern of investment and return associated with the system over time. As with the payback analysis, companies typically look at cash flow to determine when they will begin to make a profit. For rapidly growing businesses or those with limited liquid assets, a cash flow analysis to helps managers to see whether a project will compete with other business activities for available cash. When management perceives a conflict, they need to determine whether to seek a loan or to delay implementation of the proposal. To analyze cash flow, divide the expected lifetime of the system into several discrete periods. Then consider the related revenues minus the costs for each period. For the most accurate results, use the net present value of the costs and benefits for each period.

■ **Break even**   The break-even point in the lifetime of a proposed system is where the costs of the old system exceed those of the proposed system. It's usefulness is limited by its omission of benefits that don't directly map to cost savings. This sort of analysis serves an organization best when there are usage-based costs that increase as system use increases. Again, the net present value of the system costs should be used.

SANDY'S SPORT SHOPS—PRESENT VALUE

Sandy explained, "See, what I've been thinking of doing is to spend a few thousand a year on advertising over the next four years. I could put ads in phone books, in a popular sports magazine, or do repeated home mailings. Based on my results in the past, I expect to earn a lot more in sales to new customers in addition to encouraging my repeat customer base to come by more often. I estimated my IRR for this project at 2.5."

"Your what?" Tim asked.

"That's internal rate of return." Sandy launched into a detailed explanation of present value and return on investment while they drove over the next several miles of winding road.

Over tofu burgers at a coast-side diner, Tim incorporated his new-found financial knowledge into a more rigorous analysis. He made the chart shown in Table 14-1 on a napkin, using a discount rate of 10% ($i = 0.10$):

TABLE 14-1   *Present Value Example*

	End of Year 1	End of Year 2	End of Year 3	End of Year 4	TOTAL
Yearly costs	16,000	1,600	1,600	1,600	
Discount rate multiplier	0.91	0.83	0.75	0.68	
Present value of costs	14,560	1,328	1,200	1,088	18,176

TABLE 14-1   *Present Value Example (Continued)*

	End of Year 1	End of Year 2	End of Year 3	End of Year 4	TOTAL
Yearly benefits	10,500	10,500	10,500	10,500	
Discount rate multiplier	0.91	0.83	0.75	0.68	
Present value of benefits	9,555	8,715	7,875	7,140	33,285

"It looks good the way you put it, Tim, but I just don't have an extra sixteen thousand lying around for me to spend on computers right now. Even if I did, I'm not sure I could get along without it for almost two years."

"But, Sandy, maybe if it makes transactions more efficient and if it's a good summer, it could even start paying for itself during summer—our peak period. Hey, we should compare these costs to your current cash registers. They're going to need maintenance too." Sandy revealed that she was paying a yearly maintenance cost of $300 per cash register and that each year, as the machines got older, the renewal costs about doubled because of increasing need for repairs.

Back in the car, while continuing on their way north, Tim thought through a quick break-even analysis and with a sinking feeling realized that the cost of the existing cash registers wouldn't be more expensive than his system. He fell silent and then, after a few miles, he fell asleep.

ANALYZING TRENDS

While collecting data about system needs over time, you will start to discover random and cyclical variations that merit further analysis. For example, a simple average of maintenance calls may not provide detailed enough information for cost flow analysis. Rapidly changing technology can make it difficult to decide whether to purchase or to lease equipment. Fluctuations in your organization's market may make it difficult to predict costs based on system usage. Your organization's income may rise or fall dramatically as well.

For projects where the amount of risk taken depends on a specific level of system usage or revenue increase, you will need to familiarize yourself with the factors that influence these trends. Financial analysts learn forecasting methods to help them understand trends and to predict the future. While no method guarantees accuracy, learning them may yield better results in your estimates of tangible and intangible costs and benefits. Since statistical analysis requires rigor and training to perform accurately, this book only brings it to your attention, rather than giving it casual coverage. If you don't have time to learn more about forecasting methods and if trend analysis forms an essential part of your project's success, consider asking a co-worker or hiring a professional to help with the task.

ESTIMATING SOFT COSTS AND HARD COSTS

Quantifying costs and converting them to cash proves easier for some costs than for others. Some people call quantifiable costs hard or tangible costs. They include the cash outlays for maintenance agreements, hardware purchases, and salaries. In contrast, a business discovers soft or intangible costs in the loss of competitive advantage, diminished productivity, or employee dissatisfaction. The soft costs can mean the difference between a highly profitable business and one that fails. However, it's harder to determine with a high degree of certainty the price of such problems in a given period of time, whether in the past or the future.

When making a system proposal that includes analysis of two or more possible scenarios, compare hard costs to hard costs and soft costs to soft costs. Separate the hard and soft costs into sections. The hard costs, if calculated carefully, have a lower risk of being wrong and should appear first. Put the soft costs in a subsequent separate section. For each cost, estimate the risk that it won't be incurred. Such treatment allows managers to understand the relative importance of the soft costs. In some cases, a business knows it has problems that are difficult to quantify, yet finds that they repeatedly surface in customer satisfaction surveys or in bad press. Relative risk factors may help management decide the best way to try resolving the issues.

FINDING HIDDEN COSTS

You can find some costs of a system easily—usually the hard costs described above. Other costs remain hidden unless you've had personal experience with them. By hidden, we know they still affect the profitability of the company, yet, looking back, the managers of the department don't exactly remember spending the money. These costs typically include staff and end-user training, installation costs, and transition costs. Also, systems management costs tend to start out hidden, but gain exposure when they skyrocket due to poorly planned projects or aging technology.

Although Systems Managers may reap short-term benefits by being able to sell projects without including these costs, they will have to live with the results. If directors don't understand how costs are related to projects, they may call for general budget cuts across the board, rather than targeting a problem area. If it becomes apparent that the costs should have been included in the proposal, the directors will fault the author of the proposal for doing unreliable work. If particularly cost-conscious project managers refuse to spend money not included in the proposal, the project may fail due to insufficient investment.

Going through detailed financial reports of the business, if available, can help you find hidden costs. Determine which accounts system expenses are charged to, and examine the expenditures in these accounts. Make sure your list of current system expenses and projected expenses includes complete and realistic estimates corresponding to your findings. Also scan through the detail of other accounts. Perhaps training costs are not usually charged to system-related accounts. These costs will need to be included in your estimate as well. It's unlikely that other departments, such as the training department, considered the costs of proposed major system changes when creating their current budgets.

Another way of finding hidden costs is to take your analysis to the people least and most likely to support changing the system. The ones who disagree with the change will find all the expenses you forgot to include for the proposed system. The ones who want the change will find all the current system expenses that you might otherwise overlook. This approach also pays off in political benefits. By including the input of your potential detractors and supporters, these people will feel partial ownership of the proposal. If the proposal succeeds, you have minimized the risk of noncooperation. As the author of the proposal, include the names of all the contributors so that management realizes that the proposal has had a broad review and may garner broad support.

SOFT BENEFITS AND HARD BENEFITS

Similar to soft and hard costs, we can consider soft and hard benefits. The hard benefits directly contribute to profit. For example, if we currently cannot keep up with the demand for our services, but a database change would result in a direct increase in productivity by 10%, then we could count on the additional profit we would make on our services. An example of a soft benefit might be the results of creating a new database system that allows service representatives to determine a customer's repair history better. The resulting customer satisfaction might pay off in repeat business, more quickly paid bills, and fewer inquires and complaint calls to customer service. Assigning exact profits to these improvements would prove difficult.

The systems analyst and accounting personnel can accurately measure and project tangible benefits in terms of dollars, resources, or time saved. Avoid the tendency to leave out soft costs. While difficult to quantify, removing these intangible benefits from a company might make it uncompetitive. Important soft benefits include

- Improving the decision-making process
- Enhancing accuracy
- Becoming more competitive
- Maintaining a good business image
- Increasing job satisfaction

As with soft costs, be sure to include hidden benefits in your proposal as well. When these benefits appear, you and your system may get credit for the improvement. Also, if a decision maker remains undecided after looking at the hard benefits, the description of the soft benefits may sway the decision in your favor.

HIDDEN BENEFITS

Like costs, assigning benefits to specific investments poses a challenge. Unlike costs, you are unlikely to stumble on benefits in an organization's financial reports. Instead, compare the way that your current system and the proposed system transform inputs to outputs. Think about efficiencies gained and knowledge gathered. Consider the following typical system benefits and determine which might apply for you:

- Increased user efficiency
- Increased user satisfaction
- Increased customer satisfaction
- Increased overall employee satisfaction
- Increased information availability (where desired)
- Increased speed of information access
- Increased accuracy of information
- Increased revenue
- Increased system reliability
- Increased customer base
- Increased competitiveness
- Increased support of planned business changes
- Reduced training costs
- Reduced workplace stress

- Reduced maintenance costs

- Reduced energy costs

- Reduced real estate requirements

- Reduced system administration time

- Increased independence from a particular vendor or diminishing market

- Improved products

- Important advancement in industry

- important service provided

MEASURING BENEFITS

To turn projected benefits into an investment in a new system, the cost savings and revenue enhancements expected from the change must be calculated. When projected improvements fall primarily into the soft category, the calculations become complex.

One way to handle this is to make high, low, and medium costs and savings estimates and determine probabilities for attaining each level. If your project will pay for itself in a reasonable amount of time, even at its lowest estimate, it will be easier to convince others to take the risk. If the project fails to appear beneficial at the highest benefit level, then you need to determine whether your estimated costs and savings are accurate or whether you failed to include any significant costs or benefits.

SANDY'S SPORT SHOPS—BENEFITS

At each of the stores where they stopped, Tim finished programming the cash registers long before Sandy finished talking to each store manager. Tim did a lot of thinking as he wandered around the stores, and came up with some other benefits to add to his analysis.

TABLE 14-2   A More Thorough Analysis

	Year 1	Year 2	Year 3	Year 4	TOTAL
Income					
More sales	8,000	9,600	11,520	13,824	
No overtime	2,500	2,500	2,500	2,500	
Save accounting time	1,000	1,000	1,000	1,000	
Reduce cash register errors	1,000	1,000	1,000	1,000	
Save time ordering merchandise	1,500	1,500	1,500	1,500	
	14,000	15,600	17,520	19,824	66,944
Discount rate multiplier	0.91	0.83	0.75	0.68	
Discounted income	12,740	12,948	13,140	13,480	52,308
Expenses					
Computers	-12,000				
Scanners	-1,000				
Modems	-1,000				
Hardware maintenance		-1,200	-1,200	-1,200	
Software	-2,000				
Software upgrades		-400	-400	400	
	-16,000	-1,600	-1,600	-1,600	-20,800
Discount rate multiplier	0.91	0.83	0.75	0.68	
Discounted expenses	-14,560	-1,328	-1,200	-1,088	-18,176
Yearly discounted cash flow	-1,820	11,620	11,940	12,392	
Cumulative cash flow	-1,820	9,800	21,740	34,132	34,132

Based on Table 14-2, Sandy realized that Tim's instincts might have been right after all. On the way back home, she and Tim did some brainstorming and came up with a plan. Providing that a more thorough analysis of costs and benefits to be done by Sandy when they got back would yield similar results, Sandy would go ahead and launch an ad campaign this year and use the increased profits to invest in a new system next year. Meanwhile, Tim would use Sandy's existing computer to come up with mailing labels for the direct mail advertisements. Tim decided that his little management lesson might go a long way toward helping him finance his remaining semesters at school.

■ EVALUATING CURRENT AND FUTURE SYSTEM ELEMENTS

Now that we have looked at general factors in a cost/benefit analysis, you can prepare a detailed inventory of items that make up your current and possible future systems. Ideally, the inventory will include both technical and financial details. The combination of both helps you see the big picture of how an information systems budget translates to organizational advances.

In the next few sections, we'll list the elements commonly found in an information system, in terms of both costs and day to day operations. For the technical part of the inventory, particular emphasis is given to the relevance of each item to SQL Server. Of course, if you're responsible for other system software, focus your inventory efforts on the elements of most significance to that software as well.

We will also look at costs in terms of proposed changes. When comparing an existing system element to a replacement that you might purchase or lease, it's important to consider the differentiating factors described in the following sections. Two similar machines from different vendors may appear to have similar costs, yet when you evaluate the other factors, which usually aren't advertised, you find the true differences in value. For example, one vendor's maintenance contract may include providing you with a loaner machine if repairs will take longer than a specified period of time. Another vendor may offer on-site training as part of the purchase price. Some of these factors may also fall into the benefits category when compared to your existing equipment.

The ideal inventory includes the following for each item:

■ Classification (hardware, software, service)

■ Make

■ Model

■ Version

■ Vendor

■ Cost of acquisition (purchase, lease, rent, license amount)

- Acquisition date

- Warranty

- Financial arrangement for acquisition (owned, leased, borrowed, or rented)

- Maintenance/license contract renewal date

- Support/service contract cost

- Compatibility with other system elements

- Status of operation (on order, operating, in storage, needs repair)

- Expected lifetime

- Physical location

- Who to contact and how to get service and support

- Support/service contract cost

- Where contract, purchase information, and correspondence about the item are filed

- Which department or person is responsible for the acquisition, maintenance, and other information about the item

- Where user and maintenance documentation for the item are stored

- Who to contact and how to get training and any associated costs

- Who provides internal user support of the item

- License restrictions (e.g., number of users, copies, export prohibitions)

- Approximate number of users of the item

- Primary business purpose of the item

- Rating of quality and reliability (to indicate whether to replace with similar or different item when it is retired)

For some systems, this inventory would take you an afternoon or two. For many, it would take longer than your lifetime. If your situation is more like the latter case, consider proposing a format like the one above as a standard for logging future equipment as a prerequisite for purchase. In fact, before the purchase is the best time for discovering all this detail. In any case, create the inventory for the most significant components for which you have responsibility.

The especially ambitious Systems Manager can consider creating graphical context diagrams that show either together or separately

- Networks
- Subnetworks
- Machine groups
- Departmental groups of computing resources

Personnel responsible for maintaining systems will find graphical documentation helpful for locating problems quickly. You might also consider purchasing software designed for this purpose.

The sections that follow may include many components that you don't consider relevant. For example, some may be tracked and controlled by another department within your organization. Only include those that have a significant impact on your results and budget. The extensiveness of the lists is meant to help you avoid surprises, in both day to day operations and implementing proposals. This chapter may also may serve as a resource when attempting to think of ways you could improve system functionality, save costs, or enhance profits.

COMPUTER HARDWARE

For tracking costs and benefits, inventory all the following over which your department has control:

- Mainframes
- Minicomputers
- Workstations and desktop computers
- Portable, laptop, and notebook computers
- High-end calculators and personal assistants
- Printers
- Plotters
- Backup devices
- Modems and fax modems
- Page scanners and optical character readers

■ Bar code scanners

■ Stocks of cords, adapters, surge protectors, supplies, and so on. (Note whether you keep a stock on hand or order as needed)

For the technical side of your inventory, you'll want to include the major functional features and subelements of the above items. For example, the performance of SQL Server depends heavily on the balance of disk I/O rate, CPU speed, memory capacity, and network speed. To analyze a problem like poor performance, you need to know the level of resource that you are starting with in each area. While considering the hardware components of your system, evaluate the volume and type of input they accept and output they generate. Inventory the features that will most affect the quality and quantity of the data processed. When determining what level of detail to record about each item, think about what those responsible for the system will need to know and do when it fails.

For SQL Server management, having the following hardware-related information available will help you handle day to day issues and avoid critical problems.

■ **Server machines** For each machine on which Sybase Servers run, find out the operating system, the type and number of CPUs, the amount of memory, and any hardware-provided fault tolerance and failover features.

■ **CPUs** A server machine may have anywhere from one to hundreds of CPUs. Typically, machines used for SQL Servers have one to six CPUs, some or all of which are dedicated to use by the Server. Generally, the use of more CPUs allows SQL Server's compute-intensive operations to go faster. Besides documenting the number of CPUs, document their type. For example, PCs typically use Intel chips or clones and Macintoshes use Motorola or PowerPC chips. An operating system or application designed to run on one chip set almost always requires different binary to run on other chips. For example, you cannot run an Ultrix version of SQL Server on DEC's OSF/1, because the former operating system runs on a MIPS chip set and the latter runs on the Alpha chip set.

■ **Memory** The performance of SQL Server depends highly on the amount of memory available to it. Although it can run on 10 MB, this rarely provides the performance required by an application. You can use a Systems Management tool like Enterprise SQL Server Monitor or performance monitors supplied with your operating system, such as vmstat (UNIX), monitor (VMS), or perfmon (Windows

NT), to determine how your memory is being used over time. Also notice how close the current configuration of your system is to using the maximum amount of memory at a given time.

■ **Disk drives**   Knowing the number and configuration of the disk drives on your server machines will serve you better than knowing anything else about your system as far as smooth SQL Server operations are concerned. First, make a list of the specifications for each drive. This includes the amount of space it gives you (after formatting), the number of cylinders and sectors, the size of the sectors, the I/O rate, the access time, and the latency and seek speeds. Also note special attributes, such as RAID. Document the number, names, and sizes of each partition on each of the disks. Finally, determine how each partition of each disk is used. Some partitions will house file systems, while others will be devoted to system uses, like swap, and others will be used by SQL Server or other applications. See Chapter 3 for more information about how each of these factors figures into SQL Server performance and Chapter 10 for how they factor into troubleshooting efforts.

■ **Fault-tolerant components**   A fault-tolerant component allows a machine to continue working even after that component has failed. Fault tolerance is commonly available for disks, controllers, and CPUs. Networks can be configured to provide fault tolerance. For disks, all writes are mirrored to two or more devices so that if one fails the other can be used without interruption. Currently, RAID provides the predominate type of disk fault tolerance. For CPUs, failover to a duplicate CPU happens as soon as a system diagnostic detects a failure in the primary. In theory, any fault-tolerant device features of your system should not affect SQL Server, since it uses operating system services to access the disk, and such devices should support all operating system services. However, in some cases, the implementation does not facilitate optimal Sybase performance. Check with your sources of technical support when purchasing a new type of technology and compatibility may be in doubt. Whenever support is not provided for a critical hardware advance, make a request with Sybase and the hardware vendor to provide it. Such features are incorporated as demand for them increases. Usually, hardware vendors will work closely with Sybase to make sure that the advanced features they offer are supported.

■ **Server operating system**   The operating system is actually software, but is so closely tied to the hardware that we cover it here. You can find a generic operating system type such as UNIX on several hardware platforms, but each hardware vendor implements and optimizes their implementation of the operating system differently. Consequently, executable programs designed for one UNIX system may not run on another. Sybase releases software designated for specific operating system implementations to take advantage of optimizations and to avoid known problems. Therefore, know exactly which operating system version is running on each Server machine.

Client machines and operating systems   The machines that serve as clients in a client/server environment are typically terminals or workstations at each employee's desk. The features of the client machines that most affect Sybase functions are the operating systems and speed of network access. Client applications that perform data pre- and postprocessing on the local workstation will require sufficient memory and CPU power as well. The needs will depend on the application, since little overhead is required for communicating with SQL server itself. Ideally, you should know the CPU type, disks, memory, and applications on each client machine. In reality, tracking these details in a client/server environment proves challenging. At a minimum, know which different operating systems (names and versions) are in use, what the three most popular client-side applications are, and the types of network connectivity provided.

Printers   Determine the number, model, and type of printers that you have available for network use. If you have a particularly print sensitive environment, try to list the page description language each printer supports (for example, Postscript or HP emulation), the amount of RAM in each, the number of pages per minute they print, the paper sizes supported, and the amount of standard-sized paper that they can hold. Standard size of course is different for your office and for your locale. Printers do not directly affect how SQL Server behaves, but they are important to the extent that your organization depends on printed reports or materials that are output from SQL Server data. For example, SQR or PowerBuilder reports often need to send output to network printers.

Modems   Many considered modems auxiliary devices until the Internet gained mass popularity. Now, modems are practically indispensable. Also, keep in mind that modems as we have known them in the 1980s and 1990s are nearly obsolete as higher-bandwidth devices come to the fore. So, regardless of where this type of technology finds you at the time that you're reading this, such devices help to connect field personnel to their offices, help remote sites to transfer daily or weekly data into central offices, help retail businesses to perform electronic banking, credit authorization, and check verification, and help private contractors to exchange information with their client organizations. Determine the number of modems, the data transmission rate, and the phone number associated with each. You may also want to keep track of the standards compatibility, such as V.34 or V.42, if you receive frequent inquiries about whether a new user will be able to use your modems effectively. At the minimum, know these details about at least one modem—the one that you will use to allow hardware and software vendors to dial in and check your system, if you have such an agreement. Not knowing the phone number associated with a modem port and constantly having to reset modems top the list of system administrator modem troubles. To minimize annoying internal support calls, label your physical phone ports with the phone numbers. Also, keep a modem `readme` file in the devices directory or some other common location that associates modem port devices with modem types, locations, and phone numbers.

■ **CD-ROM drives**   At the time of this writing, most major software companies, including Sybase, use compact disks as the distribution medium for products and documentation. Workstations also come with CD-ROM drives as standard equipment. Until electronic distribution becomes the norm, know enough about your systems' CD-ROM capabilities to be able to install new software and to take advantage of CD-ROM-based knowledge bases. Keep track of CD-ROM drive speeds and manufacturers, since differences between these cause most compatibility problems. Differences in drive speed, usually designated as *double, triple,* or *quadruple,* do not always cause problems, but in some cases they can. If you're having persistent read problems, find out the speed and make tested by the producer of the CD-ROM. Besides speed, support of various protocols, such as ISO 9660 and High Sierra, is also important. The good news is that, for much CD-ROM based data, you can copy the data from the CD-ROM to a hard disk location so that it's necessary to have only one machine with a particular type of CD-ROM drive connected to the network in order for all users of that network to have access to the data.

■ **Backup devices**   Backup devices include a variety of tape formats, such as 1/4 inch, 8 millimeter, 4 millimeter, 9-track tape (nearly obsolete for many years, but popular because of its reliability and ubiquity). Floppy drives can also be considered backup devices, as can WORM (Write Once, Read Many times) drives. These devices, although considered peripherals, are essential for keeping backup copies of your data, both from SQL Server databases and on your file systems. You will also use them to restore data at some point in your career. Without doubt, know the location, format, speed, and capacity of each type of backup device. It is best to have more than one backup drive so that, if one fails, you will still be able to back up and recover from the other. SQL Server communicates with the backup drive directly and via the `console` (version 4.9.2 and earlier) utility or by using Backup Server (System 10 and later). Not all backup devices are compatible with SQL Server, so before relying on one to restore a backup, be sure to test it.

■ **Other peripherals**   Inventory any other specialized peripherals that you may have for data input or output, such as fax cards, bar code readers, scanners, and OCRs. Typically, a specialized interface program delivers the output from these devices to an intermediate format, which later processes them for storage in SQL Server or other data repositories. These devices rarely have a direct impact on how SQL Server performs. On the other hand, if they generate a lot of input data for SQL Server, they may become critical. For example, learning that a new store plans to install 10 additional bar code scanners may signal you that you will need to be prepared to transmit and save that much more into your databases. Data-generating devices may also stimulate a need for different types of reports or a specialized archival procedure.

COMPUTER SOFTWARE

After cataloging your hardware, make an inventory of the software that relies on it. Knowing which software users expect you to support pays off especially well. For example, if you find that a particular application generates more support calls than another, consider investing in more documentation for it or replacing it with a more user-friendly application.

Inventory any of the following software that you might consider in your baseline analysis or in a proposal:

- Operating systems
- Groupware (e.g., HTTP servers)
- Word processors
- Spreadsheets
- Database servers
- Database clients (tools)
- Middleware
- Accounting programs
- CAD programs
- Compilers
- Utilities
- APIs (libraries)
- Specialized device drivers
- Systems maintenance software

For the technical inventory, find out the important ways in which software interacts with the rest of the system. For example, if you take responsibility for an existing machine and SQL Server, find out everything you can about the processes running on the machine, and know what each one does. Include all demons, batch jobs, background processes, DLLs, and/or NLMs. Make sure that everything that is using resources that SQL Server could otherwise use is justified in doing so. Make sure that none of the processing running will compromise SQL Server performance, integrity, or security to a critical extent.

The following list outlines the more common applications that share environments with Sybase software.

■ **Database software** Database systems tend to compete with each other for disk space, CPU, and memory. Know all the types of database software licensed for use in your organization, such as Sybase SQL Server, Oracle, DB2, and RDB. Also include all database systems that are being used on PCs, such as Watcom, Microsoft Access, or Microsoft SQL Server. Optimally, your list will indicate which database servers are run on which server machines in your organization, the primary purpose of each database server, the approximate number of users, the disk space requirements, and the memory requirements. If your organization has developed any data servers and data stores in house, such as those written using the Open Server API, document them as well. Where different RDBMSs share resources, document their requirements in a central location. Also document their function and critical differences, since one day someone will wonder why everything can't be standardized under one application.

■ **Middleware and gateways** The term *middleware* is a term that has gained popularity recently to describe software that sits between the client and the server software. Gateway programs allow you to share data between database systems, frequently on different platforms, or between a database system and some other application that processes database records directly. These programs are also referred to as middleware. On your list of such programs, include the hardware, software, and network dependencies. Whenever the version of one of these components changes, the middleware may also need changing. Make documenting these a priority, since these types of programs are often invisible to the Systems Manager until they're broken.

■ **Compilers and interpreters** People commonly think of compilers and interpreters as programming languages, but a compiler is really a program that allows you to create new programs by transforming source code in a particular language to an executable form. C, C++, FORTRAN, COBOL, and Pascal are all compilers. Some Lisp and BASIC implementations are interpreters. Implementations of languages differ between versions and vendors. Many compilers come with development environments that further distinguish different vendors' offerings. Documenting the locations of all the compilers and interpreters available on your system will help new developers to become productive. If you plan to develop Open Client, Open Server, or Embedded SQL programs, you will probably use a C or Ada compiler. These APIs are certified and supported for use with certain versions of compilers, although they may work on others as well.

■ **Database clients (tools)**   Applications classified as database tools allow you to manipulate data before inputting it to a database or after outputting it. Many tools, such as PowerBuilder, SQR, and Visual Basic, provide you with simple interfaces that quickly enable you to write data entry programs or to generate specialized reports. Include in your software inventory all such tools and their purpose. In many computer environments, several available tools provide overlapping or duplicate functionality. Duplicate tools usually cost less than retraining a developer only familiar with a particular tool. Sometimes vendors bundle tools free with other programs. Also, developers find many tools, such as Sybperl, on the Internet. Finally, some tools may be developed in house for specialized purposes. The cost of supporting tools usually outweighs the cost of acquiring them. If responsibility for all tool-related inquiries rests with you, you may want to estimate the support, training, and documentation requirements of each so that you can attempt to influence your budget when the time comes. Tools typically need upgrading when the data format or database version changes. Operating system upgrades or networking changes may also necessitate tool upgrades. Try to list the approximate number of users of each tool as well.

■ **Utilities**   Utilities and tools share many of the same qualities. Typically, however, an application provides a specific data processing function, while a utility provides more general-purpose services. Systems Managers use utilities widely for scripting, conversion between data formats, viewing and changing graphics, file transfer, and data compression. Often such utilities can be obtained for free by downloading them from the Internet or another public network. Because they are ubiquitous and easily obtained, keeping an accurate inventory of each is rarely possible. Instead, consider keeping a list of the following details for the 10 most popular utilities: purpose, type of input accepted and output generated, where they can be found on the system, where the documentation is, and which version of each is available. Attempting to regulate the use and storage of these utilities in a large organization with a lot of programmers is futile and counterproductive. Most allow someone to do something more quickly than otherwise possible. Instead, consider providing consulting about selected utilities, and leave users to support themselves if they decide to use alternative solutions.

■ **APIs or libraries**   Vendors sell object or source code libraries, often called APIs, that consist of prepackaged functions that developers can plug into their applications. For example, the Sybase Open Client and CT-LIB libraries provide object code for functions typically used when writing routines to access and store data in a SQL Server. Using code libraries leverages productivity by freeing developers from writing and debugging commonly needed code. To make the most of your libraries, be sure to document for each the associated languages: functionality, versions, code library location, and documentation location. Make this information centrally available to your programmers and keep it up to date. If the libraries consist of source code, use a source code control system to manage modifications.

NETWORK AND TELECOMMUNICATIONS

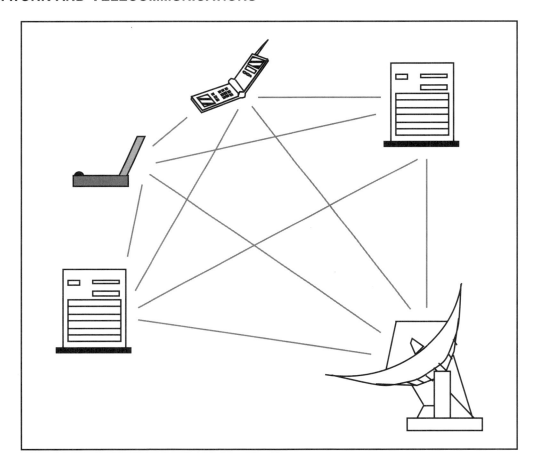

Figure 14.2 Client/server computing requires a network, but the network doesn't necessarily require wires.

With global networking becoming ever more important to organizations in the twenty-first century, you may want to consider upgrading your communications lines or your internal wiring from twisted pair to optical fiber. Increased communications or data transfer speeds directly improve distributed transaction rates and worker productivity. If you anticipate increased loads on the corporate WAN due to business changes, consider the cost of upgrading the bandwidth of your current network access.

A telecommunications cost analysis should include items such as the following:

- Network equipment (repeaters, routers, bridges, gateways)
- Network security devices
- Terminal servers
- Network software
- Computer-related telephone equipment
- Installation of phone lines for modems
- Installation of wiring for networks
- Leased line charges for WANs
- Global network access charges
- Telephone charges
- Hardware maintenance
- Systems maintenance

Most Systems Managers could attest that a computer network does the most to enhance the productivity of all employees except the Systems Managers. The multitude of connections and possible paths through a network make it difficult to maintain and troubleshoot. Yet the network must function and must function well at all times. A slow network can turn all the fast CPUs, fast disk drives, and expansive RAM into wasted investments.

To help you analyze the shape of your system—where it undergoes most stress and where it is underutilized—identify the distribution of computing by servers and clients. Knowing which servers receive and transmit the most client activity will automatically give you an understanding of which part of the network you must pay the most attention to. An underutilized network may indicate training needs or possible resources that you could redeploy elsewhere.

Networks can be grouped into three types depending on their reach:

- **Local area networks (LANs) and subnetworks (subnets)**   A LAN or subnet typically connects a subset of the machines on a network. LANs or subnets are connected to each other by way of gateways, bridges, and routers.

- **Wide area networks (WANs)**   A WAN spans two or more sites. It relies on a combination of wires, satellites, and other long- and short-distance transmission technologies to carry signals between buildings and across state and provincial borders. Usually, a WAN uses private high-speed data lines leased from a telecommunications company.

- **Global public networks**   In this book, we use the term global public networks to refer to networks such as the Internet that service millions of people and organizations around the world. These networks function not to facilitate a single business or organization, but to facilitate a public community of computer users. At the moment, everyone seems to be converging on the Internet and abandoning the smaller, previously separate networks like AOL and Fidonet. However, in the event that a traffic jam on the Internet spawns the reemergence of separate nets in the next few years, we shall refer to this type of network generically as a global network.

Sybase software can play a role in each type of network. Usually those who manage SQL Servers don't also have to manage the network, so the information you maintain about the network can be brief. However, just so that you know who to call and what to say when there's trouble, do find out this critical information:

- The names and types of LANs, WANs, and global networks that you have access to

- The network topology (at least a big picture view)

- The names and versions of network protocols used

- Which machines are network server machines

- Which applications are served from the which machines

- The names, network addresses, and administrators of critical machines that support the networking. These include the server that supports your DNS or NIS databases, your firewall, your mail server, and network administration servers that contain other information system databases.

610

- The names, phone numbers, and email addresses of the people responsible for your routers and gateways, since when these go down, everyone feels the pain

- The telecommunications services used by your department and the associated expenses

It is especially important to know about all global networks that your organization has connections to. There are three crucial reasons for this. First, you need to know whether your customers can send information to you electronically and whether your employees can send information to them. If so, it is wise to document what company information can and cannot be shared and the procedures for how this is to be handled and by whom. Corporations are finding great cost savings by providing customer interaction mediated by electronic networks, rather than by paper and phones. You will probably be asked to provide such services in the next few years if you haven't already.

Next, you need to know if you have access to the wealth of technical information and programs available. This type of access can mean the difference between being down for a day and being down for a week. Many computer companies, including Sybase, use public network forums to provide technical support information for their products.

Finally, connection to a public network brings with it an element of risk. If you are connected to the Internet, it can be possible for people to gain unauthorized access to your system. This is due to the lack of robustness in network and operating system software. Even with a room full of security experts working around the clock, your system can still be insecure. The most secure system is one that is not connected to a network at all. However, most large companies appear to have decided that the benefits of Internet service outweigh the possible risk of a break-in.[1]

---

[1] I am an ardent supporter of the Internet, yet remain skeptical that corporations have really assessed and responded to the risks appropriately. I think most just hope nothing bad will happen. At some point as the Internet expands, some bad incidents will happen, and corporations will take this risk more seriously. Try not to be the example for everyone.

PEOPLE

To complete your picture of your system, you must know your people-related costs. Also, you need to know who your users are, who is responsible for keeping your system running well, and who is responsible for paying for upgrades and additions.

When analyzing proposals, remember that any system change affects the work of people. People can cause a project to fail if they refuse to adopt the new system, or they can make it exceed expectations by finding new uses for the technology. Rather than using a list, the next few sections describe the less obvious costs and benefits that surface in relation to how people interact with computer systems, especially when these systems are changed.

Productivity Loss and Gain

Employees complain of productivity loss due to system inefficiencies. If, for example, data entry clerks must run reports manually because no batch job has been written to automate the process, their time to run the report can be charged against the system as a productivity cost.

Similarly, people encounter productivity losses due to system administration and support backlogs. If critical tasks become delayed because they are waiting for the services of systems personnel, you can consider the wait time a productivity loss.

By reviewing the productivity losses that people encounter with the existing system, you may be able to project corresponding productivity increases that you can include as expected benefits in proposals to change the system. Such estimates belong in the "intangibles" section of an analysis, since implementation quality and user acceptance factors influence actual productivity gains.

Cost of Managing People during System Changes

The people-related aspects of a project deserve as much attention as the technical aspects. If users receive the following prepa-

612

ration for a system change, the project has a high chance of efficient implementation and ultimate success at meeting its goals. Users should

- Help to define requirements and request features
- Understand when the change will occur
- Know what changes to expect
- Receive good training in advance
- Receive good documentation

Plan for the costs of providing such support. Projects missing such preparation have a higher risk of failure. Users may decide to stick to old, manual systems, only take advantage of a small percentage of the new functionality, or reject the system by not using it or leaving the organization or department. If they don't understand how to use the new system, they may introduce data entry errors or waste time using inefficient methods. The costs of overcoming such problems after the fact are much higher than planning to meet user needs ahead of time.

To facilitate the change, you might also include miscellaneous expenses for maintaining good morale in your budget. You could plan transition parties, T-shirts, or even a day off during system installation. While the project is in development, you may also need to pay your staff overtime and buy them lunch or dinner for agreeing to work late nights and weekends. During implementation, you can arrange informal gatherings for users in which you make experts available to handle questions and answers about the system. You can provide food and beverage and plan it during lunch to provide incentive to attend. Include such costs in any proposal to change a widely used information system.

Cost of Organizational Changes

A major change, such as a move from mainframe computing to network-based computing, often necessitates an organizational change. The organization may need to redeploy employees of the information systems department as computing power is being shifted. Eliminating data entry work will also mean finding new jobs for people.

Any cost/benefit analysis in a proposal should include the possibilities and costs of making such changes. Check with the organization's personnel and legal departments to determine the company's traditions, guidelines, and responsibilities in this area. If a job position changes because of a system change, plan on helping affected people to learn to do new jobs, or find them other jobs outside the company. If you give such displacement casual treatment, you or your company may earn a damaged reputation, bad press, or lawsuits, as well as losing peace of mind.

Calculate the job placement, retraining, and legal costs for the options that you decide on and include them in your analysis.

Consulting

For organizations that use external consultants for systems support, include the current average cost of consulting in a baseline analysis.

When bringing in consultants to help plan and implement new projects, establish your cost expectations clearly. Consulting needs tend to expand to fill any budget. Make preliminary estimates of the services required and the amount you are willing to pay for them. Chapter 12 discusses evaluating whether to use consultants when implementing projects.

Training

Think about the training requirements for having your users make full use of your system. Chapter 13 discusses the subject of creating a training plan as part of a project plan

Training costs include

■ Keeping the skills of the IT professionals up to date

■ Teaching new IT personnel how to maintain existing systems

■ Teaching IT personnel how to use and maintain new systems

- ■ Training users to use the existing system
- ■ Providing support and help-desk services
- ■ Acquiring manuals and tutorials
- ■ Training rooms
- ■ Training equipment
- ■ Hiring outside instructors

For transitions, you will need to meet two training objectives. First, expose users to the new features of the new system. Second, provide comparisons that show the new and the old ways to accomplish each critical system task. Finally, remember to plan for the costs of providing duplicate training sessions or computer- or video-based training so that new employees and employees who were on vacation, leave, or business trips during regular training sessions can make up for the missed opportunity. If you are part of an organization with many offices that a system change will affect, plan on how you will provide training to each location. On-site training will be more expensive but also more effective than video- or computer-based training.

Internal Support

When purchasing a new system, vendors often bundle support and licensing with the initial purchase. In some cases, only one or two people are authorized to call for support. Your needs may go far beyond this. Systems with many components need support for problems with interactions between components. Vendors typically resist resolving problems when they suspect that the fault lies in another vendor's product. In-house support people usually investigate and diagnose problems to isolate exactly which component has failed before calling the vendor help line. Keep track of the costs of such internal support.

Your analysis of support costs for proposed changes should include transition support and ongoing support. Compare ongoing support costs for both the existing system and proposed changes. Include transition support as part of the new system cost. When you introduce a new system, users will need support for performing their usual tasks in new ways and for handling unexpected gaps in training or in functionality. If the system offers significantly more power and flexibility, support costs might include providing consulting about the new technical opportunities open to users. Finally, even the best planned systems have bugs and problems. Support needs usually peak during system implementation and fall as support personnel learn the most frequent problems and solutions.

In-house Maintenance

If you maintain part or all of your system in house, account for these costs:

- **Salaries and overhead of systems personnel**   Include the salary paid to the employees, plus payroll taxes, insurance, office space, and other benefits.

- **Overtime**   Overtime salary costs may be required for personnel who must work nights and weekends to perform tasks that are better done during nonbusiness hours.

- **Downtime**   Usually calculated as loss of productivity of people who depend on the system. It may also include the loss of revenue if the computer system is directly related to sales. Include downtime for both routine systems maintenance and problems.

- **Travel**   If there are fewer systems people than there are sites in your organization with computers, it is likely the systems people will need to travel to set up new offices and sometimes to troubleshoot problems.

For proposals, remember that the maintenance needs of a new system are much higher during project development and implementation. Consultants, student interns, or other temporary help might be hired during the project to assist with systems management. Figure the cost of this possible addition to your staff.

Documentation

In addition to acquiring enough copies of software documentation for all users, you may also incur the cost of ordering supplementary documentation for ongoing needs. You may need additional reference documents for training and employee development and for an in-house library. To facilitate comparisons with older systems, CD-ROM documentation products should be included under documentation rather than software.

Having determined the costs associated with people, also document the functional aspects of their interaction with the information system. At minimum, include the following:

■ **Roles and responsibilities** In one document, outline the roles and responsibilities that people serve in your information systems organization. A second document should associate roles with people currently holding these positions. Don't link specific people to specific duties without an intervening "generic" list of responsibilities. This helps a business avoid becoming so dependent on one person that the absence of that person, by vacation, leave, or resignation, results in a significant loss of business productivity, revenue, or security. A second reason is to prevent people from feeling trapped in a specific role. Most people will tire of having responsibility for only one task and will want their job to include more authority or creativity as they progress in skill and experience. Clearly documented roles and career paths simplify hiring new people and distributing tasks. Clarifying who is responsible for which systems allows you to see any gaps or possible security imbalances. Finally, keeping job descriptions generic allows people to feel confident that they can go on vacation without everything falling apart. Along with roles and responsibilities, document the structure of the information systems organization. A chart or symbolic list should show how people are supervised, how they are assigned to projects or departments, and who they go to discuss personnel matters. If a system change under consideration will affect one or more subsystems, a manager should be able to look at this document and determine the other managers to consult about analyzing and preparing for the change.

■ **Career paths** A Systems Manager should interview—formally or informally—all direct reports and other key personnel to determine their career goals. This will yield several layers of insight. First, you will know who is most likely to be enthusiastic (or reluctant) about a proposed task in a particular area of interest. Second, you may learn who to groom as your successor, presuming that you want to advance past your current position at some point. Third, it will become clear what it will take to motivate your employees. Next, you can anticipate their training needs and possibly how soon you will need to replace them if they're not really interested in their current jobs. Finally, your employees will give you more loyalty, respect, and cooperation if you help them attain their goals.

617

■ **Users**   Consider an information systems department's users as its customers. Without them, you are out of business.[2] Treat users with respect and patience. A Systems Manager should know on a monthly basis how many users are depending on the system, the service level that they require, what they like most about the system, and where they think it needs the most improvement. Surveys can yield this valuable information. While budgets may or may not come directly from users, they influence each other, their bosses, and their friends, who may be in a position to allocate resources. While you can't hope to provide everything that your users want, you can publish documents about what services you do provide, what your budget constraints are, and what you would need to provide the most desired services. Given this information, your users will be able to help you to serve them, rather than resent you for your failure to do so. Beyond this broad information, try to document the configuration of user accounts, the number of users each major component of the current system can support, and the average cost of supporting each user. Ideally, maintain a list correlating workstations with users so that, if you see particularly high system usage coming from particular users and/or workstations, you can find out what they are doing and if there's a better way to do it. Likewise, if there are workstations that rarely access the system, you can determine by interview whether they don't need their workstation or whether they are unable or unwilling to use it for some reason.

■ **Financiers and managers**   Finally, you must know who paid for the existing system and who can be persuaded to pay for upgrades and expansions. These people influence the quality of systems management service that you can provide. If you develop your relationships with them such that you impress on them your concern for both empowering users and contributing to the bottom line, you will be able to get budget for the changes that you want to make. If the company suddenly starts losing money or making less than expected, the budget and expenses will be examined line by line. If your department has large expenses in proportion to the rest of the business, you will be asked to justify them. If your budget is proportionally larger than that for the rest of the organization, you may be asked to make greater sacrifices. To best prepare for hard times, be aware of where the expenses are in your system, what each budget item buys, and what the visible and invisible effects of cuts would be. Even if your company does lose money during your tenure, having this level of understanding

---

[2]As Ben von Ullrich says, the users are the heart and soul of the system. Often, when nothing else can motivate you to care about computers for one more minute, a desperate human voice on the phone can remind you of the joy of being able to help someone in need.

about the business of your department will mark you as someone who takes responsibility for the financial well-being of the company.

OPERATIONAL COSTS

Some costs that you encounter are associated more with the operation of the entire system than with a particular element. When creating your inventory or proposal, consider the costs in this section.

Supplies

While the cost of supplies may be negligible or beyond the scope of your authority, give it thought in case you use a particular supply heavily in your system. Also, some models of hardware use different supplies than others, radically affecting the cost. Examples from the recent past include the differences in fax paper and in plotter paper. If your machine required coated paper for most cases, your supply costs were higher than machines that could use regular bond paper.

Consider these supplies:

■ Computer paper

■ Plotter paper

■ Toner

■ Backup media

■ Floppy diskettes

■ Supplies for specialized equipment such as hand-held printers

Outside Service and Support

For some parts of the system, you will pay for service by entering into yearly service contracts. In exchange, you are free to call the service center during certain hours to fix problems and answer questions. In some cases you pay extra for emergencies that you must have handled outside of regular business hours. When calculating this kind of service charge, include both the cost of the service agreement and an estimated number of emergency calls that you might make.

For other parts of the system, you may opt to pay for service on an as-needed basis. Try to find a few years' worth of data for components with this type of service arrangement. During the first year or two of a piece of hardware, for example, you rarely need to call unless it's the first model ever produced, in which case you may be helping to work out design bugs. During years 3 and 4, you typically encounter more hardware errors, and thereafter you may find the on-site service calls doubling. If this cost is for a significant portion of your system, determine an average number of calls over the lifetime of the component, and look for a trend in the number of calls over time. Based on the machine's age, you may find it worthwhile to reconsider maintenance arrangements.

License Agreements

Vendors charge for software licenses on a one-time basis, on a periodic (monthly or yearly) basis, or on a usage basis. When evaluating proposals, be sure to inquire about the licensing arrangement. The difference between one-time licensing and usage licensing can affect your cash flow, the project payback period, and the break-even point in relation to the current system.

Power Usage

Electricity often hides in another budget than the information system department's, but should be considered when evaluating new systems. The power requirements of older, large computers usually dwarf that of newer, smaller replacements. The opposite is true for replacing old desktop computers with new ones. Include the cost of backup power supply equipment if necessary.

Air Conditioning

Older and larger systems often require dedicated air-conditioning not needed for more recent system configurations. For analysis purposes, operating costs for these systems should include the cost of the air conditioner, its maintenance, and the cost of the power consumed.

If you are moving away from centralized computing toward desktop computing, the air-conditioning requirements will change. You will not need to invest as much into maintaining a controlled environment for PCs and minicomputers since they can generally tolerate wider temperature and humidity extremes. However, PCs on everyone's desks will increase the amount of heat in everyone's office and work space, putting more of a load on the central HVAC system.

Resale, Trade-ins, and Charitable Donations

When replacing part of a system, you may be able to reduce costs by selling, trading in, or donating old equipment. Usually, a vendor will offer to take a trade-in if you are upgrading to another one of their products. Reselling pays off if the technology you are replacing is still in commercial demand. Some maintenance companies even pay for elements of broken equipment that they could use for replacement parts in another system. You may be able to get tax relief by donating unsalable technology to a school or another not-for-profit agency.

Departmental Cross Charges

In corporations, overhead-related departments, such as Human Resources, often charge other departments for their services based on a ratio, such as head count. In these organizations, IT departments typically make and receive such cross charges. Knowing these costs will be important if a new system is anticipated to result in reduced or increased charge from another department. Also, a reduction in your cost of operation may mean that you can reduce the amounts you charge or change the way that you allocate charges. An increase in the services that you provide may mean an increase in your cash flow from other departments.

Courier and Transportation Charges

Organizations with many offices or sites incur courier and transportation charges for computer equipment, tapes, bookkeeping materials, and other items that cannot be transmitted over a WAN. Since a change in business or a change in the information system can affect these costs, include them in your baseline analysis. Consider them also when evaluating proposals that include expansion of a LAN or WAN or a reduction or increase in the needs for replacing equipment at remote sites.

When proposing the replacement of large equipment, remember to arrange for the disposal of the old system. In some cases, you need to pay the transportation charges and, in others, the receiving party absorbs them.

Security

Depending on the security measures taken in your organization, you may incur system costs for security personnel, locks, safes, encryption devices, shredders, and isolating machines or data. Feature any similar expenses used for ensuring security of your data, equipment, and facilities in a special section of your cost analysis. The benefits of such investments tend to remain hidden until a crisis occurs. Tracking historical incidents can help you to assign risk factors to each possible security breach. You can then use this information to estimate appropriate levels of investment.

Other Overhead

Think of any other overhead that you might need to factor into your analysis. Examples of specialized overhead might be special service agreements, legal costs, or document management systems. These types of costs will depend on your organization and environment.

TRANSITION COSTS

In addition to the costs of new equipment, you must incorporate the cost of the change from old system components to new ones in an analysis of a proposal. The more accurately you plan and budget for the change, the greater your chances of a successful implementation. In this section, we will examine common change-over costs.

Running Parallel Systems

If you run the old and new systems parallel while verifying the stability of the new system, you will incur the costs of running both for the transition period. The easiest way to account for this cost is to determine the cost of running the old system for the planned period of time and add it to the cost of making the change.

If running both systems in parallel would generate excessively costly or inconvenient difficulties, plan on the alternative "light switch" approach. In this case, you "switch off" the old system and "switch on" the new one at the same time. This approach involves considerably higher risk, so you need a solid plan for rolling back to the old system if necessary. Prepare a contingency plan for handling serious problems found in the new system at change-over time. Then estimate the costs associated with the contingency plan. Also, evaluate the possible costs of initial downtime of the new system. Even if you plan your transition carefully, you still face the possibilities of a flaw in a brand-new disk drive or memory card. When risks and associated costs of failure are high, arrange for 24-hour support of key systems during the transition period and include those costs in your analysis.

Data Conversion, Transfer, and Archival

When system changes involve changes to data formats, you must perform one or more of three major data operations:

■ **Conversion**   Copy and convert all or part of the data from the old format to the new

■ **Transfer**   Transfer all or part of the data from the old system to the new

■ **Archival**   Archive all data transferred in the old and new formats

Backing up data in the new format allows you to avoid reconverting data if a failure occurs in the new system shortly after implementation.

Also, consider transferring and archiving historic data in the new format if it will become impossible to access it in the old format. Chapter 12 discusses data conversion and storage issues in more detail.

Facilities Changes

If you plan to change system hardware, think about whether you will need to rearrange office space to accommodate it. Mainframes and 9-track tape libraries require real estate that may be freed up if a new system is put in place. Departments incurring cross charges based on facilities usage may count this result among the benefits of the project.

When a proposal calls for putting more CPU power on every person's desk, have an electrician prepare an estimate for rewiring work spaces to allow more outlets with higher ratings. Also, desktop systems often cause requirements for space on or around each person's desk to increase.

In your analysis, include any changes in the number of dedicated workspaces for systems personnel and temporary space requirements for consultants and training.

If you anticipate major changes, consult with the people in your organization responsible for office space. After management accepts the proposal, you won't want to surprise the facilities department with radical changes in their work. Also, they make complex inventories and cost analyses of their own and will use their expertise to make much more realistic projections than you could. They will also know about special lease arrangements or legal issues that could affect your ability to carry out your plans in the expected time frame.

Taxes and Depreciation

Corporations pay business taxes on the value of their fixed assets. A computer is considered an asset rather than an expense. In recognition of the fact that an asset loses value over time, a mechanism called depreciation is used to calculate the loss in value of the asset for tax purposes. The depreciation amount is then charged as an expense. Calculation of depreciation varies depending on corporate factors and the type of the asset. Consult with your accountant or controller to see what tax implications might result from making major system changes. Sometimes they are quite significant.

Procedure Manual Suggestions

○ Format for Cost/Benefit Analysis

⇒ Create a standard format for the cost/benefit portion of system proposals that helps people to remember to consider all relevant considerations.

⇒ Document the costs and benefits of most concern to the organization so that proposals are sure to include estimates for these.

⇒ Make sure there are sections for

- Hard costs
- Soft costs
- Hard benefits
- Soft benefits
- Hardware
- Software
- Personnel expenses
- Transition expenses
- Security system expenses

○ Evaluating Proposals

→ Document any organizational expectations that have been set for equipment lifetime, payback period, and discount rate for money.

→ Set requirements that certain calculations must be made for a proposal to be reviewed.

→ Based on past experience, document the minimum ROI or IRR that must be met for a proposal to succeed.

→ Include a review procedure to make sure that at least one person besides the creator checks the calculations and the assumptions in the proposal.

○ Hardware and Software Acquisition and Support

→ Write a policy for tracking your technology investments.

→ Include a template for recording all the essential technical information needed to provide support and all the financial data needed to provide proper accounting.

→ In addition to physical specifications, include

- Default configurations

- Instructions for changing configurations (both technical and procedural)

- Instructions for monitoring performance

- Automatic batch (cron) jobs that run in association with the software or hardware

- Contact people responsible for support

→ Consider writing a policy for analyzing support needs and costs at least twice yearly to verify that the support strategy selected is working. Include the use of user satisfaction surveys as part of the policy if you need to discover primary areas of concern.

APPENDIX

A

Sybase Products
and Services
Overview

Sybase sells over 30 different products. While this book focuses on SQL Server, Systems Managers may have responsibility for or interest in other Sybase products. If you don't know what information system problems other products solve, this appendix will introduce you by way of an overview. Sybase has renamed some products and others have commonly known abbreviations. The alternative identifiers are given in parentheses in the product heading. At the time of this writing, several new Internet and WWW-related products are in development They are not described here. See the Sybase and Powersoft WWW sites for the most current descriptions of these products.

Sybase products described in this section fall into the categories of servers, tools, and middleware. Servers perform centralized computation and data manipulation, supporting many clients simultaneously. Servers usually require the expertise of an IT professional for maintenance and support. IT professionals may also provide consultation to developers. Tools generally enable the creation of client software, which centers around interaction with end users who we might not expect to have IT expertise. Middleware sits between clients and servers and provides more complex interactions than those provided by direct client/server connections. Middleware also requires management by a trained IT professional. When vendors propose new middleware, developers propose extensions, or people ask for help, a Systems Manager and a Network Manager usually need to get involved. In the final section, Services, we review the types of services Sybase supplies for helping customers to implement successful information systems.

■ SERVER AND SERVER ADMINISTRATION PRODUCTS

Sybase server and server administration products generally provide you with event-driven database services. Clients log into a server or request information from it. The server detects the request and returns the appropriate information using the Sybase Tabular Data Stream (TDS) protocol.

SECURE SQL SERVER

The National Computer Security Center's (NCSC's) Trusted Computer System Evaluation Criteria (TCSEC), also known as the Orange Book, defines security based on seven levels of trust in order, with D as the least trusted and A1, the most. Secure SQL Server is rated at the B1 level. SQL Server 10 is rated at C2. Sybase built Secure SQL Server on the System 10 foundation of code and then modified it to provide mandatory access control (MAC) features and comprehensive auditing capabilities. This means that the features of SQL Server 10 not related to security can be found in Secure SQL Server, and those related to security have been enhanced or changed to meet B1 criteria.

SQL Server, as well as most operating systems, provide security based on discretionary access control (DAC). This means that access is granted to an object at the discretion of those who already have access. As soon as one person gives someone else access, then two people have the power to grant access. In such a system, an organization can lose control of its sensitive information quickly. A trusted system at the B1 level or above must provide mandatory access control (MAC). This means that the Server associates each object (such as tables and procedures) and each subject (users) with a security label. The trusted system grants access to objects by comparing labels of objects and subjects. Users may not change their own access level nor change the labels associated with other subjects or objects.

A trusted system ranks information and people by an access hierarchy and by information categories. The hierarchy is

- Top secret
- Secret
- Confidential
- Unclassified

Each piece of information, such as a document or database table, has an associated hierarchy and is categorized based on a topic, such as *computer networks* or *military supplies.*

For each information category, a subject can have access up to a particular hierarchy level. For example, a subject might have top secret clearance for a computer category, but only have access to unclassified information about military supplies. Subjects may not read information above their clearance level in a category, nor may they write information at a level below their level in a category.

Secure SQL Server is designed to be run on a secure operating system and integrates with the operating system's label system.

AUDIT SERVER

The Sybase Audit Server, used in conjunction with the System 10 auditing features, provides enhanced access control to Servers in high-security environments. It is transparent to users and can be made inescapable, even for System Administrators. The Audit Server is designed to have minimal impact on system performance.

SQL ANYWHERE (WATCOM SQL SERVER)

Developed by Powersoft, the Watcom SQL Server is a 32-bit ANSI-standard RDBMS. It requires minimal hardware resources, so you can use it as a PC or laptop. SQL Anywhere provides installation, tuning, and administration features that don't require IT expertise. The Server includes transaction processing, referential integrity, stored procedures, triggers, and cascading updates and deletes. Users without IT experience could use a SQL Anywhere database as a test environment, as a data preprocessing environment, as a collection tool that later uploads data to a central RDBMS, or as a user's personal data processing environment. Some PowerBuilder kits include a copy of SQL Anywhere.

OPEN SERVER (SERVER LIB)

Open Server is an API that organizations can use to integrate almost any data source, with a server application and/or a client application. You can write a program with the Open Server library that acts like a SQL Server, but provides processing not available in SQL Server, such as access to flat files. You can also write a middleware application with Open Server that sits between a client and a server, providing processing, such as string manipulation, before storing data in the server. The most common application of Open Server is to facilitate communication between different database products on heterogenous computers and networks. For example, you could write an Open Server application that reads a stock feed, consolidates the information, and then stores it in a SQL Server for later analysis.

The Open Server API provides the following built-in functionality:

- Supports multiple client or Server connections
- Supports multiple logical connections on a single network connection to increase network efficiency
- Returns data a record at a time in the TDS format used by SQL Server
- Manages a task queue

■ Passes requests and parameters to foreign applications through a user handler

■ Collects and processes responses from user handlers

■ Converts returned data to a format compatible with client applications

Sybase provides sample Open Server code with the product, so you can compile the example and see how it works and how to extend its functionality.

SYBASE MPP (NAVIGATION SERVER)

Sybase MPP, formerly known as Navigation Server, provides an extension of SQL Server functionality by using parallel processing to work with terabytes of data on tens or hundreds of CPUs. It can support thousands of transactions per second and thousands of users. Organizations that need mainframe-level processing power, but don't want to support or pay for mainframes, may want to investigate Sybase MPP.

Sybase MPP provides all the usual RDBMS services, including queries, data modification, and data maintenance. Navigation Server uses standard SQL and Sybase Open Client and Open Server interfaces, so it can communicate with other Sybase products or with other RDBMSs by using Sybase middleware. The Sybase MPP Server is composed of several SQL Servers, each running on its own CPU. To other applications, Sybase MPP looks like a single server. The MPP Server translates the SQL input by the user into parallel SQL. Both read and write operations are parallelized.

To use terms commonly used for parallel systems, Sybase MPP has a message-based, shared-nothing architecture. This means that each component operates independently of the others, which minimizes contention and allows good scalability. Sybase MPP meets the parallel processing goals of providing scale up and speed up. Scale up means that as you increase database size you can increase the number of transactions correspondingly and maintain the same throughput. Speed up means that as you increase the number of CPUs that the system can use you can reduce the response time for handling queries.

The MPP Server partitions tables horizontally, such that the first N records are managed by one CPU and SQL Server, the next N by another CPU and Server, and so on. You can control how data are partitioned. You can partition based on a range of values, such as the alphabetical value of a column in a table. You can also partition using a hash function that keys values numerically. Finally, you can assign particular tables to certain partitions.

SQL Server Monitor

SQL Server Monitor allows Systems Managers to observe run-time characteristics of Sybase SQL Servers. SQL Server maintains several run-time counters that SQL Server Monitor reports on. These counters provide information designed to be useful for performance evaluation and tuning, charge-back accounting and capacity planning. SQL Server Monitor displays information from counters so that you can isolate problems more quickly and determine which types of SQL Server configuration and tuning will result in the best performance.

SQL Server Manager (SA Companion)

SQL Server Manager provides a graphical user interface on a PC platform (such as Microsoft Windows) for administering local or remote SQL Servers. SQL Server Manager gives you a simple way to add and drop logins and users, reconfigure the server, and perform backups. It also provides a very useful facility for saving an entire database schema and generating the DDL commands necessary to re-create it. For those new to SQL Server, SQL Server manager can be a useful way to manage data before all the ins and outs of Transact-SQL administration commands and procedures have been mastered.

Enterprise SQL Server Manager (ESSM)

Enterprise SQL Server Manager works like SQL Server Manager, but it gives you control over several systems simultaneously. Consider using ESSM for managing systems with more than a hundred users. Based on the Tivoli Management Framework, on its way to becoming an X/Open standard, ESSM supports the Simple Network Management Protocol (SNMP). You can integrate ESSM with third-party tools for managing other system components using SNMP APIs. ESSM has an object-oriented architecture and a GUI interface. It runs in Microsoft Windows and Motif environments.

With ESSM, you can administer many SQL Servers in a single operation, such as adding a login to 10 servers at once. You can do any Server management functions with ESSM, such as setting up databases, devices, users, tables, and stored procedures.

An administration policy feature allows you to set and enforce database policies and procedures. For example, you can set a password expiration interval as a default so that it is normally enforced for all systems managed with ESSM. You can also create configuration change profiles that automatically propagate SQL Server changes throughout an organization. A scheduling service gives you a way to get automatic notification or trigger automatic action at certain times of day, at certain time intervals, or based on certain events. You can use a built-in scripting facility to record and save a series of GUI actions as a script. You can then edit the scripts, play them, or schedule them for later execution.

ESSM also provides monitors for observing run-time server status, such as the amount of space per segment and the number of active connections. Performance tuning monitors display CPU usage, cache hits, network I/O, and locks.

SYBASE IQ (IQ ACCELERATOR, IQA)

The Sybase IQ product is an optional extension to SQL Server that provides special indexing for enhancing queries in large databases. Sybase IQ uses bitwise indexing technology that improves performance for ad hoc queries and reporting in decision support (DSS) environments. For a complex query workload, a Sybase SQL Server with Sybase IQ can be over 500 times faster than SQL Server alone and over 200 times faster than DB2 on a mainframe.

In bitwise indexes, data values are represented as bits in the index. For example, a 1 would indicate a true value for a specific field. During a query, a process only accesses the indexes on the fields needed. It never goes to the tables for information. bitwise indexing allows indexing of all data and datatypes and eliminates table scans. The indexes are more compact and are faster to build than regular SQL Server indexes. Sybase IQ works well for large read-only databases or databases updated only infrequently, such as by a nightly, weekly, or monthly refresh.

■ TOOLS

Tools allow you to provide alternative database interfaces to users, suited for a particular purpose. For example, PowerBuilder helps a developer to build and deploy a database application quickly. SQR helps IT professionals to develop complex reports based on centralized databases, which administrators can subsequently run as needed.

POWERBUILDER

PowerBuilder is an object-oriented tool for developing database applications. It includes a development environment with an extensible object-oriented language, a built-in help system, and a debugger. You can use PowerBuilder to build Microsoft Windows applications supporting DDE, OLE 2.0, and configurable tool bars. Applications are considered to be objects and are stored in PowerBuilder Library files. These library files allow users to share reports and forms. Supplied object templates such as window objects and menu objects help new users to create projects quickly. Using various PowerBuilder Painters, you can create common application functionality.

INFOMAKER

InfoMaker is the reporting tool provided with some of the PowerBuilder product kits. InfoMaker lets users create their own reports without first having to master SQL. InfoMaker allows users to define SQL Statements to extract particular information from a database and then graphically arrange the presentation of that information.

PowerBuilder and InfoMaker objects can be stored in executable files or as true OLE 2.0 objects for Microsoft Windows.

SQR WORKBENCH

SQR Workbench is a report-writing tool for multi-RDBMS environments with a heterogeneous network of server machines and workstations. It includes a procedural language that you can use to report data from one or more databases. SQR supports procedures and a parameter-passing mechanism so that you can create modular applications and share common modules among reports. SQR also has built-in support for multidimensional arrays, providing the type of access that users have traditionally relied on cursors to provide. In-memory table lookups from these arrays can improve search performance. SQR can also be used for nonreport functions, such as database updates, table creation and deletion, interactive ad hoc query functions, and batch programming.

The SQR language can access Sybase, DB2, ORACLE, Rdb, INGRES, and INFORMIX databases. Users can utilize native RDBMS features, and integrate SQR reports with other applications using the SQR API. A run-time version of SQR allows developers to precompile reports, which can be executed as a single command by end users.

SQL DEBUG

SQL Debug offers a transparent debugging environment so that you can intercept and debug Transact-SQL code from any Open Client connection to a SQL Server even if you don't have access to the client source code. With SQL Debug, the client connects to the Debug Server, rather than directly to the SQL Server. SQL Debug captures the SQL code that the client sends to the server, passes the client requests to the SQL Server, and returns the results to the client application. SQL Debug is based on the Open Server API. During database development, you can use SQL Debug instead of adding print statements and other debugging constructs to the source code to determine the cause of unexpected behavior. SQL Debug runs in the X11 and Motif environments and includes the usual debugging features, such as step-level execution, conditional traces, breakpoints, and variable examination and control. It has a point and click interface that includes display windows for code, status, debug commands, and results. A button panel provides frequently used commands. You can also add or redefine buttons, menu items, and function keys to customize the interface.

SYBOOKS

SyBooks is Sybase's interactive software-based documentation, which allows users to access the documentation online and search it using keywords and Boolean operators. The tool displays documents in two windows. One window contains the table of contents, and the other window contains the content pages of the document. By clicking on a table of contents entry in one window, you can immediately go to the section in the content window. SyBooks is delivered on CD-ROM and over the Internet (by the time this book is published).

SYBASE KNOWLEDGE INTERACTIVE LEARNING SYSTEM (SKILS)

The SKILS product provides users with interactive multimedia training for Sybase products. It incorporates animation, audio, and imaging. Currently, it is delivered on CD-ROM, but it may be distributed over the Internet in the future. The SKILS software allows users to learn Transact-SQL and basic System Administration without going to off-site training.

ANSWERBASE

AnswerBase is a knowledge base containing thousands of technical documents. While the interface is not as good as that for SyBooks, AnswerBase contains almost all Sybase documents, including Release Bulletins and Tech Notes for almost all supported versions of the software. The CD-ROM is updated quarterly and is full-text searchable. For example, you might someday receive a *kiconfig*[1] error and you might not know where to find it described in the hundreds of Sybase documents, whitepapers, and newsletters in your office. You can enter that term in AnswerBase's full-text search window and immediately see all document titles that refer to it, click on a likely match, and see the term highlighted on the associated page. Documents are displayed in WYSIWYG format, so the electronic copies look just like the hardcopy versions.

■ MIDDLEWARE

Middleware is any of a variety of software products that operate between client applications and back-end services. Enterprise CONNECT is the Sybase family of interoperability products. This includes Open Client, Open Server, Embedded SQL, Net-Library, XA-Library, all the mainframe gateway products, and all the OmniSQL gateways.

Many third-party gateway and data access products also operate as middleware. They provide an interface that clients can use to request data operations in a common format, and they interface with the data sources to satisfy these requests. One common feature of middleware is that it provides a barrier between applications and Servers. The Server can be moved, reconfigured, or replaced without requiring changes in the client applications.

REPLICATION SERVER

Replication Server allows you to maintain synchronized copies of distributed data at multiple sites. Replication Server makes copies of a primary database's transaction log, sends it to other databases, and triggers the other databases to replay the log to synchronize their copy of the data with the primary copy. With replication, you can audit updates, reduce data for reporting pur-

---

[1] A kiconfig error usually means that your SQL Server failed to open your master device.

poses, and create specialized servers for complex, user-generated, ad hoc queries. Replication Server is transaction based, so integrity is enforced across systems. A store and forward capability guards data against the consequences of network failure. Using a subscriptions feature, a replicated copy of a table may contain a subset of the rows in a table.

Resources or targets for replicated data do not need to be SQL Server RDBMSs. The Replication Server interface allows non-Sybase data servers to be included in a replicated system. A data source need not be a database. Applications can convert data feeds, real-time information, or application input into a format that can be replicated and given to users through their usual client connections to SQL Server systems.

REPLICATION SERVER MANAGER

Replication Server Manager is a systems management tool that allows you to configure, monitor, and manage Replication Server operation on all the servers involved.

OPEN CLIENT (DB-LIB AND CT-LIB)

Sybase's Open Client consists of several libraries of routines, programming services, and run-time services used to develop client applications. Open Client and Open Server are the foundation libraries on which the Sybase open architecture is built. Almost every Sybase product uses Open Client or Open Server API. Open Client allows custom programs, Sybase tools, and non-Sybase products to communicate with SQL Server, with OmniSQL Gateway, or with applications using Open Server. Open Client can request data or services over a network and provide other run-time functions, such as establishing connections and sending and receiving data.

You can use Open Client to port applications across platforms without rewriting any of the database access functions. You can also use the Open Client API to send commands in any SQL dialect to non-Sybase RDBMSs.

EMBEDDED SQL (ESQL)

Embedded SQL precompilers provide a preprocessing mechanism so that you can embed SQL Statements directly into programs written in the ANSI/ISO-standard C and COBOL programming languages. ESQL allows you to use Transact-SQL extensions to standard SQL, including stored procedures. After you have written C or COBOL source code that includes SQL statements, you use the Embedded SQL precompiler to process the application and generate a version of the program that the host language compiler can understand.

Embedded SQL statements can contain the following types of identifiers:

- Names of SQL Server objects, such as database, table, and column names

- Transact-SQL variable names and aliases

- Embedded SQL names for cursors, dynamic SQL statements, and dynamic descriptors and connections

- Host variable identifiers such as variable names, statement labels, and routine names

Embedded SQL, SQL Server, and Transact-SQL identifiers must conform to the rules for SQL Server identifiers. For host language identifiers, Embedded SQL respects the naming conventions of the host language.

ADA WORKBENCH

Ada Workbench provides a development environment and subroutine libraries for generating Ada language applications that access SQL Server data for the Motif or Microsoft Windows environments. You can port applications to different GUIs, platforms, and operating environments. The Sybase Open Client 10 in Ada Workbench extends multithreading to client applications so that you can take advantage of Ada's tasking capabilities.

NET-LIBRARIES

The Net-Library products provide modules that allow clients and servers to connect via widely used networking protocols. By specifying a particular Net-Library at run time, users can choose network protocols as needed. Net-Library supports TCP/IP, DECnet, and SPX/IPX, so you can provide connectivity to client workstations with the most common network software and adapter cards.

XA-LIBRARY

XA-Library implements the X/Open XA standard interface between transaction processing monitors and Sybase Servers. In conjunction with Open Client, XA-Library allows transaction monitors such as CICS/6000, Encina, Tuxedo, and Top End to coordinate transactions that span multiple RDBMSs, nonrelational data sources, system resources, and printers. You can also use XA-Library to provide two-phase commit transactions among heterogeneous data sources.

INFORMATIONCONNECT GATEWAYS

The InformationCONNECT product set is a series of gateways that provides read/write access to heterogeneous relational and nonrelational data sources. External data sources include host data files or tables in database systems.

Using these products, you can transfer the contents of one table into a new one on another supported remote Server using a SELECT INTO statement. You can also use any tool that works with any of the database systems as a way to access all the other database systems as well. If for example, you have a home-grown application that only works for input with a proprietary database system, you can use a Sybase-compatible tool for reporting those data. You can also access nonstandard capabilities of a remote server by using the pass-through mode. Mainframe APIs supply linkage with data behind IBM's mainframe transaction monitors (CICS and IMS).

InformationCONNECT modules include

- AS/400
- DB2
- DEC/RMS
- Informix
- Ingres
- ISAM
- Microsoft SQL Server
- Oracle
- Rdb
- Teradata
- DB2/CICS
- DB2/DRDA
- DB2/IMS
- SQL/DS (VM)
- SQL/DS (VSE)

Using InfoHub (described later), InformationCONNECT products can also access

- ADABAS/CICS
- VSAM/CICS
- IDMS/CICS
- IDMS/DB/CICS

NET-GATEWAY

Net-Gateway is an intermediate networking product that allows customers to connect their LAN-based Sybase clients and servers to IBM SNA LU6.2 networks. The Net-Gateway makes the IBM mainframe look like another server within the system. A protocol converter allows system administrators to control network clients' access to the mainframe to prevent unauthorized access. If you use the Open Server for CICS product, Net-Gateway can connect a LAN and SNA.

OPEN SERVER FOR *CICS* AND OPEN SERVER FOR *IMS/TM*

The Open Servers for CICS and IMS/TM allow users to run applications on workstations, PCs, and Macintoshes to get high-performance read/write access to data that reside on the mainframe. Users on IBM 3270 terminals and users of CICS applications can request data and services from Sybase's SQL Server or any other data source through the Open Server. You can use these Open Server products to connect with open gateway for DB2 so that data can be transported between DB2 and Sybase servers. Open Server for CICS includes developer programming libraries necessary to developing applications that access all MVS data, applications, and services and to provide the data to any Open Client system on the network.

INFOPUMP

InfoPump is a LAN-based server process integrated with InformationCONNECT gateways that allows data copies to be scheduled, transformed, and moved between mainframe data sources and networked DBMSs. Administrators can use InfoPump to access data on multiple sources and move them to multiple targets with one request. Bulk transfers can be executed on a periodic basis or at a specified time. During the transfer, InfoPump manipulates, translates, and cleans the data to move them into the server on the LAN. Heterogeneous data from tables can be consolidated into a single table.

InfoPump natively accesses the Sybase SQL Server and Lotus Notes databases. When used in conjunction with an Information-CONNECT Gateway, InfoPump can access a variety of LAN, midrange, and mainframe databases, including ORACLE, AS/400, and DB2. InfoPump also works with InfoHub (described next), allowing direct SQL access to nonrelational host data.

INFOHUB

InfoHub provides turnkey access to most major nonrelational data sources on the mainframe. It works with InformationCON-

NECT gateways to provide a database interface for VSAM, IMS, IDBMS, Adabase, sequential files, or DB2 data so that Open Client applications can access these sources.

■ SERVICES

Sybase provides financial, consulting, and educational services, technical support services, information services, a testing program for certifying Sybase professionals, and a program for Sybase business partners. In general, Sybase consulting and training services are recommended when your in-house experts don't have time to start another project without dropping an existing mission-critical project.

SYBASE FINANCIAL SERVICES, INC. (SFSI)

A wholly owned Sybase subsidiary, SFSI provides customers with numerous financing and leasing options for optimizing the return on their investment in Sybase software. SFSI can set up custom payment plans, capital and operating leases, and lease-versus-buy comparisons. SFSI can help you to analyze your return on investment and your purchase alternatives so that you can get the best cash flow and financial reporting possible and minimize tax consequences.

ENTERPRISE SERVICES

Enterprises Services consists of business process consulting services, Sybase systems development services, and training. The Sybase Enterprise Services division employs over 1000 professional consultants. All these consultants have database experience and use a common Sybase methodology for their work.

The Sybase Business Consulting Group within Enterprise Services provides business process reengineering. The group has a track record of successfully reengineering multinational organizations. The consultants that make up the group all have expertise as senior managers. They use an enterprise modeling method called the Enterprise Work Architecture. It presents a clear picture of business interactions with customers, partners, and suppliers and delivers a complete specification of the requirements for implementing a business strategy. The specification includes skills, processes, roles, activities, and systems, and it helps to design consistent processes throughout an organization.

The Professional Services group in Enterprise Services has developed and uses two methodologies for helping customers to achieve results. The first is the Sybase Architecture Framework for the Enterprise (SAFE). The application of SAFE creates a blueprint of an enterprise, including roles, activities, skills, and information needs. This approach includes data architecture, application architecture, technology architecture, and support architecture. The Sybase Development Framework (SDF) complements the SAFE architecture, providing an iterative design approach, rather than using the "waterfall" model. The four basic elements of application development are identifying needs, designing functional components, constructing the components, and evaluating the results.

The training organization of Enterprise Services delivers courses at all levels, both for managers, end users, developers, administrators, and designers. You can choose from a variety of class formats, including lectures, seminars, video, and computer-based products. Custom courses can be designed for an organization and delivered in house if requested. Sybase classes are translated into multiple languages, so they can be taught in the student's language. Instructors are all Sybase Certified Professionals, which means that they have passed a certifying exam that ensures a basic level of understanding. Sybase trainers are also typically consultants, so they not only provide the advantage of book learning, but of real-world experience.

CUSTOMER SERVICE AND TECHNICAL SUPPORT (CS&S)

Customer Service and Support answers basic service requests, such as helping you to get new software tapes or CD-ROMs, answering general inquires, and maintaining the support contact list for your site. Technical Support responds to requests for technical assistance. CS&S also interacts with development engineering to promote features requested by customers, manage the beta program, and provide information services such as creating the AnswerBase CD-ROM, technical newsletters, and the CS&S WWW site. Sybase offers several levels of technical support services so that you only pay for the amount of support you need. The basic plan allows you to access technical support during the regular business hours in your time zone and includes enhancement releases, maintenance releases, and the AnswerBase CD-ROM. You can purchase more expensive plans that allow you to call technical support 7 days a week, 24 hours a day. At the high end, the Alliance Program gives you a dedicated expert to answer questions at the Sybase support center.

SYBASE CERTIFIED PROFESSIONAL PROGRAM (CSP)

The Sybase Certified Professional Program is a series of independently administered, statistically valid examinations that verify a person's competence with client/server technology. The CSP program lets professionals measure how well they understand Sybase, lets managers know whether their education investments have paid off, and lets organizations know that the consultants they hire have a solid understanding of Sybase systems.

OPEN SOLUTIONS PROGRAM (PARTNERS, VARS, ISVS)

Sybase maintains close working relationships with VARs, systems integrators, and hardware vendors via the Sybase Open Solutions Program (also called the Partners program). Sybase works with close to 2000 systems integrators, software tools, and application partners. These vendors are required to become CSP members so that their customers and Sybase's know that they are working with people who have a consistent level of understanding about Sybase. The Open Solutions Program provides technical, sales, marketing, and finance assistance. Open Solutions developers can purchase discounted software, receive expert technical support, have access to online product information, access the Sybase certification lab, and receive training discounts.

The Sybase sales force also works with partners to refer sales, close joint deals, and provide account management.

SYBASE WORLD WIDE WEB SITE (WWW, "HOME PAGE")

The Sybase WWW site at *http://www.sybase.com*, which is available to anyone with Internet access, provides information and services that customers, potential customers, stockholders, and others might find useful. The information on the WWW site changes on a weekly basis.

Bibliography

A lot of the knowledge that led to this book came from taking classes, reading email, having conversations with engineers, having conversations with customers, hacking software, reading code, and observing people in action. Besides all that, I have read more books and magazines than you really want to see in a list at the end of a book. So here I'll just describe a few of the inputs into my career and this book.

■ FAVORITES

When you're frustrated, depressed, or simply tired of the state of the industry, read one of these.

Brooks, Frederick P., Jr., *The Mythical Man-Month, Essayson Software Engineering*. Reading, Mass.: Addison-Wesley Publishing Co., Inc., 1975. Don't let the publishing date or humble title fool you. Pick up this book read it straight through, even if you think it will push your project schedule out a day or two. You'll be able to make up that time and more if you take heed of the lessons here.

Norman, Donald A., *The Design of Everyday Things*. Garden City, N.Y.: Doubleday, 1988. Technology doesn't have to bring on the downfall of society, but you can see how it could. This book makes clear several of the problems that give technology a bad name and reveals the secrets of intuitive design.

Weinberg, Gerald M., *Becoming a Technical Leader, An Organic Problem-solving Approach*. New York.: Dorset House Publishing, 1986. Had a tough day of fighting political battles? Read one of the best books that specifically addresses the challenges of managing people and software at the same time.

White, Julie, *Image and Self-projection for Today's Professional Woman*, Audio Cassette Recording, four tapes. Boulder, Colo.: Career Track Publications, 1986. If you think you've hit a glass ceiling in a male-dominated environment, try to find this set of tapes. White gives you hints and inspiration to make small changes in your work style that yield huge rewards.

Yourdon, Edward, *Techniques of Program Structure and Design*. Upper Saddle River, N.J.: Prentice Hall, 1975. If you learned programming "on the fly," take a step back and learn the art and science from a master.

Zinsser, William, *On Writing Well, An Informal Guide to Writing Nonfiction*. New York: Harper & Row, Publishers, Inc., 1976. If you want to write with strength and grace, start by reading Zissner.

■ BECOMING AN EXPERT

For general reference purposes, see if you can find some of these. If you can't make time to read them straight through, keep them around as references for crunch times.

Burch, John G., *Systems Analysis, Design, and Implementation.* Boston: South-Western Publishing Company, Boyd & Braser division, 1992. If you need a thorough systems analysis reference work, find this one. Organized as a textbook, it presents all the terminology and techniques that you'll want to know about.

Date, C. J., *An Introduction to Database Systems.* Reading, Mass.: Addison-Wesley Publishing Co., Inc., 1995. If you plan to spend time with relational databases, plan to read this book by the man who's name is practically synonymous with the topic.

DePree, Max, *Leadership Is an Art.* New York: Bantam Doubleday Dell Publishing Group, Inc., Doubleday, 1989. If you're looking for a short, highly readable tutorial on bottom-up management, read this one.

Drucker, Peter F., *Managing for the Future, the 1990s and Beyond.* New York: Penguin Books USA, Inc., Dutton Signet, 1992. Any book you read by Drucker will give you valuable insights into why corporate America works the way it does. This book discusses where we are headed in terms of the configuration of our companies as well as the organization of our work.

Frank, Milo O., *How to Get Your Point Across in 30 Seconds—or Less.* New York: Simon & Schuster, Inc., 1986. The draft of Sybase Systems Management was much longer before I read Frank's book!

Illingworth, Valerie, Edward L. Glaser, and I. C. Pyle, eds., *Dictionary of Computing.* New York: Oxford University Press, 1983. Track down the "real" meanings of the lingo that gets scattered about as if it were confetti at a parade. Can you write clear, accurate, and concise code if you can't describe it clearly, accurately, and concisely?

Kendall, Kenneth E., and Julie E. Kendall, *Systems Analysis and Design.* Upper Saddle River, N.J.: Prentice Hall, 1988. Here's a blend of theory and practical, human perspective in a highly readable textbook format. A unique and informative perspective on decision making in organizations adds sense to the way different members of an organizational hierarchy work with software.

649

Wall, Larry, *Perl*. Sebastopol, CA: O'Reilly & Associates, Inc., 1990. Even if you don't ever want to learn the Perl language, this book will still teach you a lot about programming. Specifically, you will learn about systems reengineering, a topic that consumes most of us at one point or another. It helps if you know one of the UNIX shells so that you can see where Wall has stripped away the nonsense and revealed the sense. And it's funny! And, well, if you love UNIX as some of us do, you may become a Larry worshipper too.

■ SYBASE

Sybase, Inc., updates its manuals often and sometimes changes the titles as well. Find the most applicable versions of these manuals to go with your version of Sybase SQL Server. At the time of this writing, Sybase supplies these manuals with SyBooks, AnswerBase, and on the WWW.

Sybase SQL Server Troubleshooting Guide. If you're going to be responsible for keeping one or more SQL Servers running, sit down with your favorite beverage and snack food and read this one cover to cover. I did several times. It's amazing how much trouble you can avoid by reading the sound advice based on real, live technical support experience that went into this book.

Sybase SQL Server Errors Manual. When you get an error that you don't understand, check here first. You will generally find out why it happened and what you can do to correct it. As with the Troubleshooting Guide, the content of this manual comes from tried and true Technical Support experience.

Sybase SQL Server Installation Manual. Here's where you'll find all the particulars about installing a SQL Server on your platform. Read it all the way through first before installing the Server. Really. How late do you want to be at work tonight anyway?

Sybase SQL Server Reference Manual (multivolume set for 10.0 and subsequent releases). In this work, you'll find the syntax of all the commands and system stored procedures. In addition, an entire section covers topics such as cursors and transactions.

Sybase SQL Server Release Bulletin. If you think something came up between the time the reference manuals went to press and the software rolled out, check here for details. You'll also find out if Sybase discovered that the latest version of an operating system or network library is or is not compatible with the Server.

Sybase SQL Server System Administration Guide and Supplements. Need to change a sort order, back up a database, or enable mirroring for the first time? You'll find descriptions, warnings and advice here. The supplements contain platform-specific information for your particular version of the Server. This can be quite useful if your UNIX guru is missing when you need to install a SQL Server.

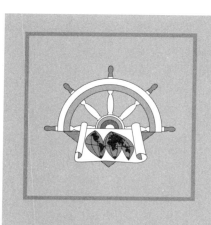

Index

Symbols

(pound sign) table name prefix 19
@@servername global variable 155

Numerics

10.1, new features
    identity in nonunique index 22
    lock escalation threshold 52
    lock wait monitoring 55
    optimizer calculates sort cost 292
    page split algorithm 127
    rows per data page 127
    size of auto identity column 22
    text information global variables 78
    transaction isolation level 0 50, 265
11.0, new features
    address lock spinlock ratio variable 236
    allow sql server async i/o variable 227
    configuration file variable 234
    configuration interface 211
    cpu grace time variable 246

deadlock checking period variable 235
deadlock retries variable 235
disk i/o structures variable 228
double precision costing by optimizer 311
dump compatibility with 10.0 65
dup_in_subquery disabled 305
event buffers per engine variable 226
executable code size variable 218
forceplan (documented) 267
freelock transfer block size variable 237
housekeeper 149
housekeeper free write percent variable 233
i/o polling process count variable 232
I/O pools 144
identity grab size variable 240
identity in nonunique index 259
lock shared memory variable 229
max async i/os per engine variable 229
max async i/os per server variable 228
max engine freelocks variable 237
max number network listeners variable 250
memory alignment boundary variable 233
named caches 140
network I/O 136

number of alarms variable 227
number of index trips variable 229
number of mailboxes variable 227
number of messages variable 227
number of oam trips variable 230
number of pre-allocated extents variable 231
number of sort buffers variable 231
o/s asynch i/o enabled variable 227
o/s file descriptors variable 229
OAM page utilization 123
optimized update algorithms 323
optimizer hints 308
page lock spinlock ratio variable 237
page utilization percent variable 230
permission cache entries variable 253
prefetch 267
runnable process search count variable 232
shared memory startring address variable 219
size of auto identity column variable 240
sort page count variable 231
spinlock configuration 54
sql server clock tick length variable 233
stack guard size variable 245
statistics subquerycache 268
subquery algorithms 303
sysattributes table 174
syslogshold table 57
table count 271
table lock spinlock ratio variable 236
table partitions 116
tcp no delay variable 250
total data cache size variable 230
user log cache size variable 250
user log cache spinlock ratio variable 251
2558 error 113, 169

A

abort tran on log full option 257
Access control, SQL Server 70
ACID test 46
Ada Workbench 639
additional network memory variable 249
address lock spinlock ratio variable 54, 236
Administrative commands, SQL Server 77
Aliases, database user 68
Aliases, for SQL Servers 152
Allocation pages 121
Allocation units 89, 119
allow nested triggers variable 240

allow nulls by default option 257
allow remote access variable 246
allow sql server async i/o variable 227
allow updates to system tables variable 224
ansi_permissions set option 264
ansinull set option 263
AnswerBase 636
Archiving 338, 349–350
arithabort set option 264
arithignore set option 265
ASCII 157
Asynchronous disk I/O 227
Attribute integrity 37
Attributes, See also Columns 8
audit queue size variable 252
Audit Server 629
Auditing 73, 200, 201, 427
    audit records in memory 252
auto identity option 22, 258

B

Backups 60–66, 389–412
    Backup Server 61, 81, 393
    backupserver executable 132
    compatibility between versions 65
    console 81
    operating system-level 394
    planning 394
    standbys 397
    third-party applications 394
    warm, configuration for 261
BCP, See Bulk Copy
Benchmarks 287
BETWEEN predicate 301
Bitmaps, understanding 203
Break-even analysis 590
Buffer manager 139
Buffer pools 144
Buffer replacement strategy 309
Buffer washing 148
Build versus buy 534
buildmaster utility 81
    and sp_configure 209
    and tempdb 108
    executable 132
    fixing configuration block 209
    function 98
    using to fix number of devices 222
Bulk copy 81, 230, 231, 393

C

Caches, named 140
Capacity planning 340
Cardinality 20
Cash flow analysis 589
Centralized systems 372
   motivation 373
chained set option 265
char_convert charset set option 272
char_convert set option 271
Character set conversion error messages 160
Character sets 156–160, 179, 242, 271, 272
charset utility 159
charsets directory 134, 159
Checkpoint 222, 256
Client/Server
   advantages 7
   architecture 5–7
close on endtran set option 265
Closure property 9
Columns
   defined 8
   external view 23–29
Communication 558, 576
Compilation, of queries 290–293, 313
   forcing 314
Complexity 376
   business operations 460
   support 473
Composite keys 21
Compression, of compiled objects 313
Configuration
   accounting 220
   ANSI compatibility 263, 264, 265, 269
   backups 225, 261
   configuration block 209
   CPU usage 220, 227, 232, 233, 242, 246, 251
      222
   cursors 269
   debugging SQL 266, 268, 269, 271
   disk usage 221, 227, 228, 229, 230, 238
   expertise levels 215
   file location 234
   for applications 266, 270, 271
   for bulk copy 230, 231
   for SQL Monitor 226
   identity columns 239, 240, 258, 259
   index creation 241
   internationalization 241, 242, 271, 272, 273

   locking 235, 236, 237
   maintenance 259, 262, 263, 273
   memory 218, 219, 227, 229, 230, 231, 233, 234, 250
   network usage 247, 248, 249, 250
   performance 267
   remote access 246, 247
   security 252, 253, 273
   Server 207–253
   sp_configure 210
   sp_dboption 255
   SQL behavior 257, 259, 264, 265, 269, 270, 271
   SQL Server 11 211
   thresholds 261
   transaction log 257, 262
   triggers 240
   user connections 229, 243, 245
   variable groups 215
   variable name changes in 11.0 212
Configuration block 98, 173
Configuration file 132, 211
   naming convention 217
configuration file variable 234
Configuration variables
   changes in 11.0 213
Configuration, database 255–263
Configuration, user environment 263–273
Connecting to SQL Server 152
   common problems 153
console utility 61, 81, 133, 393
Constraints (SQL Server object) 40, 188
   and business rules 189
   check 40
   foreign key 40
   primary key 40
   references 40
   unique 40
Consultants 535
Conventions used in this book xxiii
Conversion, data 353–354
Coordination 553
Copying data 355–357
Correlation columns and variables 304
Corruption, See Data, threats
Cost/benefit analysis 488, 581–597
   air conditioning 620
   analyzing trends 591
   analyzing variations 586
   consulting 614
   departmental charges 621
   documentation 616

estimating costs 592
evaluating benefits 594
expected lifetime 585
facilities 624
hardware 600
hidden benefits 595
hidden costs 593
license agreements 620
maintenance 616
measuring benefits 596
methods 588
power usage 620
productivity change 612
running parallel systems 623
security 622
service and support 619
supplies 619
support 615
taxes and depreciation 625
training 614
transition 612
Covering (queries and indexes) 278
cpu accounting flush interval variable 220
cpu grace time variable 246
CPU usage 135–137
  *See also Configuration
  affinity 315
  and housekeeper 150
  monitoring 332
Crisis
  affect on priorities 494
  avoiding 476
CT-Lib 638
cursor rows set option 269

D

Data
  archiving 349–350
  conversion 353–354
  eliminating duplication 347
  estimating storage requirements 340–346
  integration 348
  migration 351–360
  multidimensional 366, 370
  protection 35–37
  replication 354–360
  roles and value 337–338
  threats to 35, 99, 395, 410, 424–428
Data cache 139, 219

Data definition commands 75
Data dictionary, See System tables
Data manipulation commands 75
Data pages 122
  allocation 123
  allocation and deallocation overhead 123
  numbering 124
  splitting 123, 126
Datatypes 24
  bit 26
  datetime 26
  decimal, fixed point 26
  floating point 25
  money 26
  performance 305
  user-defined 26
Data warehouses 360–365
  creating 362
  data quality 364
Database Consistency Checker, See DBCC
Database objects 111–112
Databases
  backing up and loading, See also
      Backups 60–66
  design 8, 515–525
  external view 15–16
  files as precursors 10
  hierarchical 10–13
  marked suspect 221
  system 105–109
dataserver executable 132
Date, C.J. 8
datefirst set option 272
dateformat set option 272
Dates 272
db_id function 76
db_name function 76
DBCC 58–60, 407–410
  and number of indexes 300
DBCC CHECKALLOC 58, 59
DBCC CHECKCATALOG 58, 60
DBCC CHECKDB 58, 59
DBCC CHECKTABLE 58, 59
DBCC INDEXALLOC 58, 59
DBCC OBJECT_STATS 55, 334
DBCC PAGE 328
DBCC TABLEALLOC 58, 59
DBCC TRACEON 59
DBCC USER_STATS 55, 334
DB-Lib 638
dbo use only option 259

ddl in tran option 259
Deadlock 48
deadlock checking period variable 235
deadlock retries variable 235
Decision support systems 365–370
default character set id variable 242
default database size variable 221
default fill factor percent variable 238
default language id variable 242
default network packet size variable 248
default sortorder id variable 241
Defaults (database object) 27
defncopy utility 81, 190
Degree of table 23
Deleted table (used in triggers) 39
Denormalization 320
Design 515–525
    applications 318
    database, and performance 318
    feasibility 528
    flexibility 524
    human-centered software 516
    innovation 525
    intuitive interfaces 521
    prototyping 526
    quality 522
    review and testing 529
    tables 320
    user input 518
    validation and verification 526
Devices, SQL Server 89, 97–98
diag directory 133
Dirty reads, See also Isolation levels 48
Disasters, planning, See Data, threats to
Disk controllers 411
Disk devices 90–97
    configuring 99–103
    cylinder zero 102
    determining device numbers 165
    mirroring 103–105, 406
    overlapping partitions 103
    partitions 90, 100
    performance 92–97
    RAID 95
    setting maximum number 221
Disk fragments 89
Disk I/O
    configuration 220
    monitoring 332
disk i/o structures variable 228
DISK INIT 98

Distributed Computing Environment Standard
    (DCE) 377
Distributed systems 371–380
Distribution pages 122, 277, 291, 295
    creation 123
    structure of 295
Documentation
    and organizational culture 504
    and sucessful projects 502
    cost/benefit analysis xxii
    creating xxii
    of vision xxii
    procedures manual xxii
    project proposal xxii
    system inventory xxii
Domains 17, 23
Downtime 416
Drucker, Peter 491
DSQUERY environment variable xxv, 152
dstartio errors 228
Dump compatibility, SQL Server 10 and 11 65
DUMP DATABASE 60, 62, 393
DUMP TRANSACTION 60, 63
    warning against WITH NO_LOG option 63
    WITH NO_TRUNCATE 63
    WITH TRUNCATE_ONLY 63
dup_in_subquery set option 269, 305

E

EBFs (Emergency Bug Fixes) 413
Embedded SQL 639
Engine freelock cache 237
Enterprise Services 643
Enterprise SQL Server Manager 632
Entities 90
Entity integrity 36
Environments, multiple SQL Server 416
Error log 132, 436–440
Error messages 176
Errors
    common in programs 530
    recovering from 410
    reporting 415
ESQL 639
ESSM 632
event buffers per engine variable 226
Exclusive page locks 49
Exclusive table lock 49
executable code size variable 218

Execution, of queries 293–294
Extents 89, 120

F

Feasibility studies 528
Feedback, in applications 517
Fields, See also Columns 8
File descriptors 136
    used by SQL Server 244
Files, SQL Server 131
    backupserver 132
    buildmaster 132
    console 133
    dataserver 132
    errorlog 132
    installmaster 133
    installmodel 133
    installpubs2 133
    interfaces 132
    isql 132
    RUNSERVER 132
    scripts directory 133
    servername.CFG 132
    servername.krg and servername.srg 132
    showserver 133
    startserver 133
    sybinit 132
Fill factor, index pages 238
fipsflagger set option 264
Float data type 25
flushmessage set option 266
Forceindex feature 309, 333
forceplan set option 309, 333
Foreign keys 21
formdef directory 134
freelock transfer block size variable 54, 237
Functions, SQL Server built-in 76

G

GAM pages 121
Global variables 77
    text information in Version 11 78
Goals 475, 481
Grey, Jim 49
Groups (SQL Server) 69

H

Heaps 32, 116
Hints 308
    buffer replacement strategy 309
    forceindex 309, 333
    forceplan 333
    prefetch 267, 308
    sp_cachestrategy 310
    table count 271, 306
Housekeeper 149, 223, 233
housekeeper free write percent variable 150, 233

I

i/o accounting flush interval variable 220
i/o polling process count variable 232
I/O pools 144
Icons xxiv
Identifiers 270
identity burning set factor variable 239
Identity columns 22, 239, 240, 273
    auto identity option 22
    gaps in values 22
    identity in nonunique index option 22
    size of auto identity column variable 22
    SYB_IDENTITY_COL identifier 22
identity grab size variable 240
identity in nonunique index option 22, 259
identity_insert set option 273
IN predicate 302
include directory 134
Indexes
    and constraints 31
    and data cache 229
    and time to run DBCC 300
    bitwise 300
    clustered 32, 297
    composite and distribution statistics 297
    covering 298
    creation of, and performance 31, 120, 231, 241
    density 277, 292
    disk placement and performance 94
    distribution pages 277
    external view 29–33
    forcing use in queries 333
    keys 297
    leaf level 32

nonclustered 32
optimizing 294–300
overflow pages 123
pages 121
purpose 30
selectivity 278, 291
space for clustered vs. nonclustered 122
statistics 295
storage space 32
structure on disk 122
unique 296
InfoHub 642
InfoMaker 634
InfoPump 642
Information systems
　analyzing storage needs 339–340
　and organizational style 478
　bottlenecks 473
　complexity 376
　data warehouses 360–365
　decision support 365–370
　definition in this book 446
　distributed and interoperable 371–380
　documentation xvi
　driving organizational changes 481
　elements of 598
　executive goals 450
　extended 386
　integration 348
　internationalization goals 457
　market goals 455
　migration 351–360
　OLAP 365–370
　operational goals 460
　organizational goals 452, 478
　productivity goals 462
　profitability goals 454
　replication 354–360
　right sizing goals 467–470
　scalability goals 471
　standards 380–385, 471
　support goals 473
　systems manager goals 450
　technology goals 463
　topology 5
　vision 448
InformationCONNECT 640
In-place updates 322
Inserted table (used in triggers) 39
installmaster script 44, 80, 133, 203
installmodel script 133

installpubs2 script 133
Integrity features, SQL Server 37–44
Intent exclusive table locks 49
Intent shared table locks 49
interfaces file 132, 152, 155
Internal rate of return 589
Internationalization 80, 156–162
　business adaptations 458
　character sets 156–160
　languages 160
　sort order 161
Internet 386, 547, 610
Interoperability 371–380, 511
Inventory, system 598–625
Isolation levels 22, 49, 265
　level 0 50, 50–52
　level 1 50
　level 3 50
isql 81
　executable 132
　password encryption 156

J

Join (relational operator) 9
Joins
　clause form 292
　forcing order 309, 333
　order of evaluation 292
　performance 306
　seeing join order 330
　set table count option 309

K

Keys 20, 186
　alternate 21
　and performance 297
　and unique indexes 21
　candidate 21
　composite 21, 278
　foreign 21
　identity columns 22
　index 29
　primary 17, 22
　sequential 22
　simple 21
　surrogate, contrived or artificial 21

L

langinstall utility 81, 160
language set option 273
languages in cache variable 161
Languages, SQL Server 160, 179, 242, 273
Leadership 553–577
Leaf pages, index 122
lib directory 134
LIKE predicate 301
Limits, SQL Server 82
LOAD DATABASE 60, 64, 393
LOAD TRANSACTION 60, 64
locales directory 134
Localization, See Internationalization
Lock escalation threshold 52–54
lock promotion HWM variable 53
lock promotion LWM variable 53
lock promotion PCT variable 53
lock shared memory variable 229
Lock wait monitoring 55
Locking 47–55, 183
   and performance 326
   configuration 265
   cursors 324
   deadlock 48
   dirty reads 48
   exclusive page locks 49
   exclusive table lock 49
   intent exclusive table 49
   intent shared table 49
   lock escalation threshold 52–54
   monitoring wait time 334
   page-level and row-level 47
   repeatable reads 48
   resource locks 49
   shared page locks 49
   spinlocks 49, 54
   update locks 49
Logical Memory Manager 139
Logical page numbers 124
Logins, SQL Server 67, 193
   automating 418–420
LRU/MRU algorithm 147, 299
   optimizer hints 309

M

Magic numbers 296
Maintainability
   and number of databases 110
   improving 412–417
Management role, in projects 553
Mandatory Access Control (MAC) 198, 628
master database 16, 105, 106, 400
max async i/os per engine variable 229
max async i/os per server variable 228
max engine freelocks variable 54, 237
max number network listeners variable 250
max online engines variable 220
MAX_ROWS_PER_PAGE clause of CREATE
   and ALTER 127
maximum network packet size variable 249
Meetings, planning 564
Memory 144
   *See also configuration, memory
   caches, description of 137
   data cache 139
   procedure cache 138, 312
   usage by SQL Server 137–150
memory alignment boundary variable 143, 233
Metrics 538
Middleware products 637
Migration of data 351–360
min online engines variable 220
Mirroring 103–105, 406
model database 16, 107
MTBF, for information systems 512
Multibyte characters 158
Multidimensional data 366, 370
Murphy's Law, SQL Server performance
   corollary 278

N

Named caches 140
   and procedure recompilation 143
   binding entities 142
   default data cache 141
   logonly cache 141
   mixed cache 141
Navigation Server 631
net password encryption 155
Net present value 588
Net-Gateway 641
Net-Libraries 640
Network
   performance 317
   software and SQL Server 153
   usage by SQL Server 151–156

Network I/O 315
    in SQL Server 11.0 136
no chkpt on recovery option 261
no free space acctg option 261
nocount set option 270
noexec set option 266
Normalization 290
NOT EXISTS 302
NOT predicate 302
NULL values 27
number of alarms variable 227
number of devices variable 221
number of extent i/o buffers variable 31, 120,
    241
number of index trips variable 229
number of languages in cache variable 242
number of locks variable 235
number of mailboxes variable 227
number of messages variable 227
number of oam trips variable 230
number of open databases variable 234
number of open objects variable 234
number of pre-allocated extents variable 231
number of remote connections variable 247
number of remote logins variable 247
number of remote sites variable 247
number of sort buffers variable 231
number of user connections variable 243

O

o/s asynch i/o enabled variable 227
o/s file descriptors variable 229
OAM Page 121
Object IDs 76, 112
object_id function 76
object_name function 76
offsets set option 271
On-Line Analytical Processing (OLAP) 365–370
ONLINE DATABASE 64, 65
Open Client 638
Open Server 630
Open Server for CICS 642
Open Server for IMS/TM 642
Open Solutions Program 645
oper_role 70
Operating system priority 315
Optimizer
    purpose 277
    seeing cost calculations 330, 331

seeing join order 330
seeing query plan 333
Optimizing queries 290–293
OR predicate 302

P

Packet batching, TCP 250
Page buffers 140
page lock spinlock ratio variable 54, 237
page utilization percent variable 123, 230
Pages 89, 121–126
    allocation and performance 230
    allocation page type 121
    associating numbers with objects 328
    distribution page type 122
    flushing to disk 149
    GAM page type 121
    image page type 122
    index page type 121
    leaf, of index 32
    OAM page type 121
    table page type 121
    text page type 122
    using fill factor to avoid splitting 239
Parameters, stored procedure 314
Parse trees 184
parseonly set option 266
Parsing, of queries 290
PARTITION clause of ALTER TABLE 117
partition groups variable 117
partition spinlock ratio variable 117
Partitions 91, 103, 116–118
    *See also Disk Devices
Passwords 67
    encrypting over network 155
    expiration 252
Payback analysis 589
Performance, SQL Server 275–334
    aggregates 308
    benchmarks 287
    BETWEEN predicate 301
    clustered indexes 297
    covering indexes 298
    CPU usage 280
    data types 305
    database and application design 280
    denormalization 320
    design factors 318
    diagnosing problems 329–334

disk usage 280
distribution statistics 295
expressions 307
functions 307
identifying key transactions 283
IN and OR predicates 302
index usage 280
indexes 294–300
in-place updates 322
joins 306
keys 297
LIKE predicate 301
local variables 307
locking 326
measuring 286
memory usage 280
network 316
network usage 280
NOT predicate 302
number of indexes 299
optimization 290–293, 300
optimizer hints 308
procedural objects 280
procedure cache 312
procedure parameters 306, 314
procedure variables 314
processing capacity 284
queries 280
requirements 510
reresolution and recompilation 313
Server activities 280
setting goals 281
SQL Server versions 280
subqueries 303
temporary tables 314
tuning process 281
types of bottlenecks 276
unique indexes 296
variables to measure 287
permission cache entries variable 253
Permissions, database objects 71, 196
Ports, network 135
PowerBuilder 634
Prefetching
    data pages 140, 267, 308
    enabling for data pages 147
    extents, during index creation 140
print recovery information variable 223
Private log cache 250
Problem solving 431–436
Procedure cache 138, 312

procedure cache percent variable 219
Procedure manual suggestions
    archiving data 387
    avoiding hard-coded limits 84
    backup and recovery 84
    consultant arrangements 550
    contacting vendors 441
    creating proposals 549
    disaster recovery 440
    disk partition use 129
    document system goals 483
    documenting a standard configuration 253
    evaluating proposals 626
    format for cost/benefit analysis 625
    hardware and software acquisition and
        support 626
    information system project standards 549
    information system solutions 483
    localization 162
    making backups of system databases 129
    managing communication between
        servers 387
    managing database configuration 273
    managing database objects 83
    managing object permissions 85
    managing roles 85
    managing server configuration 254
    managing space with segments and
        thresholds 129
    managing stored procedures 85
    managing the model database 128
    managing the sybsecurity database 128
    managing user-defined datatypes 33
    managing user-defined messages 205
    naming conventions 551
    notifying users about down time 440
    notifying users of system changes 578
    organizational structure 484
    passwords 441
    programming standards 550
    project document storage 578
    recommended communication methods 578
    reporting errors 440
    requests for information systems changes 548
    starting and stopping SQL Server 83
    system timing considerations 549
    upgrades 441
Processes
    operating system 135
    SQL Server engine 135
    user 135

procid set option 266
Productivity 490
Products, Sybase 627–643
Project (relational operator) 9
Project plan 531
Projects
    and resistance to change 575
    build versus buy 534
    communication 558, 576
    costs and benefits 488
    delays 572
    design 515–525
    documents 502
    efficiency versus productivity 490
    evaluating ideas 487
    failure 487
    getting approval 506
    implementation 531
    initiating 500
    leadership 553–577
    managing expectations 574
    meetings 564
    metrics 538
    motivating team 562
    plan and schedule 531
    proposals 505
    requirements 508–515
    scope 492
    selecting a leader 557
    team building 560
    technical support 544–548
    time management 567–571
    timing 499
    to deal with personnel problems 495
    training 539–542
    transition support 543
    types to avoid 493
    use of consultants 535
Proposals 505
Prototyping 526
public (SQL Server group) 194

Q

Qualifications 291
Quality, designing in 522
Queries
    compilation 290–293
    covering 298
    execution 293–294

    normalization 290
    optimizing 290–293
    parsing 290
    performance 300
    resolution 290
Query port 135
quoted_identifier set option 270

R

RAID 95
Raw partitions, See also Disk devices 100, 227
read only option 261
Recompilation
    See Compilation, of queries
reconfigure command 217
Records, See also Rows 8
Recovery 55–58, 389–412
    *See also Backups
    and named caches 147
    and number of databases 110
    printing transaction information 223
recovery interval in minutes variable 222
References, See also Keys, foreign 21
Referential integrity 36
Reformatting strategy 292
Relational Database Management Systems 8–14
Relational model 17
Relational operators 9, 301
Relational properties 17
Relations, See also Tables 8, 17
Remote procedure calls 154
remote server pre-read packets variable 247
Repeatable reads, See also Isolation levels 48
Replication 354–360
    and data transformation 359
    and datatypes 359
    backups 393
    methods 355–357
    topography 358
Replication Server 637
Replication Server Manager 638
Requirements
    and design 515
    competitive differentiation 514
    distributed processing 512
    interoperability 511
    networks 513
    performance 510
    profit improvement 514

reliability 511
scalability 512
security 514
service and support 513
solve the problem 509
standards 515
systems management 513
Resolution 290, 313
Resource locks 49
Response time, transaction 287
Restrict (relational operator) 9
Return on investment 589
Right sizing, computers 467–470
role set option 273
Roles, SQL Server 69–70, 195, 196, 273
rowcount set option 269
Rows
    defined 8
    external view 20–23
    internal view 126–128
    number per page 127
RPCs, See Remote procedure calls
Rules (SQL Server object) 38
run_value column, sysconfigures 174
runnable process search count variable 232
RUNSERVER file xxv, 132

S

SA Companion 632
sa login account 69
sa_role 70
Sandy's Sport Shops
    backup scenarios 391
    benefits 596
    constraints 41
    data storage methods 11
    data types 26
    defaults 27
    introduction to examples 5
    maintenance 587
    NULLs 28
    present value 590
    rules 38
    segments 114
    stored procedures 42
    Tim's cost/benefit analysis 583
    transactions 45
    triggers 39
SARGs 290

scalar values 9
Schemas 33
scripts directory 133
Sectors 91
Secure SQL Server 628
Security 66–73
    access control 70
    aliases 68
    auditing 73, 200, 201
    database object permissions 71
    groups 69
    improving 424–428
    login accounts 67
    related system tables 191
    requirements 514
    roles 69–70, 273
    SQL Server 10 features 66
    SQL Server features 426
    sybsecurity database 109
    user accounts 68
    using view mechanism 72
Segments 90, 112–116
select into/bulkcopy option 262
self-recursion set option 270
Server, as synonym for SQL Server 89
SERVERNAME xxv
SET CHAR_CONVERT 159
SET LANGUAGE 159
Set processing 9
Shared memory files 132
shared memory starting address variable 219
Shared page locks 49
Short circuiting 278
showplan set option 266, 333
showserver utility 81, 133, 202
single user option 262
Site handlers 247
size of auto identity column variable 22, 240
SKILS 636
Snapshot tables 18
Sort order 159, 161, 241
    and clustered indexes 32
sort page count variable 231
Sorting, optimization 292
sp_addalias 194
sp_addlanguage 160
sp_addmessage 178
sp_addremotelogin 155
sp_addsegment 113
sp_addserver 155
sp_addthreshold 113, 170

sp_addtype 26
sp_adduser 155
sp_bindcache 142
    and locking 143
sp_binddefault 27
sp_cacheconfig 141
sp_cachestrategy 310
sp_checkreswords 79
sp_chgattribute 176
sp_clearstats 193
sp_configure 174
    general usage 210
    new syntax in 11.0 216
sp_dboption 255
sp_depends 188
sp_displaylevel 215
sp_helpcache 143
sp_helpprotect 197
sp_helptext 190, 202
sp_logiosize 145
sp_monitor 136, 285, 331
sp_poolconfig 144–145
sp_primarykey 20
sp_procqmode 305
sp_recompile 139
sp_serveroption 156
sp_setpglockpromote 52
sp_spaceused
    interpreting output 121
sp_unbindcache 142
sp_unbindcache_all 143
sp_who 420
Space usage
    by system tables 344–345
    by transaction logs 345
    by user tables and indexes 341–344
Spinlocks 49, 54
spt_ tables 225
spt_monitor 331
SQL 73–81
    standards 7
SQL Anywhere 630
SQL Debug 635
SQL Monitor 136, 285, 331, 632
    configuration 226
sql server clock tick length variable 233
SQL Server Manager 632
SQR Workbench 635
sso_role 70, 73
stack guard size variable 245
stack size variable 245

Stack space 245
Standards 380–385
    DCE 377
    reasons for lack of 382
    related to information systems 383
    shaping a strategy 385
Standby environments 397
startserver utility 82, 133
statistics io set option 268, 332
statistics subquerycache set option 268
statistics time set option 268, 332
Status values 203
Stored procedures 41–44
    creating, system 74
    deleting text of 191
    parameters 314
    performance 306, 311
    system 42
    variables in 314
string_rtruncation set option 271
Subqueries 269, 303
Support
    help desks 545
    providing 544–548
    user groups and conferences 547
    WWW 547
swapping, OS level 229
SWRs 413
SYB_IDENTITY_COL 22
Sybase Certified Professional Program 645
SYBASE environment variable xxv, 131, 152
Sybase Financial Services, Inc. 643
Sybase IQ 31, 300, 365, 633
Sybase MPP 631
Sybase Technical Support 644
Sybase WWW site 646
sybinit 132
SyBooks 636
sybsecurity database 16, 109
sybsystemprocs database 16, 108
sysalternates 194
sysattributes 174
sysauditoptions 201
sysaudits 109, 200, 427
syscharsets 159, 179
syscolumns 185
syscomments 190
sysconfigures 173, 174
sysconstraints 188
syscurconfigs 174
sysdatabases 166

sysdepends 188
sysdevices 165
sysengines 173
sysindexes 118, 187
syskeys 186
syslabels 198
syslanguages 160, 178
syslocks 183
sysloginroles 195
syslogins 193
syslogs 57, 171
syslogshold 57
sysmessages 176
sysobjects 182
syspartitions 117
sysprocedures 31, 184
sysprocesses 199
sysprotects 68, 196
sysreferences 189
sysremotelogins 198
sysroles 196
syssegments 168
sysservers 154, 164
syssrvroles 196
System catalogs, See System tables
System databases 105–109
    master 16, 105, 400
    model 16, 107
    sybsecurity 16, 109
    sybsystemprocs 16, 108
    tempdb 16, 107
System stored procedures
    creating 106
System tables 16, 18
    *See also individual table names
    direct updates 201
    modifying 224
    status columns 203
system wide password expiration variable 252
Systems Managers xvi, 447
    career advancement goals 475
    crisis avoidance goals 476
    goals 474
    roles 553
systhresholds 169
systypes 181
sysusages 125, 167
sysusermessages 177
sysusers 68, 194

T

table count set option 271, 309
table lock spinlock ratio variable 54, 236
Table partition 90
Tables
    base 18
    definition 8
    derived 18
    external view 17–20
    heaps 32
    pages 121
    partitions 116–118
    snapshot 18
    system 18
    temporary 19, 314
    user 18
    work 19
Tabular Data Stream 152
tape retention in days variable 225
tcp no delay variable 250
TDS, See Tabular Data Stream
Team building 560
Technical support 413
tempdb database 16, 107
    and complex queries 107
    keeping in RAM 108
Temporary tables 19, 314
termdef directory 134
Testing 529
Text/Image data type 122, 270
    storage on disk 122
textsize set option 270
Three-tier architecture 375
Thresholds 170, 403–406
Throughput 287
Time management 567–571
time slice variable 242
Time-slice errors 243
Timestamps 56, 261
total data cache size variable 230
total memory variable 218
TPC-C benchmark 287
Trace flags 58
    1213 55
    1610 250
    241 313
    302 330
    310 331
    3604 59
    3605 59

5101 and 5102 316
    replaced by variables in version 11 214
    using 329
Training 539–542
Transaction log 56–58, 171
    binding to memory 145
    configuration 257
    determining when dumped last 166
    invalidation 401
    logging process 45
    truncating on checkpoint 263
Transaction Processing Performance
      Council 288
Transactions 44–47
    ACID test 46
    isolation levels, See Isolation levels
Transact-SQL 73–81
Transition support 543
Triggers 38, 240, 270
Troubleshooting 431–436
trunc log on chkpt option 223, 263
Tuples, See also Rows 8

U

Unicode 158
Unique indexes 296
UNPARTITION clause of ALTER TABLE 117
Update locks 49
UPDATE STATISTICS 295
upgrade version variable 226
Upgrades 429–431
    organizational impact 464–467
    possible performance changes 311
User accounts, database 68
User connections 136
    limited by file descriptors 68
    managing 420–423

User databases 109–111
User log cache 250
user log cache size variable 250
user log cache spinlock ratio variable 251
User tables 18
User-defined datatypes 181
User-defined messages 177, 178
Users, SQL Server 194
Utilities, SQL Server 81–82

V

Variables
    and performance 307
    in stored procedures 314
Views 18
Virtual page numbers 124, 165
Virtual Server Architecture 135
VLDB
    data warehouses 360–365
    decision support 365–370
    OLAP 365–370

W

WAITFOR 227
Wash size configuration, for buffer pools 148
Watcom 630
WITH SORTED_DATA option of CREATE
    INDEX 31
Work tables 19
write-ahead logging 46
WWW, See Internet

X

XA-Library 640

PHYSICAL DATABASE DESIGN FOR SYBASE SQL SERVER

Rob Gillette ▲ *Dean Muench* ▲ *Jean Tabaka*

ISBN: 0-13-161523-8

Physical Database Design for Sybase SQL Server from Prentice Hall PTR and Sybase Worldwide Professional Services presents practical technical methods within a new application development methodology, optimized for heterogeneous, client/server environments. This Sybase Development Framework (SDF) methodology replaces the traditional "Waterfall" approach with an incremental, interactive approach, modeled in spiral. Physical database design is one of the activities within the SDF.

This practical workbook guides you from the logical model of a database to a physical, implementable representation of the database. Each chapter presents a particular design activity as a series of ordered steps that precisely describe the tasks that need to be performed.

This book can be used as a reference by programmers and database administrators who have completed and implemented a physical database design but who now need to revise it because of additional or altered performance, space, security, or integrity issues. Since the tasks outlined can be used either in the SDF methodology or in other development methodologies, the book is also of greater value to protect managers seeking to identify all the activities needed to plan the physical database design phase of a development project.

The activities presented in this book have been carefully tested in the field by the Sybase Worldwide Professional Services Group. Members of this group are Sybase consultants and architects who assist key Sybase clients in implementing SQL Server based information management solutions.

SYBASE, INC. *is a leading vendor of client/server software and services for building online, enterprise-wide information systems.*

Prentice Hall Worldwide Ordering Information

All Prentice Hall books are available at technical bookstores and participating Magnet Stores worldwide. To locate the store nearest you fax 201-236-7123 or http://www.prenhall.com/.

**Direct from the Publisher
(USA only)**
Single Copy Sales (Visa/Master Card/American Express, Checks or Money Orders only)
Tel: 515-284-6761
Fax: 515-284-2607
Toll-Free: 800-811-0912

Corporate Accounts (Quantity/Bulk Orders totaling 10 or more books.
Purchase orders only — No credit cards)
Tel: 201-236-7156
Fax: 201-236-7141
Toll-Free: 800-382-3419

Government Agencies
Prentice Hall Customer Service
Toll-Free: 800-922-0579

College Professors
(Desk/Review Copies)
Toll-free: 800-526-0485
International Inquiries

Canada
Prentice Hall Canada, Inc.
Tel: 416-293-3621
Toll-Free: 800-263-6051
(Outside Toronto)
Fax: 416-299-2529
or 416-293-5646

**UK, Europe, and North Africa
Simon & Schuster International, Ltd.**
Tel: 881900
Fax: 882277
Country Code: 441
Area/City Code: 442

India and Middle East
Prentice Hall of India, Private, Ltd.
Tel: 332-9078 or 332-2779
Fax: 371-7179
Country Code: 91
Area/City Code: 11

Singapore and Southeast Asia
Simon & Schuster (Asia) PTE., Ltd.
Tel: 278-9611/Fax: 271-1179
or 273-5002
Country Code: 65
Area/City Code: None

**Australia/New Zealand
Prentice Hall of Australia, PTY, Ltd.**
Tel: 939-1333
Fax: 938-6826
Country Code: 61
Area/City Code: 2

**Latin America, Mexico,
the Caribbean, Japan**
(Plus all other countries not mentioned above)
International Customer Service,
Old Tappan, NJ USA
Tel: 201-767-4900
(Latin America and Mexico)
Tel: 201-767-4991 (Caribbean)
Tel: 201-767-4992 (Japan)
Tel: 201-767-4990 (All others)
Fax: 201-767-5625